T0212064

# Lecture Notes of the Institute for Computer Sciences, Social Informatics and Telecommunications Engineering    251

## Editorial Board

Ozgur Akan
  *Middle East Technical University, Ankara, Turkey*
Paolo Bellavista
  *University of Bologna, Bologna, Italy*
Jiannong Cao
  *Hong Kong Polytechnic University, Hong Kong, Hong Kong*
Geoffrey Coulson
  *Lancaster University, Lancaster, UK*
Falko Dressler
  *University of Erlangen, Erlangen, Germany*
Domenico Ferrari
  *Università Cattolica Piacenza, Piacenza, Italy*
Mario Gerla
  *UCLA, Los Angeles, USA*
Hisashi Kobayashi
  *Princeton University, Princeton, USA*
Sergio Palazzo
  *University of Catania, Catania, Italy*
Sartaj Sahni
  *University of Florida, Florida, USA*
Xuemin Sherman Shen
  *University of Waterloo, Waterloo, Canada*
Mircea Stan
  *University of Virginia, Charlottesville, USA*
Jia Xiaohua
  *City University of Hong Kong, Kowloon, Hong Kong*
Albert Y. Zomaya
  *University of Sydney, Sydney, Australia*

More information about this series at http://www.springer.com/series/8197

Limin Meng · Yan Zhang (Eds.)

# Machine Learning and Intelligent Communications

Third International Conference, MLICOM 2018
Hangzhou, China, July 6–8, 2018
Proceedings

 Springer

*Editors*
Limin Meng
Zhejiang University of Technology
Hangzhou Shi
China

Yan Zhang
Department of Networks
Simula Research Laboratory
Oslo
Norway

ISSN 1867-8211 ISSN 1867-822X (electronic)
Lecture Notes of the Institute for Computer Sciences, Social Informatics
and Telecommunications Engineering
ISBN 978-3-030-00556-6 ISBN 978-3-030-00557-3 (eBook)
https://doi.org/10.1007/978-3-030-00557-3

Library of Congress Control Number: 2018954076

© ICST Institute for Computer Sciences, Social Informatics and Telecommunications Engineering 2018,
corrected publication 2020
This work is subject to copyright. All rights are reserved by the Publisher, whether the whole or part of the
material is concerned, specifically the rights of translation, reprinting, reuse of illustrations, recitation,
broadcasting, reproduction on microfilms or in any other physical way, and transmission or information
storage and retrieval, electronic adaptation, computer software, or by similar or dissimilar methodology now
known or hereafter developed.
The use of general descriptive names, registered names, trademarks, service marks, etc. in this publication
does not imply, even in the absence of a specific statement, that such names are exempt from the relevant
protective laws and regulations and therefore free for general use.
The publisher, the authors and the editors are safe to assume that the advice and information in this book are
believed to be true and accurate at the date of publication. Neither the publisher nor the authors or the editors
give a warranty, express or implied, with respect to the material contained herein or for any errors or
omissions that may have been made. The publisher remains neutral with regard to jurisdictional claims in
published maps and institutional affiliations.

This Springer imprint is published by the registered company Springer Nature Switzerland AG
The registered company address is: Gewerbestrasse 11, 6330 Cham, Switzerland

# Preface

We are delighted to introduce the proceedings of the 2018 European Alliance for Innovation (EAI) International Conference on Machine Learning and Intelligent Communications (MLICOM 2018). This conference has brought together researchers, developers, and practitioners around the world who are leveraging and developing potential intelligent solutions for future mobile communications and networks. We hope the integrating of machine learning algorithms into communication systems will improve the QoS and make the systems smart, intelligent, and efficient.

The technical program of MLICOM 2018 consisted of 66 full papers in oral presentation sessions at the main conference tracks. The conference tracks were: Track 1, Machine learning; Track 2, Intelligent positioning and navigation; Track 3, Intelligent Multimedia Processing and Security; Track 4, Wireless Mobile Network and Security; Track 5, Cognitive Radio and Intelligent Networking; Track 6, Intelligent Internet of Things; Track 7, Intelligent Satellite Communications and Networking; Track 8, Intelligent Remote Sensing, Visual Computing and Three-Dimensional Modeling; Track 9, Green Communication and Intelligent Networking; Track 10, Intelligent Ad-hoc and Sensor Networks; Track 11, Intelligent Resource Allocation in Wireless and Cloud Networks; Track 12, Intelligent Cooperative Communications and Networking; Track 13, Intelligent Computing and Caching; Track 14, Intelligent Signal Processing in Wireless and Optical Communications; Track 15, Intelligent Radar Signal Processing. Aside from the high-quality technical paper presentations, the technical program also featured four keynote speeches. The four keynote speeches were Prof. Xuemin (Sherman) Shen from the University of Waterloo, Canada, Prof. Nei Kato from the Tohoku University, Japan, Prof. Qinyu Zhang from the Harbin Institute of Technology, China, and Prof. Liping Qian from the Zhejiang University of Technology, China.

Coordination with the steering chairs, Prof. Imrich Chlamtac, Prof. Xin Liu, and Prof. Xin-Lin Huang, was essential for the success of the conference. We sincerely appreciate their constant support and guidance. It was also a great pleasure to work with such an excellent Organizing Committee team who worked hard to organize and support the conference and, in particular, the Technical Program Committee, led by our TPC co-chairs, Prof. Yan Zhang, Prof. Bo Ji, Prof. Shuai Han, and Prof. Liping Qian who completed the peer-review process of technical papers and created a high-quality technical program. We are also grateful to the conference managers, Katarina Antalova, Radka Pincakova, and Jana Štefaňáková, for their support and to all the authors who submitted their papers to the MLICOM 2018 conference.

We strongly believe that MLICOM conference provides a good forum for all researcher, developers, and practitioners to discuss all science and technology aspects that are relevant to machine learning and intelligent communications. We also expect that the future MLICOM conferences will be as successful and stimulating, as indicated by the contributions presented in this volume.

August 2018　　　　　　　　　　　　　　　　　　　　　　　　Limin Meng
　　　　　　　　　　　　　　　　　　　　　　　　　　　　　　　Yan Zhang

# Organization

## Steering Committee

### Steering Committee Chair

Imrich Chlamtac       University of Trento, Italy, and EAI

### Steering Committee Co-chair

Xin Liu       Dalian University of Technology, China

### Steering Committee Member

Xin-Lin Huang       Tongji University, China

## Organizing Committee

### General Chairs

Limin Meng       Zhejiang University of Technology, China
Yan Zhang       University of Oslo, Norway

### General Co-chairs

Su Hu       University of Electronic Science and Technology of China, China
Yuan Wu       Zhejiang University of Technology, China
Weidang Lu       Zhejiang University of Technology, China

### Technical Program Committee Chairs

Yan Zhang       University of Oslo, Norway
Bo Ji       Temple University, USA
Shuai Han       Harbin Institute of Technology, China
Liping Qian       Zhejiang University of Technology, China

### Web Chair

Liang Huang       Zhejiang University of Technology, China

### Publicity and Social Media Chair

Qing Pan       Zhejiang University of Technology, China

### Sponsorship and Exhibits Chair

Hong Peng       Zhejiang University of Technology, China

**Publications Chair**

Yu Zhang                    Zhejiang University of Technology, China

**Local Chairs**

Weidang Lu                  Zhejiang University of Technology, China
Liang Huang                 Zhejiang University of Technology, China

**Conference Manager**

Katarina Antalova           EAI - European Alliance for Innovation

# Technical Program Committee

## Machine Learning

Xinlin Huang                Tongji University, China
Liang Huang                 Zhejiang University of Technology, China
Huasen Wu                   Twitter, USA

## Intelligent Positioning and Navigation

Mu Zhou                     Chongqing University of Posts and Telecommunications,
                              China
Zhian Deng                  Harbin Engineering University, China
Zhiguo Shi                  Zhejiang University, China

## Intelligent Multimedia Processing and Security

Fen Hou                     University of Macau, Macau, SAR China
Hangguan Shan               Zhejiang University, China

## Wireless Mobile Network and Security

Kuan Zhang                  University of Nebraska-Lincoln, USA
Shijun Lin                  Xiamen University, China
Xiaojie Fang                Harbin Institute of Technology, China

## Cognitive Radio and Intelligent Networking

Weidang Lu                  Zhejiang University of Technology, China
Xin Liu                     Dalian University of Technology, China
Huiming Wang                Xian Jiaotong University, China

## Intelligent Internet of Things

Kaikai Chi                  Zhejiang University of Technology, China
Yongliang Sun               Nanjing Tech University, China
Ruilong Deng                University of Alberta, Canada

## Intelligent Satellite Communications and Networking

| | |
|---|---|
| Kanglian Zhao | Nanjing University, China |
| Haibo Zhou | Nanjing University, China |
| Shaohua Wu | Harbin Institute of Technology, China |

## Intelligent Remote Sensing, Visual Computing and Three-Dimensional Modeling

| | |
|---|---|
| Shifang Xu | Shanghai Institute of Technology, China |
| Guodao Sun | Zhejiang University of Technology, China |

## Green Communication and Intelligent Networking

| | |
|---|---|
| Yu Zhang | Zhejiang University of Technology, China |
| Nan Zhao | Dalian University of Technology, China |

## Intelligent Ad-hoc and Sensor Networks

| | |
|---|---|
| Jian Qiu | Hangzhou Dianzi University, China |
| Zhenyu Na | Dalian Maritime University, China |
| Danyang Qin | Heirongjiang University, China |

## Intelligent Resource Allocation in Wireless and Cloud Networks

| | |
|---|---|
| Caihong Kai | Hefei University of Technology, China |
| Nan Cheng | University of Waterloo, Canada |
| Suzhi Bi | Shenzhen University, China |

## Intelligent Cooperative Communications and Networking

| | |
|---|---|
| Deli Qiao | East China Normal University, China |
| Xuewen Liao | Xi'an Jiaotong University, China |
| Shan Zhang | University of Waterloo, Canada |
| Min Jia | Harbin Institute of Technology, China |

## Intelligent Computing and Caching

| | |
|---|---|
| Ju Ren | Central South University, China |
| Juan Liu | Ningbo University, China |
| Wei Wang | Zhejiang University, China |
| Zheng Chang | University of Jyvaskyla, Finland |

## Intelligent Signal Processing in Wireless and Optical Communications

| | |
|---|---|
| Qingjiang Shi | Nanjing University of Aeronautics and Astronautics, China |
| Tong Ye | Shanghai Jiaotong Univeristy, China |
| Shaohua Hong | Xiamen University, China |
| Jing Xu | Zhejiang University, China |

## Intelligent Radar Signal Processing

Yujie Gu            Temple University, USA
Weijie Xia          Nanjing University of Aeronautics and Astronautics, China
Xiaolong Chen       Naval Aviation University, China

# Contents

## Intelligent Ad-hoc and Sensor Networks

## Intelligent Resource Allocation in Wireless and Cloud Networks

## Intelligent Signal Processing in Wireless and Optical Communications

**Intelligent Cooperative Communications and Networking**

**The Second Round**

# Machine Learning

# Gun Identification Using Tensorflow

Mitchell Singleton, Benjamin Taylor, Jacob Taylor,
and Qingzhong Liu$^{(\boxtimes)}$

Department of Computer Science, Sam Houston State University,
Huntsville, TX 77341, USA
{mitchellsingleton, benjamin. taylor,
jacobtaylor, liu}@shsu. edu

**Abstract.** Automatic video surveillance can assist security personnel in the identification of threats. Generally, security personnel are monitoring multiple monitors and a system that would send an alert or warning could give the personnel extra time to scrutinize if a person is carrying a firearm. In this paper, we utilize Google's Tensorflow API to create a digital framework that will identify handguns in real time video. By utilizing the MobileNetV1 Neural Network algorithm, our system is trained to identify handguns in various orientations, shapes, and sizes, then the intelligent gun identification system will automatically interpret if the subject is carrying a gun or other objects. Our experiments show the efficiency of implemented intelligent gun identification system.

**Keywords:** Tensorflow · Gun detection · Video surveillance

## 1 Introduction and Background

Automatic video surveillance is utilized by many people and organizations in the video surveillance category of their physical security protocol. CCTV and webcams are used in many products, from specialized doorbells with cameras and microphones that allow for two-way communication and recording when an event is triggered, or Closed-Circuit Television's (CCTV) which are used to aid security personnel in preventing or helping mitigate an incident. These systems use video in some form of method to record what the camera sees. While it may be easy for a homeowner to review a single system that has 1 or 2 cameras, the task becomes an arduous and tedious even when combing through multiple video streams if they implement a larger array of cameras. Depending on an organization's footprint and their implementation of their physical security plan, security personnel may be monitoring 100's of video streams [1, 2]. These streams should be prioritized in order of importance to determine the number of personnel needed and how many streams can be observed per personnel.

Recently, there has been an increasing number of incidents involving handguns in various situations. To detect handguns, in [3], several models were utilized to detect pistols. These models used the VGG-16 based classifier and then classified the detection of the gun with either the sliding window or the region proposal approach. The authors went with the region proposal approach due to its faster detection speed –

© ICST Institute for Computer Sciences, Social Informatics and Telecommunications Engineering 2018
L. Meng and Y. Zhang (Eds.): MLICOM 2018, LNICST 251, pp. 3–12, 2018.
https://doi.org/10.1007/978-3-030-00557-3_1

but also tested against the sliding window approach. To achieve a real-time outdoor concealed-object detection with passive millimeter wave imaging [4], the authors used a passive millimeter wave (MMW) imaging system ran at or around 94 GHz with 1 Hz frame rate. To attain automatic recognition, they used both global (aligning the body and the background together) and local (inside of the body is processed) segmentation levels to find the concealed objects. To automatically detect firearms and knives in a CCTV image, the authors in [1] used an approach utilizing MPEG-7 visual descriptions and a principal component analysis (PCA). They took each frame and removed everything except the foreground of the image which included the erosion and dilation. To detect weapons in surveillance camera images [5], the authors improved detecting weapons in CCTV via the Histogram of Oriented Gradients (HOG) method for classification. In [6], a framework was developed to identify general objects in video using still image processes along with object tracking through the 4th dimension of time. In [7], a real-time detection, tracking and classification of natural video was examined. The method uses background subtraction and maximally stable extremal region (MSER) detection. However the method didn't successfully reach real-time. Recently a method to detect visual gun by using Harris interest point was proposed [2], the author uses a visual gun detection based on FREAK descriptor to recognize guns. The system processes an image, performs color segmentation, performs a boundary extraction and compares against a similarity higher than 50% and then executes an alarm. This algorithm was accurate 84.26% of the time and shows promise.

In this paper, we focus on detecting guns vs no guns. We propose a detection method that is built on a lean convolutional neural network optimized for speed. This paper is organized into four additional sections. Section 2 explains the definitions and tools where we will explain the CNNs and tools used to train our algorithm. Section 3 describes the methodology and the effectiveness of our algorithm, followed by our conclusions in Sect. 4.

## 2 Definitions and Tools

Tensorflow (https://www.tensorflow.org/) is a platform that is based on dataflow graphs and is useful in training with deep neural networks [8]. Tensorflow was created by Google and it is used in their native applications and in dozens of machine learning projects such as: facial recognition, image processing, speech recognition, and extracting information such as license plate numbers. Tensorboard, a web application, is a visualization for understanding Tensorflow trainings and monitoring the training progress in a web browser [9]. It showcases visualizations such as: graphs, scalars, and images. Tensorboard shows cross entropy and accuracy depicted into a graph for convenient visualization of training results. Tensorboard can be started from an Anaconda prompt and uses port 6006 on the localhost for its process.

OpenCV (https://opencv.org/) is an open source computer vision library that contains image processing functions and over 2,500 algorithms used for things like facial recognition [10]. OpenCV can accelerate CUDA and OpenCL GPUs. OpenCV supports deep learning platforms like Tensorflow. OpenCV is built using a layering process. You have the OS, then the languages and algorithms, the core of OpenCV, and at the bottom the hardware acceleration layer (HAL) [11].

MobileNet is a collection of vision models for Tensorflow that are mobile-oriented and used to enhance visual recognition [12]. It is essentially a convolutional neural network (CNN). MobileNet, unlike a typical CNN, separates the convolution into a $3 \times 3$ depth wise convolution and a $1 \times 1$ pointwise convolution. The reason MobileNet is used more than a traditional CNN is the computation time is much quicker with their architecture, however the accuracy can be slightly lower. Depending on the architecture, such as MobileNet_0.50.224 or 0.50.192, it can change the width multiplier and the image resolution. The image resolution is the 192 or 224 and the width multiplier is the .50. This will help the object detection computation time of the image processing the smaller the image resolution. The width multiplier can be ranged from 0.25, 0.50, 0.75, and 1.0. The image resolution can be 128, 160, 192, or 224.

ImageNet (http://www.image-net.org/) is a very large dataset of images (over 14 million) with about 22,000 categories and are collected by human labelers [13]. ImageNet compiles hundreds of thousands of thumbnails and URLs of images just like Google, a search engine, does. ImageNet is organized via synsets which is a concept of WordNet. ImageNet was created to be utilized by researchers as a primary resource for images.

Anaconda (https://www.anaconda.com/) is used for large quantities of data processing, predictive analytics, and scientific computing [14]. It has over 1000 packages in its repository that can be installed, 150 of which come pre-installed with Anaconda. It is an open-source distribution of Python used to ease and simplify package administration and distribution. The packages are managed by a package management system within anaconda called conda.

Nvidia Compute Unified Device Architecture (CUDA) is utilized by many as their primary method to process images because it essentially groups the cores of GPUs into a vector and can then be programmed to decrease processing time on the large sets of data versus CPUs that do not run on a parallel throughput architecture [15].

Shi-Tomasi corner point detection is an enhancement to the Harris corner detector. The way Harris corner detection works is that the pixel is calculated and if above a precise value then it's marked as a corner. To score it, two eigen values are used to check if it's a corner during detection and then inputted into a function which manipulates them. Shi-Tomasi decided to enhance this method and only rely on the two eigen values, not the entire Harris formula. This is because their model relies solely on the tracker's accuracy [16].

## 3    Methodologies

The dataset pictures were gathered from the Sun database [17], Internet Movie Firearm Database [18], Pixabay [19], ImageNet [20] and reduced in number to 3363 gun images and 11834 non-gun images. The dataset was trained several times adding or removing pictures from the datasets to improve accuracy.

The method utilized in this paper was to retrain multiple object detection models (inception_v3, MobileNet_0.50_192, MobileNet_0.50_224, MobileNet_1.0_224) for a binary classification of an object into either gun or no gun using a training dataset composed of firearms and non-firearm pictures. See Fig. 1 for the MobileNet architecture training flow chart.

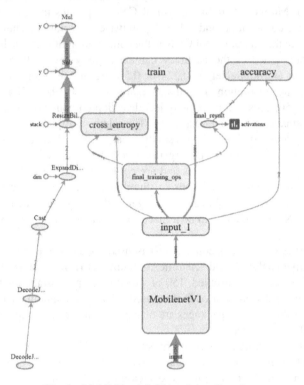

**Fig. 1.** MobileNet 1.0 224 training flowchart

The use of Tensorboard allowed watching the progress of the retraining and in Figs. 2 and 3 the visualization of the progress of the retraining can be seen from step 60 to step 4000 respectively.

Once the retraining was complete, Shi Tomasi key point detection was used to identify the parts of a picture that should be looked at by the binary classification. The assumption being that the key points would be less than the number of sliding windows across the whole picture.

The key point locations are then each used to crop out a section of the image and the retrained model is called to determine if the cropped section contains a gun or not. If a gun is found, then the cropped section has a rectangle drawn on the picture in the same location as the cropping. In the next section, we will review the results of our current models and some examples of identified pictures in the gun category and correctly identified pictures in the non-gun category.

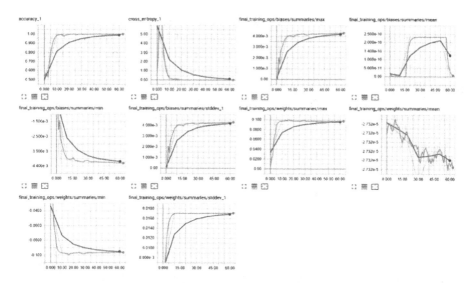

**Fig. 2.** Starting out the retraining

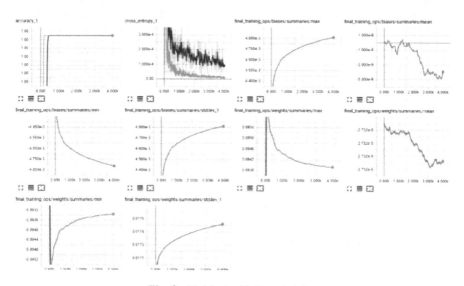

**Fig. 3.** Finished with the retraining

## 4   Results

The gun detection was trained and tested on the following datasets described in Sect. 3. The images detected in a fast method and we would like to expand upon static images to real time video as our algorithm is improved. MobileNet was trained in various step counts and tested for accuracy. In one training iteration, we trained 3000 steps as seen in Table 1 and resulting in 97.89% accuracy. In another iteration, we trained the

MobileNet 1.0 224 model 5000 steps and the accuracy increased to 100%. Our most accurate training algorithm was trained on 795 guns and 3944 non-guns. Testing using the results from this training resulted in the least false-positives compared to our dataset that included more pictures in the gun dataset. Results from this iteration of testing gave a 96% accuracy when testing against non-gun photos with the guns filtered at 89%. When testing against photos with guns, we have an accuracy of 86.67% out of 30 photos. These calculations can be referenced in Table 1 (Fig. 4).

**Table 1.** Model detection results

|         | Pictures | Correct | Incorrect | Correct |
|---------|----------|---------|-----------|---------|
| Non-gun | 25       | 24      | 1         | 96%     |
| Gun     | 30       | 26      | 4         | 86.67%  |

| Name | Smoothed | Value | Step | Time | Relative |
|------|----------|-------|------|------|----------|
| ⬤ mobilenet_1.0_224\train | 0.9969 | 1.000 | 2.999k | Fri Dec 1, 21:34:34 | 6m 9s |
| mobilenet_1.0_224\validation | 0.9889 | 0.9900 | 2.999k | Fri Dec 1, 21:34:34 | 6m 9s |

**Fig. 4.** MobileNet 1.0 224 retraining results

Our theory is accuracy will go up if we can preprocess the images with by subtracting the background, but this will have to be completed in another project. Some photos were missed because there is a limit of 25 corners maximum per image. Increasing this number will increase the amount of time the image must be processed, but we believe this will be minimized by removing or subtracting the background. Increasing the quality of our gun data set should improve the accuracy of the gun detection rate and will allow us to increase from 89% sensitivity without increasing false alarms, which can lead to alarm fatigue. We have included examples of correctly identified guns in Figs. 5, 6, and 7. The detection algorithm perform a gray transform. In Fig. 5, there were three positive hits. The background was uniform and the detection could identify the gun at least 3 times. It also correctly did not detect a gun on the subject's face, hair, earing, or shoulder. In Fig. 6, the subject had multiple hits on

**Fig. 5.** Successful detection of a gun

various parts of the gun. In future iterations of the code, we will want to decrease the output of overlapping gun identifiers. If it finds multiple positive hits within x pixels, then either combine or ignore x screen draws.

**Fig. 6.** Successful detection of a gun

In Fig. 7, you will see multiple identifiers on the base of the gun, on the barrel of the gun, and on a pistol like device in the bottom left corner. The background is the most difficult of the three different gun detection examples as the bricks do have similar hard angles that can be found in a gun. None of the bricks were identified as a gun so we are happy to report the background training with multiple forms of background photos in non-gun dataset has improved upon our earlier training and results. Again, we believe minimizing the number of identified boxes will clean up the display and will aid in the time of displaying the results in real time when this algorithm is improved and created for a real-time video system.

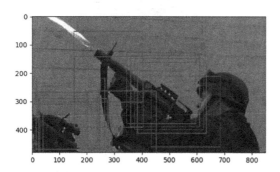

**Fig. 7.** Successful detection of a gun

We have also included correctly identified photos with no guns in Figs. 8 and 9. In Fig. 8, there are multiple hard edges in the grill and around the tires that have a gun shape. The algorithm was smart enough to not incorrectly give a false positive in all the dots that were run against. Other thing to note in the picture is the background was uniform with only having shadows at the bottom of the car. The shadows did not affect the detection of the algorithm and it performed its output correctly.

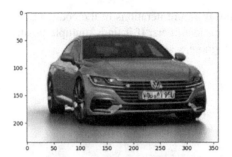

**Fig. 8.** Successful non-detection of a gun

Finally, our last example is shown in Fig. 9. In this example, the clouds and background did not affect the performance of the non-gun identification. The glasses and shadows in the pictures were also not a problem with the non-gun identifications.

**Fig. 9.** Successful non-detection of a gun

## 5   Conclusions and Future Work

By looking at the presented photos we have successfully re-trained an existing MobileNet Neural Network of varying granularity.

The assumption that using key points alone would allow testing fewer places in an image proved to be inaccurate and was problematic when a test picture had more key points than the maximum amount defined for detection or when there were many key points that were detected in the same place. It was observed that in some cases so many key points were detected on non-gun objects that the gun never got assigned a key point and thus a gun was never classified because that area in the image was not evaluated. It was also observed that when many key points were detected in the same place on a gun that the classification was ran on the same area of the picture for multiple overlapping classifications of gun.

One way to work around this issue would be to increase the maximum number of key points, however without any mitigation this would cause the total number of places in the picture needing to be looked at for classification to increase and remove the benefit of using the key point detection to decrease the instances of classification versus a sliding window over the whole picture.

Adding a processing step after the key point detection to remove key points by using a geometric density algorithm would allow keeping the number of classifications to a minimum. For example, in our test pictures, many of our key points are close enough that any gun detection boxes are overlapping.

Using a second step to remove key points would benefit both busy test pictures where the maximum number of key points was preventing a gun object from getting any key points and non-busy test pictures where all the key points are close to each other.

Adding another pre-processing step to remove the backgrounds would greatly increase the gun detection and decrease the false-positives. Finally, obtaining more pictures and continually training the dataset will allow it to continually learn and be more accurate.

To conclude, we have presented an early gun identification algorithm that we believe can be improved upon to allow detection of guns in images, video, and other applications. The goal is to give security personnel extra time to respond to a real gun alert.

# References

1. Grega, M., Matiolański, A., Guzik, P., Leszczuk, M.: Automated detection of firearms and knives in a CCTV image. Sensors **16**, 1–16 (2016). https://doi.org/10.3390/s16010047. ISSN 1424-8220
2. Tiwari, R.K., Verma, G.K.: A computer vision based framework for visual gun detection using harris interest point detector. Procedia Comput. Sci. **54**, 703–712 (2015). https://doi.org/10.1016/j.procs.2015.06.083
3. Olmos, R., Tabik, S., Herrera, F.: Automatic Handgun Detection Alarm in Videos Using Deep Learning. arXiv:170205147 cs (2017)
4. Yeom, S., et al.: Real-time outdoor concealed-object detection with passive millimeter wave imaging. Opt. Express **19**, 2530–2536 (2011). https://doi.org/10.1364/OE.19.002530
5. Vajhala, R., Maddineni, R., Yeruva, P.R.: Weapon Detection in Surveillance Camera Images (2016)
6. Kang, K., Ouyang, W., Li, H., Wang, X.: Object Detection from Video Tubelets with Convolutional Neural Networks. Presented at the June (2016)
7. Ray, L., Miao, T.: Towards Real-Time Detection, Tracking and Classification of Natural Video. Presented at the June (2016)
8. Abadi, M.: TensorFlow: learning functions at scale. In: Proceedings of the 21st ACM SIGPLAN International Conference on Functional Programming, p. 1. ACM, New York (2016)

9. Angermueller, C., Pärnamaa, T., Parts, L., Stegle, O.: Deep learning for computational biology. Mol. Syst. Biol. **12**, 878 (2016)
10. Pulli, K., Baksheev, A., Kornyakov, K., Eruhimov, V.: Real-time computer vision with OpenCV. Commun. ACM. **55**, 61–69 (2012). https://doi.org/10.1145/2184319.2184337
11. Kaehler, A., Bradski, G.R.: Learning OpenCV 3: Computer Vision in C++ with the OpenCV Library. O'Reilly Media, Sebastopol (2016)
12. Howard, A.G., et al.: MobileNets: Efficient Convolutional Neural Networks for Mobile Vision Applications. arXiv:170404861 cs (2017)
13. Krizhevsky, A., Sutskever, I., Hinton, G.E.: ImageNet classification with deep convolutional neural networks. Commun. ACM **60**, 84–90 (2017). https://doi.org/10.1145/3065386
14. Kadiyala, A., Kumar, A.: Applications of Python to evaluate environmental data science problems. Environ. Prog. Sustain. Energy **36**, 1580 (2017)
15. Saha, M.D., Darji, M.K., Patel, N., Thakore, D.: Implementation of image enhancement algorithms and recursive ray tracing using CUDA. Procedia Comput. Sci. **79**, 516–524 (2016). https://doi.org/10.1016/j.procs.2016.03.066
16. Shi, J., Tomasi, C.: Good Features to Track. Cornell University, Ithaca (1993)
17. Xiao, J., Hays, J., Ehinger, K.A., Oliva, A., Torralba, A.: Sun database: large-scale scene recognition from abbey to zoo. In: 2010 IEEE Conference on Computer Vision and Pattern Recognition (CVPR). pp. 3485–3492. IEEE (2010)
18. Internet Movie Firearm Database. http://www.imfdb.org/
19. Pixabay. https://pixabay.com
20. Deng, J., Dong, W., Socher, R., Li, L.-J., Li, K., Fei-Fei, L.: Imagenet: a large-scale hierarchical image database. In: IEEE Conference on Computer Vision and Pattern Recognition, CVPR 2009, pp. 248–255. IEEE (2009)

# A Research of Network Applications Classification Based on Deep Learning

Hong Shao, Liujun Tang, Ligang Dong[⊠], Long Chen, Xian Jiang,
and Weiming Wang

School of Information and Electronic Engineering, Zhejiang Gongshang
University, Hangzhou 310018, China
1564027103@qq.com, tlj2016@126.com,
{donglg,jiangxian,wmwang}@zjgsu.edu.cn,
smllchuju@163.com

**Abstract.** Nowadays, the huge traffic generated by a growing number of network applications occupies enormous network bandwidth and increases the burden of network management. The ability to identify and categorize network applications accurately is crucial for learning network traffic conditions, finding people's online behavior and accelerating the development of the Internet. The prior traffic classification methods often have unstable recognition rate and high computational complexity, which affects the network traffic management and application categories monitoring. Therefore, this paper proposes a method of using the deep learning technology to classify network applications. First, we propose a network application classification model based on Deep Belief Network (DBN). Then we construct a DBN-based model suitable for network applications classification with the Tensorflow framework. Finally, the classification performances of this DBN-based model and the BP-based model are compared on the real data sets. The experimental results show that the applications classification model based on DBN has higher classification accuracy for P2P applications.

**Keywords:** Deep learning · Deep belief network
Network applications classification

## 1 Introduction

According to the Visual Networking Index (VNI) report, from 2016 to 2021, global IP traffic is likely to triple, with an average annual increase of 1.2 ZB to 3.3 ZB. The majority of IP traffic is from P2P network applications. The increase of P2P network applications will inevitably generate huge traffic and occupy tremendous network bandwidth, which will exacerbate the problem of network congestion and eventually aggravate the burden of network management. Being able to identify and categorize network applications accurately is extremely important for learning the state of network traffic and accelerating the development of the internet.

The existing methods for P2P applications classification have certain limitations. Even the learning-based applications classification method, with better classification

© ICST Institute for Computer Sciences, Social Informatics and Telecommunications Engineering 2018
L. Meng and Y. Zhang (Eds.): MLICOM 2018, LNICST 251, pp. 13–21, 2018.
https://doi.org/10.1007/978-3-030-00557-3_2

performance, has unstable recognition rate and high computational complexity, which affect the management of network traffic and the monitoring of application categories.

Aiming at the deficiency of existing network applications classification technologies, and in order to learn the characteristics of network traffic data fully and improve the accuracy of network application classification, this paper proposes a network application classification model based on Deep Belief Networks (DBN). The original DBN model was proposed by Hinton [3] which can not only realize the automatic learning of characteristics but also learn the essential features that characterize the data and overcome the difficulty in the training through the method of layer-by-layer initialization. The utilization of DBN technique for characteristic classification and recognition has obvious advantages.

The remainder of this paper is structured as follows: Sect. 2 reviews the studies on network applications classification. Section 3 uses the Tensorflow framework to build the DBN model, including the construction of data sets and the determination of model parameters. Section 4 uses the DBN model to learn the traffic characteristic based on the constructed train data sets; then utilizes test datasets to analyze the classification accuracy of this model; and compares the result with that of the BP-based model at the same condition. The last chapter is the summary of this article.

## 2 Related Research

In view of the rapid growth of network traffic in the future, the majority of traffic is from the P2P applications. Recently, the most popular network classifications method is the method based on machine learning [6]. In 2005, Zuev et al. [9]. utilized the naive Bayesian method to extract the network traffic characteristics for training, but the classification accuracy of this method was only about 60%. Subsequently, Huang et al. [5] used KNN (k-Nearest Neighbor) algorithm to conduct experimental research on network traffic classification, and the classification accuracy can reach 90%. However, once the data packets are coming, all the streams in the train set will be calculated, so that the performance of classification is poor. In 2009, Xu et al. [1] used the C4.5 decision tree to classify network traffic, and the classification accuracy could reach 94%. However, the C4.5 decision tree classification method needs more traffic characteristics and data groups, and has high computational complexity, which hinders the further research. In 2015, Hong et al. [8] utilized the SVM algorithm to classify the P2P traffic, and the accuracy of that is only about 80%.

According to the demonstration above, this paper proposes a method of using the deep learning technology to construct a DBN model which is suitable for network application classification.

## 3 Network Applications Classification Model Based on DBN

In order to classify the existing network applications accurately, this paper proposes the network application classification model based on DBN. This section selects a framework to build a DBN-based model for applications classification. First, we use the

TensorFlow framework to initialize a DBN model. Second, we use the pre-process datasets to make it suitable for applications classification. Furthermore, we determine the number of hidden nodes and hidden layers of this DBN-based model through experiments. Then, we use the training datasets to train the DBN-based model until this model with better parameters, and the process of which include the unsupervised training [11] and the supervised training [12]. Finally, utilize the test dataset to evaluate the classified effect of the DBN-based model.

## 3.1   Data Pre-processing

The public dataset provided by LiWei et al. [4] is the only available dataset for UDP traffic that contains traffic data from P2P applications and non-P2P applications. Therefore, we select the UDP public data set provided by LiWei et al. as the experimental dataset. The dataset includes the feature sets and tag sets. The feature sets contain 9 kinds of features extracted from the data stream such as the port number, the stream size. The tag sets involve 6 applications like P2P. The feature sets and tag sets are presented in Tables 1 and 2.

**Table 1.** Features of the dataset

| Source port number | Destination port number | Total number of packets (bidirectional) |
|---|---|---|
| The minimum packet size (Client -> server) | The minimum packet size (Server side -> client side) | Client sends the first packet size (after receiving the server to return data) |
| The maximum packet size (Client -> server) | The maximum packet size (Server side -> client side) | The maximum number of consecutive packets the client sends to the server |

**Table 2.** Applications of the label set

| P2P | Services | Attack |
|---|---|---|
| Multimedia | VOIP | Game |

The initial DBN model is built by the Tensorflow framework, and the appropriate number of hidden layers and hidden layer nodes are determined by datasets. Before the experiment, we need to standardize those two datasets mentioned above.

1. Feature normalization

The values of nine features in above datasets are integers among 0 and 65535. The mean and variance of each feature are different, therefore, all the input features are normalized to the range of [0, 1] with Eq. (1), in which $x_i$ represents the original network traffic data, and $x_{max}$ and $x_{min}$ represent the maximum and minimum traffic respectively.

$$X_i' = \frac{X_i - X_{min}}{X_{max} - X_{min}} \tag{1}$$

2. Label coding

When the DBN model is applied to the classification study, the Softmax regression model [9] will be adopted at the final output layer of the model. The Softmax model classifies different objects by assigning probabilities. A neuron node in the model output layer corresponds to a label type. Label sets are expressed by one-hot encoding [10] as shown in Table 3 below.

**Table 3.** Dataset encoding

| Label | Attack | Services | P2P | Multimedia | VOIP | Game |
|---|---|---|---|---|---|---|
| Number | 1 | 2 | 3 | 4 | 5 | 6 |
| Coding | 000001 | 000010 | 000100 | 001000 | 010000 | 100000 |

The public data sets provided by LiWei et al. have 774141 streams, including 54,659 streams from P2P applications accounting for 7.1%. The dataset is divided into 10 sub-datasets (i.e., Dataset1–Dataset10). Among, the Dataset1 and Dataset2 which contain labels are as unsupervised training datasets; the Dataset3 which contain labels are as used in the supervised fine-tuning phase; the Dataset4–Dataset10 which contain labels are as test datasets. The number of streams contained in every dataset and that of P2P traffic are shown in Table 4 below.

**Table 4.** Details of sub-datasets

| Sub-datasets | 1 | 2 | 3 | 4 | 5 | 6 | 7 | 8 | 9 | 10 |
|---|---|---|---|---|---|---|---|---|---|---|
| P2P | 3567 | 4857 | 3632 | 4431 | 3949 | 3656 | 4472 | 9339 | 8472 | 8606 |
| Total | 60000 | 60000 | 60000 | 60000 | 60000 | 60000 | 60000 | 120000 | 120000 | 114013 |

### 3.2    Determination of the Model Parameters

Before the unsupervised training of DBN-based model, we need to determine the number of hidden nodes and hidden layers. The number of hidden nodes will affect the model on the abstract expression of features and the number of hidden layers will be directly related to the depth of the DBN-based model. And the increase of the number of hidden layers is conducive to a more comprehensive study on the characteristics. Since the problem of taking the number of different nodes and different hidden layers into account together is complicated, this section will firstly determine the number of hidden nodes when the model contains two hidden layers. When the number of hidden nodes is decided, we will determine the appropriate number of hidden layers.

### Determination of the Number of Hidden Nodes

Based on the first step, we can obtain the range of the number of hidden nodes with the formula 2. After several times of experimental comparison about the classification effect among models which vary in the number of hidden nodes, we can eventually acquire the number of hidden nodes corresponding to the model with the best classification performance; and put it as the numerical value for later experiment.

We select the DBN-based model only containing 2 hidden layers as initial model. We get the range of n is [1, 15] based on the calculation. In order to perform fully comparable experiment, we selected another 6 points, which is 16, 20, 21, 22, 26, 30.

$$n = \sqrt{m+p} + a \qquad (2)$$

In the equation above, "m" represents the number of input feature; "p" stands for the number of output label; "n" is the number of hidden layer nodes, and a symbolizes an integer within [1, 10].

When there is difference in the number of different hidden layer nodes, the overall classification accuracy of the model will be variant as shown in Fig. 1 below. The sum of the unsupervised and supervised training time of the model is used as the total training time of the model. The total training time of the models containing different number of hidden nodes is compared and shown in Fig. 2 below.

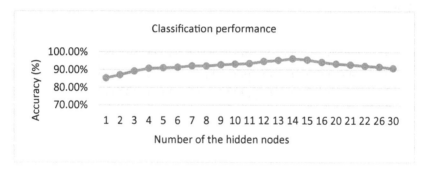

**Fig. 1.** The classification performance of the models with different number of hidden nodes

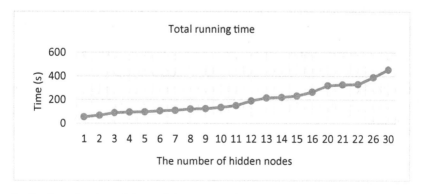

**Fig. 2.** Total running time of the models corresponding to the different number of hidden nodes

As can be seen from Fig. 1, with the increase of the number of hidden nodes, the classification accuracy of the model grows roughly. When n = 14, the classification accuracy of the model reach in 96%. From Fig. 2, we can learn that the total running time of the model generally shows an upward trend along with the growth of the number of hidden nodes. When n = 14, the total running time of the model is about 221 s, which is a bit higher than that of the nearby hidden nodes, but the classification accuracy at this time is the highest. Therefore, the number of hidden layer nodes in the DBN model is set to 14 preparing for subsequent experiments.

**Determination of the Number of Hidden Layers**
The number of hidden layers will directly affect the depth of the DBN model. The researchers [7] proved that the accuracy of the classification can be further improved by increasing the number of hidden layers of the DBN model to improve the abstraction ability of the data features. But not the more the number of hidden layers is, the better the classification effect [2] will be.

According to the analysis before, the number of hidden nodes of the model is set to 14. We will train the model respectively with different number of hidden layers, from 1 to 6. By having train on DBN-based models containing different number of hidden layers, we can obtain a group of corresponding DBN-based models. Then, we use the test datasets-Dataset4–Dataset10 to test the classification ability of those DBN models. The experimental results of DBN models with different number of hidden layers are shown in Table 5.

**Table 5.** The performance of the DBN-based models with different number of hidden layers

| The number of hidden layers | Classification accuracy | Running time (s) |
| --- | --- | --- |
| 1 | 90.2% | 221.9 |
| 2 | 95.1% | 335.1 |
| 3 | 95.4% | 546.8 |
| 4 | 96.9% | 601.2 |
| 5 | 94.7% | 693.8 |
| 6 | 93.6% | 842.5 |

As what's shown in Table 5, the total running time of the models increases with the growth of the number of hidden layers, but the classification accuracy does not always increase. When the number of hidden layers is 4, the classification accuracy of the model reaches in 97%, and the total running time at this time is 601.2 s. Therefore, we choose to construct a DBN-based model with 4 hidden layers.

Through the analysis of many experimental results, this paper will construct a DBN-based model that contains 4 hidden layers and every hidden layer contains 14 hidden nodes.

### 3.3   Training Phase of the Model

The process of training the constructed DBN-based model is as follows. The first step is the unsupervised training with unlabeled-datasets based on the initial model. Then Dataset3 (including tag) are used to adjust the model. That is, the weights trained in the unsupervised phase are transferred to the BP neural network for fine-tune of the DBN-based model. As a result, a fully trained DBN-based model is obtained preparing for the later evaluation.

## 4   Performance Evaluation

### 4.1   Experimental Environment

The experimental platform for this paper is an Intel Core i5 processor with a 3.3 GHz, 14.0 GB memory on a HP computer running window 10 (64 bit) operating system. This paper uses the TensorFlow framework to build the DBN-based model, in which all DBN-based algorithms are implemented in Python language.

Specific version of the software tools used herein is Tensorflow 1.2.1, Python 3.5.1.

### 4.2   Performance Comparison

In this section, we will compare the classification performance of the DBN-based model with that of the BP-based model. To make the comparison more accurately, we utilized the same method demonstrated in Sect. 3.2 to build a BP-based model in the same condition, including dataset and building process. Through several experiments, we finally construct a BP-based model with two hidden layers and every hidden layer contains 14 hidden nodes.

For the DBN-based model and BP-based model trained by public datasets, Dataset4–Dataset10 are utilized as the test datasets to test the performance of two models respectively. The comparison results of classification precision of the two models are presented in Fig. 3.

It can be seen from the figure above that due to the different distribution of network applications in each data set, the classification results of the same model are different. For the comparison between the classification precision of P2P application in Fig. 3, every precision value of the DBN-based model is higher than that of BP-based model, and the precision of DBN-based model is up to 98%.

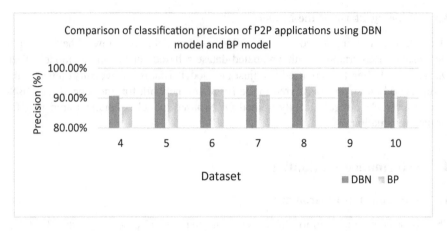

**Fig. 3.** Comparison of classification precision of P2P applications

# 5  Summary

In order to improve the classification accuracy of network applications and resolve the deficiency of existing network applications classification technology, this paper proposes a network applications classification model based on DBN. This model improves the accuracy of traditional network applications classification models. To make it more persuasive, we compare the classification results between DBN-based model and BP-based model in the same condition. Finally, we found the network application classification model based DBN has higher classification accuracy.

**Acknowledgement.** This work was supported by a grant from the Key Research and Development Program of Zhejiang (No. 2017C03058), Zhejiang Provincial Key Laboratory of New Network Standards and Technologies (NNST) (No. 2013E10012).

# References

1. Xu, P., Lin, S.: A method to classify network traffic with the C4.5 decision tree. Chin. J. Comput. **20**(10), 2692–2704 (2009)
2. Yu, K., Jia, L., Chen, Y., et al.: The yesterday, today and tomorrow of deep learning. J. Comput. Res. Dev. **50**(9), 1799–1804 (2013)
3. Hinton, G., Salakhutdinov, R.: Reducing the dimensionality of data with neural networks. Science **313**(5786), 504–507 (2006)
4. http://www.tensorfly.cn/tfdoc/tutorials/mnist_beginners.html
5. Internet assigned numbers authority [EB/OL] (2008). http://www.iana.org
6. Lu, G., Zhang, H.L., Ye, L.: P2P traffic identification. J. Softw. **22**(6), 1281–1298 (2011)
7. Ruijuan, Z., Jing, C., Mingchuan, Z., et al.: User abnormal behavior analysis based on neural network clustering. J. China Univ. Posts Telecommun. **23**(3), 29–44 (2016)
8. Wang, D., Zhang, L., Yuan, Z., et al.: Characterizing application behaviors for classifying P2P traffic. In: International Conference on Computing, Networking and Communications, pp. 21–25. IEEE (2014)

9. Zuev, D., Moore, A.W.: Traffic classification using a statistical approach. In: Dovrolis, C. (ed.) PAM 2005. LNCS, vol. 3431, pp. 321–324. Springer, Heidelberg (2005). https://doi.org/10.1007/978-3-540-31966-5_25
10. Wang, X., Li, Y.: The Introduction and Improvement of EDA, p. 225. Xidian University Press, Xi'an (2005)
11. Le, Q.V.: Building high-level features using large scale unsupervised learning. IEEE (2013)
12. Oravec, M., Podhradsky, P.: Medical image compression by backpropagation neural network and discrete orthogonal transforms. WIT Trans. Biomed. Health **4** (1970)

# Real-Time Drone Detection Using Deep Learning Approach

Manjia Wu[1]([envelope]), Weige Xie[1,2], Xiufang Shi[1,2], Panyu Shao[1,2], and Zhiguo Shi[2]

[1] State Key Laboratory of Industrial Control Technology,
Zhejiang University, Hangzhou, China
manjiawu@gmail.com
[2] College of Information Science and Electronic Engineering,
Zhejiang University, Hangzhou, China

**Abstract.** The arbitrary use of drones poses great threat to public safety and personal privacy. It is necessary to detect the intruding drones in sensitive areas in real time. In this paper, we design a real-time drone detector using deep learning approach. Specifically, we improve a well-performed deep learning model, i.e., You Only Look Once, by modifying its structure and tuning its parameters to better accommodate drone detection. Considering that a robust detector needs to be trained using a large amount of training images, we also propose a semi-automatically dataset labelling method based on Kernelized Correlation Filters tracker to speed up the pre-processing of the training images. At last, the performance of our detector is verified via extensive experiments.

**Keywords:** Drone detection · Deep learning · Visual detection

## 1 Introduction

In recent years, with the continuous development of related technologies, drone companies such as DJI, Parrot, and 3DRobotics are rapidly developing. And because of the low price and user-friendly operation, drones have been widely used in both military and civilian areas and meet an explosive growth of consumption. According to the Federal Aviation Administration (FAA), the purchases of drones were 1.9 million in 2016 and may increase to 4.3 million by 2020 [1].

However, the rapid development and widespread application of drones also bring various hidden dangers, such as public safety, personal safety, personal privacy, and so on. The occurrences of accidents caused by the illegal fly of drones become more frequent. Therefore it is necessary to regulate the fly of drones. A few companies like DJI, set up no-fly zones to ensure the safety in some sensitive areas, such as airports, prisons. But the effect of no-fly zones is very limited. It is therefore significant to implement real-time drone detection to give warning accurately in time.

© ICST Institute for Computer Sciences, Social Informatics and Telecommunications Engineering 2018
L. Meng and Y. Zhang (Eds.): MLICOM 2018, LNICST 251, pp. 22–32, 2018.
https://doi.org/10.1007/978-3-030-00557-3_3

Many existing techniques, e.g., radar, radio frequency, acoustic [2–4] and optical sensing techniques can be used for drone detection [5,6]. Because of high detection accuracy and long effective range, video-based detection has attracted many research interests [7,8] and has great potential for drone detection. In our work, we employ video-based detection based on deep learning approach which is a powerful tool in the computer vision area.

Drone detection is essentially an object detection problem. In early years, video-based object detection is by extracting discriminant features such as Local Binary Pattern (LBP) [9], Scale Invariant Feature Transform (SIFT) [10], Histogram of Oriented Gradient (HOG) [11] and Speeded Up Robust Features (SURF) [12] then using these features to train the detector. In 2012, Krizhevsky et al. [13] showed the amazing power of the convolutional neural network (CNN) in the ImageNet grand challenge. Since then, the developments and applications of deep learning methods increase rapidly. There are several variants in CNNs such as the R-CNN [14], SPPNet [15] and Faster-RCNN [16]. Since these networks can generate highly discriminant features, their performances are far beyond the traditional object detection techniques. In 2015, Redmon et al. [17] raised up a new approach of object detection called You Only Look Once (YOLO), which takes object detection as a regression problem with a single neural network. YOLO can achieve very fast detection, i.e., 67 frames per second (FPS) and can realize real-time detection. Moreover, compared with many detectors based on deep learning, YOLO has much lower requirement on computer configuration, which needs normally 4 GB GPU-RAM or even 1GB GPU-RAM for the tiny model. Therefore, we choose YOLO as the model in the detection of drones.

In our work, we develop a drone dataset called Anti-Drone Dataset, including 49 videos. And we use Kernelized Correlation Filters (KCF) tracker [18] to label the videos in the dataset without manually labelling which saves a lot of time and avoids manual errors. Then we improve the traditional YOLO model by adjusting key parameters such as the resolution of input image and the dimension of anchor box. Afterwords, we train the detector using both Anti-Drone Dataset and manually labelled dataset from the Internet and evaluate the detector's performance on these two drone datasets. Apart from that, we deploy our drone detector in Yuquan campus of Zhejiang University and conduct experiments to verify the feasibility of the detector in real world.

The rest of this paper is organized as follows. The drone datasets and labelling method are introduced in Sect. 2. The detection model and its improvement are described in Sect. 3. Experiments are shown in Sect. 4. Conclusion is given in Sect. 5.

## 2   Drone Dataset and Labelling

The establish of drone detector using YOLO requires labelled drone dataset for training. In the following we will introduce the drone datasets and the labelling method.

## 2.1   Drone Dataset

In this paper, we utilize two datasets for training: one is a public-domain drone dataset, the other one is a dataset built by ourselves.

**Public-Domain Drone Dataset.** For our training and testing work, we use a public-domain drone dataset, USC Drone Dataset [19], which consists of 30 YouTube video sequences and captures different drone models with various appearance. And the dataset is rich in diversity with different environments including both indoor and outdoor environments, such as grassland, courtyard, warehouse and so on. Some samples in the dataset is shown in Fig. 1. These video clips have a frame resolution of $1280 \times 720$ and their duration time is about one minute. Some video clips contain more than one drone, while not all of them are marked out. Furthermore, some shoots are discontinuous.

**Fig. 1.** Some samples from USC drone dataset

**Anti-drone Dataset.** A wide variety dataset is one of the essential conditions to training a robust detector based on neural-network. And as the number of existed drone dataset is very limited, we build a dataset and label it. We shoot 49 experimental videos by HIKVISION DS-2DF7330IW Network PTZ camera, as shown in Fig. 2(a). In these videos, there are three drone models, MAVIC PRO, PHANTOM 2 and PHANTOM 4, as shown in Fig. 2(b), (c), (d).

(a) HIK camera    (b) MAVIC PRO   (c) PHANTOM 2   (d) PHANTOM 4

**Fig. 2.** Equipment used in the experiment

The frame resolutions are $2048 \times 1536$ and $1024 \times 768$ respectively in main stream and sub stream. The frame rate is 24 FPS. To shoot these video clips, we consider comprehensively about shooting backgrounds, camera angles and magnifications, weather conditions, day or night. The videos are designed to capture real-world drone attributes such as fast motion, extreme illumination, small size and occultation. Several examples are shown in Fig. 3.

**Fig. 3.** Anti-drone dataset

## 2.2  Dataset Labelling

For drone detection, labelling the drones' locations especially in the videos is a labor intensive and tedious task. And the accuracy is also affected by manual errors. Motivated by the above observations, we use the KCF tracking algorithm to semi-automatically label these videos. The KCF tracker is widely used tracker and achieves very appealing tracking performance both in accuracy and speed because of the introduction of ridge regression and circulant matrix theory, which can efficiently enhance the discriminative ability of correlation filter-based algorithm.

Our basic idea is labelling the drone locations in the first frame and then obtaining next frames automatically by using KCF tracking algorithm. Our goal is to label a large number of videos in a short time with high accuracy. Due to the characteristics of the tracking algorithm, we have cut videos to ensure the drones appear all the time. With this method, we have labelled 60 videos without marking every frame manually and saved a lot of time. And in order to balance the number of videos in different background scenes and shooting conditions, we select the same number of frames for each scenario.

## 3  Real-Time Detection Model

In this section, we present a deep convolution neural network model, YOLOv2 [20], which is the state-of-the-art on standard detection tasks. Then we propose a new model for real-time drone detection by modifying the structure and tuning parameters of YOLOv2, which makes the model better adapt to the drone detection.

## 3.1 YOLOv2

YOLOv2 frames object detection as a regression problem to spatially separate bounding boxes and associate class probabilities, which is different from prior object detection repurposing classifiers to perform detection. YOLOv2 only uses a single neural network to predict bounding boxes and class probabilities directly from the whole image in one round evaluation. Since the whole detection pipeline is a single network, it can be optimized end-to-end directly on detection performance, which makes the detection extremely fast. The flowchart of YOLOv2 is shown in Fig. 4.

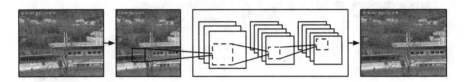

**Fig. 4.** YOLO detection system. (1) resize the input image to $416 \times 416$, (2) run a single convolutional network on the image, (3) threshold the resulting detections by non-max suppression.

**Network Design.** The network in our model is based on Darknet19 [20], which uses mostly $3 \times 3$ filters following with $1 \times 1$ filters for compressing features. The whole network for detection is obtained by removing the last convolutional layer of Darknet19, adding three $3 \times 3$ convolution layers with 1024 filters and $1 \times 1$ convolution layer with 30 filters at the end of network. There is also a passthrough layer from the last $512 \times 3 \times 3$ layer to the last but one convolution layer, which enables the model to have fine grain features, as shown in Fig. 5.

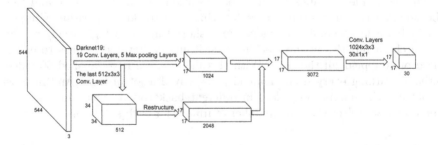

**Fig. 5.** The passthrough layer of the network. We combined the last $512 \times 3 \times 3$ convolution layers with the last but one convolution layer to make the model have fine grain feature.

**Final Prediction of the Network.** YOLOv2 models detection as a regression problem. Firstly, YOLOv2's convolutional layers downsample the image. With a $416 \times 416$ input image, we get an output feature map of $13 \times 13$. Secondly, sliding window sampling is performed on the feature map, and each center predicts $k$ anchor boxes with different sizes and aspect ratios. Thirdly, the anchor box simultaneously predicts the class probability and coordinates. So the prediction should be a $13 \times 13 \times k \times (classes + coordinates + confidence)$ tensor. As drone detector only detects one class object and predicts 5 anchor boxes for every center, the final prediction of model is $13 \times 13 \times 30$ as shown in Fig. 6.

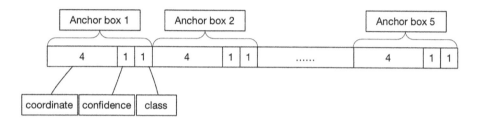

**Fig. 6.** The final prediction of model for drone detection

As shown in Fig. 6, the network predicts 5 bounding boxes at each cell. For each bounding box, it predicts 4 coordinates, $t_x, t_y, t_w, t_h$, and confidence reflecting how confidently the box contains an object and how accurately the box locates.

$$confidence = Pr(Object) \times IOU(box, object) \qquad (1)$$

If no object exists in certain cell, $Pr(Object) = 0$ and $confidence = 0$. Otherwise if an object exists, $Pr(Object) = 1$ and confidence score equal to the IOU between the predicted box and the corresponding cell.

### 3.2 Improvement

**Resize Image.** The purpose of our real-time drone detection is to detect drones for early warning. For the sake of real-time and accurate detection of drones, we resize images to higher resolution to adapt to small objects.

As objects tend to occupy the center of the image, it would be better to have a single location right at the center to predict these objects instead of four locations nearby. So we need an odd number of locations. In the original network of YOLO, the convolutional layers downsample the image by a factor of 32. With a $416 \times 416$ input image, we get an output feature map of $13 \times 13$. Therefore, we modify the network to make the input image resized as $416 \times 416$, $480 \times 480$, $544 \times 544$, $608 \times 608$ or $672 \times 672$, while ensuring an odd number of feature map locations. However, the higher resolution the feature map is, the more time may be spent to detect per image. We evaluate different resolutions with precision and recall, shown in Fig. 7(a). The valid dataset is composed of images with small object which is smaller than $56 \times 32$ in full image of $2048 \times 1536$. And in order to consider both precision and recall, we use $F1\_score$ to value the detection performance.

$$F1\_score = \frac{1}{2}(Precision + Recall) \qquad (2)$$

Processing speed is shown in Fig. 7(b). We choose $544 \times 544$ as a good tradeoff between time complexity and high $F1\_score$.

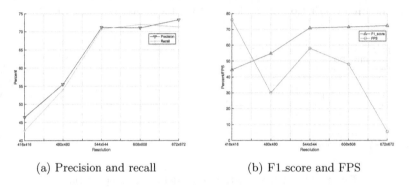

(a) Precision and recall          (b) F1_score and FPS

**Fig. 7.** Resize resolution. We resize input image in different resolution to get better detection performance for small target and guarantee the real-time.

**Anchor Box Prior Dimension.** The second improvement of our model is to adjust the pre-defined anchor box's dimensions to make the network more adaptive to drone detection. We use k-means++ proposed by Arthur et al. [21] to cluster the box dimensions in our dataset. As our goal is to get better IOU scores which is effected by box dimensions and locations, the distance function is

$$d(box, centroid) = 1 - IOU(box, centroid) \qquad (3)$$

We try different numbers of clusters with k-means++ algorithm. The $Avg\_IOU$ corresponding different numbers is shown in Fig. 8. From Fig. 8, we can see that as the amount of clusters increases, the ascension of the curve becomes less. And it is obvious that more anchor boxes means more complex the model is. Therefore, in order to keep balance between model complexity and high recall, we consider that the inflection point of the curve is the optimal number of clusters. We choose $k = 5$ in our detection model and the anchor box dimensions are (3.2896, 3.5241), (0.7357, 0.7050), (7.4209, 5.8418), (1.6510, 1.6501), (11.2494, 11.4231) for $544 \times 544$ feature map.

## 4    Experiments

### 4.1    Experimental Environment

We implement network training and evaluation on a computer server. The configuration of this server is shown in the first three rows of Table 1. And the

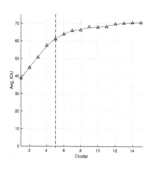 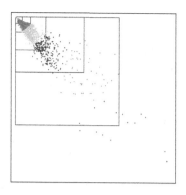

**Fig. 8.** Cluster anchor boxes. We cluster bounding boxes in dataset to get better anchor box dimension priors. The left image shows the curve of average IOU with various numbers for clusters. And the right image shows anchor boxes when $k = 5$.

configuration of our drone detection system is shown in the last three rows of Table 1.

**Table 1.** Experiment platform configuration

| Computer server | GPU | 2 × TITAN X Pascal |
|---|---|---|
| | CPU | 2 × Intel(R) Xeon(R) CPU E5-2640 v4 @ 2.40 GHz |
| | System | 64-bit, Ubuntu 14.04.5 |
| Drone detection system | GPU | NVIDIA GeForce GTX 1050 |
| | CPU | Inter(R) Core(TM) i7-7700K CPU @ 4.20 GHz |
| | System | 64-bit, Windows 10 |

## 4.2   Pre Training

The pre-training of the network is an important part of object detection. But pre-training will cost a lot of time and have high requirements for computer configuration. Therefore, we use the weights of Darknet19 which has been pre-trained with the standard ImageNet 1000 class classification dataset for 160 epochs.

## 4.3   Training for Detection

We train the network using USC Drone Dataset from the Internet and Anti-Drone Dataset labelled by KCF tracker. We divide datasets by 3:1 for training and testing. And we train the network with a starting learning rate of $10^{-3}$ and change it when the iteration step is 100, 25000 or 35000. Then we set momentum weight decay as 0.0005 which prevents overfitting. As attitudes and conditions of drones are varying from moment to moment, we generate new images for training in every iteration with *angle* = 5, *saturation* = 1.5, *exposure* = 1.5, *hue* = .1, which is in order to gain more robust model. These weights are evaluated by precision and recall. The results with different iterations shown in Fig. 9. As the curve shows, we choose the weights when the iteration is 3600 with recall of 85.44% and precision of 88.35%.

## 4.4   Evaluation

We evaluate the detector by the precision-recall curve. Precision is the fraction of detected region proposals which are true positive. Recall is the fraction of true positive which are detected. The effectiveness of KCF labelled dataset is illustrated in Fig. 9. In the figure, we compare the performances of the detector trained by only Public-Domain drone dataset and the detector trained by the dataset which combines the USC Drone Dataset with Anti-Drone Dataset. We can see that when we set the threshold as 0.2, the detector trained by the combined dataset is better than USC only detector. The IOU of the detector trained by the combined dataset is 60.59%, which is however a bit lower than that of USC only (62.44%).

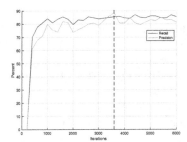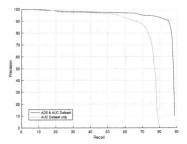

**Fig. 9.** Experiment results. The left figure shows the change of precision and recall as iterations increase. The right figure shows comparison of the drone detector trained by only USC dataset and combined with KCF labelled dataset.

**Verification with Practicality of Detector.** In order to verify that our detector can be used in an actual system while ensuring real-time performance and with low system cost, we implement detector on different GPU-RAM configurations. With GPU-RAM 4 GB, the processing speed is 33 FPS. With GPU-RAM 2 GB, the processing speed can achieve 19 FPS. Although it is a bit slower than the video frame rate (24 FPS), it's still useful as we can detect drones by frame skip. Therefore, our detector can be applied to an actual detection system, which can realize real-time detection with low system cost.

## 5   Conclusion

The video-based real-time drone detection using deep learning approach was implemented in this work. We firstly developed a dataset, which is semi-automatically labelled by KCF tracker instead of manually labelling. Then we improved the YOLOv2 model by modifying the structure with the resolutions of input images and adjusting parameters of the dimension of anchor box. The designed drone detector is trained using both our own Anti-Drone Dataset and the public domain dataset from the Internet. Extensive experiments showed that the detector can achieve real-time detection with high accuracy.

**Acknowledgments.** This work was supported by NSFC under Grant 61772467, Zhejiang Provincial Natural Science Foundation of China under Grant LR16F010002, 973 Project under Grant 2015CB352503, the Fundamental Research Funds for the Central Universities (2017XZZX009-01), and China Postdoctoral Science Foundation funded project.

# References

1. Wargo, C., Snipes, C., Roy, A., Kerczewski, R.: UAS industry growth: forecasting impact on regional infrastructure, environment, and economy. In: 2016 IEEE/AIAA 35th Digital Avionics Systems Conference (DASC), pp. 1–5. IEEE (2016)
2. Chang, X., Yang, C., Wu, J., Shi, X., Shi, Z.: A surveillance system for drone localization and tracking using acoustic arrays. In: 2018 IEEE 87th Vehicular Technology Conference (2018)
3. Chang, X., Yang, C., Shi, X., Li, P., Shi, Z., Chen, J.: Feature extracted DOA estimation algorithm using acoustic array for drone surveillance. In: 2018 10th IEEE Sensor Array and Multichannel Signal Processing Workshop (2018)
4. Yang, C., Wu, Z., Chang, X., Shi, X., Wo, J., Shi, Z.: DOA estimation using amateur drones harmonic acoustic signals. In: 2018 10th IEEE Sensor Array and Multichannel Signal Processing Workshop (2018)
5. Shi, X., Yang, C., Xie, W., Liang, C., Shi, Z., Chen, J.: Anti-drone system with multiple surveillance technologies: architecture, implementation, and challenges. IEEE Commun. Mag. **56**(4), 68–74 (2017)
6. Chen, J., Kang, H., Wang, Q., Sun, Y., Shi, Z., He, S.: Narrowband internet of things: implementations and applications. IEEE Internet Things J. **4**(6), 2309–2314 (2017)
7. Sevil, H.E., Dogan, A., Subbarao, K., Huff, B.: Evaluation of extant computer vision techniques for detecting intruder sUAS. In: 2017 International Conference on Unmanned Aircraft Systems (ICUAS), pp. 929–938. IEEE (2017)
8. Hwang, S., Lee, J., Shin, H., Cho, S., Shim, D.H.: Aircraft detection using deep convolutional neural network in small unmanned aircraft systems. In: 2018 AIAA Information Systems-AIAA Infotech@ Aerospace, p. 2137 (2018)
9. Ojala, T., Pietikainen, M., Harwood, D.: Performance evaluation of texture measures with classification based on kullback discrimination of distributions. In: Proceedings of the 12th IAPR International Conference on Pattern Recognition, 1994. Vol. 1-Conference A: Computer Vision & Image Processing, vol. 1, pp. 582–585. IEEE (1994)
10. Lowe, D.G.: Distinctive image features from scale-invariant keypoints. Int. J. Comput. Vis. **60**(2), 91–110 (2004)
11. Dalal, N., Triggs, B.: Histograms of oriented gradients for human detection. In: CVPR, vol. 1, pp. 886–893. IEEE Computer Society (2005)

12. Bay, H., Ess, A., Tuytelaars, T., Van Gool, L.J.: Speeded-up robust features (SURF). Comput. Vis. Image Underst. **110**(3), 346–359 (2008)
13. Krizhevsky, A., Sutskever, I., Hinton, G.E.: Imagenet classification with deep convolutional neural networks. In: NIPS, pp. 1106–1114 (2012)
14. Girshick, R.B., Donahue, J., Darrell, T., Malik, J.: Rich feature hierarchies for accurate object detection and semantic segmentation. In: CVPR, pp. 580–587. IEEE Computer Society (2014)
15. He, K., Zhang, X., Ren, S., Sun, J.: Spatial pyramid pooling in deep convolutional networks for visual recognition. In: Fleet, D., Pajdla, T., Schiele, B., Tuytelaars, T. (eds.) ECCV 2014. LNCS, vol. 8691, pp. 346–361. Springer, Cham (2014). https://doi.org/10.1007/978-3-319-10578-9_23
16. Ren, S., He, K., Girshick, R., Sun, J.: Faster R-CNN: towards real-time object detection with region proposal networks. In: NIPS, pp. 91–99 (2015)
17. Redmon, J., Divvala, S.K., Girshick, R.B., Farhadi, A.: You only look once: unified, real-time object detection. In: CVPR, pp. 779–788. IEEE Computer Society (2016)
18. Henriques, J.F., Caseiro, R., Martins, P., Batista, J.: High-speed tracking with kernelized correlation filters. IEEE Trans. Pattern Anal. Mach. Intell. **37**(3), 583–596 (2015)
19. Usc drone dataset. https://chelicynly.github.io/Drone-Project/
20. Redmon, J., Farhadi, A.: YOLO9000: better, faster, stronger. In: CVPR, pp. 6517–6525. IEEE Computer Society (2017)
21. Arthur, D., Vassilvitskii, S.: k-means++: the advantages of careful seeding. In: SODA, pp. 1027–1035. SIAM (2007)

# Deep Reinforcement Learning-Based Task Offloading and Resource Allocation for Mobile Edge Computing

Liang Huang, Xu Feng$^{(\boxtimes)}$, Liping Qian, and Yuan Wu

College of Information Engineering, Zhejiang University of Technology,
Hangzhou 310023, China
{lianghuang,lpqian,iewuy}@zjut.edu.cn, xfeng_zjut@163.com

**Abstract.** We consider a mobile edge computing system that every user has multiple tasks being offloaded to edge server via wireless networks. Our goal is to acquire a satisfactory task offloading and resource allocation decision for each user so as to minimize energy consumption and delay. In this paper, we propose a deep reinforcement learning-based approach to solve joint task offloading and resource allocation problems. Simulation results show that the proposed deep Q-learning-based algorithm can achieve near-optimal performance.

**Keywords:** Mobile edge computing · Deep reinforcement learning
Task offloading · Resource allocation · Deep Q-learning

## 1 Introduction

Mobile edge computing (MEC) provides a distributed computing environment for mobile users [1], such that users are able to offload their computing tasks to MEC servers. When tasks are offloaded, users can obtain higher quality of service (QoS) the adequate cloud resources. But when users offload their tasks to the cloud, the quality of service will be interfered because of the existence of communication delay.

Offloading data to the MEC system is convenient for mobile devices. [2] investigated data offloading from mobile devices to MEC system and proposes a coalitional game-based pricing scheme. A reformulation-linearization-technique-based branch-and-bound (RLTBB) method is proposed in [3] to minimize the energy consumption on mobile devices. When there are two mobile devices energized by wireless power transfer (WPT) in MEC system, [4] minimized the total transmit energy of access point (AP) by a two-phase method. Multi-user MEC systems with one task per user are addressed in [5] and [6]. [7] proposed an advanced algorithm multi-user multi-task offloading (MUMTO) to solve joint offloading decision and resource allocation in multi-user multi-tasking mobile edge computing system.

© ICST Institute for Computer Sciences, Social Informatics and Telecommunications Engineering 2018
L. Meng and Y. Zhang (Eds.): MLICOM 2018, LNICST 251, pp. 33–42, 2018.
https://doi.org/10.1007/978-3-030-00557-3_4

To minimize the weighted sum of the costs of computation and communication energies as well as transmission and processing delays, we concentrate on searching the optimal offloading decision and resource allocation for all users. Specifically, we propose a deep reinforcement approach, which is an enhanced version of Q-learning. We use deep Q network on behalf of Q value-action function [8]. Deep Q network has already been also used in the cache-enabled opportunistic IA wireless networks [9]. With this advanced reinforcement learning algorithm, the almost optimal binary offloading decision and resource allocation will be found all at once. Simulation results show that the reinforcement learning-based algorithm obtains the almost optimal offloading decision and resource allocation under varieties of parameter settings.

The rest of this paper is organized as follows. In Sect. 2, system model and problem formulation are presented. Deep Q network algorithm is presented in Sect. 3. In Sect. 4, simulation results are discussed. Finally, we present conclusions in Sect. 5.

## 2 System Model and Problem Formulation

### 2.1 Mobile Edge Offloading

We consider an ordinary cloud access network composed by one AP, one edge server and $N$ mobile users, where each user has $M$ independent tasks. The AP is wired to the edge server, and mobile users are connected to the edge server by wireless channels. The system model is shown in Fig. 1. Every task of each user can be processed locally or offloaded to the edge server. Let $x_{nm}$ denote the offloading decision of task $m$ of user $n$, where $x_{nm} = 0$ denotes that task $m$ of user $n$ is processed locally and $x_{nm} = 1$ denotes that task $m$ of user $n$ is offloaded.

### 2.2 Cost of Remote Processing

The input data size of task $m$ of user $n$ is denoted by $L_{nm}^{d}$ while the output data size is denoted by $L_{nm}^{u}$. When mobile users offload their tasks to the edge server, the energy consumption of task $m$ of user $n$ is divided into two parts, data transmission and receiving, which are denoted by $E_{nm}^{t}$ and $E_{nm}^{r}$, respectively. For the wireless transmission among mobile users and the edge server, we denote the uplink and downlink bandwidths assigned to user $n$ by $C_n^u$ and $C_n^d$. The uplink transmission time is denoted by $T_{nm}^{u} = L_{nm}^{u}/C_n^u$, accordingly, and the downlink transmission time is denoted by $T_{nm}^{d} = L_{nm}^{d}/C_n^d$. The values of $C_n^u$ and $C_n^d$ are limited by the abilities of the corresponding wireless links, and the total uplink and downlink bandwidths are denoted by $C^U$ and $C^D$, respectively.

The cloud processing time is denoted by

$$T_{nm}^{C} = \frac{L_{nm}^{d} N_{nm}^{C}}{f^c} \tag{1}$$

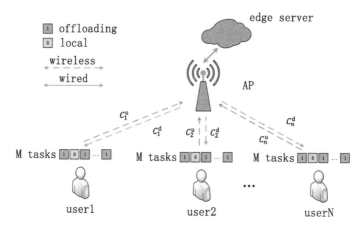

**Fig. 1.** System model

The cloud processing rate $f^c$ is pre-fixed for every user. The size of $T_{nm}^C$ only lies on the size of each task of mobile users. In this paper, $N_{nm}^C$ denotes the number of processing cycles for every input data. When some or all tasks of user $n$ are offloaded to the remote cloud, the system utility cost is denoted by $C_{nm}^c$. Because of the overlaps in the time of communication and processing, for making it acceptable, the offloading decision is set to be the offloading delay. Thus, we first provide the worst-case delay formulation:

$$T_n^W \triangleq \sum_{m=1}^{M} \left(T_{nm}^u + T_{nm}^d + T_{nm}^C\right) x_{nm}, \forall n, \tag{2}$$

which is a summation of all delays of transmission and processing.

### 2.3 Cost of Local Processing

When task $m$ of user $n$ is decided to be processed locally, the corresponding energy consumption per data bit is denoted by $e_l$. Therefore, the energy consumption of task $m$ of user $n$ is denoted by $E_{nm}^l = L_{nm}^d e_l$, where the local processing time per data bit is denoted by $t_l$. Thus, the processing time consumption of task $m$ of user $n$ is denoted by $T_{nm}^l = (L_{nm}^d + L_{nm}^u)t_l$.

### 2.4 Problem Formulation

We aim to reduce the total energy cost and keep the quality of service of every user at the same time. Our objective is to minimize the weighted sum of the costs of computation and communication energies as well as transmission and processing delays. The optimization problem is given as follows:

$$\min_{x_{nm}, C_n^u, C_n^d} \sum_{n=1}^{N} \left[ \sum_{m=1}^{M} (E_{nm}^l(1 - x_{nm}) + E_{nm}^c x_{nm}) + \omega_n \max\{T_n^L, T_n^W\} \right], \quad (3)$$

$$\text{subject to: } \sum_{n=1}^{N} C_n^u \leq C^U, \tag{4}$$

$$\sum_{n=1}^{N} C_n^d \leq C^D, \tag{5}$$

$$C_n^u, C_n^d, \geq 0, \forall n, \tag{6}$$

$$x_{nm} \in \{0, 1\}, \forall n, m, \tag{7}$$

where

$$E_{nm}^c \triangleq (E_{nm}^t + E_{nm}^r + \lambda C_{nm}^c), \tag{8}$$

and

$$T_n^L \triangleq \sum_{m=1}^{M} T_{nm}^l(1 - x_{nm}). \tag{9}$$

In the formula above, $E_{nm}^c$ is the weighted sum of transmission energy, receiving energy, and system utility cost when task $m$ of user $n$ is offloaded to the remote cloud. $\lambda$ is the corresponding weight, $T_n^L$ is the processing delay when task $m$ of user $n$ is processed locally, and $\omega_n$ is the weight between energy consumption and processing delay in the whole system cost. The uplink and downlink bandwidth are limited by constraints (2) and (3).

It is difficult to solve the mixed-integer programming problem in (3) in a general way. In the next section, we propose a reinforcement learning algorithm based on deep Q network.

## 3   Deep Reinforcement Learning

### 3.1   Deep Q Network

Reinforcement learning is a machine learning algorithm, composed by an environment and an agent. The agent is a brain, which selects the most appropriate action from the state given by the environment. The role of the environment is to generate the state of the next step and the reward generated after the action is taken by the agent. Then, the agent updates its parameters according to the reward, so as to improve its prediction accuracy. Deep Q network is an advanced reinforcement learning algorithm, which is evolved from Q-learning, by replacing the Q table of Q-learning with a deep neural network. It can solve complex problems with lager state space. The Q-function is updated as:

$$Q^\theta(s_t, a) = r(s_t, a) + \gamma \max Q'(s_{t+1}, a'; \theta'), \tag{10}$$

where $s_t$ is the system state at time shot $t$, and $r(s_t, a)$ is the reward after the agent choices action $a$ at state $s_t$. $Q^\theta(s_t, a)$ is the Q value under selecting action $a$ at state $s_t$. The larger $Q^\theta(s_t, a)$ is, the more reward to taking action $a$ in its current state $s_t$.

## 3.2 Formulation of the Network's Optimization Problem

In our system, there are $N$ mobile users, each with $M$ tasks, and each task can be offloaded to the remote server. Each user's task size is different. When the task is offloaded to the remote server, the corresponding speed may be different, and there is a limit to their uplink and downlink direction. To minimize energy consumption, we use deep Q network to find the almost optimal offloading decision $x_{nm}$ of task $m$ of user $n$ as well as resource allocation $C_n^u$ and $C_n^d$ of user $n$. $x_{nm}$, $C_n^u$ and $C_n^d$ are programmed into the system state as input for Q network. The output of the Q network is the Q value of the corresponding action. Each time the agent chooses the appropriate action with respect to the Q value. The execution result of the action is to make corresponding adjustment to offloading decision $x_{nm}$ and resource allocation $C_n^u$ and $C_n^d$.

In deep Q network, there are two networks, specifically, an evaluation network and a target network. Their inputs are the current state and the next state after the action execution respectively. The output of the target network that has been modified by reward will be used as a label of evaluation network. Then, a gradient descent algorithm is applied to the error between them. By continuously reducing the error and updating the parameters of the evaluation network, it can predict more accurately. The structures of the evaluation network and the target network are completely consistent but with different parameters. After every other $N$ cycles, all the parameters of evaluation network will be assigned to the target network to cut off the relevance between them.

There is a replay memory structure in the deep Q network. The system records a memory $(s_t, a_t, r_t, s_{t+1})$ every step after performing an action. During the network training, a small batch of memory is extracted from the memory pool, so that the Q network can learn the previous experience. An $\varepsilon$-greedy policy is used to determine the intensity of exploration and learning, i.e., how likely it is to take advantage of existing knowledge or to try new actions. The training process of deep Q network is described in Algorithm 1.

In order to get the optimal offloading decision and resource allocation, we need to appropriately design the system state, action and reward mechanism, which are described below:

**System State.** The current state of the system $x(t)$ represents the location of the agent, determined by the state of $N$ users and their $M$ tasks. The system state at time slot $t$ is defined as,

$$s(t) = \{x_{11}(t), x_{12}(t) \ldots x_{ij}(t) \ldots x_{NM}(t), C_1^u(t), C_1^d(t) \ldots C_l^u(t),$$
$$C_l^d(t) \ldots C_N^u(t), C_N^d(t)\} \tag{11}$$

The system state is consisted of two parts, offloading decision $x_{nm}$ of task $m$ of user $n$ and resource allocation $C_n^u$ and $C_n^d$ of user $n$. The offloading decision $x_{ij}(t) \in \{0,1\}$, where $i = 1, 2, \ldots N$, $j = 1, 2, \ldots M$. The subscript $l$ stands for the $l$th user, and $l = 1, 2, \ldots N$. The number of system states is proportional to the number of users. When the number of system states is very large, the advantage of replacing Q-function with Q network emerges.

**System Action.** Each action of the system determines which of the user's tasks are processed in the remote server, and what are their speed assignments when they are processed in the remote server. The selected action $a(t)$ of the agent is denoted by

$$a(t) = \{a_1(t), a_2(t) \ldots a_k(t) \ldots a_{NM}(t), a_1(t), a_2(t) \ldots a_g(t) \ldots a_{2N}(t)\} \quad (12)$$

We first pull all the tasks in the system into one dimension. $a_k(t)$ represents the decision of the $k$th task i.e., $a_k(t) = 1$ represents processing in the remote server, and $a_k(t) = 0$ represents local processing. $a_g(t)$ represents the speed distribution when processing in the remote server. Speed adjustment is achieved by stride, they meet the condition $\sum_{g=1}^{N} a_g(t) \leq C_U$ when the action adjusts the uplink speed. This restriction also occurs when the downlink speed is adjusted.

**Reward Function.** System rewards represent our optimization goals. We save the calculation result $S_{t-1}$ of formula (4) with the current parameter, before executing the action. After executing the action, we get the latest calculation result $S_t$, if $S_t$ is smaller than $S_{t-1}$ we give a positive reward $r(t) = +1$, if $S_t$ is bigger than $S_{t-1}$ we give a negative reward $r(t) = -1$, otherwise, $r(t) = 0$. This allows the agent to constantly search the optimal offloading decision and resource allocation to minimize total energy consumption.

## 4    Performance Evaluation

We use TensorFlow to evaluate the performance of deep reinforcement learning. Then, Matlab is used to demonstrate greedy algorithm performance. We assume that the number of mobile users $N = 5$, and the number of tasks for each user $M = 4$. Detailed parameters for reinforcement learning are listed in Table 1. We set the local computation time of the mobile device as $4.75 \times 10^{-7}$ s/bit, and processing energy consumption as $3.25 \times 10^{-7}$ J/bit. We assume that the input data size of all tasks is randomly distributed between 10MB and 30MB, and the output data size is randomly distributed between 1MB and 3MB.

In the simulations, we set both the uplink bandwidth and the downlink bandwidth limit between the user and the edge server as 150 Mbps. The receiving energy consumptions and transmission energy consumptions of the mobile device are both $1.42 \times 10^{-7}$ J/bit. The CPU rate of remote cloud sever is $10 \times 10^9$

**Table 1.** Parameter values used in the simulations

| Parameter | Value | Description |
|---|---|---|
| Episode | 4000 | Number of main cycles |
| Replay memory size | 2000 | The size of memory pool |
| Frequency of learning | 5 | How often the training step is performed |
| Mini-batch size | 32 | How many memories are used for each training step |
| Learning rate | 0.0001 | The learning rate of Adam optimizer |
| Reward decay | 0.9 | The degree of emphasis of previous experience |
| $\varepsilon$-greedy increment | 0.005 | The growth rate of $\varepsilon$-greedy at every training step |
| Max $\varepsilon$-greedy | 0.9 | The maximum of $\varepsilon$-greedy |
| Target network update frequency | 50 | How many steps the target network is updated |
| Pre-training steps | 200 | How many memories are stored before the training begins |

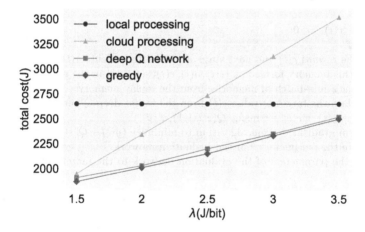

**Fig. 2.** The total cost under different $\lambda$ (J/bit)

cycle/s. When a mobile user's task is offloaded to the cloud, the system utility cost is denoted by

$$C_n^c = D_n^d + \frac{\varphi_1}{f^c} + \frac{\varphi_2}{C^U} + \frac{\varphi_3}{C^D} \qquad (13)$$

where $\varphi_1 = 10^{18}$bit×cycle/s and $\varphi_2 = \varphi_3 = 10^{16}$bit×bps. We further set $\lambda = 2.5 \times 10^{-7}$ J/bit, and $\omega_n = 1$ J/s refer to [7].

We compare the proposed algorithm with local processing only algorithm, cloud processing only algorithm, and greedy algorithm. The local processing only

**Algorithm 1. Deep reinforcement learning algorithm in task offloading and resource allocation**

---

1: **Initialization:**
2:    Initialize the evaluation and target Q network parameters with $\theta$.
3:    Initialize replay memory.
4: **for** episode $k \leq 1, 2, \ldots, K$ **do**
5:    **if** $mod(k, 100) == 0$ **then**
6:        Change the initialization to the current best result.
7:    **end if**
8:    Choose a random probability number $p$.
9:    **if** $p < \varepsilon$ **then**
10:        $a^*(t) = arg \max_a Q(s, a; \theta)$.
11:    **else**
12:        Choose $a(t)$ randomly.
13:    **end if**
14:    Calculate $S_t$ according to (3)
15:    **if** $S_t < S_{t+1}$ **then**
16:        Set $r(t) = 1$
17:    **else if** $S_t > S_{t+1}$ **then**
18:        Set $r(t) = -1$
19:    **else**
20:        Set $r(t) = 0$
21:    **end if**
22:    Get the reward $r(t)$ and next state $s(t + 1)$ after execute $a(t)$.
23:    Save this memory formed as $(s(t), a(t), r(t), s(t + 1))$ in the replay memory.
24:    Extract a min-batch of memories from the replay memory.
25:    Calculate the target Q-value $y(t)$ from the target deep-Q network,
$$y(t) = r(t) + \gamma \max_{a'} \hat{Q}(s(t + 1), a'; \theta^-).$$
26:    Perform gradient descent algorithm to minimize $(y(t) - Q(s(t), a(t); \theta))^2$.
27:    Update the parameters $\theta$ of the evaluation network.
28:    Copy the parameters of the evaluation network to the target network, every $S$ step.
29: **end for**

---

method means that all user tasks are processed locally. The cloud processing only method processes all user tasks in the cloud. The greedy algorithm means that all the offloading decision combinations are enumerated to select the optimal policy. Greedy method is time-consuming, but the optimal solution can be found. In our simulations, each simulation result is obtained through 100 repetitions, but the data size of each input and output is randomly generated.

The system total cost under different weights $\lambda$ is shown in Fig. 2. The deep reinforcement learning algorithm can get the almost optimal solution, where the gap between the deep reinforcement learning and greedy algorithm is very small. As $\lambda$ increases, all user tasks tend to be processed locally.

The performance of the system cost with different learning rate is plotted in Fig. 3. Convergence process is faster when the learning rate is 0.001, compared

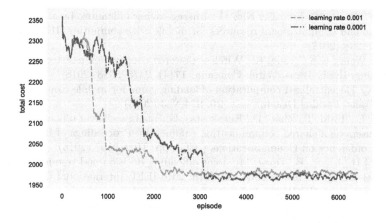

**Fig. 3.** Convergence performance under different learning rate

to the case when the learning rate is 0.0001. However, when the learning rate increases, it is more possible to find the local optimal solution instead of the global optimal. Hence, we need to choose an appropriate learning rate with respect to dedicated situations.

## 5   Conclusion

In a mobile edge computing system that every user has multiple tasks being offloaded to edge server via wireless networks, all users occupy the common communication resource when their tasks are offloaded. In order to minimize the total consumption of computation and communication energies cost, and transmission delays between mobile users and AP as well as processing delays on local devices and could, we use deep reinforcement learning to find the near optimal offloading decision and resource allocation. Compared with greedy algorithm, reinforcement learning method can find an almost optimal solution.

**Acknowledgments.** This work was supported in part by the National Natural Science Foundation of China under Grant 61572440 and Grant 61502428, in part by the Zhejiang Provincial Natural Science Foundation of China under Grants LR17F010002 and LR16F010003, in part by the Young Talent Cultivation Project of Zhejiang Association for Science and Technology under Grant 2016YCGC011.

## References

1. Liu, J., Zhang, Q.: Offloading schemes in mobile edge computing for ultra-reliable low latency communications. IEEE Access **6**, 12825–12837 (2018)
2. Zhang, T.: Data offloading in mobile edge computing: a coalition and pricing based approach. IEEE Access **6**, 2760–2767 (2018)

3. Zhao, P., Tian, H., Qin, C., Nie, G.: Energy-saving offloading by jointly allocating radio and computational resources for mobile edge computing. IEEE Access **5**, 11255–11268 (2017)
4. Hu, X., Wong, K.K., Yang, K.: Wireless powered cooperation-assisted mobile edge computing. IEEE Trans. Wirel. Commun. **17**(4), 2375–2388 (2018)
5. Chen, X.: Decentralized computation offloading game for mobile cloud computing. IEEE Trans. Parallel Distrib. Syst. **26**, 974–983 (2015)
6. Meskar, E., Todd, T., Zhao, D., Karakostas, G.: Energy efficient offloading for competing users on a shared communication channel. In: Proceedings of IEEE International Conference on Communications (ICC), pp. 3192–3197 (2015)
7. Chen, M.H., Liang, B., Dong, M.: Joint offloading decision and resource allocation for multi-user multi-task mobile cloud. In: 2016 IEEE International Conference on Communications (ICC), Kuala Lumpur, pp. 1–6 (2016)
8. Mnih, V., Kavukcuoglu, K., et al.: Human-level control through deep reinforcement learning. Nature **518**(7540), 529–533 (2015)
9. He, Y., et al.: Deep-reinforcement-learning-based optimization for cache-enabled opportunistic interference alignment wireless networks. IEEE Trans. Veh. Technol. **66**(11), 10433–10445 (2017)

# RFID Data-Driven Vehicle Speed Prediction Using Adaptive Kalman Filter

Anqi Feng$^{(\boxtimes)}$, Liping Qian, and Yupin Huang

College of Information Engineering, Zhejiang University of Technology,
Hangzhou 310023, China
aqfeng_zjut@163.com, lpqian@zjut.edu.cn, yphuang_zjut@163.com

**Abstract.** This paper focuses on the design of radio frequency identification (RFID) data-driven vehicle speed prediction method using adaptive Kalman filtering. First of all, when the vehicle moves through a RFID tag, the reader needs to acquire the state information (i.e., current speed and time stamp) of the last vehicle across the tag, and meanwhile transmits its state information to this tag. Then, the state space model can be formulated according to the acquired state information. Finally, the adaptive Kalman filtering algorithm is proposed to predict and adjust the speed of vehicles. Adaptive Kalman filtering algorithm achieves the adaptive updating of variable forgetting factor by analyzing the error between the expected output value and the actual output value, so as to achieve the online updating of the prediction model. The numerical results further show that compared with the conventional Kalman filtering algorithm, the proposed algorithm can increase the speed prediction accuracy by 20%. This implies that the proposed algorithm can provide the better real-time effectiveness for the practical implementation.

**Keywords:** Speed prediction · RFID · Data acquisition · Adaptive Kalman filter

## 1 Introduction

Nowadays, with the increasing popularity of vehicles, the vehicle driving is suffering serious traffic problems, such as traffic road congestion, road traffic collision and road traffic incidents, et al. At present, drivers often rely on personal driving experience and visual responses evaluate the driving state of the front vehicle, but there is still visual blind area and experience error phenomenon. In order to alleviate traffic pressure and reduce the incidence of accidents, it is of practical importance to improve the driving safety by accurately predicting the speed of vehicles.

Currently, the main way to get the running speed of vehicles is based on laser velocity measurement [1], radar speed measurement [2], ultrasonic speed measurement [3–5], visual speed measurement [6], or GPS speed measurement [7,8]. All of the above methods are performed in the context of wireless communication. They are mainly applied to traffic intensive areas, traffic accident

© ICST Institute for Computer Sciences, Social Informatics and Telecommunications Engineering 2018
L. Meng and Y. Zhang (Eds.): MLICOM 2018, LNICST 251, pp. 43–51, 2018.
https://doi.org/10.1007/978-3-030-00557-3_5

prone areas, urban central areas, parking lots, and crossroads. In these places, the speed of vehicle is predicted in real time through wireless sensing to avoid traffic accidents. However, when applied to complex terrain roads (e.g., U/Z shaped roads), there will be a lot of prediction errors. In the U/Z-shaped Road, there will be no vehicle in front of the rear vehicle to be scanned in the turn, and thus the wrong judgment leads to the occurrence of traffic accidents. Also, in the complex terrain roads, it is unrealistic to make the network stable communication. This implies that in some roads, vehicle communication may be delayed or even fails. To this end, a method based on radio frequency identification (RFID) is proposed in this paper.

As a new wireless communication technology, the RFID system consists of three parts: the RFID tag, the reader and the antenna. When the vehicle runs in the RFID environment, the wireless radio frequency method is used to carry out non-contact and bidirectional data transmission between the reader and the tag, in order to achieve target identification and data exchange. At present, RFID technology has been applied in many fields, such as automatic train identification management [9], automatic identification, sorting, transport management of aviation passenger baggage [10], highway toll and intelligent transportation system [11], taxi management, bus hub management [12] and railway locomotive identification system etc [13]. With the rapid development of RFID technology, the traffic management, traffic flow and vehicle safety have been guaranteed.

In different traffic scenario, different communication systems and modeling methods will make the speed prediction results diverse. The authors in [14] proposed a method of measuring and maintaining vehicle road distance based on RFID system. The simulation results show that the system can achieve high safety level while maintaining the comfort of the driver. A tracking and location algorithm of wMPS system based on small multiplier Kalman filter was proposed in [15], which reduced the nonlinear error and improved the accuracy of tracking and positioning in motion. According to [16], a vehicle speed prediction method based on Fuzzy Markovian model and autoregressive model was proposed to solve the vehicle fuel control design problem. This method poses some advantages in state recognition mapping, resolution elimination, dimensionality reduction, and improvement of prediction accuracy.

This paper focuses on the design of RFID data-driven vehicle speed prediction method using adaptive Kalman filter for inferior or complex roads, such as tunnels, caves and high bridges. The method combines the known environmental characteristics and equidistant distribution of data in a certain number of data acquisition points, that is, RFID tags. The RFID tags are placed on the surface of the road to store vehicle status information (i.e., current speed and times tamp). Then, the vehicle reader uses radio frequency to read the vehicle information from the tag and feedback its state information to the tag. Finally, the vehicle uses adaptive Kalman filter with variable forgetting factor to update the vehicle speed estimation. Adaptive Kalman filtering algorithm achieves the adaptive updating of variable forgetting factor by analyzing the error between the expected output value and the actual output value, so as to achieve the online updating of the prediction model. Through the simulation analysis, it can be seen that compared with the conventional Kalman filter method, the proposed method is better to reduce the error and improve the accuracy.

The rest of this paper is organized as follows. In Sect. 2, we describe the system framework and model establishment. Speed prediction algorithm based on adaptive Kalman filter is presented in Sect. 3. The simulation results and analysis are presented in Sect. 4. Finally, Sect. 5 concludes the paper.

## 2   System Framework and Model Establishment

### 2.1   System Framework

The RFID system is deployed on the pavement of tunnels, caves and bridge roads that GPS signals cannot cover. It consists of three parts: the RFID tag, the reader and the antenna. The corresponding RFID system model is shown in Fig. 1.

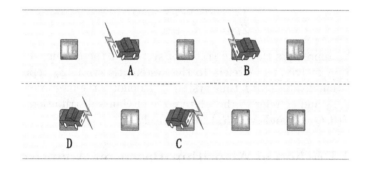

**Fig. 1.** RFID system model (Color figure online)

In Fig. 1, the block on the road is the RFID tag, which identifies the vehicle attached to it and stores the related state information of the vehicle. The vehicle front bumper equipped with the reader (two pieces of red blocks in front of the car), which is used to read the state information from the tag, and write the own state information to the tag. Antenna (yellow lightning) is used to achieve target recognition and data exchange, so that drivers can know the relevant state information of vehicles ahead of time, and better take safety measures.

The speed prediction of vehicles based on adaptive Kalman filter in RFID environment works as follows: ① the vehicle uses the logo of the RFID tag as well as the reading and writing of the reader to effectuate the data collection; ② the speed of vehicle is predicted by adaptive Kalman filter algorithm; ③ the velocity prediction value is corrected to make the velocity prediction close to the true value.

## 2.2  System Modeling

The RFID system consists of high-speed vehicles and a number of RFID tags (passive tags) deployed by a large line equidistant. Considering the RFID system set up on the roads, tunnels and bridge roads, the speed of vehicles basically the same, so the formula for displacement and speed are denoted by:

$$x_k = x_{k-1} + v_{k-1}\Delta(t) \tag{1}$$

$$v_k = v_{k-1} \tag{2}$$

Where $x_k$ denotes the displacement of the vehicle at $k$ time, $\Delta(t)$ denotes sample time interval, $v_k$ denotes the vehicle speed at $k$ time. In the static RFID system, the high-speed vehicle as the research target. When the vehicle arriving at the $X_k$ of each state, each tag can establish relatively efficient data transmission with it [17]. After the completion of the data transfer, we can obtain the vehicle speed $v_k$ and sample time $t_k$. Then, the above calculation formula (1) (2) are transformed into a state space model. Therefore, the equation of state and the measurement equation in the RFID system can be expressed as:

$$X_k = AX_{k-1} + \omega_{k-1} \tag{3}$$

$$Z_k = CX_k + \epsilon_k \tag{4}$$

Where $X_k$ represents the state vector of system at the $k$ time, $A$ and $C$ are state transition matrix, $\omega_{k-1}$ refers to the systematic error, $Z_k$ represents the state observational values for $k$ time systems, $\epsilon_k$ denotes the measurement error. Note that, $\omega_{k-1}$ and $\epsilon_k$ refer to the white noise of Gauss distribution, which are subject to $N(0, Q_{k-1})$ and $N(0, R_k)$, respectively.

# 3  Speed Prediction Algorithm Based on Adaptive Kalman Filter

In this paper, the adaptive forgetting factor $\mu_k$ is introduced on the basis of the time updating of the conventional Kalman filter algorithm. It changes the value of the error covariance matrix $\overline{P}_k$ when the time updated, thus enhancing the influence of the current data and keeping the data in the latest state. At the same time, according to the state equation and the measurement equation, an improved Kalman filter algorithm, namely the adaptive Kalman filter algorithm [18,19], is established. The improved Kalman filter algorithm:

(1) Time update (prediction stage)
  ① The state value $\overline{X}_k$ of the $k$ time is predicted by the modified state value $X_{k-1}$ of the $k-1$ time

$$\overline{P}_k = AX_{k-1} \tag{5}$$

② The error covariance matrix $\overline{P}_k$ of the $k$ time is predicted by the modified error covariance matrix $P_{k-1}$ of the $k-1$ time

$$\overline{P}_k = \mu_k AP_{k-1}A^T + Q \tag{6}$$

(2) Measurement update (correction stage)

① Calculation of Kalman gain $K_k$ based on the error covariance $\overline{P}_k$ of the $k$ time prediction and the measurement noise $R$

$$K_k = \overline{P}_k C^T (C\overline{P}_k C^T + R)^{-1} \tag{7}$$

② Introduce the state observation value $Z_k$ of the system, then obtain the optimal state value $X_k$ of the current time with using the state value $\overline{X}_k$ of the $k$ time prediction.

$$X_k = \overline{X}_k + K_k(Z_k - C\overline{X}_k) \tag{8}$$

③ Update the error covariance, get the $P_k$ value, prepare for the new error covariance at the next time.

$$P_k = (I + K_k C)\overline{P}_k \tag{9}$$

where the defined parameters [20] are shown in Table 1.

**Table 1.** Variables used by adaptive Kalman filter algorithm

| | |
|---|---|
| $Q$ | Covariance matrix of system noise |
| $R$ | Covariance matrix of measurement noise |
| $\overline{X}_k$ | The priori estimate of state at $k$ time |
| $X_k$ | The posterior estimate of state at $k$ time |
| $\overline{P}_k$ | The priori estimated error covariance matrix for $k$ time |
| $P_k$ | The posterior estimated error covariance matrix for $k$ time |
| $Z_k$ | Observation sample value at $k$ time |
| $K_k$ | Kalman gain at $k$ time |
| $A, C$ | State transition matrix |
| $I$ | Unitary matrix |
| $\mu_k$ | Adaptive forgetting factor |

In the RFID environment, the dynamic requirement is very high for the high-speed vehicles. Therefore, when the parameters change little, we use a larger adaptive forgetting factor $\mu_k$ to increase the intensity of the prediction. When the parameters vary greatly, the small adaptive forgetting factor is used to enhance the identification accuracy. The formula for the adaptive forgetting factor is used in this paper as follows:

$$\mu_k = \max\{1, tr(G_k)/tr(H_k)\} \tag{10}$$

$$G_k = M_k - CQC^T - R \tag{11}$$

$$M_k = \begin{cases} 0.5e_k e_k^T, & k = 1 \\ \frac{\mu_{k-1} e_k e_k^T}{1 + \mu_{k-1}}, & k > 1 \end{cases} \tag{12}$$

$$e_k = Z_k - C\overline{X}_k \tag{13}$$

$$H_k = CAP_{k-1}A^T C^T \tag{14}$$

With the increase of driving distance, the new error $e_k$ becomes bigger and bigger. While introducing the adaptive forgetting factor $\mu_k$, it can reduce the error between observation value and prediction value. At the same time, $\overline{P}_k$ value satisfies symmetry and positive definite, improving the dynamic performance of the system. The process of speed prediction operation for high-speed mobile vehicles based on adaptive Kalman filter in the RFID environment as follows:

---

**Algorithm. The steps of vehicle speed prediction based on adaptive Kalman filter**

---

1: **Initialization:**
   Initialize state transition matrix $A$ and $C$.
   Initialize covariance matrix $P_{k-1}$, $Q$, $R$.
   Initialize adaptive forgetting factor $\mu_{k-1}$.
2: **Collect initial data $v_{k-1}$ and $t_{k-1}$**
3: **Update adaptive forgetting factor $\mu_k$**
4: **Time update:**
   Calculate the state prediction value $\overline{X}_k$.
   Calculate the error covariance matrix $\overline{P}_k$.
5: **Measurement update:**
   Calculate Kalman gain $K_k$ for the first moment.
   Introduce the state observation value $Z_k$.
   Calculate the optimal velocity $X_k$.
   Update the error covariance matrix $P_k$.
6: **Next sample:**
   let $K = K + 1$, repeat the above operation step 2.3.4, until the vehicle driven out of the RFID system.

---

## 4   Simulation Results

In this paper, the simulation experiment is carried out by using MATLAB. The simulation environment is set to a tunnel road with a length of 0.5 km, as well as 75 linear isometric distribution of RFID tags on the surface of the road. According to the national standards of highway tunnel speed and safe distance, the safe distance is set to 100 m. At the same time, according to scientific knowledge: The nerve response time of normal people is 0.3–0.5 s; The effective time of braking is 1.2–1.5 s [21,22]. So it is set in the vehicle speed relatively constant to 80 km/h forward, and in the course of the driving process every 0.3 s to carry out a communication with RFID tag, to achieve data exchange. It is assumed that the initial state of the iterative estimate is $(0, 80/3.6)^T$.

**Speed Prediction Results Analysis:** Figures 2 and 3 shows the vehicle speed prediction results using the conventional Kalman filter and adaptive Kalman filter, respectively. It can be seen that in comparison with conventional Kalman filter (KF), adaptive Kalman filter (AKF) is expected to provide the better real-time effectiveness. The "blue dotted line" denotes the actual running speed of vehicles, and the "red real line" denotes the estimated running speed of vehicles based on the filtering method. According to the comparison of the two lines, the more close the "blue dotted line" and the "red line" position, it shows that the speed of the method is better.

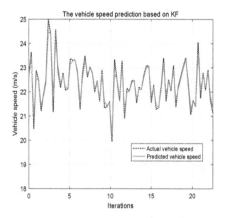

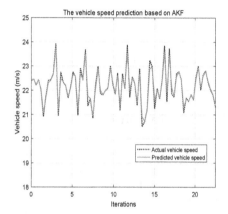

**Fig. 2.** Speed prediction effect of Kalman filter (Color figure online)

**Fig. 3.** Speed prediction effect of adaptive Kalman filter (Color figure online)

**Speed Error Results Analysis:** In the simulation experiment, the actual operation speed of vehicles and the estimated speed are calculated to observe the speed error of the vehicle passing through each RFID tag. Thus, the Kalman filtering algorithm and the adaptive Kalman filtering algorithm are compared to analyze the error results. The vehicle speed error effect as shown in Figs. 4 and 5.

From Fig. 4, we can see that in the whole iteration process, the maximum error between the actual speed of vehicles and the estimated speed based on KF is ±0.6, and fluctuates on this. From Fig. 5, it can be seen clearly that during the whole iteration process, the maximum error between measured and estimated values of vehicle speed decreased from ±0.6 to ±0.4, and the fluctuation range is decreased by 20%, and the convergence effect is improved. Comparison between Figs. 4 and 5, we can know that in the RFID environment, the error based on the AKF is lower than the error based on the KF. The reason is that it introduces adaptive forgetting factor, reduces memory length of filter, makes full use of "present" measurement data, improves dynamic performance of filter, and better reflects real-time validity.

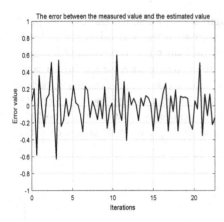

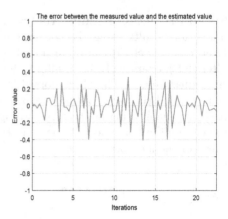

**Fig. 4.** Speed error effect of Kalman filter

**Fig. 5.** Speed error effect of adaptive Kalman filter

## 5    Conclusion

In this paper, a speed prediction method based on adaptive Kalman filter is proposed to predict the speed of vehicles. This method provides a possibility to record and predict the speed of vehicles under harsh environment, bend, downhill and other conditions. The simulation results justify that the speed prediction result based on adaptive Kalman filter is more close to the real value than based on conventional Kalman filter. Meanwhile the convergence effect of the filter improved, the fluctuation range decreased, effectively overcome the adverse effect caused by the process error and measurement error. This implies that the proposed algorithm can provide the better real-time effectiveness for the practical implementation.

**Acknowledgement.** This work was supported in part by the National Natural Science Foundation of China under Project 61379122, Project 61572440, and Project 61502428, and in part by the Zhejiang Provincial Natural Science Foundation of China under Project LR16F010003, and Project LR17F010002.

## References

1. Yang, M., Dong, B., Wang, H., et al.: Laser radar based real time ego-motion estimation for intelligent vehicles. In: IEEE Intelligent Vehicle Symposium, vol. 1, pp. 44–51 (2002)
2. Floudas, N., Polychronopoulos, A., Amditis, A.: A survey of filtering techniques for vehicle tracking by radar equipped automotive platforms. In: International Conference on Information Fusion, vol. 2, pp. 25–28 (2005)
3. Zamiri, S., Reitinger, B., Grun, H., et al.: Laser ultrasonic velocity measurement for phase transformation investigation in titanium alloy. In: IEEE International Ultrasonics Symposium, pp. 683–686 (2013)

4. Titov, S.A., Maev, R.G., Bogachenkov, A.N.: An ultrasonic array technique for velocity of bulk waves and sample thickness measurement. In: IEEE International Ultrasonics Symposium, pp. 2384–2387 (2010)
5. Kalashnikov, A.N., Challis, R.E.: Errors and uncertainties in the measurement of ultrasonic wave attenuation and phase velocity. IEEE Trans. Ultrason. Ferroelectr. Freq. Control **52**, 1754–1768 (2005)
6. Shen, Q., Ban, X.-J., Chang, Z., et al.: On-line detection and temporal segmentation of actions in vidio based human-computer interaction. Chin. J. Comput. **38**(12), 2477–2487 (2015)
7. Kloos, G., Guivant, J.E., Worrall, S., et al.: Wireless network for mining applications. In: Australasian Conference on Robotics and Automation, Canberra, Australia, December 2004
8. Yoon, J.-H., Peng, H.: A cost-effective sideslip estimation method using velocity measurements from two GPS receivers. IEEE Trans. Veh. Technol. **63**, 2589–2599 (2014)
9. Bhavsar, S.S., Kulkarni, A.N.: Train collision avoidance system by using RFID. In: International Conference on Computing, Analytics and Security Trends, pp. 30–34 (2016)
10. Li, J., Jin, M., Luan, S.: Intriduction radio frequency identification technology. Comput. Knowl. Technol. **6**(15), 4238–4240 (2010)
11. Liu, W., Ning, H., Wang, B.: REID antenna design of highway ETC in ITS. In: International Symposium on Antennas, Propagation and EM Theory, pp. 1–4 (2006)
12. Guo, Y., Zhao, Z.: Design of school bus passengers' identity authentication system based on RFID. In: IEEE International Conference on Communication Problem-Solving, pp. 412–415 (2015)
13. Lee, L.T., Tsang, K.F.: An active RFID system for railway vehicle identification and positioning. In: International Conference on Railway Engineering - Challenges for Railway Transportation in Information Age, pp. 1–4 (2008)
14. Huo, Y., Lu, Y., Cheng, W., et al.: Vehicle road distance measurement and maintenance in RFID systems on roads. In: 2014 International Conference on Connected Vehicles and Expo, pp. 30–36 (2014)
15. Qiong, D., Yang, X., Zhu, J.: Study on tracking algorithm for wMPS based on least square Kalman filter. Chin. J. Sens. Actuators **25**(2), 236–239 (2012)
16. Jing, J., Filev, D., Kurt, A., et al.: Vehicle speed prediction using a cooperative method of fuzzy Markov model and auto-regressive model. In: 2017 IEEE Intelligent Vehicles Symposium, pp. 881–886 (2017)
17. Chen, X., Ling, Y., Chen, M.: Mobile robot localization algorithm based on gaussian mixture consider Kalman filter in WSNs environment. Chin. J. Sens. Actuators **30**(1), 133–138 (2017)
18. Welch, G., Bishop, G.: An Introduction to the Kalman Filter. University of North Carolina at Chapel Hill, vol. 8, no. 7, pp. 127–132 (2006)
19. Sun, Y., Zhang, C.: Research on the detection method of airport pavement joint seeper based on Kalman filter. Chin. J. Sens. Actuators **30**(8), 1204–1208 (2017)
20. Heidari, A., Khandani, A.K., Mcavoy, D.: Adaptive modelling and long-range prediction of mobile fading channels. IET Commun. **4**, 39–50 (2010)
21. Cai, X., Cai, M., Zhang, Y.: Research on driver reaction time in internet of vehicles environment. J. Comput. Appl. **37**(S2), 270–273 (2017)
22. Yang, L., Xing, C., Zhao, H.: Study on driver's reaction time (DRT) during car following. Comput. Technol. Autom. **34**(3), 33–37 (2015)

# Speed Prediction of High Speed Mobile Vehicle Based on Extended Kalman Filter in RFID System

Yupin Huang$^{(\boxtimes)}$, Liping Qian, and Anqi Feng

College of Information Engineering, Zhejiang University of Technology,
Hangzhou 310023, China
yphuang_zjut@163.com, lpqian@zjut.edu.cn, aqfeng_zjut@163.com

**Abstract.** The traditional speed prediction generally utilizes GPS and video images, and thus the prediction accuracy is heavily dependent on environmental factors. To this end, through using RFID (Radio Frequency Identification) data, this paper proposes a vehicle speed prediction algorithm based on Extended Kalman Filter (EKF). Specifically, the proposed algorithm works as follows. First, the RFID reader equipped in the vehicle acquires the state information of tags deployed on the road. Second, The data processing module equipped in the vehicle demodulation and decoding these information. At the same time, the RFID reader sends information to the RFID label after the current information is encoded and modulated. Third, the vehicle predicts the vehicle speed based on the EKF through establishing the state space model with acquired state data. The simulation results show that the proposed algorithm can effectively predict the vehicle speed at 0.6 s.

**Keywords:** Radio frequency identification · Speed prediction
Extended Kalman filter

## 1 Introduction

With the rapid development of society and economy and the improvement of people's living standards, vehicles have become indispensable means of transport for people's daily travel. Traffic congestion and traffic accidents have become more and more common, and meanwhile traffic environment has also gradually deteriorated. The paradigm of intelligent transportation system (ITS) has been proposed as a promising solution to cope with the increasingly serious traffic problems. The ITS can effectively integrate information, data transmission, electronic sensing, computer and other technologies into the entire ground transportation management system to achieve real-time, accurate, efficient, large-scale and comprehensive traffic intelligence management. Among them, tracking and predicting the speed of vehicle ahead is indispensable, and has been widely used in the design of vehicle control plane. The speed prediction of vehicle ahead can

© ICST Institute for Computer Sciences, Social Informatics and Telecommunications Engineering 2018
L. Meng and Y. Zhang (Eds.): MLICOM 2018, LNICST 251, pp. 52–59, 2018.
https://doi.org/10.1007/978-3-030-00557-3_6

make the driver acquire more informed judgments and actions, and increase the driver's warning time and greatly reduce the probability of a traffic accident. Therefore, it is very important to track and predict the speed of vehicle ahead accurately in real time.

At present, most speed prediction methods are based on the video image speed measurement. In [1], the author proposes a new virtual loops of video speed detection method, which has the ability to judge the type of vehicle according to the characteristic curve and advantage of this method is the processing time shortened. The work [2] systematically designs a novel license plate detection method based on a texture classifier specialized, which has the ability to capture the gradient distribution characteristics of character strokes that make the license plate letters.

In recent years, although the accuracy of video velocimetry has become higher and higher, there are still limitations. For example, the video velocimetry depends largely on the camera's resolution and the corresponding image processing algorithms. At the same time, the high cost of the camera renders it not be widely used in roads.

As environmental factors have less impact on radio frequency identification technology, and its convenience and low cost have also been widely used in daily life. Some scholars do a lot of research on radio frequency identification. RFID technology has been used in the railway industry which can track the trains moving on the same track to prevent head on collisions as well as rear end collision [3]. In [4], the RFID tag system was proposed for bicycle deployment, and the label installation method and label content setting are specifically described. The authors in [5] analyzed the influence of the relative position of readers and tags on the read error and the read rate through experiments, and proposed a method of calculating the range of the readable area of the RFID reader on the pavement. To reduce the cost of RFID system safety certification, the authors in [6] propose a lightweight RFID mutual authentication protocol with cache in the reader (LRMAPC), to store the recent visited key of tags, so that recent visited tags can be authenticated directly in the reader.

Based on the above research, in order to improve the speed tracking accuracy and fast effectiveness, this paper designs an algorithm based on RFID EKF to track the speed of high-speed mobile vehicles. The simulation shows that this method can reduce the system cost to a great extent under the RFID environment, also can predict the speed of target vehicle fast and effectively, ensures the vehicle running safety, and reduce the probability of traffic accidents.

## 2    System Model Design

### 2.1    Model Architecture

In this paper, we propose a EKF-based vehicle speed prediction algorithm by using RFID. The proposed algorithm works as follows. First, the RFID reader equipped in the vehicle acquires the state information of tags deployed on the road. Second, the data processing module is equipped in the vehicle demodulation and decode these information. At the same time, the RFID reader sends information to the label after the current information are encoded and modulated. Then, the vehicle predicts the vehicle speed based on the EKF through establishing the state space model with acquired state data. Among them, the model shown in Fig. 1.

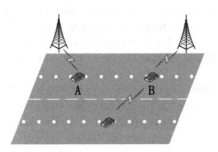

**Fig. 1.** RFID system model

In Fig. 1, the RFID tag (white point and passive tag) is deployed on a straight road. Part of the label memory is fixedly stored with its own information, traffic information and road speed limit information. The other part stores the status information of the vehicle, and the status information includes the current speed and the current time of the vehicle. Own status information encoding Modulation by the vehicle reader through the 24-bit EPC code to write the label. RFID reader installed in the middle of the front bumper of the vehicle, when the vehicle passes the label, each vehicle will first read the information in the label, and then the vehicle will replace their status information in the label status information. Considering the limitation of storage capacity of the RFID tag, the tag store only the most recent vehicle status information. As shown in Fig. 1, $A$ car now stores the status information in the RFID tag, and the $B$ car reads the status information and overwrites its own status information (i.e., $V_k$ and $T_k$). In addition, $V_k$ and $T_k$ are the speed and time the vehicle passes the $k^{th}$ label, respectively. Among them, we focus on speed prediction in this paper, so we assumed that there will be no communication interference between vehicles and the state demodulation and decoding will be completed in an instant.

## 2.2  System Modeling

The RFID system model mainly includes high-speed vehicles, RFID tags deployed at the same road distance, and RFID readers mounted on the bumper of the vehicle. The design criteria of our model are stated as follows [7]: (1) Each RFID tag should be covered by no more than one RFID readers read area at any instant of time. (2) Each RFID readers read area should cover no more than one tag at any instant of time. (3) If a vehicle is in a lane, the vehicle should be able to read tags that are deployed in the lane. (4) If a vehicle can read a tag, at least half of its body should be in the lane where the tag is deployed. (5) If less than half of a vehicle is in a lane, the vehicle should not be able to read any tag in the lane. (6) The label spacing is set to 3 m.

RFID systems can be set up in tunnels, overpasses and other harsh environments. Considering that the change of historical speed determines its future state to a great extent, we only need to collect the historical information of speed and track the speed of vehicle A. Therefore, the state equation and observation equation of the vehicle speed in the RFID system are as follows:

$$\begin{cases} x_k = g(x_{k-1}) + w_{k-1}; \\ z_k = H(x_k) + v_k. \end{cases} \tag{1}$$

In Eq. (1), $x_k$ is the state vector of the system at time $k$, which indicates the true speed of the vehicle at the $k$ time; $g(x_{k-1})$ and $H(x_k)$ are non-linear functions; $w_{k-1}$ is the system noise; $z_k$ is observed value of the system at time $k$, which represents the measured speed of the vehicle at time $k$; $v_k$ is the measurement error. Here, $w_{k-1}$ and $v_k$ are both Gaussian distributed white noise with mean zero.

## 3 Vehicle Speed Estimation Algorithm Based on Extended Kalman Filter

The core of EKF algorithm is to linearize the nonlinear system. Specifically, the nonlinear function is expanded by Taylor and first order linearization is truncated, ignoring the rest of higher-order terms, so that the nonlinear problem is transformed to linear. Second-order truncation [8] can reduce the estimation error caused by linearization and greatly increases the number of iterations of the data. Therefore, this paper selects the EKF algorithm under first-order truncation.

The EKF algorithm must first be linearized preprocessing, let $g(x_{k-1})$ Taylor expand at $\overline{x}_{k-1|k-1}$, $H(x_k)$ Taylor expand at $\overline{x}_{k|k-1}$:

$$\begin{cases} g(x_{k-1}) = g(\overline{x}_{k-1|k-1}) + A_{k-1}y_{k-1} + \Delta t_1; \\ A_{k-1} = g'(x_{k-1}); \\ y_{k-1} = x_{k-1} - \overline{x}_{k-1|k-1}; \\ H(x_k) = H(\overline{x}_{k|k-1}) + C_k(x_k - \overline{x}_{k-1|k-1} + \Delta t_2; \\ C_k = H'(\overline{x}_{k|k-1}). \end{cases} \tag{2}$$

Here, $A_{k-1}$ and $C_k$ are Taylor coefficients at the k − 1th moment and Jacobian matrix at the kth moment, respectively, $\overline{x}_{k-1|k-1}$ is the optimal estimation of the state at the $k - 1$th moment, $\overline{x}_{k|k-1}$ is the predicted value of state at the

$k$th moment, $y_{k-1}$ is estimation error at the $k-1$th moment, $\Delta t_1$ and $\Delta t_2$ are higher-order infinitesimals, and $y_k$ is the error between the measured and a priori values at time $k$.

Ignoring higher-order infinitesimals, and Take Eq. 2 into Eq. 1:

$$\begin{cases} x_k = g(\overline{x}_{k-1|k-1}) + A_{k-1}y_{k-1}; \\ z_k = \overline{H}_{k|k-1} + C_k(x_k - \overline{x}_{k-1|k-1}) + v_k; \\ A_{k-1} = g'(u_{k-1}). \end{cases} \tag{3}$$

The EKF algorithm will have little difference in form from Kalman filtering (KF) after linearizing the nonlinear system. The EKF algorithm is also divided into the forecasting process and the updating process. The EKF algorithm [9–11] is as follows:

Calculate the prior predictive value $\overline{x}_{k|k-1}$ at time $k$:

$$\overline{x}_{k|k-1} = f(\overline{x}_{k-1|k-1}) \tag{4}$$

Calculate a priori error covariance matrix $P_{k|k-1}$

$$P_{k|k-1} = A_k P_{k-1|k-1} A_k^T + Q \tag{5}$$

Calculate the approximate optimal Kalman gain $K_k$

$$\overline{K}_k = P_{k|k-1} C_k^T (C_k P_{k|k-1}^T C_k^T + R)^{-1} \tag{6}$$

Calculate the optimal state estimate $\overline{x}_{k|k}$ at time $k$

$$\overline{x}_{k|k} = x_{k|k-1} + \overline{K}_k(z_k - H(\overline{x}_{k|k-1})) \tag{7}$$

Calculate the a-posteriori error covariance matrix $P_{k|k}$ of the best estimate at time $k$

$$P_{k|k} = (I - K_k C_k)P_{k|k-1} \tag{8}$$

Where $I$ is the identity matrix. Theoretically, $A_{k-1}$ and $C_k$ are Jacobian matrices for solving $g(x_{k-1})$ and $H(x_k)$ respectively. Considering the difficulty of actual calculation, Taylor's first-order truncation approximation, so the approximate Kalman gain is obtained; Since the distance between RFID tags is set at 3 m, the time between two labels passing through a high-speed vehicle (20 m/s or more) is relatively small, In reality, few people change acceleration many times in a very short period of time, which is good for suppressing the divergence of EKF linearization.

The specific algorithm of speed prediction in this paper is as follows:

---

**Algorithm 1. Speed prediction specific algorithm**

---

 1:   Initialize variables and  $k = 1$.
 2:   According to the formula 2~3, the EKF algorithm pretreatment.
 3:   Read the initial status flow $(V_{k-1}$ $and$ $T_{k-1})$ in the RFID tag.
 4: **if** the vehicle does not travel out of the deployment of the RFID system of the road **then**
 5:     Calculated to $A_{k-1}$, $y_{k-1}$,$C_{k-1}$,$K_k$ and other variables.
 6:     According to the formula 4   5,Calculate $\overline{x}_{k|k-1}$ and $P_{k|k-1}$.
 7:     According to the formula 6   8,Calculate $K_k\overline{x}_{k|k}$ and $P_{k|k-1}$.
 8:     Vehicles to the next RFID label.
 9:     K=K+1.
10: **end if**

---

# 4 Simulation

## 4.1 Simulation Settings

In order to test the practicality and effectiveness of this tracking system, we simulated the deceleration mode. The deceleration mode means that the vehicle A moves with a speed at $25/m$, then it decelerates with an acceleration at $a = -3\,\mathrm{m/s^2}$. In order to more intuitively determine the effectiveness and rapidity of the system, set the vehicle B from $20\,\mathrm{m/s}$ to start tracking vehicle A. And set the initial distance of vehicles A and vehicles B to $1000\,\mathrm{m}$ to prevent vehicle collision.

The simulation experiment in this paper adds the real speed information plus Gaussian random noise with mean zero and variance 1 as the velocity observation, and adds the real time information to Gaussian random noise with mean zero and variance 0.5 as the time observation. The tool used in the simulation experiment is MATLAB R2016a.

## 4.2 Simulation Results Analysis

The mean square error of speed is introduced as the evaluation index. The mean square error is defined as follows:

$$MSE = \frac{1}{N}\sum_{k=1}^{N}(X(k) - \overline{X}(k))^2 \tag{9}$$

Where $N$ is the number of simulations; $k$ is the $k$th simulation; $X(k)$ is the true state value of the target at the $k$th moment; and $X(k)$ is the state of the filtered estimate at the $k$th moment.

Since the deceleration process is more important than the acceleration process while the vehicle is traveling, we only consider the deceleration process. On the other hand, the acceleration process can be seen as the opposite of the deceleration process. When there is a special situation in front of the vehicle,

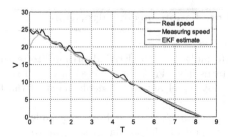

**Fig. 2.** Speed comparison chart

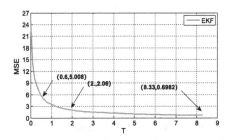

**Fig. 3.** RFID system model

the vehicle should quickly decelerate to ensure safety. Simulation diagram shown in Figs. 2 and 3.

From Fig. 2 it is clear that the extended Kalman filter algorithm can track the target vehicle speed from the initial velocity of 20 m/s in about 0.6 s. Then, even if there is a measurement error in the status information, the speed tracking target can be corrected well. On the other hand, since the label spacing is fixed and the vehicle speed varies, the sampling time in the simulation is not fixed, which results in a longer sampling period during deceleration. The specific formula is as follows.

$$\begin{cases} D_{tag} = v_{b,i}t_i + \frac{1}{2}at_i^2; \\ a = \frac{\sum F}{m} \end{cases} \tag{10}$$

Where $D_{tag}$ is the spacing of labels; $v_B$ is the speed at which vehicle B reaches the $i$th label; $t_i$ and $a$ are respectively the sampling time and acceleration of the vehicle B from the $i$th tag to the $(i+1)$th tag; $m$ is the mass of the vehicle, set to 1.5 tons.

As shown in Fig. 3, the initial tracking speed of the vehicle is 20 m/s. With the EKF algorithm, the mean square error of speed drops sharply in 0.6 s and slowly decreases in 0.6 s to 2 s, which shows that the algorithm can predict the target speed quickly and effectively.

# 5   Conclusion

In this paper, For the phenomenon that the GPS signal cannot work normally because of the environment, an RFID road system based on extended Kalman filter for tracking and predicting high-speed moving vehicles is established in this paper. The results show that the EKF algorithm can predict the vehicle real-time status and parameter changes through the established vehicle driving model. Specifically, the algorithm effectively predicts vehicle speed at $0.6\,s$ as the vehicle decelerates.

**Acknowledgement.** This work was supported in part by the National Natural Science Foundation of China under Project 61379122, Project 61572440, and Project 61502428, and in part by the Zhejiang Provincial Natural Science Foundation of China under Project LR16F010003, and Project LR17F010002.

# References

1. Liang, W., Junfang, S.: The speed detection algorithm based on video sequences. In: 2012 International Conference on Computer Science and Service System, Nanjing, pp. 217–220 (2012)
2. Luvizon, D.C., Nassu, B.T., Minetto, R.: A video-based system for vehicle speed measurement in urban roadways. IEEE Trans. Intell. Transp. Syst. **18**(6), 1393–1404 (2017)
3. Malakar, B., Roy, B.K.: Survey of RFID applications in railway industry. In: 2014 First International Conference on Automation, Control, Energy and Systems (ACES), Hooghy, pp. 1–6 (2014)
4. Penttila, K., Sydanheimo, L., Kivikoski, M.: Performance development of a high-speed automatic object identification using passive RFID technology. In: Proceedings of 2004 IEEE International Conference on Robotics and Automation, ICRA 2004, vol. 5, pp. 4864–4868 (2004)
5. Lee, E.K., Yoo, Y.M., Chan, G.P., et al.: Installation and evaluation of RFID readers on moving vehicles. In: International Workshop on Vehicular Ad Hoc Networks, Vanet 2009, Beijing, China, DBLP, pp. 99–108, September 2009
6. Li, C.T., Lee, C.C., Weng, C.Y., et al.: Towards secure authenticating of cache in the reader for RFID-based IoT systems. Peer-to-Peer Netw. Appl. **11**, 1–11 (2017)
7. Cheng, W., Cheng, X., Song, M., Chen, B., Zhao, W.W.: On the design and deployment of RFID assisted navigation systems for VANETs. IEEE Trans. Parallel Distrib. Syst. **23**(7), 1267–1274 (2012)
8. Yang, S., Baum, M.: Second-order extended Kalman filter for extended object and group tracking. In: 2016 19th International Conference on Information Fusion (FUSION), Heidelberg, pp. 1178–1184 (2016)
9. Zeng, C., Li, W.: Application of extended Kalman filter for tracking high dynamic GPS signal. In: 2016 IEEE International Conference on Signal and Image Processing (ICSIP), Beijing, pp. 503–507 (2016)
10. Jiang, K., Zhang, H., Lin, J.: $NH_3$ coverage ratio estimation of diesel-engine SCR systems by a dual time-scale extended Kalman filter. IEEE Trans. Veh. Technol. **67**(4), 3625–3629 (2018)
11. Jiang, Z., Zhou, W., Li, H., Mo, Y., Ni, W., Huang, Q.: A new kind of accurate calibration method for robotic kinematic parameters based on the extended Kalman and particle filter algorithm. IEEE Trans. Ind. Electron. **65**(4), 3337–3345 (2018)

# Mobility Prediction Based on POI-Clustered Data

Haoyuan Chen[1,2], Yali Fan[1,2], Jing Jiang[1,2], and Xiang Chen[1,2,3(✉)]

[1] School of Electronics and Information Technology, Sun Yat-sen University,
Guangzhou 511400, China
chenxiang@mail.sysu.edu.cn
[2] Key Lab of EDA, Research Institute of Tsinghua University in Shenzhen (RITS),
Shenzhen 518075, China
[3] Starway Communications Inc., Guangzhou 510663, China

**Abstract.** Predicting users' mobility trajectories is significant for service providers, such as recommendation systems for tourist routing, emergency warning, etc. However, the former researchers predict the next location merely by observing the past individual trajectories, which usually performs in the accuracy of trace prediction. In this paper, POIs (Points of Interest) information is used to adjust the weight parameters of the predicted results, and the rationality and precision would be improved. The cellular towers are firstly classified into seven types of functional area through POIs. Then the target user's next possible functional area could be speculated, which acts as a supervision of the ultimate prediction outcome. We use the DP (Dirichlet Process) mixture model to identify similarity between different users and predict users' locations by leveraging these similar users. As is shown in the results, the methods proposed above are highly adaptive and precise when being utilized to predict users' mobility trajectories.

**Keywords:** Point of interest · Clustering
Mobility trajectory prediction

## 1 Introduction

It has been a hot topic of study for human behaviors and locations. Some government workers initially used census data to roughly locate the scope of citizens' movement [1], which cost a lot of time and money. As a result, its practicability is imprecise. Some researchers used the phone call records to obtain individual locations [2]. This approach, disappointingly, is seldom put into practice because of high sparsity between two neighboring phone calls, which results in low accuracy of users' location prediction during the time without making phone calls. The current study mainly focuses on cellular network data [3], which possesses the following characteristics: (1) frequent accesses within minutes; (2) improved spatial granularity as a result of the development of cellular

© ICST Institute for Computer Sciences, Social Informatics and Telecommunications Engineering 2018
L. Meng and Y. Zhang (Eds.): MLICOM 2018, LNICST 251, pp. 60–72, 2018.
https://doi.org/10.1007/978-3-030-00557-3_7

infrastructure; (3) easily available records which are saved once when interactions between phones and bases occur. Therefore, analyzing cellular network data or wireless network data facilitates the study of individual trajectories.

Many researchers have conducted researches on user trajectories based on cellular network data or mobile network data. For instance, Bagrow et al. studied the collective response to emergencies [4,5]. Shibasaki et al. predicted the collective movement of people in rare crowding incidents [6]. Shimosaka et al. took advantage of Bilinear Poisson regression model to predict population movement in cities [7]. Some methods of trajectory prediction are roughly similar [8–11], which merely use the target user's personal history trajectories to predict the user's next most likely position. Long-time phone data from users is applied to obtain the high accuracy. However, it is hard to collect such big amount of data in reality, let alone users may conceal their data due to privacy protection, which results in insufficient data quantity and low prediction accuracy. McInerney et al. [12] mainly paid attention to resemblance in users' temporal patterns with the help of Bayesian mobility model. Jeong et al. [13] proposed an improved algorithm named Cluster-Aided Mobility Predictor (CAMP), which predicts the next most likely position of a target user using the historical trajectories of all users within a certain range. As an advance processing, this algorithm relies on the clustering techniques to discover the similarity between the user behavior profiles from the training dat. The limitation of this algorithm is that the data source is single because it only used the mobile trajectories of users drawing out from cellular network data. Meanwhile, the method of judgment is also single when selecting the best prediction outcome. Therefore, another dimension's data may be needed in order to aid the prediction.

Points of interest (POI) gathered from the map reflects certain socioeconomic activity and functional attributes, such as restaurants, playgrounds, schools, etc. The function type [3] of a certain cell can be obtained by dealing with the POI information in the cell. Furthermore, human behaviors are also closely related to these cells' functions. Recently, researchers have conducted numerous studies on POI information. [14] and [15] provided personal recommendations to users based on the POIs of the places users have visited. Carmo et al. [16] solved the problem of overlapping symbols in POI visualization. Therefore, the mobility trajectories of the user among base stations can be interpreted as the mobility trajectories among functional areas, which indicates that this dimension of data regarding functional areas is suitable to assist the trajectory prediction. Combining the prediction of the user's next functional area with the prediction of the next base station, the rationality and accuracy of the prediction result can be promoted.

Our contributions consist of two aspects:

- To the best of our knowledge, it is the first time to use POIs to categorize bases and study users' trajectories in terms of base station types. This step is crucial in our algorithm since it resolves a challenging problem. Since different users' set of locations vary a lot, i.e., the range of one person's movement have little overlap with that of another person's movement, discovering parallelism among users is difficult. However, if we map bases into 7 functional types of bases, the similarity of human mobility pattern is easier to identify.

– In addition, it is the first time that the CAMP algorithm is applied to users' mobility trajectories among bases as well as trajectories in terms of base types. Judging users' locations according the prediction of the user's next functional area and that of the next base station, the prediction result could be more accurate and credible.

The rest of this paper is structured as follows. In Sect. 2, the collection of POI data and processing methods of attaining corresponding function type of each base station are introduced. In Sect. 3, we transform users' trajectories by mapping the base station into base station types and predict the next possible base station type of a certain user through DP mixture model. The prediction results and discussions are given in Sect. 4. After showing our prediction results and discussing our ideas for future work in Sects. 5, the related works from three aspects are displayed in Sect. 5. We conclude this paper in Sect. 6.

## 2   POI Clustering

In this section, the collection of POI data and processing methods of attaining corresponding function type of each base station will be explained in detail.

### 2.1   TF-IDF Processing

TF-IDF, a statistical method, is utilized to reflect the importance of a word in a document. The importance of a word is measured from two aspects. On one hand, the importance of a word is in proportion to the frequency of the word appearing in the document. On the other hand, it is inversely proportional to the frequency of the word appearing in the corpus. TF (Term Frequency), refers to the frequency of occurrence of a word in all words in a file; IDF (Inverse Document Frequency) is the reverse file frequency, which means the logarithm of ratio between the total number of files and the number of files containing the specific word. The idea of IDF is to accentuate the significance of specific words to categorize documents, and to reduce the importance of commonly used terms in documents. In other words, if a word frequently appears in a document, the term may be a commonly used word and is slight when distinguishing different documents. If a word frequently appears only in one or a few documents, then the word is likely to be a jargon, in other words, a "label" in a specific field. Therefore, IDF is a measure of the universal importance of words and reflects the effectiveness of words to distinguish documents.

The value of TF-IDF is the product of TF and IDF, which can be perceived as the adjustment of TF by taking IDF as the weight. The purpose of this method is to highlight important words and deemphasize the secondary words.

POI data can reflect the function of an area and can be attained from API mapping service providers. However, an area may contain multiple types of POIs which makes it confusing. Therefore, preprocessing the data is highly necessary. Among the POI data utilized in this study, there are mainly 21 kinds of POIs, including: food, hotel, shopping, entertainment, sports, schools, attractions, tourism development, finance, office buildings, companies, shopping malls, factories, industrial areas, science and technology parks, economic development areas, high-tech development areas, residential areas, living services, townships and villages. Then these kinds of POIs can be grouped into 7 categories based on the classic functional area classification [17,18]: residential, recreational, commercial, industrial, educational, scenic and suburban areas as showing in Table 1.

**Table 1.** The POI categories and taxonomies

| Number | Function | Type |
|---|---|---|
| 1 | Residential | Residential areas, living services |
| 2 | Recreational | Food, hotel, shopping, entertainment, sports |
| 3 | Commercial | Finance, office buildings, companies, shopping malls |
| 4 | Industrial | Factories, industrial areas, science and technology parks, economic development zones, high-tech development zones |
| 5 | Educational | Schools |
| 6 | Scenic | Attractions, tourism development |
| 7 | Suburban | Townships and villages |

In order to correctly measure the importance of a POI within a cell area, TF-IDF is performed to process the classified POI information. In the calculation process, for a given area unit $a \in A$, where A refers to the set of all regional units, the number of POIs in each POI category is counted, and then we can calculate the POI vectors: $[TF - IDF_1^a, TF - IDF_2^a, \ldots, TF - IDF_i^a, \ldots, TF - IDF_7^a]$, where $TF - IDF_i^a$ represents the TF-IDF value of the $i$-th POI in region $a$. It can be calculated as follows:

$$IDF_i^a = log(\frac{A}{R}),$$ (1)

$$TF - IDF_i^a = n_i^a \cdot \frac{IDF_i^a}{N^a},$$ (2)

where R represents the number of regional units that contain the $i$-th POI in A; $n_i^a$ is the number of POIs contained in the $i$-th POI category in unit $a$; $N^a$ refers to the total number of POIs in unit $a$.

The corresponding TF-IDF Vector for each area is obtained, which contains a total of 7 attribute values, and each value represents the importance of its corresponding function in this area.

## 2.2   K-Means Clustering

The K-Means method is one of the most widely used partition-based clustering algorithms. Its basic idea is as follows: firstly, a K value is selected, which represents the number of clustering centroid points; secondly, the data points in space are allocated to the same category when their nearest centroids are the same according to Euclidean Distance; thirdly, according to the clustering result, the position of the centroid of each cluster is updated, and the data points in the space are redivided to generate K new clusters. The iteration continues until the centroid position is no longer changed.

After clustering TF-IDF Vectors of all cell area units, then we map the area units into seven functional types, we can get "base station type" of each cell area unit. The clustering results are shown in Fig. 1. As can be observed from the figure, the number of area units marked as "entertainment" is the largest, accounting for 41.78% of all area units; the total proportion of area units marked as "residential" and "entertainment" is 68.84%. This clustering result indicates that the functions of the region we study are biased toward housing and entertainment.

Next, the base stations appearing in the cellular network data can be mapped to the 7 base station types. The track of the users based on the base station types can be generated, which may reflect the daily mobility patterns of users. For example, the track of a user based on the base station types might be: industrial area - commercial area - entertainment area - residential area. For all users, their trajectories for base station type may be analogous.

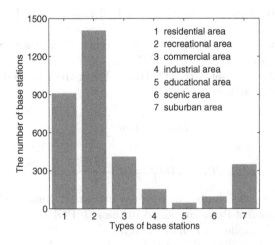

**Fig. 1.** The results of clustering POI of base stations

# 3   Trajectory Prediction Method Based on Dirichlet Process Mixture Model

Our goal is to predict the next location for a certain user at a given time on the basis of POI data as well as all users' past trajectories. The set of users is denoted by U. Assuming that the set of locations in all trajectories is $\mathcal{L}$, and its size is L. The trajectory of a user u is denoted by $x^u = (x_1^u, \ldots, x_{n^u}^u)$, where $x_t^u$ means the $t$-th location that user $u$ visits and $n^u$ means the total length of the track. $x_{n^u}^u$ is where $u$ currently locates. Since we are studying the patterns of users' behavior moving from one base to another, we impose $x_t^u \neq x_{t+1}^u$. In other words, two consecutive locations on the user's trajectory must be different.

Next additional notations are introduced as follows,

$$n_{i,j}^u = \sum_{t=1}^{n^u-1} \mathbb{I}(x_t^u = i, x_{t+1}^u = j), \tag{3}$$

where $n_{i,j}^u$ represents the number of transitions for user u from location $i$ to location $j$.

Similarly,

$$n_i^u = \sum_{t=1}^{n^u} \mathbb{I}(x_t^u = i). \tag{4}$$

We assume that a user's trajectory is a order-1 Markov chain. The user's trajectory is drawn from the transition kernel $\theta^u = (\theta_{i,j}^u)_{i,j \in L} \in [0,1]^{(L \times L)}$ where $\theta_{i,j}^u$ means the probability that user $u$ shift from $i$ to $j$. Thus, the probability of observing trajectory of user $u$ is as follows,

$$P_{\theta^u}(x^u) := \prod_{t=1}^{n^u-1} \theta_{x_t^u, x_{t+1}^u}^u. \tag{5}$$

We assume that the transition kernels of different users are independently generated from the same distribution $\mu$. In other words, users' trajectories are drawn from the hierarchical model: for all $u \in U$, $\theta^u \sim \mu$, $X^u \sim P_{\theta^u}$.

Our model is applicable to predict locations of users with rather short trajectories since similarities between different users' mobile habits are taken into account. As we know, a few analogous kernels may generate many different users' trajectories. That is, the distribution $\mu$ might be composed of a few clusters. Our goal is to find these user clusters and to predict individual trajectory based on all users' trajectories from the same cluster. Our data includes trajectories of 1000 users, while the total number of base stations is more than 3000. The number of users is smaller than that of base stations. In order to discover existing parallelism among users, we transform users' trajectories by mapping the base station into base station types. We can better characterize the similarity between different users.

Bayesian nonparametric inference [19] is adopted in this paper since the number of clusters is not obtainable before clustering. The number of clusters is flexible which could increase as input data grow. Thus, the number of clusters is a posteriori parameter which is updated in the computation procedure.

In this model, we approximate the distribution $\mu$ of transition kernels by computing $g$ iteratively. When computing $g$, Dirichlet Process (DP) mixture model which is applied in the CAMP algorithm proposed by Jaeseong et al. is adopted. Refer to the work of Jeong et al. [13] for a more exhausted description of the CAMP algorithm. The procedure of the algorithm is outlined in Algorithm 1.

The algorithm of Gibbs Sampler is used to attain independent samples of the allocation of users to clusters. The algorithm of Update DP algorithm is used to update two parameters of DP mixture model, $\alpha$ and $G_0$, according to the results of Gibbs Sampler [20]. These two algorithms are shown as Algorithms 2 and 3 respectively.

## 4   Simulation Results and Discussions

Our experimental dataset is the trajectories of 1000 users during one week from a metropolis in China provided by the Ministry of Education-China Mobile Research Fund "DPI & Pipeline Big Data". There are totally 3363 base stations appearing in the trjectories of these 1000 users. According to the locations of these base stations, we first ultilize Voronoi polygons to obtain their coverage area as is shown in Fig. 2 (left). We refer to the base station coverage area obtained in this way as the Voronoi area of the base station. Specifically, for any Voronoi area, the Euclidean distance of any point in it from its base station is always closer than that from other base stations. Then we calculate the area

---

**Algorithm 1. CAMP**

---

**Input:** $x^U$, K, $B$, $M$
**Output:** $\hat{\theta}^u, \hat{x}^u$
1:   Step 1: Updates of $G_0$ and $\alpha$
2:   **function**
3:       $G_0^1 \leftarrow Uniform\,(\Theta), \alpha_1 \leftarrow 1$
4:       **for** $k = 0 \ldots K - 1$ **do**
5:           **for** $b = 1 \ldots B$ **do**
6:               $c^{U,b,k} \leftarrow GibbsSampler\left(x^U,\ G_0^k,\ \alpha_k,\ M\right)$
7:           **end for**
8:       **end for**
9:   **end function**
10:  Step 2: Last sampling and prediction
11:  **function**
12:      **for** $b = 1 \ldots B$ **do**
13:          $c^{U,b,k} \leftarrow GibbsSampler\left(x^U,\ G_0^k,\ \alpha_k,\ M\right)$
14:      **end for**
15:      Compute $\hat{\theta}^u$ and $\hat{x}^u$
16:      $\theta^u = \frac{1}{B}\sum_{b=1}^{B} E_g[\overline{\theta}^{c^{u,b,K}}|x^{c^{u,b,K}}] = \frac{1}{B}\sum_{b=1}^{B} \frac{\int_\theta \theta \cdot P_\theta(x^{c^{u,b,K}})G_0^K(d\theta)}{\int_\theta P_\theta(x^{c^{u,b,K}})G_0^K(d\theta)}$
17:      $\hat{x}^u = argmax_j \hat{\theta}^u_{x^u_{n^u},j}$
18:  **end function**

---

**Algorithm 2.** Gibbs Sampler

**Input:** $x^U, G_0, \alpha, M$
**Output:** $c^U$
1: **function**
2:     $\forall u \in U, c^u \leftarrow c_1, n_{c_1, -u} \leftarrow |U| - 1; N \leftarrow 1; c^U = \{c_1\}$
3:     **for** $i = 1 \ldots M$ **do**
4:         **for** $u \in U$ **do**
5:             $c^u \leftarrow c^u \{u\}$
6:             $\beta_{new} \leftarrow z\frac{\alpha}{\alpha+|U|-1} \int_\theta P_\theta(x^u)G_0(d\theta)$
7:             $\beta_c \leftarrow z\frac{n_{c,-u}}{\alpha+|U|-1} \int_\theta P_\theta(x^u)G_0(d\theta|x^c), \forall c \in c^{U\setminus\{u\}}, G_0(d\theta|x^c) = \frac{\int \theta_{i,j}P_\theta(x^u)\mu(d\theta)}{\int P_\theta(x^u)\mu(d\theta)}$
8:             In the above expressions, z is a normalizing constant selected to satisfy:
9:             $\beta_{new} + \sum c \in c^{U\setminus\{u\}}\beta_c = 1;$
10:            With probability $\beta_{new}$ do:
11:                $c_{N+1} \leftarrow \{u\}; c^U \leftarrow c^U \cup \{c_{(N+1)}\}; N \leftarrow N + 1;$
12:            With probability $\beta_c$ do:
13:                $c^u \leftarrow c; c \leftarrow c \cup \{u\}; n_{c, -v} \leftarrow n_{c, -v} + 1, \forall v \neq u.$
14:        **end for**
15:    **end for**
16: **end function**

**Algorithm 3.** Update DP

**Input:** $x^U, G_0^k, \{c^{U,b,k}\}_{b=1,\ldots,B}$
**Output:** $G_0^{k+1}, \alpha_{k+1}$
1: Compute $G_0^{k+1}(.)$ and $\alpha_{k+1}$ as follows
2: **function**
3:     $G_0^{k+1}(.) = \frac{1}{B} \sum_{b=1}^{B} \sum_{c \in c^{U,b,k}} \frac{n_{c,b,k}}{|U|} G_0^k(.|x^c)$
4:
5:     $\alpha_{k+1} = \arg\min_{\alpha \in R} \left| \sum_{i=1}^{|U|} \frac{\alpha}{\alpha+i-1} - \frac{1}{B} \sum_{b=1}^{B} N_b \right|$
6:
7: **end function**
8: where $n_{c,b,k}$ is the size of cluster $c \in c^{(U,b,k)}$, and $N_b$ is the total number of (non-empty) clusters in $c^{U,b,k}$.

covered by each base station and also get the corresponding Cumulative Distribution Function (CDF)) curve as is shown in Fig. 2 (right). From Fig. 2 (right), we can see that 50% base stations cover less than 0.78 square kilometers. By analyzing the user trajectories, we attain the transition kernels for each user. Then the probability distribution that all users move among different base stations is obtained as is shown in Fig. 3. As can be observed, both residential area and entertainment area are visited most frequently when individuals shift among base stations. In particular, both educational and scenic areas have a high degree of relevance to entertainment area. When predicting the base station type of the next location of 596 users by cluster-aided mobility prediction algorithm, 310 users are predicted accurately and the accuracy rate reaches 52%. These results are higher than previous research on mobility prediction.

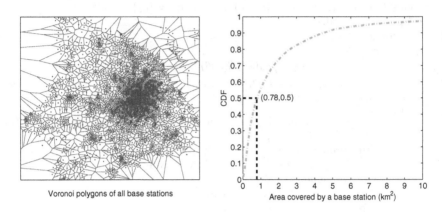

**Fig. 2.** All base stations' coverage area obtained through Voronoi diagram (left) and the corresponding CDF curve (right)

Issue concerning large population is one of the most challenging problems for the society today. Recently, the accelerated urbanization has exacerbated urban problems. Researches about urban population may bring about new insights for urban problems. It is known that the distribution of population in cities within 24 h may vary greatly. It is of great significance to foresee the aggregation of the population concerned in advance since the corresponding early warning mechanism [21]. which has been put forward will be more effective.

Xu et al. used the cellular network data to estimate Real-time population [3]. Their idea is to use the number of users connected to base stations sampled at given time. Then a specific model between the sampled population and the actual population is established. In the model put forward, the source of the sample data is exactly the number of connections detected by the base station at that moment. However, if a user's device is not connected to the base station at the sampling time, but actually they are in the base station area, they are omitted. The location of users who does not interact with base stations may be estimated, taking advantage of the trajectory prediction method proposed in this paper. Based on our research, historical cellular data for all users and POI information can assist the prediction on where a particular user may appear in the future. Therefore, for those who are leaved out at the sampling time, we can predict their most likely position. Fusing this forecast data with the sample data together as the observed data can increase its proximity with the actual population in the sample data, and the accuracy of the population distribution estimation may be promoted. Given that all of these data sources are real-time, predicting the population's dynamic distribution is highly practical.

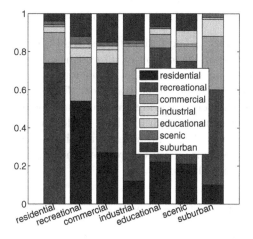

**Fig. 3.** The transition probability distribution of users from different types of bases

# 5 Related Work

With the development of the communication industry and the proliferation of smartphones, an abundance of temporal and spatial information regarding users' location are accessible to researches and are intensively studied by researches, which have brought about fruitful insights on human mobility behavior. Related work from three aspects will be introduced as followings.

## 5.1 Various Data Types Generated from Smartphones

A variety of data types can be generated from a smartphone, e.g. GPS traces, connection records generated from Apps, cellular data collected by base stations, etc. Fang et al. detected popular user mobility patterns by transforming the GPS trajectories into POI trajectories [22]. Wirz et al. predicted crowd density and crowd velocity before serious crowding evens occurred with a dataset of volunteers who reported their surrounding environment periodically utilizing smartphones [23]. Noulas et al. successfully predicted certain users' activities by formulating their communication patterns using their check-in data generated from a special App [24]. Calabrese et al. proposed a new real-time system to estimate urban traffic using a dataset of network bandwidth usage records [25]. These data above needs to be collected from certain volunteers through Apps or GPS sensors on their smartphones, which costs a great deal of time and money, resulting in small number of attendees and low reliability of human mobility patterns. By contrast, the real cellular data could be collected by base stations without installing additional hardware or software on smartphones and they can provide almost continuous trajectories of enough users with large amounts of information, which makes human mobility patterns exploiting credibly possible.

## 5.2  Researches Based on Trajectories of Users

As more user trajectories are accessible to researches, exploration of human's mobility pattern and recommendation of interesting places based on their trajectories are boosted. Isaacman et al. [26] manage to discover important places of a person according to the individual trajectory. Fan et al. [6] speculate users' collective movement when encountering unusual crowd incident. Zheng et al. [27] built a tree-based hierarchical graph (TBHG) model to recommend interesting locations to users. Yoon et al. [28] propose an algorithm that takes advantage of multiple users' trajectories in a city to provide itinerary tour routing for those who are not familiar with the city.

## 5.3  Intensive Study on Human Mobility Prediction

As for the methods of trajectory prediction, Zonoozi et al. [29] developed a mathematical formulation to track mobile movement systematically. Calabrese et al. [30] put forward an idea that utilizing geographical features of collective behavior such as land use, POI could be effective regarding mobility prediction.

# 6  Conclusion

In this paper, POI information of the cellular towers is taken into consideration to adjust the weight parameters of the predicted results, and the rationality and precision are improved significantly. The POIs information is utilized to divide cellular towers into seven categories, which makes it achievable to predict the target users' next possible function area. The DP mixture model is applied to identify similarity between different users, and the resemblance of the users is used to predict the users' locations precisely. The experimental results verify the performance of our proposed scheme, and the proposed method is highly adaptive and precise when being utilized to predict users' mobility trajectories.

**Acknowledgements.** The work is supported in part by the NSFC (No. 61501527), Science, Technology and Innovation Commission of Shenzhen Municipality (No. JCYJ20170816151823313), Guangdong Innovative and Entrepreneurial Research Team Program (No. 2013D014), State's Key Project of Research and Development Plan (No. 2016YFE0122900-3), the Fundamental Research Funds for the Central Universities, Guangdong Science and Technology Project (No. 2016B010126003), and 2016 Major Project of Collaborative Innovation in Guang-zhou (No. 201604046008).

# References

1. Perangkaan, M.J.: 1980 population and housing census of Malaysia. General report of the population census, vol. 1, Kuala Lumpur, Malaysia (2005)
2. Deville, P., et al.: Dynamic population mapping using mobile phone data. Proc. Nat. Acad. Sci. U.S.A. **111**(45), 15888–15893 (2014)

3. Xu, F., Zhang, P., Li, Y.: Context-aware real-time population estimation for metropolis. In: 2016 ACM International Joint Conference on Pervasive and Ubiquitous Computing, Heidelberg, pp. 1064–1075. ACM (2016)
4. Bagrow, J., Wang, D., Barabasi, A.L.: Collective response of human populations to large-scale emergencies. PLoS ONE **6**(3), e17680 (2011)
5. Bengtsson, L., Xin, L., Thorson, A., Garfield, R., Schreeb, J.V.: Improved response to disasters and outbreaks by tracking population movements with mobile phone network data: a post-earthquake geospatial study in Haiti. PLoS Med. **8**(8), e1001083 (2011)
6. Fan, Z., Song, X., Shibasaki, R., Adachi, R.: CityMomentum: an online approach for crowd behavior prediction at a citywide level. In: 2015 ACM International Joint Conference on Pervasive and Ubiquitous Computing, Osaka, pp. 559–569. ACM (2015)
7. Shimosaka, M., Maeda, K., Tsukiji, T., Tsubouchi, K.: Forecasting urban dynamics with mobility logs by bilinear poisson regression. In: 2015 ACM International Joint Conference on Pervasive and Ubiquitous Computing, Osaka, pp. 535–546. ACM (2015)
8. Chon, Y., Shin, H., Talipov, E., Cha, H.: Evaluating mobility models for temporal prediction with high-granularity mobility data. In: 2012 IEEE International Conference on Pervasive Computing and Communications, Lugano, vol. 25, pp. 206–212. IEEE (2012)
9. Song, L., Kotz, D., Jain, R., He, X.: Evaluating next-cell predictors with extensive Wi-Fi mobility data. IEEE Trans. Mob. Comput. **5**(12), 1633–1649 (2006)
10. Scellato, S., Musolesi, M., Mascolo, C., Latora, V., Campbell, A.T.: NextPlace: a spatio-temporal prediction framework for pervasive systems. In: Lyons, K., Hightower, J., Huang, E.M. (eds.) Pervasive 2011. LNCS, vol. 6696, pp. 152–169. Springer, Heidelberg (2011). https://doi.org/10.1007/978-3-642-21726-5_10
11. Jacquet, P., Szpankowski, W., Apostol, I.: An universal predictor based on pattern matching: preliminary results. IEEE Trans. Inf. Theory **48**(6), 1462–1472 (2002)
12. Mcinerney, J., Zheng, J., Rogers, A., Jennings, N.R.: Modelling heterogeneous location habits in human populations for location prediction under data sparsity. In: ACM International Joint Conference on Pervasive and Ubiquitous Computing, Zurich, pp. 469–478. ACM (2013)
13. Jeong, J., Leconte, M., Proutiere, A.: Cluster-aided mobility predictions. In: IEEE INFOCOM 2016-The 35th Annual IEEE International Conference on Computer Communications, San Francisco, vol. 18, pp. 1–9. IEEE (2016)
14. Yao, Z., Fu, Y., Liu, B., Liu, Y., Xiong, H.: POI recommendation: a temporal matching between POI popularity and user regularity. In: 2016 IEEE 16th International Conference on Data Mining, Barcelona, pp. 549–558. IEEE (2017)
15. Zhang, Z., Liu, Y., Chen, H., Liu, Q.: POI recommendation with geographical and multitag influences. In: International Conference on Behavioral, Economic and Socio-Cultural Computing (BESC), Durham, pp. 1–6. IEEE (2017)
16. Carmo, M.B., Afonso, A.P., Ferreira, A., Claudio, A.P., Silva, G.: PoI awareness, relevance and aggregation for augmented reality. In: 2016 IEEE 20th International Conference on Information Visualisation, Lisbon, pp. 300–305. IEEE (2016)
17. Yuan, J., Zheng, Y., Xie, X.: Discovering regions of different functions in a city using human mobility and POIs. In: 18th ACM SIGKDD International Conference on Knowledge Discovery and Data Mining, Beijing, pp. 186–194. ACM (2012)
18. Mimno, D., Mccallum, A.: Topic models conditioned on arbitrary features with dirichlet-multinomial regression. In: 2008 24th Conference on Uncertainty in Artificial Intelligence, arXiv. 1206.3278v1, pp. 411–418 (2012)

19. Ferguson, T.S.: A Bayesian analysis of some nonparametric problems. Ann. Stat. **1**(2), 209–230 (1973)
20. Gershman, S.J., Blei, D.M.: A tutorial on Bayesian nonparametric models. J. Math. Psychol. **56**(1), 1–12 (2012)
21. Gonzalez, M.C., Hidalgo, C.A., Barabasi, A.L.: Understanding individual human mobility patterns. Nature **453**(7196), 779–782 (2008)
22. Fang, Z., Ma, C., Wang, X., Qu, J.: Mining popular mobility patterns from user GPS trajectories. In: 2016 9th International Conference on Service Science, Chongqing, pp. 180–181. IEEE (2016)
23. Wirz, M., Franke, T., Roggen, D., Mitleton-Kelly, E., Lukowicz, P., Troster, G.: Inferring crowd conditions from pedestrians' location traces for real-time crowd monitoring during city-scale mass gatherings. In: 2012 IEEE 21st International Workshop on Enabling Technologies: Infrastructure for Collaborative Enterprises, Hammamet, pp. 367–372. IEEE (2012)
24. Noulas, A., Mascolo, C., Frias-Martinez, E.: Exploiting foursquare and cellular data to infer user activity in urban environments. In: 2013 IEEE 14th International Conference on Mobile Data Management, Milan, vol. 1, pp. 167–176. IEEE (2013)
25. Calabrese, F., Colonna, M., Lovisolo, P., Parata, D., Ratti, C.: Real-time urban monitoring using cell phones: a case study in Rome. IEEE Trans. Intell. Transp. Syst. **12**(1), 141–151 (2011)
26. Isaacman, S., et al.: Identifying important places in people's lives from cellular network data. In: Lyons, K., Hightower, J., Huang, E.M. (eds.) Pervasive 2011. LNCS, vol. 6696, pp. 133–151. Springer, Heidelberg (2011). https://doi.org/10. 1007/978-3-642-21726-5_9
27. Zheng, Y., Zhang, L., Xie, X., Ma, W.Y.: Mining interesting locations and travel sequences from GPS trajectories. In: 18th International Conference on World Wide Web, Madrid, pp. 791–800. ACM (2009)
28. Yoon, H., Zheng, Y., Xie, X., Woo, W.: Smart itinerary recommendation based on user-generated GPS trajectories. In: Yu, Z., Liscano, R., Chen, G., Zhang, D., Zhou, X. (eds.) UIC 2010. LNCS, vol. 6406, pp. 19–34. Springer, Heidelberg (2010). https://doi.org/10.1007/978-3-642-16355-5_5
29. Zonoozi, M.M., Dassanayake, P.: User mobility modeling and characterization of mobility patterns. IEEE J. Sel. Areas Commun. **15**(7), 1239–1252 (1997)
30. Calabrese, F., Lorenzo, G.D., Ratti, C.: Human mobility prediction based on individual and collective geographical preferences. In: 2010 13th International IEEE Conference on Intelligent Transportation Systems, Funchal, pp. 312–317. IEEE (2010)

# A Research on the Identification of Internet User Based on Deep Learning

Hong Shao, Liujun Tang, Ligang Dong[(✉)], Long Chen, Xian Jiang,
and Weiming Wang

School of Information and Electronic Engineering,
Zhejiang Gongshang University, Hangzhou 310018, China
1564027103@qq.com, tlj2016@126.com,
{donglg,jiangxian,wmwang}@zjgsu.edu.cn,
smllchuju@163.com

**Abstract.** In the environment of big data, analyzing internet user behavior has become a research hot spot. By profiling the normal online behavior data of network users to learn their online habits and preferences, is not only helpful to provide network users with more efficient and personalized network services, but also to update the network security policies. Because there is no identification of network users in network management, network administrators need to develop and deliver relevant network services manually to user base on the network user Internet Protocol (IP) address. Therefore, this paper proposes the utilization of deep learning technology to identify network user automatically after fully understand the behavior of network user. At the first, a network identification model based on Deep Belief Network (DBN) is proposed. Then, we apply the Tensorflow framework to construct a DBN model suitable for network user identification. Finally, an experiment with real data set was undertaken upon the model to verify its accuracy on identifying network users. It is found that DBN-based identification model can achieve a high classification accuracy of user identity by constructing deep network structure.

**Keywords:** Deep learning · Deep belief network · User behavior profile

## 1 Introduction

Today, in the environment big data, profiling network users' behavior has attracted many research organizations and network security researchers. By analyzing the traffic characteristics of network users, it is possible to understand their online behavioral habits and preferences, so as to provide the network users with more efficient and personalized network services and bring about a better using experience. Meanwhile, it can also provide a basis for updating network security policies.

This work was supported by a grant from the Key Research and Development Program of Zhejiang (No. 2017C03058), Zhejiang Provincial Key Laboratory of New Network Standards and Technologies (NNST) (No.2013E10012).

© ICST Institute for Computer Sciences, Social Informatics and Telecommunications Engineering 2018
L. Meng and Y. Zhang (Eds.): MLICOM 2018, LNICST 251, pp. 73–80, 2018.
https://doi.org/10.1007/978-3-030-00557-3_8

At present, the research on behavioral profiling of internet users mainly focuses on two directions [13]: abnormally behavior analysis and normal behavioral preference profile. Abnormal behavioral analysis of network users is to find the data information that does not within "normal behavioral pattern" scale. Accordingly, we can achieve the goal to maintain network security and prevent potential threats. Another research direction–analysis of network user behavioral preference has been widely developed on the internet. The purpose of this analysis is mainly to provide users with accurate marketing service and then produce network service [2] of high quality.

Most of the research on network users' behavior is to make required statistic or predictive analysis upon their normal online behavioral data, except of making automatic identification of network users. When developing and issuing network services strategy, they need to do this manually according to the network user's IP address. However, the user's IP address may change dynamically, which requires network administrators to identify artificially. This obviously increases the workload of network administrators. Besides, excessive human intervention will increase the probability of making mistake in managing network. Therefore, this paper proposes the applying of deep learning technique to identify network users automatically.

The remainder of the paper is structured as follows: Sect. 2 reviews the related research on network behavioral profiling. Section 3 explains the network identification model based on Deep Belief Network (DBN) [12], including its training phase and classification phase. The details about how to use the Tensorflow framework [6] to build the DBN-based model, how to construct data set and how to determine model parameters are presented in Sect. 4, followed by an experiment in Sect. 5-examining the classification accuracy of the model with test dataset. The last section is the conclusions of this article.

## 2 Related Research

At present, the research on behavioral profile of internet users mainly focuses on two fields: abnormal behavior and normal behavioral preferences. The common method of profiling network users' behavior is using cluster to profile. Celebi [4] improved the performance of the k-means clustering algorithm by applying windowing techniques to the clustering process. Tan [11] introduced an implicit semi-Markov model into a piece-wise k-means algorithm to train the algorithm. Ayeldeen [3] utilized vocabulary-similarity based k-means algorithm to improve the accuracy of estimation of the similarity. Ruijuan [10] proposed a user abnormal behavior profiling approach based on neural network clustering to solve the over-fitting and flooding of feature information. Guan [5] proposed and implemented to profile user behavioral preferences based on Hadoop distribution platform. Researchers [9] proposed a personalized service pattern of library that can capture readers' characteristics accurately. This pattern can provide readers with efficient and economical personalized service and have a high user satisfaction. Ma and other researchers [1] proposed an improved BP [8] neural network algorithm based on artificial bee colony algorithm, which can improve the efficiency and accuracy of profiling different users' behavior effectively.

This paper proposes for the first time to apply deep learning technology to learn the underlying relationships among user's behavior characteristics, so as to achieve a high identification precision of network user. Whilst it may provide a reference for further study about applying deep learning technology to network users' behavior analysis.

## 3    Construction of Users' Identification Model

This section bases on the TensorFlow framework to build a DBN-based model for network users identification. Its structure is divided into four parts: data collection, data pre-processing, determination of the model-parameters and training of the DBN-based model. First, construct an initialized DBN-based model with the TensorFlow. Second, we determine the number of hidden nodes and hidden layers of the DBN-based model through experiments. Then use the training dataset to train the DBN-based model, including unsupervised training [7] and supervised training [8]. After training, we obtain the DBN-based model with better weight parameters. Finally, utilize the test dataset to evaluate the classified effect of the DBN-based model. The input of the model is real network traffic data of a college. The output of the model are three categories, representing teachers, postgraduates and undergraduates respectively.

### 3.1    Data Collection

In this experiment, the traffic data from college's user generated over a seven-day period was used as the dataset utilized by the network user identification model based on deep learning. In order to profile the behavioral characteristics of network users better, we will use sFlow art to collect network traffic data. The dataset is then divided into seven sub-sets (i.e., the Dataset1–Dataset7); each data set contains 50000 streams.

### 3.2    Data Pre-processing

Since the network traffic data may present problems in format, information integrity and so on, the raw network traffic information we obtained can't be used directly as the input for the research model. So firstly, this experiment processes the packet by cleaning data noise, filling missing value and operating redundant data; These datasets contain features and tags. Eigenvalues of high quality are the premise of model classification experiments; the quality of feature values will directly affect the classification effect of the model. When examining the identification performance of the model, we need to compare the output of the model with the tags of the test dataset. Therefore, we have to normalize the feature sets and carry on one-hot encoding upon the tag sets to make the dataset suitable for the input of the model. Then use the processed data-Dataset1–Dataset2 as the unsupervised training data set (without labels) for model; select a single Dataset3 set of data (including tag) for supervised fine-tune phase; Dataset4–Dataset7 are used as the test data set (with label) for examining model performance.

Features of the datasets are as those extracted in reference [3] of its network user behavioral profiling. See features detail in Table 1.

**Table 1.** Features of experimental dataset

| Time stamp | Source IP address | Destination IP address |
|---|---|---|
| Agreement type | Flow size | |

We select 3 types of identities: teachers, graduates and undergraduates as the data label; we collect 15 IPs previously, 5 IPs of each identity-type. The specific data is as the Table 2 below.

**Table 2.** Experimental tag

| Teacher | | Postgraduate | | Undergraduate | |
|---|---|---|---|---|---|
| Label | IP | Label | IP | Label | IP |
| 1 | 10.20.0.161 | 6 | 10.20.216.158 | 11 | 10.20.3.168 |
| 2 | 10.20.0.164 | 7 | 10.20.216.21 | 12 | 10.20.3.172 |
| 3 | 10.20.0.200 | 8 | 10.20.216.77 | 13 | 10.20.3.173 |
| 4 | 10.20.216.31 | 9 | 10.20.216.67 | 14 | 10.20.3.174 |
| 5 | 10.20.1.42 | 10 | 10.20.216.78 | 15 | 10.20.3.184 |

### 3.3  Determination of the Model Parameters

Before the unsupervised training of DBN-based model, we need to determine the number of hidden nodes and hidden layers. The number of hidden layer nodes will affect the model's effect on the abstract expression of features; the number of hidden layers will be directly related to the depth of the DBN-based model. And the increase in the number of hidden layers is conducive to a more comprehensive study of the characteristics. Since the problem of taking the number of different nodes and different hidden layers into account together is complicated, this section will firstly study the determination of the number of suitable hidden nodes when the model contains two hidden layers. Then, when the number of hidden nodes is appropriate, we study the appropriate number of hidden layers.

**Determination of the Number of Hidden Nodes**

At the first step, we can obtain its value in a range with reference to empirical formula (e.g., formula 1) that conventional neural networks utilized for determining the number of hidden nodes of each layer. Through several times of experimental comparison about the classification effect among models which vary in the number of hidden nodes, we can eventually acquire the number of hidden nodes corresponding to the model with the best classification performance; put it as the numerical value for later experiment.

We select the DBN-based model only containing 2 hidden layers as initial model. After calculating with the formula 1 we get the range of n, [1, 14]; we set numerical values of n as consecutive integer in the range of 1 to 14. In order to perform fully comparable experiment, we selected another 6 points-16, 20, 21, 22, 26, 30.

$$n = \sqrt{m+p} + a \qquad (1)$$

In the equation above, "m" represents the number of input feature items; "p" stands for the number of output label items; "n" is the number of hidden layer nodes, and a symbolizes an integer within [1, 10].

When there is difference in the number of different hidden layer nodes, the overall classification accuracy of the model will be variant; the result is shown in Fig. 1 below. The sum of the unsupervised and supervised training time of the model is used as the total training time of the model. The total training time of the models containing different number of hidden nodes is compared and shown in Fig. 2 below.

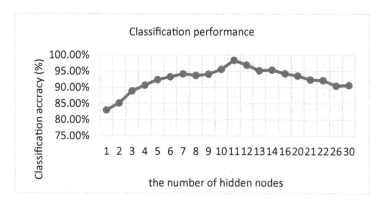

**Fig. 1.** The classification performance of the models with different number of hidden nodes

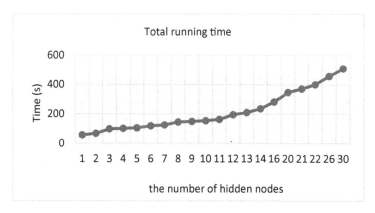

**Fig. 2.** Total running time of the models corresponding to the different number of hidden nodes

As what's shown in Fig. 1, in the range of [1, 7], the classification accuracy rate of the model grows rapidly, and then slows down. When n = 11, the classification accuracy of the model reached a maximum of about 98.4%.

On the basis of the result in Fig. 2, we may come to the conclusion that with the growth in the number of hidden nodes, the total run-time of the models is increasing. Especially when n > 11, its total run-time would be in a faster growing trend. Due to this, we set the number of hidden layer nodes applied to the DBN-based model to 11 (i.e., n = 11).

**Determination of the Number of Hidden Layers**
The number of hidden layers will directly affect the depth of the DBN model. The researchers [10] proved that the accuracy of the classification can be further improved by increasing the number of hidden layers of the DBN model to improve the abstraction ability of the data features. But not the more the number of hidden layers is, the better the classification effect will be.

According to the analysis before, the number of hidden nodes of each layer is set to 11. We will train the model respectively with different number of hidden layers, from 1 to 6. By having train on DBN-based models containing different number of hidden layers, we can obtain a group of corresponding DBN-based models. Then use the test dataset-Dataset 4–Dataset7 (Including tags) to examine those DBN-based models respectively; analyze the classification accuracy and total running time of different models so as to select the proper number of hidden layers corresponding to the model that achieves better classification effect as the final number of hidden layers for the DBN-based model. Table 3 shows the details about the classification accuracy and total running time of different numbers of hidden layers.

It can be seen from the table above that the total running time of every DBN-based models with 11 nodes of each hidden layer increases as the number of hidden layers grows. However, the classification accuracy of models increases first and then decreases with the increase of the number of hidden layers. When the number of hidden layers is n = 4, the classification accuracy of the model reaches the highest value of about 98%. And when n = 4, the running time of model is about 502 s. The time consumption is not big. Therefore, this chapter determines to build a DBN-based model with 4 hidden layers.

**Table 3.** Performance of the models

| The number of hidden layers | Classification accuracy | Running time (s) |
|---|---|---|
| 1 | 93.2% | 201.1 |
| 2 | 95.1% | 308.7 |
| 3 | 96.4% | 446.5 |
| 4 | 98.1% | 502.2 |
| 5 | 96.7% | 593.7 |
| 6 | 94.6% | 742.2 |

As the demonstration above, through the analysis of many experimental results, this paper finally determines to train the DBN-based model with 4 hidden layers and 11 hidden nodes of each hidden layer.

### 3.4 Training Phase of the Model

Process training on the constructed DBN-based model. The first step is to carry on unsupervised training with unlabeled-datasets, constructing a model initially. Then utilize Dataset3 (including tag) to adjust the model after being processed unsupervised training. That is, the weights trained in the unsupervised phase are transferred to the BP neural network for reverse fine-tuning of the DBN-based model. As a result, a fully trained DBN-based model is obtained which means we have constructed a complete identification model based on DBN.

## 4 Performance Examination of the Model

### 4.1 Experimental Environment

The experimental platform for this paper is an Intel Core i5 processor with a 3.3 GHz, 14.0 GB memory on a HP computer running window 10 (64 bit) operating system. This paper uses the TensorFlow framework to build the DBN-based model, in which all DBN-based algorithms are implemented in Python language.

Specific version of the software tools used herein is Tensorflow1.2.1, Python3.5.1.

### 4.2 Experimental Data and Results

In this experiment, we collect the data according to the method described in Sect. 3.1, and then pre-process the collected data according to the method in Sect. 3.2 of this paper. Thereafter, 4 labeled datasets-Dataset4–Dataset7 are utilized as the test dataset to process validation on previously trained DBN-based model. Figure 3 presents the results about classification accuracy of the model we come to.

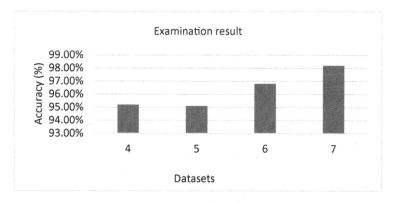

**Fig. 3.** Examination result

From the Fig. 3 above it may be seen, for different sets of data, the classification precision of the same model is various. This is the result of the difference in distribution of network user categories each dataset contained. It can be learned from the figure that the DBN-based model has a classification accuracy of over 95% for these four data sets and a maximum of 98%. Experimental results show that DBN-based model has a high accuracy for network user identification.

## 5 Conclusions

Aiming at the deficiencies of prior art in network users' identification, combining with the current prevalence of deep learning, this paper presents a study on DBN-based network users' identification. Deep learning technology is applied to identify network users and to find the underlying relationships among the behavioral characteristics of network users. Thus, improve the accuracy of network user identification. And utilizes the real traffic data of a college as the research object. The final experimental results show that the DBN-based model can achieve a high classification accuracy of network users.

## References

1. Ma, J., Zhou, G., Xu, B., et al.: A microblog user impact analysis method based on the diffusion of topic. Univ. Inf. Eng. **14**(6), 735–742 (2013)
2. Zhou, J.: Network User Behavior Analysis for SDN Firewall. Zhejiang Gongshang University (2017)
3. Ayeldeen, H., Hassanien, A.E., Fahmy, A.A.: Lexical similarity using fuzzy Euclidean distance. In: 2014 International Conference on Engineering and Technology (ICET), pp. 1–6. IEEE, (2014)
4. Celebi, M.E., Kingravi, H.A., Vela, P.A.A.: A comparative study of efficient initialization methods for the k-means clustering algorithm. Expert Syst. Appl. **40**(1), 200–210 (2013)
5. Guan, J., Yao, S., Xu, C., Zhang, H.: Design and implementation of network user behaviors analysis based on hadoop for big data. In: Batten, L., Li, G., Niu, W., Warren, M. (eds.) ATIS 2014. CCIS, vol. 490, pp. 44–55. Springer, Heidelberg (2014). https://doi.org/10.1007/978-3-662-45670-5_5
6. Huang, S., Chen, K., Liu, C., et al.: A statistical-feature-based approach to internet traffic classification using machine learning. In: International Conference on Ultra Modern Telecommunications & Workshops, pp 1–6. IEEE (2009)
7. Le, Q.V.: Building high-level features using large scale unsupervised learning. In: 2013 IEEE International Conference on Acoustics, Speech and Signal Processing, pp. 8595–8598. IEEE (2013)
8. Oravec, M., Podhradsky, P.: Medical image compression by backpropagation neural network and discrete orthogonal transforms. WIT Trans. Biomed. Heal. **4** (1970)
9. Paik, J.H.: A novel TF-IDF weighting scheme for effective ranking, pp. 343–352 (2013)
10. Ruijuan, Z., Jing, C., Mingchuan, Z., et al.: User abnormal behavior analysis based on neural network clustering. J. China Univ. Posts Telecommun. **23**(3), 29–44 (2016)
11. Tan, X., Xi, H.: Hidden semi-Markov model for anomaly detection. Appl. Math. Comput. **205**(2), 562–567 (2008)
12. Hinton, G., Osindero, S.: A fast learning algorithm for deep belief nets. Neural Comput. **18**(7), 1527–1554 (2006)
13. Dong, F.: Studies and utilization on network users' behavior analysis. Xidian University (2005)

# Intelligent Positioning and Navigation

# An Improved Constrained Least Squares Localization Algorithm in NLOS Propagating Environment

Yejia Yin[1], Jingyu Hua[1(✉)], Fangni Chen[1], Weidang Lu[1],
Dongming Wang[2], and Jiamin Li[2]

[1] College of Information Engineering, Zhejiang University of Technology,
Hangzhou 310023, China
eehjy@163.com
[2] National Mobile Communications Research Laboratory,
Southeast University, Nanjing 210096, China

**Abstract.** The non-line-of-sight (NLOS) error is a major error source in wireless localization. Therefore, an improved constrained least-squares (CLS) algorithm is put forward to tackle this issue, where the positioning problem is formulated as a mathematical programming problem. And then, the cost function of the optimization is studied and a new one is proposed. Finally, through the presented optimization, we try to minimize the positioning influence of NLOS errors. Moreover, the studied method does not depend on a particular distribution of the NLOS error. Simulation results show that the positioning accuracy is significantly improved over traditional CLS algorithms, even under highly NLOS conditions.

**Keywords:** Wireless localization · Non-line-of-sight error
Constrained least squares · Time of arrival

## 1 Introduction

With the rapid developments of mobile Internet, smart city and intelligent home, the wireless positioning technology had been an unprecedented strong concern. The wireless positioning systems in cellular networks usually located a mobile station (MS) by measuring radio signals between the MS and base stations (BS), which was specifically necessary for the safety-aided positioning system. Generally, the localization methods might concern the received signal strength (RSS) [1], time of arrival (TOA), time difference of arrival (TDOA), angle of arrival (AOA), or hybrid of them [2, 3]. Since the TOA method is most popular and simple [4], we focus on this kind of method in our study.

If a line of sight (LOS) propagation exists between the MS and BSs, a high localization accuracy can be achieved [5]. However, the wireless network (including the cellular network) propagation may be affected by a lot of obstacles so as to cause the signal refraction and scattering in the event of obstacles, i.e., the non-line-of-sight (NLOS) propagation. There had been some literatures on how to mitigate NLOS errors,

© ICST Institute for Computer Sciences, Social Informatics and Telecommunications Engineering 2018
L. Meng and Y. Zhang (Eds.): MLICOM 2018, LNICST 251, pp. 83–91, 2018.
https://doi.org/10.1007/978-3-030-00557-3_9

such as the two-step maximum-likelihood (ML) algorithm [6], which produced high accuracy when the NLOS error is not significant [7, 8]. Besides, a robust NLOS error mitigation method via second-order cone relaxation was studied in [9], where the worst NLOS error model was chosen as the Gaussian distributions. In general, the algorithms mitigating NLOS errors could be divided into two classes. The first one was to identify BS with LOS or NLOS propagation, and then exploited only the LOS BS to estimate the MS position [10]. However, this kind of algorithm usually required three more LOS BSs. The second kind of algorithm was to employ the optimization theory to find the optimal solution of MS position, as those done in [9, 11], where the performance improvements was limited if the NLOS distribution was unknown [12].

In order to tackle above issues, we propose an improved constraint least-squares (CLS) algorithm, where the geometric relations between MS and BS are employed as the constraints and a new cost function is presented as well. The whole localization problem is formulated as an optimization problem. Besides, a grouping operation is proposed to further improve the localization performance. Thus our contributions lie on two aspects, i.e., the new CLS model and the grouping improvement. The simulation results show that the proposed algorithm is superior to the traditional methods.

## 2  Basic Model

### 2.1  NLOS Measurement Model

The TOA method measures the range between each BS and the MS which is to be located. By incorporating the influences of NLOS propagation, we define the ranging measurement as

$$r_i = d_i + NLOS_i + n_i, \ i = 1, 2, 3 \ldots, M \tag{1}$$

where $M$, $NLOS_i$ and $n_i$ represent the BS number, the NLOS error and the measurement noise, respectively. (here the measured noise value is much smaller than the NLOS error) Note that the noise is modeled as a zero-mean Gaussian process with standard deviation $\sigma$. In (1), we have

$$d_i = \sqrt{(x - x_i)^2 + (y - y_i)^2}, \ i = 1, 2, 3 \ldots M \tag{2}$$

where $(x_i, y_i)$ and $(x, y)$ denote the coordinate of $i$-th BS and the targeted MS.

### 2.2  The Constrained Least Squares Algorithm

In order to mitigate the influence of NLOS error, the traditional algorithm based on the optimization theory try to find an optimal solution within the feasible range (FR), i.e.,

$$\begin{array}{l} \text{minimize} \quad function(X) \\ \text{subject to} \quad constraints \end{array} \tag{3}$$

where *function*$(X)$ represents the cost function. Generally, different cost functions lead to different positioning accuracy.

If it is in the LOS environment, we have

$$r_i = d_i = \sqrt{(x - x_i)^2 + (y - y_i)^2} \tag{4}$$

It is equivalent to

$$r_i^2 - K_i = -2x_i x - 2y_i y + x^2 + y^2 \tag{5}$$

where $K_i = x_i^2 + y_i^2$.

Taking into account of NLOS environment, we have

$$d_i = \alpha_i r_i \tag{6}$$

Where $\alpha_i \leq 1$. Hence, the following expression can be derived as

$$r_i^2 - K_i \geq -2x_i x - 2y_i y + x^2 + y^2 \tag{7}$$

It's matrix form can be written as

$$\mathbf{h} \geq \mathbf{Gz}$$

where

$$\mathbf{h} = \begin{bmatrix} r_1^2 - K_1 \\ r_2^2 - K_2 \\ \vdots \\ r_M^2 - K_M \end{bmatrix}, \mathbf{G} = \begin{bmatrix} -2x_1, -2y_1, 1 \\ -2x_2, -2y_2, 1 \\ \vdots \\ -2x_M, -2y_M, 1 \end{bmatrix}, \mathbf{z} = \begin{bmatrix} x \\ y \\ R \end{bmatrix} \tag{8}$$

where $R = x^2 + y^2$ in theory. But this equation will be broken in real-world applications due to the influence of NLOS error and measurement noise. Accordingly, next section we will propose a new cost function in the CLS localization.

In traditional CLS algorithm [14], the localization problem was expressed as:

$$\min_{\mathbf{z}} \quad (\mathbf{h} - \mathbf{Gz})^T \mathbf{\Psi}^{-1} (\mathbf{h} - \mathbf{Gz})$$
$$subject \quad to \tag{9}$$
$$\mathbf{Gz} \leq \mathbf{h}$$

Where $\mathbf{\Psi} = E[\psi \psi^T] = 4c^2 \mathbf{BQB}$, $\mathbf{B} = diag(d_1, \dots, d_M)$

$$\mathbf{Q} = diag(\sigma_1^2, \dots, \sigma_M^2).$$

Here $\mathbf{Q}$ represents the measurement error variance. As we know, in reality the entries in the diagonal of $\mathbf{B}$ are unknown. Therefore, we can use measured values instead of the true values for estimating, then using this initial solution and afterwards get a further accurate result iterationly until it reaches convergence.

## 3  Improved Constrained Least-Squares Algorithm

### 3.1  The New Cost Function in CLS Mode

As indicated previously, if the cost function of (9) is changed, the resulted new optimization problem will produce different positioning accuracy. Moreover, we have mentioned that R equals $x^2 + y^2$ in theory, but the non-ideal factors, such as NLOS error and measurement noise, make the equation be broken. Besides, the higher extent of non-ideal factor lead to the larger deviation. Hence, our study takes into consideration a novel cost function as:

$$function = \mathbf{z}^T \mathbf{p} \mathbf{z} + \mathbf{q} \mathbf{z} \tag{10}$$

where

$$\mathbf{p} = \begin{bmatrix} 1 & 0 & 0 \\ 0 & 1 & 0 \\ 0 & 0 & 0 \end{bmatrix}, \mathbf{q} = \begin{bmatrix} 0 & 0 & -1 \end{bmatrix}, \mathbf{z} = (x, y, R)^T \tag{11}$$

Here $\mathbf{z}$ is a vector containing unknowns, then the improved CLS algorithm can be rewritten as:

$$\begin{aligned} \min_{\mathbf{z}} \quad & \mathbf{z}^T \mathbf{p} \mathbf{z} + \mathbf{q} \mathbf{z} \\ subject \quad to \quad & \\ & \mathbf{G} \mathbf{z} \le \mathbf{h} \end{aligned} \tag{12}$$

Figure 1 presents a preliminary performance for (12), where the standard deviation of measurement noise is 20 m and the NLOS error is uniformly distributed in 0–300 m. We can compare the positioning accuracy of the constrained least squares algorithm under two different objective functions. After simulation comparison, we clearly see that the performance of model (12) outperforms that of model (9). For example, when the cumulative distributed probability is 0.9, the localization error of model (12) is about 180 m, while it is 240 m for model (9).

Figure 2 further compares the performance of two CLS methods. However, we find different observations from those of Fig. 1. From Fig. 2, we explicitly see that these two methods produce nearly the same performance, which means that the proposed new cost function is not suitable for three more BSs.

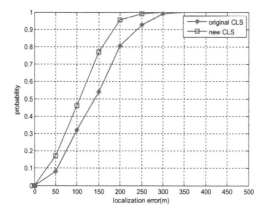

**Fig. 1.** Comparisons of two CLS methods: three BSs

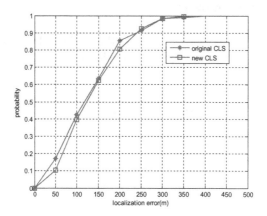

**Fig. 2.** Comparisons of two CLS methods: four BSs

### 3.2 The Grouping Improvement

According to the above analysis and observation, we must release the limitation of BS number for model (12). A simple grouping method can be applied here, i.e.,

(1) Participating the BSs into $N$ three-BS groups. In our study, $N = C_5^3$.
(2) Estimating MS positions for every BS groups through the linear line of position (LLOP) algorithm [14].
(3) Calculating the cost function (10) for each BS group.
(4) Sorting the cost function values.
(5) Choosing five BS groups with least costs. Since each BS group produces a MS position estimation, there are five MS estimates:

$$
\begin{aligned}
MS_1 &: (\hat{x}_1, \hat{y}_1),\\
MS_2 &: (\hat{x}_2, \hat{y}_2),\\
MS_3 &: (\hat{x}_3, \hat{y}_3),\\
MS_4 &: (\hat{x}_4, \hat{y}_4),\\
MS_5 &: (\hat{x}_5, \hat{y}_5),
\end{aligned}
\tag{13}
$$

(6) Averaging all MS estimates to obtain the final MS estimation, i.e.,

$$
\begin{aligned}
\hat{x} &= \frac{\hat{x}_1 + \hat{x}_2 + \hat{x}_3 + \hat{x}_4 + \hat{x}_5}{5}\\
\hat{y} &= \frac{\hat{y}_1 + \hat{y}_2 + \hat{y}_3 + \hat{y}_4 + \hat{y}_5}{5}
\end{aligned}
\tag{14}
$$

## 4 Simulation and Analysis

In the simulations, we concern the classical five BS topology [11]. Moreover, we divide this topology into two cases to study effects of BS number:

- Case 1: three BSs at

$$
(0,0), (1/2 \cdot r, \sqrt{3}/2 \cdot r), (r, 0)
$$

- Case 2: five BSs at

$$
\begin{aligned}
&(0,0), (1/2 \cdot r, \sqrt{3}/2 \cdot r), (r, 0),\\
&(-r, 0), (-1/2 \cdot r, \sqrt{3}/2 \cdot r)
\end{aligned}
$$

where $r$ denotes the cell diameter, and it is 1000 meters in our simulations. Note that the topology of case 1 is the same as that applied for Figs. 1 and 2. Moreover, the standard deviation of measured noise leads to $\sigma = 20$ m, and the NLOS error is modeled as a random variable uniformly distributed in 150– 450 m. We must point out that the NLOS scenario employed here is much worse than that in Fig. 1. Besides, the MS position is randomly produced in the area enclosed by the base stations.

There are four algorithms are compared, such as the TOA least squares (TOA LS) algorithm, the TOA CLS algorithm, the range scaling algorithm (RSA) [15] and the proposed algorithm. The simulation results are shown as follows, where each simulation includes two hundred runs.

We can see from Fig. 3 that the proposed method has more than 90% probability that the positioning error is less than 300 m, which has higher accuracy than the original CLS method, and produces similar performance of the RSA method. However, since the NLOS error is obviously enlarged, the CDF of Fig. 3 is much worse than that in Fig. 1. Hence, we need more BSs to combat the serious NLOS corruption.

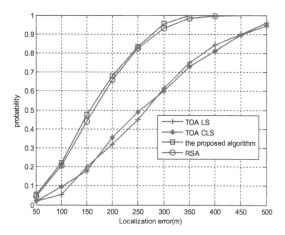

**Fig. 3.** Probability performance comparisons: three BSs

Figure 4 shows the CDF performance at five-BS topology. From it, we explicitly see that the increase of BS number significantly improve the proposed algorithm, while the RSA method remains nearly invariable CDF. We can concluded from Fig. 1 plus Fig. 4 that the increase of BS number can make the proposed algorithm be workable with more NLOS corruptions.

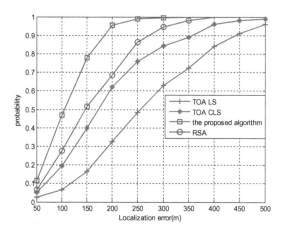

**Fig. 4.** Probability performance comparisons: five BSs

Next we will address the influence of the maximal NLOS error in case 2, where we denote the maximal NLOS error as the variable MAX. Then MAX takes value from 200–500, and the standard deviation of measured noise remains 20 m.

Figure 5 compares the root-mean-square-error (RMSE) of different methods, where the proposed method performs the best among all methods. Moreover, the results demonstrate that the CLS method is better than the RSA method for a smaller MAX.

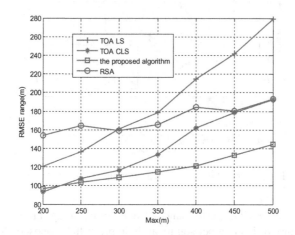

**Fig. 5.** RMSE comparisons for different MAX: five BSs.

## 5   Conclusion and Discussion

This paper proposes an improved CLS method to estimate the MS position in the wireless network, where the cost function is modified compared with the conventional CLS method. Moreover, a grouping method is proposed to further improve the CLS method.

Through the analysis and comparison of the above simulation results, we can see the proposed method's positioning accuracy outperforms the other three methods, especially for the scenarios with serious NLOS corruptions and large BS numbers.

**Acknowledgement.** This paper was sponsored by the National NSF of China No.61471322.

## References

1. Yan, Y.: Efficient convex optimization method for underwater passive source localization based on RSS with WSN. In: Proceedings of the 2012 IEEE International Conference on Signal Processing, Communication and Computing, pp. 171–174 (2012)
2. Gong, X., Ning, Z., Guo, L., et al.: Location-recommendation-aware virtual network embedding in energy-efficient optical-wireless hybrid networks supporting 5G models. IEEE Access **4**, 3065–3075 (2016)
3. Gong, X., Zhang, Q., Guo, L.: Optical-wireless hybrid virtual network embedding based on location recommendations. In: International Conference on Transparent Optical Networks, pp. 1–4. IEEE (2016)

4. Wu, N., Xiong, Y., Wang, H., et al.: A performance limit of TOA-based location-aware wireless networks with ranging outliers. IEEE Commun. Lett. **19**(8), 1414–1417 (2015)
5. Ke, W., Wu, L.: Constrained least squares algorithm for TOA-based mobile location under NLOS environments. In: International Conference on Wireless Communications, NETWORKING and Mobile Computing, pp. 1–4. IEEE (2009)
6. Chan, Y.T., Hang, H.Y.C., Ching, P.C.: Exact and approximate maximum likelihood localization algorithms. IEEE Trans. Veh. Technol. **55**(1), 10–16 (2006)
7. Zhang, J., Dong, F., Feng, G., et al.: Analysis of the NLOS channel environment of TDOA multiple algorithms. In: Sensors, pp. 1–4. IEEE (2016)
8. Zhong, Z., Jeong, J., Zhu, T., et al.: Node localization in wireless sensor networks. In: Handbook on Sensor Networks, pp. 535–563 (2014)
9. Zhang, S., Gao, S., Wang, G., et al.: Robust NLOS error mitigation method for TOA-based localization via second-order cone relaxation. IEEE Commun. Lett. **19**(12), 2210–2213 (2015)
10. Li, X., Cai, X., Hei, Y., Yuan, R.: NLOS identification and mitigation based on channel state information for indoor WiFi localization. IET Commun. **11**(4), 531–537 (2017)
11. Zheng, X., Hua, J., Zheng, Z., Zhou, S., Jiang, B.: LLOP localization algorithm with optimal scaling in NLOS wireless propagations. In: Proceedings of the 2013 IEEE 4th International Conference on Electronics Information and Emergency Communication, Beijing, pp. 45–48 (2013)
12. Li, X., Cao, F.: Location based TOA algorithm for UWB wireless body area networks. In: IEEE, International Conference on Dependable, Autonomic and Secure Computing, pp. 507–511. IEEE (2014)
13. Wang, X., Wang, Z., O'Dea, B.: A TOA-based location algorithm reducing the errors due to non-line-of-sight (NLOS) propagation. J. China Inst. Commun. **52**(1), 112–116 (2003)
14. Zheng, X., Hua, J., Zheng, Z., et al.: LLOP localization algorithm with optimal scaling in NLOS wireless propagations. In: IEEE International Conference on Electronics Information and Emergency Communication, pp. 45–48. IEEE (2014)
15. Wu, S., Li, J., Liu, S., et al.: Improved and extended range scale algorithm for wireless cellular location. IEEE Commun. Lett. **16**(2), 196–198 (2012)

# Intelligent Multimedia Processing and Security

# Fast Inter Prediction Mode Decision Algorithm Based on Data Mining

Tengrui Shi[1,2], Xiaobo Guo[2], Daihui Mo[3,4], and Jian Wang[1(✉)]

[1] Nanjing University, NJU,
Nanjing 210023, Jiangsu, People's Republic of China
wangjnju@nju.edu.cn
[2] Science and Technology on Information Transmission and Dissemination
in Communication Networks Laboratory, The 54th Institute of CETC,
Shijiazhuang 050081, Hebei, People's Republic of China
[3] Department of Electronic Engineering, Tsinghua University,
Beijing 100084, People's Republic of China
[4] Academy of Military Sciences PLA China,
Beijing 100091, People's Republic of China

**Abstract.** The HEVC greatly improves coding efficiency. However, this is accompanied by an increase in the complexity of the coding calculation, which is higher than H.264. We find that there are several features that are highly correlated with the CU's best split decision in inter prediction. As a result, we choose decision trees to solve the splitting decision problem. We implement the decision trees on official software HM16.2 and test the algorithm on the testing set. Experiments indicate that the fast decision algorithm improve the coding performance more efficiently than some existing algorithms.

**Keywords:** HEVC · Inter prediction · Data mining · Decision trees

## 1  Introduction

The performance of HEVC in many aspects is better than previous standards with more flexible data structures and other new technologies [1]. The improved intra prediction and inter prediction technology has greatly improved accuracy in sample prediction and so on. Nevertheless, these improvements result in a significant increase in coding computational complexity [2].

For each frame of the input encoder, it is divided into some block CTUs (Coding Tree Units). The coding trees are used to divide CTUs into multiple CUs (coding units). CU is the leaf node of a coding tree, and a CU can contain one or more PUs(prediction unit). There are nine division modes in the inter mode, including three square shapes (MSM, 2Nx2N, NN), two rectangular shapes (2NN, N2N), and four asymmetrical shapes (2NnU, 2N nD, nL2N, nR2N) which are presented in Fig. 1.

© ICST Institute for Computer Sciences, Social Informatics and Telecommunications Engineering 2018
L. Meng and Y. Zhang (Eds.): MLICOM 2018, LNICST 251, pp. 95–102, 2018.
https://doi.org/10.1007/978-3-030-00557-3_10

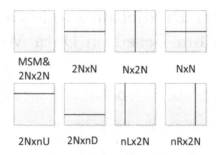

**Fig. 1.** PU partition modes

In this paper, we make use of a few new features and Correa's original features to establish four decision trees which are aimed to determine whether CU is segmented into smaller PUs in inter prediction. The reminder is arranged as follows: Sect. 2 introduces our motivation and overview of related work. Section 3 presents the fast decision algorithm with decision trees. Section 4 shows the experimental results. Finally, we do a summary of the full text in Sect. 5.

## 2 Motivation and Related Work

Numerous papers have studied the algorithms on reduction of computation complexity of HEVC encoders. By using top omitting and bottom pruning, Guo [3] present an algorithm based on subtree distribution. Xiong [4] proposed an algorithm based on SAD estimation. Zhong [5] proposed an algorithm about CU segmentation between adjacent frames. However, all these works bring about losses related to R-D efficiency, and the losses can not be ignored.

All prediction modes are performed in the encoder, and eventually the division between the modes is not equal. Figure 2 is a graph of the probability distribution of each mode of the CU. The figure indicates that most of $8 \times 8$ and $16 \times 16$ CUs are encoded as MSM. All modes are tested, which wastes a lot of time. Nevertheless, the increase of R-D costs is great, when we directly delete other modes from Table 3 in Sect. 4. If we can precisely predict the split situation of CU, once the prediction results that the current CU has to be encoded as only one PU, the remaining partition modes can be directly ignored without being tested. This will effectively reduce the coding time for inter prediction without significantly affecting coding efficiency.

Related research was proposed by Correa [8,9] and Li [10], which used machine learning to reduce the computational the coding complexity. They conducted some data analysis and selected some of the features associated with CU splitting. Finally, they used machine learning as a tool to leverage these features to build decision trees which could predict whether each CU would be split into smaller PUs. This algorithm selects some more comprehensive features, reducing the computational complexity while maintaining a low loss of R-D efficiency.

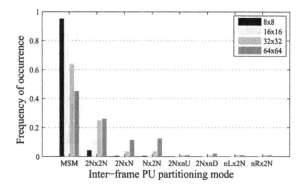

**Fig. 2.** Partition modes in inter prediction

# 3   Fast Algorithm Based on Data Mining

## 3.1   Data Analysis and Optimization

Data Mining is a procedure of analyzing multiple data, and gathering it into valuable information and modes. Supervised learning is one class of data mining [11], which is in connection with the involving algorithm in this paper. Decision trees [12] are models built through predictive Supervised Learning.Decision trees are built by using C4.5 algorithm [13] to obtain encoding optimization.

The encoding features are revealed in this subsection by presenting a series of statistics, and we optimized these features to obtain four accurate decision trees.

In order to obtain features that contribute to CU splitting decisions, many attributes are listed below. In [8,9], Correa thinks that some features (2Nx2N and MSM mode RD cost, 2Nx2N and MSM mode residue cost, the RD cost ratio between 2Nx2N and MSM mode, and splitting decision in CU of previous tree depth) are highly correlated with the split situation. Besides those mentioned by Correa, we found that the lower of MSM mode RD-cost and the lower of 2Nx2N mode RD-cost, the MV of 2Nx2N PU mode and the MV of MSM PU mode are highly correlated with the best PU partition decision.

We use the relevant features in 1616 CU of the FourPeople sequence as an example for analysis. As shown in Fig. 3, whether it is the MSM mode or the 2Nx2N mode, the RD cost of CU that is not divided into multiple PUs is much smaller than which is divided into multiple PUs. It is undeniable that the range of the rate distortion value is closely related to the features of test sequences such as resolution, texture information, motion information and so on. Therefore, we need to normalize these features. We can find that when the ratio is smaller, the likelihood of no-splitting is higher in Fig. 4 which is similar to other size CUs.

We found MV plays an important role in the PU mode selection. To simplify the calculation of the absolute MV, we only use the absolute values of the x and y MV directions, as shown in (1). $MV_x$ means the horizontal value of MV, and $MV_y$

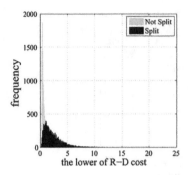

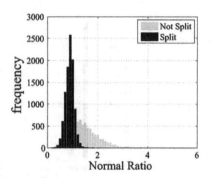

**Fig. 3.** The lower of RD cost

**Fig. 4.** Normal ratio

means the vertical value of MV, and we need to normalize these features. From Figs. 5 and 6, it is noticed to the normalized $MV_{abs}$ present a high correlation with CU-splitting. At last, we decide to combine the features of MV and the lower of normalized MSM mode and normalized 2Nx2N mode RD-cost in our algorithm.

$$MV_{abs} = |MV_x| + |MV_y| \tag{1}$$

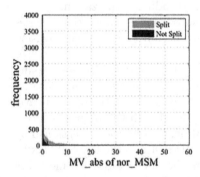

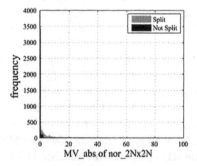

**Fig. 5.** CU not splitting and MV of normal MSM

**Fig. 6.** CU not splitting and MV of normal 2Nx2N

### 3.2   Implementation of Decision Trees

The features chosen by previous analysis are as follows abs_2Nx2N_var (absolute 2Nx2N residue variance), nor_2Nx2N_var (normalized 2Nx2N residue variance), abs_mv_MSM (absolute MSM $MV_{abs}$), nor_mv_MSM (normalized MSM $MV_{abs}$), abs_mv_2Nx2N (absolute 2Nx2N $MV_{abs}$), nor_mv_2Nx2N (normalized 2Nx2N $MV_{abs}$) and Nei_Depth (the CU depth).

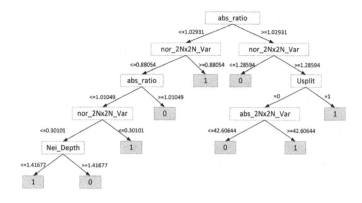

**Fig. 7.** $32 \times 32$ decision tree

Four different decision trees are built from four kinds of different sizes CUs in inter prediction. For fairness [14], we randomly select a data set, half of which consists of splitting CU and the other consists of no-splitting CU from the training sequence data set in Table 2. We use WEKA [15] to build decision trees. Figure 7 displays the obtained $32 \times 32$ decision tree. We have a test on the accuracy of the decision trees to evaluate these trees. From Table 1, we find they have high accuracy, but the decision tree of $64 \times 64$ is relatively less accurate than other trees because $64 \times 64$ decision tree has no Usplit attribute. The decision trees are within six layers with low complexity, so computational complexity can be hardly increased when we apply the decision trees into HM encoder.

**Table 1.** The accuracy of my decision trees

| CU size | Accuracy | Node num | Leave num | Layer |
|---------|----------|----------|-----------|-------|
| $64 \times 64$ | 76.96% | 15 | 8 | 5 |
| $32 \times 32$ | 81.33% | 17 | 9 | 6 |
| $16 \times 16$ | 85.47% | 19 | 10 | 6 |
| $8 \times 8$ | 89.35% | 11 | 6 | 5 |

## 4  Experimental Results and Analysis

### 4.1  Experimental Environment

On the latest version of the official reference software HM16.2, we applied this decision algorithm. In the following, we list computer parameters: CPU of i7-7700, frequency of 3.6 GHz and system of win10.

The video coding standard gives us a series of standard video sequences. These video test sequences are divided into two parts: train set (BlowingBubbles,

RaceHorses, BQMall, SlideShow, Johnny, BasketballDrive, ParkScene, Traffic) and test set (BQSquare, BasketballPass, BasketballDrill, fourpeople, SlideEditing, Catus, BQTerrace, PeopleOnStreet). In experiments, we use low delay configuration. Each test sequence selected four QPs (22, 27, 32 and 37) to encode them respectively, so that we can get average data among the four conditions for every test sequence.

In order to evaluate this algorithm proposed, we compare three encoder versions: the original HM16.2, the simple HM16.2 and the modified HM16.2 with only MSM and 2Nx2N modes enabled. Finally we used CCR and BD-rate to make a comparison among these algorithms.

## 4.2   Experimental Results

The results of 8 sequences encoded with the simple encoders are shown in Table 2. The results of 8 sequences encoded with our proposed encoders are presented in Table 3.

From Table 2, the simple encoder increases average BD-rate by 4.08%, and reduces encoding time by 55.94% in contrast to the original HM 16.2 software model. From Table 3, our proposed algorithm increases average BD-rate by 0.25% and reduces encoding time by 30.18% compared to the original HM 16.2 software model. Average BD-rate of our proposed is 16.32 times smaller than simple algorithm. The BD-rate/CCR of the proposed encoder is 7.3 times smaller than the simple. The BD-PSNR/CCR is 10 times smaller than the simple, which means that our proposed algorithm reduces complexity efficiently with negligible loss.

**Table 2.** The simple method

| Sequence | CCR(%) | BD-rate(%) | BD-PSNR(%) | BD-rate/CCR(%) | BD-PSNR/CCR(%) |
|---|---|---|---|---|---|
| BasketballPass | 56.35 | 7.64 | −0.33 | 13.56 | −0.59 |
| BQSqure | 55.615 | 5.99 | −0.22 | 10.77 | −0.40 |
| BasketballDrill | 52.3 | 2.16 | −0.081 | 1.132 | −0.15 |
| FourPeople | 56.85 | 2.699 | −0.081 | 4.132 | −0.15 |
| SlideEditing | 57.065 | 2.18 | −0.31 | 3.82 | −0.68 |
| Cactus | 56.6 | 2.96 | −0.06 | 5.23 | −0.11 |
| BQTerrace | 57.02 | 3.33 | −0.056 | 5.84 | −0.1 |
| PeopleOnstreet | 57.34 | 3.23 | −0.14 | 5.63 | −0.24 |
| Average | 55.94 | 4.08 | −0.18 | 7.3 | −0.33 |

**Table 3.** Our proposed method

| Sequence | CCR(%) | BD-rate(%) | BD-PSNR(%) | BD-rate/CCR(%) | BD-PSNR/CCR(%) |
|---|---|---|---|---|---|
| BasketballPass | 31.50 | 0.40 | −0.016 | 1.3 | −0.051 |
| BQSqure | 20.45 | 0.21 | −0.0090 | 1.0 | −0.044 |
| BasketballDrill | 28.15 | 0.22 | −0.0081 | 0.76 | −0.029 |
| FourPeople | 38.13 | 0.22 | −0.0063 | 0.57 | −0.017 |
| SlideEditing | 45.02 | −0.053 | 0.0060 | −0.12 | 0.013 |
| Cactus | 28.05 | 0.29 | −0.0057 | 1.0 | −0.020 |
| BQTerrace | 26.55 | 0.23 | −0.0043 | 0.85 | −0.016 |
| PeopleOnstreet | 23.61 | 0.53 | −0.024 | 2.2 | −0.10 |
| Average | 30.18 | 0.25 | −0.0084 | 1.0 | −0.033 |

# 5  Conclusion

In this paper, we introduce Data Mining briefly and regard CU-splitting problem as classification problem. Then we decide to use decision trees to solve the classification problem. Finally, the algorithm is proposed in HM16.2 and we perform experiments related to the test sequences. Based on the above experimental results, we find that this fast decision algorithm can effectively shorten the encoding time and has little effect on the encoding performance.

# References

1. Ohm, J., Sullivan, G.J., Schwarz, H., Tan, T.K., Wiegand, T.: Comparison of the coding efficiency of video coding standards including high efficiency video coding (HEVC). IEEE Trans. Circ. Syst. Video Technol. **22**, 1669–1684 (2012)
2. Bossen, F., Bross, B., Suhring, K., Flynn, D.: HEVC complexity and implementation analysis. IEEE Trans. Circ. Syst. Video Technol. **22**, 1685–1696 (2012)
3. Guo, L., Zhou, L., Tian, X., Chen, Y.: Adaptive coding-unit size selection based on hierarchical quad-tree correlations for high-efficiency video coding. J. Electron. Imaging **24**, 023036–023036 (2015)
4. Xiong, J., Li, H., Meng, F., Wu, Q., Ngan, K.N.: Fast HEVC inter CU decision based on latent SAD estimation. IEEE Trans. Multimed. **17**, 2147–2159 (2015)
5. Zhong, G.Y., He, X.H., Qing, L.B., Li, Y.: Fast inter-mode decision algorithm for high-efficiency video coding based on similarity of coding unit segmentation and partition mode between two temporally adjacent frames. J. Electron. Imaging **22**, 381–388 (2013)
6. Fernández, G., Cuenca, P., Barbosa, L.O., Kalva, H.: Very low complexity MPEG-2 to H.264 transcoding using machine learning. In: Proceedings of the 14th Annual ACM International Conference on Multimedia, pp. 931–940 (2006)
7. Van, L.P., et al.: Fast transrating for high efficiency video coding based on machine learning. In: 2013 20th IEEE International Conference on Image Processing (ICIP), pp. 1573–1577 (2013)

8.  Correa, G., Assuncao, P., Agostini, L., da Silva Cruz, L.A.: A method for early-splitting of HEVC inter blocks based on decision trees. 2014 Proceedings of the 22nd European Signal Processing Conference (EUSIPCO), pp. 276–280 (2014)

9.  Correa, G., Assuncao, P.A., Agostini, L.V., da Silva Cruz, L.A.: Fast HEVC encoding decisions using data mining. IEEE Trans. Circuits Syst. Video Technol. **25**, 660–673 (2015)

10. Li, K., Wang, J.: Fast CU-splitting decisions based on data mining. In: IEEE International Conference on Consumer Electronics-China, pp. 1–5 (2017)

11. Fayyad, U., Piatetsky-Shapiro, G., Smyth, P.: From data mining to knowledge discovery in databases. AI Mag. **17**, 37 (1996)

12. Shan, S.: Decision tree learning. In: Shan, S. (ed.) Machine Learning Models and Algorithms for Big Data Classification, vol. 36, pp. 237–269. Springer, Boston (2016). https://doi.org/10.1007/978-1-4899-7641-3_10

13. Quinlan, J.R.: C4. 5: Programs for Machine Learning. Morgan Kaufmann, Los Altos (1993)

14. Orriols-Puig, A., Bernadó-Mansilla, E.: The Class imbalance problem in UCS classifier system: a preliminary study. In: Kovacs, T., Llorà, X., Takadama, K., Lanzi, P.L., Stolzmann, W., Wilson, S.W. (eds.) IWLCS 2003–2005. LNCS (LNAI), vol. 4399, pp. 161–180. Springer, Heidelberg (2007). https://doi.org/10.1007/978-3-540-71231-2_12

15. Russell, I., Markov, Z.: An introduction to the WEKA data mining system. In: ACM SIGCSE Technical Symposium on Computer Science Education, pp. 742–742 (2017)

# Wireless Mobile Network and Security

# Smartphone Application Identification by Convolutional Neural Network

Shuang Zhao$^{(\boxtimes)}$ and Shuhui Chen

College of Computer, National University of Defense Technology, Changsha, China
Zhaos_abby@163.com, shchen@nudt.edu.cn

**Abstract.** Mobile traffic has received much attention within the field of network security and management due to the rapid development of mobile networks. Unlike fixed wired workstation traffic, mobile traffic is mostly carried over HTTP/HTTPS, which brings new challenges to traditional traffic identification methods. Although there have been some attempts to address this problem with side-channel traffic information and machine learning, the effectiveness of these methods majorly depends on predefined statistics features. In this paper, we presented an approach based on convolutional neural network without explicit feature extraction process. And owing to no payload inspection requirement, this method also works well even encrypted traffic appears. Six instant message applications are used to verify our approach. The evaluation shows the proposed approach can achieve more than 96% accuracy. Additionally, we also discussed how this approach performed under real-world conditions.

**Keywords:** Application identification
Convolutional neural network · Mobile traffic · Encrypted traffic
Network management

## 1 Introduction

With the proliferation of mobile devices and applications, the composition and diversity of network traffic changes tremendously. SmartInsights [1] points out that mobile devices dominate total minutes spent online and Apps drive dominant share of mobile time in all markets. China Statistical Report on Internet Development [2] reports that mobile internet users account for 96.3% of internet users in China. Consequently, mobile traffic has overtaken traditional workstation traffic and occupied a major portion of network traffic. Therefore, mobile traffic monitoring becomes a real concern for individuals, business and related organizations.

For instance, with the aid of mobile traffic identification technology, ISP could figure out which application is using the most bandwidth. Intrusion detection system could identify malicious traffic, and enterprises could identify and limit the use of related apps during office hours. It is worth mentioning that only passive traffic monitor is required during the analysis process.

© ICST Institute for Computer Sciences, Social Informatics and Telecommunications Engineering 2018
L. Meng and Y. Zhang (Eds.): MLICOM 2018, LNICST 251, pp. 105–114, 2018.
https://doi.org/10.1007/978-3-030-00557-3_11

There are some problems when handling mobile traffic by traditional identification methods. Unlike traditional workstation traffic, mobile traffic has some special characteristics: (1) Mobile traffic is mostly carried over HTTP/HTTPS which indicates that port-based identification method nearly useless. (2) The effectiveness of DPI-based methods is diminishing because of encrypted HTTPS traffic. (3) Traditional workstation traffic has too coarse-grained identification targets such as protocols or services, while mobile traffic is required to match with Apps or even particular activities. (4) Technologies include clouding host, CDN (content distribution network), and third libraries also make server domain less reliable and the generated traffic more similar. (5) Mobile App markets grow fast, and Apps update frequently, so the identification method must be scalable. These features reveal that it is necessary to propose new identification methods for dealing with mobile traffic.

In recent years, some notable work has used machine learning and traffic patterns leaked through side-channel information such as packet sizes or time-related features to identify traffic [3–5]. These methods only employ traffic statistics features and do not involve payload, thus overcoming the problems raised by random ports and encryption techniques. However, the effectiveness of these methods depends on the handcrafted features heavily. On the one hand, it's difficult to extract abstract traffic features manually. On the other hand, the classifier's ability is limited by distinguishing all applications with the same set of features, given that different application has different distinguishable features. In addition, most features are complete flow related making real-time identification impossible.

To solve the mentioned problems, in this paper, we propose a real-time mobile traffic identification approach based on two-dimensional convolutional neural network (2D-CNN). This method only needs raw data as input without decrypting traffic. And 2D-CNN could extracts features automatically. The main process is as follows. The raw traffic is first separated into flows according to 5-tuple (SrcIp, DstIp, SrcPort, DstPort, protocol), and then only the application layer data of the first five packets with at least a byte of TCP data payload is reserved. Next, the data is transformed into a two-dimensional image as the 2D-CNN model' input. In the end, 2D-CNN model gives the prediction.

The main contributions of our work are as follows. Firstly, we present a real-time mobile traffic identification method based on 2D-CNN, which omits the feature extraction process and regardless of whether traffic is encrypted. Secondly, the experimental results show that the proposed method performs better than the state-of-the-art method Random Forest. Afterwards we also propose validation threshold to reduce the false positive rate. Finally, we discuss the influence of background traffic on model accuracy.

The rest of this paper is organized as follows. Section 2 reviews related work. Section 3 describes the proposed approach including data collection and model architecture. Section 4 presents results of the experiments and outlines the post-validation method. The influence of background traffic is discussed in Sect. 4.3. Section 5 concludes the paper.

## 2   Related Work

Current mainstream research of mobile traffic identification could be categorized into two categories. First one is to generate unique App signatures by tokens such as User-Agent field in HTTP requests. The Other one focuses on machine learning.

Xu et al. [6] used User-Agent field in HTTP requests to differentiate apps and analyze the resource usage. Dai et al. [7] automatically generated apps' fingerprints by domain name and HTTP request tokens. AppPrint [8] also discovered apps' signatures by parameters in URL or cookies. The limitation of these methods is that it only works for HTTP traffic which provides these specific tokens. Additionally, they also cannot distinguish between the traffic generated by the same third-party effectively.

Thanks to not needing to inspect the payload of traffic, machine learning-based identification method doesn't have the problems of the above work. Wang et al. [9] identified 13 apps by Random Forest with packets size and interval time features were used. Taylor et al. [10] applied Random Forest to identify 110 apps. They proposed burst modeling traffic and employed packet sizes as features. This work also attempted to identify ambiguous traffic that shared among apps. Hasan et al. [11] extracted the packet sizes patterns of the traffic produced by the first 20s when apps launched and identified thousands of apps. However, the features used in the above work have obvious concrete sense, whereas the more abstract features are overlooked.

As a kind of machine learning algorithm, the neural network has the advantage of extracting features automatically. A few impressive studies have applied CNN to classify mobile traffic. Chen et al. [12] encoded HTTP requests plain text and trained a 2D-CNN model to identify 20 apps. Deep Packet [13] employed stacked autoencoder and 1D-CNN to identify and characterize mobile traffic. Wang et al. [14] considered mobile traffic as a sequential data and therefore utilized 1D-CNN as the classification model. Work [15] comes closer to the work in this paper, which uses 2D-CNN to classify malware traffic. But we design a different processing method to generate the input data.

## 3   Methodology

### 3.1   Data Collection

To validate the proposed approach, a local dataset is collected by our lab members during one month. We selected 6 popular Android instant messaging applications, and captured these Apps' traffic by Tpacketcapture [16]. Then Network-Log [17] is used to label the traffic accurately. Figure 1 depicts the procedure of data preprocessing.

Firstly, packets are split into flows according to the 5-tuple with the timeout set to 90s according to experience. Considering apps could use long connection, so a long connection would be separated into several flows due to the timeout limitation. We would retain flows which without SYN handshake, but flows which have less than two packets with payload are removed. Secondly, flow is converted into an image which can be easily calculated in the 2D-CNN model. To identify a flow rapidly, we only employ first five payload carried packets' application layer data. The reason for retaining only the application layer data is that the link header does not have App-related information, and IP address and ports are also not reliable. Then, given that the MTU is mostly set to 1500 bytes, so each packet's payload can be represented as a 1 * 1500 bytes vector. Zero padding and Truncation are used if needed. To preserve packet's direction information, the bytes from client to server are normalized to [128, 255] and bytes in the other direction are normalized to [0, 127]. Finally, five packets are sequentially combined to a 5 * 1500 2D-vector, and converted to an 87 * 87 image with normalized to range [0, 1]. The details of this dataset after preprocessing are shown in Table 1.

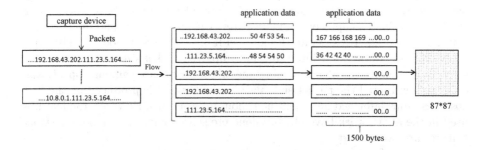

**Fig. 1.** The procedure of converting raw traffic to CNN input data

**Table 1.** The processed results of local dataset

| Application | Flow size |
| --- | --- |
| ChaoXin | 7185 |
| DingTalk | 5936 |
| MoMo | 8000 |
| TanTan | 7962 |
| WeChat | 7991 |
| YiXin | 7779 |

### 3.2 2D-CNN Architecture

2D-CNN has been successfully applied in the field of image processing. It mainly includes convolution and sampling layer, which can extract the abstract features within structured data and then identify the targets. After sufficient experiments and careful parameters tuning, the 2D-CNN model proposed in this paper is illustrated in Fig. 2, which contains two convolution layers and three full connection layers. Table 2 gives the detailed parameters of each layer.

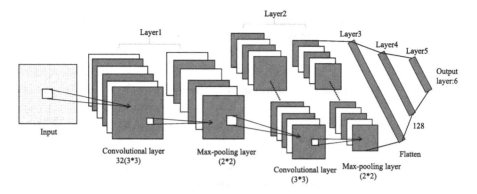

**Fig. 2.** The procedure of converting raw traffic to 2D-CNN input data

**Table 2.** Parameters of 2D-CNN model

a) Convolution layer parameters

| Layer | Activation Function | Filter | Max-pooling | Dropout |
|-------|---------------------|--------|-------------|---------|
| 1 | ReLU | 32(3*3) | 2*2 | / |
| 2 | ReLU | 64(3*3) | 2*2 | 0.25 |

b) Full connection layer parameters

| Layer | Node | Activation Function | Dropout |
|-------|------|---------------------|---------|
| 3 | Flatten | ReLU | / |
| 4 | 128 | ReLU | 0.25 |
| 5 | 6 | Softmax | / |

## 4    Experiments and Evaluations

We use the mentioned local dataset to evaluate our approach and compare with the results of the stat-of-the-art method Random Forest. 80% of the dataset are randomly sampled as training set and the rest is test set.

2D-CNN model is implemented using Keras library [18] with TensorFlow as backend. Training batch size is set to 64, loss function and optimizer use cross entropy and Adadelta optimizer built in Keras. The final model is obtained after 100 epochs.

Random Forest is implemented by data mining tool Weka [19]. Like the input data preprocessing of 2D-CNN, at most first five payload carried packets are used to extract 37 statistical features for each flow, as listed in Table 3. Since

Random Forest itself has the function of feature selection, no feature selection is performed. The final model contains 100 trees and the rest of the parameters remain the default of Weka.

**Table 3.** Features used in random forest

| Feature type | Description | Number |
|---|---|---|
| Port | Port number in unidirection | 2 |
| Packet size | First three payload carried packets size in unidirection. Min, Max, Mean, Std Dev of payload carried packets size in unidirection and flow | 18 |
| Inter-packet Time | Max, Min, Mean, Std Dev of inter packet time in unidirection and flow | 12 |
| Packets | Packets number transferred in unidirection. The ratio of the payload carried packets transferred in unidirection | 4 |
| Bytes | The ratio of volume bytes transferred in two directions | 1 |

## 4.1   Local Dataset Evaluation

Four evaluation metrics including recall, precision, F-measure and overall accuracy are used. The results show that the overall accuracy of 2D-CNN model is 96.94%, and Random Forest is 96.08%. Tables 4 and 5 display the experimental results of 2D-CNN model and Random Forest. Table 6 shows the confusion matrix of two models.

From the above Tables, we can observe that the performance of 2D-CNN in each class higher than that of Random Forest, which indicates 2D-CNN could extract more abstract and effective features.

**Table 4.** Results of 2D-CNN model

| Apps | Precision | Recall | F-measure |
|---|---|---|---|
| ChaoXin | 97.22% | 95.21% | 96.20% |
| DingTalk | 91.79% | 97.10% | 94.37% |
| MoMo | 98.67% | 97.56% | 98.11% |
| TanTan | 97.69% | 98.55% | 98.11% |
| WeChat | 98.27% | 96.61% | 97.43% |
| YiXin | 96.94% | 96.44% | 96.69% |
| Mean | 96.76% | 96.91% | 96.83% |

**Table 5.** Results of random forest model

| Apps | Precision | Recall | F-measure |
|------|-----------|--------|-----------|
| ChaoXin | 95.9% | 94.4% | 95.1% |
| DingTalk | 92.5% | 95.1% | 93.8% |
| MoMo | 97.2% | 96.8% | 97.0% |
| TanTan | 96.8% | 97.7% | 97.2% |
| WeChat | 97.5% | 96.4% | 96.9% |
| YiXin | 95.7% | 95.7% | 95.7% |
| Mean | 95.93% | 96.02% | 95.95% |

**Table 6.** Confusion matrix of 2D-CNN model/random forest model

| True | Pred | | | | | |
|------|---------|----------|---------|---------|---------|---------|
|  | ChaoXin | DingTalk | MoMo | TanTan | WeChat | YiXin |
| ChaoXin | 1331/1320 | 42/37 | 3/9 | 11/16 | 3/3 | 8/13 |
| DingTalk | 10/25 | 1140/1117 | 3/7 | 3/5 | 7/5 | 11/15 |
| MoMo | 5/6 | 10/14 | 1561/1548 | 11/14 | 3/9 | 10/9 |
| TanTan | 3/8 | 6/5 | 6/7 | 1566/1552 | 6/8 | 2/9 |
| WeChat | 5/3 | 19/14 | 7/11 | 7/10 | 1537/1533 | 16/20 |
| YiXin | 15/15 | 25/20 | 2/10 | 5/7 | 8/15 | 1490/1478 |

## 4.2 Post-validation

It's worth noting that the last layer in the CNN model uses softmax as the activation function, i.e., softmax function is used to output the probability of each class. Therefore, the output of the last layer could represent the confidence of the prediction.

From this perspective, we calculate the probability distribution of the predictions on the local data set as shown in Fig. 3. We can see that above 90% of true positive instances have a confidence value higher than 0.9. On the contrary, most false predictions have lower confidence value. Thus, we could use confidence threshold to further confirm the prediction. If confidence is lower than the threshold, CNN model could refuse to give a prediction.

We set the confidence threshold to 0.85, and retest the test set on the 2D-CNN model. The experiment shows that the average precision is 99.15%, average recall is 99.11%, and average F-measure is 99.13%. Due to the rejection of the sample with low confidence, flow coverage decreases to 93.67%. However, this trade-off is desirable for the scenarios where concentrate on accuracy or app coverage rather than flow coverage.

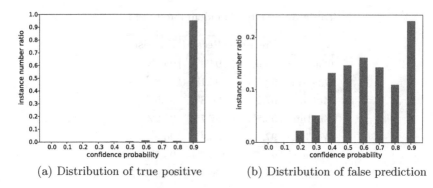

(a) Distribution of true positive     (b) Distribution of false prediction

**Fig. 3.** Confidence probability distribution

## 4.3   Influence of Background Traffic

In real world, network traffic is dominated by the background traffic rather than the target traffic. We examine the impact of background traffic on classifier performance in this section. Based on the original output classes, we add a class Other, and all non-target traffic belongs to Other. Therefore, the classifier can handle background traffic.

Then we add 52853 background flows to the mentioned local dataset and retrained the 2D-CNN model. The confidence threshold is configured to 0.85. The results show that the average precision, recall and F-measure are 97.69%, 97.71%, 97.7% respectively. And the flow coverage is 93.64%. The confusion matrix is shown in Fig. 4.

From the above experimental results, it can be concluded that under the influence of background traffic, the performance of the classifier will decrease. Furthermore, it can be speculated that the accuracy of the classifier will become lower as time goes on because the background traffic set used in the training phrase is incomplete. Therefore, it is necessary to continuously monitor the classifier's performance and update the model with new traffic samples.

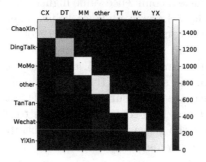

**Fig. 4.** Confusion matrix of 2D-CNN with identifying other class

# 5  Conclusion

Traditional traffic identification methods have been unable to handle mobile traffic effectively. In this paper, we have studied the efficiency of 2D-CNN model to address the mobile traffic identification. Our results proved that 2D-CNN is an effective approach and superior to the state-of-the-art method Random Forest. In addition, we found that the 2D-CNN model can satisfy the requirement of the scenario where focus on accuracy simply by setting a confidence threshold. At the end of the paper, we also discussed the impact of background traffic on classifier performance. As future work we will continue to further study how to handle background traffic and automatically identify new traffic classes.

# References

1. Mobile Marketing Statistics compilation. https://www.smartinsights.com/mobile-marketing/mobile-marketing-analytics/mobile-marketing-statistics/
2. The 40th China Statistical Report on Internet Development. http://cnnic.cn/hlwfzyj/hlwxzbg/hlwtjbg/201708/P020170807351923262153.pdf
3. Gerard, D., Arash, L., Mamun, M., Ali, G.: Characterization of encrypted and VPN traffic using time-related features. In: The International Conference on Information Systems Security and Privacy, Italy, pp. 94–98 (2016)
4. Zhang, J., Chen, X., Xiang, Y., Zhou, W.-L., Wu, J.: Robust network traffic classification. J. IEEE/ACM Trans. Netw. **23**(4), 1257–1270 (2015)
5. Taylor, V., Spolaor, R., Conti, M., Martinovic, I.: AppScanner: automatic fingerprinting of smartphone apps from encrypted network traffic. In: IEEE Symposium on Security and Privacy, pp. 439–454 (2016)
6. Xu, Q., Ermanet, J., Gerber, A., Mao, Z., Pang, J., Venkaraeaman, S.: Identifying diverse usage behaviors of smartphone apps. In: Proceedings of the 2011 ACM SIGCOMM conference on Internet measurement conference, Berlin, pp. 329–344 (2011)
7. Dai, S.-F., Tongaonkar, A., Wang, X.-Y., Nucci, A., Song, D.: NetworkProfiler: towards automatic fingerprinting of Android apps. In: Proceeding IEEE INFOCOM, Italy, pp. 809–817 (2013)
8. Miskovic, S., Lee, G.M., Liao, Y., Baldi, M.: AppPrint: automatic fingerprinting of mobile applications in network traffic. In: Mirkovic, J., Liu, Y. (eds.) PAM 2015. LNCS, vol. 8995, pp. 57–69. Springer, Cham (2015). https://doi.org/10.1007/978-3-319-15509-8_5
9. Wang Q.-L., Yahyavi, A., Kemme, B., He, W.-B.: I know what you did on your smartphone: inferring app usage over encrypted data traffic. In: Communications and Networking Symposium, pp. 433–441 (2015)
10. Taylor, V., Spolaor, R., Conti, M., Martinovic, I.: Robust smartphone app identification via encrypted network traffic analysis. J IEEE Trans. Inf. Forensics Secur. **13**, 63–78 (2018)
11. Alan, F., Kaur, J.: Can android applications be identified using only TCP/IP headers of their launch time traffic? In: Wireless Network Security, pp. 61–66 (2016)
12. Chen, Z.-Y., Yu, B.-W., Zhang, Y., Zhang, J.-Z., Xu, J.-D.: Automatic mobile application traffic identification by convolutional neural networks. In: Trustcom/bigdatase/ispa, pp. 301–307(2017)

13. Lotfollahi, M., Zade, R., Siavoshani, M., Saberian, M.: Deep Packet: A Novel Approach for Encrypted Traffic Classification Using Deep Learning. arXiv (2017)
14. Wang, W., Zhu, M., Wang, J.-L., Zeng, X.-W., Yang, Z.-Z.: End-to-end encrypted traffic classification with one-dimensional convolution neural networks. In: IEEE International Conference on Intelligence & Security Informatics, pp. 43–48. IEEE Press, Beijing (2017)
15. Wang, W., Zhu, M., Zeng, X.-W., Ye, X.-Z., Sheng, Y.-Q.: Malware traffic classification using convolutional neural network for representation learning. In: 2017 International Conference on Information Networking, pp. 712–717. IEEE Press, Da Nang (2017)
16. TPacketCapture. https://play.google.com/store/apps/details?id=jp.co.taosoftware.android. Packetcapture
17. Pragmatic Software, Network Log. https://play.google.com/store/apps/details?id=com.googlecode.networklog
18. Keras: The Python Deep Learning library. https://keras.io/
19. Weka 3: Data Mining Software in Java. https://www.cs.waikato.ac.nz/ml/weka/

# Joint D2D Cooperative Relaying and Friendly Jamming Selection for Physical Layer Security

Yijie Luo[1($\boxtimes$)], Yang Yang[1], Yanlei Duan[2], and Zhengju Yang[2]

[1] Army Engineering University of PLA, Nanjing, China
yijieluo@sina.com, sheep_1009@163.com
[2] Troop of PLA, Kunming, China
duanyanlei2008@163.com, yangzhengju1001@126.com

**Abstract.** D2D communications are emerging technologies to improve spectrum efficiency, energy efficiency as well as physical layer security of cellular networks. In most research, D2D users, considered as friendly jammers, can improve the information security of cellular networks. D2D users can also work as cooperative relays between the eNB and the cellular user (CU) to increase the transmission rate and improve the security capacity simultaneously. Considering there exists an active eavesdropper in the cellular network, which can attack as a passive eavesdropper or an active jammer, joint D2D cooperative relaying and friendly jamming selection can enhance the secrecy achievable rate or the transmission rate of CU. We formulate a Stackelberg game between different intelligent agents, and derive the mixed-strategy equilibrium (MSE) via a hierarchical learning algorithm based on Q-learning. Simulation results show that the strategic selections of D2D users and the active eavesdropper are convergent, and the proposed algorithm has a better performance than the random selection method.

**Keywords:** D2D communications · Cooperative relaying · Friendly jamming
Active eavesdropper · Stackelberg game · Q-learning

## 1 Introduction

D2D communications, owing to its potential ability to realize low-latency and high-data-rate communications and bring higher spectrum and energy efficiency, are considered as a disruptive technology direction of 5G mobile communication systems [1, 2]. Most of researches of D2D communications focus on resource allocation and interference avoidance [3, 4]. While introducing D2D communications to cellular networks, security problem becomes more and more important. In [5], secrecy energy efficiency of the cellular user and the D2D user was improved by the proposed power control algorithm based on Stackelberg game. In [6, 7], considering power control, access control and D2D pair selection, a joint mechanism was proposed to enhance secrecy performance. Furthermore, the cooperation among cellular users and D2D users was formulated as a coalitional game, and both social welfare and system secrecy rate were improved via proposed algorithms. In these works, D2D users were always considered to be friendly jammers to enhance system achievable secrecy rate by

© ICST Institute for Computer Sciences, Social Informatics and Telecommunications Engineering 2018
L. Meng and Y. Zhang (Eds.): MLICOM 2018, LNICST 251, pp. 115–126, 2018.
https://doi.org/10.1007/978-3-030-00557-3_12

deteriorating the wiretap channel. There were also some works considering D2D users to be cooperative relays in cellular networks, while not in the physical layer security aspect. In [8], cooperation schemes in the form of relaying or jamming between cellular and D2D users was discussed, and three cooperative frameworks were proposed and compared. Considering the channel estimation error and the interference between different D2D users, a joint beamforming design of base station and D2D relay user was proposed in [9]. In [10], joint mode selection, resource assignment and power allocation scheme of D2D users were studied and the joint relay and jamming scheme outperformed conventional D2D directly or relay communication schemes.

In fact, cooperative relaying can enhance achievable secrecy rate by improving the transmission rate of legitimate users. Joint cooperative relaying and friendly jamming selection is widely applied to improve physical layer secrecy performance in all kinds of wireless networks [11–14]. In [11], the reliable-and-secure connection probability (RSCP) and the reliability-security ratio (RSR) were introduced and analyzed in different relaying and jamming cooperation schemes with channel state information (CSI) feedback delays. In [12], the ergodic secrecy rate (ESR) was maximized and joint power allocation and relay selection scheme was presented. In [13], considering intermediate nodes working as relays or jammers, two relay and jammer selection approaches were proposed to minimize secrecy outage. In [14], the scheme that source node communicating with destination node securely via cooperative relay and cooperative jammer selection was considered, and a particle swarm optimization approach was proposed to enhance overall secrecy achievable rate. Whereas few works on D2D relay-assisted secrecy cellular communications is under studied. So we consider introducing joint cooperative relaying and friendly jamming selection strategies to D2D communications for physical layer security improvement. In our former work [15], we consider single D2D user to work as a cooperative relay or a friendly jammer to enhance secrecy achievable rate of the cellular user, a non-cooperative game between the D2D user and the active eavesdropper was formulated and the mixed-strategy Nash equilibrium (MSNE) was derived via the fictitious play-based algorithm [16].

In this paper, we go further to consider multiple D2D users underlaying cellular networks where there exists an intelligent attacker (active eavesdropper), who has the dual ability of either passively eavesdropping or actively jamming cellular links. Due to the mutually opposite interest of the legitimate user and the attacker, a Stackelberg game is formulated between them. To be specific, the legitimate user is modeled as the leader and the active eavesdropper is the follower. The legitimate user firstly selects a "best" D2D user to work as a cooperative relay and leaving other D2D users to work as friendly jammers. Then the active eavesdropper selects passively eavesdropping or actively jamming as follows. We analyze the existence of MSE of the Stackelberg secrecy game and achieve a MSE using a hierarchical Q-learning algorithm with which the legitimate user and the attacker can update their strategies. The contributions of the paper are as follows: (1) compared with our former work, we consider multiple D2D users cooperation rather than single D2D user access, (2) we propose a joint friendly jammer and cooperative relay selection scheme to retain the diversity gain, enhance physical layer security and increase transmission opportunity of D2D users to the utmost, (3) The proposed hierarchical learning algorithm based on Q-learning significantly outperforms the random selection method.

The rest of this paper is organized as follows. In Sect. 2, the system model is described and the secrecy rate under different schemes is analyzed. In Sect. 3, utility functions of cellular networks and the active eavesdropper are designed and a Stackelberg game between them is formulated. Then the Q-learning based algorithm is proposed to find the MSE and simulation results are analyzed and discussed in Sect. 4. And conclusions are drawn in Sect. 5 finally.

## 2  System Model and Problem Formation

We consider a single cell scenario, where there is an evolved Node B (eNB), a cellular user, $N$ D2D users and an active eavesdropper, which are equipped with a single antenna and operate in a half-duplex mode, as shown in Fig. 1. The eNB, the cellular user and the active eavesdropper are denoted as $B$, $C$ and $A$ respectively. All the $N$ D2D users form the set of $\mathcal{N}$, one of D2D users is denoted as $n_i \in \mathcal{N}$. Furthermore, we assume that the eNB can establish the direct cellular link to the cellular user, and select only one D2D transmitter to relay confidential data to the destination cellular user, while other $N - 1$ D2D users transmit their own data through direct D2D channels in the underlay way, respectively. And assumed that the attacker can work in two modes: (1) passively overhearing the confidential information transmitted from the eNB and the relay D2D transmitter; (2) actively jamming signals received by cellular user.

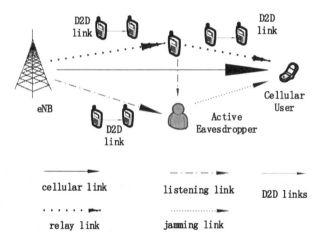

**Fig. 1.** System model

Suppose that the transmission power of the eNB, the jamming power of the active eavesdropper and the transmission (or relaying) power of the $ith$ D2D transmitter are denoted by $P_B$, $P_J$ and $P_i$, respectively. The channel gain between the eNB and the cellular user, between the eNB and the active eavesdropper, and between the cellular user and the active eavesdropper, are denoted by $h_{BC}$, $h_{BA}$ and $h_{AC}$, respectively. The channel gain between the eNB and the $ith$ D2D transmitter, between the active eavesdropper and the *ith* D2D transmitter, between the *ith* D2D transmitter and the cellular user, between the *ith* D2D transmitter and the *jth* D2D receiver are denoted by $h_{Bi}$, $h_{Ai}$, $h_{iC}$ and $h_{ij}$, respectively. And the background additive white Gaussian noise is denoted by $N_0$.

## 2.1  Secrecy Achievable Rate of Cellular User When Passively Eavesdropped

Because the active eavesdropper works in a half-duplex mode, it can't eavesdrop and jam simultaneously. Therefore, we first consider it works as a passively eavesdropper. It is assumed that the eNB can transmit the confidential information not only through the direct cellular link to the cellular user, but also through the selected D2D transmitter to relay. In the first phase, the confidential information is transmitted from the eNB to the D2D transmitter (suppose that it is the *ith* D2D transmitter); while in the second phase, the selected *ith* transmitter relays the received information to the cellular user. Meanwhile the confidential information transmission is performed through the direct cellular link during the two phases. Hence the signal-to-interference-plus-noise-power-ratio (SINR) for the direct cellular link and the direct eavesdropping link are expressed as

$$\xi_1 = \frac{P_B |h_{BC}|^2}{\sum\limits_{j=1,j\neq i}^{N-1} P_j |h_{jC}|^2 + N_0} \tag{1}$$

and

$$\phi_1 = \frac{P_B |h_{BA}|^2}{\sum\limits_{j=1,j\neq i}^{N-1} P_j |h_{jA}|^2 + N_0} \tag{2}$$

respectively.

If the eNB selects the *ith* D2D transmitter to be the relay node, and the relay node employs Amplify and Forward (AF) protocol to forward the message. It is also assumed that the eavesdropper is mainly interested in the confidential information, so it wiretaps the cellular link and relaying link where the confidential information going through. Then the SINR for the relay cellular link and the relay eavesdropping link are

$$\xi_2 = \frac{\gamma_{1E} \cdot \gamma_{2E}}{\gamma_{1E} + \gamma_{2E} + 1} \tag{3}$$

where $\gamma_{1E} = \dfrac{P_B |h_{Bi}|^2}{\sum\limits_{j=1,j\neq i}^{N-1} P_j |h_{ij}|^2 + N_0}$, $\gamma_{2E} = \dfrac{P_i |h_{iC}|^2}{\sum\limits_{j=1,j\neq i}^{N-1} P_j |h_{jC}|^2 + N_0}$,

and

$$\phi_2 = \frac{\psi_1 \cdot \psi_2}{\psi_1 + \psi_2 + 1} \tag{4}$$

where

$$\psi_1 = \frac{P_B|h_{Bi}|^2}{\sum\limits_{j=1, j\neq i}^{N-1} P_j|h_{ij}|^2 + N_0}, \psi_2 = \frac{P_i|h_{iA}|^2}{\sum\limits_{j=1, j\neq i}^{N-1} P_j|h_{jA}|^2 + N_0}$$

respectively. Therefore the achievable rate of CU and the wiretap rate of the eaves-dropper are expressed as

$$R_R(i, E) = \frac{1}{2}\log_2(1 + \xi_1 + \xi_2) \tag{5}$$

and

$$R_E(i, E) = \frac{1}{2}\log_2(1 + \phi_1 + \phi_2) \tag{6}$$

respectively. Then the achievable secrecy rate of CU is expressed as

$$R(i, E) = [R_R(i, E) - R_E(i, E)]^+ \tag{7}$$

where $[\cdot]^+ = \max\{\cdot, 0\}$.

## 2.2    Transmission Rate of Cellular User When Actively Jammed

If the attacker chooses the active jamming mode, the transmission signals of D2D users are not friendly at all but harmful to the cellular user for introducing more extra interference. While compared with working as cooperative relays, D2D users prefer to work as friendly jammers to transmit their own data. Therefore, we consider the scheme that the eNB selects a "best" D2D transmitter to relay data to the cellular user, and other D2D pairs transmit their own data. It can retain the diversity gain, eliminate the interference to the cellular link and increase transmission opportunity of D2D users to the utmost.

Under this scheme, the SINR of CU for the direct cellular link when jammed by the active eavesdropper is

$$\omega_1 = \frac{P_B|h_{BC}|^2}{P_J|h_{AC}|^2 + \sum\limits_{j=1, j\neq i}^{N-1} P_j|h_{jC}|^2 + N_0} \tag{8}$$

The SINR for the relaying cellular link when jammed by the active eavesdropper is

$$\omega_2 = \frac{\gamma_{1J} \cdot \gamma_{2J}}{\gamma_{1J} + \gamma_{2J} + 1} \tag{9}$$

where

$$\gamma_{1J} = \frac{P_{Bi}|h_{Bi}|^2}{P_J|h_{Ai}|^2 + \sum\limits_{j=1,j\neq i}^{N-1} P_j|h_{ij}|^2 + N_0}, \quad \gamma_{2J} = \frac{P_i|h_{iC}|^2}{P_J|h_{AC}|^2 + \sum\limits_{j=1,j\neq i}^{N-1} P_j|h_{jC}|^2 + N_0}.$$

Hence when the active eavesdropper selects actively jamming, the achievable rate of the CU is expressed as

$$R(i,J) = \frac{1}{2}\log_2(1 + \omega_1 + \omega_2) \tag{10}$$

Let $a = E, J$, then the utility function of the legitimate user is

$$U(i,a) = R(i,a) \tag{11}$$

While the utility function of the active eavesdropper is

$$U_A(i,a) = \{ \begin{array}{l} -R(i,E), a = E \\ -R(i,J) - c_J P_J, a = J \end{array} \tag{12}$$

where $c_J$ represents a cost factor on the power level used by the active eavesdropper when it chooses actively jamming.

## 3 Stackelberg Game Formulation

In this section, a Stackelberg game is formulated to characterize the interaction between legitimate users and the active eavesdropper. Specifically, the legitimate user first selects the "best" D2D transmitter to maximize its utility function, which acts as the leader, whereas the active eavesdropper selects attacking modes subsequently to minimize its jamming cost, which is the follower. The strategy of the legitimate user is the probability of selecting which D2D user to relay its message to the cellular user and leaving other D2D users to transmit their own data to be friendly jammers. The probability of selecting the $ith$ D2D user is denoted by $p_{n_i}$, and let $\mathbf{P}_n = [p_{n_1}, p_{n_2}, \ldots, p_{n_N}]$ be a mixed strategy of the legitimate user in the set of all feasible strategies $\mathcal{P}_n := \{p_{n_i} \in \mathbb{R}_+ : \sum_{n_i \in \mathcal{N}} p_{n_i} = 1\}$. While the active eavesdropper's strategy is the probability of selecting passively eavesdropping or actively jamming. Let $p_E$ and $p_J$ be the eavesdropping probability and jamming probability respectively, $\mathbf{P}_A = [p_E, p_J]$ is an admissible mixed strategy of the active eavesdropper and $\mathcal{P}_A$ is the set of admissible mixed strategies, defined by $\mathcal{P}_A := \{p_E, p_J \in [0,1]^2 : p_E + p_J = 1\}$. Then average utilities of the legitimate user and the active eavesdropper are expressed as:

$$\overline{U}(\mathbf{P}_n, \mathbf{P}_A) = \mathbb{E}_{\mathbf{P}_n, \mathbf{P}_A}(U(i,a)) \tag{13}$$

$$\overline{U_A}(\mathbf{p}_n, \mathbf{P}_A) = \mathbb{E}_{\mathbf{P}_n, \mathbf{P}_A}(U_A(i,a)) \tag{14}$$

**Proposition 1.** Let $\mathcal{G} = \{\{B, A\}, \mathcal{N}, \{a\}, \overline{U}, \overline{U_A}\}$ be the game described in Sect. 3, the Stackelberg game admits a MSE $(\mathbf{P}_n^*, \mathbf{P}_A^*)$, which satisfies the following set of inequalities:

$$\overline{U}(\mathbf{P}_n^*, \mathbf{P}_A^*) \geq \overline{U}(\mathbf{P}_n^*, \mathbf{P}_A), \forall \mathbf{P}_A \in \mathcal{P}_A \tag{15}$$

$$\overline{U}_A(\mathbf{P}_n^*, \mathbf{P}_A^*) \geq \overline{U}_A(\mathbf{P}_n, \mathbf{P}_A^*), \forall \mathbf{P}_n \in \mathcal{P}_n, n_i \in \mathcal{N} \tag{16}$$

**Proof.** Since every finite strategy game has a MSE [17], we can achieve the above outcome on existence of the MSE of the Stackerlberg game. ∎

The MSE of the game defines a state in which no player, including the legitimate user and the active eavesdropper, has an incentive to change its strategies.

## 4 Algorithm Description

In this section, we will study the MSE of the proposed secrecy game. Based on Q-learning algorithm [18, 19], we propose a hierarchical algorithm to find an MSE of the game $\mathcal{G}$. Firstly, the legitimate user makes its strategic decisions according to its policy $\mathbf{P}_n(k)$, which is the mixed strategy of D2D users in the $k$th epoch. And then the active eavesdropper updates its Q value in the $t$th iteration as follows:

$$Q_{A,m}(t+1) = (1 - \kappa_A^t)Q_{A,m}(t) + \kappa_A^t U_A(t), \tag{17}$$

where $\kappa_A^t \in [0, 1)$ is the learning rate of the active eavesdropper, and $\sum_{t=0}^{\infty} \kappa_A^t = \infty$, $\sum_{t=0}^{\infty} (\kappa_A^t)^2 < \infty$. The attacker's strategy is updated according to:

$$p_{A,m}(t+1) = \frac{\exp[Q_{A,m}(t)/\tau_0]}{\sum\limits_{r \in \mathcal{A}} \exp[Q_{A,r}(t)/\tau_0]}, \tag{18}$$

where $\tau_0$ controls the tradeoff of exploration-exploitation.

Then the Q value of the legitimate user is updated as:

$$Q_{B,n}(k+1) = (1 - \kappa_B^k)Q_{B,n}(k) + \kappa_B^k U(k), \tag{19}$$

where $\kappa_B^k \in [0, 1)$ is the learning rate of the legitimate user, and $\sum_{k=0}^{\infty} \kappa_B^k = \infty$, $\sum_{k=0}^{\infty} (\kappa_B^k)^2 < \infty$. Then the probability of selecting the relay is updated according to

$$p_{B,n}(k+1) = \frac{\exp[Q_{B,n}(k)/\tau_0]}{\sum\limits_{w \in \mathcal{N}} \exp[Q_{B,w}(k)/\tau_0]} \tag{20}$$

**Theorem 1.** The proposed hierarchical learning algorithm can discover a MSE strategy of the secrecy game.

**Proof.** For brevity, the convergence of the proposed hierarchical algorithm can be found in [20] and it is a MSE of the secrecy game. ∎

Then this algorithm is summarized in Table 1.

**Table 1 .**

| TABLE I. **ALGORITHM 1:** PROPOSED HIERARCHICAL LEARNING ALGORITHM BASED ON Q-LEARNING |
| --- |
| 1: **initialization:** |
| 2:     set $t = 0$, $k = 0$ , $Q$ values of the eNB and the attacker |
| 3:     set initial selecting probabilities $p_{n_i} = \dfrac{1}{N}, n_i \in N$ |
| 4:     set initial attacking probabilities $p_E = p_J = \dfrac{1}{2}$ |
| 5: **end initialization** |
| 6: According to the policy $\mathbf{P}_n(k)$ of the legitimate users in the $k$th epoch, the eNB selects a D2D transmitter from the D2D users' set $\mathcal{N}$ . |
| 7: The active eavesdropper's learning process. |
| 8: **innerloop** |
|     (1)   According to the policy $\mathbf{P}_A(t)$ in the $t$th slot, the active eavesdropper selects its attacking strategy from the set $\mathcal{A}$ . |
|     (2)   The active eavesdropper calculates its utility function $U_A(t)$ in the $t$th slot. |
|     (3)   According to (17) , the active eavesdropper updates its Q values and according to (18), it updates its attacking policy. |
| 9:     set t=t+1, and until the stopping criterion hold. |
| 10: **end inner loop** |
| 11: The legitimate user calculates its utility function $U(k)$ in the $k$th epoch. |
| 12: According to (19), the legitimate user updates its Q values and according to (20), it updates its relay selection probability. |
| 13: Go to 6, and until the stopping criterion hold. |

## 5 Simulation and Numerical Analysis

For our simulations, we consider a D2D underlay cellular network composed of a square area of 1 km * 1 km with the eNB located at the center and the cellular user and all the D2D users are randomly located on the square area of 0.5 km * 0.5 km centered by the eNB, while the active eavesdropper is randomly located between the square area of 0.5 km * 0.5 km and 1 km * 1 km. In these simulations, a path loss model is adopted, and the path loss exponent is set as $\alpha = 3$. The transmit power of the eNB and D2D users are set as $P_B = 1\,\text{W}, P_i = 100\,\text{mW}$, and the jamming power of the active eavesdropper is set as $P_J = 100\,\text{mW}$, respectively. The jamming cost is set as $c_J = 1$, and the noise level is set as $N_0 = 10^{-10}\,\text{W}$.

In Fig. 2, the update of the active eavesdropper's attacking mode selection probability in the first epoch is presented, while in Fig. 3, the convergent process of the D2D relay selection over epoch numbers is showed. From these figures, we have found that the selection probability of the legitimate user (or the active eavesdropper) converges to a stationary mixed strategy very soon. In Fig. 4, it is compared with the random selection algorithm (RSA) to evaluate the proposed hierarchical learning algorithm based on Q-learning (HLA). In RSA, the legitimate user and the active eavesdropper randomly select their actions from their strategy sets at each time. It clearly shows that the proposed HLA presents a significant better performance gain than RSA at all sizes of D2D users. And it also shows that the average expected utility of CU decreases as the number of D2D users increases, and the gaps between different algorithms will be narrowed. That is because the more D2D users, the larger interference they induce to the CU, and they lower the transmission rate of the CU dramatically.

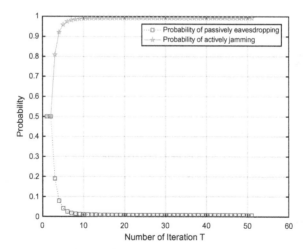

**Fig. 2.** The convergent process of the active eavesdropper's attacking mode selection.

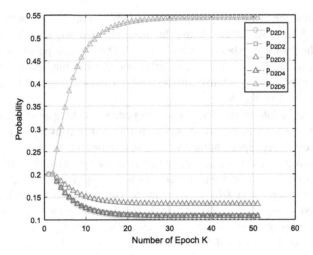

**Fig. 3.** The convergent process of D2D relay selection.

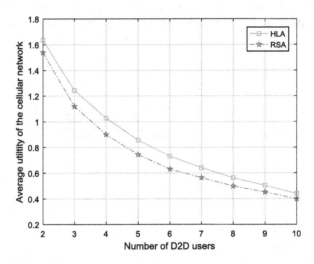

**Fig. 4.** Average utility function of the cellular network vs. number of D2D users

# 6    Conclusions

In this paper, we have formulated a Stackelberg game between the legitimate user and the active eavesdropper. Firstly, the eNB works as the leader, select a "best" D2D user to work as the cooperative relay and others as friendly jammers to improve physical layer security of cellular networks, then the active eavesdropper, working as the follower, selects the passive eavesdropping or the active jamming mode to lower the overall secrecy rate or transmission rate of cellular networks. To solve this problem, we have employed a hierarchical learning algorithm based on Q-learning using which the legitimate user and the active eavesdropper can reach a MSE through a small number of iterations. The results have shown that the proposed algorithm enables the legitimate user to significantly improve its average expected utility either the achievable secrecy rate of the cellular link when eavesdropped or the transmission rate when jammed.

# References

1. Federico, B., Robert, W.H., Angel, L., Thomas, L.M., Petar, P.: Five disruptive technology directions for 5G. IEEE Commun. Mag. **52**(02), 74–80 (2014)
2. Shaoyu, L., Chunche, C., Fanmin, T., Tienchen, H.: 3GPP device-to-device communications for beyond 4G cellular networks. IEEE Commun. Mag. **54**(03), 28–35 (2016)
3. Zhenyu, Z., Mianxiong, D., Kaoru, O., Jun, W., Takuro, S.: Energy efficiency and spectral efficiency tradeoff in device-to-device (D2D) communications. IEEE Commun. Lett. **3**(05), 485–488 (2014)
4. Lili, W., Rose, Q.H., Yi, Q., Geng, W.: Enable device-to-device communications underlaying cellular networks: challenges and research aspects. IEEE Commun. Mag. **52** (06), 90–96 (2014)
5. Wanbing, H., Wei Z., Wei B., Yueming C., Xinrong G., Junyue Q.: Improving physical layer security in underlay D2D communication via stackelberg game based power control. In: 2016 IEEE International Conference on Computer, Information and Telecommunication Systems (CITS), pp. 1–5. IEEE Press, Kunming (2016)
6. Rongqing, Z., Xiang, C., Liuqing, Y.: Joint power and access control for physical layer security in d2d communications underlaying cellular networks. In: 2016 IEEE International Conference on Communications (ICC), pp. 1–6, IEEE Press, Kuala Lumpur (2016)
7. Rongqing, Z., Xiang, C., Liuqing, Y.: Cooperation via spectrum sharing for physical layer security in device-to-device communications underlaying cellular networks. IEEE Trans. Wirel. Commun. **15**(8), 5651–5663 (2016)
8. Yang, C., Tao, J., Conggang, W.: Cooperative device-to-device communications in cellular networks. IEEE Wirel. Commun. **22**(3), 124–129 (2015)
9. Yi, Q., Ming, D., Meng, Z., Hui, Y., Hanwen, L.: Relaying robust beamforming for device-to-device communication with channel uncertainty. IEEE Commun. Lett. **18**(10), 1859–1862 (2014)
10. Tuong, D.H., Long, B.L., Tho, L.N.: Joint mode selection and resource allocation for relay-based d2d communications. IEEE Commun. Lett. **21**(2), 398–401 (2017)
11. Lei, W., Yueming, C., Yulong, Z., Weiwei, Y., Lajos, H.: Joint relay and jammer selection improves the physical layer security in the face of CSI feedback delays. IEEE Trans. Veh. Technol. **65**(8), 6259–6274 (2015)
12. Chao, W., Huiming, W., Xia, X.: Hybrid opportunistic relaying and jamming with power allocation for secure cooperative networks. IEEE Trans. Wirel. Commun. **14**(2), 589–605 (2015)
13. Hui, H., Lee, S., Guobing, L., Junli, L.: Secure relay and jammer selection for physical layer security. IEEE Signal Process. Lett. **22**(8), 1147–1151 (2015)
14. Ning, Z., Nan, C., Ning, L., Xiang, Z., Jon, W.M., Xuemin (Sherman), S.: Partner selection and incentive mechanism for physical layer security. IEEE Trans. Wirel. Commun. **14**(8), 4265–4276 (2015)
15. Yijie, L., Yang, Y., Cui, L.: Research on physical layer security in D2D enabled cellular networks with an active eavesdropper. Signal Proccesing (accepted)

16. Fudenberg, D., Levine, D.K.: The Theory of Learning in Games. MIT Press, Cambridge (1998)
17. Han, Z., et al.: Game Theory in Wireless and Communication Networks. Cambridge University Press, Cambridge (2012)
18. Watkins, C.J.C.H., Dayan, P.: Q-learning. Mach. Learn. **8**, 279–292 (1992)
19. Luliang, J., Fuqiang, Y., Youming, S., Yuhua, X., Shuo, F., Alagan, A.: A hierarchical learning solution for antijamming stackelberg game with discrete power strategies. IEEE Wirel. Commun. Lett. **6**(6), 818–821 (2017)
20. Sastry, P.S., Phansalkar, V.V., Thathachar, M.: Decentralized learning of nash equilibria in multi-person stochastic games with incomplete information. IEEE Trans. Syst. Man Cybern. **24**(5), 769–777 (1994)

# Variable Tap-Length Blind Equalization for Underwater Acoustic Communication

Zhiyong Liu[1,2(✉)], Yinyin Wang[1], and Fan Bai[1]

[1] School of Information and Electrical Engineering,
Harbin Institute of Technology (Weihai), Weihai 264209,
People's Republic of China
lzyhit@aliyun.com, wcuteyy@163.com, 694683139@qq.com
[2] Key Laboratory of Science and Technology on Information Transmission
and Dissemination in Communication,
Shijiazhuang 050081, People's Republic of China

**Abstract.** In view of the characteristics of underwater acoustic channel, a blind equalization algorithm for underwater acoustic communication based on variable tap length is proposed. On the basis of the normalized modified constant modulus algorithm (MCMA), the algorithm adjusts the length of the tap through the update algorithm to realize the blind equalization of the underwater acoustic channel. The simulation shows that the algorithm adaptively adjusts the length of the taps to the optimal. Compared with the traditional blind equalization algorithm, the performance of the system is improved.

**Keywords:** Underwater acoustic communication · Equalizers
Modified constant modulus algorithm (MCMA) · Variable tap-length

## 1 Introduction

In the underwater acoustic communication system, the communication quality of the underwater acoustic channel is greatly affected due to the existence of poor inter symbol interference (ISI). In order to overcome this weakness, channel equalization is commonly used in underwater acoustic communication systems to reduce ISI [1–5]. The traditional linear equalizer works by sending known training sequences. However, in the complex and time-varying underwater acoustic channels, the training sequence extraction fails due to the serious distortion of the receiving waveform, and the training sequence is sent periodically to cause the channel bandwidth waste and reduce equalizer performance. Therefore, the channel is equalized using a blind equalization

The work was supported by Shandong Provincial Natural Science Foundation of China (ZR2016FM02), National Natural Science Foundation of China (61201145), the Graduate Education and Teaching Reform Research Project in Harbin Institute of Technology (JGYJ-201625) and the Foundation of Key Laboratory of Communication Network Information Transmission and Dissemination.

© ICST Institute for Computer Sciences, Social Informatics and Telecommunications Engineering 2018
L. Meng and Y. Zhang (Eds.): MLICOM 2018, LNICST 251, pp. 127–135, 2018.
https://doi.org/10.1007/978-3-030-00557-3_13

technique that only needs to the received signal and statistical characteristics of transmitted signal.

Godard proposed a constant modulus algorithm (CMA) [6], which is simple and easy to implement, but the convergence rate is slow. In this connection, scholars have proposed a number of corresponding improved algorithms. The author in [7], proposed orthogonal constant modulus algorithm. Because the orthogonalization matrix is needed in the iterative process, the computation is heavy, when the signal dimension is large. In [8], the squared norm of the input signal is used as the normalization factor to improve the convergence speed. Due to the phase error of the equalized output signal constellation, MCMA proposed in [9] can achieve blind equalization and carrier recovery simultaneously. All of the above researches are based on fixed tap blind equalization. Due to the time-varying of underwater acoustic channels, the traditional fixed tap-length blind equalization cannot determine the optimal tap length, and is not suitable for complex and variable underwater acoustic channels.

In this paper, to solve the above problems, combined with the normalized MCMA, a blind equalization algorithm based on variable tap length is proposed, which adaptively adjusts to the optimal tap length and improves the performance of the system.

## 2   System Model

In Fig. 1, $a(n)$ is transmission sequence, $h(n)$ is the underwater acoustic channel impulse response, which is obtained from the BELLHOP model, $n(n)$ is the additive white Gaussian noise, and received signal can be seen in the following equations:

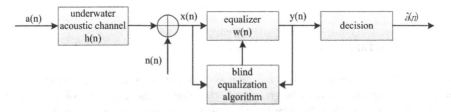

**Fig. 1.** The equivalent baseband model of a blind equalization system

$$x(n) = \sum_{i=0}^{N-1} h(i)a(n-i) + n(n) \tag{1}$$

And the output of the equalizer is expressed as the following formula

$$y(n) = X^T(n)W(n) \tag{2}$$

where $W(n) = [w_0(n), w_1(n), \ldots, w_{N-1}(n)]^T$ is the weight vector and $X(n) = [x(n), x(n-1), \ldots, x(n-N+1)]^T$ represents the input signal vector. In addition, $N$ indicates the length of the equalizer.

This paper, we use normalized MCMA, the cost function of it is as follows:

$$J(n) = J_R + jJ_I = E\left\{(y_R^2(n) - R_{2R})^2\right\} + jE\left\{(y_I^2(n) - R_{2I})^2\right\} \tag{3}$$

where $y_R(n)$ and $y_I(n)$ represent the real and imaginary parts of the equalizer output, respectively. $R_{2R}$ and $R_{2I}$ are the real and imaginary parts of the input signal statistics. The transmitted signal constant modulus:

$$R_{2R} = \frac{E\{a_R^4(n)\}}{E\{a_R^2(n)\}} \tag{4}$$

$$R_{2I} = \frac{E\{a_I^4(n)\}}{E\{a_I^2(n)\}} \tag{5}$$

We use the random gradient descent method for the derivation of the cost function and seek the minimum, thus we get the error signal of MCMA and divide it into the real part and the imaginary part.

$$e_R(n) = y_R(n)(y_R^2(n) - R_{2R}) \tag{6}$$

$$e_I(n) = y_I(n)(y_I^2(n) - R_{2I}) \tag{7}$$

The normalized iterative recursive formula of the tap weight vector is

$$W(n+1) = W(n) + \frac{\mu}{\delta + X^T(n)X(n)} e(n)X^*(n) \tag{8}$$

where $\mu$ is step-size, $\delta$ is some small constant. $e(n)$ is an error signal, the formula is as follows:

$$e(n) = e_R(n) + je_I(n) \tag{9}$$

The MCMA algorithm equalizes the real and imaginary parts of the output signal separately. Since the MCMA algorithm utilizes the amplitude and phase information of the received signal, it can well solve the problem of phase deflection or offset after equalization (Fig. 2).

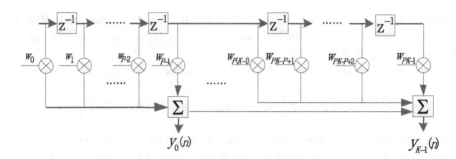

**Fig. 2.** Segmented equalizer with K segments of P taps

## 3   Variable Tap Length-Based MCMA (VT-MCMA)

The received signal is equalized by the VT-MCMA, finally recover the signal. The idea of VT-MCMA is to use a piecewise filter, that is, to divide a FIR filter with M taps into K segments, each of which contains P taps $(M = PK)$. Each segment produces an estimate of the transmitted signal $y_m(n)$ $(1 \leq m \leq K)$:

$$y_m(n) = X^T(n)W_m(n) \tag{10}$$

where $W_m(n)$ is the weight vector in segment m. The Eq. (11) is a normalized weight vector equation:

$$W_m(n+1) = W_m(n) + \frac{\mu}{\delta + X^T(n)X(n)} e_m(n)X^*(n) \tag{11}$$

where $\mu$ is step-size, $\delta$ is some small constant to avoid diverging the algorithm when the $X(n)$ is zero. * represents conjugate transpose operation. The real and imaginary part of the error signal for each segment can be expressed as:

$$e_{mR}(n) = y_{mR}(n) \times \left| y_{mR}(n)^2 - R_{2R} \right| \tag{12}$$

$$e_{mI}(n) = y_{mI}(n) \times \left| y_{mI}(n)^2 - R_{2I} \right| \tag{13}$$

We let $y_{mI}(n)$ and $y_{mR}(n)$ denote the real and imaginary parts of the output $y_m(n)$ signal respectively. In addition, we denote the real and imaginary parts of the input signal statistics using $R_{2R}$ and $R_{2I}$ respectively. Then the error signal formula of each segment is as follows:

$$e_m(n) = e_{mR}(n) + je_{mI}(n) \tag{14}$$

The mean square error (MSE) can be calculated by error signal of each segment.

$$MSE_m(n) = E\{|e_m(n)|^2\} = \frac{\sum\limits_{i=1}^{n} e_m(i)^2}{n} \tag{15}$$

We define the accumulated squared error (ASE) for each segment as:

$$A_m(n) = \sum_{i=1}^{n} e_m(i)^2 \tag{16}$$

The tap-length of equalizer can be adjusted with the following length update algorithm.

$$A_L(n) = \sum_{i=1}^{n} \beta^{n-i} \left| e_L(n)^2 \right| \tag{17}$$

$$A_{L-1}(n) = \sum_{i=1}^{n} \beta^{n-i} \left| e_{L-1}(n)^2 \right| \tag{18}$$

If:

$$A_L(n) \leq \alpha_{up} A_{L-1}(n) \tag{19}$$

then increase one segment.
   Else if:

$$A_L(n) \geq \alpha_{down} A_{L-1}(n) \tag{20}$$

remove one segment.
   Form the tap-length algorithm, we can see that if $A_L(n)$ is much smaller than $A_{L-1}(n)$, then adding taps can obviously improve the system performance. If $A_L(n)$ is close to or even greater than $A_{L-1}(n)$, then the increase of taps has no effect on system performance or even deteriorates the performance of the system. Where $\beta(\beta \leq 1)$ is forgetting factor, its roles is to weight the importance of the previous segment and the current segment. $\alpha_{up}$ and $\alpha_{down}$ are parameters that change the frequency of the tap update. L indicates the current active segment.

## 4   Simulation Results

Simulation build underwater acoustic channel from BELLHOP model. The carrier frequency is 12 kHz. The distance between transmitter and receiver is 100 m, they all located at a depth of 10 m. Wave height is 0.2 m. The transmitted sequences are 1000 bits. The variable tap length method has an initial tap length of 1 and a tap length increment of 4, the transmitted signal is modulated by 4QAM.

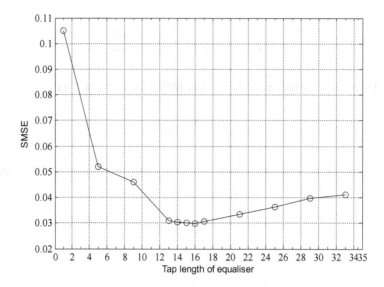

**Fig. 3.** The influence of the tap-length on SMSE

First, we simulate the tap length of the system performance, and determine the optimal tap length. Set the number of packets transmitted in the simulation to 300. Signal to noise ratio (SNR) is set to 15 dB. Herein, we define optimal tap length is the minimum tap length which close to the minimum steady mean square error (SMSE). The tap length is an important parameter affecting the SMSE. It can be seen from Fig. 3 that the system can achieve the minimum SMSE when the tap length is 16, but when

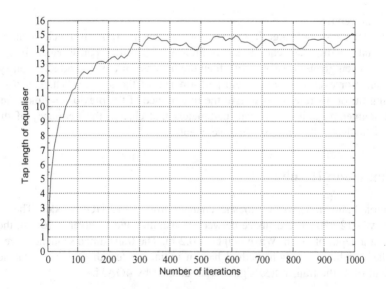

**Fig. 4.** Tap-length variation curve

the tap length is 13, it can not only achieve the near minimum SMSE, but also reduce the tap length, which reduces the arithmetic operation, so the optimal tap length is 14.

Next, we evaluated the tap length adjustment capability of the improved method. Set the channel conditions as in Fig. 3. Figure 4 shows the equalizer tap length adjustment curve. It can be seen from the Fig. 4 that the tap length can converge to 14. Therefore, the proposed method can converge to the optimal tap length.

To evaluate the performance of the proposed blind equalization algorithm, we compared its bit error rate (BER) performance and convergence performance with the fixed tap length-based MCMA (FT-MCMA). Simulation using Monte-Carlo method, the number of packets transmitted 400.

The BER performance of the proposed VT-MCMA and existing FT-MCMA is shown in Fig. 5. It can be seen from the figure that the proposed method can achieve better BER performance. This is because the FT-MCMA can not predict the optimal tap length, resulting in the new system performance is limited. However, the proposed method can converge to the optimal tap length through adaptive algorithm, so as to improve BER performance.

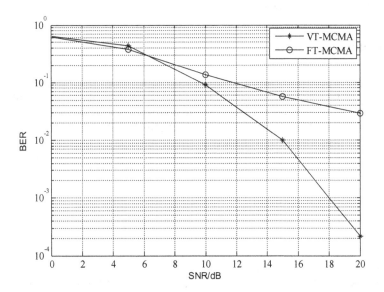

**Fig. 5.** Bit error rate performance comparison (SNR = 15 dB)

Finally, we compare the convergence performance, the simulation results shown in Fig. 6. It can be seen from the figure that VT-MCMA approaches the convergence speed of the traditional FT-MCMA. When reaching steady state, VT-MCMA achieves a smaller SMSE.

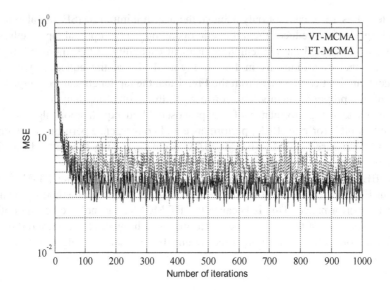

**Fig. 6.** Convergence curve comparison

## 5  Conclusion

The traditional FT-MCMA affected by the tap length, there will be a waste of computing and system performance constraints. Based on this improvement, this paper proposes VT-MCMA. It adopts the length updating algorithm, which can adaptively adjust to the optimal tap length according to the underwater acoustic channel environment. The feasibility of this method is proved through simulation, and its performance is compared with the existing FT-MCMA to verify the system performance is improved.

## References

1. Treichler, J.R., Agee, B.G.: A new approach to multipath correction of constant modulus signals. IEEE Trans. Acoust. Speech Sig. Process. **31**(2), 459–472 (1983)
2. Nandi, A.K.: Blind Estimation Using Higher-Order Statistics. Kluwer Academic Publishers (2010)
3. Silva, M.T.M., Arenas-Garcia, J.: A soft-switching blind equalization scheme via convex combination of adaptive filters. IEEE Trans. Sig. Process. **61**(5), 1171 (2013)
4. Xia, M., Rouseff, D., Ritcey, J., Zou, X., Polprasert, C., Xu, W.: Underwater acoustic communication in a highly refractive environment using SC-FDE. IEEE J. Oceanic Eng. **39**(3), 491–499 (2014)
5. Khalid, S.S., Abrar, S.: Blind adaptive algorithm for sparse channel equalization using projections onto $l_p$-ball. Electron. Lett. **51**, 1422–1424 (2015)
6. Godard, D.N.: Self-recovering equalization and carrier tracking in two-dimensional data communication systems. IEEE Trans. Commun. **28**, 1867–1875 (1980)

7. Guo, Y., Fang, D., Liang, C.: An orthogonal effective constant modulus algorithm. J. Beijing Univ. Posts Telecommun. **25**(1), 30–33 (2002)
8. Abdaoui, A., Laot, C.: Blind DFE based on NLMS algorithm with generalized normalized gradient descent regularization. In: Proceedings of the Oceans 2009, Biloxi, pp. 123–127 (2009)
9. Oh, K.N., Chin, Y.O.: Modified constant modulus algorithm: blind equalization and carrier phase recovery algorithm. In: IEEE International Conference on Communications, pp. 498–502 (1995)

# Random Sequence Generation Algorithm for Multi-chaotic Systems

Xiaodi Chen and Hong Wu[(✉)]

College of Electronic Engineering, Heilongjiang University,
150080 Harbin, China
2002060@hlju.edu.cn

**Abstract.** The characteristics of chaotic signals, such as pseudorandom and non long term predictability, make it suitable for application to information encryption, digital watermarking and so on. Nevertheless, since the chaotic system is often characterized by its characteristics, attackers can take advantage of these known features to reduce the difficulty of attacks. In contrast, the characteristics of multi-chaotic systems are not uniform, and the complexity of generating sequences is higher than that of single-chaos systems. Hence, the multi-chaotic system increases the security of the sequence to some extent. Therefore, we design a random sequence generation algorithm consisting of multiple chaotic systems that is a chaotic sequence generation algorithm combining Logistic map and Cubic map. And we analyze the sequence of new generation whose the performance, so we can conclude that the new algorithm has better randomness.

**Keywords:** Multi-chaos system · Logistic map · Cubic map
Chaotic sequence · Randomness

## 1 Introduction

The ideal chaotic sequence is not periodic, but in the actual application, as the computer or digital signal processor is through finite word length adder, multiplying unit to realize chaotic iteration [1], and all the data are stored in a finite word length unit, resulting in error. And it triggers the simulated chaotic orbit to deviate from the real chaotic orbit, thus resulting in the short-period phenomenon of chaotic sequence. This short-period phenomenon is more than apparent in the system using rarely single chaos mapping [2]. Therefore, we use double-precision floating-point arithmetic and compound chaotic system to improve the dynamic characteristics of chaotic system caused by finite precision. That is to say that we use a chaotic sequence generation algorithm which combines logistic map and cubic map. This paper first analyzes the characteristics of cubic mapping and logistic mapping through the comparison of histogram, correlation and balance, and subsequently analyzing whether the improved algorithm is more cyclical than that of logistic sequence from theoretical and experimental standpoints.

© ICST Institute for Computer Sciences, Social Informatics and Telecommunications Engineering 2018
L. Meng and Y. Zhang (Eds.): MLICOM 2018, LNICST 251, pp. 136–143, 2018.
https://doi.org/10.1007/978-3-030-00557-3_14

## 2  Performance Analysis of Chaotic System

The classical one dimensional chaotic logistic mapping which is widely studied and applied for its simple form and the ability to produce the complex structure of the random sequence. Cubic mapping has the same advantages as logistic mapping, but little attention which has been paid. The following comparison of the logistic mapping and the cubic mapping which reveals that the cubic mapping can be widely used in the domain of encryption.

The logistic mapping is defined as $x_{k+1} = \mu x_k(1 - x_k)$, the range of $x_k$ is 0 to 1, and the range of the bifurcation parameter $\mu$ is 3.56994 to 4 [3].

The definition of the cubic mapping is that $x_{k+1} = ax_k^3 - bx_k$, the range of b is 2.3 to 3, and when a is 4, the range of $x_k$ is −1 to 1 [4].

The parameter range of logistic mapping is about 0.43, and the parameter of cubic mapping whose the range is about 0.7. In contrast, we can see that the parameter range of cubic mapping is larger. The maximum Lyapunov exponent of the logistic mapping is 0.6920, while the cubic mapping whose the maximum Lyapunov exponent is 1.0980 [5], and there is a stronger chaotic characteristic compared with the logistic mapping. The logistic mapping parameter $\mu$ is 4, and the cubic mapping parameter a is 4 and b is 3, and the initial values of the two mappings are all 0.1. After the comparison of histogram, correlation and balance, so the cubic mapping and logistic mapping whose the characteristics are analyzed.

### 2.1  Histogram Characteristics

Figure 1 is the state diagrams of logistic mapping and cubic mapping. As can be seen from the figure, the state values of cubic mapping which are approximately random and have no apparent periodicity. In Fig. 1(a) and (b), the horizontal axis which represents the frequency and the vertical axis which represents the sequence value.

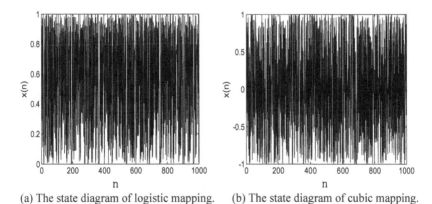

(a) The state diagram of logistic mapping.    (b) The state diagram of cubic mapping.

**Fig. 1.**  The state diagrams of logistic sequence and cubic sequence.

## 2.2    Sequence Correlation Analysis

The autocorrelation of sequences reflects the degree of correlation between the sequences generated by the same function at different moments and which is defined as [6]:

$$R_{XX}(m) = \frac{1}{N} \lim_{N \to \infty} \sum_{i=0}^{N-1} x_i x_{i+m} - \bar{x}^2. \tag{1}$$

The mean value of the ideal cubic mapping sequences which is 0, so 0 is taken as the threshold, and the cubic real value sequences which are digitized into the 0/1 sequences according to the binary decision method [7]:

$$d_k = \begin{cases} 0 & x_k \leq 0 \\ 1 & x_k > 0 \end{cases}. \tag{2}$$

Similarly, the mean 1/2 of the logistic mapping sequences which is used as threshold, and subsequently the logistic real value sequences are digitized into 0/1 sequences:

$$d_k = \begin{cases} 0 & x_k \leq 1/2 \\ 1 & x_k > 1/2 \end{cases}. \tag{3}$$

According to the formula (1), the autocorrelation coefficients of the logistic mapping and the cubic mapping are calculated respectively, and the results of MATLAB simulation are shown in Fig. 2. It can be seen that the cubic mapping has the same good autocorrelation with the logistic mapping. The transverse axis of the (a) and (b) of Fig. 2 is the correlation interval, and the longitudinal axis is the correlation coefficient value.

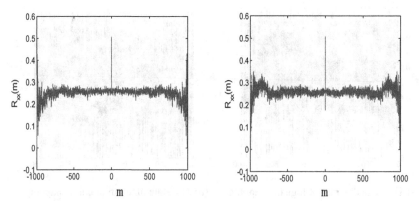

(a) Autocorrelation function of logistic sequence. (b) Autocorrelation function of cubic sequence.

**Fig. 2.** Autocorrelation function figures of logistic sequence and cubic sequence.

## 2.3   Analysis of Balancing Characteristics

Another criterion for the randomness of the testing sequence which is the balance test, that is whether the number of 0 in the statistical series is balanced by the number of 1 [8]. The statistical results show Table 1.

**Table 1.** Comparison of balancing characteristics.

| The name of the sequence | The statistics of balance | Sequence length N | | |
|---|---|---|---|---|
| | | 2000 | 5000 | 10000 |
| Logistic chaotic sequence | The number of 0 | 1007 | 2527 | 5102 |
| | Ratio | 0.5035 | 0.5054 | 0.5102 |
| | The number of 1 | 993 | 2473 | 4898 |
| | Ratio | 0.4965 | 0.4946 | 0.4898 |
| Cubic chaotic sequence | The number of 0 | 1002 | 2528 | 5011 |
| | Ratio | 0.5010 | 0.5056 | 0.5011 |
| | The number of 1 | 998 | 2472 | 4989 |
| | Ratio | 0.4990 | 0.4944 | 0.4999 |

From the analysis of the table, it can be seen that the numbers of 0 and 1 of the cubic chaotic sequence are nearly equivalent to the numbers of 0 and 1 of the logistic chaotic sequence. Although both sequences which are well balanced, the cubic mapping that is slightly more balanced.

Based on the above analysis, it can be found that cubic mapping has the same characteristics as logistic mapping, and which is superior to logistic mapping relating to balance. Consequently, it is of research value to apply cubic mapping to the field of information encryption.

# 3   Design of Chaotic Sequence Algorithm

From the above analysis, we know that due to the limitation of computer accuracy, accordingly the randomness of chaotic system can not achieve ideal conditions, and there will be the minor-cycle phenomenon. Consequently, we propose a hypothesis that multiple chaotic systems are combined and the parameters of the system are mutually restricted to form a compound chaotic system with variable parameters. Thus, the complexity of the sequence which is increased and the minor-cycle phenomenon is improved. Since cubic mapping which has the same good features as logistic mapping, so we can select cubic mapping and logistic mapping to generate random sequences. At the same time, it provides theoretical support for the improved composite chaotic system due to the superposition of chaotic system [9].

(1)   The initial values and parameters of the logistic mapping are given, and the first layer of chaotic sequences which is generated by the iteration of the logistic mapping: $\{x_{k0}|\ k = 0, 1, 2, ..., M\}$.

(2) Each $x_{k0}$ which is used as the initial value of the cubic mapping to iterate out a sequence of length N. A total of M $x_{k0}$ generated M chaotic sequences, and which were connected in series to get the sequence of the second layer:$\{x_{ki}|\ k = 0, 1, 2, ..., M;\ i = 0, 1, 2, ..., N\}$.

(3) In accordance with the value of $x_{k0}$ and the value of $x_{kN}$ which is iterated out as initial value, the parameter $\mu$ of logistic mapping and the parameter a of cubic mapping which are dynamically transformed according to the following method to form a mutual control chaotic system.

$$\mu = \begin{cases} 3.9 & x_{kN} \geq 0 \\ 4 & x_{kN} < 0 \end{cases}. \tag{4}$$

$$a = \begin{cases} 1 & x_{k0} \geq 0.5 \\ 4 & x_{k0} < 0.5 \end{cases}. \tag{5}$$

(4) Discard the antecedent sequence of each subsystem iteration to ensure that the system enters chaos state.

(5) Give the system a different initial value $y_{00}$ and repeat the above steps to generate a compound sequence $\{y_{ki}\}$.

(6) Select 0 as the threshold, according to the binary decision method to chaotic sequence $\{x_{ki}\}$, $\{y_{ki}\}$ to obtain a binary sequence $\{X_{ki}\}$ and $\{Y_{ki}\}$.

(7) Exclusive-OR of $\{X_{ki}\}$ and $\{Y_{ki}\}$ which yields a random sequence for encryption $\{Z_{ki}\}$.

# 4  Performance Analysis and Comparison of Algorithms

## 4.1  Periodicity Analysis

From the theoretical and experimental point of view, we will analyze whether the hybrid sequence generated by the improved algorithm is more periodic than the logistic sequence.

(1)  Theoretical analysis

The improved algorithm is compounded by two chaotic systems with different initial values by XOR generated mixed sequence, and each of the composite chaotic system is composed of several different initial cubic subsystems, the period of the chaotic sequence produced by each compound system must be larger than the period of each subsystem generation sequence, and two composite systems by XOR the operation once again expand the cycle, due to the XOR operation is to add operation, the two systems are independent of each other, the number of states experienced from a certain state to recovering this state can only be the least common multiple of two composite system periods [10].

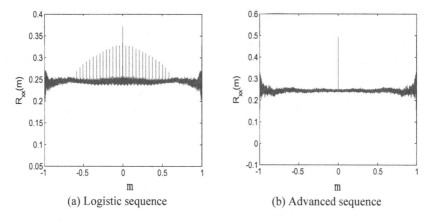

(a) Logistic sequence                    (b) Advanced sequence

**Fig. 3.** Autocorrelation function figures of logistic sequence and advanced sequence

(2)  Experimental analysis

Provided that a sequence is periodic, so its autocorrelation function which is also cyclical and has the same period as the sequence, so we can use the autocorrelation function to test the periodicity of the improved sequence. When the accuracy is $10^{-8}$, logistic sequence and mixed chaotic sequence with length of $10^4$ are respectively calculated whose the autocorrelation according to formula (1), and Fig. 3 is the relation graph between correlation interval and autocorrelation function. The horizontal axis of (a) and (b) of Fig. 3 is related interval, and whose the vertical axis is all autocorrelation function value. Logistic sequences have apparent short-period phenomena under low-precision conditions. Nevertheless, the autocorrelation function of the sequence generated by the improved algorithm in this paper is closer to the $\delta$ function, which avoids the short-period phenomenon and the randomness of the sequences is better [11].

## 4.2  Key Space Analysis

In this algorithm, the key is the initial value $x_{00}$ and $y_{00}$ of two systems, and the value range of $x_{00}$ and $y_{00}$ is 1 to 2, and the key space is 1032 when the computing precision is $10^{-16}$. As a result $\log_2 10^{32} \approx 106$, a 106 bits key is sufficient to resist the exhaustive attack.

## 4.3  Randomness Test

There are many relevant theories and methods for testing the randomness of sequences, such as the Menezes test [12], the NIST test, the Helsinki test [13] and so on. Among the test methods, the NIST test is universally accepted [14]. NIST test by the United States National Institute of Standards and Technology research and development of randomness test system, due to the perfect function, it has been widely used. It includes approximate entropy, block frequency, cumulative sums, spectrum test (FFT), frequency test, linear complexity, longest run, nonoverlapping template, overlapping template, random excursions, random excursions variant, binary matrix rank test rank, run, serial, universal, and a total of 15 tests. Test results return P-value, the value range of the significant level of $\alpha$ is 0.001 to 0.01, if so P-value $\geq \alpha$, through the test, and conversely, if P-value $< \alpha$, subsequently did not pass the test, generally take $\alpha = 0.01$ [15].

NIST tests which are carried out on the single logistic chaotic sequence and the chaotic sequence generated by the improved algorithm, and the results show Table 2.

**Table 2.** NIST test results of logistic sequences and complex sequences.

| Test item | Logistic sequences P-value | Whether to pass the test | Complex sequences P-value | Whether to pass the test |
|---|---|---|---|---|
| Frequency | 0.173900 | Yes | 0.726265 | Yes |
| Block frequency | 0.547993 | Yes | 0.649631 | Yes |
| Runs | 0.855063 | Yes | 0.924797 | Yes |
| Approximate entropy | 0.552590 | Yes | 0.691964 | Yes |
| Cumulative sums | 0.132336 | Yes | 0.831463 | Yes |
| Longest run | 0.103811 | Yes | 0.808232 | Yes |
| Rank | 0.239974 | Yes | 0.696357 | Yes |
| FFT | 0.036674 | Yes | 0.353091 | Yes |
| Nonoverlapping template | 0.029912 | Yes | 0.906058 | Yes |
| Overlapping template | 0.616504 | Yes | 0.184802 | Yes |
| Universal | - | No | 0.825677 | Yes |
| Linear complexity | 0.842133 | Yes | 0.789689 | Yes |
| Random excursions | - | No | 0.184802 | Yes |
| Random excursions Variant | - | No | 0.759490 | Yes |
| Serial | 0.624629 | Yes | 0.293907 | Yes |

## 5  Summary

In this paper, we study that the digital chaotic system, compare the performance of cubic mapping with logistic mapping, and point out that its superior performance in quite a few aspects is also suitable for the application in the field of encryption. A new improved combinatorial chaotic system is proposed, in which the output of the first level chaotic system is taken as the initial input of the next level chaotic system and the chaotic system parameters which are controlled according to the output iteration value of each stage. Combining with the theory and experiment, the performance of the new algorithm is analyzed. It can be seen that the new algorithm can improve the short-period phenomenon effectively, resist the exhaustive attack and have good stochastic behavior.

# References

1. Vattulainen, I., Kankaala, K.: Physical models as tests of randomness. Phys. Rev. E **52**, 3205–3214 (2013)
2. Li, T.Y., Yorke, J.A.: Entropy and chaos. Adv. Math. **3**, 122–128 (2010)
3. Zhang, Y.P., Zuo, F.: A new image encryption algorithm based on multiple chaos system. In: International Symposium on Electronic Commerce and Security, vol. 142, pp. 347–350 (2017)
4. Li, S.J., Cai, Y.L.: Problems with computerized chaos in finite computing precision. Comput. Phys. Commun. **153**, 52–55 (2016)
5. Xue, K.P., Hong, P.L.: Security improvement on an anonymous key agreement protocol based on chaotic maps. Commun. Nonlinear Sci. Number. Simulat. **17**, 2969–2977 (2012)
6. Short, K.M.: Signal extraction from chaotic communications. Int. J. Bifurcat. Chaos **7**, 1579–1997 (2010)
7. Zhai, Y.K., Lin, X.Y.: Improving image encryption using multi-chaotic map. In: Workshop on Power Electronics and Intelligent Transportation System, vol. 106, pp. 143–148 (2015)
8. Habutsu, T., Nishio, Y., Sasase, I., Mori, S.: A secret key cryptosystem by iterating a chaotic map. In: Davies, D.W. (ed.) EUROCRYPT 1991. LNCS, vol. 547, pp. 127–140. Springer, Heidelberg (1991). https://doi.org/10.1007/3-540-46416-6_11
9. Alvarez, G., Pastor, G.: Chaotic cryptosystems. IEEE Secur. Technol. **67**, 332–338 (2012)
10. Diffie, W., Hellman, M.: New directions in cryptography. IEEE Trans. Inf. Theory **22**, 644–654 (2015)
11. Shannon, C.E.: Communication theory of secrecy systems. Bell Syst. Tech. J. **28**, 656–715 (2016)
12. Kocarev, L.: A brief overview. IEEE Circ. Syst. Mag. **1**, 11–21 (2010)
13. Sabery, K.M., Yaghoobi, M.: A new approach for image encryption using chaotic logistic map. In: 2008 International Conference on Advanced Computer Theory and Engineering, vol. 177, pp. 585–590 (2013)
14. Akhavan, A., Samsudin, A.: A symmetric image encryption scheme based on combination of nonlinear chaotic maps. J. Franklin Inst. **348**, 1797–1813 (2011)
15. Lian, S.: Efficient image or video encryption based on spatiotemporal chaos system. Chaos Solitons Fractals **40**, 2509–2519 (2014)

# VulAware: Towards Massive-Scale Vulnerability Detection in Cyberspace

Zhiqiang Wang[1], Pingchuan Ma[1(✉)], Ruming Wang[2], Shichun Gao[1],
Xuying Zhao[1], and Tao Yang[3]

[1] Beijing Electronic Science and Technology Institute,
Beijing 100070, People's Republic of China
wangzq@besti.edu.cn, 20162308@mail.besti.edu.cn
[2] Hainan University, Haikou 570100, People's Republic of China
[3] Key Lab of Information Network Security of Ministry of Public Security,
Shanghai 200000, People's Republic of China

**Abstract.** Due to the delay of threat warning and vulnerability fixing,
the critical servers in cyberspace are under potential threat. With the
help of vulnerability detection system, we can reduce risk and manage
servers efficiently. To date, substantial related works have been done,
combined with unenjoyable performance. To address these issues, we
present VulAware, which is a distributed framework for detecting vulnerabilities. It is able to detect remote vulnerabilities automatically. Finally,
empirical results show that VulAware significantly outperforms the state-
of-the-art methods in both speed and robustness.

**Keywords:** Cyber security · Vulnerability detection
Network attack · Security vulnerability

## 1 Introduction

With the widely-using of Internet technology, cyber security is now of great significance to state security and social stability. Hence, the confidentiality, availability, and integrity of information system are faced with more and more threats
and challenges. CNVD[1] had disclosed 10,822 vulnerabilities in 2016 at the 33.9%
year-on-year growth. According to the report by CNCERT/CC[2] in 2016, about
40,000 IP address have attacked and created backdoor over 82,000 sites at the
9.3% year-on-year growth.

As cyber security situation becomes rigorous, the existing methods deal ineffi-
ciently with massive hosts in cyberspace. As a result, there is a great requirement
of high-performance framework for detecting vulnerabilities. Hence, we proposed
a distributed framework for detecting vulnerabilities, where load-balancing and
efficient scheduling are realized to enhance vulnerability detector's performance

---

[1] China National Vulnerability Database.
[2] National Internet Emergency Centre.

© ICST Institute for Computer Sciences, Social Informatics and Telecommunications Engineering 2018
L. Meng and Y. Zhang (Eds.): MLICOM 2018, LNICST 251, pp. 144–149, 2018.
https://doi.org/10.1007/978-3-030-00557-3_15

and efficiency. And ablation studies show our framework outperforms other baselines. Cyber security situation can be further enhanced, and thus the process of discovering vulnerability can be accelerated, which makes active defence come true.

The sections of this paper is as follows: In Sect. 2, We review and analyze some related works and their problems. In Sect. 3, we introduce the proposed distributed vulnerability detection framework. In Sect. 4, we evaluate the performance and accuracy of the developed prototype system. At last, we discuss our work in Sect. 5.

## 2    Related Works

As is mentioned in Ref. [7], researchers have proposed several approaches, including front-end detection [4,6], remote detection [3,8]. However, as cyberspace becomes more and more complicated, these approaches suffer from several limitations, such as poor adaptability, scalability and performance.

Reference [6] developed a generic web vulnerability scanner called "SecuBat" that analyses websites aimed at finding SQL injection and XSS vulnerabilities automatically. However, the module can only be used to identify individual vulnerability and can't deal with various web applications.

References [4,5] proposed a new way to infer web applications' internal state machine, which drives a black-box web application vulnerability scanner. The scanner, according to the awareness of state, generates fuzzing test cases toward a web page and automatically discover vulnerabilities. But their approach suffers from a severe problem: they don't fully support the web applications based on Ajax and the number of these web applications is sharply increasing.

In addition, Ref. [6] as well as Refs. [4,5] only supportted front-end vulnerability discovery. Server-end vulnerabilities are not considered in their approaches.

Reference [8] proposed a distributed module aimed at vulnerability scanning, which improves the efficiency of vulnerability discovery. Using PoC to provide an in-depth detection to remote hosts, the module extends standard vulnerability databases and registers the vulnerabilities' description, classification and test. The module overcomes the limitation of single machine deployment. Still Ref. [8] highly relies on the central server and can't resist any accident. Thus, hardly can high availability be ensured when deployed in a large scale, according to the disadvantaged architecture.

Reference [3] proposed a security scanning system based on C/S architecture. It works at server side and designs a unified interface to describe vulnerability. The system realized expansion of external vulnerabilities. However, similar to Refs. [3,8] didn't realize a distributed system.

While great progress has made in the existing works, many problems remain to be solved, including unpractical deployment modes and poor scalability. Directed at the problems mentioned above, we carried out our research which will be described in the following sections.

# 3   Architecture

Typical conventional tools for detecting vulnerabilities run with other security tools, such as firewalls, IDS and authentication devices. (See Fig. 1) Due to poor performance and lack of scalability, conventional tools are disadvantaged when encountered in high-loading situation.

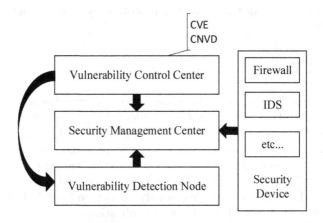

**Fig. 1.** Conventional architecture

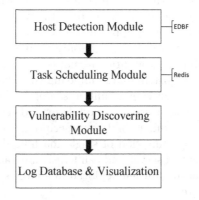

**Fig. 2.** The Architecture of VulAware

To address these challenges, we design a distributed framework called "VulAware", which decouples every components. VulAware is based on Producer-Consumer model and connected by a distributed queue. The advantage is that accident of any individual node wouldn't directly impact on runtime systems. VulAware includes host detection module, task scheduling module, vulnerability discovering module, log database and visualization module. (See Fig. 2) Similar to web crawler, the host detection module generates detection tasks. Task scheduling module is a task queue based on Redis[3], which serves as a bridge between vulnerability and host detection module. Vulnerability discovering module simulates attack behaviours with an objected-oriented method. The log database will save the test results as a log, and visualization module will show the results in a chart.

## 3.1   Host Detection Module

As a fundamental component of VulAware, host detection module generates the initial data in order to create further tasks. Firstly, the module renders remote pages by chrome-headless[4] and parses the elements of the pages in the Dom-tree. Secondly, it matches the URLs with the same origin. Thirdly, with distributed Bloom Filter, it removes the duplicated URLs. Finally, it adds available URLs into the task queue.

According to Refs. [1,2], Bloom Filter is an algorithm proposed by Burton H. Bloom in 1970, used to test a series of messages one-by-one for membership in a given set of messages. Compared to conventional algorithms, such as HashMap, it is of excellent time-space performance at the time complexity of $O(1)$. However, the length of binary vector must be fixed before using it. As a result, with the growth of data set, the accuracy would sharply decrease, and the existing algorithms can't handle dynamic data set. Meanwhile, the single machine deployment can't handle retrieval in a massive scale.

To address the inability of existing algorithms, we designed EDBF (Extendable Distributed Bloom Filter) which is formed by several sub-filters (the number of sub-filters is based on the error rate and initial capacity). Each sub-filter is a distributed Bloom Filter of fixed capacity, and the distributed filter contains an improved Bloom Filter and remote storage module. EDBF can add sub-filters automatically to meet the requirements of data set and error rate. Additionally, the data in each sub-filter will be saved on more than one machine and automatically synchronize among every node. Furthermore, atomic operation contributes to data persistence and load balancing. Faced with massive data, EDBL realizes both steady performance and high availability. EDBF transforms URL into a value of 256 Bits with HASH256 and thus check the vector from sub-filter to remove the duplicated URLs.

## 3.2   Task Scheduling Module

The task scheduling module is a bridge in the framework, which passes through the total process of VulAware. The module is a task queue based on Redis which is an open-source in-memory database project. After collected by host detection module, tasks are added to the task queue, and the vulnerability detection module will pull from the queue and detect the specific hosts.

---

[3] https://redis.io.

[4] https://developers.google.com/web/updates/2017/04/headless-chrome.

### 3.3 Vulnerability Discovering Module

Vulnerability discovering module is the core module of VulAware. After getting a task from the task scheduling module, it will verify remote hosts, recognize their service, retrieve services in the database, run PoC, and finally analyze the response of hosts.

The existing methods tend to simulate an attack to remote hosts by sending a specific packet and assess whether remote hosts have security vulnerabilities based on the response of hosts. For the sake of compliance with penetration test, we delete the sensitive codes and test remote hosts with the guarantee of availability.

## 4     Evaluation and Empirical Result

### 4.1 Result

The framework runs on a virtual machine platform based on five vSphere ESXi servers (32 Cores, 128 GB Memory). We deploy several virtual machines (Ubuntu 16.02), and each machine is connected with 1 GB local area network. To evaluate the performance of our framework, we implement the prototype system based on Docker. We build the vulnerable testing environments in different scales.

Struts 2 is an open-source web application framework for developing Java EE web applications and has a history of critical security bugs. Hence, we deployed a schedule app and a management platform based on Struts2 and tested these two web applications. According to the results, VulAware has found 6 vulnerabilities in schedule app within 4 s and 73 vulnerabilities in management platform within 114 s.

### 4.2 Evaluation

In the ideal network environment, we compare VulAware to Refs. [3,4,6,8]. In terms of distribution, Refs. [3,8] and VulAware realize distributed deployment. And in the view of robustness, VulAware is of high robustness and able to meet any accident of individual node due to Docker[5] which performs virtualization also known as containerization. In term of scalability, we simulate attack behaviours by objected-oriented methods and resolve the problem, and Ref. [8] can detect external vulnerabilities by developing plugins of their detecting module. Last but not least, when it comes to data processing ability, due to EDBF, we break through the bottleneck of massive data. Reference [3,4,8] consider little of wide-scale deployment and can't handle this situation. (See Table 1).

Overall, VulAware can detect web applications' vulnerabilities in a brief time and is advantaged in availability and reliability.

---

[5] https://www.docker.com.

**Table 1.** Evaluation.

| Research | Distributed | Robustness | Scalability | Speed |
|----------|-------------|------------|-------------|-------|
| This paper | Y | High | High | High |
| Reference [6] | N | Low | Low | Low |
| Reference [4] | N | Low | Low | Low |
| Reference [8] | Y | Low | High | Low |
| Reference [3] | Y | Low | Low | Low |

# 5  Conclusion

We design and implement a distributed framework for detecting vulnerabilities and enhance the disadvantages of conventional tools, and can scan massive cyber hosts quickly. Due to the distributed deployment, it can handle any accident of individual node. Thus, high robustness and stability are achieved. Generally, VulAware mitigates the security risk in cyberspace, speeds up the process of vulnerability response, and finally the security of information system is improved from the perspective of attackers.

Despite the enormous performance, VulAware still has some limitations. It can only detect known vulnerabilities which are in the database. In the future, we would research on discovering web application vulnerabilities automatically.

**Acknowledgment.** Our research is supported by Key Lab of Information Network Security of Ministry of Public Security, Open Project Foundation of Information Technology Research Base of Civil Aviation Administration of China (NO. CAAC-ITRB-201705), Beijing Common Construction Project (2017), National Innovation and Start-up Training Program (201710018026).

# References

1. Bloom, B.H.: Space/time trade-offs in hash coding with allowable errors. Commun. ACM **13**(7), 422–426 (1970)
2. Broder, A., Mitzenmacher, M.: Network applications of bloom filters: a survey. Internet Math. **1**(4), 485–509 (2004)
3. Chen, T.M., Cai, J.M., Jiang, R.R., Feng, X.C.: Design of network security scanning system based on plug-in. Comput. Eng. Des. (2004)
4. Doupé, A., Cavedon, L., Kruegel, C., Vigna, G.: Enemy of the state: a state-aware black-box vulnerability scanner. In: USENIX Security Symposium (2012)
5. Doupé, A., Cova, M., Vigna, G.: Why Johnny can't pentest: an analysis of black-box web vulnerability scanners. In: Kreibich, C., Jahnke, M. (eds.) DIMVA 2010. LNCS, vol. 6201, pp. 111–131. Springer, Heidelberg (2010). https://doi.org/10.1007/978-3-642-14215-4_7
6. Kals, S., Kirda, E., Kruegel, C., Jovanovic, N.: SecuBat: a web vulnerability scanner. In: International Conference on World Wide Web, pp. 247–256 (2006)
7. Liang, L., Zhang, Y., Gao, Y., Qian, X.: Research and implementation of a vulnerability detection and initiative recover system model. Comput. Eng. **3**(3), 1–7 (2004)
8. Zhan, S.: Research and application of distributed vulnerability scanning model. Ph.D. thesis, Guangdong University of Technology (2013)

# Cognitive Radio and Intelligent Networking

# Optimization in Cognitive Radio Networks with SWIPT-Based DF Relay

Jie Zhang[1(✉)], Weidang Lu[1], Hong Peng[1], Zhijiang Xu[1], and Xin Liu[2]

[1] College of Information Engineering, Zhejiang University of Technology, Hangzhou 310023, China
393707734@qq.com
[2] School of Information and Communication Engineering, Dalian University of Technology, Dalian 116024, China

**Abstract.** Energy-constrained relay networks are normally powered by a fixed energy, which limits the runtime of networks. Energy harvesting (EH) with simultaneous wireless information and power transfer (SWIPT) is hopeful to increase the life of energy-limited relay networks. We investigate the optimization problem about power splitting ratio for SWIPT-based decode-and-forward (DF) relay in cognitive radio networks (CRNs). Secondary relaying node (SRN) harvests energy from secondary source node (SSN) then use the energy to assist forwarding SSN information to the secondary destination node (SDN). We maximize throughput of secondary users (SUs) if the interference caused by SU to the primary users (PUs) is under the threshold. Some opinions are provided through theory analysis and simulation results.

**Keywords:** Energy harvesting · SWIPT · Decode-and-forward
Power splitting · Cognitive radio networks

## 1 Introduction

With the increasing popularity of wireless system, radio spectrum becomes more rare. However, FCC reports that the spectrum is not utilized validly [1]. Considering the challenges of low efficiency of spectrum utilization, the wireless networks should have Intelligent network information perception, flexible spectrum management and dynamic network reconfiguration abilities.

Cognitive Radio (CR), as an intelligent wireless system, enables the wireless devices can not only perceive the information rapidly but also to adjust the dynamic parameters. Ordinarily, CR allows SUs linking to the bands to improves the utilization efficiency if only they do not have large impact on the performance of PUs. In a CR network, the transmit power, power splitting ratio and energy harvesting are important factor which need to be optimized to obtain the maximum throughput. Therefore, many studies have focused on these aspects underlay CRNs [2–4]. In [2], the authors analyzed the interrupt probability and spatial throughput. Also, they derived the optimal transmission power and density of SN nodes. In [3], a harvested energy-throughput trade-off optimization

© ICST Institute for Computer Sciences, Social Informatics and Telecommunications Engineering 2018
L. Meng and Y. Zhang (Eds.): MLICOM 2018, LNICST 251, pp. 153–161, 2018.
https://doi.org/10.1007/978-3-030-00557-3_16

problem was formulated and a closed-form solution was obtained. The SU's transmit power allocation was optimized to maximize the throughput [4].

Radio-frequency (RF) energy harvesting is an increasingly popular research due to the fact that it's a practical way to increase energy-limited wireless networks life. The common energy harvesting depends on ambient energy sources like wind and geothermal, which are not always available. RF attracts considerable research interests since it owns several favorable properties including availability and controllability. Meanwhile, RF signal is able to transfer information and energy simultaneously. Thus, interest has risen greatly in regard to powering mobile networks by EH from electro-magnetic waves propagation in radio-frequency (RF) signals.

A lot methods have been studied recently [5–7], the authors in [5] devised receiver architectures for simultaneous wireless information and power transfer (SWIPT) systems. In [6], the receiver operates switch between energy harvesting (EH) and information decoding (ID) as time-switching (TS) mode, or share the input signal into ID and EH as power-splitting (PS). Power-splitting SWIPT is applied in traditional networks like MISO systems in [7] where optimizes efficiency of transmission energy.

The applications of RF in the acquisition of harvesting energy and transferring data were summed by Mohjazi et al. at [8]. And there are many researches studied SWIPT in CRNs, [9] propose that collaboration between primary and secondary systems can increase the spectrum efficiency in CRNs. In [10], authors consider a novel cooperative cognitive radio network,which is made up of full-duplex-enabled energy access points which receive primary signal in first slot, and perform decode-and-forward relaying in second slot. But CRNs with power-splitting SWIPT under multi-user condition have not been studied well. The research on SWIPT has enough possible uses, like wireless powered cognitive cellular networks, where are supposed to get information and energy simultaneously in [11].

In the article, we derive the maximum throughput expression in SWIPT-Based DF with energy harvesting by taking into account relay node interference. The closed-form expressions of power splitting ratio about the optimal value is derived. The structure of this article is as follows:

- First, we consider the interference at PUs to derive the maximum throughput expression of SWIPT-Based DF with energy harvesting.
- Second, an algorithm is given to obtain the closed-form optimal value of power splitting ratio in same transmit power.
- Third, we show that there our proposed algorithm slightly superior than the exhaustive search method.

The other of article is that Sect. 2 describes the system model in CRNs with energy harvesting relay node and the formulation for the optimization problem. Section 3 presents the algorithm to solve the optimization problem. Simulation results are given in Sect. 4. In Sect. 5, we summarize this article.

## 2  System Model and Problem Formulation

### 2.1  System Model

In Figure we describe a distributed cognitive relay radio network. The primary network has a pair of PUs, include a transmitter (PT) and a receiver (PR). The secondary network consists of a source node (SSN), a DF relay node (SRN), and a destination node (SDN). All nodes have single-antenna. Because the direct connection between SSN and SDN is assumed not to exist due to poor fading conditions or obstacles, we suppose that SSN can only communication with SDN through SRN. We consider that the secondary nodes can transmit data in the same spectrum licensed to the primary network subject to interference constraint at the primary receiver (Fig. 1).

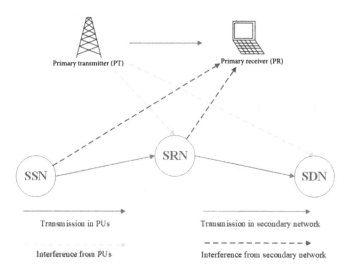

**Fig. 1.** System model

The PT's transmission will interfere the secondary network. The channel coefficient between any terminal a and b are expressed as $h_{a,b} = g_{a,b}d_{a,b}^{-m/2}$, where $d_{a,b}$ is the distance between $a$ and $b$, $m$ is the path loss exponent, $g_{a,b} \sim CN(0, \mu)$ is rayleigh fading coefficient where $\mu = 1$.

The relaying communication has two equal slots. SSN sends the signal to SRN in first slot, so the signal at SRN is represented as

$$y = \sqrt{P_s}x_s h_{SSN,SRN} + \sqrt{P_p}x_p h_{PT,SRN} + n_a \tag{1}$$

where $P_s$ and $P_p$ are the transmission power of SSN and PT. $x_s$ and $x_p$ are the signals from SSN and PT, $n_a \sim CN(0, \sigma_a^2)$ is additive white Gaussian noise (AWGN) at SRN.

In the article, we fix $P_s$ with $P_{\max}$ which limits maximum transmit power for SSN and the interference from SSN to PR is less than $I_{th}$. Thus, $P_s$ is given by

$$p_s = \min(p_{\max}, \frac{I_{th}}{|h_{SSN,PR}|^2}) \tag{2}$$

The received signal has two parts at SRN. One part $\lambda(0 \le \lambda \le 1)$ uses for energy harvesting, the other $(1 - \lambda)$ is used for information decoding. The harvested energy can be expressed as

$$E = \frac{1}{2}\eta\lambda(P_s|h_{SSN,SRN}|^2 + P_p|h_{PT,SRN}|^2 + \sigma_a^2) \tag{3}$$

where $\eta(0 < \eta < 1)$ is the conversion efficiency. We suppose all the harvesting energy forwarding SSN's information. So, SRNs power can be expressed as

$$P_{sr} = \frac{E}{\frac{1}{2}} = \eta\lambda(P_s|h_{SSN,SRN}|^2 + P_p|h_{PT,SRN}|^2 + \sigma_a^2) \tag{4}$$

The baseband signal of the information receiver is represented as

$$y_{sr} = \sqrt{(1-\lambda)}y + n_b = \sqrt{(1-\lambda)}(\sqrt{P_s}x_s h_{SSN,SRN} + \sqrt{P_p}x_p h_{PT,SRN} + n_a) + n_b \tag{5}$$

where $n_b \sim CN(0, \sigma_b^2)$ is the noise from RF band to baseband [12].

From (5), we deduce the SINR at SRN as followed

$$SINR_{SRN} = \frac{(1-\lambda)P_s|h_{SSN,SRN}|^2}{(1-\lambda)(P_p|h_{PT,SRN}|^2 + \sigma_a^2) + \sigma_b^2} = \frac{-A\lambda + A}{-B\lambda + C}P_s \tag{6}$$

where $A = |h_{SSN,SRN}|^2$, $B = P_s|h_{PT,SRN}|^2 + \sigma_a^2$, $C = P_p|h_{PT,SRN}|^2 + \sigma_a^2 + \sigma_b^2$.

In the second slot, SRN send the signal from SSN through the DF relaying protocol, and the received signal at SDN is indicated as

$$y_{sd} = \sqrt{P_{sr}}x_s h_{SRN,SDN} + \sqrt{P_p}x_p h_{PT,SDN} + n_c \tag{7}$$

where $n_c \sim CN(0, \sigma_c^2)$ is AWGN at SDN.

Substituting (4) to (7), we can get

$$y_{sd} = \sqrt{\eta\lambda(P_s|h_{SSN,SRN}|^2 + P_p|h_{PT,SRN}|^2 + \sigma_a^2)}x_s h_{SRN,SDN} + \sqrt{P_p}x_p h_{PT,SDN} + n_c \tag{8}$$

From (8), we can deduced the SINR at SDN as following

$$SINR_{SDN} = \frac{\eta\lambda(P_s|h_{SSN,SRN}|^2 + P_p|h_{PT,SRN}|^2 + \sigma_a^2)|h_{SRN,SDN}|^2}{P_p|h_{PT,SDN}|^2 + \sigma_c^2} = \frac{(DP_s + E)\lambda}{F} \tag{9}$$

where $\quad D = \eta|h_{SSN,SRN}|^2|h_{SRN,SDN}|^2, \qquad E = \eta(P_p|h_{PT,SRN}|^2 + \sigma_a^2)|h_{SRN,SDN}|^2,$
$F = P_p|h_{PT,SDN}|^2 + \sigma_c^2.$

So the SDNs throughput is given by

$$R_d = \min(\frac{1}{2}\log_2(1 + SINR_{SRN}), \frac{1}{2}\log_2(1 + SINR_{SDN})) \tag{10}$$

## 2.2 Problem Formulation

During two time slots, the interference from SRN to PR is represented as

$$I_{sr} = P_r|h_{SRN,PR}|^2 = \eta\lambda(P_s|h_{SSN,SRN}|^2 + P_p|h_{PT,SRN}|^2 + \sigma_a^2)|h_{SRN,PR}|^2 \tag{11}$$

The optimization problem is formulated as

$$OP1: \quad \max_{\lambda} R_d \tag{12}$$

$$\text{s.t.} \quad C1: I_{sr} \leq I_{th} \tag{13}$$

$$C2: \lambda \in [0,1] \tag{14}$$

where C1 denote that the interference from the secondary network to primary network should not be larger than *Ith*. C2 denotes the limit of $\lambda$. Because $\log(x)$ is an increasing function of $x$, OP1 could turn to OP2.

$$OP2: \quad \max_{\lambda} SINR \tag{15}$$

$$\text{s.t.} \quad C1 - C2 \tag{16}$$

where $SINR = min(SINR_{SRN}, SINR_{SDN})$

## 3 Optimization for Problem with Fixed Transmission Power

We can know the first derivative of (6) with $\lambda$

$$\frac{dSINR_{SRN}}{d\lambda} = \frac{A(B-C)}{(-B\lambda + C)^2}P_s \tag{17}$$

From (6) and (14), we can easily know that $B < C$ and $\lambda \in [0,1]$, so $\frac{dSINR_{SRN}}{d\lambda} < 0$ and $SINR_{SRN}$ is monotone decreasing function with $\lambda$. From (9), we know $SINR_{SDN}$ is monotone increasing function with $\lambda$.

$$SINR_{SRN}(1) = \frac{APs}{C} > 0 \tag{18}$$

$$SINR_{SRN}(1) = 0 \tag{19}$$

$$SINR_{SDN}(0) = 0 \tag{20}$$

$$SINR_{SDN}(1) = \frac{DPs + E}{F} > 0 \tag{21}$$

From (20) to (23), we know that there is only one point of intersection when C4 satisfies, and the throughput reach the maximum when $\frac{-A\lambda + A}{-B\lambda + C} P_s = \frac{(DP_s + E)\lambda}{F}$. So we can obtain

$$\lambda^* = \frac{(CDP_s + CE + AFP_s) - \sqrt{x(P_s)}}{2(BDP_s + BE)} \tag{22}$$

where $x(P_s) = (CDP_s + CE + AFP_s)^2 - 4(BDP_s + BE)AFP_s$. From C2, we have

$$\lambda \le \lambda_{th} = \frac{I_{th}}{GP_s + H} \tag{23}$$

where $G = \eta |h_{SSN,SRN}|^2 |h_{SRN,PR}|^2$, $H = \eta(\sigma_a^2 + P_p |h_{PT,SRN}|^2)|h_{SRN,PR}|^2$.
The optimal value of $\lambda$ is given by

$$\lambda = \begin{cases} \lambda^* = \frac{(CDP_s + CE + AFP_s) - \sqrt{x(P_s)}}{2(BDP_s + BE)} & if\ \lambda_{th} > \lambda^* \\ \lambda_{th} = \frac{I_{th}}{GP_s + H} & if\ \lambda_{th} \le \lambda^* \end{cases} \tag{24}$$

## 4　Simulation Result and Discussion

Unless noted, we postulate that the path loss exponent $m = 3$, the distance $d_{SSN,SRN} + d_{SRN,SDN} = 2$, $d_{PT,SRN} = d_{PT,SDN} = d_{SSN,PR} = d_{SRN,PR} = 2$, the efficiency of energy harvesting $\eta = 0.8$, PT's transmission power $Pp = 2\,W$, the maximum transmission power of SSN $Pmax = 2\,W$. Noise variances $\sigma_a^2 = \sigma_b^2 = \sigma_c^2 = 0.01$. There are averaged over 50,000 channel for all simulations.

In Fig. 2, we get the relationship between the throughput and $d_{SSN,SRN}$. We can easily find that the throughput of secondary network decreases with the farther distance from SRN to SSN. The reason is that the power received at SRN will be reduced cause of the path loss, which means the harvested energy reduce. And we can know that with $Ith$ getting larger, the throughput of SUs gets larger. With $Ith$ larger, the transmission power becomes larger. It will show in Fig. 3.

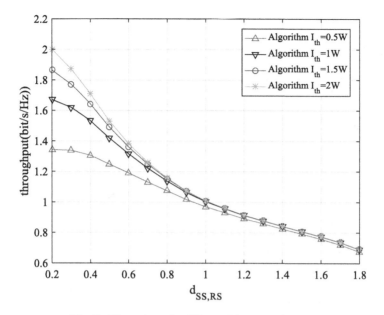

**Fig. 2.** Throughput for different *Ith* versus $d_{SSN,SRN}$

Figure 3 proves the algorithm proposed, where the distance from SSN to SRN is set to be 1 as well as SRN and SDN. Figure 3 proves that SUs reaches the maximum throughput with optimal $\lambda$ than other ratio.

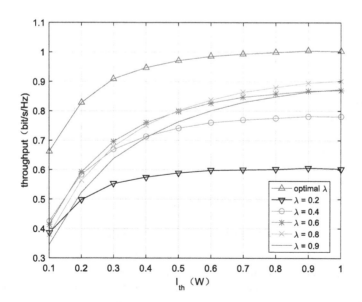

**Fig. 3.** Throughput with different $\lambda$ versus *Ith*

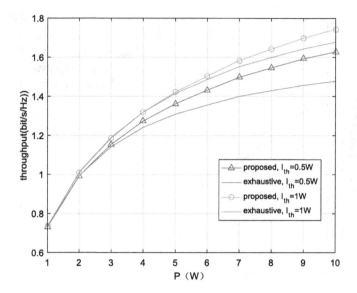

**Fig. 4.** Throughput with different *Ith* and algorithm versus $P_s$

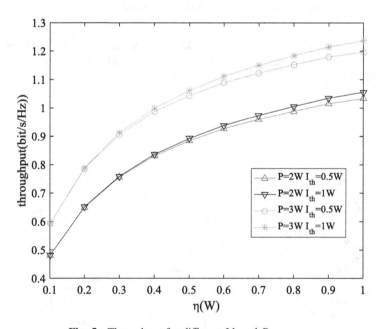

**Fig. 5.** Throughput for different *Ith* and $P_s$ versus $\eta$

Figure 4 shows the throughput versus transmission power. In Fig. 4, we can know that the throughput increases along with the growth of $P_s$. Under the same premise, the proposed algorithm is slightly better than exhaustive algorithm.

Figure 5 shows the throughput for different *Ith* and $P_s$ versus $\eta$. We find that the throughput increases when $\eta$ increases which means the harvested energy for forwarding information become more.

# 5 Conclusion

In the article, we study the maximum throughput for the DF in CRNs with SWIPT-enable relaying node. SRN harvests energy from SSNs and utilizes it to forward SSNs information. Considering the constraints of interference at PU as well as SU, we give an algorithm to solve the optimization problem with fixed transmission power. It is supposed to get the max throughput ensuring that interference is less than threshold. The simulation results verify the effectiveness of the optimized program.

# References

1. FCC Spectrum Policy Task Force: Report of the spectrum efficiency working group. Technical report ET Docket No. 02-135, Federal Communications Commission, Washington, D. C. (2002)
2. Lee, S., Zhang, R., Huang, K.: Opportunistic wireless energy harvesting in cognitive radio networks. IEEE Trans. Wirel. Commun. **12**(9), 4788–4799 (2013)
3. Zheng, M., Xu, C., Liang, W., Yu, H.: Harvesting-throughput tradeoff for RF-powered underlay cognitive radio networks. Electron. Lett. **52**(10), 881–883 (2016)
4. Lozano, A., Tulino, A.M., Verdú, S.: Optimum power allocation for parallel Gaussian channels with arbitrary input distributions. IEEE Trans. Inf. Theory **52**(7), 3033–3051 (2006)
5. Zhang, R., Ho, C.K.: MIMO broadcasting for simultaneous wireless information and power transfer. IEEE Trans. Wireless Commun. **12**(5), 1989–2001 (2013)
6. Bi, S., Ho, C.K., Zhang, R.: Wireless powered communication: opportunities and challenges. IEEE Commun. Mag. **53**, 117–125 (2015)
7. Vu, Q.D., Tran, L.N., Farrel, R., Hong, E.K.: An efficiency maximization design for SWIPT. IEEE Signal Process. Lett. **22**, 2189–2193 (2015)
8. Mohjazi, L., Dianati, M., Karagiannidis, G.K., Muhaidat, S.: RF-powered cognitive radio networks: technical challenges and limitations. IEEE Commun. Mag. **53**, 94–100 (2015)
9. Zheng, G., Ho, Z., Jorswieck, E.A., Ottersten, B.: Information and energy cooperation in cognitive radio networks. IEEE Trans. Wirel. Commun. **62**, 2290–2303 (2014)
10. Xing, H., Kang, X., Wong, K.-K., Nallanathan, A.: Optimizing DF cognitive radio networks with full-duplex-enabled energy access points. IEEE Trans. Wireless Commun. **16**, 4683–4697 (2017)
11. Tuan, P.V., Koo, I.: Robust weighted sum harvested energy maximization for SWIPT cognitive radio networks based on particle swarm optimization. Sensors **17**(10), 2275 (2017). https://doi.org/10.3390/s17102275
12. Nasir, A.A., Zhou, X., Durrani, S., Kennedy, R.A.: Throughput and ergodic capacity of wireless energy harvesting based DF relaying network. In: Proceedings of the IEEE ICC, pp. 4066–4071 (2014). https://doi.org/10.1109/ICC.2014.6883957

# Real-Valued Orthogonal Sequences for Ultra-low Overhead Channel Estimation in MIMO-FBMC Systems

Su Hu[1(✉)], Jing Zhang[1], Wanbin Tang[1], Zilong Liu[2], Pei Xiao[2],
and Yuan Gao[3(✉)]

[1] National Key Laboratory on Communications,
University of Electronic Science and Technology of China, Chengdu 611731, China
husu@uestc.edu.cn
[2] Institute of Communication Systems, 5G Innovation Centre, University of Surrey,
Guildford GU2 7XH, UK
[3] Department of Electronic Engineering, Tsinghua University, Beijing 100084, China
yuangao08@tsinghua.edu.cn

**Abstract.** Multiple-input multiple-output filterbank multicarrier communication (MIMO-FBMC) is a promising technique to achieve very tight spectrum confinement (thus, higher spectral efficiency) as well as strong robustness against dispersive channels. In this paper, we present a novel training design for MIMO-FBMC system which enables efficient estimate of frequency-selective channels (associated to multiple transmit antennas) with only one non-zero FBMC symbol. Our key idea is to design real-valued orthogonal training sequences (in the frequency domain) which displaying zero-correlation zone properties in the time-domain. Compared to our earlier proposed training scheme requiring at least two non-zero FBMC symbols (separated by several zero guard symbols), the proposed scheme features ultra-low training overhead yet achieves channel estimation performance comparable to our earlier proposed complex training sequence decomposition (CTSD). Our simulations validate that the proposed method is an efficient channel estimation approach for practical preamble-based MIMO-FBMC systems.

**Keywords:** Filterbank multicarrier · MIMO-FBMC
Channel estimation · Preamble · Real-valued orthogonality
Zero-correlation zone sequences

## 1 Introduction

Future wireless communications must be highly spectral efficient. For multicarrier communications, we require waveform pulses with ultra-tight spectrum confinement as well as efficient channel estimation scheme having ultra-low training overhead. As an enhanced modulation scheme to orthogonal frequency-division multiplexing (OFDM), filterbank multicarrier (FBMC) systems employing offset quadrature amplitude modulation (OQAM), called OFDM/OQAM

© ICST Institute for Computer Sciences, Social Informatics and Telecommunications Engineering 2018
L. Meng and Y. Zhang (Eds.): MLICOM 2018, LNICST 251, pp. 162–171, 2018.
https://doi.org/10.1007/978-3-030-00557-3_17

or FBMC/OQAM, achieves very high spectrum efficiency and have attracted increased research attention in recent years [1].

Aiming to eliminate the intrinsic imaginary interference incurred from adjacent symbols, a number of training schemes and associated estimation methods for preamble-based FBMC systems have been proposed [2–6]. These methods, however, generally suffer from heavy training overhead, especially when the number of transmit antennas becomes large. For improved channel estimation performance, there are three obstacles to be attacked: (1), inter-carrier interference (ICI) and inter-symbol interference (ISI); (2), correlation properties of orthogonal sequences could be damaged by the intrinsic imaginary interference; (3), the "real-field orthogonality" (which is pertinent to FBMC) generally prevents the use of any channel estimation methods which require the "complex-field orthogonality".

Recently, a training method called complex training sequence decomposition(CTSD) [7], which requires two non-zero FBMC symbols for channel estimation in MIMO-FBMC has been proposed. CTSD is specifically designed to facilitate the reconstruction of the complex-field orthogonality of MIMO-FBMC signals by superimposing different training sequences over the air (based on code-division multiplexing, CDM). This paper aims to improve our earlier proposed CTSD by designing real-valued orthogonal sequences for novel training scheme with one FBMC symbol only.

The paper is organized as follows: Sect. 2 presents the system model of FBMC systems and introduces the constraint conditions for channel estimation in MIMO-FBMC systems. In Sect. 3, we present a design of training symbols having real-valued orthogonality and capability of interference self-cancellation, followed by detailed description of corresponding training scheme. Numerical simulations are presented in Sect. 4. In the end, this paper is summarized in Sect. 5.

## 2 System Model and Constraint Conditions

### 2.1 System Model

In this paper, we consider an equivalent FBMC baseband model with $M$ subcarriers, where the subcarrier spacing is $1/T$ with $T$ being complex symbol interval. The equivalent discrete-time FBMC signal is expressed as [8]

$$s(l) = \sum_{n \in \mathbb{Z}} \sum_{m=0}^{M-1} a_{m,n} \underbrace{j^{m+n} e^{j2\pi ml/M} g\left(l - n\frac{M}{2}\right)}_{g_{m,n}(l)}, \tag{1}$$

where $j = \sqrt{-1}$, $a_{m,n}$ is the real-valued offset QAM symbol transmitted over the $m$th subcarrier and the $n$th time-slot, and $T/2$ is the interval of real-valued symbols. Meanwhile, $g(l)$ is the employed symmetrical real-valued prototype filter impulse response with length of $L_g = KM$ and $K$ is the overlapping factor.

$g_{m,n}(l)$ represents the synthesis basis which is obtained by the time-frequency translated version of $g(l)$.

Let $\mathbf{h} = [h(0), h(1), \cdots, h(L_h - 1)]^T$ be the discrete impulse response of a multipath fading channel, where $L_h$ denotes the maximum channel delay. According to (1), the baseband received signal therefore can be written as

$$r(l) = \sum_{\tau=0}^{L_h-1} h(\tau) s(l - \tau) + \eta(l), \qquad (2)$$

where $\eta(l)$ denotes the complex additive white gaussian noise with zero mean and variance of $\sigma^2$. The demodulation of received signal at the $(m, n)$ th time-frequency lattice provides a complex symbol given as

$$y_{m,n} = \sum_{l=-\infty}^{\infty} r(l) g\left(l - \frac{nM}{2}\right) e^{-j2\pi ml/M} j^{m+n}. \qquad (3)$$

We assume the symbol interval is much longer than the maximum channel delay spread, i.e., $L_h \ll L_g$. Therefore, the channel may be viewed as frequency flat at each subcarrier over the prototype filter over any time interval $[l, l + L_h]$, i.e., $g(l) \approx g(l + \tau)$, for $\tau \in [0, L_h]$. Hence, $y_{m,n}$ in (3) can be simplified to

$$y_{m,n} = H_{m,n} a_{m,n} + \underbrace{\sum_{(p,q) \neq (m,n)} H_{p,q} a_{p,q} \zeta_{m,n}^{p,q}}_{I_{m,n}} + \eta_{m,n}, \qquad (4)$$

where $H_{m,n}$ denotes the channel frequency response at the $(m, n)$ th lattice, and $I_{m,n}$ and $\eta_{m,n}$ are the intrinsic interference and noise terms, respectively.

The above FBMC formulation in SISO scenario may be easily extended to MIMO-FBMC systems. Consider an $N_T \times N_R$ MIMO-FBMC system, the received signal in each receive antenna $k = 1, 2, \cdots, N_R$ can be expressed as

$$y_{m,n}^k = \sum_{i=1}^{N_T} \left\{ H_{m,n}^{k,i} a_{m,n}^i + \sum_{(m,n) \neq (p,q)} H_{p,q}^{k,i} a_{p,q}^i \zeta_{m,n}^{p,q} \right\} + \eta_{m,n}^k, \qquad (5)$$

where $H_{m,n}^{k,i}$ denotes the channel frequency response from the $i$th transmit antenna to the $k$th receive antenna, and $\eta_{m,n}^k$ denotes the corresponding noise component in the $k$th receive antenna.

## 2.2   Constraint Conditions

Preamble design in MIMO-FBMC system needs to satisfy several constraint conditions presented below.

(1): Compared with CP-OFDM system with complex-field orthogonality, the orthogonality of FBMC system only maintains in real-field. Recalling from PHY-DYAS European project [9], one needs to deal with intrinsic imaginary interference from any lattice point $(m, n) \neq (p, q)$, even passing through a distortion-free channel. Hence, it is ideal to have zero (or close to zero) $I_{m,n}$ in Eq. (3) by proper training design.

(2): To separate the transmission data from different antennas properly, the training set $S = \{S_1, S_2, \cdots, S_K\}$, each sequence having length $L$, is required to be a zero-correlation-zone $(K, L, Z)$ sequence set [7], which is defined as follows.

$$
\begin{aligned}
&(1), \ R_{S_\mu, S_\mu}(\tau) = 0, \ 1 \le \mu \le K \text{ and } 1 \le |\tau| < Z; \\
&(2), \ R_{S_\mu, S_\nu}(\tau) = 0, \ \mu \ne \nu \text{ and } 0 \le |\tau| < Z;
\end{aligned}
\tag{6}
$$

where $R_{S_\mu, S_\nu}(\tau)$ denotes the periodic cross-correlation function between sequences $S_\mu$ and $S_\nu$ at time-shift $\tau$ (see [7] for detailed definition).

(3): To overcome the drawback of CTSD which requires two non-zero FBMC symbols for efficient training, it is ideal to design a ZCZ training set each sequence consists of purely real-valued elements in the frequency domain.

## 3   Efficient Preamble-Based Channel Estimation for MIMO-FBMC System

Motivated by the inefficient channel estimation approach above-mentioned and special attributes of the MIMO-FBMC system, our idea is to form orthogonal sequences set which has real-field orthogonality and interference self-cancellation capability.

### 3.1   Preamble Design of Real-Valued Orthogonal Sequences

Based on the constraint conditions stated in the above, we present below a ZCZ sequence set each sequence having purely real-valued elements in the frequency-domain:

**STEP 1:** Let $\mathbf{M} = [M(0), M(1), \cdots, M(N-1)]$ which is a real-valued unimodular sequence satisfying certain correlation properties. Consider the following sequence in the frequency-domain.

$$
\begin{aligned}
\mathbf{A}_1 &= [A_1(0), A_1(1), \cdots, A_1(2N-1)]_{1 \times 2N} \\
&= [M(0), 0, M(1), 0, \cdots, M(N-1), 0]_{1 \times 2N}.
\end{aligned}
\tag{7}
$$

**STEP 2:** Apply IDFT to $\mathbf{A}_1$. Since $\mathbf{A}_1$ is obtained by inserting zeros into $\mathbf{M}$ in the frequency-domain, the time-domain sequence can be expressed as $\alpha_1 = [\alpha_1(0), \alpha_1(1), \cdots, \alpha_1(2N-1)]_{1 \times 2N} = [\beta; \beta]$, where $\beta = [\alpha_1(0), \cdots, \alpha_1(N-1)]_{1 \times N}$. Then, we have

$$
\begin{aligned}
\alpha_1(t) &= \frac{1}{\sqrt{2N}} \sum_{K=0}^{2N-1} A_1(k) \exp\left(\frac{j2\pi kt}{2N}\right) \\
&= \frac{1}{\sqrt{2N}} \sum_{K=0}^{N-1} M(k) \exp\left(\frac{j2\pi kt}{N}\right) = \frac{1}{\sqrt{2}} \text{IDFT}(M).
\end{aligned}
\tag{8}
$$

It can be easily proved that the periodic autocorrelation function (PACF) of $\alpha_1$ is zero except at the time-shift of $N$ (i.e., the middle time-shift position).

Consider the following time-shifted version of $\alpha_1$ which is defined as

$$\alpha_2 = T^{N/2}(\alpha_1) = [\alpha_1(3N/2), \alpha_1(3N/2+1), \cdots, \alpha_1(3N/2-1)]_{1\times 2N}, \quad (9)$$

where $T^\tau(\cdot)$ denotes the right-cyclically shifted version of $(\cdot)$ for $\tau$ positions. Note that a time domain shift corresponds to a phase rotation in the frequency domain. It can be easily proved that the corresponding frequency domain sequence is $\mathbf{A}_2 = [A_2(0), A_2(1), \cdots, A_2(2N-1)]_{1\times 2N}$, where

$$A_2(k) = \exp(-\frac{j\pi k}{2})A_1(k) = \begin{cases} (-1)^{k/2}A_1(k), & k \text{ is even;} \\ 0, & \text{otherwise} \end{cases} \quad (10)$$

In this way, two columns of real-valued training sequences have been obtained.

**STEP 3:** Choose another seed sequence $\mathbf{M}'$ satisfying certain correlation properties as that of $\mathbf{M}$. By STEP 1, we obtain the third real-valued training sequence $\mathbf{A}_3$ whose time-domain dual is expressed as $\alpha_3$.

**STEP 4:** Following STEP 2, $\alpha_4$ is obtained by applying right-cyclic shift of $N/2$ to $\mathbf{A}_3$. Therefore, four ZCZ training sequences can be obtained. Next, we verify the orthogonality of these sequences.

Let us recall the original sequence $\mathbf{M}$ and the newly designed sequence $\mathbf{A}_1$. Since the frequency-domain preamble sequences are obtained by inserting zeros, the time-domain sequence $\alpha_1$ is formed by cascading two identical sequences $\beta$, i.e. $\alpha_1 = [\beta; \beta]$.

$$R_{\alpha_1,\alpha_1}(\tau) = \sum_{n=0}^{2L-1} \alpha_1(n)(\alpha_1(n+\tau))^* = 2\sum_{n=0}^{L-1} \beta(n)(\beta(n+\tau))^* = 2R_{\beta,\beta}(\tau) \quad (11)$$

So, if $\mathbf{M}$ is a ZCZ sequence of length $N$, $\alpha_1$ will be a ZCZ sequence of length $2N$. By calculating their related properties, we assert that $\{\alpha_1, \alpha_2, \alpha_3, \alpha_4\}$ is a $(4, 2N, N/2)$ ZCZ sequences set.

$$\begin{array}{ll} (1) & R_{\alpha_i,\alpha_i}(\tau) = 0,\ 1 \le i \le 4 \text{ and } 1 \le |\tau| < N \\ (2) & R_{\alpha_i,\alpha_j}(\tau) = 0,\ i \ne j \text{ and } 0 \le |\tau| < N/2 \end{array} \quad (12)$$

In this paper, we select the first two columns of a Hadamard matrix as "seed" sequences $\mathbf{M}$ and $\mathbf{M}'$ to generate our training sequences.

## 3.2   Efficient Channel Estimation

Once $N_T$ sequences are generated, they will be simultaneously transmitted over $N_T$ transmit antennas. Our proposed method suppresses the ISI by inserting $G$ zero symbols as shown in Fig. 1. Because of zero insertion in the training sequences, ICI can be substantially suppressed. In addition, the proposed method takes up only one non-zero FBMC symbol (in contrast to two non-zero FBMC

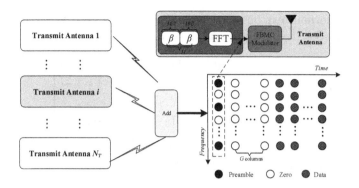

**Fig. 1.** Proposed preamble structure in MIMO-FBMC system with $N_T$ transmit antenna.

training symbols in CTSD [7]) and therefore, about half training overhead can be saved.

For an $N_T \times N_R$ MIMO-FBMC system, there are $N_T N_R$ independent channels to be measured, in which every channel is modelled as a finite impulse response filter with $L_h$ taps. For ease of analysis, we assume that $N_T = N_R$ and the channel is quasi-static. The key idea is to use the real-valued orthogonal sequences to estimate the time-domain channel coefficients. The channel impulse response can be expressed as

$$\mathbf{h}_{i,k} = [h_{i,k}(0), h_{i,k}(1), \cdots, h_{i,k}(L-1)]^T, \tag{13}$$

$\mathbf{h}_{i,k}$ represents the channel impulse response vector from the $i$-th ($i = 1, 2, \cdots, N_T$) transmit antenna to the $k$-th ($k = 1, 2, \cdots, N_R$) receive antenna. Similar to SISO-FBMC system, the demodulation of the received signal at the $(m, n)$th time-frequency lattice in the kth receive antenna associated to $\mathbf{A}_i$ can be written as

$$y_k(m) \approx \sum_{i=1}^{N_T} \sum_{\tau=0}^{L_h-1} A_i(m)e^{-j2\pi m\tau/M} h_{i,k}(\tau) + \eta_k(m). \tag{14}$$

For the ease of expression, let $\mathbf{W}_M = e^{-j2\pi/M}$. Note that $A_i(m) = \sum_{n=0}^{M-1} \alpha_i(n)\mathbf{W}_M^{m,n}$, and let $n' = n + \tau$. Then (14) can be rewritten as (15), where $(\cdot)_M$ represents the modulo M operation.

$$y_k(m) = \sum_{\tau=0}^{L_h-1} \left( \sum_{i=1}^{N_T} \left( \sum_{n'=0}^{M-1} \alpha_i(n'-\tau)_M W_M^{mn'} \right) h_{i,k}(\tau) \right) + \eta_k(m). \tag{15}$$

The above formula can be written in matrix form as $\mathbf{y}_k = \mathbf{WSh}_k + \eta_k$, where $\mathbf{S} = [\mathbf{S}_1, \mathbf{S}_2, \cdots, \mathbf{S}_{N_T}]^T$, $\mathbf{h}_k = [h_{1,k}, h_{2,k}, \cdots, h_{N_T,k}]^T$,

$$\mathbf{S}_i = \begin{bmatrix} \alpha_i(0) & \alpha_i(M-1) & \cdots & \alpha_i(M-L_h+1) \\ \alpha_i(1) & \alpha_i(0) & \cdots & \alpha_i(M-L_h+2) \\ \vdots & \vdots & \ddots & \vdots \\ \alpha_i(M-1) & \alpha_i(M-2) & \cdots & \alpha_i(M-L_h) \end{bmatrix}. \tag{16}$$

Here, $\mathbf{S}_i, i = 1, 2, \cdots, N_T$ are $M \times L_h$ matrices shown as (16), where the matrix $\mathbf{W}$ is an FFT matrix. Applying IFFT to $\mathbf{y}_k$, we obtain

$$\mathbf{r}_k = \frac{1}{M}\mathbf{W}^H \mathbf{y}_k = \mathbf{Sh}_k + \mathbf{w}_k, \tag{17}$$

where

$$\mathbf{w}_k = [\omega_k(0), \omega_k(1), \cdots, \omega_k(M-1)]^T, \quad \omega_k(n) = \frac{1}{M}\sum_{m=0}^{M-1} \eta_k(m)e^{j2\pi mn/M}. \tag{18}$$

Since in general the rank of $S$ is equal to the number of columns for $M > L_h$, the linear least square channel estimator for the $k$th receive antenna is shown as

$$\tilde{\mathbf{h}}_k = [\tilde{h}_{1,k}, \tilde{h}_{2,k}, \cdots, \tilde{h}_{N_T,k}]^T = (\mathbf{S}^H\mathbf{S})\mathbf{S}^H\mathbf{r}_k. \tag{19}$$

If the noise terms satisfy zero-mean white normal distribution, one can see that the channel estimator is unbiased, which means $E[\tilde{h}_k] = h_k$. And thus the channel estimation MSE can be defined as

$$MSE = \mathrm{E}\left[(h_k - \tilde{h}_k)^H (h_k - \tilde{h}_k)\right] = 2\sigma^2 \mathrm{Tr}((\mathbf{S}^H\mathbf{S})^{-1}), \tag{20}$$

where $\mathrm{E}(\cdot)$ denotes the expectation and $\mathrm{Tr}(\cdot)$ denotes the matrix trace operation.

## 4    Simulation Result

In this section, we calculate the spectrum efficiency of different systems and evaluate the performance of our proposed channel estimation method in terms of mean square error (MSE) of channel estimation.

### 4.1    Comparison of Spectrum Efficiency

The normalized spectrum efficiency $\gamma$ of MIMO-FBMC system compared with ideal MIMO-OFDM system with no overhead (i.e., no guard time interval and no frequency-domain training symbols) are

$$\gamma_{FBMC} = \frac{N_D}{N_D + N_P} \times 100\% \quad \gamma_{OFDM} = \frac{M}{N_{CP} + M} \times 100\%, \tag{21}$$

where $N_D$ and $N_P$ denote the number of data and training symbols, and $N_{CP}$ denotes the length of the cyclic prefix, respectively.

For a MIMO-OFDM system, every distinct ZCZ sequence is sent in a different transmit antenna and superimposed within the same time-frequency resource, leading to $N_P = 1$ complex-valued symbols. The main wasting of spectrum lies in CP (1/4 or 1/8 of a symbol). In contrast, a non-CP MIMO-FBMC system relies on well-localized time-frequency pulse shaping filter to suppress the effect of dispersive channel. Both the IAM and ICM require $N_T(G + 1)$ real-valued symbols. Obviously, an increasing $N_T$ will lower the system spectrum efficiency.

Our earlier proposed CTSD is a code–division multiplexing based channel estimation whose training overhead has nothing to do with the number of $N_T$. But its preamble data has complex-value in the frequency domain and this means it requires at least two FBMC symbols as well as $3G$ columns of zeros. In this paper, our proposed method only requires one FBMC training symbol and G zero symbols. Because of this, our proposed channel estimation scheme owns higher spectrum efficiency, as shown in Table 1.

**Table 1.** Spectrum efficiency comparison ($N_D = 50$)

|  | MIMO-OFDM | | MIMO-FBMC ($G = 3$) | | |
| --- | --- | --- | --- | --- | --- |
|  | CP = 1/8 | CP = 1/4 | IAM & ICM | CTSD | Proposed |
| $N_T = 2$ | 88.9% | 80% | 92.6% | 90.1% | 96.2% |
| $N_T = 4$ | 88.9% | 80% | 86.2% | 90.1% | 96.2% |
| $N_T = 8$ | 88.9% | 80% | 75.8% | 90.1% | 96.2% |

## 4.2   Numerical Simulations

MIMO-FBMC systems employing the pulse shaping filter in the PHYDYAS project with 256 subcarriers are considered. Moreover, multipath channels are adopted, each having $L_h$ sample-paced fading coefficients, in which the channel tap coefficients are assumed to be independent complex Gaussian random variables with uniformly distributed phases and Rayleigh distributed envelopes. The transmitted power from each transmit antenna is assumed to be same.

Figure 2 shows the MSE performance of the proposed channel estimation method with different guard interval $G$, antenna number $N_T$ and multipath channels number $L_h$. It is shown that increasing $N_T$ and $L_h$ will lower the estimation performance. The MSE floors at high SNR region for $G = 1, 2$ appearing in our proposed method are mainly caused by the residual ISI from neighboring training- or data- symbols and interference from quasi-orthogonal sequences. But when $G = 3$ increases, the MSE floor at high SNR region disappears.

Figure 3(a) compares our proposed method with IAM and ICM. Note that training symbols in IAM or ICM are sent in turn over different transmit antennas and thus the MSE for each method is equivalent to that in SISO scenario. One can see that, the performance of our proposed method is better than ICM. IAM shows a better performance because of the interference approximation and more preamble resourse.

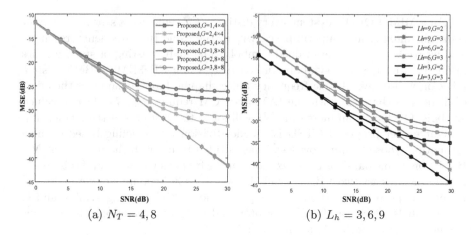

**Fig. 2.** MSE performance comparison of the proposed method in different situations.

Figure 3(b) compares our proposed channel estimation with CTSD. For both methods, the average power of the training sequences (preamble symbol and the guard interval) is one. According to the simulation result, the MSE performance of our proposed method is better than CTSD. That's because there are two real-valued symbols in CTSD to be calculated and thus larger amount of interference incurred, but the proposed method has only one.

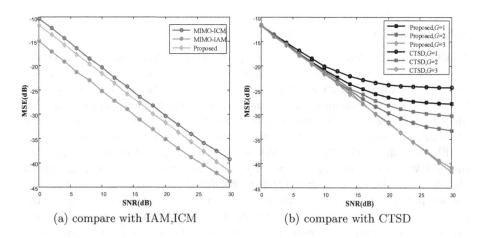

**Fig. 3.** MSE performance comparison between our proposed method and the former methods.

# 5 Conclusion

In this paper, we have presented an efficient channel estimation scheme in MIMO-FBMC systems. Our proposed training scheme is based on "real-valued orthogonal sequences" and allows simultaneous transmission of preambles over one FBMC symbol, regardless of the number of transmit antennas. Compared to our previously proposed CTSD training scheme in [7], the overall training overhead is reduced by half. Numerical simulation results have shown that our proposed training scheme strikes a good tradeoff between channel estimation performance and training overhead.

**Acknowledgement.** The work of S. Hu is jointly supported by the MOST Program of International S&T Cooperation (Grant No. 2016YFE0123200), Science and Technology on Electronic Information Control Laboratory (Grant No. 6142105040103) and Fundamental Research Funds for the Central Universities (Grant No. ZYGX2015J012). The work of Z. Liu and S. Hu was supported in part by National Natural Science Foundation of China (Grant No. 61750110527, Grant No. 61471100/61701503), Research Fund for International Young Scientists. The work of Z. Liu and P. Xiao was also supported in part by European Commission under the 5GPPP H2020 Clear5G Project (Grant No. 761745). The support of members at 5GIC of the University of Surrey (www.surrey.ac.uk/5gic) during this work is also acknowledged.

# References

1. Gao, X., Wang, W., Xia, X., Au, E.K.S., You, X.: Cyclic prefixed OQAM-OFDM and its application to single-carrier FDMA. IEEE Trans. Commun. **59**(5), 1467–1480 (2011)
2. Du, J.: Pulse shape adaptation and channel estimation in generalized frequency division multiplexing systems. Licentiate thesis, KTH (2008)
3. Lele, C., Javaudin, J.-P., Legouable, R., Skrzypczak, A., Siohan, P.: Channel estimation methods for preamble-based OFDM/OQAM modulations. Eur. Trans. Telecommun. **19**, 741–750 (2008)
4. Lele, C., Siohan, P., Legouable, R.: 2dB better than CP-OFDM with OFDM/OQAM for preamble-based channel estimation. In: IEEE International Conference on Communications, Beijing, China, pp. 1302–1306, May 2008
5. Kang, S.W., Chang, K.H.: A novel channel estimation scheme for OFDM/OQAM-IOTA system. ETRI J. **29**(4), 430–436 (2007)
6. Kofidis, E., Katselis, D., Rontogiannis, A., Theogoridi, S.: Preamble based channel estimation in OFDM/OQAM systems: a review. Signal Process. **93**(7), 2038–2054 (2013)
7. Hu, S., Liu, Z.: Training sequence design for efficient channel estimation in MIMO-FBMC systems. IEEE Access **5**, 4747–4758 (2017)
8. Hu, S., Wu, G., Li, T., Xiao, Y., Li, S.: Preamble design with ICI cancellation for channel estimation in OFDM/OQAM system. IEICE Trans. Commun. **E93–B**(1), 211–214 (2010)
9. PHYDYAS European project. www.ict-phydyas.org

# A Novel Spectrum Allocation Scheme in Femtocell Networks Using Improved Graph Theory

Feng Li, Lili Yang$^{(\boxtimes)}$, Jiangxin Zhang, and Li Wang

College of Information Engineering, Zhejiang University of Technology,
Hangzhou 310023, China
yll@zjut.edu.cn

**Abstract.** In this paper, we propose a novel spectrum allocation scheme by using graph coloring and taking QoS thresholds into account. The goal of our proposed method is to reduce interference among femtocells deployed densely and improve spectral efficiency after reaching user's QoS threshold. We design an interference-based graph model by detecting terminals' transmit power between femtocell stations and classifying the interference levels according to the coloring algorithm. Spectrum resource is allocated based on the QoS requirement of each user in a centralized way. The simulation results show that when the scheme is deployed in femtocells with high density, it can effectively reduce the interference within same layer and improve system capacity along with spectrum efficiency.

**Keywords:** Femtocell · Spectrum allocation · Graph theory

## 1 Introduction

Research shows that in recent years, the worldwide mobile data traffic has surged 13 times [1]. Other outcomes present that about two-thirds of mobile phone communications and over 70% of data traffic occur indoors [2]. Therefore, the indoor coverage quality of wireless signal becomes critical for user's experience. However, the macro base station usually cannot satisfy users' requirements for indoor traffic. Besides, mobile operators need to meet the requirement of customer service quality at a lower cost. Femtocell, as a low-power base station, becomes an ideal solution to enhance user's service experience indoor. In general, users can install the femtocell station in their rooms according to various needs. It is a mobile base station with high service quality, low power consumption, high stability and small coverage. It can provide consumers with good network services and transmission quality in given region. On the other hand, the application of femtocells also requires to solve many challenges [3]. As the distance between each household is always very close, the interference between them becomes very heavy especially when the density of the femtocells increases. Hence, it is worth to study how to mitigate the interference between femtocells within the same layer while ensuring the QoS requirements of all the users involved.

The same-layer interference between adjacent femtocells can be restrained by rational spectrum allocation scheme. In [4], the author adopted a spectrum allocation

© ICST Institute for Computer Sciences, Social Informatics and Telecommunications Engineering 2018
L. Meng and Y. Zhang (Eds.): MLICOM 2018, LNICST 251, pp. 172–180, 2018.
https://doi.org/10.1007/978-3-030-00557-3_18

scheme which clusters the base stations. The control center of the femtocell networks uses the weighted interference map to allocate the base stations to the user groups and then authorizes the sub-bands to the base stations in dynamic way. The key point of this method is SINR-based clustering. In [5], the control center of the femtocell networks used the vertex coloring algorithm of graph theory, allocating sub-bands to each base station, and its sub-bands were not used by neighboring base stations. However, neither [4] nor [5] take into account the load of each base station. The spectrum allocation scheme proposed in [6] had deficiencies in sub-band allocation, although it can overcome the above disadvantages.

In this paper, we propose a spectrum resource allocation scheme that combines graph theory and QoS. The scheme is based on the coloring algorithm in the graph theory to realize the grouping of the base station, and then allocates spectrum resources according to the user's QoS requirements. Specifically, each base station classifies the base stations with large interference as interference neighbors and reports them to the center base station. And the center base station establishes the interference graph according to these interference relations, uses a specific algorithm to color. Base stations with the same color are grouped in the same group and reuse the same frequency. Different groups of base stations use mutually orthogonal sub-bands, thus greatly reducing the interference in the same layer and also improving the spectrum utilization and the femtocell network capacity.

The remainder of this article is organized as follows. In Sect. 2, we introduce the system model. Section 3 describes the spectrum resource allocation scheme that combines graph theory and QoS. In Sect. 4, the simulation results and analyses are introduced. Finally, we conclude this paper in Sect. 5.

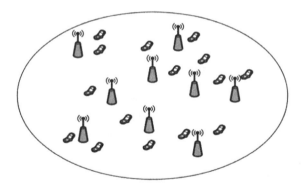

**Fig. 1.** System model of femtocell networks

## 2 System Model

In this paper, we consider downlink transmission based on orthogonal frequency division multiple access (OFDM), as shown in Fig. 1. Femtocell and macrocell use different spectrum resources so that the cross-layer interference in the femtocell network can be ignored. The femtocell system controller (FSC) is a central controller that controls the configuration and status of femtocell base stations (FBSs) in the network. Throughout the femtocell network, the FSC controls numbers of FBSs, $N = \{1, 2, \ldots, N\}$, which are randomly placed in each building and have a maximum coverage radius of $Rc$. Each activated FBS $i(i \in N)$ service has a set of FUEs within its coverage, $Ki = \{1, 2, \ldots, ki\}$, all of which are random locations. In the femtocell networks, the user number can be expressed as

$$K = \sum_{i=1}^{i=N} K_i \tag{1}$$

Femtocell base stations are densely deployed, so there exists a heavy interference between them. We must identify each FBS interference neighbors. For example, for user FUE $k$ in FBS $i$, if the interference of FBS $j$. user FUE $k$ exceeds the threshold $\gamma_{th}$, the FBS $j$ and FBS $i$ are mutually interference neighbors.

$$\frac{\sum_{k=1}^{k=k_i} P_i g_{i,k}}{\sum_{k=1}^{k=k_i} P_j g_{j,k}} < \gamma_{th} \quad i \neq j \in N \tag{2}$$

where $P_i$ is the transmit power of FBS $i$, $g_{i,k}$ is the channel gain between FBS $i$ and FUE $k$. Then, the signal-to-interference and noise ratio (SINR) of user FUE $k$ in FBS $i$ can be expressed as

$$\gamma_{ik} = \frac{P_i g_{i,k}}{\sum_{i \neq j} P_j g_{j,k} + \sigma_k^2} \tag{3}$$

where $\sigma_k^2$ is white noise power. We assume that the total spectral bandwidth of the system in the femtocell network is $B$. FSC divides $B$ into a group of same sub-bands of bandwidth, $S = \{1, 2, \ldots, S\}$, and their bandwidth is $B_S$. Then, given a specific $\gamma_{ik}$, the spectral efficiency (in $bps/Hz$) of FBS $i$ to FUE $k$ in the unit bandwidth can be given as

$$R_{ik} = \begin{cases} 0 & for \quad \gamma_{ik} < \gamma_{min} \\ \alpha \ log_2(1 + \gamma_{ik}) & for \quad \gamma_{min} < \gamma_{ik} < \gamma_{max} \\ R_{max} & for \quad \gamma_{max} < \gamma_{ik} \end{cases} \tag{4}$$

where $\gamma_{min}$ is minimal SINR. We set $\gamma_{min} = -1\,dB$, $\gamma_{max} = 19.5\,dB$ as maximal SINR. $\alpha = 0.6$ denotes the attenuation factor.

In order to meet the QoS needs of each user, the base station serving the user must provide sufficient bandwidth. In this article, FBS $i$ must provide enough subbands for the FUE $k$ it serves. The demand sub-band for each FBS $i$ is given by the following formula

$$r_{ik} = R_{ik} B_S \tag{5}$$

$$B_{ik} = \frac{Q_r}{r_{ik}} \tag{6}$$

$$B_i = \left\lceil \sum_{k=1}^{k=k_i} B_{ik} \right\rceil, \forall i \in N \qquad (7)$$

where $r_{ik}$ is the reachable rate of FBS $i$ to FUE $k$ in a sub-band under a specific $\gamma_{ik}$. $Q_r$ is the QoS requirement of user FUE $k$, $B_{ik}$ is the required bandwidth of FUE $k$ for each user served by FBS $i$. $B_i$ denotes the desired bandwidth for FBS $i$.

## 3 Combining Graph Theory and QoS Spectrum Resource Allocation Scheme

In this section, we propose a spectrum allocation scheme (CGQR) that combines graph theory and QoS. The scheme is composed of three steps: Interference graph formation and coloring; base station grouping based on the coloring result; the allocation of spectrum resources.

- Step 1: Interference graph formation and coloring

    In this step, we first obtain the interference graph of the base station according to the formula (2), establish the adjacency matrix, and utilize the graph theory algorithm for the vertex shading.

(1) When the FSC detects FBS activation, the active base station reports its neighbor list to the FSC. FSC constructs the interference graph $G = (V, E)$, $V$ represents the set of vertices of FBS, and $E$ represents the set of edges of the interference between two FBSs. We represent the relationship between base stations as a binary matrix, i.e. the adjacency matrix $W$. This matrix can be expressed as $W = [\omega_{ij}]_{N \times N}$.

$$\omega_{ij} = \begin{cases} 1 & \textit{FBS } i \textit{ and FBS } j \textit{ are neighbors} \\ 0 & \textit{Otherwise} \end{cases} \qquad (8)$$

    Where $\omega_{ij} = 1$ indicates that the base station FBS $i$ and FBS $j$ are mutually interference neighbors. Otherwise, interference can be tolerated.

(2) After the interference graph is established, we will use the DSATUR algorithm [7] to color the vertices in the graph. The algorithm has two important parameters: vertex saturation $C$ and vertex degree $\theta$. $\theta_f$ represents the number of adjacent vertices of different colors, and $\theta$ represents the number of adjacent vertices. Note that the colors of adjacent vertices are different.

- Step 2: Group base stations based on the coloring result

    In this step, we group the base station based on the coloring result in the previous step. Base stations with the same color are grouped in the same group, otherwise, grouped in different groups. After grouping, there are k groups, $G = \{1, 2, \ldots, k\}$.

- Step 3: Allocation of spectrum resources

After all the base station have been grouped, find the desired bandwidth for each group:

$$B_k = \sum_{i \in G_k} B_i \qquad (9)$$

where $G_k$ is the set of base stations in the $k$ th group. Since the number of users in each base station may be different and the QoS of each user may be different, the average required bandwidth for each group is

$$B_{ak} = \frac{B_k}{n_k} \qquad (10)$$

where $n_k$ is the number of FBS in the $kth$ group. Then, the actual bandwidth allocated to each team is

$$B_{cak} = S * \frac{B_{ak}}{\sum_{k \in G} B_{ak}} * B_S \qquad (11)$$

Although the bandwidth allocated to each base station may be less than its required bandwidth, it minimizes interference and meets its QoS needs, as well as increasing spectrum efficiency. Of course, the above spectrum resource allocation scheme needs to satisfy the condition of $|C| < S$.

## 4   Numerical Results

In this section, we simulate the scheme proposed in the third part and analyze the numerical results. Regarding the simulation environment, we use the downlink transmission in the femtocell network. The femtocell network model used in this paper is a $5 \times 5$ grid. Use a non-interference single story apartment building, this floor a total of 25 apartments, an area of 10 m × 10 m. One FBS is deployed randomly in each apartment. FSC can control all FBS in this layer and coordinate resource sharing between FBS. The activation probability of FBS is $P_a$. For example when $P_a = 0.2$, 5 of 25 FBS are activated and their positions are randomly distributed. We assume that there is only the same layer of interference between these FBS, so the impact from the macro base station can be ignored. The SINR threshold $\gamma_{th}$ we use to construct the interference graph is set to 4.4 dB. The simulation parameters are given in Table 1.

**Table 1.** Simulation parameters

| | |
|---|---|
| System bandwidth | 10 MHz |
| Carrier frequency | 2 GHz |
| Number of available sub-bands | 50 |
| Sub-band bandwidth | 180 kHz |
| FBS coverage radius | 20 m |
| Coverage of the building | 50 m * 50 m |
| Minimum distance between FBSs | 2 m |
| FBS transmission power | 20 dBm |
| Path loss | 127 + 30log10(r/1000) r/m |
| Noise power density | −174 dBm/Hz |
| Minimum distance between FBS and FUE | 0.2 m |

Compare our proposed spectrum resource allocation plan (CGQR) with two scenarios:

- ASR: All FBS reuse all sub-bands, all spectrum reuse;
- SEDR: After FBS is grouped, the number of sub-bands allocated to each group is the ratio of the total number of sub-bands to the number of groups, that is, spectrum evenly distributed reuse;

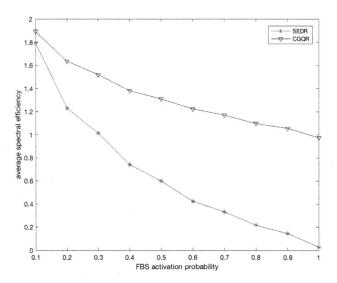

**Fig. 2.** Average spectral efficiency with activation probability

Average spectral efficiency: We compare the spectral efficiency between the three schemes. Since both CGQR and SEDR use the coloring algorithm in Sect. 3, the grouping results are the same. Therefore, only the average spectral efficiency between

CGQR and ASR is compared. We assume that all FBSs in the femtocell network use closed access mode and only serve FUE within their apartment. For the sake of simplicity, let's assume that the number of fuels in each apartment is 1 and the QoS needs are all 384 kbps. As shown in Fig. 2, the spectral efficiency of the three schemes shows a decreasing trend due to the increase of femtocell base station density, but the CGQR curve will drop slowly, especially when $P_a$ increases. Femtocell base station density increases, the interference between them also increases, our scheme has obvious advantages in anti-interference aspect. Therefore, our proposed scheme can significantly improve the average spectral efficiency of the femtocell network when the femtocell network density is high.

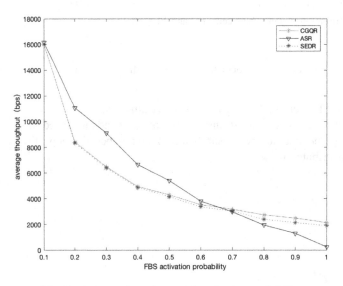

**Fig. 3.** Average throughput with activation probability

Average Throughput: We still assume that the number of FUEs in each apartment is 1, which all require 384 kbps for QoS. As shown in Fig. 3, when $P_a$ is small, since the femtocell base station has a small density, and the ASR can use all the sub-bands, the interference at the same layer is light, so the throughput is better than the solution we propose. As $P_a$ increases, the femtocell base station density increases, and the average throughput of CGQR and SEDR begins to be greater than the ASR. Because our solution is based on QoS allocated on demand, and SEDR is evenly distributed, do not have the flexibility. So our scheme is slightly better than SEDR in the case of strong interference. Therefore, our proposed scheme is superior to the other two schemes when the femtocell base station density is high.

Femtocell Network Capacity: We continue to set the number of FUEs in each apartment to 1, which all require 384 kbps for QoS. As shown in Fig. 4, as the number of activated base stations in the femtocell network increases, the network capacity in the ASR scheme becomes larger, reaching a peak when $P_a = 0.4$. After that, as the

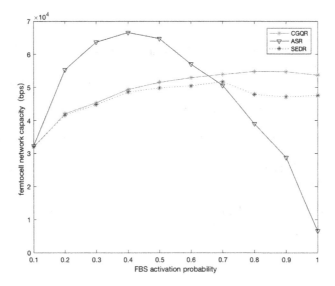

**Fig. 4.** Femtocell network capacity with activation probability

femtocell base station density increases, and the interference in the same layer becomes larger, the capacity of the network begins to drop drastically. The network capacity of CGQR and SEDR has been on a steady upward trend. In particular, the solution proposed by us has almost no fluctuation in the upward trend of network capacity, indicating that CGQR has obvious advantages over the other two schemes in terms of anti-interference. When the base station density becomes larger and the number of users increases, the total capacity of the proposed scheme in the network is obviously better than the other two schemes.

## 5   Conclusions

In this paper, we propose a spectrum resource allocation scheme which adopts graph theory and takes QoS requirement into account. The base stations in femtocell networks are first analogized to the vertices in the graph theory and then colored. The base stations with the same color are grouped, and then sub-bands are allocated to each group of base stations according to the QoS requirement of each FUE. The simulation results show that when the system load becomes larger, the anti-interference ability, system throughput and spectrum efficiency of our proposed scheme are better than the other traditional methods. Besides, there are still many shortcomings in our algorithm which need to be solved in future work.

# References

1. Cisco Visual Networking Index: Global mobile data traffic forecast update. In: Whitepaper, February 2013
2. Zhou, X., Feng, S.L., Ding, Y., et al.: Game-theoretical frequency reuse algorithm in femtocell network. J. Commun. **36**(2), 137–143 (2015)
3. Andrews, J.: Seven ways that hetnets are a cellular paradigm shift. IEEE Commun. Mag. **51** (3), 136–144 (2013)
4. Uygungelen, S., Auer, G., Bharucha, Z.: Graph-based dynamic frequency reuse in femtocell networks. In: Proceedings of the 2011 IEEE VTC-Spring, pp. 1–6 (2011)
5. Kim, S., Cho, I.: Graph-based dynamic channel assignment scheme for femtocell networks. IEEE Commun. Lett. **17**(9), 1718–1721 (2013)
6. Demestichas, P., Georgakopoulos, A., Karvounas, D., et al.: 5G on the horizon: key challenges for the radio-access network. IEEE Veh. Technol. Mag. **8**(3), 47–53 (2013)
7. Brelaz, D.: New methods to color the vertices of a graph. Commun. ACM **22**(4), 251–256 (1979)

# Distributed Channel Allocation for Wireless Mesh Networks Based on Hypergraph Interference Model

Chen Pan, Yunpeng Cheng, Ducheng Wu$^{(\boxtimes)}$, Lei Zhao, and Yuli Zhang

College of Communication Engineering, Army Engineering University of PLA,
Haifuxiang 1st, Nanjing 210007, China
panchenlgdx@163.com, ypcheng@yahoo.com, wuducheng@foxmail.com,
johnson-007@163.com, yulipkueecs08@126.com

**Abstract.** Wireless mesh networks (WMNs) are widely used to expand the current wireless network coverage. In this paper, we present a hypergraph-based channel selection method to allocate channels, which can be used to alleviate the accumulative interference from multiple weak interfering links in WMNs. Firstly, we build the ternary interference hypergraph model for all links in a WMN. Then we present a interference mitigating hypergraph game to solve the distributed channel selection problem. It is proved that the proposed game is an exact potential game with at least one Nash equilibrium (NE). Finally, a best reply (BR) based channel selection algorithm for the interference mitigating hypergraph game is presented to obtain NEs. Simulation results show that the presented channel selection method with hypergraph model has a lower global accumulate protocol interference than the existing method with binary graph model.

**Keywords:** Wireless mesh networks
Channel allocation · Hypergraph · Potential game

## 1 Introduction

Wireless mesh networks (WMNs) are widely used to expand the current wireless network coverage, which consist of mesh routers and mesh clients [1]. The interference caused by multiple links simultaneous transmitting is one of the major reasons of the capacity reduction in WMNs [2]. When multiple neighboring wireless links occupy a same channel to transmit, they would cause serious mutual interference and cannot transmit data simultaneously. The link-layer binary conflict graph is often utilized to model the interference between the logical links in WMNs [3,4]. In a link-layer binary conflict graph, vertices are the logical links. And the edge between two vertices reflects the interfere relationship between these two corresponding links who cannot transmit information at the same time.

© ICST Institute for Computer Sciences, Social Informatics and Telecommunications Engineering 2018
L. Meng and Y. Zhang (Eds.): MLICOM 2018, LNICST 251, pp. 181–189, 2018.
https://doi.org/10.1007/978-3-030-00557-3_19

However, it is clear that several weak interfering links of a certain link may cause strong interference together to that link [5]. When the cumulative interference power exceeds a threshold, it can produce bad influence on quality of service (QoS) of that certain link. The binary edge of the traditional conflict graph ignores the accumulative effect of multiple weak interfering links in above case. Hence, there is need to consider the influence of cumulative interference from multiple sources to the links. Hypergraph model is an appropriate mathematics tool to analyze the effect of accumulative interference. Some existing works studied the resource allocation of wireless networks based on hypergraph model [5–8]. The same problem also exists in WMNs. However, there is no existing work studying the hypergraph based multi-channel selection in WMNs.

In this paper, we present a hypergraph-based channel selection method to mitigate interference in WMNs. Firstly, we construct the ternary interference hypergraph according the interferer identification of each link in the mesh network. Then a interference mitigating hypergraph game is proposed to allocate channel distributedly. The proposed game is proved to be an exact potential game with at least one pure strategy Nash equilibrium (NE). Finally, a best reply (BR) algorithm for the interference mitigating hypergraph game is presented to achieve NEs. It can be found from simulation results that the presented hypergraph-based channel selection method has a lower global interference in contrast with the traditional binary conflict graph method.

## 2   System Model and Problem Formulation

The model of a multi-channel wireless mesh network is considered with $N$ stationary mesh routers. These mesh routers are denoted by $\mathcal{N} = \{1, 2, \ldots, N\}$. In this paper the expression of nodes and mesh routers are utilized interchangeably. It is assumed that $C$ orthogonal frequency channels, $\mathcal{C} = \{1, 2, \ldots, C\}$, are dedicated to the information transmission of the mesh network.

It is assumed that all node transmit information with a same transmission power $P_{tr}$. For an available link $(m, n)$, the received power at the receiver of link $(m, n)$ should exceed a certain power threshold $\gamma_{tr}$, thus we have $P_{tr}d(n,m)^\alpha > \gamma_{tr}$. Here $d(n, m)$ is the range of node $n$ and node $m$, $\alpha$ is the fade loss factor. The maximal communication range can be denoted as $D_{tr} = \sqrt[\alpha]{\gamma_{tr} P_{tr}^{-1}}$. Then the networks logical topology can be predetermined. We assume that each link is symmetric and the set of all mesh links is denoted by $\mathcal{L}$ (There are $L$ links in $\mathcal{L}$). In this work, we focus on the problem of channel allocation and interference mitigation without considering the interface constraints.

### 2.1   Binary Conflict Graph

The interference threshold of the received power of each node is denoted by $\gamma_{int}$, and the interference range is $D_{int} = \sqrt[\alpha]{\gamma_{int} P_{tr}^{-1}}$, $D_{tr} < D_{int}$. Then a binary

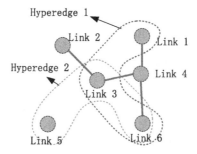

**Fig. 1.** Illustration of hypergraph interference model.

variable $I(\rho, \varrho)$ can be used to represent the interference relationship of two links $\rho = (m, n)$ and $\varrho = (m', n')$ $(\rho, \varrho \in \mathcal{L}, \rho \neq \varrho)$,

$$I(\rho, \varrho) = \begin{cases} 1, & P_{tr}\check{d}(\rho, \varrho)^\alpha \geq \gamma_{int} \\ 0, & P_{tr}\check{d}(\rho, \varrho)^\alpha < \gamma_{int}, \end{cases} \tag{1}$$

where $\check{d}(\rho, \varrho) = \min(d(m, m'), d(n, m'), d(m, n'), d(n, n'))$ is the distance between links $\rho$ and $\varrho$. It is clear that $I(\rho, \varrho) = I(\varrho, \rho)$. The set of binary mutual interfering links of $\rho$ is $\Phi_\rho = \{\varrho : I(\rho, \varrho) = 1\}$.

A binary conflict graph $G(\mathcal{L}, \mathcal{I})$ can be used to model interference in the mesh network, where each vertex $l \in \mathcal{L}$ corresponds to link $l$ and each edge $I(l, l') \in \mathcal{I}$ corresponds to the binary interference link relationship of links $l$ and $l'$. Because the binary interference link relationship is symmetric, the binary conflict graph $G(\mathcal{L}, \mathcal{I})$ is also symmetric.

## 2.2 Hypergraph Interference Model

The binary conflict graph can only models the strong interference relationship between two links and does not consider the accumulative effect of the power from multiple weak interfering sources which may constitute a strong interferer. To capture the influence of accumulative interference, the definition of hypergraph is given as follows.

**Definition 1.** Hypergraph $\Gamma = (\mathcal{L}, \mathcal{E} = (e_i)_{i \in \Lambda})$, which is on a finite set $\mathcal{L}$ ($\Lambda$ is a finite set of indexes), is a group $(e)_{i \in \Lambda}$ of subsets of $\mathcal{L}$. Here $(e)_{i \in \Lambda}$ is a hyperedge of hypergraph $\Gamma$.

According to above the definition, it can be found that hyperedge can comprise a subset of vertex set $\mathcal{L}$ with multiple vertices. As shown in the Fig. 1, in the given hypergraph there are 6 vertices, 4 two-verticed edge and 2 hyperedges, i.e., $(3, 1, 6)$ and $(3, 5, 6)$. Similar to [5], random hypergraph is constructed with the maximum cardinality of hyperedges $Q = 3$ in this work. It can be found from existing works [6–8] that $Q = 3$ can reach a tradeoff between computation complexity and network performance in most wireless networks.

In the mesh network, when the cumulative interferences from multiple weak interfering links $(\rho, \varrho)$ to a certain link $\tau = (m, n)$ is above a threshold, it can cause a conflict to the link $\tau = (m, n)$, i.e., $(\tau, \rho, \varrho)$ form a hyperedge $(\tau \neq \rho \neq \varrho)$.

Then a ternary variable $H(\tau, \rho, \varrho)$ can be used to represent the interference relationship of two links the hyperedge $(\tau, \rho, \varrho)$,

$$
H(\tau, \rho, \varrho) = \begin{cases} 1, & P_{tr}\bar{d}(m, \rho)^\alpha + P_{tr}\bar{d}(m, \varrho)^\alpha \geq \gamma'_{int} \text{ or} \\ & P_{tr}\bar{d}(n, \rho)^\alpha + P_{tr}\bar{d}(n, \varrho)^\alpha \geq \gamma'_{int} \\ 0, & \text{else,} \end{cases} \tag{2}
$$

where $\bar{d}(m, \rho)$ is the minimum range between node $m$ and the nodes in link $\rho$ and $\gamma'_{int}$ is the cumulative interference threshold. It is clear that the hyperedge interference link relationships and the hypergraph are asymmetric, i.e., there may be $H(\tau, \rho, \varrho) \neq H(\rho, \tau, \varrho)$. The set of interfering hyperedges of $\tau$ is $\Psi_\tau = \{(\tau, \rho, \varrho) : H(\tau, \rho, \varrho) = 1\}$. The set of hyperedge interfered links of $\rho$ is $\Omega_\rho = \{\tau : H(\tau, \rho, \varrho) = 1\}$.

## 2.3   Problem Formulation

For the link $\tau$, its channel strategy is denoted as $a_\tau \in C$. Then the accumulate protocol interference of link $\tau$ is expressed as:

$$
T_\tau(a_\tau, a_{-\tau}) = \sum_{\rho \in \Phi_\tau} \delta(\tau, \rho) + \sum_{(\tau, \rho, \varrho) \in \Psi_\tau} \delta(\tau, \rho)\delta(\tau, \varrho), \tag{3}
$$

where $\delta(\tau, \rho)$ is the indicator function as follows:

$$
\delta(\tau, \varrho) = \begin{cases} 1, & a_\tau = a_\varrho \\ 0, & a_\tau \neq a_\varrho, \end{cases} \tag{4}
$$

The global accumulate protocol interference level of the mesh network can be written as :

$$
Y(a) = \sum_{\tau \in \mathcal{L}} T_\tau(a_\tau, a_{-\tau}), \tag{5}
$$

where $a = \{a_\tau\}_{\tau \in \mathcal{L}}$ the channel selection profile of the network. The multi-channel allocation in the mesh network is formulated as the following optimization problem

$$
\min_a Y(a). \tag{6}
$$

It is clear that the above non-linear programming problem is NP-hard [9]. It cannot achieve the optimal solution by the traditional convex optimization algorithms, like gradient descent algorithm.

# 3  Interference Mitigating Hypergraph Game

## 3.1  Game Model

To solve (6), any direct search method would incur super high complexities. Considering the distributive and autonomous decision making of the router pairs of links, we propose an interference mitigating hypergraph game approach for wireless mesh network multi-channel allocation.

The game is denoted as $\mathcal{G} = \{\mathcal{L}, \mathcal{A}, \Gamma, \{u_\tau\}_{\tau \in \mathcal{L}}\}$, where $\mathcal{L}$ is link player set, $\mathcal{A}$ is the nodes strategy space, $\Gamma$ is the hypergraph topology of the network, $u_\tau$ is the utility of link $\tau$. The utility function is defined as follows:

$$u_\tau(a_\tau, a_{-\tau}) = -\{T_\tau(a_\tau, a_{-\tau}) + \sum_{\rho \in \Phi_\tau \cup \Omega_\tau} T_\rho(a_\rho, a_{-\rho})\}. \tag{7}$$

Each player's objective is to maximize its utility as follows:

$$\max_{a_\tau \in \mathcal{A}_\tau} u_\tau(a_\tau, a_{-\tau}), \quad \tau \in \mathcal{L}. \tag{8}$$

## 3.2  Analysis of NE

Nash equilibrium (NE) is a kind of stable solution being widely used in game models.

**Definition 2.** An action selection profile $a*$ is a pure strategy NE if and only if no player can improve its utility by deviating unilaterally, i.e.,

$$u_\tau(a_\tau*, a_{-\tau}*) \geq u_\tau(a_\tau, a_{-\tau}*), \forall \tau \in \mathcal{L}, \forall a_\tau \in \mathcal{A}_{a_\tau}, a_\tau* \neq a_\tau. \tag{9}$$

**Theorem 1.** The presented interference mitigating hypergraph game $\mathcal{G}$ is an exact potential game [10]. The optimal channel allocation strategy, which can achieve the global network hypergraph interference minimization, is a pure strategy NE of the game at least.

*Proof.* The potential function can be constructed as follows:

$$\varphi(a) = -Y(a) = -\sum_{\tau \in \mathcal{L}} T_\tau(a_\tau, a_{-\tau}). \tag{10}$$

It is shown that the potential function is equal to the negative value of the global interference level. Then we analyze the changes of the potential function after an arbitrary player $\tau$ unilaterally changes its action selection from $a_\tau$ to $\bar{a}_\tau$, which is given by

$$\begin{aligned}
&\varphi(\bar{a}) - \varphi(a) \\
&= -\sum_{l \in \mathcal{L}} T_l(\bar{a}) - (-\sum_{l \in \mathcal{L}} T_l(a)) \\
&= \{u_\tau(\bar{a}_\tau, a_{-\tau}) - u_\tau(a_\tau, a_{-\tau})\} \\
&\quad + \sum_{l \in \mathcal{L}/\{\tau \cup \Phi_\tau \cup \Omega_\tau\}} \{-T_l(\bar{a}) + T_l(a))\}.
\end{aligned} \tag{11}$$

where $\bar{a}$ is obtained from $a$ by replacing $\tau$'s action from $a_\tau$ to $\bar{a}_\tau$. It can be concluded that the action of link $\tau$ cannot influence the accumulate protocol interference of each link $l \in \mathcal{L}/\{\tau \cup \Phi_\tau \cup \Omega_\tau\}$, i.e.,

$$T_l(\bar{a}) = T_l(a)), \forall l \in \mathcal{L}/\{\tau \cup \Phi_\tau \cup \Omega_\tau\}. \tag{12}$$

Thus, when link $\tau$ takes an action unilaterally, the varying value of the potential function is the same as the varying value of the utility function given in (7), i.e.,

$$\varphi(\bar{a}) - \varphi(a) = u_\tau(\bar{a}_\tau, a_{-\tau}) - u_\tau(a_\tau, a_{-\tau}). \tag{13}$$

Therefore, based on the definition of the potential game, it is obvious that $\mathcal{G}$ is a potential game. Theorem 1 to prove based on these properties.

---

*Algorithm 1. Best reply (BR) based channel selection algorithm*

---

**Step 1:** Initially, each link randomly selects a channel. The initial channel selection profile is $a[0]$, $a_l[0] \in \mathcal{C}$, $\forall l \in \mathcal{L}$.
**Step 2:** At iteration $t$, randomly select a link $l$, and find the best reply of link $l$ and update the channel selection profile:

$$\begin{aligned} a_l[t+1] &= \arg \max\{u_l(a_l, a_{-l}[t])\}, a_l \subset \mathcal{C}, \\ a_{l'}[t+1] &= a_{l'}[t], l' \neq l. \end{aligned} \tag{14}$$

**Step 3:** If $t$ exceeds the predetermined maximum iteration number, stop; otherwise go to Step 2.

---

### 3.3   Best Reply Based Channel Selection Algorithm

According to Theorem 1, it is cleat that when a link improves it utility (7) unilaterally, the value of the potential function will also be improved and the global interference level will be decreased. Thus, best reply (BR) algorithm can be applied to achieve NE of the interference mitigating hypergraph game $\mathcal{G}$ as shown in Algorithm 1, which is a very effective negotiation mechanism in the distributed selection problem. The proposed BR based channel selection algorithm converges to a pure strategy NE of the game $\mathcal{G}$ in finite steps [11].

## 4   Simulation Result

In the following simulation study, the size of the network field is $40\,\mathrm{m} \times 80\,\mathrm{m}$ and there are 19 routers randomly located in the area, as shown in Fig. 2. The communication range is uniformly set as $D_{tr} = 10\,\mathrm{m}$, and the interference range is uniformly set as $D_{int} = 20\,\mathrm{m}$. The path fade loss is $\alpha = -2$ and the transmission power is $P_{tr} = 40\,\mathrm{mW}$. We set a same interference threshold for both the direct strong interference and the cumulative interference, i.e., $\gamma_{int} = \gamma'_{int}$.

The convergence curve of Algorithm 1 is shown in Fig. 3 (with 5 available channels $C = 5$). It can be found that Algorithm 1 need about 60 iterations to achieve the convergence.

We analyze the performance of the global accumulate protocol interference level with proposed hypergraph-based channel selection method and traditional binary conflict graph-based method. Here, we change the number of available channels, i.e., $C = 3, 4, 5, 6, 7$. It is shown from Fig. 4 that the global accumulate protocol interference achieved by the proposed hypergraph-based method is much smaller than the traditional graph-based method. From the figure, we can also find that the global accumulate protocol interference decreases with the increase of the number of available channels.

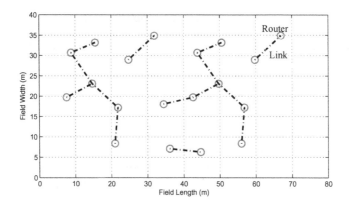

**Fig. 2.** The topology of the mesh network.

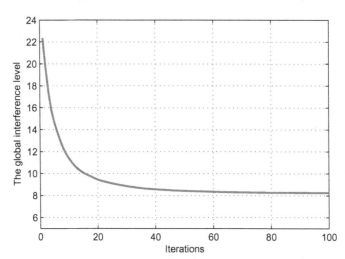

**Fig. 3.** The convergence curve of Algorithm 1.

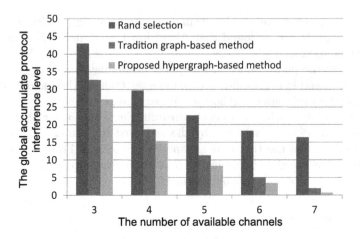

**Fig. 4.** The global accumulate protocol interference when varying the number of channels.

## 5    Conclusion

In this paper, we focused on the problem of distributed multichannel allocation in WMNs. We presented a hypergraph-based channel selection method to allocate channels in WMNs. Firstly, we constructed the ternary interference hypergraph for each link. Then we presented a interference mitigating hypergraph game to solve the channel selection problem distributedly. It was proved that the proposed game is an exact potential game with one NE at least. Finally, a best reply (BR) based channel selection algorithm for the interference mitigating hypergraph game was presented to achieve NEs. It could be found from simulation results that the presented hypergraph-based channel selection method could achieve lower global accumulate protocol interference performance than the method with traditional graph. Next, we will study channel and interface joint allocation problems with the interference hypergraph model in WMNs.

**Acknowledgment.** This work was supported by the National Science Foundation of China under Grant No. 61771488, No. 61671473, No. 61631020 and No. 61401508, the in part by Natural Science Foundation for Distinguished Young Scholars of Jiangsu Province under Grant No. BK20160034, and in part by the Open Research Foundation of Science and Technology on Communication Networks Laboratory.

## References

1. Pathak, P.H., Dutta, R.: A survey of network design problems and joint design approaches in wireless mesh networks. IEEE Commun. Surv. Tutor. **13**, 396–428 (2011)
2. Tang, J., Xue, G., Zhang, W.: Interference-aware topology control and QoS routing in multi-channel wireless mesh networks. In: MobiHoc (2005)

3. Chen, L., Low, S., Doyle, J.: Joint congestion control and media access control design for ad hoc wireless networks. In: Proceedings of IEEE INFOCOM, Miami, FL, March 2005
4. Rad, A.H.M., Wong, V.W.S.: Joint channel allocation, interface assignment and MAC design for multi-channel wireless mesh networks. In: INFOCOM 2017 (2007)
5. Feng, J., Tao, M.: Hypergraph-based frequency reuse in dense femtocell networks. In: IEEE ICCC 2013, pp. 537–542 (2013)
6. Zhang, H., Song, L., Han, Z.: Radio resource allocation for device-to-device underlay communications using hypergraph theory. IEEE Trans. Wirel. Commun. **15**(7), 4852–4861 (2018)
7. Sarkar, S., Sivarajan, K.N.: Hypergraph models for cellular mobile communication systems. IEEE Trans. Veh. Technol. **47**(2), 460–471 (1998)
8. Li, Q., Negi, R.: Maximal scheduling in wireless ad hoc networks with hypergraph interference models. IEEE Trans. Veh. Technol. **61**(1), 297–310 (2012)
9. Cormen, T.H., Leiserson, C.E., Rivest, R.L., Stein, C.: Introduction to Algorithms, 2nd edn. MIT Press, Cambridge (2001)
10. Xu, Y.H., Wang, J.L., Wu, Q.H.: Opportunistic spectrum access in cognitive radio networks: global optimization using local interaction games. IEEE J. Sel. Top. Signal Process. **6**(2), 180–194 (2012)
11. Young, H.P.: Strategic Learning and Its Limits. Oxford University Press, Oxford (2005)

# Physical Violence Detection with Movement Sensors

Liang Ye[1,2(✉)], Le Wang[1], Peng Wang[1,3], Hany Ferdinando[2,4],
Tapio Seppänen[5], and Esko Alasaarela[2]

[1] Communication Research Center, Harbin Institute of Technology,
Harbin 150080, China
yeliang@hit.edu.cn, 1659412561@qq.com,
wphitstudent@163.com
[2] Optoelectronics and Measurement Techniques Laboratory,
Department of Electrical Engineering, University of Oulu, 90570 Oulu, Finland
{hferdina,esko.alasaarela}@ee.oulu.fi
[3] China Electronics Technology Group Corporation, Nanjing 210012, China
[4] Department of Electrical Engineering, Petra Christian University,
Surabaya 60236, Indonesia
[5] Department of Computer Science and Engineering, University of Oulu,
90570 Oulu, Finland
tapio@ee.oulu.fi

**Abstract.** With the development of movement sensors, activity recognition becomes more and more popular. Compared with daily-life activity recognition, physical violence detection is more meaningful and valuable. This paper proposes a physical violence detecting method. Movement data of acceleration and gyro are gathered by role playing of physical violence and daily-life activities. Time domain features and frequency domain ones are extracted and filtered to discribe the differences between physical violence and daily-life activities. A specific BPNN trained with the L-M method works as the classifier. Altogether 9 kinds of activities are involved. For 9-class classification, the average recognition accuracy is 67.0%, whereas for 2-class classification, i.e. activities are classified as violence or daily-life activity, the average recognition accuracy reaches 83.7%.

**Keywords:** Physical violence detection · Activity recognition
Movement sensor

## 1 Introduction

In recent years, movement sensor techniques have developed very rapidly. Benefit from this, activity recognition based on movement data becomes more and more popular. Commonly used movement sensors are accelerometers and gyroscopes, and the corresponding data are acceleration and gyro, respectively.

Existing activity recognition research work mainly focuses on the recognition of daily-life activities. For example, Cheng et al. [1] recognized daily-life activities of standing, sitting, walking, turning left, turning right, going upstairs, going downstairs,

© ICST Institute for Computer Sciences, Social Informatics and Telecommunications Engineering 2018
L. Meng and Y. Zhang (Eds.): MLICOM 2018, LNICST 251, pp. 190–197, 2018.
https://doi.org/10.1007/978-3-030-00557-3_20

jogging, and jumping. Nakano *et al.* [2] recognized daily-life activities of walking, walking upstairs, walking downstairs, sitting, standing, and lying. Hegde *et al.* [3] recognized daily-life activities of lying down, sitting, standing, walking driving, descend stairs, ascend stairs, and cycling.

In 2014, Alasaarela [4] argued that activity recognition with movement sensors can also be used for school violence detection, i.e. with wearable movement sensors such as smartphones embedded with accelerometers and gyroscopes, one can detect school violence events. As members of his research group, Ye *et al.* [5] designed their first experimental classifier FMT (Fuzzy Multi-Threshold) with some simple activities. Later they [6] involved more kinds of activities and different ages of actors and actresses, and designed a more compatible Instance-Based classifier. Besides movement features, physiological features such as ECG (electrocardiogram) [7, 8] and HRV (heart rate variability) [9] were also used for school violence detection, but they are not considered in this paper.

As a continuation, this paper improves the authors' previous work by involving more features and designing a more proper classifier. Besides, more kinds of activities are tested compared with the authors' previous work. The remainder of this paper is organized as follows: Sect. 2 describes the extracted movement features; Sect. 3 describes the classifier and the training method; Sect. 4 shows the simulation results; Sect. 5 draws a conclusion.

## 2 Movement Features Extraction

Movement data of physical violence and daily-life activities are gathered by role playing. Nine kinds of activities are acted, namely beating, pushing, pushing down, walking, running, jumping, falling down, playing, and standing. The first three kinds of activities are physical violence events, and the remaining six are daily-life activities. A Butterworth filter is used before feature extraction to remove high frequency jitters.

The authors' previous work [5, 6] only extracted time domain features of the activities, but this paper extract both time domain features and frequency domain ones. The extracted time domain features are given in Table 1, whereas the extracted frequency domain features are shown in Table 2.

In this experiment, the $y$-axis is the vertical direction, so the horizontal combined vector means the combination of the $x$-axis and the $z$-axis. The combined vector means the combination of all the three axes. MAD is the Median Absolute Deviation, and $MAD = \text{median}(|x_i - \text{median}(X)|)$, where $X = \{x_1, x_2, \ldots, x_n\}$. *VarDir* describes the change of horizontal movement direction, and $Area_y$ is the accumulation of movement jitter in the vertical direction [6].

The frequency domain features are extracted by FFT (Fast Fourier Transform). The maximum or minimum of the frequency means the frequency with the maximum or minimum amplitude. The horizontal combined vector and the combined vector have the same meanings with those of the time domain feature vectors.

There are altogether 41 features (23 time domain features and 18 frequency domain features) extracted for classification. However, since the authors' purpose is to apply the physical violence detecting algorithm on a smartphone for pratical use, the

**Table 1.** Extracted time domain features

| Feature | Meaning | From |
|---------|---------|------|
| $Mean_y$ | Mean of the $y$-axis | Acceleration |
| $Mean_{Hori}$ | Mean of the horizontal combined vector | Acceleration |
| $Mean_{Gyro}$ | Mean of the combined gyro | Gyro |
| $MAD_y$ | MAD of the $y$-axis | Acceleration |
| $MAD_{Hori}$ | MAD of the horizontal combined vector | Acceleration |
| $MAD_{Gyro}$ | MAD of the combined gyro | Gyro |
| $Max_y$ | Maximum of the $y$-axis | Acceleration |
| $Max_{Hori}$ | Maximum of the horizontal combined vector | Acceleration |
| $Max_{Gyro}$ | Maximum of the combined gyro | Gyro |
| $Min_y$ | Minimum of the $y$-axis | Acceleration |
| $Min_{Hori}$ | Minimum of the horizontal combined vector | Acceleration |
| $Min_{Gyro}$ | Minimum of the combined gyro | Gyro |
| $Max_{diff(y)}$ | Maximum of the differential of the $y$-axis | Acceleration |
| $Max_{diff(Hori)}$ | Maximum of the differential of the horizontal combined vector | Acceleration |
| $Mean_{diff(y)}$ | Mean of the differential of the $y$-axis | Acceleration |
| $Mean_{diff(Hori)}$ | Mean of the differential of the horizontal combined vector | Acceleration |
| $Max_{diff(Gyro)}$ | Maximum of the differential of the combined gyro | Gyro |
| $Mean_{diff(Gyro)}$ | Mean of the differential of the combined gyro | Gyro |
| $ZCR_x$ | Zero cross rate of the $x$-axis | Acceleration |
| $ZCR_y$ | Zero cross rate of the $y$-axis | Acceleration |
| $ZCR_z$ | Zero cross rate of the $z$-axis | Acceleration |
| $VarDir$ | Variation of the horizontal movement direction | Acceleration |
| $Area_y$ | Accumulation of movement jitter of the $y$-axis | Acceleration |

**Table 2.** Frequency domain features

| Feature | Meaning | From |
|---------|---------|------|
| $Max_{fy}$ | Maximum of the $y$-axis | Acceleration |
| $Max_{fHori}$ | Maximum of the horizontal combined vector | Acceleration |
| $Max_{fGyro}$ | Maximum of the combined gyro | Gyro |
| $Min_{fy}$ | Minimum of the $y$-axis | Acceleration |
| $Min_{fHori}$ | Minimum of the horizontal combined vector | Acceleration |
| $Min_{fGyro}$ | Minimum of the combined gyro | Gyro |
| $MAD_{fy}$ | MAD of the $y$-axis | Acceleration |
| $MAD_{fHori}$ | MAD of the horizontal combined vector | Acceleration |
| $MAD_{fGyro}$ | MAD of the combined gyro | Gyro |
| $Mean_{fy}$ | Mean of the $y$-axis | Acceleration |
| $Mean_{fHori}$ | Mean of the horizontal combined vector | Acceleration |
| $Mean_{fGyro}$ | Mean of the combined gyro | Gyro |
| $Energy_{fy}$ | Energy of the $y$-axis | Acceleration |
| $Energy_{fHori}$ | Energy of the horizontal combined vector | Acceleration |
| $Energy_{fGyro}$ | Energy of the combined gyro | Gyro |
| $Center_{fHori}$ | Main lob center frequency of the horizontal combined vector | Acceleration |
| $Center_{fy}$ | Main lob center frequency of the $y$-axis | Acceleration |
| $Center_{fGyro}$ | Main lob center frequency of the combined gyro | Gyro |

dimension of the feature vector should be as low as possible. In this paper, the authors choose the Wrapper method [10] for feature selection.

The authors firstly designed the entire classification system, including data gathering, data pre-processing, feature extraction, and the classifier. A specific BPNN (Back Propagation Neural Network) [11] works as the classifier. Then the authors use this system to find out the best feature combination with the Wrapper method. In each iteration, Wrapper adds or removes features, and compares the classification results. Finally, Wrapper selects 11 features, including 7 time domain features, namely $Mean_{Gyro}$, $Max_{Gyro}$, $Max_{diff}(y)$, $Max_{diff(Gyro)}$, $ZCR_x$, $ZCR_y$, and $VarDir$, and 4 frequency domain features, namely $MAD_{fHori}$, $MAD_{fGyro}$, $Mean_{fHori}$, and $Energy_{fy}$.

## 3 Classifier Design

In the authors' previous work, the first classifier FMT was discarded in the second experiment because it was difficult to find unified thresholds for the actors and actresses of different ages due to strength difference. However, the second Instance-Based classifier could not distinguish the activities of pushing down and falling down very well. Therefore, the authors decide to find a more proper classifier. By comparing the advantages and disadvantages of some commonly used classifiers, e.g. Bayesian, SVM, KNN and KNN-based, the authors finally choose BPNN for this work. BPNN is particularly suitable for solving complex problems with non-linear relationship between the extracted features and classification results. Figure 1 shows the architecture of a classical BPNN, where $p$ is the input, $w$ is the weight, $b$ is the bias, $f$ is the transfer function, and $a$ is the output.

The parameter setting of BPNN is a key factor which affects the classification performance. Normally, the number of inputs of the network equals to the dimension of the input feature vector. In this paper, it is 11. The number of neurons of the output layer equals to the number of target classes, i.e. 9 in this paper. The number of neurons of the hidden layer should be set larger than the square of the sum of the input and the output dimensions empirically. Other parameters, e.g. the number of hidden layers, the transfer functions of the hidden layers and the output layer, will be set experimentally according to the simulations.

For training BPNN, this paper chooses the Lenvenberg-Marquardt (L-M) method [12]. Compared with other training methods such as the Newton method and the Gradient Descent method, the L-M method can avoid calculating a Hessian matrix which will cause large computational cost. Instead, the Hessian matrix is approximated by $\mathbf{H} = \mathbf{J}^T\mathbf{J}$ with the gradient $\mathbf{g} = \mathbf{J}^T\mathbf{e}$ where $\mathbf{J}$ is a Jacobian matrix containing the first order derivative of the training error $\mathbf{e}$. In each iteration, $x_{k+1} = x_k - [\mathbf{J}^T\mathbf{J} + \mu I]^{-1}\mathbf{J}^T\mathbf{e}$.

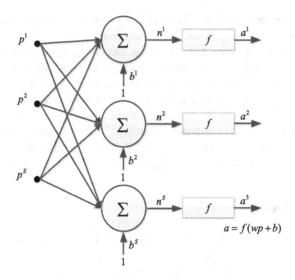

$$a = f(wp + b)$$

**Fig. 1.** Architecture of a classical BPNN

## 4 Simulations

The authors recorded altogether 1160 fragments of the 9 kinds of activities, and the amount of each kind was similar. The movement sensors (accelerometers and gyroscopes) were fixed on the actors' and actresses' waists. Ten-fold cross validation was used for the simulations, i.e. the authors split each kind of activity into 10 groups, 9 of which were used as the training set whereas the remaining 1 as the testing set. Repeat this procedure 10 times and change the testing set each time. The final result was the average of the 10 results.

Then the authors set the parameters of BPNN experimentally: there are 6 neurons in the hidden layer; the transfer function of the hidden layer is logsig, whereas that of the output layer is purelin. Figure 2 shows the architecture of this specific BPNN.

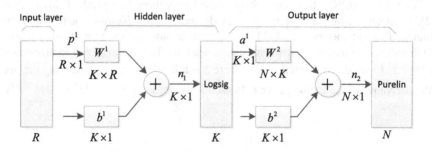

**Fig. 2.** Architecture of the employed BPNN

Firstly, the 9 kinds of activities were classified into 9 classes. The confusion matrix is given in Table 3.

**Table 3.** Confusion matrix of 9-class classification (%)

| Classified as | Beat | Push | Push down | Walk | Run | Jump | Fall down | Play | Stand |
|---|---|---|---|---|---|---|---|---|---|
| Beat | **50.0** | 10.0 | 13.3 | 0.0 | 3.3 | 0.0 | 3.3 | 20.0 | 0.0 |
| Push | 8.3 | **68.3** | 8.3 | 0.0 | 1.7 | 6.7 | 6.7 | 0.0 | 0.0 |
| Push down | 0.0 | 3.3 | **40.0** | 10.0 | 0.0 | 3.3 | 10.0 | 23.3 | 10.0 |
| Walk | 2.5 | 1.3 | 7.5 | **43.8** | 0.0 | 0.0 | 0.0 | 42.5 | 2.5 |
| Run | 0.0 | 1.4 | 0.0 | 0.0 | **91.4** | 5.7 | 0.0 | 0.0 | 1.4 |
| Jump | 0.0 | 0.0 | 0.0 | 0.0 | 12.5 | **87.5** | 0.0 | 0.0 | 0.0 |
| Fall down | 0.0 | 20.0 | 6.7 | 0.0 | 0.0 | 0.0 | **66.7** | 6.7 | 0.0 |
| Play | 4.2 | 5.0 | 15.0 | 5.8 | 0.0 | 2.5 | 4.2 | **60.8** | 2.5 |
| Stand | 0.0 | 0.0 | 1.1 | 1.1 | 0.0 | 0.0 | 0.0 | 3.3 | **94.4** |

Then, considering the theme of this paper, i.e. physical violence detection, the 9 kinds of activities are classified into 2 classes, namely physical violence and daily-life activities, respectively. Table 4 shows the 2-class classification confusion matrix.

**Table 4.** Confusion matrix of 2-class classification (%)

| Classified as | Physical violence | Daily-life activity |
|---|---|---|
| Physical violence | **71.7** | 28.3 |
| Daily-life activity | 11.2 | **88.8** |

Table 4 shows an intuitional result of the proposed violence detecting method, and Table 3 may tell some details of it. Violent activities of beating and pushing down are likely to be misclassified as the daily-life activity of playing, and daily-life activities of falling down and playing are likely to be misclassified as violenct activities of pushing and pushing down, respectively, because these kinds of activities have similar strenghth and suddenness especially when playing contains confrontational actions.

The average accuracy of the proposed method is about 83.7%, which outperforms the authors' previous Instance-Based method by 3.7%. The first method FMT is uncomparable because it is hardly possible to find unified thresholds for actors and actresses of different ages due to strength difference.

# 5  Conclusion

This paper proposed a physical violence detecting method. The movement data were gathered by movement sensors by means of role playing. Both time domain features and frequency domain features were extracted and filtered to describe the differences between physical violence and daily-life activities. A specific BPNN trained with the L-M method worked as the classifier. Ten-fold cross validation was performed for simulation. The average classification accuracy was 83.7%, which showed an improvement compared with the authors' previous work.

**Acknowledgements.** This paper was supported by the National Natural Science Foundation of China (61602127), and partly supported by the Directorate General of Higher Education, Indonesia (2142/E4.4/K/2013), and the Finnish Cultural Foundation, North Ostrobothnia Regional Fund.

The authors would like to thank Tuija Huuki, Vappu Sunnari, Seppo Laukka and Antti Siipo from University of Oulu, Finland, teachers Taina Aalto and Pekka Kurttila and principal Maija Laukka from Oulunlahti School, Finland, pupils from 2nd and 6th grades of Oulunlahti School, Tian Han and Zhu Zhang from Harbin University of Science and Technology, China, Yubo Zhang, Jifu Shi and Zhi Xun from Harbin Institute of Technology, China for their assistance to this work.

# References

1. Cheng, L., Yu, Y., Liu, X., Su, J., Guan, Y.: Recognition of human activities using fast and adaptive sparse representation based on wearable sensors. In: 2017 16th IEEE International Conference on Machine Learning and Applications, pp. 944–949 (2017)
2. Nakano, K., Chakraborty, B.: Effect of dynamic feature for human activity recognition using smartphone sensors. In: 2017 IEEE 8th International Conference on Awareness Science and Technology (iCAST), pp. 539–543 (2017)
3. Hegde, N., Bries, M., Swibas, T., et al.: Automatic recognition of activities of daily living utilizing insole based and wrist worn wearable sensors. IEEE J. Biomed. Health Inform. **99**, 1–9 (2018)
4. Ye, L., Ferdinando, H., Alasaarela, E.: Techniques in pattern recognition for school bullying prevention: review and outlook. J. Pattern Recognit. Res. **9**(1), 50–63 (2014)
5. Ye, L., Ferdinando, H., Seppänen, T., Alasaarela, E.: Physical violence detection for school bullying prevention. Adv. Artif. Intell. **2014**, 1–9 (2014)
6. Ye, L., Ferdinando, H., Seppänen, T., et al.: An instance-based physical violence detection algorithm for school bullying prevention. In: 2015 International Wireless Communications and Mobile Computing Conference (IWCMC), Dubrovnik, Croatia, pp. 1384–1388 (2015)
7. Ferdinando, H., Ye, L., Han, T., et al.: Violence detection from ECG signals: a preliminary study. J. Pattern Recognit. Res. **12**(1), 7–18 (2017)
8. Ferdinando, H., Seppänen, T., Alasaarela, E.: Enhancing emotion recognition from ECG signals using supervised dimensionality reduction. In: Proceeding of 6th International Conference on Pattern Recognition Applications and Methods (ICPRAM), 24–26 February 2017, Porto, Portugal, pp. 112–118 (2017)
9. Ferdinando, H., Ye, L., Seppänen, T., et al.: Emotion recognition by heart rate variability. Aust. J. Basic Appl. Sci. **8**(10), 50–55 (2014)

10. El Aboudi, N., Benhlima, L.: Review on wrapper feature selection approaches. In: 2016 International Conference on Engineering and MIS (ICEMIS), pp. 1–5 (2016)
11. Huang, Z., Wang, W.: Multi-sensor fusion based on BPNN in quadruped ground classification. In: 2017 IEEE International Conference on Mechatronics and Automation (ICMA), pp. 1620–1625 (2017)
12. Bengang, W., Xinye, W., Zhoufei, Y., et al.: A method of optimized neural network by L-M algorithm to transformer winding hot spot temperature forecasting. In: 2017 IEEE Electrical Insulation Conference (EIC), pp. 87–91 (2017)

# Joint Resource Allocation for Wireless Energy Harvesting Based on DF Relaying

Tian Nan$^{(\boxtimes)}$, Weidang Lu, and Zhijiang Xu

College of Information Engineering, Zhejiang University of Technology,
Hangzhou 310023, China
15757175896@163.com

**Abstract.** In this paper, a spectrum sharing protocol of cognitive radio (CR) based on joint resource allocation is proposed. The problem of spectrum access for one-way relaying *CR* networks using decode-and-forward (DF) relaying protocols is investigated. Specifically, in the first phase, the primary transmitter (*PT*) sends its own signal to primary receiver (*PR*) and cognitive transmitter (*CT*). Then, *CT* divides the received signal into two portions, which are used to decode information and harvest energy, respectively. In the second phase, the accessed bandwidth of *CT* is divided into two parts. One of the bandwidth is used to forward *PT's* signal to *PR* with the harvested energy. *CT* can use the other of bandwidth to send *CT's* signal to the cognitive receiver (*CR*) by using its own energy. The main object is to maximize cognitive system transmission rate by jointly optimizing the power splitting ratio and bandwidth allocation while satisfying the constraint of primary transmission rate.

**Keywords:** Energy harvesting · Power splitting · Bandwidth allocation
Spectrum access

## 1 Introduction

Since wireless communication facilitates people's communication, they want to have higher transmission rate of wireless communication. In order to meet people's needs, we need higher transmission rates, that is, we need more spectrum resources. However, the spectrum resource in nature is limited, and existing fixed spectrum allocation has more or less wastes in time and space, which restricts the development of wireless communications. Cognitive radio (*CR*) can advance the efficiency of spectrum utilizing by admitting cognitive system to access the licensed spectrum of the primary system while persevering in the interference restriction of the primary systems [1].

With the advantages of expanding coverage of the system and improving reliability of the link, cooperative diversity technology has wide applications in the spectrum access of cognitive radio [2–4]. In distributed spectrum sharing protocols with cooperative relay, the cognitive transmitter uses a part of its power to transmit the primary signal. As a reward, it can transmit its own signal to cognitive receiver by using the remainder [5–7]. In the spectrum access protocol, the cognitive transmitter plays the role of relay, to help reach the target rate of primary system with a part of sub-carriers to transmit the primary signal, while the rest are used for transmitting its signal [8–10].

© ICST Institute for Computer Sciences, Social Informatics and Telecommunications Engineering 2018
L. Meng and Y. Zhang (Eds.): MLICOM 2018, LNICST 251, pp. 198–205, 2018.
https://doi.org/10.1007/978-3-030-00557-3_21

Simultaneous wireless information and power transfer (SWIPT) [11] is the product of wireless energy transmission combined with wireless information transmission, which can realize the parallel transmission of information and energy. A relay can harvest energy from the received signal,and forward the received signal to the destination [12, 13]. By optimizing some practical parameters in [14], SWIPT proposes a general framework to maximize network performance. A cooperative SWIPT scheme based on time switching (TS) protocol was presented to maximize the energy-delivery efficiency in wireless sensor networks (WSNs) with multiple nodes [15]. However, there are some flaws in the articles above. Such as, the cognitive user utilizes the same bandwidth to send signal of the primary and cognitive users, which will result in grave interference between the primary and cognitive system.

A spectrum sharing protocol of cognitive radio based on DF relaying is proposed in this paper. Specifically, the accessed bandwidth of cognitive system is divided into two parts. One part is used to send primary signal with the harvested energy, and the other part is used to transmit its own signal by using its own energy. Therefore, independent bandwidth is used to send primary and cognitive signal without interference. We study the joint power splitting ratio and bandwidth allocation optimization to obtain the maximum value of cognitive system transmission rate under the constraint of primary target rate $R_T$. The simulation results show that the primary and cognitive performance is improved.

The remaining part of this paper is arranged as follows. In Sect. 2, we introduce the components of the system model and the definition of various parameters. In Sect. 3, we propose the formulation and solution of the problem. In Sect. 4, Simulation results explain the performance of the proposed spectrum sharing protocol and power allocation algorithm. Finally, in Sect. 5, we give the conclusion of this paper.

## 2 System Model

We consider a cognitive radio system make up a primary system and a cognitive system, which is shown in Fig. 1. The primary system is composed of a primary transmitter ($PT$) and a primary receiver ($PR$) which supports the relaying functionality and operates on a licensed spectrum $W$. The cognitive system is made up of a cognitive transmitter ($CT$) and a cognitive receiver ($CR$), which transmits signal by looking for the chance to get the licensed spectrum. $CT$ has the function of energy harvesting, which will acquire and store the energy from the received signal.

We assume that the channel in this system is Rayleigh flat fading channel, $h_1, h_2, h_3$ and $h_4$ denote the channel coefficients of the links $PT \rightarrow PR$, $PT \rightarrow CT$, $CT \rightarrow PR$ and $CT \rightarrow CR$, respectively. $d_1, d_2, d_3$ and $d_4$ denote the distance of the links $PT \rightarrow PR$, $PT \rightarrow CT$, $CT \rightarrow PR$ and $CT \rightarrow CR$, respectively. We have $h_i \sim CN(0, d_i^{-v})$, $i = 1, 2, 3, 4$, where $v$ is the path loss exponent. $\gamma_i = |h_{i,k}|^2$ denotes the instantaneous channel gain of $h_i$. We also assume that all the channel coefficients are constant throughout the whole process. Generally, we assume that all the noise terms are additive white Gaussian noise with a mean of zero and a variance of $\sigma^2$.

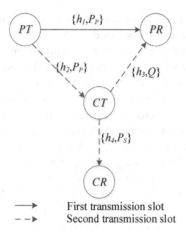

Fig. 1. System model.

We separate the transport process of the system into two phases. firstly, *PT* sends signal to *PR* and *CR* by using its power $P_p$. *CT* uses one of the received signal to decode information and the other to harvest energy. Secondly, *CT* forward the receives signal to *PR*. As a reward, *CT* can send its own signal to *CR* with the remaining bandwidth by using its transmit power $P_c$.

## 3 The Problem Formulation and Solution

Firstly, we consider that there is no cognitive system access, *PT* sends its signal to *PR* directly. The achievable rate of *PR* can be written as

$$R_D = W \log_2\left(1 + \frac{\gamma_1 P_P}{\sigma^2}\right) \tag{1}$$

When the primary rate $R_D$ falls below the target rate $R_T$, *PR* will seek cooperation with surrounding cognitive users to help transmit the primary signal.

In the first phase, *PT* transmits its signal to *PR* and *CT*. *CT* uses $\alpha(0 < \alpha < 1)$ fraction of the primary power for decoding information and utilizes the remainder for harvesting energy. Therefore, the rates of $PT \rightarrow PR$ and $PT \rightarrow CT$ links can be expressed as

$$R_d = \frac{1}{2} W \log_2(1 + \frac{\gamma_1 P_P}{\sigma^2}) \tag{2}$$

$$R_p^1 = \frac{1}{2} W \log_2(1 + \frac{\alpha \gamma_2 P_P}{\sigma^2}) \tag{3}$$

The energy collected by $CT$ can be expressed as

$$Q = \varepsilon(1 - \alpha)\gamma_2 P_P \tag{4}$$

where $\varepsilon$ is a constant representing the loss factor for converting energy into electricity.

In the second phase, $CT$ utilizes a part of the bandwidth $bW(0 < b < 1)$ to transmit $PT's$ signal with the collected energy $Q$. If $CT$ decodes successfully, the primary rate can be expressed as

$$R_p^2 = \frac{1}{2}bW \log_2\left(1 + \frac{\varepsilon(1 - \alpha)\gamma_2\gamma_3 P_P}{\sigma^2} + \frac{P_P\gamma_1}{\sigma^2}\right) + \frac{1}{2}(1 - b)W \log_2\left(1 + \frac{P_P\gamma_1}{\sigma^2}\right) \tag{5}$$

After two phases, the achievable rate of $PR$ can be expressed as

$$R_P = \min\{R_p^1, R_p^2\} \tag{6}$$

Meanwhile, $CT$ sends its own signal to $CR$ with the remained bandwidth $(1 - b)W$ and cognitive power. Therefore, the rate of $CR$ can be expressed as

$$R_c = \frac{1}{2}(1 - b)W \log_2\left(1 + \frac{\gamma_4 P_c}{\sigma^2}\right) \tag{7}$$

## 3.1  Problem Formulation

With the objective of maximize the cognitive rate $R_c$ by joint optimization of power $\alpha$ and bandwidth $b$ while ensuring the primary rate $R_P$ can achieve the target rate $R_T$. The optimization problem can be written as:

$$\max_{\alpha, b} R_c = \frac{1}{2}(1 - b)W \log_2\left(1 + \frac{\gamma_4 P_c}{\sigma^2}\right) \tag{8}$$

$$\text{s.t.} \begin{cases} R_p \geq R_T \\ 0 < \alpha < 1 \\ 0 < b < 1 \end{cases} \tag{9}$$

## 3.2  Problem Solution

Substituting (3), (5), (6) into the first condition of (9), we can obtain

$$\frac{1}{2}W \log_2(1 + \frac{\alpha\gamma_2 P_P}{\sigma^2}) \geq R_T \tag{10}$$

$$\frac{1}{2}bW \log_2\left(1 + \frac{\varepsilon(1 - \alpha)\gamma_2\gamma_3 P_P}{\sigma^2} + \frac{P_P\gamma_1}{\sigma^2}\right) + \frac{1}{2}(1 - b)W \log_2\left(1 + \frac{P_P\gamma_1}{\sigma^2}\right) \geq R_T \tag{11}$$

Convert the format (10) and (11), we can obtain

$$
\begin{cases}
\alpha \geq \dfrac{\sigma^2 M}{\gamma_2 P_P} \\[2mm]
b \geq \dfrac{2R_T - W \log_2(1 + \frac{P_P \gamma_1}{\sigma^2})}{W \log_2(1 + \frac{\varepsilon(1-\alpha)\gamma_2\gamma_3 P_P}{\sigma^2 + P_P \gamma_1})}
\end{cases}
\tag{12}
$$

where $M = 2^{2R_T/W} - 1$.

We have the constraint of $0 < b < 1$, and can obtain

$$
\alpha \leq 1 - \frac{\sigma^2 M - \gamma_1 P_P}{\varepsilon \gamma_2 \gamma_3 P_P}
\tag{13}
$$

$$
\frac{1}{2} W \log_2 \left( 1 + \frac{\gamma_1 P_P}{\sigma^2} \right) < R_T
\tag{14}
$$

In (12) and (7), we can know that $b$ monotonically increases with $\alpha$ and $R_c$ monotonically decreases of $b$, respectively. Therefore, the joint optimization problem of power $\alpha$ and bandwidth $b$ can be expressed as

$$
b^* = \frac{2R_T - W \log_2(1 + \frac{P_P \gamma_1}{\sigma^2})}{W \log_2(1 + \frac{\varepsilon(1-\alpha)\gamma_2\gamma_3 P_P}{\sigma^2 + P_P \gamma_1})}
\tag{15}
$$

$$
\alpha^* = \frac{\sigma^2 M}{\gamma_2 P_P}
\tag{16}
$$

Substituting $\alpha^*$ into (15), the optimal $b^*$ can be expressed as

$$
b^* = \frac{2R_T - W \log_2(1 + \frac{P_P \gamma_1}{\sigma^2})}{W \log_2(1 + \frac{\gamma_3 \varepsilon(P_P \gamma_2 - \sigma^2 M)}{\sigma^2 + P_P \gamma_1})}
\tag{17}
$$

## 4   Simulation Results

We consider $PT$, $PR$, $CT$ and $CR$ are in a two-dimensional $X - Y$ plane, where $PT$ and $PR$ are located at points $(0,0)$ and $(1,0)$, respectively, thus $d_1 = 1$. $CT$ moves on the positive $X$ axis from, its coordinate is $(d_2, 0)$. $CR$ is located at point $(1, -0.5)$. Thus, $d_3 = 1 - d_2$, and $d_4 = \sqrt{d_2^2 + 0.25}$. The path loss exponent denotes $v = 4, \sigma^2 = 1, R_T = 2.5 \, \text{bps/Hz}, P_P = 6 \, \text{dB}, P_c = 10 \, \text{dB}, W = 1$.

Figure 2 presents the value of $R_p$ and $R_C$ versus $d_2$ in a transmission process. In Fig. 2, we can find that $R_p = R_T, R_C > 0$ when $CT$ moves in the access domain of $[0, 0.595]$. We can also find that when $CT$ moves in the access domain of $[0.596, 1]$, $R_p = R_D, R_C = 0$, which indicates that $CT$ can't operate on the primary spectrum. This is because that when $CT's$ location is aloof from $PT$, the $SNR$ of $PT \rightarrow CT$ link is worse and then the harvested energy $Q$ at $CT$ will be less and less. It will lead to $CT$ can't help the value of $R_p$ to reach the target rate $R_T$. Hence, the cognitive system will not be admitted to operate on the spectrum of primary system.

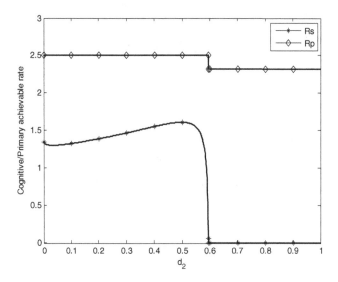

**Fig. 2.** Value of $R_P$ and $R_c$ versus $d_2$.

Figure 3 presents the value of $R_C$ versus $P_c$ with different $R_T$ when $CT$ in the access domain. From Fig. 3, we can observe that the rate of the cognitive system increases with the increase of the cognitive transmit power $P_c$, which is because $CT$ only uses $P_c$ to send cognitive signal in the access domain. Figure 4 presents the value of $R_C$ versus $d_2$ with different $R_T$. From Fig. 4, we can observe that when $CT$ is not in access domain, the rate of the cognitive system increases first, and then decreases as $d_2$ increase. When $CT$ is not in access domain, the rate of the cognitive system would become zero. It is because that the $SNR$ of $PT \rightarrow CT$ link is worse when $CT's$ location is too close or too far away from $PT$. We can also discover from the following figures that the cognitive rate $R_C$ will decrease as the target rate $R_T$ increase. It is because that when $R_T$ gets larger, $CT$ will use more bandwidth to transmit $PT's$ signal to reach the target rate $R_T$, which leads to less bandwidth being left to send its own signal.

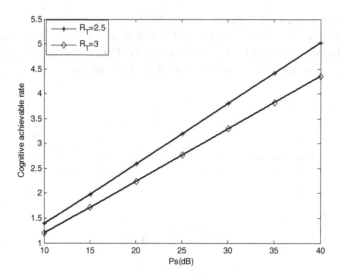

**Fig. 3.** Value of $R_c$ versus $P_c$ with different $R_T$

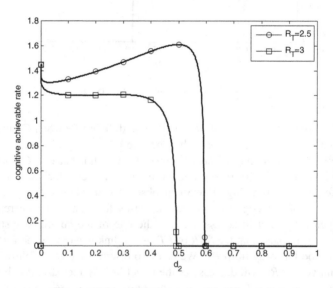

**Fig. 4.** Value of $R_c$ versus $d_2$ with different $R_T$

## 5    Conclusion

A spectrum sharing protocol of cognitive radio based on DF relaying is proposed in this paper. Specifically, *CT* decodes information and harvests energy with the received signal. Then, the accessed bandwidth of *CT* is divided into two parts. One part is used to forward $PT's$ signal to *PR* with the energy $Q$, and the other part is used to transmit

$CT's$ signal to $CR$ by using its own energy. There will be no interference between primary and cognitive systems. Joint power splitting ratio and bandwidth allocation is studied to maximize the value of $R_C$ while satisfying the constraint of primary transmission rate. Simulation results show that the proposed joint optimization strategy is beneficial to both the cognitive and primary system.

# References

1. Haykin, S.: Cognitive radio: brain-empowered wireless communications. IEEE J. Sel. Areas Commun. **23**(2), 201–220 (2005)
2. Sendonaris, A., Erkip, E., Aazhang, B.: User cooperation diversity part I and part II. IEEE Trans. Wirel. Commun. **51**(11), 1927–1948 (2003)
3. Zhong, B., Zhang, Z., Zhang, D., et al.: Partial relay selection in decode and forward cooperative cognitive radio networks over rayleigh fading channels. In: International Conference on Information and Communications Technologies, pp. 152–157 (2014)
4. Li, Y., Zhang, Z., Zhang, X., et al.: Best relay selection in decode and forward cooperative cognitive radio relay networks over Rayleigh fading channels. In: International Conference on Information and Communications Technologies. IET, pp. 152–157 (2013)
5. Han, Y., Pandharipande, A., Ting, S.H.: Cooperative decode-and-forward relaying for secondary spectrum access. IEEE Trans. Wirel. Commun. **8**(10), 4945–4950 (2009)
6. Han, Y., Pandharipande, A., Ting, S.H.: Cooperative spectrum sharing via controlled amplify-and-forward relaying. In: 2008 IEEE 19th International Symposium on Personal, Indoor and Mobile Radio Communications, PIMRC 2008, pp. 1–5. IEEE (2008)
7. Li, S., Mitra, U., Ratnam, V., et al.: Jointly cooperative decode-and-forward relaying for secondary spectrum access. In: Information Sciences and Systems, pp. 1–6. IEEE (2012)
8. Lu, W.D., Gong, Y., Ting, S.H., Wu, X.L., Zhang, N.T.: Cooperative OFDM relaying for opportunistic spectrum sharing: protocol design and resource allocation. IEEE Trans. Wirel. Commun. **11**(6), 2126–2135 (2012)
9. Lu, W.D., Wang, J.: Opportunistic spectrum sharing based on full-duplex cooperative OFDM relaying. IEEE Commun. Lett. **18**(2), 241–244 (2014)
10. Wang, L., Tang, Y., Luo, W., et al.: Resource allocation in OFDM-based cooperative cognitive radio networks with two-way amplify-and-forward relay. In: International Conference on Wireless Communications, NETWORKING and Mobile Computing. IET, pp. 1–6 (2015)
11. Varshney, L.R.: Transporting information and energy simultaneously. In: IEEE International Symposium on Information Theory, pp. 1612–1616. IEEE (2008)
12. Liu, Y., Wang, X.: Information and energy cooperation in OFDM relaying: protocols and optimization. IEEE Trans. Veh. Technol. **65**(7), 5088–5098 (2015)
13. Liu, Y., Wang, X.: Information and energy cooperation in OFDM relaying. In: IEEE International Conference on Communications, pp. 2506–2511. IEEE (2015)
14. Lu, W.D., Zhang, Y.J., Wang, M.Y., Liu, X., Hua, J.Y.: Cooperative spectrum sharing in OFDM two-way relay systems with bidirectional transmissions. IEEE Commun. Lett. **21**(6), 1349–1352 (2017)
15. Kisseleff, S., Chen, X., Akyildiz, I.F., Gerstacker, W.H.: Efficient charging of access limited wireless underground sensor networks. IEEE Trans. Commun. **64**(5), 2130–2142 (2016)

# Optimal Power Splitting of Cognitive Radio Networks with SWIPT-Enabled Relay

Yuanrong Lin$^{(\boxtimes)}$, Weidang Lu, Hong Peng, and Jingyu Hua

College of Information Engineering, Zhejiang University of Technology,
Hangzhou 310023, China
452147635@qq.com

**Abstract.** Cognitive radio (CR), as an intelligent spectrum sharing technology, can improve utilization of spectrum by sharing the licensed spectrum bands with secondary users (SUs) as long as do not have harmful effect on primary users (PUs). Simultaneous wireless information and power transfer (SWIPT) combines wireless information transmission (WIT) technology and wireless power transfer (WPT) technology, which harvesting energy from ambient RF signals. In this paper, we consider amplify-and-forward (AF) cognitive radio networks (CRNs) with SWIPT-enabled secondary relay node. We aim to maximize the throughput of secondary network in considering the interference caused by the transmitted signal of secondary relay node to PUs, and derived the closed-form expression of the optimal power splitting ratio. Simulation results demonstrate the performance of the optimal power splitting ratio.

**Keywords:** Simultaneous wireless information and power transfer
Cognitive networks · Amplify-and-forward · Throughput

## 1 Introduction

In recent years, with the rapid increase of the wireless devices, spectrum scarcity becomes the bottleneck for the development of wireless communication. However, most licensed spectrum bands are usually under-utilized while the unlicensed spectrum bands are becoming increasingly crowded [1]. Cognitive radio (CR), as an intelligent spectrum sharing technology, can improve utilization of spectrum by sharing the licensed spectrum bands with secondary users (SUs) as long as do not have harmful effect on primary users (PUs) [2, 3].

Energy harvesting (EH), as an economical and feasible technology to prolong the lifetime of energy-constraint networks has drawn significantly attention. In addition to the traditional energy resources, such as solar [4], radio-frequency (RF) signal as a new resource which can carry energy and information at the same time. Simultaneous wireless information and power transfer (SWIPT) combines wireless information transmission (WIT) technology and wireless power transfer (WPT) technology, which harvesting energy from ambient RF signals [5]. Compare with the traditional EH technology, SWIPT does not affected by weather and geographical location. Moreover, the node that utilizes the SWIPT can receive information while harvesting energy to sustain itself. Due to these advantages, SWIPT has attracted great attention [6–10].

© ICST Institute for Computer Sciences, Social Informatics and Telecommunications Engineering 2018
L. Meng and Y. Zhang (Eds.): MLICOM 2018, LNICST 251, pp. 206–215, 2018.
https://doi.org/10.1007/978-3-030-00557-3_22

Varshney firstly proposed the idea of SWIPT assuming that the receiver can decode the carried information from the signal that used for EH in [6]. However, this assumption is unachievable in practice due to the limitation of circuit [7]. Two practical receiver architectures named time switching (TS) and power splitting (PS) respectively was proposed in [8]. Recently, SWIPT also has been proposed in cooperative relaying networks [9, 10]. [9] considered introducing SWIPT to amplify-and-forward (AF) co-operative relaying networks, in which two relaying protocols for SWIPT were studied. In [10], three power transfer policies were proposed for two-way relaying networks, where the performances of throughput for different policies were analyzed.

Recently, to combine the merits of two technology, SWIPT has been introduced into cognitive radio networks (CRNs) [11–13]. [11] studied the policy of channel selection to maximize SU's throughput, in which the RF-powered CRN contains multiple PUs allocated with different channels. [12] analyzed the performance of outage probability for CRNs with SWIPT-enabled relay, while did not obtain the closed-form expression of the optimal TS ratio. [13] derived the approximate expressions of ergodic sum-rate and throughput for AF underlay CRNs, in which relay uses PS receiver architecture to harvest energy. However, the interference caused by the transmitted signal of secondary relay node to PUs.

In this paper, we derived the closed-form expression of the optimal power splitting ratio for AF CRNs with SWIPT-enabled secondary relay node. The main contributions of this paper can be summarized as follows: First, unlike the aforementioned work [13], we maximize the throughput of secondary network in considering the interference caused by the transmitted signal of secondary relay node to PUs as well as PU to secondary network. Second, we derived the closed-form expression of optimal power splitting ratio rather than the simulation like [12]. Finally, the simulation result demonstrates that the optimal power splitting ratio we obtained can maximize the throughput of secondary network.

The remainder of the paper is organized as follows. Section 2 describes the underlay AF CRN with SWIPT-enabled secondary relay node and formulate the optimization problem. Section 3 solves the optimization problem and obtains the closed-form expression of the optimal power splitting ratio. The simulation results are presented and discussed in Sect. 4. Finally, we conclude the paper in Sect. 5.

## 2  System Model and Problem Formulation

### 2.1  System Model

As illustrated in Fig. 1, we consider an underlay AF CRNs with SWIPT-enabled secondary relay node, where consists of a primary network and a secondary network. The primary network consists of a pair of PUs, i.e., a primary transmitter (PT) and a primary receiver (PR), respectively. There are three node which are respectively source node (SN), SWIPT-enabled relay node (RN) and destination node (DN) in the secondary network. We assume that SN can transmit the signal to DN only with the help of RN due to there is no direct link between SN and DN. The channel coefficient from any terminal $i$ to $j$ is denoted as $h_{i,j} \sim CN(0, d_{i,j}^{-m})$, where $d_{i,j}$ is the distance between $i$ and $j$, $m$ is the path loss exponent.

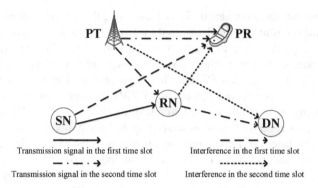

**Fig. 1.** System model.

The cooperative communication takes place in two equal phases. In the first phase, PT uses transmission power $p_p$ to transmit the signal $x_p$ to PR and will cause the interference to RN. For the underlay mode, the interference from SN to PR should not excessed the threshold $I_{th}$. Moreover, we denote the maximal transmission power at SN as $P_{max}$. Then, the transmission power of SN can be written as

$$p_s = \min \left( \frac{I_{th}}{\left| h_{SN,PR} \right|^2}, P_{max} \right) \tag{1}$$

SN uses the transmission power $p_s$ to transmit the signal $x_s$ to RN, and the received signal at the RN is expressed as

$$y = \sqrt{p_s} x_s h_{SN,RN} + n_a + \sqrt{p_p} x_p h_{PT,RN} \tag{2}$$

where $n_a \sim N(0, \sigma_a^2)$ is the additive white Gaussian noise (AWGN) at RN.

The RN splits the received signal into two parts with the power allocation ratio $\lambda (0 \leq \lambda \leq 1)$, one part is used for the energy harvesting and the other part $(1 - \lambda)$ for information processing. The energy harvested at RN can be expressed as

$$E = \frac{1}{2} \eta \lambda (P_s \left| h_{SN,RN} \right|^2 + \sigma_a^2 + P_p \left| h_{PT,RN} \right|^2) \tag{3}$$

where $0 < \eta < 1$ is the energy conversion efficiency. RN utilize all of the energy harvested in the first phase to help forward SN's information, then the transmission power of RN is

$$p_r = E/(1/2) = \eta \lambda (p_s \left| h_{SN,RN} \right|^2 + \sigma_a^2 + p_p \left| h_{PT,RN} \right|^2) \tag{4}$$

In the second phase, PT uses transmission power $p_p$ to transmit the signal $x_p$ to PR and will cause the interference to DN. RN utilizes the AF relaying protocol to forward SN's information, and the transmission signal is given by

$$y_r = \phi(\sqrt{(1-\lambda)}y + n_b) \tag{5}$$

where $n_b \sim N(0, \sigma_b^2)$ is the noise caused by the signal conversion from RF band to baseband [9], $\phi$ is the amplification coefficient and can be written as

$$\phi = \sqrt{\frac{p_r}{(1-\lambda)\left(p_s|h_{SN,RN}|^2 + \sigma_a^2 + p_p|h_{PT,RN}|^2\right) + \sigma_b^2}} \approx \sqrt{\frac{\eta\lambda}{1-\lambda}} \tag{6}$$

The received signal at DN is written as

$$y_d = y_r h_{RN,DN} + n_c + \sqrt{p_p} x_p h_{PT,DN} \tag{7}$$

where $n_c \sim N(0, \sigma_c^2)$ is AWGN at DN.

Substituting (2), (5) and (6) into (7), we have

$$\begin{aligned}
y_d = &\sqrt{\eta\lambda p_s} h_{SN,RN} h_{RN,DN} x_s \\
&+ (\sqrt{\eta\lambda p_p} h_{PT,RN} h_{RN,DN} + \sqrt{p_p} h_{PT,DN}) x_p \\
&+ \sqrt{\frac{\eta\lambda}{1-\lambda}} h_{RN,DN} \left(\sqrt{1-\lambda} n_a + n_b\right) + n_c
\end{aligned} \tag{8}$$

From (8), we can obtain the SINR at DN as following

$$\gamma = \frac{-A\lambda^2 + A\lambda}{-B\lambda^2 + (B+C-D)\lambda + D} \tag{9}$$

where $A = \eta p_s|h_{SN,RN}|^2|h_{RN,DN}|^2$, $B = \eta p_p|h_{RN,DN}|^2|h_{PT,RN}|^2 + \eta|h_{RN,DN}|^2\sigma_a^2$, $C = \eta|h_{RN,DN}|^2\sigma_b^2$, $D = p_p|h_{PT,DN}|^2 + \sigma_c^2$.

Thus, the throughput at DN is given by

$$R_d = \frac{1}{2}\log_2(1+\gamma) \tag{10}$$

## 2.2 Problem Formulation

In the second phase, the interference from RN to PR is written as

$$I_r = p_r|h_{RN,PR}|^2 = \eta\lambda\left(p_s|h_{SN,RN}|^2 + \sigma_a^2 + p_p|h_{PT,RN}|^2\right)|h_{RN,PR}|^2 \tag{11}$$

Thus, the optimization problem can be formulated as

$$OP1 : \max_{\lambda} R_d \tag{12a}$$

$$s.t. \, C1 : I_r \leq I_{th} \tag{12b}$$

$$C2 : \lambda \in [0, 1] \tag{12c}$$

where $C1$ denotes that the interference from RN to PR should not excessed the threshold $I_{th}$. $C2$ shows the practical constraint of $\lambda$.

Since $\log(x)$ is monotonically increasing with $x$, the object function can omit log. Then, we can transform the optimization problem above into the following problem

$$OP2 : \max_{\lambda} \gamma \tag{13}$$

$$s.t. \quad C1, C2$$

## 3  Optimal Solution

Take the first derivation of (5) with $\lambda$, we have

$$\frac{d_\gamma}{d_\lambda} = \frac{A(D-C)\lambda^2 - 2AD\lambda + AD}{\left[-B\lambda^2 + (B+C-D)\lambda + D\right]^2} \tag{14}$$

Since the denominator of $\frac{d_\gamma}{d_\lambda}$ is always positive, $\frac{d_\gamma}{d_\lambda}$ is positive or negative just depends on $f(\lambda) = A(D-C)\lambda^2 - 2AD\lambda + AD$. Furthermore, we can find that for the different relative values of $C$ and $D$, $f(\lambda)$ has different forms with $\lambda$. Thus, we should analyze the constraint of $\lambda$ as well as the relative values of $C$ and $D$ to obtain the optimal value of $\lambda$.

**Condition 1.** When $D < C$

Obviously, $f(\lambda)$ is a quadratic function of $\lambda$, and solve the equation $f(\lambda) = 0$ we can obtain two different roots which respectively written as

$$\lambda_1 = \frac{2AD - 2A\sqrt{CD}}{2A(D-C)} = \frac{D - \sqrt{CD}}{D - C} \tag{15}$$

$$\lambda_2 = \frac{2AD + 2A\sqrt{CD}}{2A(D-C)} = \frac{D + \sqrt{CD}}{D - C} \tag{16}$$

Moreover, we have

$$f(1) = A(D - C) - 2AD + AD = -AC < 0 \tag{17}$$

$$f(0) = AD > 0 \tag{18}$$

It is obvious that $0 < \lambda_1 < 1$ and $\lambda_2 < 0$. Moreover, combine (17), (18) and the constraint $C2$ we can know that $\gamma$ reaches the maximum when $\lambda = \lambda_1$ and for $\lambda < \lambda_1$, $\gamma$ is monotonically increasing with $\lambda$; for $\lambda \geq \lambda_1$, $\gamma$ is monotonically decreasing with $\lambda$. Moreover, we also should consider the constraint C1, and we have

$$\lambda \leq \lambda_{th} = \frac{I_{th}}{E + F} \tag{19}$$

Where $E = \eta p_s |h_{SN,RN}|^2 |h_{RN,PR}|^2$, $F = \eta(\sigma_a^2 + p_p |h_{PT,RN}|^2) |h_{RN,PR}|^2$. Thus, the optimal $\lambda$ is given by

$$\lambda^* = \begin{cases} \lambda_1 = \frac{D - \sqrt{CD}}{D - C} & \text{if } \lambda_{th} > \lambda_1 \\ \lambda_{th} = \frac{I_{th}}{E + F} & \text{if } \lambda_{th} \leq \lambda_1 \end{cases} \tag{20}$$

**Condition 2.** When $D > C$

With the similar analysis as above, we can obtain the optimal $\lambda$ as

$$\lambda^* = \begin{cases} \lambda_1 = \frac{D - \sqrt{CD}}{D - C} & \text{if } \lambda_{th} > \lambda_1 \\ \lambda_{th} = \frac{I_{th}}{E + F} & \text{if } \lambda_{th} \leq \lambda_1 \end{cases} \tag{21}$$

**Condition 3.** When $D = C$

Obviously, $f(\lambda)$ is a linear function of $\lambda$, and we have

$$f(1) = -2AD + AD = -AD < 0 \tag{22}$$

$$f\left(\frac{1}{2}\right) = -2AD * \frac{1}{2} + AD = 0 \tag{23}$$

$$f(0) = AD > 0 \tag{24}$$

Combining (22), (23), (24) and the constraint $C2$ we can know that $\gamma$ reaches the maximum when $\lambda = \frac{1}{2}$ and for $\lambda < \frac{1}{2}$, $\gamma$ is monotonically increasing with $\lambda$; for $\lambda \geq \frac{1}{2}$, $\gamma$ is monotonically decreasing with $\lambda$. Moreover, we also should consider the constraint $C1$ as above. Thus, the optimal $\lambda$ is given by

$$\lambda^* = \begin{cases} \frac{1}{2} & \text{if } \lambda_{th} > \frac{1}{2} \\ \lambda_{th} = \frac{I_{th}}{E + F} & \text{if } \lambda_{th} \leq \frac{1}{2} \end{cases} \tag{25}$$

From the analyses in Condition 1 to Condition 3, we can know that when $D \neq C$, the optimal $\lambda$ is given by

$$\lambda^* = \begin{cases} \lambda_1 = \frac{D-\sqrt{CD}}{D-C} & \text{if } \lambda_{th} > \lambda_1 \\ \lambda_{th} = \frac{I_{th}}{E+F} & \text{if } \lambda_{th} \leq \lambda_1 \end{cases} \tag{26}$$

When $D = C$, the optimal $\lambda$ is given by

$$\lambda^* = \begin{cases} \frac{1}{2} & \text{if } \lambda_{th} > \frac{1}{2} \\ \lambda_{th} = \frac{I_{th}}{E+F} & \text{if } \lambda_{th} \leq \frac{1}{2} \end{cases} \tag{27}$$

## 4  Simulation Results and Discussion

We assume that the path loss exponent $m = 3$, the distance $d_{SN,RN} + d_{RN,DN} = 2$, $d_{PT,RN} = d_{PT,DN} = d_{SN,PR} = d_{RN,PR} = 2$, the energy harvesting efficiency $\eta = 0.8$, the transmission power of PT $p_p = 2W$ the maximum transmission power of SN is set to $P_{max} = 2W$. For simplicity, the power of noise is set to $\sigma_a^2 = \sigma_b^2 = \sigma_c^2 = 0.01$. Simulation results are generated by averaging 10,000 channel realizations.

Figure 2 shows the throughput of secondary network versus $d_{SN,RN}$ with different $I_{th}$. In Fig. 2, we can observe that there is no performance gap when compared with exhaustive search method. Figure 2 also shows that when RN moves far away to SN, less energy that utilized to help SN forward the information can be harvested at RN, so that the throughput of the secondary network decreases. From Fig. 2, we can observe

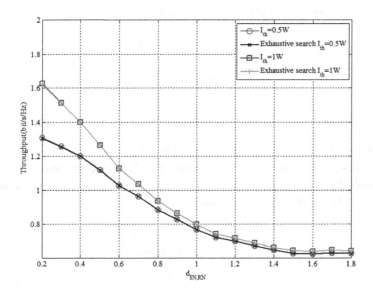

**Fig. 2.** Throughput versus $d_{SN,RN}$.

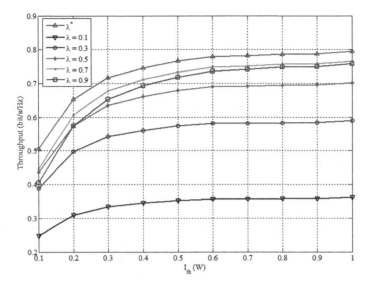

**Fig. 3.** Throughput for different $\lambda$ versus $I_{th}$.

that secondary network obtains larger throughput with larger $I_{th}$ due to PR can allow more interference form the secondary network with larger $I_{th}$, which is also showed in Fig. 3. Figure 3 presents the throughput versus $I_{th}$ with different $\lambda$. The distance $d_{SN,RN}$ is set to be 1. Figure 3 also demonstrates the performance of the optimization, we can find that the throughput of secondary network obtains maximum value with $\lambda^*$.

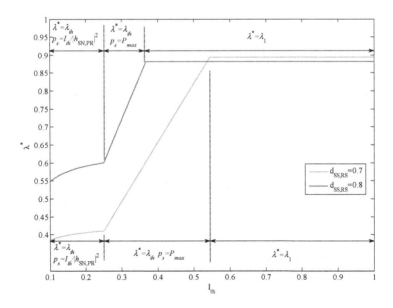

**Fig. 4.** The optimal value of $\lambda$ versus $I_{th}$.

$\lambda^*$ versus $I_{th}$ with different $d_{SN,RN}$ is presented in Fig. 4. First, $I_{th}$ is too small to makes $p_s = \min\left(\dfrac{I_{th}}{\left|h_{SN,PR}\right|^2}, P_{max}\right) = \dfrac{I_{th}}{\left|h_{SN,PR}\right|^2}$, at this point, $\lambda^* = \lambda_{th}$ and $\lambda^*$ increases nonlinearly with $I_{th}$. Then, $I_{th}$ increase and makes $p_s = \min\left(\dfrac{I_{th}}{\left|h_{SN,PR}\right|^2}, P_{max}\right) = P_{max}$, at this point, $\lambda^* = \lambda_{th}$ and $\lambda^*$ increases linearly with $I_{th}$. Finally, $\lambda^*$ will equal to $\lambda_1$ and will no longer change.

## 5  Conclusion

We consider an underlay AF CRNs with SWIPT-enabled secondary relay node and aim to maximize the throughput of the secondary network in considering the interference caused by the transmitted signal of the secondary relay node to PUs as well as PU to secondary network. We derived the closed-form expression of $\lambda^*$ which can obtain the maximum throughput more effectively than the simulation. Moreover, the results show that when RN moves far away to SN, less energy that utilized to help SN forward the information can be harvested at RN, so that the throughput of the secondary network decreases. Our results also demonstrate the performance of the optimization.

## References

1. Wang, J., Ghosh, M., Challapali, K.: Emerging cognitive radio applications: a survey. IEEE Commun. Mag. **49**(3), 74–81 (2011)
2. Haykin, S.: Cognitive radio: brain-empowered wireless communications. IEEE J. Sel. Areas Commun. **23**(2), 201–220 (2005)
3. Wang, B., Liu, K.: Advances in cognitive radio networks: a survey. IEEE J. Sel. Top. Signal Process. **5**(1), 5–23 (2011)
4. Ho, C.K., Zhang, R.: Optimal energy allocation for wireless communications with energy harvesting constraints. IEEE Trans. Signal Process. **60**(9), 4808–4818 (2012)
5. Lu, X., Wang, P., Niyato, D., Kim, D.I., Han, Z.: Wireless networks with RF energy harvesting: a contemporary survey. IEEE Commun. Surveys Tuts. **17**(2), 757–789 (2015)
6. Varshney, L.R.: Transporting information and energy simultaneously. In: Proceedings of IEEE ISIT, pp. 1612–1616 (2008)
7. Zhou, X., Zhang, R., Ho, C.K.: Wireless information and power transfer: architecture design and rate-energy tradeoff. IEEE Trans. Commun. **61**(11), 4754–4767 (2013)
8. Zhang, R., Ho, C.K.: MIMO broadcasting for simultaneous wireless information and power transfer. IEEE Trans. Wirel. Commun. **12**(5), 1989–2001 (2013)
9. Nasir, A.A., Zhou, X., Durrani, S., Kennedy, R.A.: Relaying protocols for wireless energy harvesting and information processing. IEEE Trans. Wirel. Commun. **12**(7), 3622–3636 (2013)
10. Liu, Y., Wang, L., Elkashlan, M., Duong, T.Q., Nallanathan, A.: Two-way relaying networks with wireless power transfer: policies design and throughput analysis. In: Proceedings of IEEE GLOBECOM, pp. 4030–4035 (2014)

11. Lu, X., Wang, P., Niyato, D., Hossain, E.: Dynamic spectrum access in cognitive radio networks with RF energy harvesting. IEEE Wirel. Commun. **21**(3), 102–110 (2014)
12. Im, G., Lee, J.H.: Outage probability of underlay cognitive radio networks with SWIPT-enabled relay. In: IEEE VTC 2015-fall (2015)
13. Singh, S., Modem, S., Prakriya, S.: Optimization of cognitive two-way networks with energy harvesting relays. IEEE Commun. Lett. **21**(6), 1381–1384 (2017)

# Deflection Angle Detection of the Rotor and Signal Processing for a Novel Rotational Gyroscope

Dianzhong Chen and Zhongzhao Zhang$^{(\boxtimes)}$

Communication Research Center, Harbin Institute of Technology,
Harbin 150001, China
dc2el2@163.com, zzzhang@hope.hit.edu.cn

**Abstract.** Differential capacitance detection, a common high resolution proof mass displacement detection scheme, is adopted in the gyroscope to measure the rotor deflection angle by installing an electrode with four poles under the rotor disk, which forms four detection capacitors and opposite ones form a differential capacitance detection pair. Theoretical inference explains the approximately proportional relationship between the capacitance difference and the rotor deflection angle. Simulation in Ansys Maxwell verifies the inference and confirms the differential capacitance detection range of the rotor deflection angle to 0–1°, limited by linearity. A signal processing system is constructed, obtaining a DC output voltage proportional to the measured input angular speed. Experiment shows the fabricated gyroscope with the designed differential capacitance detection pairs exhibits excellent performance with the resolution and the bias stability of 0.1 °/s and 0.5 °/h, respectively.

**Keywords:** Rotational gyroscope · Differential capacitance detection pair

## 1 Introduction

Gyroscope, angular speed sensor, has found applications in areas such as navigation, attitude control of aircraft, stability control systems in cameras, game controllers, automotive electronics, for instance, electronic stability program (ESP) [1]. Vibratory gyroscope and rotational gyroscope are the two main categories, based on Coriolis principle and precessional principle, respectively [2, 3]. The former has inherent problem of cross-talk between drive-mode vibration and sense-mode vibration, which restricts the performance [4, 5]. Small volume rotational gyroscope, mainly including magnetically suspended gyroscopes (MSG) and electrostatically suspended gyroscopes (ESG), with a rotor processing a large moment of inertia, exhibits higher performance than vibratory gyroscope. Researches on rotor suspension structures [3, 6], driving schemes [7, 8], pick up circuits [9, 10] and control electronics [11–14] to MSGs and ESGs have been conducted to improve measurement accuracy. Stability of rotor suspension has become a major constraint for further performance improvement of MSGs and ESGs.

© ICST Institute for Computer Sciences, Social Informatics and Telecommunications Engineering 2018
L. Meng and Y. Zhang (Eds.): MLICOM 2018, LNICST 251, pp. 216–226, 2018.
https://doi.org/10.1007/978-3-030-00557-3_23

To obtain stable rotor support, a contacting low-friction rotor support structure with a water-film bearing is designed in the proposed gyroscope [15]. When sensing an input angular speed, rotor will deflect a certain angle proportional to the angular speed under the act of Coriolis torque, magnetic self-restoring torque and damping torque [16]. Thus, the measurement accuracy of rotor deflection angle is the critical point that determines performance of the gyroscope. Differential capacitance detection is a classic scheme for proof mass displacement measurement and for the proposed gyroscope, rotor deflection angle is detected by four capacitors formed by the rotor disk and four sectorial poles on a detection electrode. Opposite capacitors form a differential capacitance pair and two pairs can measure the rotor deflection angle at any direction of the stator plane (which is also the rotor plane when no input angular speed acts on the gyroscope). The gyroscope structure is illustrated and the operational principle of the proposed gyroscope is explained in Sect. 2. From analysis in Sect. 2, it is known that when sensing an input angular speed, rotor deflects an angle proportional to the angular speed with small amplitude harmonic vibration. Section 3 explains the principle of differential capacitance detection and defines the measurement angle range limited by the linearity of differential capacitance detection through simulation in Ansys Maxwell. Section 4 introduces the signal processing system and in Sect. 5, performance parameters of the gyroscope are tested. Section 6 summarizes the paper.

## 2 Operational Principle of the Gyroscope

### 2.1 Structure Design

The structure of the fabricated gyroscope is illustrated in Fig. 1. Figure 1(a) is a cross-section view by SolidWorks with a top-view of the detection electrode with four poles and Fig. 1(b) is a photograph of the fabricated gyroscope with the upper bronze shell open. Rotor is composed of a ball by stainless steel at the center and a ring-shaped disk by 2J85 grade permanent magnet, magnetized at the parallel direction, glued to the great circle. The diameter of the rotor ball, which is equal with the inner diameter of the rotor disk is 3 mm. The outer diameter and the thickness of the rotor disk are 10.8 mm and 0.5 mm, respectively. The stator, with 12 ring-distributed poles, is of the same thickness with rotor disk. A stable rotating magnetic field is produced by the stator to drive the rotor to a rated spinning speed of 10000 rpm. With no input angular speed acting on (zero state), the rotor disk and the stator are parallel. A detection electrode with four poles is installed to the lower supporting pillar (Fig. 1(a)), parallel to the rotor disk at zero state (with a distance of 100 µm). Each pole and the rotor disk construct a capacitor, and opposite ones compose a differential capacitor pair. Conducting oil is filled in the cavity of the upper supporting pillar and modulation signal $V_{mod}$ (2 V, 15 kHz) is added through the upper supporting pillar, conducting oil, rotor ball to differential capacitor pairs. Two differential capacitor pairs detect the rotor deflection angle at the rotor plane which is perpendicular to the measurand of the input angular speed. For gyroscope, a higher angular momentum ($H$), which is proportional to rotor spinning speed, will produce a larger Coriolis torque under the same input angular speed, thus leading to a larger sensitivity. To obtain a high $H$, a superhydrophobic surface is fabricated on the rotor ball and deionized water is filled in the cavity of the lower supporting pillar to form a water-film bearing under centrifugal force when rotor is actuated. With the rated driving current, steady-state spinning speed of the rotor with a superhydrophobic surface increases 12.4% [15].

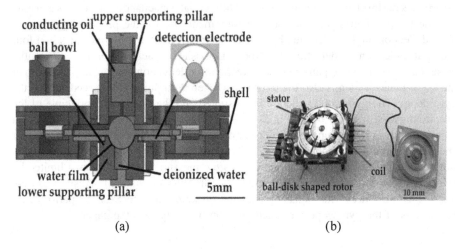

(a)                                        (b)

**Fig. 1.** (a) Cross-section view of the gyroscope; (b) Photograph of the gyroscope.

## 2.2    Sensing of Input Angular Speed

Schematic diagram for dynamics analysis of the gyroscope is as Fig. 2. Stator and rotor are fixed at the coordinates of $X_0Y_0Z_0$ and $XYZ$ (without spinning motion), respectively. When the gyroscope senses an input angular speed at the $X_0Y_0Z_0$ plane, a proportional Coriolis torque $M_G$ will act on the rotor, deflecting the rotor disk off the $X_0Y_0Z_0$ plane. For high relative magnetic permeability of the rotor disk and the stator (silicon steel sheets) compared with air, most of the magnetic energy is within the air gap. Tendency to keep total magnetic energy of the system as lowest produces a magnetic self-restoring torque ($M_c$) proportional to rotor deflection angle ($\varphi$), as inferred in [16]. Damping torque ($M_d$) at the $X_0Y_0$ plane exerted by the water-film bearing to the rotor ball is proportional to rotor precessional angular speed [16]. For high amplitude of $H$, nutation, which is low in amplitude and will attenuate fast, is neglected and dynamic equations for the rotor in the $X_0Y_0$ plane are as below:

$$M_{Gy} + M_{cy} + M_{dy} = \left(H\omega_x - H\dot{\beta}\right) - C_y\alpha - D_y\dot{\alpha} = 0, \qquad (1)$$

$$M_{Gx} + M_{cx} + M_{dx} = \left(-H\omega_y - H\dot{\alpha}\right) + C_x\beta + D_x\dot{\beta} = 0, \qquad (2)$$

where for the symmetrical structure of the gyroscope, letting self-restoring coefficient $C = C_x = C_y = M_c/\varphi$, damping coefficient $D = D_x = D_y = M_d/\omega$. Under step inputs of $\omega_x$, $\omega_y$ with amplitudes of $A_x$, $A_y$, solutions of (1) (2) give:

$$\alpha(t) = \frac{H}{C}A_x + \frac{H}{C}\sqrt{A_x^2 + A_y^2}\,e^{-\frac{CD}{H^2+D^2}t}\sin\left(\frac{CH}{H^2+D^2}t + \varphi + \pi\right), \tag{3}$$

$$\beta(t) = \frac{H}{C}A_y + \frac{H}{C}\sqrt{A_x^2 + A_y^2}\,e^{-\frac{CD}{H^2+D^2}t}\cos\left(\frac{CH}{H^2+D^2}t + \varphi + \pi\right), \tag{4}$$

in which $\varphi = arctan(A_x/A_y)$. (3) (4) reflect dynamic response of the rotor responding to a step angular speed input ($\omega_x$, $\omega_y$) at the $X_0Y_0$ plane. Self-restoring torque ($M_c$) is a periodic restoring torque with the expression of $M_c = (C_1 + C_2\sin(4\pi f t + \psi))\varphi$ ($C_1 = 0.0219$, $C_2 = 0.0083$) [16]. Through inference, taking periodic self-restoring effect into account, expressions (3) (4) can be modified as [16]:

$$\alpha(t) = \frac{H}{C_1}\left(1 + \left(-\frac{C_2}{C_1}\right)\sin(4\pi ft + \psi)\right)\left[A_x + \sqrt{A_x^2 + A_y^2}\,e^{-\frac{C_1 D}{H^2+D^2}t}\sin\left(\frac{C_1 H}{H^2+D^2}t + \phi + \pi\right)\right], \tag{5}$$

$$\beta(t) = \frac{H}{C_1}\left(1 + \left(-\frac{C_2}{C_1}\right)\sin(4\pi ft + \psi)\right)\left[A_y + \sqrt{A_x^2 + A_y^2}\,e^{-\frac{C_1 D}{H^2+D^2}t}\cos\left(\frac{C_1 H}{H^2+D^2}t + \phi + \pi\right)\right], \tag{6}$$

in which $C_2/C_1 = 0.0083/0.0219 = 0.379$, $f$ (167 Hz) is the driving frequency. Expressions (5) (6) indicate that the rotor will spiral at the angular speed of $C_1 H/(H^2 + D^2)$ with the radius attenuation rate of $C_1 D/(H^2 + D^2)$, to a dynamic equilibrium position of ($\alpha = HA_x/C_1$, $\beta = HA_y/C_1$) with harmonic angular vibration at the frequency of $2f$ within the range of $C_2 H/C_1^2$. Thus, it can be concluded that dynamic equilibrium deflection angles $\alpha$, $\beta$ are proportional to measurands of input angular speeds $\omega_x$, $\omega_y$.

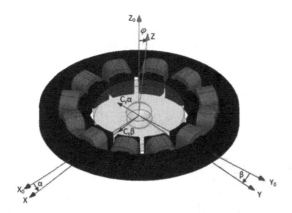

**Fig. 2.** Schematic diagram for dynamics analysis of the gyroscope.

## 3   Deflection Angle Detection by Differential Capacitance Pairs

Capacitive detection is adopted in the design and four poles on the electrode under the rotor disk form four capacitors with the disk. Two capacitors in $X_0$ or $Y_0$ direction form a detection pair. The detection schematic diagram is shown in Fig. 3. The inner radius $R_i$, outer radius $R_o$ of the sector pole are the inner and outer radii of the rotor disk. The central angle of one pole, the distance between the pole and the rotor are set as $2\theta_0$ and $h$. When the rotor deflect an angle of small value $\vec{\varphi} = \alpha\vec{Y} + \beta\vec{X}$, letting $g(\theta) = \alpha\cos\theta + \beta\sin\theta$, the expression of $C_{X+}$ and $C_{X-}$ are:

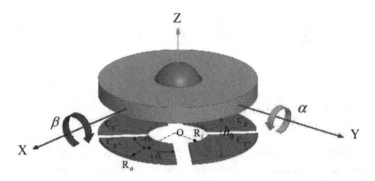

**Fig. 3.**  Capacitive detection schematic diagram.

$$C_{X^+} = \varepsilon \int_{-\theta_0}^{\theta_0} \int_{R_i}^{R_o} \frac{r d\theta dr}{h_0 - rg(\theta)} = \varepsilon \int_{-\theta_0}^{\theta_0} \left[ \frac{R_o - R_i}{-g(\theta)} - \frac{h_0}{g^2(\theta)} \ln \frac{h_0 - R_o g(\theta)}{h_0 - R_i g(\theta)} \right] d\theta, \quad (7)$$

$$C_{X^-} = \varepsilon \int_{-\theta_0}^{\theta_0} \int_{R_i}^{R_o} \frac{r d\theta dr}{h_0 + rg(\theta)} = \varepsilon \int_{-\theta_0}^{\theta_0} \left[ \frac{R_o - R_i}{g(\theta)} - \frac{h_0}{g^2(\theta)} \ln \frac{h_0 + R_o g(\theta)}{h_0 + R_i g(\theta)} \right] d\theta. \quad (8)$$

Expanding expressions (7) (8) with Taloy's series gives:

$$C_{X^+} = \varepsilon \int_{-\theta_0}^{\theta_0} \sum_{n=2}^{\infty} \frac{R_o^n - R_i^n}{n h_0^{n-1}} g^{n-2}(\theta) d\theta$$

$$= \varepsilon \left[ \frac{\theta_0 (R_o^2 - R_i^2)}{h_0} + \frac{R_o^3 - R_i^3}{3 h_0^2} \int_{-\theta_0}^{\theta_0} g(\theta) d\theta + \frac{R_o^4 - R_i^4}{4 h_0^3} \int_{-\theta_0}^{\theta_0} g^2(\theta) d\theta + \dots \right], \quad (9)$$

$$C_{X^-} = \varepsilon \int_{-\theta_0}^{\theta_0} \sum_{n=2}^{\infty} (-1)^n \frac{R_o^n - R_i^n}{n h_0^{n-1}} g^{n-2}(\theta) d\theta$$

$$= \varepsilon \left[ \frac{\theta_0 (R_o^2 - R_i^2)}{h_0} + \frac{R_o^3 - R_i^3}{3 h_0^2} \int_{-\theta_0}^{\theta_0} g(\theta) d\theta + \frac{R_o^4 - R_i^4}{4 h_0^3} \int_{-\theta_0}^{\theta_0} g^2(\theta) d\theta - \dots \right]. \quad (10)$$

For $\alpha$, $\beta$ are of small values and $g(\theta) = \alpha cos\theta + \beta sin\theta$, items with integration of high orders of $g(\theta)$ are omitted. Then, Eqs. (9), (10) become:

$$C_{X^+} = \frac{\varepsilon\theta_0\left(R_o^2 - R_i^2\right)}{h_0} + \frac{\varepsilon\left(R_o^3 - R_i^3\right)}{3h_0^2}\int_{-\theta_0}^{\theta_0} g(\theta)d\theta = C_{X_0^+} + \frac{2\alpha\varepsilon\left(R_o^3 - R_i^3\right)sin\theta_0}{3h_0^2},$$

(11)

$$C_{X^-} = \frac{\varepsilon\theta_0\left(R_o^2 - R_i^2\right)}{h_0} - \frac{\varepsilon\left(R_o^3 - R_i^3\right)}{3h_0^2}\int_{-\theta_0}^{\theta_0} g(\theta)d\theta = C_{X_0^-} - \frac{2\alpha\varepsilon\left(R_o^3 - R_i^3\right)sin\theta}{3h_0^2}, \quad (12)$$

where $C_{X_0^+}$, $C_{X_0^-}$ are the initial capacitance of $C_{X^+}$, $C_{X^-}$ at zero state. Though the expressions of the two initial capacitance are the same, fabrication and assembling errors will cause inequality between them and the right expression in (11) and (12) are more accurate. Therefore, the changed capacitance caused by rotation angles of $\alpha$ and $\beta$ are:

$$\Delta C_{X^+} = C_{X^+} - C_{X_0^+} = \frac{2\varepsilon\left(R_o^3 - R_i^3\right)sin\theta_0}{3h_0^2}\alpha = G_d\alpha \qquad (13)$$

$$\Delta C_{X^-} = C_{X^-} - C_{X_0^-} = -\frac{2\varepsilon\left(R_o^3 - R_i^3\right)sin\theta_0}{3h_0^2}\alpha = -G_d\alpha \qquad (14)$$

The coefficient of $G_d$ is the amplification factor of differential capacitance. From expressions (13) and (14), it can be pointed out that the changed capacitance $\Delta C_{X^+}$ and $\Delta C_{X^-}$ are proportional to angle $\alpha$ and irrespective to $\beta$. The conclusion is based on the precondition that $\alpha$, $\beta$ are of small values and high order items in (9) and (10) are omitted. To identify the rotor deflection angle range, within which errors of linear approximation in (11) (12) are acceptable, capacitance differences between $C_{X^+}$ and $C_{X^-}$ under rotate_Y_angle ($\alpha$) range of 0°–2° are simulated in ANSYS Maxwell (Fig. 4). It can be seen that the linearity of differential capacitance deteriorates with the increase of rotor deflection angle and the range of rotor deflection angle is limited to 0°–1°.

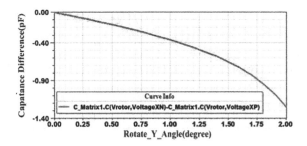

**Fig. 4.** Capacitance difference between $C_{X^+}$ and $C_{X^-}$ under rotate_Y_angle ($\alpha$) from 0° to 2°.

## 4  Differential Signal Processing

To detect the capacitive change, a high frequency sinusoidal modulation signal $V_{mod}$ (2 V, 15 kHz) is added to four capacitors through the rotor ball. Circuit through $C_X$ pair ($C_{X+}$ and $C_{X-}$) or $C_Y$ pair ($C_{Y+}$ and $C_{Y-}$) is induced to differential amplifier circuit. Proportional amplifier circuit is applied to amplify the signal to an appropriate amplitude. The signal detection block diagram is shown in Fig. 5. The processing system for $C_X$ pair and $C_Y$ pair are the same and the following derivation takes $C_X$ pair, which senses X axis input angular speed, for example. In the circuit, resisters $R_1$, $R_2$, $R_3$, $R_4$ satisfy:

$$\frac{R_2}{R_1} = \frac{R_4}{R_3} = G_{op3}. \tag{15}$$

$C_{f+}$ and $C_{f-}$ are adjusted to satisfy:

$$\frac{C_{X_0^+}}{C_{f+}} = \frac{C_{X_0^-}}{C_{f-}}, \tag{16}$$

so that the zero state output voltage is zero. Then the output signal before HPF is:

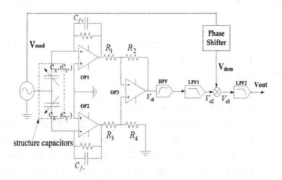

**Fig. 5.**  Signal detection and processing system.

$$V_{o1} = G_{op3}V_{mod}\left(\frac{C_{X+}}{C_{f+}} - \frac{C_{X-}}{C_{f-}}\right) = G_{op3}V_{mod}\left(\frac{C_{X_0^+} + \Delta C_{X+}}{C_{f+}} - \frac{C_{X_0^-} + \Delta C_{X-}}{C_{f-}}\right) \tag{17}$$

Taking (13), (14), (16) into (17), the following equation can be derived:

$$V_{o1} = G_{op3}V_{mod}G_d\alpha\left(\frac{1}{C_{f+}} + \frac{1}{C_{f-}}\right) \tag{18}$$

Equation (18) reveals that an AC output voltage of, proportional to rotational angle $\alpha$, is obtained. High pass filter (HPF) after $V_{o1}$ filters out low frequency offset drift and 1/f noise first. Then low pass filter 1 (LPF1) filters out modulated signal of high frequency mechanical vibration (indicated in (5) and (6)) and nutation, obtaining $V_{o2}$. Afterwards, $V_{o2}$ is demodulated by multiplier. Set the expression of $V_{o2}$ as:

$$V_{o2} = GV_{mod}\alpha = G\alpha V_m \cos(\omega_c t + \varphi_0),  \tag{19}$$

where $G = G_{op3}G_d\left(\frac{1}{C_{f+}} + \frac{1}{C_{f-}}\right)$, $V_m$ is the amplitude of $V_{mod}$ and $\omega_c$ is the angular frequency of $V_{mod}$. Demodulation signal $V_{dem}$ after phase shifter is expressed as $V_m \cos(\omega_c t + \varphi_1)$. Then, $V_{o3}$ is:

$$\begin{aligned} V_{o3} &= V_{o2} \times V_{dem} = G\alpha V_m \cos(\omega_c t + \varphi_0) \times V_m \cos(\omega_c t + \varphi_1) \\ &= 0.5GV_m^2\alpha[\cos(2\omega_c t + \varphi_0 + \varphi_1) + \cos(\varphi_0 - \varphi_1)] \end{aligned}  \tag{20}$$

It reveals that $V_{o3}$ is composed of a DC signal, amplitude of which is sensitive to phase difference between $V_{o2}$ and $V_{dem}$, and an AC signal with the frequency of $\omega_c/\pi$. In the experiment, phase shifter is adjusted until maximum DC offset signal in $V_{o3}$ is obtained. Finally, AC component in $V_{o3}$ is filtered by LPF2, and $V_{out}$ is a DC signal proportional to rotor deflection angle $\alpha$ in amplitude.

## 5   Measurement and Discussion

To observe the spectral characteristic of $V_{out}$, cut-off frequency of LPF2 is set as 50 Hz initially. Spectral analysis result is as Fig. 6, in which, 12 Hz, 167 Hz ($f$), 334 Hz ($2f$) components are observed. Parameters $C_1$, $D$ have been identified through curve fitting in [16] to be 0.02017, $2.971 \times 10^{-5}$, respectively, and H (under rated driving speed of 10000 rpm) is calculated to be $2.784 \times 10^{-4}$. Then, rotor spiraling rate $(C_1H/(2\pi(H^2 + D^2)))$ indicated in expressions (5) (6) is calculated to be 11.4 Hz, which accounts for the first peak of spectral density in Fig. 6. It is analyzed in Sect. 2.2 that the rotor will vibrate at frequency $2f$ during precessional motion, which accounts for the third peak of spectral density in Fig. 6. Spectral component of the second peak ($f$) derives from asymmetrical fabrication error, which brings mechanical vibration at the driving frequency ($f$). To filter out these noises (12 Hz, 167 Hz, 334 Hz), cut-off frequency of LPF2 is set as 10 Hz finally. For LPF, a lower cut-off frequency will cause a longer response delay, thus increasing response time of the gyroscope.

Performance parameter test is conducted by putting the proposed gyroscope on a rate table. Input angular speeds within the measurement range of $-30$ °/s to 30 °/s (limited by the non-linearity of differential capacitance detection) with 5° intervals are given and output voltages are linear fitted in Matlab (Fig. 7(a)). Sensitivity and non-linearity within the measurement range are identified as 0.0985 V/(°/s) and 0.43%, respectively. Responses to exponentially-distributed input angular speeds from $-0.00625$ °/s to $-1.6$ °/s are tested and marked in Fig. 7(a). Analysis to these data reveals that the resolution of the gyroscope is 0.1 °/s. Bias stability test is done to the

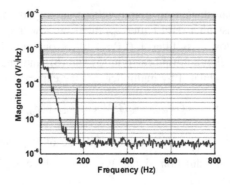

**Fig. 6.** Spectral density of $V_{out}$.

gyroscope (testing outputs of the gyroscope under 0 input angular speed) for half an hour. Allan derivation curve is plotted as Fig. 7(b), which identifies the bias stability to be 0.5 °/h.

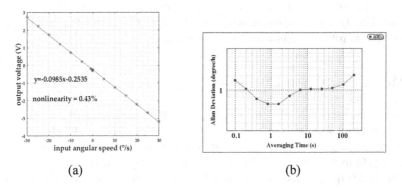

(a)                                                        (b)

**Fig. 7.** (a) Input-out characteristic of the proposed gyroscope; (b) Allan deviation curve.

## 6   Conclusions

Differential capacitance detection is adopted in the proposed rotational gyroscope with a specially designed ball-disk shaped rotor. A detection electrode with four sectorial poles is installed under the rotor disk to form 2 differential capacitance detection pairs, measuring the rotor deflection angle at the direction of the stator plane. Through theoretical inference, it is known that, firstly, capacitance difference of opposite detection capacitors (a differential capacitance detection pair) is approximately proportional to the rotor deflection angle at the perpendicular direction; and secondly, linear relationship of differential capacitance to rotor deflection angle deteriorates with the increase of the angle. Through simulation in Ansys Maxwell, non-linearity is acceptable when rotor deflection angle is within 1°, which restricts gyroscope measurement range to −30 °/s–30 °/s. A modulation signal (2 V, 15 kHz) is added to differential capacitors to obtain an AC signal, proportional to the rotor deflection angle in amplitude. By multiplying the modulation signal after a phase shifter, AC signal is demodulated and a proportional output DC signal ($V_{out}$) is obtained, finally. Through spectral analysis, cut-off frequency of LPF before $V_{out}$ is confirmed as 10 Hz. Gyroscope performance parameters of sensitivity, non-linearity, resolution, and bias stability are tested to be 0.0985 V/(°/s), 0.43%, 0.1 °/s, 0.5 °/h, respectively.

**Acknowledgement.** The work presented in this paper was supported by National Nature Science Foundation of China under Grant No. 91438205.

# References

1. Saukoski, M., Aaltonen, L., Salo, T., Halonen, K.A.I.: Interface and control electronics for a bulk micromachined capacitive gyroscope. Sens. Actuators A **147**(1), 183–193 (2008)
2. Liu, K., et al.: The development of micro-gyroscope technology. J. Micromech. Microeng. **19**, 113001 (2009)
3. Xia, D., Yu, C., Kong, L.: The development of micromachined gyroscope structure and circuitry technology. Sensors **14**, 1394–1473 (2014)
4. Saukoski, M., Aaltonen, L., Halonen, K.A.I.: Zero-rate output and quadrature compensation in vibratory MEMS gyroscopes. IEEE Sens. J. **7**, 1639–1651 (2007)
5. Elsayed, M., Nabki, F., Sawan, M., El-Gamal, M.: A 5 V MEMS gyroscope with 3 aF/°/s sensitivity, 0.6°/√hr mechanical noise and drive-sense crosstalk minimization. In: Proceedings of the 2011 International Conference on Microelectronics (ICM), Hammamet, Tunisia, 19–22 December 2011, pp. 1–5 (2011)
6. Cui, F., Liu, W., Chen, W.-Y., Zhang, W.-P., Wu, X.-S.: Hybrid microfabrication and 5-DOF levitation of micromachined electrostatically suspended gyroscope. Electron. Lett. **47**, 976–978 (2011)
7. Wu, H.M., Yang, H.G., Yin, T., Zhang, H.: Stability analysis of MEMS gyroscope drive loop based on CPPLL. In: Proceedings of the 2011 Asia Pacific Conference on Microelectronics and Electronics, Macao, China, 6–7 October 2011, pp. 45–48 (2011)
8. Mo, B., Liu, X.W., Ding, X.W., Tan, X.Y.: A novel closed-loop drive circuit for the micromechined gyroscope. In: Proceedings of the 2007 IEEE International Conference on Mechatronics and Automation, Harbin, China, 5–8 August 2007, pp. 3384–3390 (2007)
9. Feng, L.H., Zhang, Z.X., Sun, Y.N., Cui, F.: Differential pickup circuit design of a kind of Z-axis MEMS quartz Gyroscope. Procedia Eng. **15**, 999–1003 (2011)
10. Fang, R., et al.: A control and readout circuit with capacitive mismatch auto-compensation for MEMS vibratory gyroscope. In: Proceedings of the 11th IEEE International Conference on Solid-State and Integrated Circuit Technology (ICSICT), Xi'an, China, 29 October–1 November 2012, pp. 1–3 (2012)
11. Aaltonerr, L., Halonen, K.A.I.: An analog drive loop for a capacitive MEMS gyroscope. Analog. Integr. Circuit Signal **63**, 465–476 (2010)
12. Cui, J., Chi, X.Z., Ding, H.T., Lin, L.T., Yang, Z.C., Yan, G.Z.: Transient response and stability of the AGC-PI closed-loop controlled MEMS vibratory gyroscopes. J. Micromech. Microeng. **12**, 1–17 (2009)
13. Yang, B., Zhou, B.L., Wang, S.R.: A precision closed-loop driving scheme of silicon micromachined vibratory gyroscope. J. Phys: Conf. Ser. **34**, 57–64 (2006)

14. Xiao, Q., Luo, Z.: Initial levitation of micromachined electrostatically suspended gyroscope with fuzzy hybrid PI controller. In: Proceedings of the International Conference on Control, Automation, Robotics & Vision, Phuket, Thailand, 13–15 November 2016 (2016)
15. Chen, D., et al.: Friction reduction for a rotational gyroscope with mechanical support by fabrication of a biomimetic superhydrophobic surface on a ball-disk shaped rotor and the application of a water film bearing. Micromachines **8**, 223 (2017)
16. Chen, D., et al.: A rotational gyroscope with a water-film bearing based on magnetic self-restoring effect. Sensors **18**(2), 415 (2018)

# Intelligent Internet of Things

# Reusing Wireless Power Transfer for Backscatter-Assisted Cooperation in WPCN

Wanran Xu$^{(\boxtimes)}$, Suzhi Bi, Xiaohui Lin, and Juan Wang

College of Information Engineering, Shenzhen University,
Shenzhen 518060, Guangdong, China
{xuwanran2016,bsz,xhlin,juanwang}@szu.edu.cn

**Abstract.** This paper studies a novel user cooperation method in a wireless powered communication network (WPCN), where a pair of closely located devices first harvest wireless energy from an energy node (EN) and then use the harvested energy to transmit information to an access point (AP). In particular, we consider the two energy-harvesting users exchanging their messages and then transmitting cooperatively to the AP using space-time block codes. Interestingly, we exploit the short distance between the two users and allow the information exchange to be achieved by energy-conserving backscatter technique. Meanwhile the considered backscatter-assisted method can effectively reuse wireless power transfer for simultaneous information exchange during the energy harvesting phase. Specifically, we maximize the common throughput through optimizing the time allocation on energy and information transmission. Simulation results show that the proposed user cooperation scheme can effectively improve the throughput fairness compared to some representative benchmark methods.

## 1 Introduction

Wireless device battery life has always been a key problem in modern wireless communication. Frequent battery replacement/recharging may bring lots of inconvenience and cause high probability of communication interruption. To overcome the above difficulties, RF-enabled wireless energy transfer (WET) technique has recently drawn greater attention [1–3], which can charge wireless devices with continuous and stable energy through the air.

One useful application of WET is wireless powered communication network (WPCN) [4–10], where wireless devices (WDs) transmit information using the energy harvested from energy node. Specifically, [4] proposed a harvest-then-transmit protocol in WPCN where one hybrid access point (HAP) with single-antenna first broadcasts energy to all users, then allows users to take turns to perform wireless information transmission (WIT). [5] studied the placement optimization when each pair of EN and AP is colocated and integrated as a hybrid access point. However, all the above works consider using a HAP for

© ICST Institute for Computer Sciences, Social Informatics and Telecommunications Engineering 2018
L. Meng and Y. Zhang (Eds.): MLICOM 2018, LNICST 251, pp. 229–239, 2018.
https://doi.org/10.1007/978-3-030-00557-3_24

performing both WET and WIT. This WPCN model will inevitable suffered from a so-called "doubly near-far" problem, such that the far user can receive less wireless power than the near user, but needs to consume more energy to transmit information for achieving the same communication performance.

To enhance user fairness, [11] proposed a two-user cooperation scheme where the near user helps relay the far user's information to the HAP. [12] considered a cluster-based user cooperation in a WPCN with a multi-antenna HAP. However, using a single HAP is the essential cause of the user unfairness problem. To further enhance system performance, [13] considered using separate EN and information AP. Specifically, the WDs first harvest energy from the EN and then use distributed Alamouti code to jointly transmit their information to the AP. Thanks to the achieved cooperative diversity gain, the cooperation scheme can effectively improve the throughput performance. However, the two WDs may need to consume considerable amount of energy and time on information exchange, which may constrain the overall communication performance of the energy-constrained devices.

Besides, a newly emerged low-cost ambient backscatter (AB) communication technique provides an alternative method to reduce such cooperation system's overhead [14–16]. Specifically, AB allows WDs to transmit information by passively backscatter environment RF signals, e.g., WiFi and cellular signals, in the neighbouring area. Several recent works have focused on improving the data rates of AB, such as applying new signal detection methods and more advanced backscattering circuit designs [15,16]. However, due to the dependency on time-varying environment RF signals, backscatter technology suffers many problems, e.g., sensitive to transmission distance and uncontrollable transmissions.

In this paper, we present a novel user cooperation method assisted by backscatter in WPCN. As shown in Fig. 1, we consider a similar setup in [13], where two devices first harvest WET from the HAP and then transmit jointly to the AP by forming a virtual antenna array. However, unlike the conventional information exchange in [13], we allow the two closely-located WDs to use backscatter communication to exchange their messages in a passive manner during the WET stage. The key contributions of this passage are summarized as follows:

1. We propose a novel user cooperation method assisted by backscatter communication during the information exchange stage. By reusing the WET signal, the proposed method can achieve simultaneous energy harvesting and information exchange, and thus potentially improves the throughput performance of the energy-constrained system.
2. We derive the individual throughput of the two WDs for the proposed backscatter-assisted cooperation method, and formulate an optimization problem that maximizes the minimum data rates (common throughput) between the two users. By optimizing the time allocation on WET and WIT, we can effectively enhance the throughput fairness of the system.
3. We show that the throughput maximization problem can be cast as a convex optimization, such that its optimum can be efficiently obtained. By comparing

with some representative benchmark methods, we show that the proposed backscatter-assisted cooperation can effectively improve the throughput performance under various practical network setups.

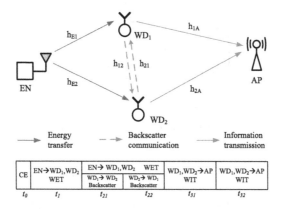

**Fig. 1.** The proposed user cooperation method and operating protocol.

## 2  System Model

### 2.1  Channel Model

As shown in Fig. 1, we consider a WPCN consisting of an EN, two WDs, and an information AP, where all the devices have single antenna each. The EN is assumed to have stable energy supply and able to broadcast RF energy at constant power $P_0$. Besides, it has a time-division-duplexing (TDD) circuit structure to switch between energy transfer and communication, e.g., for performing channel estimation. The two WDs have no other embedded energy source thus need to harvest RF energy for performing information transmission to the AP.

The circuit block diagram of a WD is shown in Fig. 2. With the two switches $S_1$ and $S_2$, a WD can switch flexibly among three operating modes as follows.

1. *RF (active) communication mode* $(S_1 = 0)$: the antenna is connected to the RF communication circuit and WD is able to transmit or receive information using conventional RF wireless communication techniques, e.g., QAM modulation and coherent detection.
2. *energy harvesting mode* $(S_1 = 1$ and $S_2$ is open): the antenna is connected to the energy harvesting circuit, which can convert the received RF signal to DC energy and store in a rechargeable battery. The energy is used to power the operations of all the other circuits.
3. *backscatter (passive) communication mode* $(S_1=1$ and $S_2$ is closed): the antenna is connected to backscatter communication and energy harvesting

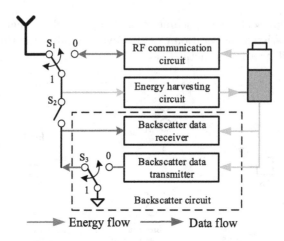

**Fig. 2.** Circuit block diagram of the RF-powered backscatter wireless device.

circuits. In this case, the WD transmits information passively by backscattering the received signal. Specifically, by setting the switch $S_3 = 0$, the impedance-matching circuit absorbs most of the received signal such that a "0" is transmitted; otherwise when $S_3 = 1$, due to the imbalance of transmission line impedance, the received signal is reflected and broadcasted by the antenna such that a "1" is transmitted. Meanwhile, non-coherent detection techniques, e.g., energy detector [17], can be used to decode backscatter transmissions from other devices.

Notice that a WD can harvest RF energy simultaneously when the backscatter circuit transmits or receives information. Specifically, as shown in Fig. 3, a power splitter is used to split the received RF signal into two parts. We denote the portion of signal power for backscatter communication by $(1 - \beta)$, where $\beta \in [0, 1]$, and the rest $\beta$ for energy harvesting (EH). The received signal is corrupted by an additive noise $N_0 \sim \mathcal{CN}(0, \sigma_0^2)$ at the receiver antenna. Besides, the power splitting circuit and the information decoding circuit are also introduced by an additional noise $N_s \sim \mathcal{CN}(0, \sigma_s^2)$, which is assumed independent of the antenna noise $N_0$. As a result, the equivalent noise power for information decoding is $(1 - \beta)\sigma_0^2 + \sigma_s^2$. The value of $\beta$ can be adjusted according to different receive signal power and is assumed constant for the time being.

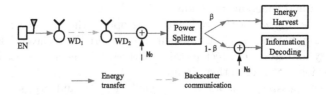

**Fig. 3.** The power splitter structure used during backscatter communication

Evidently, backscatter communication does not need to generate RF carrier signals locally and insteads using simple energy encoding/decoding circuits, thus is more energy-efficient than conventional active wireless communication. However, its application is often limited by the strength of the ambient RF signal and its short communication range (within a couple of meters) due to the weak signal strength after reflection. In the following, we propose a method to reuse WET to achieve controllable backscatter communication in WPCN.

## 2.2 Protocol Description

We consider a block fading channel model where all the channels are reciprocal and the channel gains remain constant during each transmission block of duration $T$. At the beginning of a transmission block channel estimation (CE) is performed within a fixed duration $t_0$. Then, a three-stage operating protocol is used in the remainder of a tagged transmission block, as shown in Fig. 1. Specifically, in the second stage, the EN continuous to broadcast energy for $t_2$ amount of time, during which the $WD_1$ and $WD_2$ take turns to backscatter their local information for $t_{21}$ and $t_{22}$ amount of time, respectively, where $t_2 = t_{21} + t_{22}$. With the power splitter structure in Fig. 3, each of the two WDs can decode information from the other's transmission and harvest RF energy simultaneously. Notice that we neglect the backscatter signal received by the AP due to the much larger distance separation between a WD and the AP in practice. In the third stage of length $t_3$, the two users transmit jointly their information to the AP. Specially, $t_{31}$ amount of time is allocated to transmit user $WD_1$'s information, and the rest of $t_{32}$ is for transmitting $WD_2$'s information. Accordingly, we have a total time constraint

$$t_0 + t_1 + t_{21} + t_{22} + t_{31} + t_{32} = T. \tag{1}$$

For convenience, we normalize $T = 1$ in the sequel without loss of generality.

We denote the complex channel coefficient between $WD_1$ and $WD_2$ as $\alpha_{12}$. Similarly, the other channel coefficients are denoted as $\alpha_{E1}$, $\alpha_{E2}$, $\alpha_{1A}$, $\alpha_{2A}$, $\alpha_{21}$. In the CE stage, user $WD_1$ and $WD_2$ broadcast their pilot signals, so that EN has the knowledge of $\alpha_{E1}$ and $\alpha_{E2}$, the AP knows $\alpha_{1A}$ and $\alpha_{2A}$, and user $WD_1$ ($WD_2$) knows $\alpha_{12}$ ($\alpha_{21}$) respectively. Then, each node feeds back their known CSI to a control point, which calculates and broadcasts the optimal time allocation $(t_1^*, t_{21}^*, t_{22}^*, t_{31}^*, t_{32}^*)$ to all the nodes in the network.

# 3    System Performance Analysis

## 3.1    Derivation of Individual Data Rate

During the WET phase, we denote the baseband equivalent pseudo-random energy signal transmitted by the EN as $x(t)$ with $E[|x(t)|^2] = 1$. The received signal at $WD_i$, $i = 1, 2$, is then expressed as

$$y_i^{(1)}(t) = \sqrt{P_0}\alpha_{Ei}x(t) + n_i(t), \tag{2}$$

where $n_i(t)$ denotes the receiver noise at $WD_i$ with $n_i(t) \sim \mathcal{CN}(0, N_0)$. It is assumed that $P_0$ is sufficiently large such that the energy harvested due to the receiver noise is negligible. Hence, the amount of energy harvested by $WD_1$ and $WD_2$ can be expressed as

$$E_1^{(1)} = P_0 \eta h_{E1} t_1, \quad E_2^{(1)} = P_0 \eta h_{E2} t_1, \tag{3}$$

where $0 < \eta < 1$ denotes the energy harvesting efficiency coefficient.

In the backscattering stage, $WD_1$ first transmits its information to $WD_2$ for $t_{21}$ amount of time. We assume a fixed data transmission rate $R_b$ bit/s, thus the duration of transmitting a bit is $1/R_b$ s. In particular, when $WD_1$ transmits a bit 0, the switch 3 is open, and $WD_2$ receives only the energy signal from the HAP and $WD_1$. Otherwise, when $WD_1$ transmits a bit 1, the received signal at $WD_2$ is a combination of both the HAP's energy and the reflected signal from $WD_1$. Those signals can be jointly expressed as

$$y_2^{(2)}(t) = \alpha_{E2} \sqrt{P_0} x(t) + B \mu_1 \alpha_{E1} \alpha_{12} \sqrt{P_0} x(t) + n_2^{(2)}(t), \tag{4}$$

where $\mu_1$ denotes the backscatter reflection coefficient of $WD_1$, and $B$ denotes the information bit transmitted by $WD_1$ through backscattering. Due to the use of the power splitter at each user, the energy and information signals received by $WD_2$ can be respectively expressed as

$$y_{2,E}^{(2)}(t) = \sqrt{\beta} y_2^{(2)}(t), \quad y_{2,I}^{(2)}(t) = \sqrt{(1-\beta)} y_2^{(2)}(t). \tag{5}$$

It is assumed that the probabilities of transmitting 0 and 1 are equal. Therefore the harvested energy by $WD_2$ can be expressed as

$$E_2^{(2)} = \frac{1}{2} \eta \beta t_{21} (E[|y_{2,0}^{(2)}(t)|^2] + E[|y_{2,1}^{(2)}(t)|^2])$$

$$= \eta \beta t_{21} P_0 [h_{E2} + \mu_1 \alpha_{E1} \alpha_{E2} \alpha_{12} + \frac{1}{2} \mu_1^2 h_{E1} h_{12}]. \tag{6}$$

Notice in (4), we assume that the signals received directly from the HAP and that reflected from $WD_1$ are uncorrelated due to the random phase change during backscatter. We denote the sampling rate of $WD_2$'s backscatter receiver as $S$, such that it sampled $N = \frac{S}{R_b}$ samples during the transmission of a bit information, where $R_b$ denotes the fixed backscatter rate in bits per second. In the following lemma, we derive the bit error rate (BER) of a backscatter receiver using an optimal energy detector.

*Lemma 3.1:* The BER of $WD_2$ for the considered backscatter communication with an optimal energy detector is

$$P_{e2} = \frac{1}{2} erfc \left[ \frac{(1-\beta) P_0 \sqrt{N}}{4(1-\beta)\sigma_0^2 + 4\sigma_s^2} (\mu_1^2 h_{E1} h_{12}) \right]. \tag{7}$$

*Proof*: The proof is omitted here due to the space limitation.

As the backscatter communication can be modeled as a binary symmetric channel, the channel capacity (in bit per channel use) of the transmission from $WD_1$ to $WD_2$ can be expressed as

$$C_2 = 1 + (1 - P_{e2}) \log_2 (1 - P_{e2}) + P_{e2} \log_2 (P_{e2}). \tag{8}$$

By symmetry, we can get the BER and channel capacity from $WD_2$ to $WD_1$ as $P_{e1}$ and $C_1$, where

$$P_{e1} = \frac{1}{2} erfc \left[ \frac{(1 - \beta)P_0\sqrt{N}}{4(1 - \beta)\sigma_0^2 + 4\sigma_s^2} (\mu_2^2 h_{E2} h_{21}) \right], \tag{9}$$

$$C_1 = 1 + (1 - P_{e1}) \log_2 (1 - P_{e1}) + P_{e1} \log_2 (P_{e1}). \tag{10}$$

As a result, the communication rates of $WD_1$ and $WD_2$ in this stage can be expressed as function of time allocation $\mathbf{t} = [t_0, t_1, t_{21}, t_{22}, t_{31}, t_{32}]$

$$R_1^{(2)}(\mathbf{t}) = R_b t_{21} C_2, \quad R_2^{(2)}(\mathbf{t}) = R_b t_{22} C_1. \tag{11}$$

In the last WIT stage, we assume that both user $WD_1$ and $WD_2$ exhaust the harvested energy, and each transmits with a constant power. Then, the transmit powers of $WD_1$ and $WD_2$ is

$$P_1 = \frac{E_1^{(1)} + E_1^{(2)}}{t_3}, \quad P_2 = \frac{E_2^{(1)} + E_2^{(2)}}{t_3}, \tag{12}$$

where $t_3 = t_{31} + t_{32}$. In this stage, the two users use Alamouti STBC transmit diversity scheme [13] for joint information transmission with $t_{31} = t_{32}$, where the achievable data rates from user $WD_1$ to AP is

$$R_1^{(3)}(\mathbf{t}) = \frac{t_3}{2} \log_2(1 + \frac{P_1 h_{1A}}{\sigma_0^2} + \frac{P_2 h_{2A}}{\sigma_0^2}). \tag{13}$$

Likewise, we have $R_1^{(3)}(\mathbf{t}) = R_2^{(3)}(\mathbf{t})$ for user $WD_2$.

### 3.2   Common Throughput Maximization

With the considered cooperation scheme, the overall achievable date rates of user $WD_1$ and $WD_2$ are

$$R_1(\mathbf{t}) = \min \left\{ R_1^{(2)}(\mathbf{t}), R_1^{(3)}(\mathbf{t}) \right\}, \quad R_2(\mathbf{t}) = \min \left\{ R_2^{(2)}(\mathbf{t}), R_2^{(3)}(\mathbf{t}) \right\}. \tag{14}$$

In this paper, we focus on maximizing the common throughput (max-min throughput) of two users by jointly optimizing the time allocated to the HAP, $WD_1$ and $WD_2$.

$$(P1) : \max_{\mathbf{t}} \min \left( R_1(\mathbf{t}), R_2(\mathbf{t}) \right)$$
$$\text{s. t. } t_0 + t_1 + t_{21} + t_{22} + t_{31} + t_{32} = 1, \tag{15}$$
$$t_1, t_{21}, t_{22}, t_{31}, t_{32} \geq 0.$$

By introducing an auxiliary variable $Z$, (P1) can be equivalently written as

$$(P2) : \max_{t,Z} Z$$
$$\text{s. t. } t_0 + t_1 + t_{21} + t_{22} + t_{31} + t_{32} = 1,$$
$$t_1, t_{21}, t_{22}, t_{31}, t_{32} \geq 0, \tag{16}$$
$$Z \leq R_1^{(2)}(\mathbf{t}), Z \leq R_2^{(2)}(\mathbf{t}),$$
$$Z \leq R_1^{(3)}(\mathbf{t}), Z \leq R_2^{(3)}(\mathbf{t}).$$

Notice that $R_1^{(3)}(\mathbf{t}), R_2^{(3)}(\mathbf{t})$ are both concave functions, therefore (P2) is a convex problem whose optimum can be efficiently solved using off-the-shelf algorithms, e.g., interior point method.

## 4    Simulation Results

In this section, we evaluate the performance of the proposed backscatter-assisted cooperation with that without backscatter in [11] (the No B.S. scheme). Unless otherwise stated, it is assumed that users are separated by 4 meters. The noise power $N_0$ is set $10^{-10}$W for all receivers, and the additional noise power for ID circuit is $N_s = 10^{-10}$W. The transmit power of EN is $P_0 = 1$W, and the wireless channel gain $h_{ij} = G_A(\frac{3*10^8}{4\pi d f_d})^\lambda$, where $ij \subset \{E1; E2; 1A; 2A; 12; 21\}$, $f_d$ denotes 915 MHz carrier frequency, $\lambda = 2.5$ denotes the path loss exponent, and we fix the antenna power gain $GA = 2$, the signal bandwidth is $10^5$ Hz, and the sampling rate $S = 6 \times 10^5$. Without loss of generality, we assume the power splitting factor $\beta = 0.7$, energy harvesting efficiency $\eta = 0.8$, and backscatter reflection coefficient $\mu_1 = \mu_2 = 0.8$.

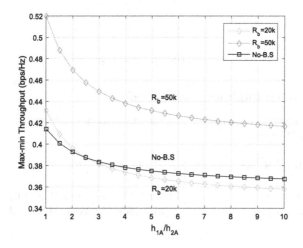

**Fig. 4.** The impact of user-to-AP channel disparity to the common throughput performance

Figure 4 shows the impact of user-to-AP channel disparity to the optimal common throughput performance. Here we set $h_{E1} = h_{E2} = 8.5 \times 10^{-5}$, fix $h_{1A} = 8.5 \times 10^{-6}$ as a constant and show the performance when $h_{2A}$ becomes smaller. Notice that when $h_{1A}/h_{2A}$ changes from 1 to 10, all the schemes show a decreasing trend in system performance, which is due to the weaker user-to-AP channel. In particular, the backscatter communication rate $R_b$ has a significantly effect on system performance. As we can see in Fig. 4, when $R_b = 50$ kbps the performance of backscatter system is similar to the case without backscattering. However, the former decrease faster than the latter, which is because the worse channel $h_{2A}$ will affect both two user's communication rate. When $R_b$ increases to 100 kbps, the system performance increases and outperforms the one without backscattering in all cases. This is because the higher backscatter communication rate can effectively reduce the time spent on cooperation, thus leaving more time on energy harvesting and information transmission to the AP.

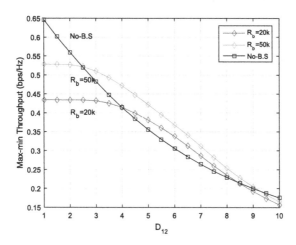

**Fig. 5.** The impact of inter-user channel to the common throughput performance

Figure 5 further studies the impact of inter-user channel strength to the throughput performance. Here we set $h_{E1} = h_{E2} = 8.5 \times 10^{-5}$, and $h_{1A} = h_{2A} = 8.5 \times 10^{-6}$. We consider the distance between $WD_1$ and $WD_2$ varies form 1 to 5 m. It is observed that the max-min throughput of all schemes decreases with $D_{12}$, due to the worse inter-user channel $h_{12}$. We can see that cooperation without backscatter performs relatively well when $d_{12}$ is small. However, as the distance between users increases, its performance quickly degrades due to the larger time and energy consumed on information exchange, and in general is worse than the proposed backscatter-assisted method, e.g., when $2 < d < 4.4$ for $R_b = 100$ kbps. When the inter-user distance becomes very large, e.g., larger than 4.4 m, the common throughputs of the backscatter-assisted cases decrease faster than the case without backscatter because of the extremely sensitivity of backscatter technique to distances. We can therefore conclude that proposed backscatter-assisted cooperation has advantage over that without backscattering when the inter-user channel is relatively weak.

## 5    Conclusion

This paper studied a novel user cooperation method in a two-user WPCN assisted by backscatter communication. In particular, the considered backscatter-assisted method reuses wireless power transfer for simultaneous information exchange during the energy harvesting phase, which can effectively save the energy and time consumed by conventional active transmission schemes. We derived the maximum common throughput of the proposed method through optimizing the time allocation on WET and WIT. By comparing with existing benchmark method, we showed that the proposed method can effectively improve the throughput fairness performance under various practical network setups.

**Acknowledgement.** The work of S. Bi was supported in part by the National Natural Science Foundation of China under Project 61501303, the Foundation of Shenzhen City under Project JCYJ20160307153818306 and JCYJ20170818101824392, the Science and Technology Innovation Commission of Shenzhen under Project 827/000212, and the Department of Education of Guangdong Province under Project 2017KTSCX163. The work of X. H. Lin was supported by research Grant from Guangdong Natural Science Foundation under the Project number 2015A030313552. X. H. Lin is the corresponding author of this paper.

## References

1. Bi, S., Ho, C.K., Zhang, R.: Wireless powered communication: opportunities and challenges. IEEE Commun. Mag. **53**(4), 117–125 (2015)
2. Bi, S., Zeng, Y., Zhang, R.: Wireless powered communication networks: an overview. IEEE Wirel. Commun. **23**(2), 10–18 (2016)
3. Lu, X., Wang, P., Niyato, D., Kim, D.I., Han, Z.: Wireless networks with RF energy harvesting: a contemporary survey. IEEE Commun. Surv. Tutor. **17**(2), 757–789 (2015)
4. Ju, H., Zhang, R.: Throughput maximization in wireless powered communication networks. IEEE Trans. Wirel. Commun. **13**(1), 418–428 (2014)
5. Bi, S., Zhang, R.: Placement optimization of energy and information access points in wireless powered communication networks. IEEE Trans. Wirel. Commun. **15**(3), 2351–2364 (2016)
6. Bi, S., Zhang, R.: Distributed charging control in broadband wireless power transfer networks. IEEE J. Sel. Areas Commun. **34**(12), 3380–3393 (2016)
7. Bi, S., Zhang, Y.J., Zhang, R.: Distributed scheduling in wireless powered communication network: protocol design and performance analysis. In: Proceedings of IEEE WiOpt, Paris, France, May 2017
8. Wang, F., Xu, J., Wang, X., Cui, S.: Joint offloading and computing optimization in wireless powered mobile-edge computing systems. IEEE Trans. Wirel. Commun. **17**(3), 1784–1797 (2018)

9. Bi, S., Zhang, Y.J.: Computation rate maximization for wireless powered mobile-edge computing with binary computation offloading. IEEE Trans. Wirel. Commun. **17**(6), 4177–4190 (2018)
10. Bi, S., Zhang, R.: Node placement optimization in wireless powered communication networks. In: Proceedings of IEEE GLOBECOM, San Diego, USA (2015)
11. Ju, H., Zhang, R.: User cooperation in wireless powered communication networks. In: Proceedings of IEEE GLOBECOM, Austin, TX, USA, pp. 1430–1435 (2014)
12. Yuan, L., Bi, S., Zhang, S., Lin, X., Wang, H.: Multi-antenna enabled cluster-based cooperation in wireless powered communication networks. IEEE Access **5**, 13941–13950 (2017)
13. Zhong, M., Bi, S., Lin, X.H.: User cooperation for enhanced throughput fairness in wireless powered communication networks. Springer Wirel. Netw. **23**(4), 1315–1330 (2017)
14. Bharadia, D., Joshi, K.R., Kotaru, M., Katti, S.: BackFi: high throughput WiFi backscatter. SIGCOMM Comput. Commun. Rev. **45**(4), 283–296 (2015)
15. Liu, V., Parks, A., Tala, V., Gollakota, S., Wetherall, D., Smith, J.R.: Ambient backscatter: wireless commumication out of thin air. In: Proceedings of ACM SIGCOMM, pp. 39–50, Hong Kong (2013)
16. Wang, G., Gao, F., Fan, R., Tellambura, C.: Ambient backscatter communication systems: detection and performance analysis. IEEE Trans. Commun. **64**(11), 4836–4846 (2016)
17. Abdulsattar, M.A.K., Hussein, Z.A.: Energy dector with baseband sampling for cognitive radio: real-time implemention. Wirel. Eng. Technol. **3**(4), 229–239 (2012)
18. Liu, L., Zhang, R., Chua, K.C.: Wireless information and power transfer: a dynamic power splitting approach. IEEE Trans. Commun. **61**(9), 3990–4001 (2013)

# Intelligent Satellite Communications and Networking

# Channel Estimation in Next Generation LEO Satellite Communicastion Systems

Zheng Pan[1], Zhenyu Na[1(✉)], Xin Liu[2], and Weidang Lu[3]

[1] School of Information Science and Technology, Dalian Maritime University,
Dalian 116026, China
nazhenyu@dlmu.edu.cn
[2] School of Information and Communication Engineering,
Dalian University of Technology, Dalian 116024, China
[3] College of Information Engineering, Zhejiang University of Technology,
Hangzhou 310058, China

**Abstract.** Low earth orbit (LEO) satellite communication systems are
the key parts of Space-Air-Ground networks. In order to deal with the
scarcity of spectrum source, generalized frequency division multiplexing
(GFDM) becomes a candidate for next generation LEO satellite systems. In LEO satellite communication systems, channel estimation is
an indispensable technique to adapt to complex satellite channel environment. Because of the non-orthogonality between GFDM subcarriers,
conventional channel estimation techniques can't achieve the desired performance. We propose a Turbo receiver channel estimation method with
threshold control to improve the channel estimation performance by utilizing the feedback information from Turbo decoder. The numerical and
analytical results show that the proposed method can achieve better
performance over LEO satellite channel.

**Keywords:** LEO · Satellite communication · GFDM
Channel estimation · Turbo coding · Threshold control

## 1 Introduction

Recently, satellite communication systems are used in almost every area all over
the world. The global satellite industry revenues have doubled in last decade.
According to the height of satellite orbit, the satellites can be divided into three
categories: geostationary earth orbit (GEO), medium earth orbit (MEO) and
low earth orbit (LEO). Compared with GEO and MEO, LEO satellites have
the advantages of lower delay, lower Doppler frequency shift and lower cost of
launch and manufacture. SpaceX and OneWeb both propose the projects of
worldwide LEO satellite constellations, they determine to launch thousands of
LEO satellites to build Space-Air-Ground networks [1–3].

Since more and more LEO satellites are launched for satellite communication,
the scarcity of spectrum source has become one of the most important problems.

© ICST Institute for Computer Sciences, Social Informatics and Telecommunications Engineering 2018
L. Meng and Y. Zhang (Eds.): MLICOM 2018, LNICST 251, pp. 243–252, 2018.
https://doi.org/10.1007/978-3-030-00557-3_25

In order to improve spectrum utilization, orthogonal frequency division multiplexing (OFDM) is used to supersede code division multiple access (CDMA) in many satellite systems [4,5]. As a key physical layer technology in 4th generation (4G) mobile communications, there are still many shortcomings need to be solved. With the development of mobile communications, some improved candidate waveforms for 5th generation (5G) are proposed [6–8]. Among these waveforms, the generalized frequency division multiplexing (GFDM) is considered as one of the optimal technique for LEO satellite communication systems. In GFDM systems, adjacent subcarriers are non-orthogonal. The modulation is based on data blocks, which contain several subsymbols and subcarriers. The non-orthogonality makes GFDM can achieve better spectrum efficiency than OFDM [9,10]. The structure of GFDM data blocks can be adjusted flexibly to adapt to different application scenarios. For the application of GFDM in satellite communication systems, the complicated satellite channel is one of the most serious obstacles. Channel estimation is the indispensable technique in satellite communication systems. In OFDM based satellite systems, channel estimation techniques have been well studied [11,12]. In [13], a general idea of separating pilot symbols from data symbols has been proposed. However, both of the pilot and data are known as the prior knowledge at the transmitter. Moreover, their channel estimation method is only suitable for nearly flat fading channels. In [14,15], an interference free pilot insertion is proposed to handle the interference from data to pilot symbols. In our prior works [16], a Turbo receiver channel estimation method is proposed in GFDM based cognitive radio networks. But as far as we know, there is no exact channel estimation technique in GFDM based LEO satellite systems. Our main contribution in this paper is to modify the Turbo receiver and calculate the threshold for channel estimation. Based on the LEO satellite channel, the performance of the least square (LS) channel estimation and the Turbo receiver channel estimation (TRCE) with threshold control (TC) is theoretically analyzed and verified by simulation.

The rest of this paper is arranged as follows: Sect. 2 describes the basic GFDM system model and the frequency domain signal processing. The TRCE with TC is proposed in Sect. 3. The orthogonal pilot insertion and LS channel estimation are also introduced in this section. Section 4 demonstrates and discusses the simulation results of the proposed channel estimation method. Section 5 is the conclusion of the paper.

## 2   System Model

The block diagram of GFDM-based satellite communication system is shown in Fig. 1. The binary source is coded by Turbo encoder to get the encoded binary source $\mathbf{b}_c$. Then $\mathbf{b}_c$ is mapped to $2^\mu$-valued complex constellation symbols by a mapper, e.g. quadrature amplitude keying (QAM) or phase shift keying (PSK). A GFDM block contains $K$ subcarriers and $M$ subsymbols, the $N = K \times M$ mapped symbols in vector $\mathbf{s}$ are given as

$$\mathbf{s} = (s_{0,0}, s_{1,0}, \cdots, s_{K-1,0}, s_{0,1}, s_{1,1}, \cdots, s_{K-1,M-1})^T. \tag{1}$$

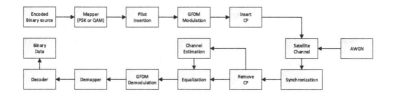

**Fig. 1.** Block diagram of GFDM-based satellite communication system.

The individual symbols $s_{k,m}$ are the transmission data symbols in $m$th subsymbol and on $k$th subcarrier. Each data symbol $s_{k,m}$ is pulse shaped by a filter impulse response

$$g_{k,m}[n] = g[(n, mK)modN]e^{-j2\pi\frac{k}{K}n}, \tag{2}$$

where $n = 0, \cdots, N - 1$ denotes the sampling index. The filter impulse response $g_{k,m}[n]$ is the time and frequency shifted version of prototype filter $g[n]$. The transmission sample of GFDM signal is given as

$$x[n] = \sum_{k=0}^{K-1} \sum_{m=0}^{M-1} g_{k,m}[n]s_{k,m}. \tag{3}$$

The time and frequency shifting of prototype filter can be integrated into a $KM \times KM$ transmission matrix as

$$\boldsymbol{A} = (\mathbf{g}_{0,0}, \mathbf{g}_{1,0}, \cdots, \mathbf{g}_{K-1,0}, \mathbf{g}_{0,1}, \cdots, \mathbf{g}_{K-1,M-1}), \tag{4}$$

where $\mathbf{g}_{k,m} = (g_{k,m}[0], g_{k,m}[1], \cdots, g_{k,m}[N-1])^T$. Based on the transmission matrix $\boldsymbol{A}$, all the GFDM modulation operations can be rewritten into

$$\mathbf{x} = \boldsymbol{A}\mathbf{s}. \tag{5}$$

**Fig. 2.** Block diagram of GFDM modulation in frequency domain.

Based on the time and frequency 2-dimensional structure of GFDM blocks, the modulation process can be implemented in frequency domain or time domain. In this paper, we focus on the frequency domain modulation mainly because the channel estimation is applied in frequency domain. As shown in Fig. 2, the modulation process is given by

$$\mathbf{x} = \boldsymbol{W}_N^H \sum_{k=0}^{K-1} \boldsymbol{C}^{(k)} \boldsymbol{\Gamma}^{(L)} \boldsymbol{R}^{(L)} \boldsymbol{W}_M \mathbf{s}_k, \tag{6}$$

where $\mathbf{s}_k$ are the data symbols on the kth subcarrier. The fast Fourier transformation (FFT) and inverse fast Fourier transformation (IFFT) processes are realized by FFT matrix $\boldsymbol{W}_M$ and IFFT matrix $\boldsymbol{W}_N^H$. Then the frequency domain data is upsampling by the repetition matrix $\boldsymbol{R}^{(L)}$. $\boldsymbol{R}^{(L)} = (\boldsymbol{I}_M\ \boldsymbol{I}_M \cdots \boldsymbol{I}_M)^T$ consists of L identity matrices with the size of $M \times M$. Each upsampled subcarrier is filtered by the filter matrix $\varGamma^{(L)} = \boldsymbol{diag}(\boldsymbol{W}_{LM}\mathbf{g}^{(L)})$. Subsequently, each subcarrier is upconverted to its respective frequency with the cyclic matrix $\boldsymbol{C}^{(k)}$. The higher and the lower spectrum components of the baseband subcarrier are converted into the passband components by the matrix $\boldsymbol{C}^{(k)}$. Similar to OFDM, CP is inserted to GFDM block before transmission to combat the inter block interference and multipath fading. Transmission over the satellite channel is modelled as $\tilde{\mathbf{y}} = \hat{\boldsymbol{H}}\tilde{\mathbf{x}} + \tilde{\mathbf{w}}$, where $\tilde{\mathbf{y}}$ is the received signal, $\hat{\boldsymbol{H}}$ is a $N + N_{CP} + N_{ch} - 1$ by $N + N_{CP}$ satellite channel convolution matrix. $N_{CP}$ is the length of CP and $N_{ch}$ is the length of channel impulse response $\mathbf{h} = (h_0, \cdots, h_{N_{ch}-1})^T$. Finally, $\tilde{\mathbf{w}}$ is the additive white Gaussian noise (AWGN). At the receiver side, we assume that the time and frequency synchronization is perfectly performed. Based on the cyclic prefix, the transmission model of the satellite channel can be simplified to

$$\mathbf{y} = \boldsymbol{H}\mathbf{x} + \mathbf{w}, \tag{7}$$

where $\boldsymbol{H}$ is the circular convolution channel matrix with the size of $N \times N$. This circular convolution matrix allows GFDM to employ zero forcing (ZF) equalization as in OFDM. The ZF channel equalization can be performed as

$$\mathbf{z} = IFFT\left(\frac{FFT(\mathbf{y})}{FFT(\hat{\mathbf{h}})}\right), \tag{8}$$

where $\hat{\mathbf{h}}$ is the channel impulse response obtained by channel estimation. Based on the prior knowledge of noise variance $\sigma_w^2$, the linear minimum mean square error (MMSE) makes a trade-off between noise enhancement and compute complexity. The MMSE frequency channel equalization is performed as

$$\mathbf{z} = IFFT[(\hat{\mathbf{H}}^H\hat{\mathbf{H}} + \sigma_w^2\boldsymbol{I}_N)^{-1})\hat{\mathbf{H}}^H], \tag{9}$$

where $\hat{\mathbf{H}}$ is the estimated channel frequency response. Derived from (6), the GFDM demodulation process can be written as

$$\hat{\mathbf{d}}_k = \boldsymbol{W}_M^H(\boldsymbol{R}^{(L)})^T\varGamma_R^{(L)}(\boldsymbol{C}^{(k)})^T\boldsymbol{W}_N\mathbf{z}, \tag{10}$$

where $\varGamma_R^{(L)}$ is the receiver filter matrix. At last, $\hat{\mathbf{d}}$ is demapped and decoded to get the binary data stream.

## 3   Channel Estimation

### 3.1   Least Square Channel Estimation

Pilot based channel estimation is to insert known pilot sequence into transmission block. Based on the received signal and known pilot sequence, the channel frequency response at pilot location can be estimated. In GFDM based LEO satellite communication system, the pilots are inserted into the first subsymbol with a specific interval $\Delta k$. In this paper, we use an orthogonal pilot insertion method. By moving the pilots to the pilot subcarriers which are orthogonal to data subcarriers, the pilots can avoid the interference from data subcarriers. The orthogonal pilot modulation is shown as follows:

$$\mathbf{x}_p = \mathbf{W}_N^H \sum_{k=0}^{K-1} \mathbf{C}^{(k)} \Gamma^{(L)} \mathbf{R}^{(L)} \Lambda \hat{\mathbf{s}}_k \qquad (11)$$

$$\Lambda = blkdiag(\mathbf{I}_n, \mathbf{W}_{M-n}), \qquad (12)$$

$\mathbf{s} = \hat{\mathbf{s}} + \check{\mathbf{s}}$ and $\hat{\mathbf{s}} \circ \check{\mathbf{s}} = \mathbf{0}_N$ is the Hadamard product of $\hat{\mathbf{s}}$ and $\check{\mathbf{s}}$. The permutation matrix $\Lambda$ can allocate the first $n$ pilot subsymbols to the subcarriers orthogonal to data subcarriers. Because of (11) and (12), the pilot can totally kept away from the inter carrier interference (ICI). The transmission signal $\mathbf{x}$ can be defined as $\mathbf{x} = \mathbf{x}_p + \mathbf{x}_d$ based on (6) and (11), where $\mathbf{x}_d$ denotes the modulated subsymbols on data subcarriers. The transmission model (7) can be written into frequency domain as

$$\mathbf{Y} = \mathbf{H}(\mathbf{X}_d + \mathbf{X}_p) + \mathbf{W}, \qquad (13)$$

where $\mathbf{Y}$ is the received signal in frequency domain. $\mathbf{X}_d$ and $\mathbf{X}_p$ are the frequency domain transmission symbols on data and pilot subcarriers. The received pilot symbols $\mathbf{Y}_{pilot}$ can be segregated from the received symbols without ICI. The LS channel estimation is used to minimize the cost function $||\mathbf{Y} - \mathbf{H}\mathbf{X}||^2$. The LS channel estimation can be expressed as:

$$\check{\mathbf{H}}_{pilot} = \frac{\mathbf{Y}_{pilot}}{\mathbf{X}_{pilot}} = \mathbf{H}_{pilot} + \mathbf{W}_{LS}, \qquad (14)$$

where $\mathbf{W}_{LS} = \frac{\mathbf{W}_{pilot}}{\mathbf{X}_{pilot}}$ is the enhanced AWGN on pilot subcarriers. In order to get the whole channel frequency response (CFR) of the satellite channel, $\check{\mathbf{H}}_{pilot}$ will be interpolation filtered at last.

### 3.2 Turbo Receiver Channel Estimation with Threshold Control

Turbo code is widely used in LEO satellite communication systems. In normal Turbo decoder, the feedback soft information is only used for iterative decoding, so the soft information is not fully utilized. We propose a TRCE with TC to make full use of the feedback soft information. The block diagram of the TRCE with TC is shown in Fig. 3. The TRCE with TC can be divided into a three-stage process.

The first stage is initial channel estimation. The CFR is initially estimated by pilot-aided channel estimation based on (14). After the equalization, the equalized symbols will enter into next stage.

The second stage is iterative channel estimation. In Turbo decoder, the external soft information is fed back in each iteration. The output log-likelihood ratio

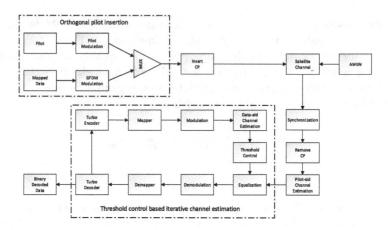

**Fig. 3.** Block diagram of Turbo receiver channel estimation with threshold control in GFDM based LEO satellite communication system.

from maximum a posteriori (MAP) decoder is encoded again for iterative channel estimation. In this stage, the rebuilt GFDM data symbols $\hat{\mathbf{X}}_{data}$ are treated as known training symbols. By applying data-aided channel estimation, the CFR at data position can be expressed as:

$$\check{\mathbf{H}}_{data} = \frac{\mathbf{Y}_{data}}{\hat{\mathbf{X}}_{data}}. \tag{15}$$

Although the data-aided channel estimation in iteration can utilize the external soft information, the imperfect decoded data will lead the estimation to a bias. If the estimated CFR is used for next iteration directly without any judgement, the accuracy of the channel estimation will deteriorate evidently. Thus, the threshold control is necessary to judge the reliability of the estimated CFR. The mean square error (MSE) of the data-aided channel estimation is given as:

$$MSE_{data} = \mathbb{E}\left[|\mathbf{H} - \check{\mathbf{H}}_{data}|^2\right] = \frac{\sigma_w^2}{|\hat{\mathbf{X}}|^2} \tag{16}$$

where $\mathbb{E}[\cdot]$ means the expectation. And the MSE of the pilot-aided channel estimation can be expressed as:

$$MSE_{pilot} = \mathbb{E}\left[|\mathbf{H} - \check{\mathbf{H}}_{pilot}|^2\right]$$
$$= \frac{1}{N}\boldsymbol{Tr}\left\{R_{hh} + F_{in}(R_{pp} + \frac{\sigma_w^2}{\sigma_x^2}\boldsymbol{I}_{N_p}F_{in}^H) - 2\boldsymbol{Re}[F_{in}R_{hp}^H]\right\}, \tag{17}$$

where $\boldsymbol{Tr}[\cdot]$ denotes the trace of matrix. $R_{hh}$, $R_{pp}$ and $R_{hp}$ represent the channel correlation matrices. $F_{in}$ is the interpolation filter matrix with the size of $N$ by $N_p$.

Based on the compare between $MSE_{pilot}$ and $MSE_{data}$, the reliability of data-aided channel estimation can be judged and the threshold $\lambda$ can be defined.

$$MSE_{pilot} \gtrless MSE_{data}$$

$$\lambda \triangleq \sqrt{\frac{\sigma_w^2}{\frac{1}{N}\boldsymbol{Tr}\left\{R_{hh} + F_{in}(R_{pp} + \frac{\sigma_w^2}{\sigma_x^2}\boldsymbol{I}_{N_p}F_{in}^H) - 2\boldsymbol{Re}[F_{in}R_{hp}^H]\right\}}}. \tag{18}$$

By means of this judgement, (14) and (15) can be integrated into:

$$\check{\boldsymbol{H}}^i(n) = \begin{cases} \dfrac{\boldsymbol{Y}_{data}(n)}{\hat{\boldsymbol{X}}_{data}^{(i)}(n)} & |\hat{\boldsymbol{X}}_{data}^{(i)}(n)| > \lambda \\ \check{\boldsymbol{H}}^{(i-1)}(n) & |\hat{\boldsymbol{X}}_{data}^{(i)}(n)| < \lambda \end{cases}, \quad n = 0, 1, \cdots, N-1, \tag{19}$$

where $i$ means the $i$th iteration. $\check{\boldsymbol{H}}^{(i-1)}$ denotes the estimated CFR of the previous iteration. Based on (19), the data-aided channel estimation is judged by TC strategy. Subsequently, the estimated CFR is fed back to equalizer for the next iteration. With the increase of the iteration number, the veracity of the channel estimation will be improved obviously.

# 4    Simulation Results

This section provides simulation results to demonstrate the validity of the TRCE with TC in the GFDM based LEO satellite communication systems. The simulation parameters are listed in Table 1. According to [17], we select the L-band LEO satellite channel in urban environment as the simulation environment. The bit error rate (BER) and MSE performances are evaluated through Monte-Carlo simulations.

**Table 1.** Simulation parameters

| Parameter | Value |
|---|---|
| Modulation mode | QPSK |
| Structure of GFDM block | K = 96, M = 7 |
| Pilot spacing | 3 |
| Pilot sequence | Zadoff-Chu |
| Channel coding | Turbo coding |
| Generating matrix | (1,1,1,1;1,1,0,1) |
| Coding rate | 1/3 |
| Number of decoder iteration | 8 |

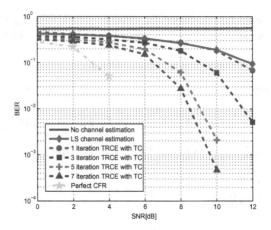

**Fig. 4.** BER performance of TRCE with TC in GFDM based LEO satellite systems.

The BER performance of the proposed TRCE with TC is shown in Fig. 4. Without channel estimation, the BER performance of GFDM based LEO satellite systems is terrible. When performing the basic LS channel estimation, the BER performance becomes better. But even when the SNR is 12 dB, the BER is still nearly $10^{-1}$. The proposed TRCE with TC has better performances within any iteration number. When only one iteration is utilized for TRCE, the BER performance only has tiny improvement than LS channel estimation. The BER performance is improved gradually as more iteration is used for TRCE.

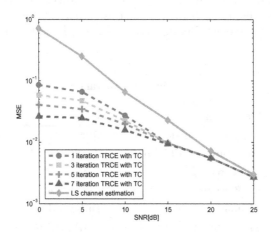

**Fig. 5.** MSE performance of TRCE with TC in GFDM based LEO satellite systems.

In Fig. 5, the MSE performances of LS channel estimation and the proposed method are evaluated. The proposed TRCE with TC significantly improves the

MSE performance compared with basic LS channel estimation. The increase of iteration number leads to better MSE performance of TRCE. When SNR is above 15 dB, the reliability of rebuilt symbols is high. Therefore, the MSE performances of TRCE with different iteration number are nearly the same.

## 5   Conclusion

We have proposed a TRCE method with TC in GFDM based LEO satellite communication systems. The LS channel estimation is used to cope with the LEO satellite channel. The GFDM receiver is modified for data-aided iterative channel estimation. A TC strategy is added to verify the credibility of rebuilt data symbols before equalization. From the simulation results we observed that TRCE with TC outperforms the basic LS channel estimation in LEO satellite channel. The BER and MSE analysis have shown that, the performance can be improved significantly by increasing the iteration number. The number of iteration which is used for TRCE can be selected flexibly to meet different demands.

**Acknowledgment.** This work was supported by the National Natural Science Foundations of China under Grant No. 61301131 and 61601221, the Natural Science Foundations of Jiangsu Province under Grant No. BK20140828, the China Postdoctoral Science Foundations under Grant No. 2015M580425 and the Fundamental Research Funds for the Central Universities under Grant No. 3132016347 and DUT16RC(3)045.

## References

1. Foreman, V.L., Siddiqi, A., De Weck, O.: Large satellite constellation orbital debris impacts: case studies of OneWeb and SpaceX proposals. In: AIAA SPACE and Astronautics Forum and Exposition, American Institute of Aeronautics and Astronautics (2017). https://arc.aiaa.org/doi/abs/10.2514/6.2017-5200
2. Babu, A., Camp, K., Price, W.: SpaceX satellite constellations. Engineering and Technology Management Student Projects (2017). https://pdxscholar.library.pdx.edu/etm_studentprojects/1191
3. Satellite Industry Association, others: State of the satellite industry report (2017). https://wwwsiaorg/wp-content/uploads/2017/10/SIA-SSIR-2017-full-2017-10-05-updatepdf. Accessed 5 Oct 2017
4. Kim, H.W., Hong, T.C., Kang, K., Kim, S., Yeo, S., Ku, B.J.: Applicability of orthogonal frequency division multiple access in satellite communication. In: 2011 IEEE 73rd Vehicular Technology Conference (VTC Spring), pp. 1–6. IEEE (2011)
5. Papathanassiou, A., Salkintzis, A.K., Mathiopoulos, P.T.: A comparison study of the uplink performance of W-CDMA and OFDM for mobile multimedia communications via LEO satellites. IEEE Pers. Commun. 8(3), 35–43 (2001). https://doi.org/10.1109/98.930095
6. Farhang-Boroujeny, B.: OFDM versus filter bank multicarrier. IEEE Signal Process. Mag. **28**, 92–112 (2011). https://doi.org/10.1109/MSP.2011.940267
7. Tao, Y., Liu, L., Liu, S., Zhang, Z.: A survey: several technologies of non-orthogonal transmission for 5G. China Commun. **12**(10), 1–15 (2015). https://doi.org/10.1109/CC.2015.7315054

8. Michailow, N., et al.: Generalized frequency division multiplexing for 5th generation cellular networks. IEEE Trans. Commun. **62**(9), 3045–3061 (2014). https://
   doi.org/10.1109/TCOMM.2014.2345566
9. Gaspar, I., Michailow, N., Navarro, A., Ohlmer, E., Krone, S., Fettweis, G.: Low
   complexity GFDM receiver based on sparse frequency domain processing. In:
   2013 IEEE 77th Vehicular Technology Conference (VTC Spring), pp. 1–6 (2013).
   https://doi.org/10.1109/VTCSpring.2013.6692619
10. Gaspar, I., Matth, M., Michailow, N., Mendes, L.L., Zhang, D., Fettweis, G.:
    GFDM Transceiver using Precoded Data and Low-complexity Multiplication in
    Time Domain. arXiv:150603350 [cs, math] (2015)
11. Liu, Y., Tan, Z., Hu, H., Cimini, L.J., Li, G.Y.: Channel estimation for OFDM.
    IEEE Commun. Surv. Tutor. **16**(4), 1891–1908 (2014). https://doi.org/10.1109/
    COMST.2014.2320074
12. Ogundile, O.O., Oyerinde, O.O., Versfeld, D.J.J.: Decision directed iterative chan-
    nel estimation and Reed-Solomon decoding over flat fading channels. IET Com-
    mun. **9**(17), 2077–2084 (2015). https://doi.org/10.1049/iet-com.2015.0234
13. Vilaipornsawai, U., Jia, M.: Scattered-pilot channel estimation for GFDM. In: 2014
    IEEE Wireless Communications and Networking Conference (WCNC), pp. 1053–
    1058 (2014). https://doi.org/10.1109/WCNC.2014.6952274
14. Ehsanfar, S., Matthe, M., Zhang, D., Fettweis, G.: Theoretical analysis and CRLB
    evaluation for pilot-aided channel estimation in GFDM. In: 2016 IEEE Global
    Communications Conference (GLOBECOM), pp. 1–7 (2016). https://doi.org/10.
    1109/GLOCOM.2016.7842323
15. Ehsanfar, S., Matthe, M., Zhang, D., Fettweis, G.: Interference-free pilots insertion
    for MIMO-GFDM channel estimation. In: 2017 IEEE Wireless Communications
    and Networking Conference (WCNC), pp. 1–6 (2017). https://doi.org/10.1109/
    WCNC.2017.7925957
16. Na, Z., et al.: Turbo receiver channel estimation for GFDM-based cognitive radio
    networks. IEEE Access **6**, 9926–9935 (2018). https://doi.org/10.1109/ACCESS.
    2018.2803742
17. Lutz, E., Werner, M., Jahn, A.: Satellite Systems for Personal and Broadband
    Communications. Springer, Heidelberg (2012). https://doi.org/10.1007/978-3-642-
    59727-5. Google-Books-ID: qXrnCAAAQBAJ

# A Novel Approach of Semi-blind Frequency Selection for HF Regional Emergency Maneuver Communication

Dai-hui Mo[1,2(✉)], Guo-jun Li[3], Xiao-fei Xu[3], Lu Tan[3], and Ya-kun Xing[3]

[1] Department of Electronic Engineering, Tsinghua University, Beijing, China
modh14@mails.tsinghua.edu.cn
[2] Academy of Military Sciences PLA China, Beijing, China
[3] HF Communications Engineering Lab of CQ, Chongqing Communication College,
Chongqing, China

**Abstract.** Shortwave regional mobile communication relies on regional ionospheric vertical detector for frequency forecast. The inherent properties of full band, high power and fixed detection result in the difficulty of real-time deployment in complex terrains. In this case, from the perspective of communication fusion detection, with comprehensive utilization of broadband passive monitoring and low SNR detection technology, we propose a semi-blind frequency selection mechanism for regional mobile shortwave communication. First, we acquire the optimal scanning frequency in the working frequency band based on the full range of passive monitoring, which abandons the electromagnetic pollution made by the full band scanning. This mechanism can act as the basis for the use of existing narrow band shortwave radio bidirectional detection. Then, we get the active optimal frequency perception based on the portable shortwave radio and the optimal frequency selection. Finally, we work out the problem of low efficiency and poor concealment in the high-power independent detection, which is of great significance to the promotion of the regional emergency mobile shortwave communication in complex environments.

**Keywords:** Cognitive radio · Active detection system
Passive frequency selection · Real-time spectrum monitoring

## 1 Introduction

China has been suffering from frequent and various natural disasters such as earthquakes and floods, resulting in great economy loss and casualties. The emergency communication is an important guarantee for punctual, efficient, safe and reliable operations in all aspects of emergency management, such as preventing preparation, monitoring, early warning, disposal rescue, rehabilitation and reconstruction. The near vertical incidence skywave (NVIS), an important regional

© ICST Institute for Computer Sciences, Social Informatics and Telecommunications Engineering 2018
L. Meng and Y. Zhang (Eds.): MLICOM 2018, LNICST 251, pp. 253–262, 2018.
https://doi.org/10.1007/978-3-030-00557-3_26

emergency communication mode, could cover 300 Km in complex terrains without blind spots or the terrains limits. In some areas like alpine canyon or jungle gully, since the satellite communication, VHF communication and other means alike are affected by the wave distance transmission, bad weather environment and many other factors, the unique characteristic of ultra-horizon transmission and mobile capabilities of shortwave NVIS communication becomes the only way of emergency mobile communication, which meets the high, middle and low altitude blindfold coverage of complex terrains reaching 300 Km.

The short wave communication [1] band ranges from 3 MHz to 30 MHz. The short wave NVIS sky wave is a propagation mode with a high elevation angle (near 90°) antenna, which needs to work below the critical layer of the ionosphere $F_2$ (f0F2), otherwise it will be penetrated by the ionosphere and the system could hardly work. The ionosphere f0F2 is directly related to the magnetic storm, absorption, solar activity, latitude, climate and so on, and changes dynamically with seasons, months and days. Therefore, in order to adapt to the time-varying dispersion characteristics of NVIS channel, shortwave NVIS communication must work out the dynamic selection problem of communication frequency. The reliability, timeliness and maneuverability of frequency selection have been the bottlenecks in the development of shortwave NVIS mobile communication.

However, long-term short-wave frequency detection system and communication system [2–4] are different from each other, whether it is an active detection method or a passive detection method, different signal waveform, transceiver and antenna equipment should be used in the communication system. On one hand, that leads to the poor applicability and feasibility of the communication frequency predicted by the detection system in the existing communication system. In addition, the active detection method has also been haunted by problems such as high power, poor mobility and electromagnetic environment pollution. On the other hand, passive detection method also has the problem of low reliability and blind coverage of the link. Based on the combination of active detection and passive detection, this paper proposes a new portable low-power semi-blind selection method suitable for shortwave NVIS sky-wave maneuvered communication. Based on real-time estimation of broadband spectrum and passive monitoring Ionospheric critical frequency, the critical frequency is used as a priori knowledge to design a narrow-band ionospheric detection window. A new low-power mobile short-wave channel detection technique suitable for existing shortwave communication equipment is proposed, which detects the narrow-band window channel characteristics in real time, and select the current optimal frequency for communication.

## 2    The Current Situation of Frequency Selection in Shortwave NVIS Communication

For a long time, the frequency planning of shortwave NVIS communication [5–7] has been mainly adopting the ionospheric vertical detector to obtain the critical frequency, realizing the shortwave communication frequency forecast on the basis of this frequency. The ionospheric vertical detector emits the radio pulses as the frequency changes with time, receiving the ionospheric reflection signals of these pulses at the same location, measuring the transmission delay of the radio and the round trip, and obtains the relationship between the reflection height and the frequency called Ionospheric high frequency chart. The ionospheric characteristic parameters of each layer such as the critical frequency and minimum frequency of $E$, $F_1$, $F_2$ and Es layers are obtained. The distribution of electron density with height can also be obtained by frequency conversion.

China Institute of Radio Propagation is the main development organization of the ionospheric vertical detector, which deployed 19 fixed detection sites in the territory, continuously detecting in the entire shortwave band (3–30 MHz) for 24 h. Detected sites transmission power is usually greater than 400 W, and some even up to 1000 W to obtain a reliable ionospheric critical frequency and other parameters. After obtaining the current ionospheric critical frequency, the available frequency forecasts are usually given at equal intervals within the range of 2 MHz below the critical frequency. Since the detection system and the communication system are independent from each other, the predicted frequency obtained by this equal interval division has not been subjected to the actual ionospheric channel test, and the availability of the prediction frequency is insufficient.

In addition, because the existing detecting sites are mostly built in the more developed large and middle-sized cities, the performance of ionospheric detection and forecasting is poor in remote areas. In order to meet the needs of the construction of emergency shortwave communication in remote mountainous areas, in recent years, many organizations such as the Institute of Radio Propagation have developed the vehicle-mounted short-wave ionospheric vertical detection equipment. However, the transmission power of this equipment is mostly above 400 W. In case of limiting energy supply in complex terrain environments such as remote mountainous areas, the application of such active detection equipment is severely limited.

Due to this situation, the Institute of Radio Propagation has recently further developed a passive and source-free detection equipment, which is used to detect ionospheric frequencies in complex terrains. The main idea of passive detections is that dozens of detecting sites are built as a beacon station, and portable ionospheric detection equipment only needs to receive the signals sent by beacon stations. The ionospheric propagation characteristic parameters away from the beacon station could be obtained by the interpolation fit. It can be seen that this passive detection method puts aside the launch part of the equipment, with the result that volume power consumption is greatly reduced, while mobility and concealment are greatly enhanced. However, the frequency of NVIS estimation, which is estimated by numerical fitting, is limited by the accuracy of the algorithm itself, and the performance of the area where the beacon information is difficult to cover (land border, ocean island reef) is obviously degraded.

In conclusion, the existing short-wave NVIS frequency detection and prediction methods [8,9] suffer from large power consumption and poor mobility (difficult to expand in complex terrains) in active detection modes, or low precision and poor practicability (cannot meet the need of remote NVIS frequency forecast) in passive detection modes.

# 3 Semi-blind Selection Methods for HF NVIS Communication

In this paper, an information processing terminal is added to the existing shortwave communication system to realize the integration of probing communication, which avoids the additional radiation interference caused by the independent detection system, reduces the system costs and enhances the applicability of the frequency selection. Because the frequency detection system has wider scanning bandwidth and higher peak power than the shortwave communication system, it is necessary to work out the problem of narrowband and low power frequency detection by frequency detection and forecasting based on the communication system. Therefore, this paper presents a short-wave NVIS semi-blind frequency detection method, using narrowband and low power to achieve short-wave NVIS communication frequency selection, which includes two steps: obtaining a priori scanning frequency based on broadband spectrum monitoring, and activating sensing channel characteristics based on low power bidirectional detection.

## 3.1 Obtain a Priori Scanning Frequency Based on Broadband Spectrum Monitoring

As the national short-wave detection station is conducted by Institute of Radio Propagation and the launch signal waveform is not open to public, other organizations cannot develop the ionospheric passive detection system. This paper uses the local short-wave signal in whole spectrum band to calculate the frequency of the energy center of the ionospheric reflection signal in local areas, which is called reflection center frequency [10] (RCF) in this paper and is based on the short-wave broadband spectrum monitoring. RCF directly reflects the best frequency of the current ionospheric NVIS propagation, and can determine the best frequency band for the current work. However, the shortwave communication is also closely related to channel interference noise, and the ionosphere has a dynamic time-varying characteristic in the short term. To achieve reliable communication, it is necessary to analyze and capture the spectrum holes in the best working frequency band for obtaining the priori scanning frequency and achieving the frequency optimization through selecting to resting channel.

With the progress of software radio technology [11], the current shortwave communication field has developed a practical full-band software receiver to record the entire shortwave 30 MHz band in real-time, hence it provides a possibility for real-time calculation of short-wave NVIS reflection center frequencies. For the widely used $G31DDC$ broadband shortwave receiver, the A/D sampler digitally processes the signal directly at the RF end with a sampling frequency of 100 MHz. According to the Nyquist sampling theorem, the A/D sampler can achieve the real-time monitoring to the occupancy situation of full- frequency band (up to 50 MHz), which in the realization is also absolutely feasible. In order to obtain a more detailed spectrum in a band occupancy situation, the sampled signals could be digitally down-converted and further processed by the IF digital signal filtering process, which helps get 20 KHz–2 MHz different band-width range of detailed spectrum after getting windowed and FFT processed once again. When the observation window bandwidth is 20 KHz, the maximum resolution could get up to 1 Hz.

After a large number of experiments, we have demonstrated that the frequency of the ionospheric reflection center RCF (some documents call it the interference center frequency) obtained by the short-wave full-band monitoring can effectively characterize the short-wave NVIS propagation characteristics, and it seems that the available frequency of the current period has good operability and high predicted accuracy [12]. The implementation method is as follows:

(1) Use the broadband receiver to scan the full range of shortwave, and record the interference energy value at each scanning frequency point;
(2) According to the $CCIR258 - 2$ report, the relationship between the median and the frequency of the anthropogenic noise figure is provided [13]. The interference energy value is corrected to minimize the effect of artifacts, since the noise is not ionized Layer reflection, if included in the calculation of RCF, will cause a greater deviation;
(3) Set the threshold based on the MUF and LUF provided by the ITS propagation model, and eliminate the effects of sudden interference and strong signal interference at the adjacent station;
(4) Calculate the reflection center frequency (RCF) value using the following formula:

$$ICF = \frac{\sum\limits_{i=1}^{n} F_i \times D(F_i)}{\sum\limits_{i=1}^{N} D(F_i)}$$

where $F_i$ is the $i$-th frequency, $D(F_i)$ is the spectral energy value of $F_i$.

(5) Make$(RCF - 1.5, RCF + 1.5)$the best working window for NVIS
(6) Frequency monitoring modules rapidly output the quiet frequency point within$(RCF-1.5, RCF+1.5)$ as a priori scanning frequency setting. Figure 1 shows the ICF measured data of the Chongqing area obtained by this method, which has a high degree of coincidence with the measured communication frequency of the Chongqing area. Through the line test of Chongqing - Beijing, Chongqing - Wuhan and other places, it is shown that the optimal frequency obtained by this method could improve the communication capability obviously when applied to the special route.

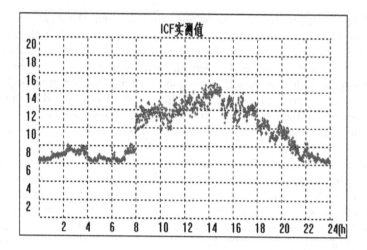

**Fig. 1.** ICF based on broadband spectrum monitoring.

## 3.2 Active Sensing Channel Characteristics Based on Low Power Bidirectional Detection

In order to utilize the existing portable shortwave communication equipment for spectrum sensing to obtain the actual propagation characteristics (including bidirectional SNR, frequency offset, delay spread, etc.) of the above mentioned NVIS channel, it is necessary to make the system operate in narrowband channel and low power mode. In this paper, adaptive multi-carrier differential frequency shift keying (ADMFSK) is used as the detection waveform, conducting forward error correction through RS code. The low signal-to-noise ratio ($-20$ db) and the harsh working conditions of the strong multipath interference (8 ms) are exchanged at lower symbol rate in exchange for low-power NVIS communication.

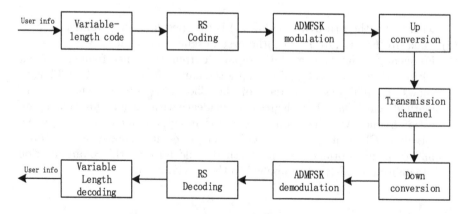

**Fig. 2.** Schematic diagram of frequency detection waveform structure.

This multi-carrier serial differential technology is particularly suitable for helicopters, unmanned aerial vehicles and other high mobility targets. The concrete implementation is shown in Fig. 2.

Due to the low signal-to-noise ratio of the application environment and the fast fading of the mobile NVIS channel, the synchronous carrier (as shown by $f_0$ in Fig. 3) is specifically set for ADMFSK modulation.

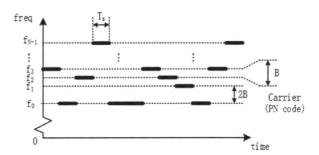

**Fig. 3.** Schematic diagram of ADMFSK modulation scheme.

On one hand, the carrier sends the preset PN code repeatedly by keying, and then performs the detection of the auto correlation peak through the receiving port to realize the group synchronization of the data. On the other hand, the received carrier frequency is used as the reference of other carriers frequency, thereby reducing the transmission frequency of the overall frequency error. The black and bold line in Fig. 3 indicates that there is a tone signal transmission over the corresponding frequency band of the time period, assuming that there are N frequency points for the transmission of the signal, where the smallest frequency point $f_0$ is used to transmit the carrier and synchronization signal, $f_1$–$f_{N-1}$ is used to transmit data, it is worth noticing that only the data on the carrier wave is 0, that can transmit data on $f_1$–$f_{N-1}$, although the design sacrifices the transmission rate, the inter-carrier interference is avoided at the same time, while the use of a separate frequency of the fundamental and synchronous PN code transmission can ensure the synchronization of the signal access on maximum priority. In addition, it can also transmit a different preset PN code to achieve a certain degree of the information encryption, while the use of PN code autocorrelation characteristics, it can use a simple autocorrelation peak to achieve rapid access and use short-term good channel environment or interference gap to operate payload transmission.

The detection waveform has a single frequency at any time and the signal phase is continuous and the amplitude remains constant, which is to say that in the entire transmission process peak-to-average ratio is kept at a relatively constant state and can improve the efficiency of transmitted signal as much as possible while ensuring that the waveform is not distorted (extended), that have a significant practical significance for the single-soldier, bicycle and other mobile users whose power and antenna efficiency are limited in bad environments.

### 3.3 HF NVIS Communication Semi-blind Selection Frequency System Program

On one hand, the semi-blind selection system in this paper mainly includes a portable computer terminal, broadband receiver and portable shortwave radio, and the system structure is shown in Fig. 4, which actively detect the frequency selection completely relying on the existing short-wave radio transceiver to the antenna, and baseband signal modulation and demodulation completely in the form of software. On the other hand, as the existing shortwave radio has no broadband receiver function, to configure a miniature shortwave broadband receiver through the USB port access to computer terminals, it is necessary to achieve a priori scanning frequency calculation.

Due to the fact that the portable radio's transmit power is 20 dB less than the ionospheric vertical detector transmitter, the detecting waveforms, used by semi-blind selection method, can reliably work in the background of −20 dB noise. In addition, due to the strong multi-path delay existing in the NVIS propagation, the long symbol width, which means low-speed communication, is exchanged

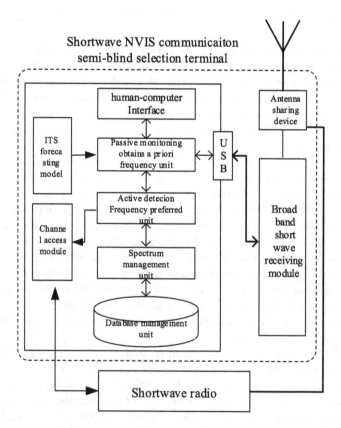

**Fig. 4.** Block diagram of short-wave NVIS communication semi-blind selection system.

for the low signal-to-noise ratio in this paper. Meanwhile, the radio channel conversion time, antenna tuning time, radio continuous transmission capacity and other factors taken into account and referring to that ionospheric vertical detector's scanning cycle usually is half an hour, the semi-blind selection method proposed in this paper actively senses to the 30 transcendental frequency of 3 MHz best working frequency band in 1 h, which means every 2 min a channel of two-way detection is completed. When 24 h of continuous detection is completed, 30 channels are obtained at each time period, and a total of 720 channels are actually transmitted.

Although the channel sensing and passive monitoring of the two modules share a pair of antennas, the hardware channel devices are independent from each other, which provide the probability for channel sensing and passive selection frequency working at the same time [14]. So the central station can use the radio station for a priori frequency active detection, and at the same time, it can also achieve a priori frequency-set real-time calculation by optimizing the timing design, the system can achieve a long term and uninterrupted exploration, as long as the prior scanning frequency informed to mobile users in real time through other means (such as Beidou SMS), and the system timing is shown in Fig. 5.

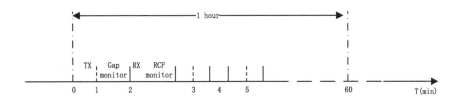

**Fig. 5.** Semi-blind selection system timing chart.

## 4    Summary

With the rapid development of cognitive radio technology, the idea of dynamic frequency optimization and distribution in the field of shortwave communication has been widely discussed and recognized. Based on the idea of cognitive software radio and the analysis of combing the main problems of current shortwave NVIS communication frequency selection, this paper proposes a portable shortwave NVIS communication semi-blind selection taking advantage of wide-band passive monitoring technology and low SNR detection technology, the composition of the system structure, waveform characteristics, working process, timing and others alike are described in detail. This semi-blind selection method, which utilizes broadband passive monitoring and radio active cognition, will be more suitable for maneuver detection of ionosphere in complex terrain environments by the deep fusion of detecting communication, and at the same time, it is helpful to avoid the problem of low communication efficiency caused by independent frequency selection system and have great significance to enhance the emergency mobile communication capability of shortwave areas in complex terrain environments.

**Acknowledgment.** This work was supported in part by the National Natural Science Foundation of China (61671452), Natural Science Foundation of Chongqing (Cstc2015jcyjBX0078, Cstc2016jcyjA0556), Chongqing Society Livelihood Security Project(cstc2016shm-szx40003) and Chongqing Industry Key Technology Innovation Project(cstc2017z-dcyzdyfx0011).

# References

1. Song, Z., Liu, Y., et. al: Cognitive Radio Technology and Application. Defense Industry Press (2012)
2. Tan, X., Lin, G.: Frequency prediction method of shortwave communication based on flight test. Radio Commun. Technol. (03) (2014)
3. Li, X.: Chirp detection technology and its application in shortwave communication. Ship Electron. Eng. (2005)
4. Yang, K., Ye, X.: Overview of shortwave channel quality assessment technology. Telecommun. Technol. **53**(8), 1113–1118 (2013)
5. Yang, Z.Z.: Study on spectrum sensing technology of shortwave network. J. Commun. Technol. **47**(11), 1318–1321 (2014)
6. Zhang, T., Liu, A., Shao, L.: Cognitive radio technology and its application in shortwave communication frequency selection. Commun. World **12**(8), 12–17 (2016)
7. Yan, J.-F., Guo, R., Tian, H.: Study on hollow rate and time-effect of short-wave dynamic spectrum based on cognition. School Sci. Technol. **33**(6), 57–60 (2011)
8. Shahid, A., Ahmad, S., Akram, A., et al.: Cognitive ALE for HF radios. In: Proceedings of Second International Conference on Computer Engineering and Applications, Bali Island Indonesia, pp. 28–33. IEEE (2010)
9. Blau, G.: Shortwave Communication Line Engineering Design. Electronic Industry Press, Beijing (1987)
10. Stewart, F.G.: Ionospheric Communications Enhanced Profile Analysis Circuit (ICEPAC) Prediction Program Technical Manual. Institute for Telecommunication Sciences, USA, pp. 46–59 (2008)
11. Hu, Z.: Modern Shortwave Communication. Defense Industry Press (2009)
12. Dai, Y.: Shortwave Digital Communication System Adaptive Frequency Selection Technology. Zhejiang Science and Technology Press
13. Li, D.: Frequency management of shortwave communication system. Radio Commun. Technol. (2009)
14. Zhang, W., Mallik, R.K., Letaief, K.B.: Cooperative spectrum sensing optimization in cognitive radio networks. In: 2008 IEEE International Conference on Communications (2008)

# Green Communication and Intelligent Networking

# A Network Coding Optimization Algorithm for Reducing Encoding Nodes

Limin Meng and Yangtianxiu Hu[(⊠)]

College of Information Engineering, Zhejiang University of Technology,
Hangzhou 310023, China
2111603007@zjut.edu.cn

**Abstract.** Network coding can effectively improve the transmission efficiency of the network, but compared with the traditional forwarding nodes, the participation of network encoding nodes will bring resource consumption. In this paper, we propose an improved algorithm of the max-flow based on the shortest path, which combines the concept of path capacity summation to achieve the maximum flow of the network, and the shortest path guarantees the minimal number of encoding nodes. The simulation results based on random network show that this algorithm can effectively reduce the encoding nodes and the consumption of network resources on the basis of realizing the maximum flow of the network.

**Keywords:** Network coding · Encoding nodes · The shortest path
Max-flow · Capacity summation

## 1 Introduction

The traditional network intermediate node has long played a role of routing forwarding until 2000 Ahlswede et al. [1] proposed the concept of network coding to break the limitations of the understanding of intermediate nodes. Intermediate nodes not only play the role of storage and forwarding, but also can encoded the information, so that the multicast network can achieve the maximum transmission traffic thus increasing the transmission rate.

But the encoding nodes are brought to the resource consumption, affecting the transmission efficiency. So, in case of maximum throughput (maximum flow), the fewer encoding are, the less resource consumption is. In the traditional network coding algorithm, encoding nodes are the intermediate nodes whose number of input links is larger than the number of output links in the work, however, in the guarantee of the maximum flow is not all such intermediate nodes need to be encoded, so there is a lot of unnecessary resource consumption. Therefore, how to ensure that maximum flow on the basis of the minimal coding node become a hot issue.

In graph theory, there are many algorithms for calculating the maximum flow of the network, which can be applied to the network coding to achieve maximum throughput. In recent years, more and more scholars have studied this aspect in more depth. Liu et al. [2] combined Dijkstra routing [3] and generic linear network coding [4] to reduce the complexity of network coding algorithm, and explained the possibility of applying

© ICST Institute for Computer Sciences, Social Informatics and Telecommunications Engineering 2018
L. Meng and Y. Zhang (Eds.): MLICOM 2018, LNICST 251, pp. 265–272, 2018.
https://doi.org/10.1007/978-3-030-00557-3_27

the knowledge of graph theory to network coding. Tao et al. [5] proposed a minimal cost network coding algorithm based on critical link, and the Dinic algorithm [6] in graph theory is applied to search of the augmented path. In [7], the Floyd algorithm [8] is applied to the path cluster search process of the polynomial time algorithm [9]. And Zhu et al. [10] proposed an algorithm to reduce the number of coding nodes on the basis of Ford-Fulkerson algorithm [11]—the maximum flow algorithm of graph theory with the new understanding of reused links and super critical nodes.

In this paper, we proposed a shortest path maximum flow network coding algorithm based on the capacity summation. When the max-flow is achieved, the number of encoding nodes can be minimized because the shortest path makes the minimal passing intermediate nodes and the selection principle of coding nodes is improved.

The rest of this paper is organized as follows. We will review some related knowledge in Sect. 2 and give our algorithm steps in Sect. 3. In Sect. 4, we will present an example to compare this improved algorithm with the Ford-Fulkerson algorithm. In Sect. 5, simulation results will be given and we can know the advantage of the improved algorithm in reducing encoding nodes. At last, Sect. 6 serves as conclusions.

## 2  Related Works

In a network $N = (V, L, C)$ [12], $V$ represents the set of nodes, including the source node set $S$, the sink node set $T$, and the intermediate node set $W$; $L$ represents the set of links between nodes and $C$ represents the capacity set. For link $l \in L, f(l)$ is called the flow on the link $l$. If $l = (v_i, v_j)$, $f(l)$ can also be recorded as $f_{ij}$. And for $v \in V$, $f^+(v) = \sum_{v_i=v} f_{ij}$ is the output flow of node $V$, $f^-(v) = \sum_{v_j=v} f_{ij}$ is the input flow of node $V$.

### 2.1  The Shortest Path

The shortest path in the graph theory is the shortest path between two mutually distinct nodes, where each link has a corresponding length. In this paper, in order to simplify the calculation, the length of each link will be united, so the shortest path from source to sink is to find a path with the minimal links in all possible cases, and thus the number of passing node is the minimal.

### 2.2  Capacity Summation

For a network, the links between each node have the corresponding capacity. If there is no link between two nodes, then there is no capacity and the capacity value is 0. The sum of all links' capacity on a path is added to obtain capacity summation.

## 2.3    Feasible Flow

If flow $f$ satisfies:

$$0 \le f(l) \le C(l), \forall l \in L \tag{1}$$

$$f^+(v) = f^-(v), \forall v \in V\{s, t\} \tag{2}$$

such a $f$ is called a feasible flow and $f$ always exists.

## 2.4    Encoding Node

The encoding node will only appear in the intermediate nodes, and the encoding node of previous algorithm judges that such a node may be an encoding node when the number of input links is greater than the number of output links– $num^-(v) > num^+(v)$. But in this paper, in addition to this encoding node conditions, we also consider that transmission information on the input link is different from that on the output link; and for each $v \in V$, $\sum_{i=1}^n f_i > \sum_{i=1}^n c_i$, $\sum_{i=1}^n f_i$ represents the total flow of all input links, and $\sum_{i=1}^n c_i$ represents the total capacity of output links.

# 3    Algorithm Process

We propose an improved algorithm based on some of the above concepts to achieve the maximum flow of the network, and the following are the implementation steps of the algorithm:

(1)    Generate a more regular network structure (single source network) by making some changes to the random network topology [13], where the source node is denoted as $S$, the sink node is denoted as $T_n(n = 1, 2, 3 \ldots)$, and the intermediate node is denoted as $V_i(i = 1, 2, 3 \ldots)$.

(2)    Initialization: Suppose that the capacity of each link in the network is $C_{ij} > 0$ (if there is no link between two nodes, then $C_{ij} = 0$), and the value of the feasible flow $f_{ij}$ is initialized to be 0.

(3)    Augmented process: The source node $S$ is sent to the adjacent node information, and then find the shortest path for augmentation from the source node $S$ to the sink nodes $T_n$. If there are multiple paths of the same length, then find the path of the maximum capacity summation for augmentation (If all the capacity summation is the same, then choose one to augment arbitrarily). If there is such an augmenting path, then go to (4), otherwise re-enter (3) until finding such an augmenting path.

(4)    Adjustment Process: The augmenting flow $\varepsilon = min_{(v_i, v_j \in V)} \{C_{ij}\}$. If the link is the forward link, then the residual flow value of the link minus $\varepsilon$. If the link is the backward link, then the residual flow value of the link plus $\varepsilon$. If a link has reached saturation after the flow adjustment, the link is not considered in the following augmenting path search.

(5)    After the end of the flow adjustment, and then re-enter (3) to search for the next augmenting path.

(6) The above process is iterated until all the augmenting paths in the network are found to reach the maximum flow, and the information of the input edge and the output edge of each intermediate nodes is recorded, and then the encoding node is judged according to the definition of the encoding node.

The complexity of the algorithm is analyzed as follows:

Assume that the number of vertices is $m$ and the number of links is $k$ in the network graph. When searching for an augmenting path, since the number of vertices of the network is $m$, the number of links included in the augmented path found by the algorithm is at most $m$. So from the source node to the sink node, it takes at most $m$ steps. And because the number of links is $k$, searching for an augmentation path takes at most $k$ times, so the complexity of finding an augmenting path is $O(k * m)$. Then in the process of modifying the flow for the augmenting link that is sought, the traffic on each edge needs to be modified and this complexity is $O(m)$. So the complexity of this algorithm is $O(k * m^2)$.

## 4  Example Analysis

Suppose there is such a network, the source node is denoted as $S$ and the sink node is denoted as $T$, and the intermediate node is denoted as $1, 2, 3, 4, 5, 6$. The connection between nodes represents a link, and the number on the link represents capacity. The network topology is shown in Fig. 1.

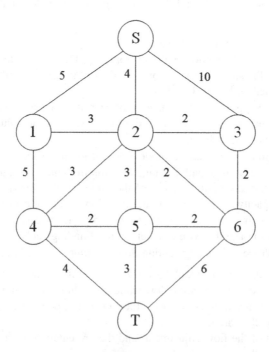

**Fig. 1.** Network topology

The implemental of the shortest path maximum flow algorithm based on the capacity summation in the network is as follows:

Find the shortest path from source node to the sink node, respectively $S \rightarrow 1 \rightarrow 4 \rightarrow T$, $\quad S \rightarrow 2 \rightarrow 4 \rightarrow T$, $\quad S \rightarrow 2 \rightarrow 5 \rightarrow T$, $\quad S \rightarrow 2 \rightarrow 6 \rightarrow T$, $S \rightarrow 3 \rightarrow 6 \rightarrow T$, where the path of the maximum capacity summation is $S \rightarrow 3 \rightarrow 6 \rightarrow T$, so this path is augmenting path and the augmenting flow $\varepsilon_1 = 2$. For the saturated link, will not be considered in the next augmenting path search. So, we can get all of the following augmentation processes, as shown in the Table 1.

**Table 1.** Augmengting process of the improved algorithm

| Serial number | Augmenting path | Augmenting flow |
|---|---|---|
| 2 | $S \rightarrow 1 \rightarrow 4 \rightarrow T$ | $\varepsilon_2 = 4$ |
| 3 | $S \rightarrow 2 \rightarrow 6 \rightarrow T$ | $\varepsilon_3 = 2$ |
| 4 | $S \rightarrow 2 \rightarrow 5 \rightarrow T$ | $\varepsilon_4 = 2$ |
| 5 | $S \rightarrow 1 \rightarrow 2 \rightarrow 5 \rightarrow T$ | $\varepsilon_5 = 1$ |
| 6 | $S \rightarrow 3 \rightarrow 2 \rightarrow 4 \rightarrow 5 \rightarrow 6 \rightarrow T$ | $\varepsilon_6 = 2$ |

Finally, all the maximum flow paths from the source node to the sink node are obtained. The maximum flow $f_{max} = \varepsilon_1 + \varepsilon_2 + \varepsilon_3 + \varepsilon_4 + \varepsilon_5 + \varepsilon_6 = 2 + 4 + 2 + 2 + 1 + 2 = 13$.

So, for a multi sink multicast network, we can extend to find out all the maximum flow paths from the source node $S$ to the sink nodes $T_n (n = 1, 2, 3 \ldots)$. And the encoding nodes in all the maximum flow paths can be found according to the definition of the encoding node.

If we do not use the improved shortest path maximum flow algorithm but use the traditional maximum flow algorithm—Ford-Fulkerson. Ford-Fulkerson algorithm is an important max-flow algorithm in the graph theory and achieves the max-flow of the network through the residual network. And then we can know the augmenting process of this network is shown in Table 2.

**Table 2.** Augmengting process of Ford-Fulkerson algorithm

| Serial number | Augmenting path | Augmenting flow |
|---|---|---|
| 1 | $S \rightarrow 1 \rightarrow 2 \rightarrow 4 \rightarrow 5 \rightarrow 6 \rightarrow T$ | $\sigma_1 = 1$ |
| 2 | $S \rightarrow 1 \rightarrow 4 \rightarrow 5 \rightarrow 6 \rightarrow T$ | $\sigma_2 = 1$ |
| 3 | $S \rightarrow 1 \rightarrow 4 \rightarrow T$ | $\sigma_3 = 3$ |
| 4 | $S \rightarrow 2 \rightarrow 4 \rightarrow T$ | $\sigma_4 = 1$ |
| 5 | $S \rightarrow 2 \rightarrow 6 \rightarrow 5 \rightarrow T$ | $\sigma_5 = 2$ |
| 6 | $S \rightarrow 2 \rightarrow 5 \rightarrow T$ | $\sigma_6 = 1$ |
| 7 | $S \rightarrow 3 \rightarrow 2 \rightarrow 5 \rightarrow 6 \rightarrow T$ | $\sigma_7 = 2$ |
| 8 | $S \rightarrow 3 \rightarrow 6 \rightarrow T$ | $\sigma_8 = 1$ |

The max-flow $f_{max} = \sigma_1 + \sigma_2 + \sigma_3 + \sigma_4 + \sigma_5 + \sigma_6 + \sigma_7 + \sigma_8 = 1 + 1 + 3 + 1 + 2 + 1 + 2 + 2 = 13$.

Although the Ford-Fulkerson algorithm can achieve the maximum flow, the number of augmenting path is larger than the number of augmenting path of the shortest path maximum flow algorithm based on the capacity summation. And with the increase of nodes, the advantages of improved algorithm are more obvious. This is because the Ford-Fulkerson algorithm is not targeted to find nodes when looking for augmenting path and needs to continue to contiguous nodes labeled, so there is redundancy and blindness. The improved algorithm is based on the principle of the shortest path—passing the least nodes—and the maximum capacity summation to select the augmenting path, so that redundancy can be reduced, and because the number of passing intermediate nodes is minimal, then the corresponding number of intermediate nodes that can become the encoding node will be reduced.

## 5  Simulation Results

In this paper, the adopted simulation tool is MATLAB 2015a, the first set of experiments is to verify the relationship between the number of augmenting paths and the number of nodes of the improved algorithm and the Ford-Fulkerson algorithm in the same case, as shown in Fig. 2. We can see that in the case of fewer nodes, the path exists in the network is limited, so the difference between the two algorithms is not

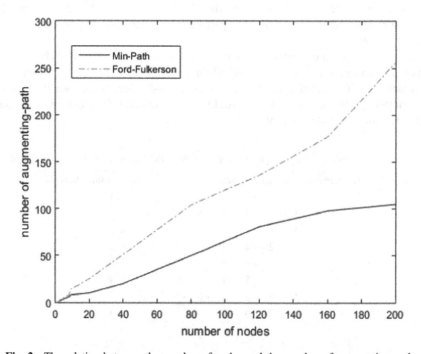

**Fig. 2.** The relation between the number of nodes and the number of augmenting paths

significant. However, as the number of nodes increases, the number of augmenting path of two algorithms is increased. But the curve of the improved algorithm is slower than that of the Ford-Fulkerson algorithm, which indicates that the larger the network size is, the more available paths are. The improved algorithm reduces redundancy so that maximum flow can be achieved with fewer augmenting paths.

In the second experiment, the relationship between the number of encoding nodes and the number of nodes is simulated, as shown in Fig. 3. Though the re-definition of encoding nodes, it can be seen that under the same conditions (the same network topology and the same capacity value on the link), the number of encoding nodes of the improved algorithm is smaller than the traditional network encoding nodes. And with the increase of the network size (the number of network nodes), this advantage is more prominent. Firstly, this is because that the shortest path means the minimal number of passing nodes, and then the definition of encoding nodes is stricter so that some unnecessary encoding nodes can be reduced.

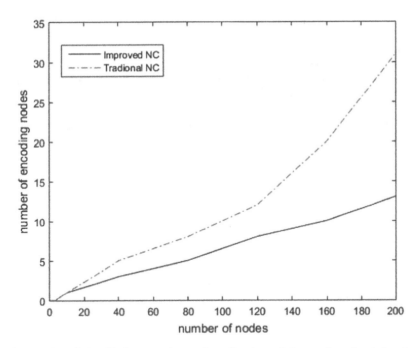

**Fig. 3.** The relationship between the number of nodes and the number of coded nodes

## 6  Conclusion

This paper aims to solve the problem of reducing the number of unnecessary encoding nodes in the network coding process, so we propose the shortest path maximum flow algorithm based on the capacity summation. Not only can achieve the maximum network flow makes the maximum throughput, but also reduces the amount of computation for encoding nodes of the network. Compared with the traditional algorithm, it has more advantages in reducing the encoding nodes, reducing the overhead of nodes, and making network coding more practical.

**Acknowledgement.** Thanks for the support of Zhejiang Provincial Key Laboratory of Communication Network Applications, National Natural Science Foundation of China (61372087) and Natural Science Foundation of Zhejiang Province (LY18F010024).

# References

1. Ahlswede, R., Cai, N., Li, S.Y.R., et al.: Network information flow. IEEE Trans. Inf. Theory **46**, 1204–1216 (2000)
2. Hu, J.X., Liu, S.Y.: Improved multicast network coding algorithm. Comput. Eng. Appl. **47** (15), 116–118 (2011)
3. Dijkstra, E.W.: A note on two problems in connection with graphs. Numer. Math. **1**(1), 269–271 (1959)
4. Yeung, R.W., Li, S.Y.R., Cai, N., et.al.: Network Coding Theory. Now Publishers Inc. (2006)
5. Tao, S.G., Huang, J.Q., Yang, Z.K., et al.: An improved algorithm for minimal cost network coding. Huazhong Univ. Sci. Tech. (Natural Sci. Edit.) **36**(5), 1–4 (2008)
6. Yefim, D.: Algorithm for solution of a problem of maximum flow in a network with power estimation. Dokl. Akad. Nauk SSSR **11**, 1277–1280 (1970)
7. Liu, J.F., Zhou, J.: Minimize coding node algorithm based on polynomial time algorithms. In: The 23rd National Conference on New Computer Science and Technology and Computer Education (2012)
8. Floyd, R.W.: Algorithm 97: shortest path. Commun. ACM **5**(6), 345 (1962)
9. Jaggi, S., Sanders, P., Chou, P.A., et al.: Polynomial time algorithms for multicast network code construction. IEEE Trans. Inf. Theory **51**(6), 1973–1982 (2005)
10. Zhu, Y.Y., Cao, Z., Zhu, L.X.: An improved encoding nodes reduction algorithm for network. Electron. Electro—opt. Syst. **3**, 47–52 (2012)
11. Ford, L.R., Fulkerson, D.R.: Maximal flow through a network. Can. J. Math. **8**, 399–404 (1956)
12. Wang, H.Y., Huang, Q., Li, C.T., et al.: Graph algorithm and its MATLAB implementation. Beijing University of Aeronautics and Astronautics Press, Beijing (2010)
13. Waxman, B.M.: Routing of multipoint connections. IEEE J. Sel. Areas Commun. **6**(9), 1617–1622 (1988)

# Backscatter-Assisted Relaying in Wireless Powered Communications Network

Yuan Zheng$^{(\boxtimes)}$, Suzhi Bi, and Xiaohui Lin

College of Information Engineering, Shenzhen University,
Shenzhen 518060, Guangdong, China
zhengyuan2016@email.szu.edu.cn, {bsz,xhlin}@szu.edu.cn

**Abstract.** This paper studies a novel cooperation method in a two-user wireless powered communication network (WPCN), in which one hybrid access point (HAP) broadcasts wireless energy to two distributed wireless devices (WDs), while the WDs use the harvested energy to transmit their independent information to the HAP. To tackle the user unfairness problem caused by the near-far effect in WPCN, we allow the WD with the stronger WD-to-HAP channel to use part of its harvested energy to help relay the other weaker user's information to the HAP. In particular, we exploit the use of backscatter communication during the wireless energy transfer phase such that the helping relay user can harvest energy and receive the information from the weaker user simultaneously. We derive the maximum common throughput performance by jointly optimizing the time duration and power allocations on wireless energy and information transmissions. Our simulation results demonstrate that the backscatter-assisted cooperation scheme can effectively improve the throughput fairness performance in WPCNs.

## 1 Introduction

Wireless communication is fundamentally constrained by the limited battery life of wireless devices. Frequent battery replacement/recharging will interrupt wireless communication and degrade the quality of communication service. Alternatively, radio frequency (RF) enabled wireless energy transfer (WET) technology can supply continuous and sustainable energy to remote WDs. Its application in wireless communication introduces a new networking paradigm, named wireless powered communication network (WPCN). Recent studies have shown that its deployment can largely reduce the network operational cost, and effectively improve the communication performance, e.g., achieving longer operating time and more stable throughput [1–7]. For example, [3] proposed a harvest-then-transmit protocol in WPCN, where one hybrid access point (HAP) with single antenna first transfer RF energy to all WDs in the downlink (DL), and then the WDs transmit information to the HAP in the uplink (UL) using their received energy in a time-division-multiple-access (TDMA) manner. It is observed in [3] that the WPCN suffers from a doubly near-far problem among WDs in different locations, where a far user from the HAP achieves low throughput because they

© ICST Institute for Computer Sciences, Social Informatics and Telecommunications Engineering 2018
L. Meng and Y. Zhang (Eds.): MLICOM 2018, LNICST 251, pp. 273–283, 2018.
https://doi.org/10.1007/978-3-030-00557-3_28

receive less energy and need more power to transmit information. To solve the doubly near-far problem and improve user fairness, several different user cooperation schemes have been proposed [8–11]. For instance, [8] proposed a two-user cooperation, where the near user helps relay the far user's information to the HAP. [9] allows two cooperating users to from a distributed virtual antenna array. [10] considered a cluster-based user cooperation, where a multi-antenna HAP applies WET to power a cluster of remote WDs and receives their data transmissions.

A major design issue of the existing user cooperation schemes is that the overhead (both energy and time) consumed on information exchange between the collaborating users. Alternatively, the recent development of ambient backscatter (AB) communication provides an alternative to reduce such collaborating overhead. Specifically, AB enables a WD to transmit information passively to another device in the vicinity by backscattering the RF signal in the environment, e.g., WiFi and cellular signals, thus achieving device battery conservation. Several recent studies have devoted to improve the data rate of AB, such as proposing new signal detection method and AB communication circuit designs [12,13]. However, the performance of conventional ambient backscatter communication greatly depends on the conditions of time-varying ambient RF signal, which is not controllable in either its strength or time availability.

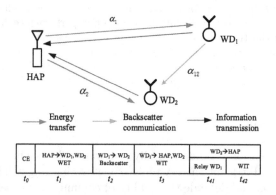

**Fig. 1.** A two-user WPCN and transmission protocol for user cooperation.

In this paper, we consider a novel user cooperation method in WPCN which uses backscatter communication. As shown in Fig. 1, we consider two wirelessly powered WDs that harvest RF energy in the DL and transmit cooperatively their information to the HAP in the UL. Unlike in conventional cooperation in WPCN where one WD transmits its information actively to the helping WD, we reuse the WET signal for achieving simultaneous information transmission in a passive manner. This largely saves the collaborating overhead. Besides, compared to conventional AB communication, the use of WET is fully controllable in the RF signal strength and transmission time. With the proposed backscatter-assisted cooperation method, we formulate a rate optimization problem that maximizes the minimum throughput between the two WDs, by jointly optimizing the system transmit time allocation and the power allocations of energy-constrained WDs. Efficient algorithm is proposed to solve the optimization optimally. Simulation results show that, compared to conventional cooperation based on active communication, the proposed passive cooperation can effectively enhance the throughput performance of energy-constrained devices in WPCN.

## 2  System Model

### 2.1  Channel Model

As show in Fig. 1, we consider a WPCN consisting of one HAP and two users denoted by $WD_1$ and $WD_2$, where the WDs harvest RF energy in the DL and transmit wireless information in the UL. It is assumed that each device is equipped with one antenna and both WET and WIT operate over the same frequency band. We assume that the channel reciprocity holds between the DL and UL, the channel coefficient between the HAP and $WD_i$ is denoted as $\alpha_i$ and the channel power gain is denoted as $h_i = |\alpha_i|^2, i = 1, 2$. Besides, the channel coefficient between $WD_1$ and $WD_2$ is denoted as $\alpha_{12}$ with the channel power gain $h_{12} = |\alpha_{12}|^2$. We assume without loss of generality that $WD_2$ has a better WD-to-HAP channel than $WD_1$, so which acts as a relay to forward the message of $WD_1$ to the HAP.

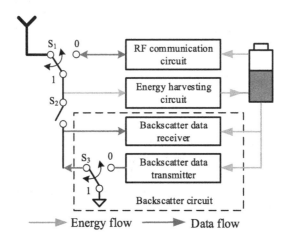

**Fig. 2.** Circuit block diagram of backscatter wireless user.

In this paper, we consider that the two WDs can transmit information in both active (RF communication) and passive modes (backscatter communication). The circuit block diagram of two users is shown in Fig. 2. With the two switches $S_1$ and $S_2$, the two WDs can switch flexibly among three operating mode as follows.

1. *Backscatter Mode* ($S_1 = 1$ and $S_2$ is closed): in this case, the antenna is connected to backscatter communication and energy harvesting circuits. A WD transmits information passively by backscattering the received RF signal. Specifically, a WD transmits "1" or "0" by switching $S_3$ between reflecting or absorbing state, respectively. Accordingly, a backscatter receiver uses non-coherent detection techniques, e.g., energy detector [14], to decode the transmitted bit. Notice that the energy consumption on the operation of backscatter transmitter can be well neglected due to the harvested energy during the absorbing state [16].

2. *RF Communication Mode* ($S_1 = 0$): the antenna is connected to the RF communication circuit and the user can transmit or receive information using conventional RF wireless communication techniques. Here, the transmission energy consumption is supplied by the RF energy harvested from the HAP.

3. *Energy-harvesting Mode* ($S_1 = 1$ and $S_2$ is open): the antenna is connected to the energy harvesting circuit, which can convert the received RF signal to DC energy and store in a rechargeable battery. The energy is used to power the operations of all the other circuits.

## 2.2  Protocol Description

As shown in Fig. 1, channel estimation (CE) is first performed with a fixed duration $t_0$, such that a central control point (such as the HAP) is aware of the channel coefficients $\{\alpha_1, \alpha_2, \alpha_{12}\}$. After CE, the system operates in four phases. In the first phase of duration $t_1$ the HAP broadcasts wireless energy in the DL with fixed transmit power $P_1$, while both the WDs harvest RF energy. In the second phase of duration $t_2$, the HAP continues to broadcast energy while $WD_1$ uses its backscatter communication circuit to transmit its information to the $WD_2$. Here, we assume the HAP neglects the backscattered signal due to the hardware constraint. Then, in the third phase, $WD_1$ operates in the conventional RF communication mode to transmit its information, using the harvested energy to $WD_2$. Notice that the HAP can overhear the RF transmission of $WD_1$ during this phase. In the last phase of length $t_4$, $WD_2$ first relays the user $WD_1$'s information to the HAP with average power $P_{41}$ over $t_{41}$ amount of time, and then transmits its own information to the HAP using its harvested energy with average power $P_{42}$ over $t_{42}$ amount of time, respectively, where $t_4 = t_{41} + t_{42}$. Notice that we have a total time constraint

$$t_0 + t_1 + t_2 + t_3 + t_{41} + t_{42} \leq T. \tag{1}$$

For convenience, we assume $T = 1$ in the sequel without loss of generality.

## 3  Throughput Performance Analysis

During the DL phase, the HAP transmits energy signal with the fixed power $P_1$ in $t_1$ amount of time. It is assumed that the energy harvested from the receiver noise is negligible. Hence, the amount of energy harvested by $WD_1$ and $WD_2$ can be expressed as [15]

$$E_1^{(1)} = \eta t_1 P_1 h_1, \; E_2^{(1)} = \eta t_1 P_1 h_2, \tag{2}$$

where $0 < \eta < 1$ denotes the energy harvesting efficiency assumed fixed and equal for each user.

In the second stage of duration $t_2$, $WD_1$ uses backscatter communication to transmit its information to $WD_2$. Let $x_2(t)$ denote the transmitted energy signal by the HAP with $E[|x_2(t)|^2] = 1$. We assume a fixed backscattering data rate $R_b$ bits/second, thus the duration of transmitting a bit is $1/R_b$ second. In particular, when $WD_1$ transmits a bit "0", $WD_2$ receives only the energy signal from the HAP

$$y_{2,0}^{(2)}(t) = \alpha_2 \sqrt{P_1} x_2(t) + n_2^{(2)}(t). \tag{3}$$

Otherwise, when $WD_1$ transmits a bit "1", the received signal at $WD_2$ is a combination of both the HAP's energy signal and the reflected signal from $WD_1$, where

$$y_{2,1}^{(2)}(t) = \alpha_2 \sqrt{P_1} x_2(t) + \mu \alpha_1 \alpha_{12} \sqrt{P_1} x_2(t) + n_2^{(2)}(t), \tag{4}$$

where $\mu$ denotes the signal attenuation coefficient due to the reflection at $WD_1$, $n_2^{(2)}(t)$ denotes the receiver noise at $WD_2$.

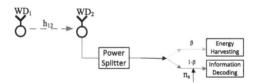

**Fig. 3.** Power splitting scheme in backscattering stage.

Specifically, as shown in Fig. 3, we apply a power splitting scheme, where the received RF signal is split into two parts. We denote $\beta \in [0,1]$ as the splitting factor, such that $\beta$ part of the signal power is harvested by the device, while the rest $(1 - \beta)$ of the signal power is used for information decoding (ID). For simplicity, $\beta$ is assumed a constant in this paper. The information decoding circuit introduces an additional noise $n_s(t)$, which is assumed independent of the antenna noise $n_2(t)$. Thus, the signal at energy decoder and information decoder can be expressed as

$$y_{2,E}^{(2)}(t) = \sqrt{\beta} y_2^{(2)}(t), y_{2,I}^{(2)}(t) = \sqrt{1 - \beta} y_2^{(2)}(t) + n_s(t), \tag{5}$$

where $y_2^{(2)}(t) = y_{2,0}^{(2)}(t)$ when sending "0" and $y_2^{(2)}(t) = y_{2,1}^{(2)}(t)$ when sending "1". Without loss of generality, we assume that "0" and "1" are transmitted with equal probability. The harvested energy by $WD_2$ can be expressed as

$$E_2^{(2)} = \eta t_2 \beta \frac{1}{2}((E[|y_{2,0}^{(2)}(t)|^2] + E[|y_{2,1}^{(2)}(t)|^2])) = \frac{1}{2}\eta t_2 \beta P_1(h_2 + |\alpha_2 + \mu\alpha_1\alpha_{12}|^2).$$
$$(6)$$

Here, we assume that the signals received directly from the HAP and that reflected from $WD_1$ are uncorrelated due the random phase change during backscatter. Meanwhile, we assume that $WD_1$ maintains its battery level unchanged during the backscatter stage, where the small amount of energy harvested is consumed on the on-off operations of the backscatter switches.

We denote the sampling rate of $WD_2$'s backscatter receiver as $NR_b$, such that it takes $N$ samples during the transmission of a bit, either "0" or "1". The following lemma derives the bit error probability (BER) of using an optimal energy detector to decode the received one-bit information.

**Lemma 1.** *The BER $\epsilon$ using an optimal energy detector for the backscatter communication is*

$$\epsilon = \frac{1}{2}erfc[\frac{(1-\beta)P_1\mu^2 h_1 h_{12}\sqrt{N}}{4((1-\beta)N_0 + N_s)}].$$
$$(7)$$

*Proof.* Due to the page limitation, the derivation is omitted here.

Then, the communication can be modeled as a binary symmetric channel, whose capacity (in bit per channel use) can be expressed as

$$C = 1 + \epsilon log\epsilon + (1-\epsilon)log(1-\epsilon).$$
$$(8)$$

Accordingly, the effective data rate from $WD_1$ to $WD_2$ is

$$R_1^{(1)}(\mathbf{t}) = CR_b t_2.$$
$$(9)$$

Within the sequel $t_3$ amount of time, $WD_1$ uses the harvested energy to actively transmit its information. By exhausting its harvested energy on WIT, the average transmit power of $WD_1$ is given by

$$P_3 = E_1^{(1)}/t_3 = \eta P_1 h_1 t_1/t_3.$$
$$(10)$$

We denote $x_3(t)$ as the complex base-band signal transmitted by $WD_1$ with $E[|x_3(t)|^2] = 1$. The received signals at $WD_2$ and the HAP in this time slot are expressed as

$$y_2^{(3)}(t) = \alpha_{12}\sqrt{P_3}x_3(t) + n_2^{(3)}(t), y_0^{(3)}(t) = \alpha_1\sqrt{P_3}x_3(t) + n_0^{(3)}(t),$$
$$(11)$$

where $n_2^3(t)$ and $n_0^{(3)}(t)$ denote the receiver noises.

During the last time slot of duration $t_4$, the $WD_2$ first relays $WD_1$'s message to the HAP and then transmits its own message. Specifically, we denote the transmit power and time for relaying $WD_1$'s message as $P_{41}$ and $t_{41}$, and those for transmitting its own message as $P_{42}$ and $t_{42}$. Then, the total energy consumed by $WD_2$ is constrained as

$$t_{41}P_{41} + t_{42}P_{42} \leq E_2^{(1)} + E_2^{(2)}.$$
$$(12)$$

Denote the time allocations as $\mathbf{t} = [t_1, t_2, t_3, t_{41}, t_{42}]$, and the transmit power values $\mathbf{P} = [P_1, P_2, P_3, P_{41}, P_{42}]$. For simplicity of illustration, we assume that the receiver noise power is $N_0$ at all receiver antennas except for the additional noise $n_s(t)$ introduced in the power splitter, whose power equals to $N_s$. Then, let $R_1^{(2)}(\mathbf{t}, \mathbf{P}), R_1^{(3)}(\mathbf{t}, \mathbf{P})$ and $R_1^{(4)}(\mathbf{t}, \mathbf{P})$ denote the achievable rates of transmitting $WD_1$'s message from $WD_1$ to $WD_2$, from $WD_1$ to the HAP, and to the HAP relayed by $WD_2$, respectively, which are given by

$$R_1^{(2)}(\mathbf{t}, \mathbf{P}) = t_3 \log_2\left(1 + \frac{P_3 h_{12}}{N_0}\right), R_1^{(3)}(\mathbf{t}, \mathbf{P}) = t_3 \log_2\left(1 + \frac{P_3 h_1}{N_0}\right), \quad (13)$$

$$R_1^{(4)}(\mathbf{t}, \mathbf{P}) = t_{41} \log_2\left(1 + \frac{P_{41} h_2}{N_0}\right). \quad (14)$$

Thus, the achievable rate of $WD_1$ within the time slot of length $T = 1$ can be expressed as [8]

$$R_1(\mathbf{t}, \mathbf{P}) = \min[R_1^{(1)}(\mathbf{t}) + R_1^{(2)}(\mathbf{t}, \mathbf{P}), R_1^{(3)}(\mathbf{t}, \mathbf{P}) + R_1^{(4)}(\mathbf{t}, \mathbf{P})], \quad (15)$$

and the achievable rate of $WD_2$ is

$$R_2(\mathbf{t}, \mathbf{P}) = t_{42} \log_2\left(1 + \frac{P_{42} h_2}{N_0}\right). \quad (16)$$

## 4    Common Throughput Maximization

In this paper, we focus on maximizing the minimum (max-min) throughput of the two users by jointly optimizing the time allocated to the HAP, $WD_1$ and $WD_2$ ($\mathbf{t}$), and power allocation $\mathbf{P}$, i.e.,

$$(P1) : \max_{\mathbf{t}, \mathbf{P}} \quad \min(R_1(\mathbf{t}, \mathbf{P}), R_2(\mathbf{t}, \mathbf{P}))$$

$$\text{s. t.} \quad (1), (10), \text{and} (12),$$
$$t_1, t_2, t_3, t_{41}, t_{42} \geq 0, \quad (17)$$
$$P_2, P_3, P_{41}, P_{42} \geq 0.$$

Noticed that if we set $t_2 = 0, t_{41} = 0$ and $P_2 = 0, P_{41} = 0$. Then (P1) reduces to the special case of WPCN without cooperation, i.e., the near user $WD_2$ does not help the far user $WD_1$ with relaying its information to the HAP.

(P1) is non-convex in the above form due to the multiplicative terms in (12). To transform (P1) into a convex problem, we introduce auxiliary variables $\tau_{41} = t_{41} P_{41}$ and $\tau_{42} = t_{42} P_{42}$. With $P_3$ in (10), $R_1^{(2)}(\mathbf{t}, \mathbf{P}), R_1^{(3)}(\mathbf{t}, \mathbf{P}), R_1^{(4)}(\mathbf{t}, \mathbf{P})$ in (13)–(14) can be re-expressed as function of $\mathbf{t}$, and $R_2(\mathbf{t}, \mathbf{P})$ in (16) can be re-expressed as function of $\mathbf{t}$ and $\boldsymbol{\tau} = [\tau_{41}, \tau_{42}]$, i.e.,

$$R_1^{(2)}(\mathbf{t}) = t_3 \log_2\left(1 + \rho_1^{(2)} \frac{t_1}{t_3}\right), R_1^{(3)}(\mathbf{t}) = t_3 \log_2\left(1 + \rho_1^{(3)} \frac{t_1}{t_3}\right), \quad (18)$$

$$R_1^{(4)}(\mathbf{t}, \boldsymbol{\tau}) = t_{41} \log_2 \left(1 + \rho_2 \frac{\tau_{41}}{t_{41}}\right), R_2(\mathbf{t}, \boldsymbol{\tau}) = t_{42} \log_2 \left(1 + \rho_2 \frac{\tau_{42}}{t_{42}}\right), \quad (19)$$

where $\rho_1^{(2)} = h_1 h_{12} \frac{\eta P_1}{N_0}$, $\rho_1^{(3)} = h_1^2 \frac{\eta P_1}{N_0}$, $\rho_2 = \frac{h_2}{N_0}$ are constant parameters.

Accordingly, by introducing another auxiliary variable $\bar{R}$, (P$_1$) can be equivalently transformed into the following epigraph form:

$$(\text{P2}) : \max_{\bar{R}, \mathbf{t}, \boldsymbol{\tau}} \quad \bar{R}$$

$$\text{s. t.} \quad t_0 + t_1 + t_2 + t_3 + t_{41} + t_{42} \le 1,$$

$$\tau_{41} + \tau_{42} \le E_2^{(1)} + E_2^{(2)}, \tag{20}$$

$$\bar{R} \le R_1^{(1)}(\mathbf{t}) + R_1^{(2)}(\mathbf{t}),$$

$$\bar{R} \le R_1^{(3)}(\mathbf{t}) + R_1^{(4)}(\mathbf{t}, \boldsymbol{\tau}),$$

$$\bar{R} \le R_2(\mathbf{t}, \boldsymbol{\tau}).$$

Notice that $R_1^{(2)}(\mathbf{t}), R_1^{(3)}(\mathbf{t}), R_1^{(4)}(\mathbf{t}, \boldsymbol{\tau})$ and $R_2(\mathbf{t}, \boldsymbol{\tau})$ are all concave functions (see the proof in [8]), therefore (P2) is a convex optimization problem, which can be easily solved by off-the-shelf convex optimization algorithms, e.g., interior point method. Then, after obtaining the optimal $\boldsymbol{\tau}^*$ and $\mathbf{t}^*$ in (P2), the optimal $\mathbf{P}^*$ in (P1) can be easily retrieved by setting $P_{41}^* = \tau_{41}^*/t_{41}^*$ and $P_{42}^* = \tau_{42}^*/t_{42}^*$.

## 5  Simulation Results

In this section, we use simulations to evaluate the performance of the proposed cooperation method. In all simulations, we use the parameters of Powercast TX91501-1W transmitter as the energy transmitter at the HAP and those of P2110 Power harvester as the energy receiver at each WD with $\eta = 0.6$ energy harvesting efficiency. Without loss of generality, it is assumed that the noise power is set $N_0 = 10^{-10}$ W for all receivers, the introduced additional noise power for ID circuit in Fig. 3 is $N_s = 10^{-10}$ W. The channel gain $h_i = G_A (\frac{3 \times 10^8}{4 \pi d_i f_c})^\lambda$, where $d$ denotes the distance separation between two devices, e.g., HAP-to-WD distance or the distance between the two WDs. $G_A = 2$ denotes the antenna power gain, $\lambda = 2$ denotes the path-loss factor, $\beta = 0.8$ denotes the power splitting factor, $\mu = 0.8$ is set as a fixed backscatter reflection coefficient and $f_c = 915$ MHz denotes the carrier frequency.

Figure 4 compares the achievable max-min throughput of different schemes when the inter-user channel $h_{12}$ varies. In this case, the HAP and the two users are assumed to lie on a straight line in which the near user WD$_2$ is in the middle with $d_{12} = d_1 - d_2$. Here, we fix $d_2 = 3$ m and vary $d_1$ from 6 to 10 m. Besides, we consider two different AB communication rates $R_b = 5$ kbps, 50 kbps. Evidently, the throughput performance decreases with $d_1$ for all the methods due to the worse inter-user channel $h_{12}$. Besides, both user cooperation methods, either with or without AB communication, outperforms the independent transmission scheme. For the two cooperation methods, when $R_b = 50$ kbps, the proposed AB-assisted cooperation outperforms the one without AB communication when $d_1 > 6.8$, but produces worse performance otherwise. Similar result is also observed when $R_b = 5$ kbps, where the proposed method has better performance when the inter-user channel is relatively weak. This is because when the far user $WD_1$ moves more away from the HAP, it suffers from more severe attenuation in both energy harvesting and information transmission to $WD_2$. Therefore, the optimal solution allocates more time to both WET and information exchange from $WD_1$ to $WD_2$ if AB communication is not used. The application of AB communication can effectively reduce the energy and time consumed on information exchange, thus can improve the overall throughput performance.

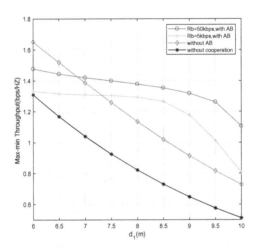

**Fig. 4.** The impact of inter-user channel ($h_{12}$) to the optimal throughput performance

Figure 5 shows the impact of the HAP-to-$WD_2$ (relaying) channel to the optimal throughput performance. Here, We set $d_1 = 9$ m, and vary $d_2$ from 3 to 5 m. Noticed that the performance of non-cooperation scheme hardly changes as $d_2$ increases, this is because its throughput is mainly constrained by the weak channel between the far user $WD_1$ to HAP. It is observed that the proposed user cooperation has better performance than the one without AB communication when the helping relay is close to the HAP ($d_2$ is small). Again, this is because when $d_2$ is small, the separation between the two WDs is large thus the inter-user channel is weak. Therefore, $WD_1$ needs to consume significant amount of energy if transmitting actively to the helping WD. The use of AB-assisted cooperation can effectively reduce the energy consumptions and thus improve the throughput performance. The simulation results in Figs. 4 and 5 demonstrate the advantage of applying AB communication to improve the throughput performance of user cooperation in WPCN under various practical setups, especially when the inter-user channel is relatively weak.

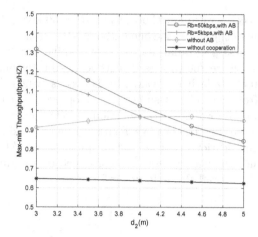

**Fig. 5.** The impact of relaying channel ($h_2$) to the optimal throughput performance

# 6 Conclusions

In this paper, we proposed a novel user cooperation method using AB communication in a two-user WPCN. In particular, we studied the maximum common throughput optimization problem of the proposed model, and proposed efficient method to obtain the optimal solution. By comparing with representative benchmark methods, we showed that the proposed AB-assisted cooperation can effectively improve the throughput fairness performance in WPCN.

**Acknowledgement.** The work of S. Bi was supported in part by the National Natural Science Foundation of China under Project 61501303, the Foundation of Shenzhen City under Project JCYJ20160307153818306 and JCYJ20170818101824392, the Science and Technology Innovation Commission of Shenzhen under Project 827/000212, and the Department of Education of Guangdong Province under Project 2017KTSCX163. The work of X. H. Lin was supported by research Grant from Guangdong Natural Science Foundation under the Project number 2015A030313552. X. H. Lin is the corresponding author of this paper.

# References

1. Bi, S., Ho, C.K., Zhang, R.: Wireless powered communication: opportunities and challenges. IEEE Commun. Mag. **53**(4), 117–125 (2015)
2. Bi, S., Zeng, Y., Zhang, R.: Wireless powered communication networks: an overview. IEEE Wirel. Commun. **23**(2), 10–18 (2016)
3. Ju, H., Zhang, R.: Throughput maximization in wireless powered communication networks. IEEE Trans. Wirel. Commun. **13**(1), 418–428 (2014)
4. Bi, S., Zhang, R.: Placement optimization of energy and information access points in wireless powered communication networks. IEEE Trans. Wirel. Commun. **15**(3), 2351–2364 (2016)

5. Bi, S., Zhang, Y.J., Zhang, R.: Distributed scheduling in wireless powered communication network: protocol design and performance analysis. In: Proceedings of IEEE WiOpt, Paris, France (2017)
6. Bi, S., Zhang, Y.J.: Computation rate maximization for wireless powered mobile-edge computing with binary computation offloading. IEEE Trans. Wirel. Commun. **17**(6), 4177–4190 (2018)
7. Bi, S., Zhang, R.: Node placement optimization in wireless powered communication networks. In: Proceedings of IEEE GLOBECOM, San Diego, USA (2015)
8. Ju, H., Zhang, R.: User cooperation in wireless powered communication networks. In: Proceedings of IEEE GLOBECOM, Austin, TX, USA, pp. 1430–1435 (2014)
9. Zhong, M., Bi, S., Lin, X.: User cooperation for enhanced throughput fairness in wireless powered communication networks. Springer Wirel. Netw. **23**(4), 1315–1330 (2017)
10. Yuan, L., Bi, S., Zhang, S., Lin, X., Wang, H.: Multi-antenna enabled cluster-based cooperation in wireless powered communication networks. IEEE Access **5**, 13941–13950 (2017)
11. Wu, Y., Chen, J., Qian, L.P., Huang, J., Shen, X.S.: Energy-aware cooperative traffic offloading via device-to-device cooperations: an analytical approach. IEEE Trans. Mobile Comput. **16**(1), 97–114 (2017)
12. Liu, V., Parks, A., Talla, V., Gollakota, S., Wetherall, D., Smith, J.R.: Ambient backscatter: wireless communication out of thin air. In: Proceedings of ACM SIGCOMM, Hong Kong, pp. 39–50 (2013)
13. Wang, G., Gao, F., Fan, R., Tellambura, C.: Ambient backscatter communication systems: detection and performance analysis. IEEE Trans. Commun. **64**(11), 4836–4846 (2016)
14. Abdulsattar, M.A.K., Hussein, Z.A.: Energy detector with baseband sampling for cognitive radio: real-time implementation. Wirel. Eng. Technol. **3**(4), 229–239 (2012)
15. Bi, S., Zhang, R.: Distributed charging control in broadband wireless power transfer networks. IEEE J. Sel. Areas Commun. **34**(12), 3380–3393 (2016)
16. Hoang, D.T., Niyato, D., Wang, P., Kim, D.I., Han, Z.: Ambient backscatter: a new approach to improve network performance for RF-powered cognitive radio networks. IEEE Trans. Commun. **65**(9), 3659–3674 (2017)

# Energy-Efficient Power Allocation Scheme Based on Discrete-Rate Adaptive Modulation in Distributed Antenna System

Xi Wang[1]([envelope]), Xiangbin Yu[1,2], Tao Teng[1], and Guangying Wang[1]

[1] College of Electronic and Information Engineering,
Nanjing University of Aeronautics and Astronautics, Nanjing 210016, China
woxiaoniu_wang@163.com
[2] National Mobile Communications Research Laboratory,
Southeast University, Nanjing 210096, China

**Abstract.** In this paper, the energy efficiency (EE) for a distributed antenna system (DAS) with discrete-rate adaptive modulation (AM) is investigated, and an optimal adaptive power allocation (PA) scheme for maximizing EE is developed. First of all, the system model of DAS based on discrete-rate AM is presented. Then, subject to transmit power per antenna and target bit error rate (BER), a constrained optimized problem is formulated to maximize EE of DAS. By solving KKT conditions, we derive the optimal solution as a closed form. The obtained closed-form expression is applicable to DAS with an arbitrary number of distributed antennas (DA) ports and general per-DA port power and target BER constraints. To illustrate the validity of the developed scheme, the exhaustive search method is used in the simulation to compare with the developed scheme. As a result, the proposed power allocation method produces the EE and spectrum efficiency (SE) identical to the exhaustive search method with remarkably reduced computational complexity. Moreover, the EE and SE of the DAS with AM increase as the target BER increases.

**Keywords:** Energy efficiency · Optimal power allocation
Discrete-rate adaptive modulation · Distributed antenna system
Spectrum efficiency

## 1 Introduction

Green communication, which pursues lower energy consumption and higher energy efficiency in wireless communication systems, has drawn increasing attention nowadays. In order to provide massive connections from various terminals, including not only smartphones but also machine-type communication devices with diverse quality of service (QoS) requirements, the 5G mobile network is required to have tremendous EE improvement. Energy efficiency (EE) is

© ICST Institute for Computer Sciences, Social Informatics and Telecommunications Engineering 2018
L. Meng and Y. Zhang (Eds.): MLICOM 2018, LNICST 251, pp. 284–292, 2018.
https://doi.org/10.1007/978-3-030-00557-3_29

defined as the ratio of the sum-rate to the total power consumption measured in bit/Hz/Joule. Various energy efficient methods have been proposed to improve the EE [1–4].

A key technology for green communication is a distributed antenna system (DAS). Compared with a conventional antenna system (CAS), which has centralized antennas at the central location, higher energy efficiency can be obtained in DAS. The reason why the distributed antenna system can achieve higher energy efficiency is that its structure makes the user closer to the antenna. Actually, the distributed antenna (DA) ports in DAS are distributed in different locations of the cell. As the locations of DA are different, the distances between the users and antennas are different, which brings different pass losses. In DAS, the large scale fading like pass loss needs to be taken into account. Consequently, compared with the CAS, where the average access distance between the user and antennas is longer, the transmit power and co-channel interference can be substantially reduced in DAS due to smaller access distance.

Adaptive modulation can select the most appropriate modulation, based on the current channel state information (CSI) [5]. It was shown that adaptive modulation can effectively improve the capacity, spectral efficiency (SE) and bit error rate (BER) performance of the system. Reference [6] demonstrated that adaptive modulation can improve the transmission rate and energy efficiency in fading channels. In [7], the performance of adaptive modulation was systematically observed in MIMO systems. The closed-form expressions of average SE and BER are given, respectively. Considering the incomplete CSI, [8] investigated the performance of adaptive modulation in a DAS, and the closed-form of the SE and average BER were presented.

However, the works above basically address the SE and BER study of DAS with AM, and the EE performance is studied less. Moreover, the superiority of power allocation (PA) is not considered, and the resultant system performance is limited. For this, we give the energy-efficient power allocation scheme with adaptive modulation in [9], but the modulation mode is based on continuous rate, that is, the modulation method continuously changes. Whereas in practice, the modulation mode need to work in discrete rate.

Motivated by the reason above, in this paper, we will study the power allocation of DAS with AM for obtaining more practical application and superior EE performance, where discrete-rate adaptive modulation and power allocation are both considered. We firstly present the system model of DAS with discrete-rate modulation. In constraint of the maximum transmit power and target BER, a constrained optimized problem is then formulated to maximize the EE of DAS. By using the KKT conditions, a general expression of optimal PA is derived. With this result, the optimal solution having closed form is further derived, and an effective algorithm is presented to achieve the optimal power allocation.

## 2  System model

We consider a downlink single cell DAS with $N$ DA ports, denoted as $DA_i, i = 1, 2, \ldots N$, and all DA ports are connected to central processing unit (CPU) via dedicated channels, such as optical fibers. Considering the implementation of mobile station (MS) as well as its limitation of volume and size, only single receive antenna is available at the MS. The location of the mobile station (MS) is random. The adaptive modulation and transmit power adjustment are performed by the CPU based on the channel information feedback. When the CSI changes, the current modulation mode and transmit power will be changed accordingly (Fig. 1).

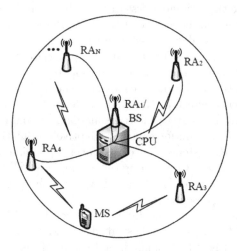

**Fig. 1.** Structure of DAS.

Assuming that both the transceiver and the receiver know the channel state information, the effective signal-to-noise ratio (SNR) at the MS can be expressed as

$$\rho = \sum_{i=1}^{N} \gamma_i P_i \tag{1}$$

where $P_i$ is the transmit power of the $i$-th DA port $DA_i$, $\gamma_i$ denotes the ratio of power gain to noise power between the $i$-th DA and MS. We take path loss, shadow fading and Rayleigh fading into account.

$$\gamma_i = \frac{d_i^{-\alpha_i} S_i |h_i|^2}{\sigma_z^2} \tag{2}$$

where $d_i$ denotes the distance between the $i$-th DA and MS, $\alpha_i$ is the path loss exponent, shadowing fading $S_i$ is a log-normal shadow fading variable with the standard deviation $\sigma_i$, $h_i$ indicates the independent and identically distributed circularly symmetric complex Gaussian channel coefficient between the $i$-th distributed antenna and MS with zero mean and unit variance, $\sigma_z^2$ represents the noise power.

Considering high efficiency, MQAM is used for the AM scheme. For the two-dimensional Gray coded MQAM modulation, the instantaneous bit error rate of the $n$-th modulation scheme under additive white Gaussian noise (AWGN) channel can be tightly approximated as [10].

$$BER_n(\rho) \simeq a_n \, erfc(\sqrt{b_n\rho}) \tag{3}$$

where $a_n$ and $b_n$ are parameters of the $n$-th MQAM modulation,$n = 1, 2, \ldots, M, erfc(\cdot)$ is a complementary error function. By setting the instantaneous bit error rate of the system equal to the target BER($BER_0$), the switching threshold of the $n$-th modulation can be given by

$$\phi_n = [erfc^{-1}(BER_0/a_n)]^2/b_n \tag{4}$$

where $erfc^{-1}(\cdot)$ denotes the inverse complementary error function. When the effective SNR falls into the n-th region, i.e., $\phi_n \leq \sum_{i=1}^{N} \gamma_i P_i \leq \phi_{n+1}$, the $n$-th MQAM modulation is employed for the current modulation mode.

## 3   Optimal Power Allocation Scheme

In this section, we will develop an optimal power allocation scheme for DAS with discrete-rate adaptive modulation by maximizing the EE, and the corresponding algorithm for calculating the PA is also presented.

The EE for DAS is defined as

$$\eta_{EE} = \frac{R}{\sum_{i=1}^{N} P_i + P_c} \tag{5}$$

where $P_c$ denotes the circuit power, which is a constant value, $R$ represents the transmission rate. Considering the discrete-rate adaptive modulation, the EE under different SNR conditions can be given by

$$\eta_{EE} = \begin{cases} 0 & \sum_{n=1}^{N} \gamma_i P_i < \phi_1 \\ \dfrac{R_1}{\sum_{i=1}^{N} P_i + P_c} & \phi_1 \leq \sum_{i=1}^{N} \gamma_i P_i < \phi_2 \\ \vdots & \vdots \\ \dfrac{R_M}{\sum_{i=1}^{N} P_n + P_c} & \sum_{i=1}^{N} \gamma_i P_i \geq \phi_M \end{cases} \tag{6}$$

where $R_n = log_2 Q_n (n = 1, 2, \ldots M)$ denotes the transmission rate of the $n$-th MQAM with size $Q_n$, and it is constant.

By maximizing the (6) subject to maximum power constraint, we can get the optimal power allocation scheme. However, we find that it is difficult to optimize the piecewise function (6) directly. For this, we firstly optimize each segment of (6) separately, and the respective results are then compared to obtain an optimal solution which corresponding to the maximum EE.

According to (6), and considering maximum power constraint, the energy efficiency optimization problem for the $n$-th modulation can be written as

$$\max_{\boldsymbol{P}(n)} \eta_{EE,n} = \frac{R_n}{\sum_{i=1}^N P_i + P_c}$$

$$s.t. \ \phi_n \leq \sum_{i=1}^N \gamma_i P_i < \phi_{n+1} \tag{7}$$

$$0 \leq P_i \leq P_{max,i}$$

where $P_{max,i}$ indicates the maximum power of the $i$-th RA. Without loss of generality, we assume that all $\gamma_i$ are different due to the structure of DAS, and they are sorted in descending order as

$$\gamma_1 > \gamma_2 > \cdots > \gamma_N \tag{8}$$

By means of the KKT conditions, we can analytically solve the optimization problem of the DAS with general per DA port power constraint. According to the KKT conditions, the optimal values $\rho_i^*$, $\kappa$, $\lambda$, $\mu_i$, $v_i$ should satisfy the following equations:

$$-\frac{R_n}{(\sum_{i=1}^N P_i^* + P_c)^2} - \kappa\gamma_i + \lambda\gamma_i + \mu_i - v_i = 0 \tag{9}$$

$$\kappa(\phi_{n+1} - \sum_{i=1}^N \gamma_i P_i^*) = \lambda(\sum_{i=1}^N \gamma_i P_i^* - \phi_n) = \mu_i P_i^* = v_i(P_{max,i} - P_i^*) = 0 \tag{10}$$

$$\kappa, \lambda, \mu_i, v_i \geq 0 \tag{11}$$

where $\kappa$, $\lambda$, $\mu_i$, $v_i$ are the Lagrangian multipliers.

According to (9–11), by means of mathematical derivation, we can obtain $\sum_{i=1}^N \gamma_i P_i^* = \phi_n$, and the corresponding general expression of the optimal power allocation for the $n$-th modulation, i.e., it is expressed as

$$\boldsymbol{P}^*(n) = [P_{max,1}, \ldots, P_{max,N_0-1}, P_{N_0}^*, 0, \ldots, 0]^T \tag{12}$$

and

$$N_0 = \max_{1 \leq k \leq N} \{j : \sum_{i=1}^{j-1} \gamma_i P_{max,i} < \xi\}$$

$$P_i^* = P_{max,i}, 1 \leq i \leq N_0$$

$$P_{N_0}^* = (\rho - \sum_{i=1}^{N_0-1} \gamma_i P_{max,i})/N_0 \tag{13}$$

The detailed derivation on Eqs. (12) and (13) is not provided because of the paper length limitation. With (12) and (13), we can calculate the EE of the system with $n$-th modulation, i.e., $\eta_{EE,n}$, $n = 1, 2, \ldots, M$. By comparing the obtained $\{\eta_{EE,n}\}$, the optimal PA and modulation mode can be attained, which corresponds to maximum $\eta_{EE,n}$. In other words, if $n^* = arg\max_{n=1,2,\ldots M}\{\eta_{EE,n}\}$, then the $n^*$-th modulation mode is selected for data transmission, and the corresponding PA is the optimal one.

Besides, considering that $\sum_{i=1}^{N}\gamma_i P_{max,i}$ is the achievable maximum SNR of the system under current channel conditions, we can determine which modulation mode can be used in the current channel by comparing this maximum SNR and the switching threshold. Namely, When $\phi_n \leq \sum_{i=1}^{N}\gamma_i P_{max,i} \leq \phi_{n+1}$, the $n$-th method of modulation will be used, and when $\phi_n > \sum_{i=1}^{N}\gamma_i P_{max,i}$, the $n$-th method of modulation will not be employed. Furthermore, when $\sum_{i=1}^{N}\gamma_i P_{max,i} < \phi_1$, even the lowest modulation will not be used, and thus the communication will be interrupted.

According to the analysis above, the algorithm of optimal power allocation for EE maximization with adaptive modulation in DAS can be summarized in Table 1.

**Table 1.** Power allocation method.

| **Algorithm 1** |
| --- |
| 1. Sort all the $\{\gamma_i, i = 1,, N\}$ in descending order; |
| 2. Calculate the switching thresholds $\{\phi_n\}, n = 1, 2, \ldots, M$, of all the modulations according to (4); |
| 3. Calculate $\sum_{i=1}^{N}\gamma_i P_{max,i}$ ; |
| 4. Initialize $n = 1, \boldsymbol{P}_{opt} = 0, \eta_{opt} = 0$; |
| 5. If $\phi_n \leq \sum_{i=1}^{N}\gamma_i P_{max,i}$ <br>     continue 6; <br> Else <br>     go to 11; <br> End |
| 6. Calculate the optimal PA for $n$-th modulation method $\boldsymbol{P}^*(n)$ according to (12) and (13); |
| 7. Calculate the EE of the $n$-th modulation method $\eta_{EE,n}$ based on $\boldsymbol{P}^*(n)$ using (7); |
| 8. If $\eta_n > \eta_{opt}$ <br>     continue 9 <br> Else step to 10; <br> End |
| 9. $\boldsymbol{P}_{opt} = \boldsymbol{P}_n$ , $\eta_{opt} = \eta_n$; |
| 10. $n = n + 1$, step to 5; |
| 11. If $n = 1$ <br>     return "communication outage"; <br> Else continue 12; <br> End |
| 12. Return the optimal power allocation $\boldsymbol{P}_{opt}$ , and maximum EE $\eta_{opt}$ . |

Moreover, it is worth mentioning that not only our proposed optimal scheme is applicable to MQAM, but also can be applied to MPSK. And what varies is only the instantaneous BER and further the switching thresholds need to be recalculated.

## 4   Simulation Results and Analysis

In this section, we evaluate the performance of the proposed scheme through computer simulations. To illustrate the validity of the scheme, an exhaustive search method, which examines all possible power allocation combinations with a resolution 0.01 in the range of 0 to $P_{max,i}$, is used to compare with the algorithm presented in Sect. 3. We choose six modulation modes for adaptive modulation in simulations, i.e., BPSK, 4QAM, 8QAM, 16QAM, 32QAM and 64QAM. For simplicity, we assume that $P_{max,i} = P_{max}, \alpha_i = \alpha = 3$, and $\sigma_i = \sigma = 8dB$ for $\forall i$ throughout the simulations. For DAS with $N$ DA ports, one DA port is set in the center of the cell located at $(0,0)$, and the others are located at $(\sqrt{3/7}R, 2\pi i/(N-1)), i = 1, 2, \ldots, N-1$. The radius of the cell $R = 1000\,\text{m}$. We set $P_{max} = 1W$ and the circuit power $P_c = 5W$ in simulation. The computer we used for simulation is an AMD 2.2-GHz dual core with 3.25 GB of RAM, and the simulation software is MATLAB 2012b.

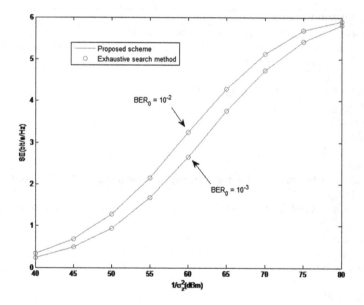

**Fig. 2.** SE of DAS with AM for different $BER_0$.

In Fig. 2, we plot the system SE as a function of the reciprocal of the maximal transmit power $1/\sigma_z^2$ for different $BER_0$ and three DA ports, where $BER_0 = 10^{-2}, 10^{-3}$. As shown in Fig. 2, the performance of the proposed scheme is identical to that of exhaustive search method, but our scheme has lower complexity than the latter. Explicitly, the running time of the proposed scheme is 0.21 s only, while the exhaustive search method needs 326 s. Hence, our scheme obviously reduces the complexity and has much less running time. Moreover, with the increase of the target BER, the SE also increases. This is due to the fact that the larger the $BER_0$ is, the lower is the BER performance requirement of the system. Thus higher order modulation mode will be selected and the resultant SE increases as well.

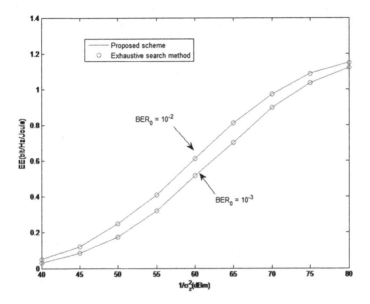

**Fig. 3.** EE of DAS with AM for different $BER_0$.

Figure 3 illustrates the EE of the DAS with AM and three DA ports for different tar-get BER, where $BER_0 = 10^{-2}, 10^{-3}$. From Fig. 3, it is found that the EE performance of the proposed scheme is same as that of exhaustive search method with substantially reduced complexity. Specifically, the running time of the proposed scheme is 0.136 s only, but the exhaustive search method needs the time of 173 s. Thus, our scheme need less time. Moreover, the system with $BER_0 = 10^{-3}$ has lower EE than that with $BER_0 = 10^{-2}$. This is because for stricter BER requirement, the lower order modulation will be adopted, which will decrease the SE and corresponding EE. Besides, the EEs of the system using the proposed scheme and the exhaustive search method both gradually improve as $1/\sigma_z^2$ increases, as expected. The reason for this result is that as $1/\sigma_z^2$ increases, the noise power decreases, the corresponding SNR increases. As a result, the system can choose a better power allocation and higher modulation scheme, which brings about larger energy efficiency.

## 5    Conclusions

In this paper, we formulated the system model of DAS based on discrete-rate adaptive modulation. We have studied the EE performance of DAS with discrete-rate AM over composite fading channels including path loss, shad-owing and Rayleigh fading. The optimal power allocation is derived by maximizing the EE in constraint of transmit power antenna and target BER of the system. By using the KKT conditions and mathematical derivation, the constrained optimized problem is solved well, and the closedform solution of PA is attained. With these results, the optimal PA can be obtained by comparing the EEs of the system with all possible modulation modes, and it corresponds to the largest EE. Based on this, a computationally efficient algorithm is presented to calculate the PA. Simulation results show that the proposed scheme produces the optimal EE performance with remarkably reduced complexity compared to the exhaustive search method. Also, the EE and SE of the DAS with AM increase as the target BER increases.

**Acknowledgement.** This work is partially supported by National Natural Science Foundation of China (61601220), Open Research Fund of National Mobile Communications Research Laboratory of Southeast University (2017D03), and Six Talent Peaks Project in Jiangsu (2015-DZXX-007).

## References

1. Kim, H., Lee, S., Song, C.: Optimal power allocation scheme for energy efficiency maximization in distributed antenna systems. IEEE Trans. Commun. **63**(2), 431–440 (2015)
2. He, C., Li, G., Zheng, F., You, X.: Energy-efficient resource allocation in OFDM systems with distributed antennas. IEEE Trans. Veh. Technol. **63**(3), 1223–1231 (2014)
3. Wu, Y., Sun, X., Tan, X.: Cooperative distributed energy generation and energy trading for future smart grid. In: IEEE Control Conference, pp. 8150–8157 (2014)
4. Zhang, J., Andrew, J.: Distributed antenna systems with randomness. IEEE Trans. Wirel. Commun. **7**(9), 3636–3646 (2008)
5. Zhou, Y., Zhong, C., Jin, S.: A low complexity multiuser adaptive modulation scheme for massive MIMO systems. IEEE Signal Process. Lett. **23**(10), 1464–1468 (2016)
6. Goldsmith, A., Chua, S.: Adaptive coded modulation for fading channels. IEEE Trans. Commun. **46**(5), 595–602 (1998)
7. Qiu, X., Chawla, K.: On the performance of adaptive modulation in cellular systems. IEEE Trans. Commun. **47**(6), 884–895 (1999)
8. Yu, X., Tan, W., Wu, B., Li, Y.: Discrete-rate adaptive modulation with variable threshold for distributed antenna system in the presence of imperfect CSI. China Commun. **11**(13), 31–39 (2014)
9. Wang, H., Yu, X., Wang, Y.: Energy-efficient power allocation scheme for DAS with adaptive modulation. In: International Conference on Wireless Communications & Signal Processing, pp. 1–5 (2016)
10. Cho, K., Yoon, D.: On the general BER expression of one and two dimensional ampli-tude modulations. IEEE Trans. Commun. **50**(7), 1074–1080 (2002)

# RETRACTED CHAPTER: A Method of Balanced Sleep Scheduling in Renewable Wireless Sensor Networks

Maohan Song[(⊠)], Weidang Lu, Hong Peng, Zhijiang Xu,
and Jingyu Hua

College of Information Engineering, Zhejiang University of Technology,
Hangzhou 310023, People's Republic of China
959708887@qq.com,
{luweid,ph,zyfxzj,eehjy}@zjut.edu.cn

**Abstract.** Energy harvesting from its environmental sources become an integral part of green cities. This paper considers a low-energy consumption Wireless Sensor Networks to improve energy utilization in green cities. By this approach, a wireless node can directly harvest energy from ambient by introducing an energy-harvesting layer on the top of traditional WSN layer. The energy harvesting layer composed of charging points (CPs) that it can harvest energy from ambient renewable energy sources (solar, vibration, light, and electromagnetic wave, etc.) transfer the harvested energy to the underlying WSN layer by wireless energy transfer. Furthermore, in order to conserve battery power in very dense sensor networks, some sensor nodes may be put into the sleep state while other sensor nodes remain active for the sensing and communication tasks. The proposed scheme applies energy informatics to increase the energy efficiency by optimizing energy harvesting time interval and energy consumption of the node for uniform data gathering over the network.

**Keywords:** Green cities · Energy informatics · Energy harvesting ·
Duty cycles

## 1 Introduction

With the rapid development in ultra-low-power computing and communication devices equipped with the capability of Energy Harvesting (EH), current networking and communication systems are evolving towards green cities concept [1–4]. Green cities play a significant role by enabling connected devices to gather data in an energy-efficient way. Recently, energy informatics technologies, which become an integral part of green smart cities, aim to increase the energy efficiency by analyzing and optimizing energy distribution and energy consumption units.

In energy constrained wireless sensor networks, it is very important to conserve energy and prolong active network lifetime while ensuring proper operations of the network. Energy Harvesting WSNs (EH-WSNs) [5–9] become an emerging approach to prolong network lifetime with harvested energy. This article considers a green WSN,

---

The original version of this chapter was retracted: The retraction note to this chapter is available at
https://doi.org/10.1007/978-3-030-00557-3_67

© ICST Institute for Computer Sciences, Social Informatics and Telecommunications Engineering 2018,
corrected publication 2020

which has two layers as follows: energy harvesting layer and traditional WSN layer equipped with the capability of energy-harvesting. In this green WSNs, the method of energy supply is extended by introducing energy harvesting layer. This energy harvesting layer consists of Charging Points (CPs) that harvest energy from multiple sources. It is assumed that these CPs will have continuous support to obtain energy. However, due to their dynamic nature, the remaining energy in energy storage may vary according to underlying system requirements. In bottom layer, wireless sensor nodes recharge their storage devices by either energy harvesting or direct connection to these CPs. By this way, the upper layer acts as energy distribution layer with CPs, whereas, the lower layer is responsible for sensing and data gathering to support the required Quality-of-Service (QoS) for End Users (EUs) in the green city paradigm.

Although ambient energy sources are infinite, dynamic nature of energy sources restricts the wide application of harvested energy towards sustainable network demand. Thus, it is an equally important issue to efficiently use the harvested energy for energy-balanced network and prolonged underlying sensor networks in green cities. The contributions of our work are summarized as follows:

A renewable WSN is considered for green cities. Furthermore, this article presents a sleep scheduling algorithm that considers the energy utilization and network throughput using energy informatics in the green cities.

The rest of this paper is organized as follows. The system model of green WSN is discussed in Sect. 2. Section 3 presents the problem formulation and proposed algorithm. The performance results and discussed are presented in Sect. 4. Finally, conclusions are drawn in Sect. 5.

## 2   System Model

### 2.1   Practical Network Model

As shown in Fig. 1, the system model of the green WSNs consist of following layers:

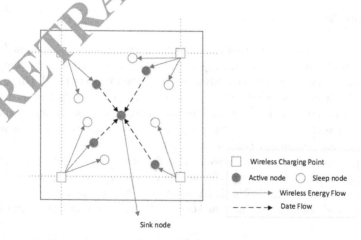

**Fig. 1.** System model of a green WSN

**(1)  Energy Harvesting Layer**

Let N be the number of Charging Points (CPs) in the energy harvesting layer. It is assumed that the power supply of these CPs is sufficient and stable. These CPs can harvest energy from environment (e.g., wind, solar, vibration, indoor light, and EM waves). For the convenience of analysis, the network space is divided into smaller square grids. In addition, the side-length of smaller square grids, L, should be less than $\sqrt{2}R$ [10]. Any CP resides on each vertex of the grid. The main function of this layer is harvest energy from environment and to provide wireless energy to wireless sensor nodes. The main notations in this paper are summarized in Table 1.

**Table 1.**  Notation definition.

| Notation | Definition |
|----------|------------|
| S | The number of wireless sensor nodes |
| N | The number of wireless charging points |
| R | Transmission radius |
| L | The side length of charging grid |
| T | The time duration of a single epoch |
| CPs | The Charging points |
| $\tau$ | The time proportion of energy harvesting |
| n | The number of contending nodes |
| D | The distance from charging point to sensor nodes |
| Q | The harvested energy per unit time |
| $\eta$ | The overall energy conversion efficiency |
| $E_u$ | The energy utilization |
| $E_{h,u}$ | The harvesting energy for the *uth* node |
| $E_{c,u}$ | The energy consumption for the *uth* node |
| $E_{res,u}$ | The residual energy for the *uth* node |
| E | The maximum storage capacity of a sensor |
| TH | The network throughput |

**(2)  Wireless Sensor Node Layer**

Consider a single-hop WSN with total S number of uniformly and randomly deployed static wireless sensor nodes. It is assumed that any wireless sensor nodes are equipped with wireless energy harvesting receiver. The location of any sensor node can be obtained. The sink node is located in the center of the network space and knows the location and IDs of all nodes. It is also assumed that each node has the same functionality and sensing capability.

## 2.2  Energy Harvesting and Energy Consumption

A time-splitting method (see Fig. 2.) is used to handle data transmission and energy harvesting. Each sensor node harvests the wireless energy during $\tau T$ interval and either sends gathered data or forwards data to the sink during the rest interval $(1 - \tau)T$, where

$0 < \tau < 1$ and T is the time duration of a single epoch. According to harvest-use-storage approach, any node first directly harvest energy to the storage unit and then use the stored energy.

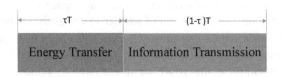

**Fig. 2.** Time allocation method about energy harvesting and data transmission

**(1) Wireless Energy Harvest.**

As each CP sends wireless energy to the sensor nodes, multiple antennas are considered in each transmitter/receiver for wireless energy transfer. Each of the sensor nodes is equipped with a diode and a low-pass filter to convert RF-signal to direct current. By the Friis transmission equation, the received power $P_r$, is calculated as [11]:

$$P_r = P_t \left(\frac{\lambda_0}{4\pi D}\right)^2 G_r G_t \qquad (1)$$

Where $P_t$ is the transmit power, D denotes the normalized distance from the CP to energy-harvesting node, wavelength $\lambda_0 = 12.2$ cm and 5.1 cm for 2.45 GHz and 5.8 GHz frequency [11], $G_r$ and $G_t$ represent gains of transmitter and receiver antenna, respectively. Finally, the harvested energy per unit time is denoted as [12]:

$$Q = \eta Pr = \eta PtD^{-\alpha} G_A \qquad (2)$$

Where $0 < \eta < 1$ is the overall receiver energy conversion efficiency, $\alpha$ is the path loss factor, and $G_A$ denotes the combined antenna gain.

**(2) Wireless Energy Consumption.**

According to the residual energy of the battery, we can dynamically schedule sensors work/sleep cycles (or duty cycles).

*Active state.*

Let $E_T(b,d)$ and $E_R(b)$ be the consumed energy for transmitting a b-bit packet within a distance d and receiving a b-bit packet, respectively, and are given as [12]: $E_T(b,d) = bE_{elec} + bd^\alpha E_{amp}$, and $E_R(b) = bE_{elec}$, where $E_{amp}$ is the energy consumed in the amplifier of the transmitter to send a packet at unit distance, and a node consumes

$E_{elec}$ to run the transceiver circuitry. Finally, the energy consumption of transmitting a b-bit packet from a node u to sink node v as $E_{c,uv}(b) = E_T(b,d) + E_R(b)$ is given as follows [12]:

$$E_{c,uv}(b) = 2bE_{elec} + bd^\alpha E_{amp} \tag{3}$$

*Sleep-stat.*

Due to most of the circuitry goes to a hibernating mode in sleep state, energy consumption is low compared to the awake-state.

## 2.3   Calculation of Throughput

Every sensor node has two states: active and sleep. When an active-node transmits or receives a packet, the contention window is fixed. The Carrier-Sense Multiple Access with Collision Avoidance (CSMA/CA) mechanism can effectively avoid this collision by randomly waiting for a period of time from 0 to W to back off. By Markov chain, we can know the probability of a station transmits in a slot: $p_0 = 2/(W+1)$, where W is a fixed contention window [13]. Then the probability of a successful transmission, i.e., $P_s$ and the average number of consecutive idle slots, i.e., $C_i$ are presented as follows [14]:

$$P_s = \frac{np_0(1-p_0)^{n-1}}{1-(1-p_0)^n} \tag{4}$$

And

$$C_i = \frac{1}{1-(1-p_0)^n} - 1 \tag{5}$$

Finally, with successful transmissions, the network throughput *TH* is expressed as:

$$TH = P_s \frac{\gamma(1-\tau)T}{(1-\tau)T + C_i}, \gamma < 1 \tag{6}$$

Where $\gamma$ is the constraint fraction reserved to packet payload field. According to [13], the approximate optimal value is $W \approx n\sqrt{2(1-\tau)T}$. So, it is observed that the maximization of the network throughput depends on the number of contending active sensor nodes n and packet transmission time $(1-\tau)T$.

## 3  Problem Statement and Algorithm

Although CPs can provide the underlying wireless sensor nodes with a sufficient and stable supply of energy, it is equally important to balance the energy consumption in WSN-layer to efficiently use the harvested energy in green-city paradigm. Sleep-scheduling, one of the efficient approaches to prolong network lifetime, can fulfill this requirement. The traditional CKN-based [15] sleep scheduling algorithm does not consider every nodes residual or consumed energy. The Energy-Consumption-based algorithm, which considers nodes residual energy to decide sleep-state and awake-state, results more awake nodes near CPs due to sufficient amount of harvested energy in nodes closer to the CPs. We know that the awake (or sleep) state occurrence of the sensor nodes is randomly distributed, however, it is not uniformly distributed, the data gathering by the awake nodes is not uniform. Thus, it is an important issue how to design a sleep scheduling algorithm based on harvested, stored, and consumed energy for uniform data collection over the network.

Besides, the energy that harvested by the sensor nodes will linearly increase if the energy harvesting duration increases, however, at the same time, overall network throughput will decrease due to less data transmission duration. Furthermore, the harvested energy in sensor nodes does not always increase the energy utilization due to the limitation of energy storage capacity of sensor nodes over the network. Thus, it is an important task to find optimum ranges of $\tau$ that balance the harvested, stored, and consumed energy and network demand in terms of throughput utilizing energy informatics towards green-city.

A sleep scheduling algorithm is proposed in green WSNs with an aim to balance network demands, residual energy, and harvested energy. The steps are presented as follows:

### 3.1  Step 1 Energy Sleep Scheduling

As shown in Algorithm 1, any node u decides itself to be in the possible set based on the remaining energy $E_{res,u}$, $E_{h,u}$ and $E_{c,u}$. In the proposed scheme, if combined the harvested and the residual energy of any node is not enough for the energy consumption due to data transmission, i.e., $E_{c,u} > (E_{res,u} + E_{h,u})$, then node u goes to the sleep-state. The optimum $\tau$ are obtained based on a throughput threshold $TH^{Threshold}$ and preferred energy utilization $E^{Threshold}$, The energy utilization $E_u$ is expressed in (7), where $A = (\eta E_{h,u} - E_{c,u}) + E_{res}$ and $B = \eta E_{h,u} + E_{res}$.

$$E_u = \frac{1}{\sum_{u=1}^{S} E_{h,u}} \left( \sum_{u=1}^{S} E_{c,u} + \sum_{\substack{u=1 \\ A < E_s \forall u}}^{S_{awake}} (\eta E_{h,u} - E_{c,u}) + \sum_{\substack{u=1 \\ A \geq E_s \forall u}}^{S_{awake}} (E_s - E_{res}) + \sum_{\substack{u=1 \\ B < E_s \forall u}}^{S_{sleep}} \eta E_{h,u} + \sum_{\substack{u=1 \\ B > E_s \forall u}}^{S_{sleep}} (E_s - E_{res}) \right)$$

(7)

| Algorithm 1: Energy-Utilization-Aware Sleep Scheduling | Algorithm 2: Update $E_{res,u}$ for Awake and Sleep Nodes |
|---|---|
| **Input:** $E_{h,u}$, $E_{c,u}$, $E_{res,u}$, $u$, $\eta$ <br><br> **Output:** $S_{awake}$, $S_{sleep}$, $TH$, $E_u$ <br><br> **begin** <br>   **for** u=1 to S **do** <br>     **if** $E_{c,u} > \left(E_{res,u} + E_{h,u}\right)$ **then** <br>       Node u goes to sleep; <br>     **else** <br>       Node u goes to awake; <br>     **end** <br>   **end** <br>   **for** $t = \tau$, $\tau \in (0,1]$ **do** <br>     Calculate the $TH$ and $E_u$ ; <br>   **end** <br>   **Update** $E_{res,u}$ for Awake and Sleep Nodes <br><br> (see Algorithm 2); <br> **end** <br> **Continue to the next epoch** | **Input:** $S_{awake}$, $S_{sleep}$, $E_{h,u}$, $E_{c,u}$, $E_{res,u}$, $\eta$, $E$ <br><br> **Output:** Update $E_{res,u}$ <br><br> **begin** <br>   **for** u=1 to $S_{sleep}$ **do** <br>     **if** $E_{h,u} + E_{res,u} < E$ **then** <br>       $E_{res,u} \leftarrow E_{h,u} + E_{res,u}$ <br>     **else** <br>       $E_{res,u} \leftarrow E$ <br>     **end** <br>   **end** <br>   **for** u=1 to $S_{awake}$ **do** <br>     **if** $E_{h,u} + E_{res,u}$ ⤷ **then** <br>       $E_{res,u} \leftarrow E_{h,u} + E_{res,u} - E_{c,u}$ <br>     **else** <br>       $E_{res,u} \leftarrow E - E_{c,u}$ <br>     **end** <br>   **end** <br> **end** |

### 3.2 Step 2 Update $E_{res,u}$ for the Awake and Sleep Nodes

For the sleep nodes, because the energy consumption is very low compared to awake-state, most of the harvested energy is stored to the storage devices with a storage conversion efficiency $\eta$. Each sleep node recharges its storage device up to the maximum capacity $E_s$. On the other hand, awake nodes use the energy for data transmission after energy storage. The Algorithm 2 presents the above steps.

## 4 Simulation Results and Discussion

Under the condition of $\tau = 0.5$, perform 100 times simulation. Then, with the current residual energy and sensor node working state, calculating the throughput and the energy utilization at different $\tau$. It is important to note that there is no need to update the residual energy at this time for the sake of accuracy of simulation.

Figure 3(a) shows the state of all nodes of initial time over the network. The sink node is located at the center of the network. The side length of the network is 480 m. It is further divided into a square grids in which the border length is 60 m. Charging Points (CPs) resides on the vertex of each square grid. Figure 3(b) shows that the state of all nodes after 100 times simulation over the network. It is clear that the probability of nodes around sink node being awake-state is higher after 100 times simulation, this is due to they have more residual energy.

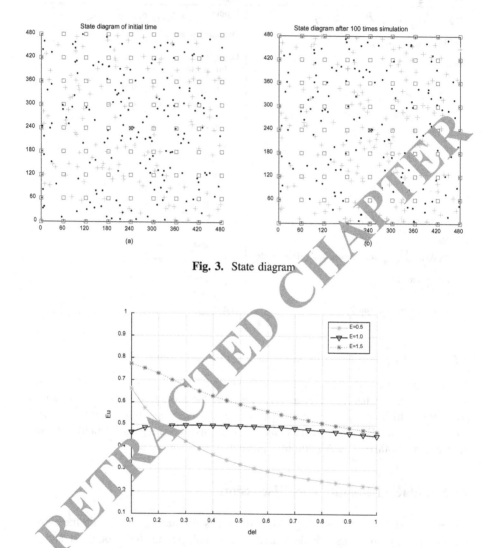

**Fig. 3.** State diagram

**Fig. 4.** The energy utilization with different storage capacity

Figures 4 and 5 show energy utilization and network throughput with different storage capacity. In Fig. 4, we can observe that the energy utilization is rapid decline with E = 0.5 J. The energy utilization with E = 1.0 J tends to be stable. Optimal energy utilization is at E = 1.5 J. In Fig. 5, no matter what the value of storage capacity is, the trend of the three curves is generally consistent. When the value of the E is given, we can get the optimal range of $\tau$.

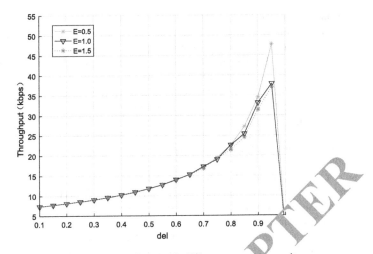

**Fig. 5.** The network throughput with different storage capacity

## 5   Conclusion

This article considers a renewable green WSNs by extending the energy harvesting capabilities for green cities. The charging points that act as energy supply points in energy harvesting layer transfer energy to the WSN layer for data gathering task. In addition, to prolong the network lifetime of WSN layer, a sleep scheduling algorithm that aims uniform data gathering over the whole network with high utilization of harvested energy is proposed. The optimum ranges of time fraction to harvest energy and data transmission duration are provided to support required QoS and high energy utilization. The extensive simulation results reflect the aim of energy informatics technologies of green WSN for green smart cities by balancing energy utilization in terms of harvested energy, consumed energy, storage energy, and network demand in terms of throughput.

## References

1. Cheng, S.: How to build a green city. IEEE Spectr. **44**(6), 26–29 (2007)
2. IEEE Standard for green smart home and residential quarter control network protocol. IEEE Std 1888.4-2016, pp. 1–32, June 2017
3. Zhu, C., Leung, V.C.M., Wang, K., Yang, L.T., Zhang, Y.: Multimethod data delivery for green sensor-cloud. IEEE Commun. Mag. **55**(5), 176–182 (2017)
4. Zhong, W., Yu, R., Xie, S., Zhang, Y., Tsang, D.H.K.: Software defined networking for flexible and green energy internet. IEEE Commun. Mag. **54**(12), 68–75 (2016)
5. Liu, J., Xiong, K., Fan, P., Zhong, Z.: RF energy harvesting wireless powered sensor networks for smart cities. IEEE Access **5**, 9348–9358 (2017)
6. Castagnetti, A., Pegatoquet, A., Le, T.N., Auguin, M.: A joint duty-cycle and transmission power management for energy harvesting WSN. IEEE Trans. Ind. Inform. **10**(2), 928–936 (2014)

7. Djenouri, D., Bagaa, M., Chelli, A., Balasingham, I.: Energy harvesting aware minimum spanning tree for survivable WSN with minimum relay node addition. In: Proceedings of IEEE Globecom Workshops (GC Wkshps), pp. 1–6, December 2016

8. Ju, H., Zhang, R.: Throughput maximization in wireless powered communication networks. IEEE Trans. Wirel. Commun. 13(1), 418–428 (2014)

9. Fang, W., Mukherjee, M., Shu, L., Zhou, Z., Hancke, G.: Energy utilization concerned sleep scheduling in wireless powered communication networks. In: Proceedings of IEEE ICC, pp. 1–6, May 2017

10. Han, G., Qian, A., Jiang, J., Sun, N., Liu, L.: A grid-based joint routing and charging algorithm for industrial wireless rechargeable sensor networks. Elsevier Comput. Netw. 101, 19–28 (2016)

11. Suh, Y.-H., Chang, K.: A high-efficiency dual-frequency rectenna for 2.45-and 5.8-GHz wireless power transmission. IEEE Trans. Microw. Theory Tech. 50(7), 1784–1789 (2002)

12. Heinzelman, W., Chandrakasan, A., Balakrishnan, H.: Energy-efficient communication protocol for wireless microsensor networks. In: Proceedings of IEEE 33rd Annual Hawaii International Conference on System Sciences, Maui, Hawaii, pp. 3005–3014 (2000)

13. Bianchi, G., Fratta, L., Oliveri, M.: Performance evaluation and enhancement of the CSMA/CA MAC protocol for 802.11 wireless LANs. In: Proceedings of IEEE PIMRC, pp. 392–396, October 1996

14. Zhu, C., Chen, Y., Wang, L., Shu, L., Zhang, Y.: SMAC-based proportional fairness backoff scheme in wireless sensor networks. In: Proceedings of ACM 6th IWCMC, June/July 2010, pp. 138–142 (2010)

15. Nath, S., Gibbons, P.B.: Communicating via fireflies: Geographic routing on duty-cycled sensors. In: Proceedings of IEEE/ACM 6th IPSN, Cambridge, MA, pp. 440–449 (2007)

RETRACTED CHAPTER

# Intelligent Ad-hoc and Sensor Networks

# Pedestrian Walking Model for Floor Plan Building Based on Crowdsourcing PDR Data

Guangda Yang[1], Yongliang Zhang[2], Lin Ma[2(✉)], and Leqi Tang[2]

[1] Mobile Communications Group Heilongjiang Co., Ltd., Harbin 150028, China
[2] Communication Research Center, Harbin Institute of Technology,
Harbin, China
malin@hit.edu.cn

**Abstract.** Indoor navigation has gained lots of interest in the last few years due to its broad application prospect. However, indoor floor plan for position display is not always available. In this paper, we utilize the crowdsourcing pedestrian dead reckoning (PDR) data got from the smart phone to build the indoor floor plan. According to the crowdsourcing PDR data, we propose new walking model that reflects the distribution of indoor pedestrian trajectory. This model is can well express the pedestrian walking pattern. In addition, the proposed model can also estimate the hallway width through the PDR data in hallway. According to the proposed model, we can draw the floor plan with the width of hallway. We have implemented the proposed algorithm in our lab and evaluated its performances. The simulation results showed that the proposed algorithm can efficiently generate the floor plan in the unknown environments with lower cost, which can contribute a lot for indoor navigation.

**Keywords:** Floor plan · Mobile crowdsourcing · IMU · PDR

## 1 Introduction

Nowadays, several candidate methods can be employed in the future indoor navigation system, such as WiFi, Bluetooth and ZigBee [1]. Though these methods are different, all they require the same information, which is floor plan. As the indoor geographic information, floor plan contains wealth of geographic information, and it is necessary for the indoor navigation service. Floor plan will be standardized processed after collecting the geographical data, so that all of the navigation and positioning services can be established in the precise geographical space model [2]. With the help of floor plan, indoor navigation system can make specific database in the offline phase [3], and also show its location and navigation estimation clearly in a smart phone in the online phase. Therefore, the complete and accurate of floor plan are the basic conditions for indoor navigation and positioning system.

However, in some cases, floor plan is not always available, which greatly limits the development of indoor navigation service. Considering about the number of buildings or floors, it is unrealistic to make floor plan by SLAM due to the inevitable cost of economic or time [4]. Therefore, we need to find an effective way to build floor plan in the unknown indoor environment. In recent years, it becomes possible to use pedestrian trajectory to indicate the indoor path.

© ICST Institute for Computer Sciences, Social Informatics and Telecommunications Engineering 2018
L. Meng and Y. Zhang (Eds.): MLICOM 2018, LNICST 251, pp. 305–316, 2018.
https://doi.org/10.1007/978-3-030-00557-3_31

The key idea of PDR algorithm is to count the step at a starting point by sensors, and combined with step estimation and heading calculation to realize the pedestrian trajectory estimation. Chen proposed a pedestrian indoor and outdoor seamless positioning method using multi-sensor positioning platform, which based on the fusion GPS and self-contained sensor [5]. Liu proposed a pedestrian positioning and navigation algorithm with a 6 degrees of freedom IMU equipment [6]. [7] proposed a system named CrowdInside, which used the crowdsourcing data to draw the indoor pedestrian trajectories through the smart phone sensors. In [8], Luo proposed an IMAP system, which can collect the smart phone sensor and construct the indoor floor map by detecting interest points, such as doors, elevators or stairs. In [9], Ma proposed a heading angle correction algorithm for PDR trajectory in the indoor corner environment. It turned the heading angle to right angle at the corner through the right angle detection algorithm. In [10], Zhou proposed a system called ALIMC, which can build an indoor floor plan in the unknown environment through an abstract link node model. However, there are still many problems remained for building the indoor floor plan with the crowdsourcing PDR data. The key problem is that all the methods stated above cannot provide the hallway width but only the indoor path. The hallway width is so important that it can help further decide the indoor structure, such as walls, doors and windows. Actually, the crowdsourcing PDR data contain lots of information about the indoor environment that are not well utilized.

Therefore, based on the crowdsourcing PDR data, in this paper, we propose a pedestrian walking model for floor plan building to provide not only the indoor path but also the hallway width. Since the crowdsourcing PDR data have inherent noise, it needs to be cleaned before building the floor plan. We assume the pedestrians prefer to walking in the long straight hallway along the central axis. And when turning happens in the corner, the pedestrians prefer to walk away from the central axis and gradually close to the corner in the rotation area. Finally, with pedestrians walk out rotation area, their path will be back to the hallway central axis again. Based on such a pedestrian walking model, we propose a crowdsourcing PDR data cleaning method. Different from the available literatures, we do non clean the PDR data based on each PDR trajectory but the trajectory point. We set up a simulation environment in our lab. And the experimental results show that the proposed method can better build indoor floor plan, substantially reduce costs. The remainder of this paper is organized as follows. Section 2 will introduce key ideas of the PDR algorithms and indoor walking model. Section 3 will introduce the proposed floor map building method based on PDR data. Section 4 will provide the implementation and performance analysis. Conclusion will be drawn in the last section.

## 2  System Model

### 2.1  PDR Overview

As a useful method to estimate the pedestrian trajectory, PDR algorithm can record the direction and distance from a known start position. The principle of the PDR algorithm is shown in Fig. 1. Each trajectory point represents the position of the pedestrian, and the line between two adjacent dots forms pedestrian trajectory.

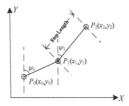

**Fig. 1.** The schematic diagram of PDR algorithm

We assume the initial trajectory point position $P_0(X_0, Y_0)$ is known. The next position is $P_1(X_1, Y_1)$, and the heading angle from $P_0$ to $P_1$ is $\psi_0$, the step length is $S(t_0)$. Then we have:

$$\begin{cases} x_1 = x_0 + S(t_0) \times \sin \psi_0 \\ y_1 = y_0 + S(t_0) \times \cos \psi_0 \end{cases} \tag{1}$$

The general relation from $P_0$ to $P_k$ is:

$$\begin{cases} x_k = x_0 + \sum\limits_{i=0}^{k-1} S(t_i) \cdot \sin \psi_i \\ y_k = y_0 + \sum\limits_{i=0}^{k-1} S(t_i) \cdot \cos \psi_i \end{cases} \tag{2}$$

Due to the traditional gyro integration method for heading calculation will lead to deviation drift, the heading angle calculation is not accurate. Therefore, we utilize the quaternion method to acquire the high-precision heading angle.

## 2.2 Heading Angle Estimation Based on Quaternion

Quaternion is a mathematical method to describe a rotation of a vector relative to a certain coordinate system. It utilizes vector and scalar to define the rotation. Vector indicates the direction of rotation axis and the direction cosine value between rotation axis and coordinate axis. Scalar indicates the cosine of rotation angle in three demission. Equation (3) represents the expression of a new vector $R(t + 1)$ getting from the vector $R(t)$ rotating at a certain angle in a reference coordinate.

$$R(t+1) = q \times R(t) \times q^{-1} \tag{3}$$

where $q = q_0 + q_1 i + q_2 j + q_3 k$, and $i, j, k$ are unit vectors for the three Cartesian axes.

An object rotation can be described with roll $\gamma$, pitch $\theta$ and yaw $\psi$. If the initial rotation at time $t_0$ is known, we have:

$$
\begin{bmatrix} q_0 \\ q_1 \\ q_2 \\ q_3 \end{bmatrix}_{t_0} = \begin{bmatrix} \cos(\gamma_0/2)\cos(\theta_0/2)\cos(\psi_0/2) + \sin(\gamma_0/2)\sin(\theta_0/2)\sin(\psi_0/2) \\ \sin(\gamma_0/2)\cos(\theta_0/2)\cos(\psi_0/2) - \cos(\gamma_0/2)\sin(\theta_0/2)\sin(\psi_0/2) \\ \cos(\gamma_0/2)\sin(\theta_0/2)\cos(\psi_0/2) + \sin(\gamma_0/2)\cos(\theta_0/2)\sin(\psi_0/2) \\ \cos(\gamma_0/2)\cos(\theta_0/2)\sin(\psi_0/2) - \sin(\gamma_0/2)\sin(\theta_0/2)\cos(\psi_0/2) \end{bmatrix} \tag{4}
$$

Then, we can use the first order Runge-Kutta to update the rotation in quaternion from $t_i$ to $t_{i+1}$:

$$
\begin{bmatrix} q_0 \\ q_1 \\ q_2 \\ q_3 \end{bmatrix}_{t_{i+1}} = \begin{bmatrix} q_0 \\ q_1 \\ q_2 \\ q_3 \end{bmatrix}_{t_i} + \frac{(t_{i+1} - t_i)}{2} \begin{bmatrix} -\omega_\gamma q_1 - \omega_\theta q_2 - \omega_\psi q_3 \\ +\omega_\gamma q_0 - \omega_\theta q_3 + \omega_\psi q_2 \\ +\omega_\gamma q_3 + \omega_\theta q_0 - \omega_\psi q_1 \\ -\omega_\gamma q_2 + \omega_\theta q_1 + \omega_\psi q_0 \end{bmatrix}_{t_i} \tag{5}
$$

The resolutions for $\gamma$, $\theta$ and $\psi$ are:

$$
\begin{cases} \gamma_{i+1} = \arctan\dfrac{2(q_2 q_3 + q_0 q_1)}{q_0^2 - q_1^2 - q_2^2 + q_3^2} \\ \theta_{i+1} = -\arcsin(2(q_1 q_3 - q_0 q_2)) \\ \psi_{i+1} = \arctan\dfrac{2(q_1 q_2 + q_0 q_3)}{q_0^2 + q_1^2 - q_2^2 - q_3^2} \end{cases} \tag{6}
$$

Thus, according to Eqs. (2) and (6), we can accurately estimate the PDR trajectory point.

## 3 Pedestrian Walking Model

### 3.1 Pedestrain Indoor Walking Habit Analysis

Generally, there are two common walking mode in the indoor environment, which are walking in straight and walking in corner. The probability model of pedestrian walking in straight is shown in Fig. 2(a). When pedestrians take turns, they tend to take "shortcut" in most cases. They will departure from the central axis and approach to the inside corner gradually. The probability model of the pedestrian walking in corner is shown in Fig. 2(b).

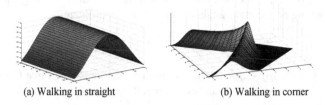

(a) Walking in straight          (b) Walking in corner

**Fig. 2.** Pedestrian walking case

Based on the analysis above, we model the pedestrian walking habit with the Erlang distribution. Either in straight case or corner case, the trajectory point distribution can be described as:

$$f(x) = \frac{\lambda(\lambda x)^{k-1}}{(k-1)!} e^{-\lambda x} \tag{7}$$

where $\lambda$ is the coefficient of Erlang, $k$ is the order. When $\lambda = 0.5$, the distribution probability is shown in Fig. 3 to describe the PDR trajectory point distribution both for walking in straight and walking in corner.

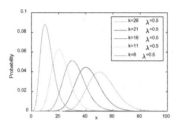

**Fig. 3.** Erlang distribution

In order to better analysis the distribution of trajectory points in corner, we illustrate a real crowdsourcing PDR trajectory points in Fig. 4, where the blue dots are PDR trajectory points and the red dash line are the hallway central. We further model the trajectory points distribution in Fig. 4 into three types of area as straight are, transition area and rotation area, which are used to describe the pedestrian walking in different cases in the hallway. We illustrated in Fig. 5.

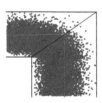

**Fig. 4.** Trajectory points distribution

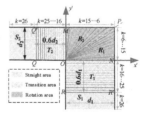

**Fig. 5.** Corner area division

As shown in Fig. 5, $S_1$ and $S_2$ are straight areas, which means pedestrian is walking in straight and does not tend to take a turn. $T_1$ and $T_2$ are the areas where pedestrian is ready to start or finish a turning. $R_1$ and $R_2$ are rotation areas, which means pedestrian is turning a corner. Suppose the hallway width of $S_1$ area and $T_1$ area are $d_1$, and the hallway width of $S_2$ area and $T_2$ area are $d_2$. The boundaries of $S$ and $T$ are $QQ'$ and $RR'$, and the boundaries of $T$ and $R$ are $OM$ and $ON$ respectively. The boundary of $R_1$

and $R_2$ is $OP$. According to our experiment results, we find that if the hallway width is $d$, pedestrian will start and finish the turning at $0.6d$. So, we set the length of $OQ$ is $0.6d_1$ and the length of $OR$ is $0.6d_2$ in transition area.

## 3.2    Pedestrian Walking Model

We assume pedestrians start from the $S_2$ area and passes through $S_2$-$T_2$-$R_2$-$R_1$-$T_1$-$S_1$ in clockwise. When they are walking in the $S_2$ area, they tend to walking in a straight central axis of hallway. Then the order of Erlang distribution is $k = 26$. When pedestrians pass $QQ'$ and walk into the $T_2$ area, their walking paths are gradually approaching to the inside corner point $O$. In this area, $k$ gradually decreases from 25 to 16, until pedestrians cross $OM$ into the $R_2$ area. When pedestrians are in turning state, their walking trajectories are gradually close to the corner point $O$. Until walking to the cross section $OP$, the pedestrians are closest to the corner $O$. The order of Erlang distribution $k$ now gradually decreases from 15 to 6. When pedestrians cross the diagonal $OP$ and continue to walk, their paths are gradually away from $O$ and return to the central axis of the hallway. The path will be back to the axis of the hallway on $RR'$. The returning process is similar to the turning process and the order $k$ is increased from 6 to 25. In this way, we divide $T_2$, $R_2$, $R_1$, and $T_1$ equally. $T_1$ and $T_2$ areas are divided into 10 segments, and the order of Erlang distribution $k$ is from 16 to 25. $R_1$ and $R_2$ areas, taking the inner corner as the center of the circle, are equal divided into 10 segments, where $k$ varies from 6 to 15. As shown in Fig. 3, the width and position of Erlang major distribution area are changes with the change of $k$. So, we introduce scaling coefficient $t$ to make the width of Erlang major distribution area consistent with the hallway cross section. And we introduce deviation coefficient $a/\lambda$ to make Erlang major distribution area corresponding to the actual location of PDR trajectory. In this way, Eq. (7) can be rewritten as follows:

$$f(x, \alpha_i, k_i) = \frac{\lambda[\lambda(tx + a/\lambda)]^{k_i-1}}{(k_i - 1)!} e^{-\lambda(tx + a/\lambda)} \tag{8}$$

$$\lambda = b\left[(d_1 \cos \alpha_i)^2 + (d_2 \sin \alpha_i)^2\right]^{-1/2} \tag{9}$$

where $a = 0.062k_i - 3.463$, $b = 0.151k_i + 2.478$.

Combining the coordinate translation and the change matrix, we can unify all cases to the coordinate system shown in Fig. 4 (Fig. 5). The coordinate translation in $S_2$, $T_2$, $R_2$, $R_1$, $T_1$, and $S_1$ is:

$$\begin{bmatrix} x' \\ y' \end{bmatrix} = \begin{bmatrix} \cos \alpha_i & -\sin \alpha_i \\ \sin \alpha_i & \cos \alpha_i \end{bmatrix} \begin{bmatrix} x \\ y \end{bmatrix} + \begin{bmatrix} 0 \\ y_{step} \end{bmatrix} \tag{10}$$

Thus, we can get the probability density distribution of trajectory point in different areas as follows:

$$f = \frac{\lambda[\lambda(10x' + a/\lambda)]^{k_i-1}}{(k_i - 1)!} e^{-\lambda(10x' + a/\lambda)} \tag{11}$$

So in different areas, we have different $a$ and $k$. In straight area $S_1$ and $S_2$:

$$\alpha_i = 0, \quad k_i = 26 \tag{12}$$

In transition area $T_2$:

$$\alpha_i = \frac{\pi}{2}, \quad k_i = 26 - \left\lceil 10 + \frac{x'}{0.06d_2} \right\rceil \tag{13}$$

In rotation area $R_2$:

$$\alpha_i = 0.1i \arctan(d_2/d_1) + \arctan(d_1/d_2), \quad k_i = 6 + i \tag{14}$$

In rotation area $R_1$:

$$\alpha_i = 0.1\, i \arctan(d_1/d_2), \quad k_i = 16 - i \tag{15}$$

where we have $i = 0,\ldots,10$. In transition area $T_1$:

$$\alpha_i = 0, \quad k_i = 26 - \left\lfloor 10 + \frac{y'}{0.06d_2} \right\rfloor \tag{16}$$

where $\alpha_i$ is the angle of rotation, $k$ is the Erlang coefficient.

In summary, the pedestrian trajectory points distribution in hallway can be expressed as follows:

$$f' = f(x', \alpha_i, k_i) \tag{17}$$

where $\alpha_i$ and $k_i$ can be summarized as follows:

$$\alpha_i = \begin{cases} 0.1i \arctan\frac{d_1}{d_2} & i = 0,\ldots,10 \\ 0.1(i-10)\arctan\frac{d_1}{d_2} + \arctan\frac{d_1}{d_2} & i = 11,\ldots,20 \\ 0 & \text{others} \end{cases} \quad k_i = \begin{cases} 16 - i & i = 0,\ldots,10 \\ i - 4 & i = 11,\ldots,20 \\ i - 5 & i = 21,\ldots,30 \\ 25 & \text{others} \end{cases} \tag{18}$$

And the step of each part can show as follows:

$$y_{step} = \begin{cases} 0 & \text{rotation area} \\ l \times n_i/n & \text{others} \end{cases} \tag{19}$$

where $l$ is the length of hallway, and $n_i/n$ is step radio.

In above equations, all the parameters are known without the hallway width $d_1$ and $d_2$. We will estimate the hallway width in the following subsection.

### 3.3   Hallway Width Estimation

Large number of experiment data show that when the pedestrians are far away from the starting point, their trajectory points will be more divergent leading to errors. There are two reasons causing errors. The first one is PDR algorithm will inherently accumulate the measurement error. With the extension of the walking distance, the error accumulation of the PDR algorithm will lead to a divergence of the trajectory. The second reason is the accumulated error generated by gyroscope of smartphone. The error caused by calculate of heading angle will lead a divergence phenomenon when the PDR trajectory passes the turning point. Thus, PDR trajectories obtained by crowdsourcing users will be partially inaccurate as shown in Fig. 6.

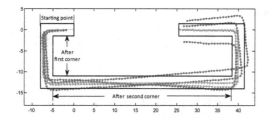

**Fig. 6.** PDR trajectory diagram

At different locations, the trajectory points distribution at the cross section of hallway are shown in Fig. 7.

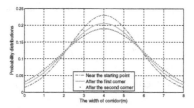

**Fig. 7.** The relationship between starting point and probability distributions

Because of the PDR error, some PDR trajectory points will be outside the real hallway. If we select these outliers to estimate the hallway width, a larger hallway width maybe got. To solve this problem, we introduce the turning factor $m$ and the correction factor $\xi$ to estimate the hallway width as:

$$d = \xi(\sigma - m \times \gamma) \tag{20}$$

where $\gamma$ is the number of corners that one PDR trajectory turns, $\sigma$ is the standard deviation of Erlang probability distribution function. On account of the standard deviation can reflect the dispersion of the random variables, we use $\sigma$ to describe the major distribution area of Erlang distribution.

As we known, though two straight hallways are connected by one corner, they do not always have the same width. We should estimate the hallway width respectively. The next step is to distinguish trajectory points which are belong to the same straight areas. As shown in Fig. 8, there are lots of PDR trajectories start nearly from the middle of the floor plan, which are actually to show pedestrians walk from the elevators. And then pedestrians turn left or right for their ways.

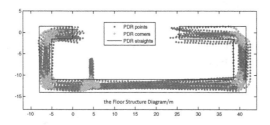

**Fig. 8.** The filter result of PDR trajectory points in corner (Color figure online)

The estimation of hallway width can be seen as the estimation of major distribution area of PDR trajectory points projected to the cross section of hallway. Therefore, we further process the PDR data of straight hallway (red point in Fig. 8) by clustering method to distinguish whether the PDR trajectory point is belong to the straight area or not. We then segment the straight hallway evenly and project the trajectory points to the hallway cross section. Therefore the histogram of occurrence is established and fitted with the Erlang distribution of $k = 26$. Finally, we can get $\sigma$ for different straight area. According to analysis of massive straight hallway PDR data, we can further get the parameter $m$ and $\gamma$.

# 4   Implementation and Performance Analysis

## 4.1   Experiment Environment

We make an experiment in our lab, which is located in Information building, Science Park of Harbin Institute of Technology, China, as shown in Fig. 9. In this building, the main experimental environment is the indoor hallway illustrated with blue part. The crowdsourcing PDR trajectory acquisition equipment are Google Nexus 4, Google Pixel and Redmi 3. We use the PDR algorithm to generate the PDR trajectories for indoor floor plan building, and the original data are collected based on the acceleration and gyro from the smartphones stated above.

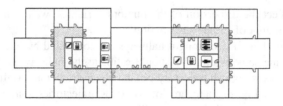

**Fig. 9.** The diagram of experimental environment in hallway (Color figure online)

## 4.2 Performance Analysis

In this experiment environment, there are 5 turnings, and there remains 6 different straight hallways as shown in Fig. 10. Different color represents the result of clustering, and the black points means the noise.

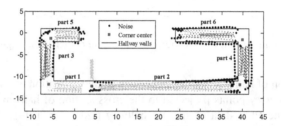

**Fig. 10.** Straight area diagram (Color figure online)

According to a large number of straight hallway data testing and simulation, we can get turning factor $m$ and correction factor $\xi$ as shown in Table 1.

**Table 1.** Results of hallway width estimation

|  | Part1 | Part2 | Part3 | Part4 | Part5 | Part6 |
|---|---|---|---|---|---|---|
| $\sigma$ | 0.660 | 0.668 | 0.863 | 0.844 | 0.960 | 1.078 |
| $m$ | 1 | 1 | 2 | 2 | 3 | 3 |
| $m \times \gamma$ | 0.216 | 0.216 | 0.432 | 0.432 | 0.648 | 0.648 |
| $\xi(\sigma - m \times \gamma)$ | 3.108 | 3.164 | 3.017 | 2.884 | 2.184 | 3.011 |

In our proposed model, the correction factor $\xi = 7$, and the turning factor $m = 0.216$. Based on the summary of Table 1, the hallway width in the 6 part are respectively 3.1 m, 3.2 m, 3.0 m, 2.9 m, 2.1 m and 3.0 m. The width we estimate is similar to the true value of hallway width except part 5. Finally, we get the floor boundary as shown in Fig. 11, and this boundary is the indoor hallway environment floor plan based on crowdsourcing PDR data.

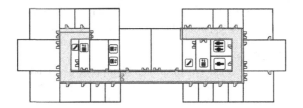

**Fig. 11.** The final generated floor plan in experiment environment

# 5   Conclusion

In this paper, we proposed a novel floor plan building method based on the crowd-sourcing PDR data. We build an indoor pedestrian walking mode, which includes walking in straight and walking in corner. Based on the analysis of the PDR trajectory points of straight hallway, the hallway width can be estimated. We use turning factor and correction factor to restore the width of the hallway well. Finally, by solving the hallway width, the contour of the PDR is generated, and the accurate indoor floor plan can be obtained. This algorithm can establish the floor plan more efficiently when lacking floor plan in an unknown indoor environment.

**Acknowledgment.** This paper is supported by National Natural Science Foundation of China (61571162), Ministry of Education - China Mobile Research Foundation (MCM20170106) and Heilongjiang Province Natural Science Foundation (F2016019).

# References

1. Purohit, A., Sun, Z., Pan, S., Zhang, P.: SugarTrail: indoor navigation in retail environments without surveys and maps. In: 2013 IEEE International Conference on Sensing, Communications and Networking (SECON), New Orleans, LA, pp. 300–308 (2013)
2. Murray, A.T.: Advances in location modeling: GIS linkages and contributions. J. Geogr. Syst. **12**(3), 335–354 (2010)
3. Fallah, N., Apostolopoulos, I., Bekris, K., Folmer, E.: Indoor human navigation systems: a survey. Interact. Comput. **25**(1), 21–33 (2013)
4. Marck, J.W., Mohamoud, A., vd Houwen, E., van Heijster, R.: Indoor radar SLAM A radar application for vision and GPS denied environments. In: 2013 European Microwave Conference, Nuremberg, pp. 1783–1786 (2013)
5. Wang, Q., Zhang, X., Chen, X., Chen, R., Chen, W., Chen, Y.: A novel pedestrian dead reckoning algorithm using wearable EMG sensors to measure walking strides. In: 2010 Ubiquitous Positioning Indoor Navigation and Location Based Service, Kirkkonummi, pp. 1–8 (2010)
6. Liu, Y., Li, S., Mu, C., Wang, Y.: Step length estimation based on D-ZUPT for pedestrian dead-reckoning system. Electron. Lett. **52**(11), 923–924 (2016)
7. Alzantot, M., Youssef, M.: CrowdInside: automatic construction of indoor floorplans. In: 20th International Conference on Advances in Geographic Information Systems (SIGSPATIAL 2012), pp. 99–108 (2012)

8. Luo, C., Hong, H., Cheng, L., Sankaran, K., Chan, M.C.: iMap: automatic inference of indoor semantics exploiting opportunistic smartphone sensing. In: 2015 12th Annual IEEE International Conference on Sensing, Communication, and Networking (SECON), Seattle, WA, pp. 489–497 (2015)

9. Ma, W., Wu, J., Long, C., Zhu, Y.: HiHeading: smartphone-based indoor map construction system with high accuracy heading inference. In: 2015 11th International Conference on Mobile Ad-hoc and Sensor Networks (MSN), Shenzhen, pp. 172–177 (2015)

10. Zhou, B., Li, Q., Mao, Q., Tu, W., Zhang, X., Chen, L.: ALIMC: activity landmark-based indoor mapping via crowdsourcing. IEEE Trans. Intell. Transp. Syst. **16**(5), 2774–2785 (2015)

# Weight Matrix Analysis Algorithm for WLAN Indoor Positioning System

Lin Ma$^{(\boxtimes)}$, Jian Li, and Yubin Xu

Communication Research Center, Harbin Institute of Technology, Harbin, China
malin@hit.edu.cn

**Abstract.** Because WLAN signal strength data is vulnerable to external interference and its validity period is short-lived, it is necessary to reconstruct radio map to improve positioning performance. We add the weight data to the original fingerprint library, which is obtained by the reliability of information. Using it, we can know the importance of neighborhood points selected in the online phase and get better positioning performance. In the positioning phase, the KD tree is added to improve the positioning efficiency of the positioning algorithm. Finally, the positioning accuracy and efficiency can be improved.

**Keywords:** Indoor positioning · WLAN · Radio map · Weight matrix analysis

## 1 Introduction

With the development of positioning technology, people use positioning more and more widely. At the same time, people's demand for indoor positioning is also increasing. At present, indoor positioning technology based on WLAN [1, 2] has made great progress in the algorithm, but it still lacks specific management and construction in the use of fingerprint database. The fingerprint database usually consists of receiving signal strength information, because the fingerprint database is continuously updated. we need to continuously update signal strength information from access point (AP). These information is the uneven distribution and different quality, therefore, it is necessary to reconstruct the fingerprint database in order to reduce the uneven distribution and the poor positioning effect caused by the poor reliability information.

At the present stage, the research on the reconfiguration of Radio map is mainly aimed at improving the positioning effect and positioning efficiency of the original positioning system [3–5], several reconstruction algorithms will be introduced below. Bong [6] proposed a method to optimize the received signal strength (RSS), through smoothing the RSS processing radio map. This method can retain the positioning accuracy, simplify radio map and improve the efficiency of online positioning. Li [7] Put forward a set of good radio map reconstruction model. Removing abnormal data, dividing the region of radio map, selecting AP [8, 9] and reducing the dimension of AP in the region, using the weighted K nearest neighbor (KNN) algorithm [10] to position, positioning time, the capacity of the database are reduced when the positioning accuracy is guaranteed.

© ICST Institute for Computer Sciences, Social Informatics and Telecommunications Engineering 2018
L. Meng and Y. Zhang (Eds.): MLICOM 2018, LNICST 251, pp. 317–326, 2018.
https://doi.org/10.1007/978-3-030-00557-3_32

Although the current reconstruction algorithm can make the original radio map get a good improvement in localization accuracy and computation time, but we can not guarantee the stability of the fingerprint database. When continuous abnormal signal is received over a period of time, that affects the accuracy of the positioning system, it is difficult to solve this problem easily by eliminating abnormal data. To solve this problem, a weight database is constructed, which is based on RSS similarity and AP and provide a positioning reference weight for the data in different time periods to assist on-line positioning and to improve the stability of radio map. In order to ensure the efficiency of database location, KD tree [11] is constructed based on RSS data and weight data. The following is the overall structure of this paper. In Sect. 2, we will introduce the overall model architecture of the indoor positioning system, and give the positioning algorithm and the specific function of the reconfiguration technology applied in the indoor positioning system and the composition of the reconstruction algorithm proposed in this paper. In Sect. 3, we will give the concrete algorithm of the reconstruction technology, including the establishment of the weight database and the construction of KD tree. In Sect. 4, we will implement the reconstruction technology, and compare it with the performance of the previous reconstruction technology. Finally, conclusion will be drawn.

## 2  Indoor Positioning System Model

Positioning based fingerprint positioning system can be divided into two phases, as shown in Fig. 1, including the offline phase and the online phase [12]. The offline phase mainly completes the establishment of radio map, and the online phase mainly completes the application of radio map to realize the matching and positioning.

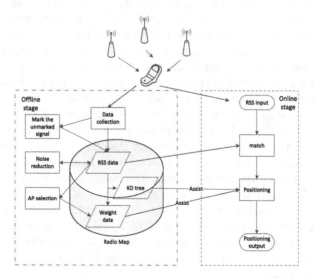

**Fig. 1.**  Positioning system based on position fingerprint

In the offline phase, the wireless base station receives a signal from a WLAN client, and the system will establish the mapping relationship between the received signal strength of all AP in the target area and the actual physical location, and we use the mapping to construct radio map. It is assumed that there are $M$ access points and location information for $N$ reference points in the positioning environment. The radio map format is constructed as follows

$$RadioMap = [L \quad S] \tag{1}$$

where $L \in R^{2 \times N}$ is the position information and contains the reference point position coordinate, and $S \in R^{M \times N}$ is the received signal strength information and contains the received signal strength of $N$ dimension. The initial radio map is of great computational complexity and poor positioning accuracy, so it is necessary to optimize the initial Radio [13] to improve the positioning efficiency of radio map. These optimization algorithms can be classified as part of the reconstruction technology, including the noise reduction, smoothing and clustering algorithms for the fingerprint library [14]. The reconstruction technology proposed in this paper is applied to the offline phase, and the reliability analysis of RSS data is carried out during the off-line updating phase, and the weighted matrix and KD tree are constructed.

In the online phase, the positioning [15] is implemented on the basis of optimized radio map. The received data is used to position mainly by using nearest neighbor method, maximum likelihood probability method, kernel function method, neural network method and support vector regression method. In the reconstruction algorithm proposed in this paper, the weight database is involved in the assisted positioning, and the weighted KNN algorithm is used. Compared to the traditional KNN algorithm, weighted KNN increases the sample weight allocation step, but this phase takes little time comparing with the classification decision phase. The weighted KNN algorithm is applied to this subject. The redistribution of weights is realized on the objective conditions in the actual environmental factors. The reconfiguration technique proposed in this paper is based on the weight database, and the weights in the database are applied to the weighted KNN algorithm to assist the on-line positioning. Formula is as follows

$$D_k = \sqrt{\sum_{i=1}^{m} \beta_i \cdot (RSS_{u,i} - RSS_{k,i})^2} \tag{2}$$

$$(x_u, y_u) = \sum_{k=1}^{n} \gamma_k \cdot \frac{1}{D_k^{\alpha}} \cdot (x_k, y_k) \tag{3}$$

where the $RSS$ is the information in the RSS database, the $\beta$ and $\gamma$ are the weights in the weight database, and $D$ is the distance between the reference points and the positioned points.

## 3  Reconstruction Technology

As mentioned above, in the online phase, the localization algorithm needs to create a weight database to assist the positioning. The reconstruction algorithm proposed in this paper consists of two parts, obtaining weights based on RSS and AP, and constructing KD tree. Through the above several algorithms, the original radio map is reconstructed, and the weight matrix and the KD tree are obtained. Finally, the reconstructed fingerprint database is combined with the weight matrix and the KD tree to Position online.

### 3.1  Weight Based on RSS

The weighting algorithm based on RSS uses the Truth Finder algorithm for reference, and obtains the reliability by comparing the similarity between RSS. Because of different mobile devices in different time periods, the reliability of accepting RSSs for each period of time is different, therefore the accuracy of the data in different time periods needs to be calculated, which can be calculated from the arithmetic mean of the probability that the data is true

$$a_w = \frac{1}{m} \sum_{k=1}^{m} p(e \le \delta) \quad w \in W \tag{4}$$

where m is the number of RSS messages obtained for each period, and the error is within the acceptable range, and $\delta$ is an acceptable error.

Obtained by the Bayesian formula

$$p(x) \propto \prod_{w \in W} \frac{a_w}{1 - a_w} \tag{5}$$

Where $w$ is a period of time, $W$ is all time periods. Let

$$c(x) = \ln \prod_{w \in W} \frac{a_w}{1 - a_w} = \sum_{w \in W} \ln \frac{a_w}{1 - a_w} \tag{6}$$

$$q = \ln \frac{a}{1 - a} \tag{7}$$

Based on (6) and (7), we can have:

$$c(x) = \sum_{w \in W} q_w \tag{8}$$

The normalized probability distribution is obtained, which is added to the weight matrix as a weight $\gamma$.

$$p(X=x) = \frac{c(x)}{\sum c(y)} \tag{9}$$

where $c(x)$ can be corrected by the similarity between RSSs, the correction process is as follows.

Signal similarity is

$$r(x,x') = \frac{xx'}{|x||x'|} \tag{10}$$

The corrected credibility is

$$c'(x) = c(x) + \sum_{e(x)=e(x')} (r(x,x')-\rho)c(x') \tag{11}$$

where $\rho$ is the similarity parameter, and by adjusting the parameter, we can get the effective weight. This parameter is selected according to the positioning environment. Eventually, the weight $\gamma$ can be obtained from the posterior probability.

### 3.2 Weight Based on AP

Taking account of the positioning environment, the performance of each AP is different. In the positioning process, the poor performance of the AP will often cause the positioning accuracy decreased. So each AP needs a weight to express its performance is good or bad in a particular environment, and we use AP selection algorithm to determine the weight.

In the AP selection algorithm, the simplest algorithm is to keep all APs as samples, but this does not play a role in improving the system. The MaxMean algorithm was proposed by Youssef. We need to average the RSS values of the signals received by all APs, and then select several APs with large RSS meanings as optional access points for that location and provide weight to these APs.

Another AP selection algorithm is the InfoGain algorithm, which is based on the gain of information entropy, which is presented by Chen of Hong Kong University of Science and Technology. Firstly, the stochastic entropy of radio map is calculated, and then the conditional entropy of different APs is calculated. The AP is sorted by calculating the difference between stochastic entropy and conditional entropy. The AP with high information entropy gain is used to construct the fingerprint library.

$$IG(AP_i) = H(G) - H(G|AP_j) \tag{12}$$

among them:

$$H(G) = -\sum_{g=1}^{n_i} p(G_g) \log_2 p(G_g) \tag{13}$$

$$H(G|AP_j) = -\sum_v \sum_{g=1}^{n_i} p(G_g, AP_j = v) \log_2 p(G_g|AP_j = v) \tag{14}$$

where $H(G)$ is the gain of the information entropy of the AP, $IG(AP_i)$ is the information entropy when there is no AP information, $p(G)$ is the information entropy for the AP information, and $p(G)$ is the probability of judging the various positions. The weight is obtained from the gain of the information entropy.

There is also a method based on the stability of the AP, firstly we use the RSS variance information to determine an amount that represents the AP stability. At the same time, considering the relationship between the intensity of the signal and the frequency of the occurrence of the signal, the energy information of the signal is reflected by a frequency. Combine two aspects to obtain the value of the AP stability as a weight. The formula is as follows

$$Sta(AP_i) = \frac{1}{\frac{1}{N}\sum_{j=1}^{N}(RSS_j - \overline{RSS})^2} \cdot \frac{N_i}{Sum_{k=1}^{n}(N_k)} \tag{15}$$

where $N_i$ is the frequency at which each AP appears.

Using the above algorithms, we can get the weight of each AP in the region, which is the weight $\beta$ mentioned above.

The weighted KNN algorithm described above requires the traversal of the entire database when we need to obtain the nearest neighbor reference point, so it takes a lot of time in the online positioning phase. The weighted KNN algorithm is combined with the KD tree and has a very high efficiency. By creating the KD tree, it can save the time of calculation.

KD tree is a high-dimensional index tree data structure, commonly used in large-scale high-dimensional data space for the nearest neighbor search and approximate nearest neighbor search, such as high-dimensional image feature vector for K proximity searching and matching in image retrieval and recognition. When a K-nearest neighbor of a reference point is required, it is only necessary to trace along the branches of the KD tree to find the nearest few data.

KD tree construction algorithm: select the dimension with the largest variance in the k-dimensional data set, and then select the median m in this dimension as pivot to divide the data into two sub-sets, while creating a tree node for storage. This step is repeated until all sub-sets can not be divided. If a subset can no longer be divided, the data in the sub-set is saved to the leaf node.

# 4 Implementation and Performance Analysis

## 4.1 Experiment Environment

The experimental environment is located at 12th floor, 2A Building, Science and Technology Park, Harbin Institute of Technology. The height of this floor is 3 m, the area is $66.43 \times 24.9$ m$^2$, with 19 laboratories and a conference room and a table tennis room. The experimental facilities were spread across the 12th floor laboratory and were fixed at a height of 2 m. The device supports IEEE 802.11 g standard, and its transmission rate is 54 Mbps. The receiver is 1.2 m from the ground.

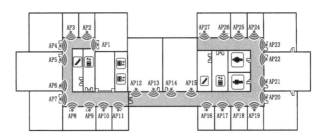

**Fig. 2.** Experiment environment

In order to test the universality of the reconstructed model, we select the 12th floor corridor as the experimental area, so that we can get more signals from the AP in the experiment, and the AP selection algorithm can be effectively tested. 27 APs evenly distribute in the laboratories, as shown in Fig. 2, to ensure that any location in the 12 layer can have more AP. Use a laptop computer as a data collector to collect fingerprint library data and test data.

In the laboratory corridor, the yellow area in the figure, evenly select the reference point within every 0.5 m, and select 823 reference points and rely on these reference points to build radio map. Firstly collect 420 data at each sampling point, and then remove the 20 data in the first and tail, and finally use the remaining 400 data to build the initial radio map to ensure that the initial radio map has a better positioning effect.

In addition to building a radio map, we also need to get the test data used in the online positioning phase. We collect the data in a random location, collected in five time periods. We collect data in five time periods, because the need for different time periods to grant different weights to the original fingerprint library and updating operation in the establishment of the RSS weight. Assume that the test data selected in the five time periods are not relevant and are randomly distributed in the positioning area. We need to collect 200 times to get the final test data in each time period, and collect data in a random location.

## 4.2  Performance Analysis

Based on different test data for several experiments, Fig. 3 is the cumulative error probability obtained three reconstruction algorithms. The reconstruction algorithm based on AP selection is the reconstruction algorithm mentioned above. Using the noise reduction algorithm and AP selection algorithm to optimize the original radio map, we can see that it can improve the positioning accuracy after removing the abnormal information and the selection of feasible AP, cumulative probability within 2 m increased by 8%. The reconstruction algorithm based on weight matrix proposed in this paper can more effectively distinguish the data confidence in each time. Compared with the noise reduction algorithm, the positioning accuracy is improved, and the cumulative probability of positioning within two meters is increased by 3%.

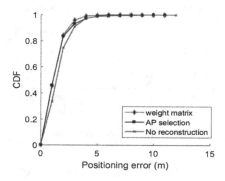

**Fig. 3.**  Different reconstruction algorithm

Next, for different noise powers, the performance of the reconstructed technique is compared. When the power spectral density is gradually increased and the system parameters are kept as the optimal parameters, the experimental comparison is carried out. Figure 4 shows the cumulative error probability of the positioning error in the environment where the noise power spectral density is increased by 3, 4 and 10. It can be seen from the trend of curve with the noise enhancement, the maximum positioning error is increasing. In the low-noise environment, the maximum positioning error of the reconstruction algorithm based on weight matrix is better than that of AP-based

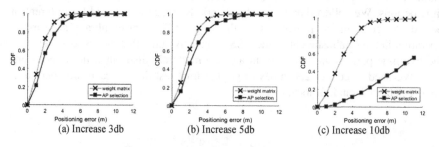

**Fig. 4.**  Different noise environments

reconstruction algorithm, and the positioning error is reduced by 3.5 m. It can be seen that the reconstruction algorithm based on AP can not guarantee the lower positioning error and can not meet the requirement of location, when the noise power spectral density is increased by 10. However, the reconstruction algorithm based on weight matrix has better positioning effect.

The positioning efficiency of the two reconstruction algorithms is compared below. Table 1 is the comparison of the positioning usage time under different fingerprint libraries. The first reconstruction scheme uses zoning to position, using multi-step positioning, which can effectively improve the positioning efficiency. The second location is the KD tree proposed in this paper. As can be seen from the experimental results, the use of KD tree can save a lot of time in the positioning phase, and with the increasing number of fingerprint libraries, the time saved is also rising compared to the former reconstruction algorithm.

**Table 1.** KD tree experiment

| Fingerprint library size (number of RSS) | 1000 | 2000 | 5000 | 10000 | 20000 |
|---|---|---|---|---|---|
| Using zoning (s) | 0.472 | 0.939 | 6.976 | 14.558 | 30.320 |
| Using the KD tree (s) | 0.145 | 0.208 | 0.283 | 0.510 | 1.068 |

# 5   Conclusion

In this paper, a new method is proposed to solve the problem that the stability of the positioning system is degraded by the long time abnormality signal of radio map. The original fingerprint library is reconstructed by constructing the weight matrix and KD tree of radio map. And we compare the performance of the reconstruction algorithm in the laboratory environment. The accumulated positioning error within two meters is increased by 11% and increased by 3% to comparing the reconstruction algorithms based on AP selection. The algorithm presented in this paper uses the weight matrix provided by RSS reliability analysis to assist in positioning, and the performance of resisting noise has been improved. In view of the positioning efficiency, the proposed positioning algorithm combined with the KD tree simplifies the complexity of the nearest neighbor search algorithm. It can be seen from the experimental results that the positioning time is shortened.

**Acknowledgment.** This paper is supported by National Natural Science Foundation of China (61571162), Ministry of Education - China Mobile Research Foundation (MCM20170106) and Heilongjiang Province Natural Science Foundation (F2016019).

# References

1. Gartner, G., Ortag, F.: Advances in location-based services. Lect. Notes Geoinformation Cartogr. **5**(8), 97–106 (2014)
2. Feng, C., Au, W.S.A., Valaee, S., et al.: Received-signal-strength-based indoor positioning using compressive sensing. IEEE Trans. Mob. Comput. **11**(12), 1983–1993 (2012)
3. Baala, O., Zheng, Y., Caminada, A.: The impact of AP placement in WLAN-based indoor positioning system. In: Eighth International Conference on Networks, pp. 12–17. IEEE Computer Society (2009)
4. Pan, J.J., Pan, S.J., Yin, J., et al.: Tracking mobile users in wireless networks via semi-supervised colocalization. IEEE Trans. Pattern Anal. Mach. Intell. **34**(3), 587–600 (2012)
5. Au, A.W.S., Feng, C., Valaee, S., et al.: Indoor tracking and navigation using received signal strength and compressive sensing on a mobile device. IEEE Trans. Mob. Comput. **12**(10), 2050–2062 (2013)
6. Bong, W., Kim, Y.C.: Reconstruction of radio map from sparse RSS data by discontinuity preserving smoothing. In: ACM Research in Applied Computation Symposium, pp. 227–231. ACM (2012)
7. Li, X., Deng, Z.: Radio map reconstruction technology in indoor fingerprint localization algorithm (2012)
8. Deng, Z., Ma, L., Xu, Y.: Intelligent AP selection for indoor positioning in wireless local area network. In: International ICST Conference on Communications and Networking in China, pp. 257–261. IEEE Computer Society (2011)
9. Umair, M.Y., Xiao, D., Li, A., et al.: Access point selection for indoor positioning in a WLAN environment using an algorithm based on RSSI and dilution of precision. Environ. Entomol. **26**(3), 91–99 (2014)
10. Yang, L., Chen, H., Cui, Q., et al.: Probabilistic-KNN: a novel algorithm for passive indoor-localization scenario. In: Vehicular Technology Conference, pp. 1–5. IEEE (2015)
11. Chen, X.K., Liu, Z.S.: K nearest neighbor query based on improved Kd-tree construction algorithm. J. Guangdong Univ. Technol. **31**, 119–123 (2014)
12. Kaemarungsi, K., Krishnamurthy, P.: Analysis of WLAN's received signal strength indication for indoor location fingerprinting. Elsevier Science Publishers B. V. (2012)
13. Lee, M., Han, D.: Voronoi tessellation based interpolation method for Wi-Fi radio map construction. IEEE Commun. Lett. **16**(3), 404–407 (2012)
14. Abubaker, M., Ashour, W.: Efficient data clustering algorithms: improvements over kmeans. Int. J. Intell. Syst. Appl. **5**(3), 37–49 (2013)
15. Wang, L., Wong, W.C.: A RSS based statistical localization algorithm in WLAN. In: International Conference on Signal Processing and Communication Systems, pp. 1–5 (2012)

# Manifold Alignment-Based Radio Map Construction in Indoor Localization

Ping Ji, Danyang Qin$^{(\boxtimes)}$, Pan Feng, and Yan Zhang

Key Laboratory of Electronic and Communication Engineering,
Heilongjiang University, No. 74 Xuefu Road,
Harbin, People's Republic of China
qindanyang@hlju.edu.cn

**Abstract.** In recent years, Wireless Access Point (WAP)-based Received Signal Strength Indication (RSSI) indoor localization technology has been of intriguing interest to deduce the coordinates of an object or an observer in the scene with RSSI being collected by various WAPs in a Range of Interest (ROI). The Radio Map construction by fingerprints is of great importance for indoor localization. Existing methods of Radio Map construction have encountered bottlenecks in this area, which will limit the application of indoor localization technology due to the deployment is massive and cumbersome. The spatial correlation between RSSI observations is adopted and the manifold alignment algorithm will be adopted to locate the user's current location without a complete Radio Map so as to reduce the requirements of the calibration fingerprints. Simulated Radio Map (SRM) scheme and Plan Coordinate (PC) scheme will be proposed and simulated separately to verify the correctness and efficiency of the proposed scheme.

**Keywords:** Indoor localization · Radio map construction · Spatial correlation
Manifold alignment

## 1 Introduction

Where is the nearest metro station? Is this product I want to buy in the supermarket? With the advent of mobile Internet, there will be more expectations for localization services. For airports, libraries, shopping malls and parking lots, localization services are expected to be more accurate and faster in such scenes.

RSSI-based localization technology can be divided into two main stages. The first stage is offline acquisition stage. It is necessary to identify a few landmarks (LM) inside the building and collect the location fingerprints of each LM in the building by the equipment. Next, the spatial coordinate data of the LM should be correlated to establish a localization fingerprint database, which is to be called Radio Map. The second stage is online localization stage. One user enters the localization area holding a mobile terminal to measure the RSSI data through the receiver equipped with WiFi. The RSSI data will be compared with the data in the manifold alignment algorithm to obtain the coordinates of the user according to the determination result.

© ICST Institute for Computer Sciences, Social Informatics and Telecommunications Engineering 2018
L. Meng and Y. Zhang (Eds.): MLICOM 2018, LNICST 251, pp. 327–337, 2018.
https://doi.org/10.1007/978-3-030-00557-3_33

The deployment of WAP is time consuming and labor intensive when put into use in larger environments such as airports and mega-stores although the Radio Map, built by fingerprinting, covers a very comprehensive set of information. Therefore, a solution that can reduce the deployment cost and workload is the key to solve the problem. The scheme proposed in this paper greatly reduces the deployment cost and users can be located without build complete Radio Map for the indoor environment. The program has taken advantage of the inherent spatial correlation reflected by the RSSI data to reduce the number of calibration fingerprints. We recall that there is a high spatial correlation between neighboring positions in the Radio Map. If a DS to reflect the mapping between each position in the target region can be obtained, the approximate location of the RSSI data source can be determined. Moreover, manifold alignment algorithm [1] will locate the collected RSSI data in real time.

The rest of the paper will be organized as follows. The current state of research will be described in Sect. 2. The basics of the manifold alignment algorithm will be introduced in Sect. 3. The SRM scheme and the PC scheme will be introduced respectively in Sect. 4. Section 5 will discuss performance evaluation and the full text will be summarized in Sect. 6.

## 2 Motivation

There are few ways to combine the Radio Map establishment and localization methods, the typical ones are multi-sensor Particle Filtering (PF) based on intelligent platform [2] and WLAN indoor localization based on Compressive Sensing (CS) [3]. The former achieved the Radio Map construction by a variety of smart phones sensor devices, simultaneously, achieved localization by PF. It is found that, however, this is a probabilistic localization method, which has complicated localization process and poor localization accuracy. The latter achieved localization by CS, which included Radio Map reconstruction under the condition of sparse Radio Map.

The unsupervised Radio Map is one of the algorithms to increase the efficiency of the Radio Map construction. Kim et al. proposed an unsupervised Radio Map construction algorithm based on the improved RSSI indoor propagation model in [4]. The measurement of RSSI adopted Client-Assistant (CA) proposed in [5]. There was high efficiency in this measurement. Nevertheless, the problems caused by a variety of different devices to collect RSSI data are inconsistent, especially due to the different sensitivity of the hardware.

In order to reduce the deployment workload and ensure the accuracy of Radio Map, the semi-supervised Radio Map construction algorithm has been proposed. Considering the deployment workload, the literatures started with reducing the number of LMs and RSSI resampled per LM. The difference is that [6] adopted Kernel Based Interpolation method to reconstruct Radio Map, and [7] adopted Linear Interpolation method to reconstruct Radio Map. However, the accuracy of the Radio Map obtained by the interpolation method was low. The other paper [8] adopted Label Propagation to learn the mapping between RSSI and unlabeled RSSI to implement Radio Map reconstruction. Although all the above algorithms can reconstruct the Radio Map, these algorithms were not used for indoor localization.

# 3   Manifold Alignment

The application of manifold alignment learning method should satisfy two conditions. First of all, it is required that the correlation between each pair of adjacent data points in both DSs, that is the neighboring correlation, will be strong. Even if the two DSs show different distributions or shapes in high-dimensional space, a common low-dimensional correlation between them should be ensured.

## 3.1   Neighborhood Weight

Manifold alignment requires two DSs to preserve neighborhood correlation in low-dimensional space. Accordingly, we select local linear embedding techniques [9].

Any high-dimensional space data point $z^{(i)}$ with $N$ adjacent data points will be described as a neighborhood DS, notes as $\mathcal{N}(i) = \left[z^{(\mathcal{N}(i,1))}, \ldots, z^{(\mathcal{N}(i,N))}\right]$. And the neighborhood weight of $z^{(i)}$ is $W_z^{(i)}$ satisfying Eq. (1).

$$W_z^{(i)} = \arg \min_{W_{ij}} \left\{ \left| z^{(i)} - \sum_{j \in \mathcal{N}(i)} W_{ij} z^{(\mathcal{N}(i,j))} \right|^2 \right\}$$
$$\text{s.t.} \sum_{j \in \mathcal{N}(i)} W_{ij} = 1 \tag{1}$$

It is easy to understand that the closer $z^{(\mathcal{N}(i,j))}$ is to $z^{(i)}$, the higher its weight $W_{ij}$ will be. For the data point $j$ not belonging to $\mathcal{N}(i)$, there will be $W_{ij} = 0$. The computing method of the neighborhood weight by the closed form solution [10] can be optimized. For any data point $i$, its distance matrix $D_i$ will be:

$$D_i = \left[ z^{(i)} - z^{(\mathcal{N}(i,1))}, z^{(i)} - z^{(\mathcal{N}(i,2))}, \ldots, z^{(i)} - z^{(\mathcal{N}(i,N))} \right]^T \tag{2}$$

Therefore, the optimized formula for $W_{ij}$ is:

$$W_{ij} = \frac{\sum_{k=1}^{N} \left\{ \left(D_i D_i^T\right)^{-1} \right\}_{jk}}{\sum_{m=1}^{N} \sum_{n=1}^{N} \left\{ \left(D_i D_i^T\right)^{-1} \right\}_{mn}} \tag{3}$$

where $\{(D_i D_i^T)^{-1}\}$ denotes the element of the inverse matrix $\left(D_i D_i^T\right)^{-1}$ at the intersection of the $u$th row and the $v$th column.

## 3.2   Manifold Alignment Structure

The source DS $\mathcal{X}$ consists of the $X$ points in $\mathbb{R}^h$, the target DS $\mathcal{Y}$ consists of the $Y$ points in $\mathbb{R}^h$, and the manifold alignment $F$ between the two DSs is expressed as:

$$F = \arg \min_{f,g}\{\lambda^x f^T L^x f + \lambda^y g^T L^y g + \mu(f - g)^T(f - g)\} \tag{4}$$

$\mathbf{f} = [f_1, \ldots, f_X]^T$ and $\mathbf{g} = [g_1, \ldots, g_Y]^T$ are two vectors belonging to $\mathbb{R}^X$ and $\mathbb{R}^Y$, respectively, and $\mathcal{P}$ is a set of point of pairs in $\mathcal{X}$ and $\mathcal{Y}$. The pairing points are points where the source and target DSs are exactly or similarly falling in low-dimensional space. $\lambda^x$, $\lambda^y$ and $\mu$ are the weight factors of different components in Eq. (4). The first term takes the minimum value to ensure that the $f_i - f_j$ is smaller, when the weight $W_{ij}$ is higher, which can preserve the neighborhood relation in $\mathcal{X}$. And it is the same with the second one. The last term is the treatment of the difference between the pairing points of $\mathbf{f}$ and $\mathbf{g}$. Then Eq. (4) can be rewritten as:

$$F = \arg \min_{f,g}\{\lambda^x f^T L^x f + \lambda^y g^T L^y g + \mu(f - g)^T(f - g)\} \tag{5}$$

where $L^x = \left[L^x_{i,j}\right] \forall i,j \in \mathcal{X}$ and satisfies:

$$L^x_{i,j} = \begin{cases} \sum_j W^x_{ij}, & i = j \\ -W^x_{ij}, & j \in \mathcal{N}_i \\ 0, & \text{otherwise} \end{cases} \tag{6}$$

In addition, since $L^y = \left[L^y_{i,j}\right] \forall i,j \in \mathcal{Y}$, in order to obtain $L^y_{i,j}$, all of $W^x_{ij}$ in Eq. (6) will be replaced by $W^y_{ij}$. Equation (5) needs to be subjected to a strict constraint of $f_i = g_i \forall i \in P$(i.e. as $\mu \to \infty$), and it is defined as $Q^x = \mathcal{X}\backslash\mathcal{P}$ and $Q^y = \mathcal{Y}\backslash\mathcal{P}$. Then the problem in Eq. (5) will be translated into solving the following eigenvalues:

$$F = \arg \min_h\left\{\frac{h^T L^z h}{h^T h}\right\} \tag{7}$$
$$\text{s.t. } h^T 1 = 0$$

where h and $L^z$ will satisfy:

$$h = \begin{bmatrix} f_\mathcal{P} = g_\mathcal{P} \\ f_{Q^x} \\ g_{Q^y} \end{bmatrix} \tag{8}$$

$$L^z = \begin{bmatrix} \lambda^x L^x_{PP} + \lambda^y L^y_{PP} & \lambda^x L^x_{PQ^x} & \lambda^y L^y_{PQ^y} \\ \lambda^x L^x_{Q^x P} & \lambda^x L^x_{Q^x Q^x} & 0 \\ \lambda^y L^y_{Q^y P} & 0 & \lambda^y L^y_{Q^y Q^y} \end{bmatrix} \tag{9}$$

$L^x_{\mathcal{I}\mathcal{J}}(L^y_{\mathcal{I}\mathcal{J}})$ is a submatrix of $L^x(L^y)$ consisting of the intersection of the row of element indices in vector $I$ and the column of element indices in vector $J$. According to the structure of $L^z$, the structure of $\mathbf{h}$ begins with the aligned element $\mathcal{P}$ in $\mathbf{f}$ and $\mathbf{g}$, then follows with the rest data points in $\mathbf{f}$, and finally ends up with the rest data points in $\mathbf{g}$.

Now, the final structure of embedded $\varepsilon$ as shown in Eq. (10), because of the DSs need to be embedded in $l$-dimensional $(l < h)$, which consists of the eigenvector $\left[ h^{(1)}, \ldots, h^{(l)} \right]$.

$$
\varepsilon = \begin{bmatrix}
f_P^{(1)} & f_P^{(2)} & \cdots & f_P^{(l)} \\
f_{Q^x}^{(1)} & f_{Q^x}^{(2)} & \cdots & f_{Q^x}^{(l)} \\
g_{Q^y}^{(1)} & g_{Q^y}^{(2)} & \cdots & g_{Q^y}^{(l)}
\end{bmatrix} \tag{10}
$$

## 4 SRM Scheme and PC Scheme

SMP and PC schemes will be introduced in detail in this section, and the spatial correlation between RSSI values will be moved to calibration fingerprints with a limited number and online RSSI observations to enable user localization.

### 4.1 SRM Offline Stage

The offline deployment stage requires the following operations:

(1) The indoor environment information is input, such as the CAD file of the building, the location and height of WAPs, and RF simulator Volcano Lab can generate the simulated Radio Map $\mathcal{S} = \left[ \left( s^{(1)}, p^{(1)} \right), \ldots, \left( s^{(\mathcal{S})}, p^{(\mathcal{S})} \right) \right]$, which contains all the grid points divided in the area.

- $s^{(i)} = \left[ s_1^{(i)}, \ldots, s_K^{(i)} \right]$ is the simulated RSSI vector for $K$ WAPs at the $i$th grid point in the area.
- $p^{(i)} = \left[ x^{(i)}, y^{(i)} \right]$ is the plane coordinate of the $i$th grid point.

(2) The SRM is regarded as a source DS to figure $W_{ij}^x$ and $L^x$ of LLE by Eq. (3) and Eq. (6) respectively. The complexity of this step is $O(S^3)$.

(3) The subset $\mathcal{C} = \left[ \left( c^{(1)}, p_c^{(1)} \right) \ldots, \left( c^{(C)}, p_c^{(C)} \right) \right]$ of $S$ is taken as a calibration measure, and all grid points in $C$ are the paired data points in manifold alignment.

- $c^{(i)} = \left[ c_1^{(i)}, \ldots, c_K^{(i)} \right]$ is the simulated RSSI vector of $K$ WAPs at the $i$th grid point in the area.
- $p_c^{(i)} = \left[ x_c^{(i)}, \ldots, y_c^{(i)} \right]$ is the plane coordinate at the $i$th grid point.

### 4.2 SRM Online Stage

During the online positioning stage, the following actions will be performed by the positioning server:

(1) The server will be received $O$ online RSSI values $\mathcal{O} = \left[ o^{(1)}, \ldots, o^{(O)} \right]$ sent by the user with $O$ localization requests.

(2) The following sets will be defined:

- The data points in set $\mathcal{P}$ are the data point of $S$ that is paired with $C$.
- The data points in set $\mathcal{Q}^x$ are the remaining parts of $S$ that cannot be paired with $C$.
- The data points in set $\mathcal{Q}^y$ are the online RSSI observations in $\mathcal{Y}$.
- $\mathcal{X} = \left[ U_{i \in \mathcal{P}} s^{(i)} \mid U_{j \in \mathcal{Q}^x} s^{(j)} \right]$ is the DS formed by rearranging the SRM vectors, the accuracy of the RSSI data will be improved at the pairing position, which is called the *source DS*.
- $\mathcal{Y} = \left[ c^{(1)}, \ldots, c^{(C)} \mid o^{(1)}, \ldots, o^{(O)} \right]$ is a new DS formed by the offline calibration fingerprint vector and the online observation RSSI vector connection, which is called the *target DS*.

The formation of the *source DS* and the *target DS* are shown in Fig. 1.

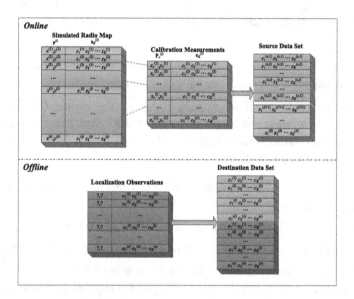

**Fig. 1.** The formation of the *source DS* and the *target DS* in SRM

(3) $W_{ij}^y$ and $L^y$ of the *target DS* are figured by Eqs. (3) and (6), separately. The complexity of this step is $O\left( (C+O)^3 \right)$.

(4) $L^z$ can be calculated by Eq. (9), and there is:

$$\lambda^x = \frac{C+O}{S+C+O}, \quad \lambda^y = \frac{S}{S+C+O} \tag{11}$$

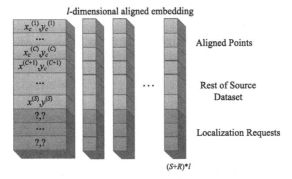

**Fig. 2.** Alignment embedded structure

(5)  The eigenvalues of $L^z$ will be calculated and the low dimensional embedding matrix $\varepsilon$ can be constructed. The alignment embedded structure is showed in Fig. 2.

- The first $C$ lines $\varepsilon_P = \left[ f_P^{(1)}, \ldots, f_P^{(l)} \right]$ correspond to the calibration fingerprint $C$.
- The next $(S - C)$ lines $\varepsilon_{Q^x} = \left[ f_{Q^x}^{(1)}, \ldots, f_{Q^x}^{(l)} \right]$ are the rest of $S$ that cannot be paired with $C$.
- The last $O$ line $\varepsilon_O = \left[ g_{Q^y}^{(1)}, \ldots, g_{Q^y}^{(l)} \right]$ indicates the online observations.

(6)  The distance will be calculated from each line in $\varepsilon_O$ to all the lines in $\varepsilon_O$ and $\varepsilon_{Q^x}$, the closest line will be find. Attach its plan coordinate to the observation, then sent to the user. The iterations will be $O\left( (C + O)^3 + (S + O)^3 \right)$.

### 4.3  PC Scheme

It is difficult to get the location and height of WAPs in large scale indoor scenes. Less environment detail will be required if plane coordinates serve as the source DS. The scheme will project the WAPs in space onto the ground to generate the plane coordinate DS as well as the spatial correlation between adjacent data points will not be changed. Plane coordinate DSs still reflect the neighborhood relationships between data points in the *source DS*, although they cannot reflect the spread of RF in space. The plane coordinate DS $S = \left[ p^{(1)}, \ldots, p^{(S)} \right]$ has been determined during the offline deployment stage. The other steps are the same as the SRM.

- In the *source DS*, the first $1\text{-}K$ elements of $\hat{p}^{(i)}$ are the same as $p^{(i)}$, and the $k$th element becomes $x/y$.
- The set $\mathcal{X} = \left[ U_{i \in P} \hat{p}^{(i)} | U_{j \in Q^x} \hat{p}^{(j)} \right]$ will be modified.

  The changed *source DS* and *target DS* are shown in Fig. 3.

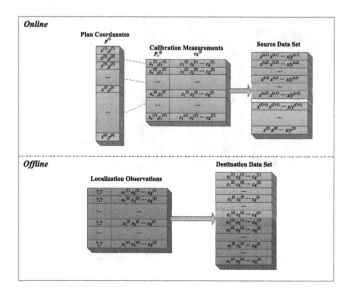

**Fig. 3.** The formation of the *source DS* and the *target DS* in SRM

## 5 Performance Analysis

Floor-7 of Physical Laboratory Building in Heilongjiang University is taken as the indoor localization test environment. As shown in Fig. 4, five WAPs are deployed along the corridor. The testing area will be divided into 219 mesh points with 1 m spacing between adjacent mesh points. In this section, the neighborhood set size, localization observations number and WAPs number will be performed based on MATLAB. The simulations reveal that the superior performance of PC to SRM.

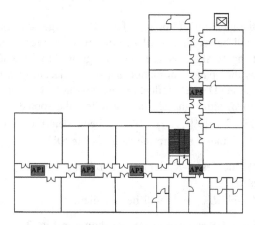

**Fig. 4.** Indoor structure plan and WAP deployment

## 5.1 Influence of Neighborhood Set Size

As shown in Fig. 5, the number of neighbors affects the performance of SRM and PC in some degree. The percentages of localization observations and calibrated fingerprints are 5% and 25%, respectively. From Fig. 5, we can find that the number of neighbors is an important factor for the localization accuracy. It is clear that when the number of neighbors is from 10 to 15 (a small number), the localization error level is greater than it is from 20 to 25 (a large number). When there are fewer neighbors, the outlier value of neighborhood has a greater influence on the result of weight. However, the localization error rises again if the neighbors number reaches 35–50 (a very large number), which indicates that each point owns many adjacent points as the number of neighbors is too large. At this point, the localization accuracy will be reduced. The concept of neighborhood dilution [11] can be used to explain this issue.

## 5.2 Influence of Localization Observations Number

The effect of the localization observations number on the average localization error performance is depicted in Fig. 6 when there are 25 neighbors and the calibration fingerprints number is 25%. The localization errors of the two schemes decrease slightly as the localization observations number increases. It is found that the average localization error is less than 3.5 m as the localization observations number increases from 1 to 50. For most indoor localization applications, the localization observations number does not have a significant impact on the localization accuracy.

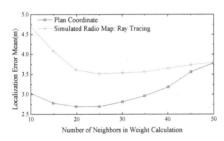 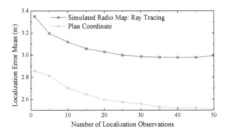

**Fig. 5.** Mean positioning error against the number of neighbors

**Fig. 6.** Mean positioning error against the percentage of localization observations

## 5.3 Influence of the Number of WAPs

The effect of the WAPs number on average localization error under different percentages of calibration fingerprints is depicted in Fig. 7 when the localization observations number is 11 and the number of neighbors is 20. SRM and PC refer to simulated radio map and plan coordinate respectively. The percent in parentheses is the calibration load. As expected, both algorithms will achieve high localization accuracy as the number of WAPs within a certain range of the number of WAPs is growing. In fact, the performance of all indoor localization scheme based on RSSI will be better as the WAPs number increases. The localization errors of the PC scheme are 5.7 m and 3.8 m, respectively, when the calibration load is 20% and the WAPs number is 3 and 4. It can be observed that, for any calibration load, the localization error of the SMP scheme is higher than PC scheme, which shows that the superior performance of PC to SRM.

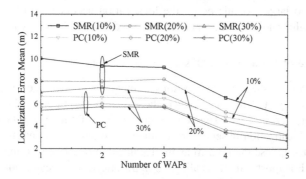

**Fig. 7.** Mean positioning error performance against the number of WAPs

## 6   Conclusion

This paper mainly solves the problem of Radio Map construction which will determine the accuracy and efficiency of the indoor localization. The RSSI values are collected by WAPs and a limited calibration load is assumed for practical deployment. The scheme proposed in this paper will reduce the number of calibration fingerprints by the spatial correlation between RSSI observations in the same indoor area. And the user's current location is located by the popular alignment algorithm without a complete Radio Map. Two schemes, SRM scheme and PC scheme, are proposed and simulated. The simulation results show that localization error can be limited from 0.4 to 0.8 compared with the complete Radio Map when the percentage of calibration fingerprints is selected from 70% to 80%. In the future, the algorithms will be studied by unsupervised manifold alignment so that reduce Calibration work of SRM and PC.

**Acknowledgement.** This work was supported by the National Natural Science Foundation of China (61771186), Postdoctoral Research Project of Heilongjiang Province (LBH-Q15121), University Nursing Program for Young Scholars with Creative Talents in Heilongjiang Province (UNPYSCT-2017125).

# References

1. Pei, Y., Kim, T.K., Zha, H.C.: Unsupervised random forest manifold alignment for lipreading. In: IEEE International Conference on Computer Vision, pp. 129–136. IEEE Computer Society, Sydney (2013)
2. Cappello, F., Sabatini, R., Ramasamy, S.: Particle filter based multi-sensor data fusion techniques for RPAS navigation and guidance. In: Metrology for Aerospace, Benevento, pp. 395–400. IEEE (2015)
3. Feng, C., Au, W.S.A., Valaee, S.: Received-signal-strength-based indoor positioning using compressive sensing. IEEE Trans. Mob. Comput. 11(12), 1983–1993 (2012)
4. Rusli, M.E., Ali, M., Jamil, N.: An improved indoor positioning algorithm based on RSSI-trilateration technique for internet of things (IOT). In: International Conference on Computer and Communication Engineering, Kuala Lumpur, pp. 72–77. IEEE (2017)
5. Liu, Y., Sheng, X., Marston, S.R.: The impact of client-side security restrictions on the competition of cloud computing services. Int. J. Electron. Commer. 19(3), 90–117 (2015)
6. Ducru, P., Josey, C., Dibert, K.: Kernel reconstruction methods for Doppler broadening temperature interpolation by linear combination of reference cross sections at optimally chosen temperatures. J. Comput. Phys. 335(2), 535–557 (2017)
7. Wu, Z., Guo, X., Huang, X.: A liver vessel skeleton line reconstruction method based on linear interpolation. In: International Conference on Virtual Reality and Visualization, Xi'an, pp. 257–260. IEEE (2013)
8. Gong, C., Tao, D., Liu, W.: Label propagation via teaching-to-learn and learning-to-teach. IEEE Trans. Neural Netw. Learn. Syst. 28(6), 1452–1465 (2017)
9. Fakhr, M.W.: Sparse locally linear and neighbor embedding for nonlinear time series prediction. In: Tenth International Conference on Computer Engineering & Systems, Cairo, pp. 371–377. IEEE (2016)
10. Chen, L., Sun, J.Q.: The closed-form solution of the reduced Fokker–Planck–Kolmogorov equation for nonlinear systems. Commun. Nonlinear Sci. Numer. Simul. 41, 1–10 (2016)
11. Barra, A., Agliari, E.: A statistical mechanics approach to autopoietic immune networks. J. Stat. Mech: Theory Exp. 51(7), 165–169 (2010)

# Research on the Contextual Information in Scene Classification

Pan Feng, Danyang Qin[✉], Ping Ji, and Jingya Ma

Key Lab of Electronic and Communication Engineering,
Heilongjiang University,
No. 74 Xuefu Road, Harbin, People's Republic of China
qindanyang@hlju.edu.cn

**Abstract.** The classical localization approaches only focus on the performance of features extracted from images but ignore contextual information hidden in the images. In this paper, it is annotated on the images and SVM model is used to classify different images for semantic localization. Supervised Latent Dirichlet Allocation (sLDA) model is introduced to obtain the annotations, and the standard SIFT algorithm is improved to extract feature descriptors. Two situations are designed for the acquisition of contextual annotations, which are to provide the accurate contextual annotations directly and to infer contextual information by sLDA model. The effect of contextual information in scene classification is simulated and verified.

**Keywords:** Contextual information · Semantic localization
Scene classification

## 1 Introduction

With the development of Artificial Intelligence (AI), the robot localization has become a research hotspot. Considering the importance of robot localization, some existing localization methods are combined to obtain better performance.

The semantics-based visual localization method is adopted in this paper, which takes use of the category labels such as "office" and "corridor" to describe the location of the robot and can be applied to many cases. [1] proposed an application of semantic localization to autopilot. As the camera is the primary information collection device of the robot, the semantic positioning can be considered as a classification problem.

To improve the precision of classification, contextual information annotations are combined with image feature descriptors. Contextual information involves multiple aspects e.g. keywords to describe images. In other fields, some papers are proposed to solve various technology problems with contextual information. Contextual

This work was supported by the National Natural Science Foundation of China (61771186), Postdoctoral Research Project of Heilongjiang Province (LBH-Q15121), University Nursing Program for Young Scholars with Creative Talents in Heilongjiang Province (UNPYSCT-2017125).

© ICST Institute for Computer Sciences, Social Informatics and Telecommunications Engineering 2018
L. Meng and Y. Zhang (Eds.): MLICOM 2018, LNICST 251, pp. 338–345, 2018.
https://doi.org/10.1007/978-3-030-00557-3_34

information can be used to monitor system intrusion from external network [2]. Filippini in [3] adopt the contextual information of user location to improve directional cell discovery.

In addition to the contextual information, the standard Scale Invariant Feature Transform (SIFT) method will also be adopted to improve the performance of image descriptors, and the sLDA model [4] is used to obtain the contextual annotations.

Three scenes will be designed and adopted to perform the simulation: (a) without contextual information; (b) providing context information annotation directly; (c) inferring contextual information by sLDA. Scene (a) represents the classic semantic localization, scene (b) will show the maximum benefit of the contextual information and scene (c) will evaluate the effective integration of contextual information.

## 2 Related Work

### 2.1 Image Feature Descriptor

Image feature descriptors are used to describe image features, such as color, shape and gradient, which are divided into local feature descriptor and global feature descriptor. In our work, we use two feature descriptors, Histogram of Oriented Gradient (HOG) [5] and Histogram of Vision Words (HoVW), which is combination of the SIFT and the Bag of Words (BoW).

The BoW process is based on cluster and takes use of the local features extracted from image as the input. Every cluster is a "word", and the whole $n$ words are defined as a whole to be a codebook. By mapping local features to words, any input image can be represented as a word bag. Finally, the word frequency histogram is calculated and it is a global feature descriptor.

In addition, different descriptor dimensions will be evaluated in the following ways: (a) Combining neighboring angles in HOG process; (b) Choosing different numbers of words in HoVW process. Finally, four dimensions of 50, 100, 200 and 300 are selected and shared by two descriptors.

### 2.2 sLDA Model

LDA is a kind of Bayesian model, which can infer the posterior distribution of hidden variables as in (1) if given a set of visual words in the image.

$$P\left(\theta_d, z_j | w_i, \alpha, \beta\right) = \frac{P\left(\theta_d, w_i, z_j | \alpha, \beta\right)}{P(w_i | \alpha, \beta)} \tag{1}$$

where $z_j$ is the topic of the visual word $w_i$ that can be observed, and is defined by $P\left(z_j | \theta_d\right)$. $Z = \{z_1, z_2, \ldots, z_k\}$, $|Z| = k$ indicating that there are k topics. $\theta_d$ is the mixture proportion of the topics in the image and it is a Dirichlet random variable. If there is $z_j$, $w_i$ can be obtained from $P\left(w_i | z_j, \beta\right)$ under multinomial distribution, where $\beta$ is a $k \times V$ matrix and $\beta_{i,j} = P(w^j = 1 | z^i = 1)$ as in (2).

$$P\left(w_i | z_j, \beta\right) = \prod_{n=1}^{N} \beta_{z_j, w_i} \tag{2}$$

$w_i$ is defined as (3):

$$P(w_i | \alpha, \beta) = \int P(\theta_d | \alpha) \left( \sum_{j=1}^{k} P(z_j | \theta_d) P\left(w_i | z_j, \beta\right) \right) d\theta_d \tag{3}$$

where $\alpha$ and $\beta$ are model parameters defined before test. $P(\theta_d | \alpha)$ is defined as (4):

$$P(\theta_d | \alpha) = \frac{\Gamma(m\alpha)}{\Gamma^m(\alpha)} \prod_{j=1}^{m} \theta_{d_j}^{\alpha-1} \tag{4}$$

While sLDA adds a response variable $y$ to LDA and jointly model the document and the response to find latent topics which can predict the response variables for unlabeled images in the future.

The response variable comes from a normal linear model $N(\eta^T \bar{z}, \sigma^2)$, where $\eta$ and $\sigma$ are the response parameters and there is $\bar{z} = 1/N \sum_{j=1}^{N} z_j$.

A graphical model representation of sLDA can be seen in Fig. 1. Top-$N$ $F$-measure in [6] is used to measure annotation performance and there is $N = 5$. The score is standardized to represent a number between 0 and 1, where the larger the number is, the stronger the relevancy will be.

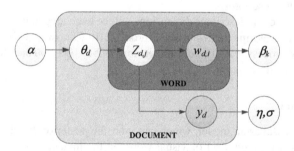

**Fig. 1.** Graphical model representation of sLDA

Table 1 shows performance comparison of sLDA and multi-label SVM in object recognition, which indicates the performance of sLDA is better than that of SVM.

### 2.3 SIFT Algorithm Optimization

Considering that SIFT cannot deal with images in many scenes well enough, such as underwater scene. An optimized SIFT is presented in this section.

**Table 1.** Object detection performance of sLDA and SVM

| Detecting object | SVM | sLDA |
|---|---|---|
| Bed | 0.5371 | 0.6322 |
| Cupboard | 0.3029 | 0.4204 |
| Keyboard | 0.5157 | 0.6846 |
| Monitor | 0.4529 | 0.6212 |
| Table | 0.3829 | 0.4843 |

Pre-filtering operation in the image by a Gabor filter can be realized as follows:

$$
\begin{aligned}
g_{x,y,\theta} &= \frac{1}{2\pi\sigma_1\sigma_2} \times \exp\left(i\frac{2\pi}{\lambda}(x\cos\theta + y\sin\theta)\right) \\
&\times \exp\left(-\frac{(x\cos\theta + y\sin\theta)^2}{2\sigma_1^2} - \frac{(y\cos\theta - x\sin\theta)^2}{2\sigma_2^2}\right)
\end{aligned}
\tag{5}
$$

where $(x, y)$ is the coordinate; $\theta$ is the orientation of the filter; $\lambda$ is the wavelength; $\sigma_1$ and $\sigma_2$ are Gaussian standard deviations taken along with the orientation $\theta$ and $\theta + \pi/2$.

To approximate the odd Gabor filter, there is $\sigma_1 = \sigma_2 = \sigma$ to make only one variable exist in the function. Odd Gabor filters approximate odd Gaussian filters where $\lambda = 6\sigma$, so it can be set as $\lambda = 6\sigma$ and being taken into (5) to generate (6). It is similar to an odd Gaussian filter.

$$
g_{x,y,\theta} = \frac{1}{2\pi\sigma^2} \exp\left(-\frac{x^2 + y^2}{2\sigma^2}\right) \sin\left(\frac{2\pi}{6\sigma}(x\cos\theta + y\sin\theta)\right)
\tag{6}
$$

As standard SIFT has a fixed threshold as 0.03, many key points in dim scenes will be eliminated. To avoid the absence of information, the threshold will be kept at 10% of the image contrast. The points below 10% are considered as the low illuminance points and are not regarded as key points.

Standard SIFT uses pixel differentiation to obtain the image derivative and further generates relative amplitude and gradient. The process will be very sensitive to noise. The pixel difference process involves high-pass filtering, amplifying high-frequency noise in it. To avoid the noise, the sobel operator is adopted to each key point.

$$
\begin{aligned}
M(x, y) &= \sqrt{D_x(x, y)^2 + D_y(x, y)^2} \\
\Theta(x, y) &= \tan^{-1}\left(D_y(x, y)/D_x(x, y)\right)
\end{aligned}
\tag{7}
$$

where the intermediate variables satisfy:

$$
\begin{aligned}
D_x(x, y) &= f_{x_{sobel}}(x, y)I(x, y) \\
D_y(x, y) &= f_{y_{sobel}}(x, y)I(x, y)
\end{aligned}
\tag{8}
$$

and

$$f_{x_{sobel}} = \begin{bmatrix} 1 & 0 & -1 \\ 2 & 0 & -2 \\ 1 & 0 & -1 \end{bmatrix}, f_{y_{sobel}} = \begin{bmatrix} 1 & 2 & 1 \\ 0 & 0 & 0 \\ -1 & -2 & -1 \end{bmatrix} \qquad (9)$$

The parameters $f_{x_{sobel}}$ and $f_{y_{sobel}}$ are the sobel operators along the orientation $x$ and $y$, and $M(x,y)$ and $\Theta(x,y)$ are value and orientation of gradient respectively. This improvement will preserve more information in the descriptors and eliminate noise.

Finally, we use Hausdorff distance [7] to computer the distance between key points. Given two sets of points $A = \{a_1, a_2, \ldots, a_m\}$ and $B = \{b_1, b_2, \ldots, b_n\}$, Hausdorff distance is calculated as follows:

$$H(A,B) = \max(h(A,B), h(B,A)) \qquad (10)$$

where $h(A,B) = \max_{a \in A} \min_{b \in B} \|a - b\|$. Hausdorff distance is more accurate than Euclidean distance between two key points and eliminates false matches. The performance comparison of SIFT before and after optimization is shown in Table 2, in which Key Points in Reference Image (KPRI), Key Points in Test Images (KPTI), Match points (Matches), Correct Match points (CMathes), Root Mean Square Error (RMSE) and Time Cost will be taken to compare based on standard and optimized SIFT.

**Table 2.** Comparison of quantitative parameters

| Algorithm | KPRI | KPTI | Matches | CMathes | RMSE | Time Cost |
|---|---|---|---|---|---|---|
| SIFT (standard) | 259 | 493 | 44 | 4 | 1.79 | 5.41 |
| SIFT (optimized) | 1464 | 2034 | 32 | 5 | 0.69 | 15.1 |

## 2.4   SVM Model

Supposing A is a series of examples and labels under unknown probability distributions, it needs to find a function that allows the most accurate determination of the class of any future example. Generally, there is:

$$f(x) = \sum_{i=1}^{l} \alpha_i y_i K(x, x_i) + b \qquad (11)$$

where $b \in R$, $b$ and $\alpha_i$ are Lagrange coefficients. Most $\alpha_i$ will become zero after training and the vector with non-zero is called support vector. $K(x_1, x_2)$ is the kernel function being selected based on specific issue.

Most classification models can solve multi-label problem, but SVM model fail to do so. Multi-label SVM classifier can be constructed by using one-versus-one or one-versus-all method [8], and the one-versus-all is adopted in the test. About the key parameter $K(x_1, x_2)$, the following two metrics are usually taken to evaluate:

- Linear kernel ($SVM_{lin}$): $K(x_1, x_2) = x_1 \cdot x_2 + coef_0$
- $\chi^2$ kernel ($SVM_{\chi^2}$): $K(x_1, x_2) = 1 - \sum_{i=1}^{n} \frac{(x_1 - x_2)^2}{\frac{1}{2}(x_1 + x_2)}$

Considering about the indoor characteristics, $\chi^2$ kernel is taken in this paper. The paper evaluates the model through 5-fold cross validation. To keep each sample distribution invariable in the test, we use stratified fold selection. In addition, the fold remains the same value during evaluation of different descriptors, and the effect of randomness is avoided.

### 2.5  Context Information

Two existing datasets are adopted to train and test the model as KTH-IDOL2 [9] and ViDRILO [10], both of which are acquired by robots in indoor environments:

- KTH-IDOL2 dataset contains 5 scenes and 3 lighting conditions
- ViDRILO dataset contains 10 scenes and the existence of 15 objects in images

The lighting condition in KTH-IDOL2 and the existence of 15 objects in ViDRILO are considered as contextual information respectively. By adding some binary numbers to descriptors, we combine context information with descriptors.

Contextual information about the objects is not exclusive and each object is a binary variable. Although the lighting conditions are unique, we choose 3 binary representations allowing more experimental variables, and 15 binary values are taken to represent objects' presences which are annotated in the ViDRLO.

## 3  Performance Evaluation

We choose HoVW and HOG as feature descriptors, and the dimensionalities are chosen for 50, 100, 200 and 300. 5-fold cross validation is used to calculate classification accuracy. In the test, image descriptors are considered to be input data of model to obtain context information.

Figure 2 shows the simulation results in three cases: (1) Free of contextual information (Baseline); (2) Providing context annotations (Ideal) directly; (3) Inferring contextual information (Realistic). Comparison and analysis from Fig. 2 can draw the following conclusions:

- Annotations in KTH-IDOL2 have no effect on scene classification, suggesting that the lighting condition has little to do with the scene category;
- Comparing HoVW and HOG, the combination with lower baseline accuracy has larger improvement space by integrating contextual information;
- When inferring contextual information, the SVM classification is less effective than scene without contextual annotations, indicating SVM is sensitive to data error;

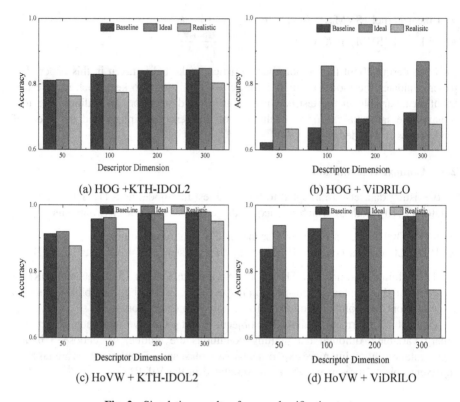

(a) HOG +KTH-IDOL2

(b) HOG + ViDRILO

(c) HoVW + KTH-IDOL2

(d) HoVW + ViDRILO

**Fig. 2.** Simulating results of scene classification tests

## 4    Conclusion

To achieve the scene classification effectively in real application, the combination of contextual information and image descriptor are proposed and evaluated in this paper. Two integration methods are adopted: one is giving accurate contextual information annotations and the other is inferring contextual information at the initial stage. The proposal is experimentally tested by using SVM classification model with two datasets and two image descriptors. It can be concluded that the contextual information is useful for classification.

The effect of context information relies on the descriptor, model and dataset. When providing contextual information directly, the classification accuracy improves; when inferring contextual information, there are some errors which make the classification result worse. In the future, we will do more experiments on new datasets, classification models and descriptors to find more effective approaches using contextual information.

# References

1. Sefati, M., Daum, M., Sondermann, B., Kreisköther, K.D., Kampker, A.: Real-time vision-aided localization and navigation based on three-view geometry. In: International Conference on Intelligent Vehicles, Los Angeles, CA, USA, pp. 13–19. IEEE (2017)
2. Anton, S.D., Fraunholz, D., Schotten, H.D., Teuber, S.: A question of context: enhancing intrusion detection by providing context information. In: International Conference on Internet of Things Business Models, Users, and Networks, Copenhagen, Denmark, pp. 1–8. IEEE (2017)
3. Filippini, I., Sciancalepore, V., Devoti, F., et al.: Fast cell discovery in mm-wave 5G networks with context information. IEEE Trans. Mob. Comput. **99**, 1 (2017)
4. Blei, D.M., Mcauliffe, J.D.: Supervised topic models. Adv. Neural. Inf. Process. Syst. **3**, 327–332 (2010)
5. Bosch, A., Zisserman, A., Munoz, X.: Representing shape with a spatial pyramid kernel. In: International Conference on Image and Video Retrieval, The Netherlands, Amsterdam, pp. 401–408. ACM (2007)
6. Wang, C., Blei, D., Li, F.F.: Simultaneous image classification and annotation. In: Computer Vision and Pattern Recognition, pp. 1903–1910 (2010)
7. Huttenlocher, D.P., Klanderman, G.A., Rucklidge, W.J.: Comparing images using the hausdorff distance. IEEE Trans. Pattern Anal. Mach. Intell. **15**(9), 850–863 (1993)
8. Rifkin, R., Klautau, A.: In defense of one-vs-all classification. J. Mach. Learn. Res. **5**, 101–141 (2004)
9. Luo, J., Pronobis, A., Caputo, B., et al.: The KTH-IDOL2 database (2006)
10. Martinez-Gomez, J., Cazorla, M., Garcia Varea, I., et al.: ViDRILO: the visual and depth robot indoor localization with objects information dataset. Int. J. Robot. Res. **34**(14), 1681–1687 (2015)

# Intelligent Resource Allocation in Wireless and Cloud Networks

# OFDM Based SWIPT in a Two-Way Relaying Network

Weilin Zhao[✉], Weidang Lu, Hong Peng, Zhijiang Xu,
and Jingyu Hua

College of Information Engineering, Zhejiang University of Technology,
Hangzhou 310023, China
1019653554@qq.com

**Abstract.** We consider a simultaneous wireless transfer of information and power in a two-way relaying network, a decode-and-forward protocol and OFDM modulation is employed. Subcarriers are divided into a couple of groups, one is for information decoding, and another is for energy harvesting. With total rate maximized, subcarrier grouping optimization is performed. And the power of subcarriers is optimized according to channel state. The performance of the optimal design is performed on different transmit conditions.

**Keywords:** SWIPT · DF · TWR network · OFDM subcarrier grouping

## 1 Introduction

Simultaneous wireless transfer of information and power (SWIPT) technology is a frontier direction of the cross-integration of wireless information transmission technology and energy harvesting technology, aiming to realize the parallel transmission of energy and information. Consequently, receiver requires information processing and energy harvesting. The splitting is achieved by time switching (TS) and power splitting (PS) as been put forward in [1, 2]. With multiple receiving antennas, antenna selection (AS) also has been proposed [1].

In addition, cooperation and relaying has been identified as an efficient solution for lengthening the distance of transmission as well as increasing stability in wireless communications [3, 4]. Combined with SWIPT, relay node could collect the energy in the RF signal sent by the source node for information collaboration, instead of consuming its own energy. There are various forms, for example, the OWR [5, 6] and TWR protocols [7, 8]. Amplify-and-Forward (AF) or Decode-and-forward (DF) relay is also an option [9].

In this paper, we address the SWIPT in a two-phase wireless network, where a relay decodes and forwarding the signals of two sources with the energy powered from them. Noting that the relay in the first phase existing interference caused by two sources using the same bandwidth to send information simultaneously. Therefore, we use interference elimination and OFDM modulation method. As a kind of mature modulation technique, OFDM technology can resist inter-symbol interference caused by channel selective fading and can flexibly allocate subcarriers and control transmission power on

© ICST Institute for Computer Sciences, Social Informatics and Telecommunications Engineering 2018
L. Meng and Y. Zhang (Eds.): MLICOM 2018, LNICST 251, pp. 349–357, 2018.
https://doi.org/10.1007/978-3-030-00557-3_35

subcarriers. And we assumed the relay node knows the subcarrier grouping condition of source node when receives information and energy, so that the relay does not need a splitter as PS protocol.

The rest of this paper is organized as follows. In Sect. 2, we introduce the system model. The problem formulation and optimal solution is depicted in Sects. 3 and 4, respectively. In Sect. 5, simulation results are proposed to illustrate the performance of the proposed OFDM based SWIPT scheme and subcarrier grouping allocation algorithm. Finally, we draw the conclusion of this paper in Sect. 6.

## 2  System Model

Relaying network system model can be seen in Fig. 1, which consists of two source nodes S1, S2, and one relay node R. The signal is OFDM modulated over K subcarriers.

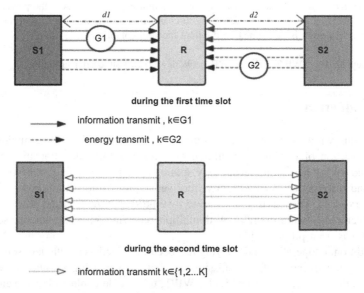

**Fig. 1.** System model

In our model, a completed transmission is composed of two time slots. During the first time slot, both source nodes transmit its signal $x_{1,k}, x_{2,k}$ over all the subcarriers. We use $k \in \{1, \ldots, K\}$ to denote the subcarriers. And $h_{1,k}$ and $h_{2,k}$ are the channel coefficient of the S1 → R link and S2 → R link, respectively. The received signal on subcarrier k at R is corrupted by noise $n_{R,k}$, which are complex Gaussian random variables, denoted by $n_{R,k} \sim CN(0, \sigma_k^2)$. The total transmit power of S1 is denoted as $p_{s1}$, and so is $p_{s2}$. The signal at DF relay can be given as:

$$y_{R,k} = h_{1,k}\sqrt{p_{s1,k}}x_{1,k} + h_{2,k}\sqrt{p_{s2,k}}x_{2,k} + n_{R,k} \tag{1}$$

The received signal is separated into a couple of groups depending on different subcarriers, information decoding group G1 and energy harvesting group G2, respectively. Where $G1 \in K$, $G2 \in K$ and $G1 \cup G2 = K$. When R uses the subcarriers in G1 to decode information, there exits interference for R receives the signal come from S1 and S2 simultaneously. To reduce the interference, when $p_{s1,k}^I \gamma_{1,k} > p_{s2,k}^I \gamma_{2,k}$, $x_{1,k}$ will be decoded priority, meanwhile, $x_{2,k}$ will be regarded as noise. $x_{2,k}$ will be decoded later, we define $\gamma_{1,k} = \frac{|h_{1,k}|^2}{\sigma_k^2}$, $\gamma_{2,k} = \frac{|h_{2,k}|^2}{\sigma_k^2}$. For simplicity, the condition $p_{s1,k}^I \gamma_{1,k} > p_{s2,k}^I \gamma_{2,k}$ could be defined as $G11$, and the condition $p_{s1,k}^I \gamma_{1,k} < p_{s2,k}^I \gamma_{2,k}$ could be defined as $G12$, $G11 \cup G12 = G1$. Therefore, achievable rate on every subcarrier k can be expressed as

$$R_{s1R,k} \begin{cases} \frac{1}{2}\ln\left(1 + \frac{p_{s1,k}^I \gamma_{1,k}}{1 + p_{s2,k}^I \gamma_{2,k}}\right), k \in G11 \\ \frac{1}{2}\ln\left(1 + p_{s1,k}^I \gamma_{1,k}\right), k \in G12 \end{cases} \tag{2}$$

$$R_{s2R,k} = \begin{cases} \frac{1}{2}\ln\left(1 + p_{s2,k}^I \gamma_{2,k}\right), k \in G11 \\ \frac{1}{2}\ln\left(1 + \frac{p_{s2,k}^I \gamma_{2,k}}{1 + p_{s1,k}^I \gamma_{1,k}}\right), k \in G12 \end{cases} \tag{3}$$

Sum achievable rate in the first phase:

$$R_{s1R} = \sum_{k \in G1} R_{s1R,k} = \sum_{k \in G11} \frac{1}{2}\ln\left(1 + \frac{p_{s1,k}^I \gamma_{1,k}}{1 + p_{s2,k}^I \gamma_{2,k}}\right) + \sum_{k \in G12} \frac{1}{2}\ln\left(1 + p_{s1,k}^I \gamma_{1,k}\right) \tag{4}$$

$$R_{s2R} = \sum_{k \in G1} R_{s2R,k} = \sum_{k \in G11} \frac{1}{2}\ln\left(1 + \frac{p_{s2,k}^I \gamma_{2,k}}{1 + p_{s1,k}^I \gamma_{1,k}}\right) + \sum_{k \in G12} \frac{1}{2}\ln\left(1 + p_{s2,k}^I \gamma_{2,k}\right) \tag{5}$$

And energy harvested at relay R can be given as

$$Q = \sum_{k \in G2} Q_k = \sum_{k \in G2} \zeta(p_{s1,k}^E |h_{1,k}|^2 + p_{s2,k}^E |h_{2,k}|^2 + \sigma_k^2) \tag{6}$$

$\zeta$ denotes the energy conversion efficiency at Relay R.

During the second time slot, R uses all the subcarriers $k' \in \{1, \ldots, K\}$ to forward signal, which is also called broadcast phase. Similarly, $h_{1,k'}$ and $h_{2,k'}$ are the channel coefficient of the link R $\rightarrow$ S1, R $\rightarrow$ S2 over subcarriers $k'$, $p_{r,k'}$ representing the transmit power of R on subcarrier $k'$. Therefore, sum achievable rate here can be seen as (7) and (8). It is worth noting that both the source node could decode the signal from the other source node since it could identify its own signal.

$$R_{Rs1} = \sum_{k'=1}^{K} \frac{1}{2} \ln\left(1 + p_{r,k'} \gamma_{1,k'}\right) \tag{7}$$

$$R_{Rs2} = \sum_{k'=1}^{K} \frac{1}{2} \ln\left(1 + p_{r,k'} \gamma_{2,k'}\right) \tag{8}$$

Through two time slots of transmission, the transmission rate of S1 to S2 through relay R can be expressed as $R_{s1}$, whose value is determined by the smaller value of $R_{s1R}$, $R_{Rs2}$ in DF relay network. Corresponding, $R_{s2}$ representing the transmission rate of S2 to S1. And $Rs$ representing the system total rate, as the following formula

$$R_{s1} = \min(R_{s1R}, R_{Rs2}) \tag{9}$$

$$R_{s2} = \min(R_{s2R}, R_{Rs1}) \tag{10}$$

$$Rs = R_{s1} + R_{s2} \tag{11}$$

## 3   Problem Formulation

In this article, our target is to maximize the system total transmission rate. Power allocation in the first time slot is determined by water-filling algorithm with minimum power limit, whose value is $p_{min}$, and $p_{r,k'}$ in the second time slot uses average power allocation as (14), which satisfies the energy constrain in relay node R.

$$p_{s1,k} = \max\{p_{min}, \frac{1}{\beta_1} - \frac{1}{\gamma_{1,k}}\}, k \in \{1, 2, \ldots K\} \tag{12}$$

$$p_{s2,k} = \max\{p_{min}, \frac{1}{\beta_2} - \frac{1}{\gamma_{2,k}}\}, k \in \{1, 2, \ldots K\} \tag{13}$$

$$P_{r,k'} = \frac{1}{K} Q \tag{14}$$

$\beta_1$, $\beta_2$ meet the power constraints $\sum_{k=1}^{K} p_{s1,k} = P_s$, $\sum_{k=1}^{K} p_{s2,k} = P_s$, respectively. The problem can be transferred into determining subcarrier grouping, and can be formulated as

$$Max \ Rs = R_{s1} + R_{s2} \tag{15}$$

$$s.t. Q \geq \sum_{k'=1}^{K} P_{r,k'} \tag{16}$$

## 4 Optimal Solution

The optimization problem in (15–16) is a non-convex problem, using exhaustive search would be rather difficult. We assumed that the "time-sharing" condition [10] is meet, which will be always satisfied when the number of subcarriers is larger. In our scenario, the dual decomposition method can be used to solve the problem in (15–16) using the following two steps.

**Step 1:** Constructing a Lagrangian function

$$min(\alpha)g(\alpha) = max \, L(G1, G2) \tag{17}$$

While

$$g(\alpha) = g(\alpha_1, \alpha_{11}, \alpha_2, \alpha_{21}, \alpha_3) = \alpha_1(R_{s1R} - R_{s1}) + \alpha_{11}(R_{Rs2} - R_{s1}) + R_{s1} + \alpha_2(R_{s2R} - R_{s2})$$
$$+ \alpha_{21}(R_{Rs1} - R_{s2}) + R_{s2} + \alpha_3 \left( Q - \sum_{k'=1}^{K} p_{r,k'} \right) \tag{18}$$

$\alpha = \{\alpha_1, \alpha_{11}, \alpha_2, \alpha_{21}\}$ are binary parameters, $\alpha \in \{0, 1\}$, satisfying $\alpha_{11} + \alpha_1 = 1$, $\alpha_{21} + \alpha_2 = 1$. If $R_{s1R} > R_{Rs2}$, $R_{s1} = R_{Rs2}$, $\alpha_1$ is supposed to be 0, and $\alpha_{11}$ is supposed to be 1. In order to get the optimal value, we relax $\alpha_1, \alpha_{11}, \alpha_2, \alpha_{21}$ to be real values in the interval [0, 1], instead of binary. Substituting it into (18), the dual function can be rewritten as (19)

$$g(\alpha_1, \alpha_2, \alpha_3) = \alpha_1 R_{s1R} + (1 - \alpha_1)R_{Rs2} + \alpha_2 R_{s2R} + (1 - \alpha_2)R_{Rs1} + \alpha_3 \left( Q - \sum_{k'=1}^{K} p_{r,k'} \right) \tag{19}$$

Using the sub-gradient based methods. The sub-gradient can be easily given as:

$$\triangle \alpha_1 = R_{s1R} - R_{Rs2} \tag{20}$$

$$\triangle \alpha_2 = R_{s2R} - R_{Rs2} \tag{21}$$

$\alpha_1, \alpha_2$, is updated by $\alpha^{t+1} = \alpha^t - \xi^t \triangle \alpha$, $\xi^t$ is the step size satisfying the diminishing policy [11]. Thus, the optimal dual variable of convergence can be obtained. And $\alpha_3$ is nearly equal constrain, so its value could be adjusted first.

**Step 2:** Assumed that we had already know $\{p_{s1,k}^*, p_{s2,k}^*, p_{r,k'}^*\}$. Substituting (12)–(14) into (19), and having mathematic transformation, we can rewrite the formula as (22). And only the first part on the right side, $F_k$, involves G1. Therefore, the optimal subcarrier group for information decoding G1 can be obtained by (24), finding all the $k \in \{1, \ldots, K\}$ makes $F_k$ positive.

$$g(\alpha_1, \alpha_2, \alpha_3) = \sum_{k \in G1} F_k^* + (1 - \alpha_1)R_{Rs2}^* + (1 - \alpha_2)R_{Rs1}^*$$
$$+ \alpha_3 \left( \sum_{k=1}^{K} Q_k^* - \sum_{k'=1}^{K} p_{r,k'}^* \right) \tag{22}$$

Where

$$F_k^* = \alpha_1 R_{s1R,k} + \alpha_2 R_{s2R,k}^* - \alpha_3 Q_k^* \tag{23}$$

$$G_1^* = \arg \max F_k^* \tag{24}$$

$$G_2^* = K - G_1^* \tag{25}$$

## 5　Simulation Results

In our article, we set the distance between two sources nodes to be 4 m. Relay R locates between S1 and S2, and the distance between R and S1 is represented as d1, as can be seen in Fig. 1. Both the total power of S1 and S2 is represented as Ps. The number of subcarriers K is 32. The harvesting conversion efficiency is set to be 1.

The channel is as Rice fading, and line-of-sight signal plays a primary role in this simulation. Channel coefficient $h_k$ could be depicted as (26). Where g1(k) and g2(k) denotes LOS deterministic component and the Rayleigh fading, respectively, and M is the Rice factor set to be 3.

$$h_k = \sqrt{\frac{M}{M+1}}g1(k) + \sqrt{\frac{1}{M+1}}g2(k) \tag{26}$$

$$|g1|^2 = -40\text{dB} \tag{27}$$

$$g2(k) \in CN(0, d^{(-v)}) \tag{28}$$

$v$ is the path-loss index, which is set to be 2, and the variance of noise is set to be-50 dBm.

Figures 2 and 3 show the power allocation of source nodes S1 and S2, respectively, when Ps = 2 w, $p_{min}$ = 0.02 w, and d1 = 1.5 m. As can be seen, subcarrier index number 7 is allocated as energy transmission, and the other subcarriers are used for information decoding. Due to the interference cancellation technique, one side will inevitably have a relatively poor SINR. Therefore, the total rate in this paper does not require the minimum decoding SINR, and the results show that the number of subcarriers used for energy is not very large.

Figure 4 shows the total rate versus relay location d1 when Ps = 2 w and 4 w. The curve is approximately axisymmetric with d1 = 2 m. The total rate reaches the lowest value when d1 is 2 m, when R is exactly at the middle of S1 and S2. When d1 is 2 m,

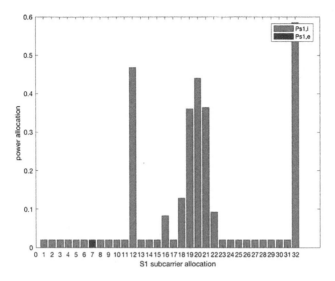

**Fig. 2.** Power allocation of S1

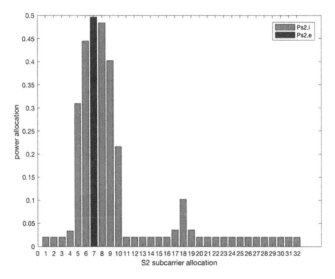

**Fig. 3.** Power allocation of S2

the two channels are similar, which is not conducive to interference cancellation. We can see that the relay location has a clear influence on the total rate.

When the transmission power becomes larger, the total rate increases, as can be seen in Fig. 5. While d1 is set as 1.3 m and 2.0 m, respectively. Both curves show an upward trend and conform to the law of Fig. 4.

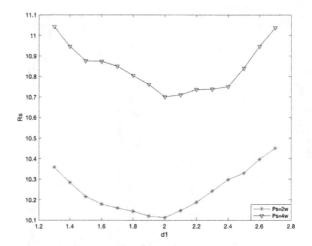

**Fig. 4.** Total rate versus relay location d1

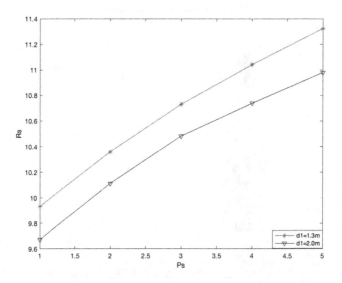

**Fig. 5.** Total rate versus transmit power.

## 6   Conclusions

In this paper, we proposed a collaborative energy and information transfer protocol for two-way DF relay network. Explicitly, the received subcarriers at R in the first time slot are divided into a couple of groups, one is for information decoding and another is for energy harvesting. Then relay R uses all the subcarriers to broadcast signal, helping achieving the information transmission of the two sources. Subcarrier grouping is optimized to maximize the total rate.

# References

1. Zhang, R., Ho, C.K.: MIMO broadcasting for simultaneous wireless information and power transfer. IEEE Trans. Wirel. Commun. **12**(5), 1989–2001 (2013)
2. Zhou, X., Zhang, R., Ho, C.K.: Wireless information and power transfer: architecture design and rate-energy tradeoff. IEEE Trans. Commun. **61**(11), 4754–4767 (2013)
3. Rankov, B., Wittneben, A.: Spectral efficient protocols for half-duplex fading relay channels. IEEE J. Sel. Areas Commun. **25**(2), 379–389 (2007)
4. Dai, M., et al.: Survey on cooperative strategies for wireless relay channels. Trans. Emerg. Telecommun. Technol. **25**(9), 926–942 (2014)
5. Nasir, A.A., Zhou, X., Durrani, S., Kennedy, R.A.: Relaying protocols for wireless energy harvesting and information processing. IEEE Trans. Wirel. Commun. **12**(7), 3622–3636 (2013)
6. Ding, Z., Perlaza, S.M., Esnaola, I., Poor, H.V.: Power allocation strategies in energy harvesting wireless cooperative networks. IEEE Trans. Wirel. Commun. **13**(2), 846–860 (2014)
7. Wen, Z., Wang, S., Fan, C., Xiang, W.: Joint transceiver and power splitter design over two-way relaying channel with lattice codes and energy harvesting. IEEE Commun. Lett. **18**(11), 2039–2042 (2014)
8. Do, T.P., Song, I., Yun, H.K.: Simultaneous wireless transfer of power and information in a decode-and-forward two-way relaying network. IEEE Press (2017)
9. Sendonaris, A., Erkip, E., Aazhang, B.: User cooperation diversity. Part I: system description. IEEE Trans. Commun. **51**(11), 1927–1938 (2003)
10. Laneman, J.N., Wornell, G.W.: Exploiting distributed spatial diversity in wireless networks. In: Proceedings Allerton Conference on Communication, Control, and Computing (2000)
11. Yu, W., Lui, R.: Dual methods for nonconvex spectrum optimization of multicarrier systems. IEEE Trans. Commun. **54**(7), 1310–1322 (2006)

# Dynamic Network Access for Multi-UAV Networks: A Cloud-Assisted Learning Algorithm

Xiaodu Liu[1](✉), Yitao Xu[1], Yanlei Duan[2], Dianxiong Liu[1], and Zhiyong Du[3]

[1] College of Communications Engineering,
Army Engineering University of PLA, Nanjing, China
lxdlgdx@163.com
[2] No. 92274 Troops of PLA, Kunming, China
[3] National University of Defense Technology, Changsha, China

**Abstract.** In this paper, we study the strategy of UAV dynamic network access in the large-scale UAVs swam. We model the master UAV providing communication coverage for the small UAVs which transformed the large-scale UAVs communication problem into the optimization problem. Compared to the traditional ground user network access, the characteristic of UAV's mobility have been considered and each UAV have chance to move to any master UAV for better service. We propose a joint optimization for the throughput and flight loss. Due to the limitation of flight loss, the UAVs can not fly to different networks many times for learning. We set up a load aggregator cloud to help the UAVs simulate the results of each decision. We propose a dynamic network access algorithm based on SLA which is proved to achieve stable solutions with dynamic and incomplete information constraint. The simulation results show that this algorithm can converge to the optimal solution. Also, it is shown that the algorithm has strong robustness and can get good utility than other algorithms regardless of how the environment changing.

**Keywords:** Dynamic network access · Multi-UAV communication
Cloud-assisted · SLA

## 1 Introduction

The application of the intelligent unmanned aerial vehicles (UAVs) is expanding with the development of the UAV technology [1]. Nowadays, large-scale UAVs and UAV-assisted communication are playing important roles in various fields. In 2017, nearly 300 UAVs flied together to create a dreamlike stage in the USA super bowl. Recently, the company EHang has also achieved the formation of 1000 UAVs. However, the focus of large-scale UAVs is more on the collaborative control [2]. UAV-assisted communication is also only considered as the air base station to assist ground communication [3–7]. However, how to solve the problem of large-scale UAVs' inter-domain communication and how to deal with the

© ICST Institute for Computer Sciences, Social Informatics and Telecommunications Engineering 2018
L. Meng and Y. Zhang (Eds.): MLICOM 2018, LNICST 251, pp. 358–369, 2018.
https://doi.org/10.1007/978-3-030-00557-3_36

relationship between the master UAV and the other small UAVs are not having clear answers. There is still relatively little research on the combination of large-scale UAVs and UAV-assisted communication.

In the large-scale UAVs scenario, the communication between UAVs is interactive, resulting in a series of coupling optimization problems. Most of the existing studies have looked at how the UAVs serving ground users. The paper [8] assigns UAV to specific region as the relay, thus enhancing the communication capability of heterogeneous wireless network. However, the work in paper [8] is limited to the uniform distribution of ground users, and does not fully consider the fairness of users' choice in the case of network congestion. In the paper [9], the base station which associated with UAV is determined with the goal of minimizing UAV's transmit power and satisfying the user's rate requirement. The UAV has been used as a mobile base station to serve ground users, and achieves the goal of maximizing the minimum throughput of each ground user by accessing different users in [10]. The authors [11] considered the multi-UAV system and added power control based on the paper [10]. Most of the current researches only consider the UAV as the aerial base station to serve the ground users. The communication problem of the UAV itself is not considered.

In order to solve the problem of large-scale UAVs communication, the relationship between the small UAV and its upper master UAV is analogous to the relationship between the user and the network in the traditional network access scenario. That is, the master UAVs provide communication coverage for the small UAVs. The network connectivity of a UAV-assisted network has been optimized in [12] and [13]. However it does not consider the situation of master UAVs assisting the small UAVs with communication. And there is a lack of research on network access in multi-UAV system. In our paper, the communication problem of the large-scale UAVs is transformed into the optimization problem of the network access. Different from the traditional network access problem, only users in the overlapping areas of the network can choose the access network [14]. Because of the mobility of the UAV, no matter where it is currently located, it can move to the range of any master UAVs to find better service. Such a scenario is more equitable than the original scenario, not just the users in the network's overlapping areas but every one has opportunity to make decisions.

We model the application scenarios as a master UAV has been crashed, and the small UAVs in it are not served. We command the access of small UAVs to other networks through ground control center. The small UAVs of other mater UAVs can also change their location for better service after receiving the impact from outside small UAVs. This brings us more challenges to the study of network access problems. How to define the flight loss of UAV is the first problem to be faced with UAV's mobility. The paper [15–17] considered the UAV energy saving communication but did not consider the flight energy required by the movement. The flight loss have been considered in [18] to solve the problem of energy-efficient UAV communication, but our paper focuses more on the completion of UAV's communication task. We combine the traditional network access throughput optimization with the flight loss of UAV which becomes a joint optimization for the throughput and flight loss. We propose a dynamic network access algorithm based on SLA [19] to find the tradeoff between throughput and UAV flight loss. Due to the limitation of flight loss, the UAVs can not fly to different networks many times for learning. We set up a load aggregator cloud to help the UAVs simulate the results of each decision. The main contributions of our work can be summarized as follows:

- We solve the problem of UAV group communication by clearing the relationship between the master UAV and the small UAV. We model the master UAV providing communication coverage for the small UAVs which transformed the large-scale UAVs communication problem into the optimization problem of the network access. We solve the problem as some master UAVs have been crashed, how the small UAVs to make decisions to guarantee the communication quality.
- We consider the characteristic of UAV's mobility and we make it possible for each UAV to move to any master UAV for better service. We combine the traditional network access throughput optimization with the flight loss of UAV which becomes a joint optimization for the throughput and flight loss.
- A dynamic network access algorithm based on SLA has been proposed to get the Nash equilibrium and find the tradeoff between throughput and UAV flight loss. Due to the limitation of flight loss, the UAVs can not fly to different networks many times for learning. We set up a load aggregator cloud to help the UAVs simulate the results of each decision.

The remainder of this paper is organized as follows. In Sect. 2, we present the system model and problem formation. In Sect. 3, we propose a cloud-assisted learning algorithm based on SLA to solve the problem. Further, we present the simulation results and performance analysis in Sect. 4. Then, we draw the conclusion in Sect. 5.

## 2    System Model and Problem Formulation

### 2.1    System Model

We consider a UAV formation consisting of $\mathcal{N} = \{1, 2, ..., N\}$ master UAVs and $\mathcal{M} = \{1, 2, ..., M\}$ small UAVs. The master UAVs provide communication coverage for the small UAVs. The small UAVs are denoted as users which share the master UAVs' resource to send information. Each small UAV has communication tasks to finish, so it must be covered by the master UAV. In this paper, we only consider the case that the number of small UAVs is much larger than the number of master UAVs, so we put three master UAVs $N_1$, $N_2$ and $N_3$ in the system which serve this areas' small UAVs. We denote two kinds of small UAVs in this system. One of them are already in the range of a master UAV, the others do not covered by any master UAVs because their master UAVs have been crashed. In traditional network access scenarios, users are not able to access the network if they are outside of the communication coverage. But this is not a question in the UAV system. Because of the dynamics of UAVs, we can deploy the small UAVs through the control center to move to the coverage of any master UAVs to get service. Due to the addition of external users, the small UAVs which originally in the range of some master UAVs may get less resources for communication. Therefore they also can move to the coverage of different master UAVs to achieve better payoff. Each small UAV has multiple available master UAVs, but the small UAVs can only access one master UAV at any time (Fig. 1).

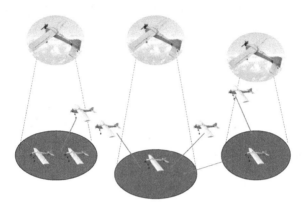

**Fig. 1.** Dynamic network access system consist of three master UAVs and two kinds of small UAVs. One of the UAVs are already in the range of a master UAV, the others do not covered by any master UAVs because their master UAVs have been crushed.

## 2.2   Problem Formulation

In our model there are two actions of each small UAV: Firstly, the small UAV is in the coverage of any master UAVs and it does not want to change the master UAV. The throughput of the small UAV accesses the network depends on a number of factors, including the physical layer data transmission rate, the load connect to the network, and the resource allocation strategy adopt by the access network. This paper considers a resource allocation strategy which based on proportional equity. Under this mechanism, the average throughput of the small UAV $m$ to access the master UAV $n$ can be achieved as [14].

$$g_m = \theta_m = \frac{w_m R_{m,n}}{W_n}, \tag{1}$$

where $R_{m,n}$ is the peak data rate between small UAV $m$ and master UAV $n$, $w_m$ is small UAV $m$'s load, and $W_n = \sum_{i \in M_n} w_i$ is the total weight of small UAVs that accessed master UAV $n$. This above model combines many practical considerations. The peek data rate $R_{m,n}$ reflects physical characteristics such as wireless channel quality and modulation encoding. Secondly, the discount factor $\frac{w_m}{W_n}$ reflect the characteristics of the users sharing the network's resources.

The user's weight can distinguish the application types of different small UAVs in the same network. Such that the reconnaissance UAV need to send some photos and videos, so it needs more resources. The attack UAV only needs to receive real-time message, so it has low throughput requirements. In conclusion, the weight of the small UAV depends on the type of the task it needs to do.

Secondly, if the small UAV is not covered by any master UAV so it needs to move to any master UAV to look for the communication service. Some small UAVs which already have master UAVs to access want to move to other master UAVs for better payoff. They all have flight loss caused by movement. The cost $E_c$ can be denoted as [17]

$$E_c = \frac{d_{m,n}}{V}(c_1 V^3 + \frac{c_2}{V}), \tag{2}$$

where $d_{m,n}$ equals to the distance between the small UAV and the communication coverage of the master UAV. That is also what we need to optimize. $V$ is a given UAV speed, $c_1, c_2$ are constant which related to the weight of the aircraft and the external wind force. The first term in the speed loss is proportional to the third power of the velocity, which is the resistance loss caused by air friction during the flight. The second inverse is the energy loss to overcome the lift. So the utility function of the small UAV $m$ to move to access the master UAV $n$ can be achieved as [8]

$$g_m = \frac{w_m R_{m,n}}{W_n} - \beta \frac{d_{m,n}}{V}(c_1 V^3 + \frac{c_2}{V}), \tag{3}$$

where $\beta$ is the normalized coefficient. The importance of flight loss can be expressed by changing the size of $\beta$. If we improve the value of $\beta$ means that we do not want the small UAV to change its location. This utility function represents the intentions of each small UAV. We must find the tradeoff between the throughput and flight loss.

We denoted the user-network correlation as $M_0$. So we defined the utility as the social welfare

$$U_{social}(M_0) = \sum_{m \in M} g_m(\theta_m, E_c). \tag{4}$$

The target of the system is to optimize the relationship between the small UAVs and the master UAVs to maximize the net utility which is denoted as

$$(P1) : \max U_{social}(M_0), \tag{5}$$

## 3   Dynamic Network Access Algorithm

### 3.1   SLA: Stochastic Learning Automata

Due to the dynamic and incomplete information constraints, most existing algorithms can not be applied [19]. Based on the SLA (Stochastic learning automata), we propose a new algorithm. Stochastic learning automata is a finite machine that interacts with an unknown environment and tries to learn the best practices provided by the environment [20]. SLA updates the selection probability dynamically through the feedback from each learning and keeps doing the probability update until users reach stable conditions. Due to the limitation of flight loss, the UAVs can not fly to different networks many times for learning. We set up a control center using the SLA algorithm to help the UAVs simulate the results of each decision. When all users converge to Nash equilibrium, the control center deploy the small UAVs to move to the coverage of the specified master UAVs to get service. So as to realize the distributed solution for the original problem.

We extend the dynamic network access game to the form of mixed strategy. We denote that $P = (p_1, ..., p_M)$ is the mixed strategy for all users, where $p_m = (p_{m1}, ...p_{mN})$ is the probability vector when small UAV $m$ access any master UAVs. And $p_{mn}$ is probability of the small UAV $m$ to access the master UAV $n$. We also denote $h_{nm}(P)$ as the average throughput of small UAV $m$ when the small UAV $m$ access the master UAV $n$ $(a_m = n)$ and other small UAVs use the mixed strategy.

$$h_{mn}(P) = u_m(a_1, ..., a_{m-1}, n, a_{m+1}, ..., a_M) \tag{6}$$

According to the number of small UAVs in each master UAV and the location of each small UAV, each small UAV can achieve random return value at the end of each time slot. The small UAV updates its mixed strategy on this basis.

## 3.2   A Cloud-Assisted Learning Algorithm Based on SLA

Due to the limitation of flight loss, the UAVs can not fly to different networks many times for learning. We set up a load aggregator cloud to help the UAVs simulate the results of each decision. Compared with the existing learning framework, UAVs in the cloud support framework do not need to actually perform frequent network switching, but only report the decision information to the cloud. There is a load aggregator cloud that is responsible for collecting decision information for all UAVs and sending "virtual network load information" to UAVs. Unlike the centralized optimization method adopted in literature [17], the network load aggregation cloud does not make any decision about the allocation of wireless resources. Therefore, the proposed cloud learning framework can also be applied to similar distributed learning algorithms (such as SLA) and improve its operational efficiency. In our paper, UAVs are willing to submit all necessary information to the cloud. Including rate information $R_{m,n}$ and demand information $\theta_m$. After collecting the UAV's information, the network load aggregation cloud represents the benefit of the UAVs, simulating multiple UAVs to run the SLA learning algorithm. The algorithm process is as follows:

The cloud-assisted learning algorithm based on SLA which we proposed has the following characteristics: (i) this algorithm is not a rigid decision, but select the strategy according to a certain probability randomly in the candidate actions; (ii) not blindly choose the optimal utility of action, but improve the access probability of which action has better payoff softly; (iii) the probability of the

---

**Algorithm 1. A Cloud-assisted Learning Algorithm based on SLA**

---

*The User Side:* .
**Step 1:** Each user $m$ access to any network and register in the load aggregator cloud.
**Step 2:** User $m$ reports to the cloud rate information $R_{m,n}$ and demand information $\theta_m$ . And wait for the network selection $a_m$ return from the cloud .
*The Load Aggregator Cloud Side:*
**Step 1:**   Receive all user reports. Maintain a cumulative decision distribution vector for each user.
**Step 2:**   Run the dynamic network access algorithm based on the SLA and update the network access probability vector until the end of a scheduled stop rule.
*The SLA part:*
*Initialize:* . Set the number of iterations k=1 and set the initial network access probability as $p_{mn}(k) = 1/N, \forall m \in \mathcal{M}, n \in \{1, ..., N\}$, then generate small UAVs $\mathcal{M} = \{1, 2, ..., M\}$ randomly within or without the range of the master UAV.
*Loop for $k = 0,1,...$*
**Step 1:** At the beginning of the time slot k, firstly the small UAV $m$ which are not in the range of any master UAVs access the master UAV $a_m(k)$ according to its current network access probability vector $p_m(k)$ . Secondly the other small UAVs do the same steps.
**Step 2:** On the basis of the network access in Step1, the UAV do the network awareness and access the master UAV. At the end of the current slot, the small UAV obtains the random return which is calculated by (3) and set the return to the small UAVs.
**Step 3:** All the small UAVs update the probability of network access according to the following rules:

$$p_{mn}(k + 1) = p_{mn}(k) + bg_m(k)(1 - p_{mn}(k)), n = a_m(k)$$
$$p_{mn}(k + 1) = p_{mn}(k) - bg_m(k)p_{mn}(k), \quad n \neq a_m(k) \tag{7}$$

where $0 < b < 1$ is the iteration step length, $g_m(k)$ is the normalized throughput.
**Step 4:** For any small UAV, the corresponding network access probability vector has an element that is close to 1, if greater than 0.99, and the algorithm go back to Step 2. Otherwise, go back to Step 2. Until all the small UAVs' network access probability are close to 1, then the algorithm ends.
*Loop end*

---

network access is updated based on the random return value of each slot. The random return is the reinforcement signal of this algorithm. Leaving the small UAVs more exploration space in the dynamic network access system, which can effectively get rid of the local optimal dilemma. According to the real-time change of the network environment, the user can improve the access probability of the current optimal decision at each time slot. So that the probability of optimal access will eventually converge.

# 4 Simulation Results and Analysis

In this scenario we generate two circular networks as the coverage of master UAVs with a diameter of 500 m. A circular network with a diameter of 300 m has been set to distinguish the different kinds of master UAVs. Then we randomly generate each 10 nodes in first two networks and 5 nodes in the third network as the small UAVs. Twenty nodes have been set as the small UAVs which are not in range of any master UAVs. The number of iterations is set as 500 in the simulation. The location of each small UAV is generated randomly each time. The distance between each small UAV and the distance from the small UAV to the network is the decisive factor of the system. We set up a control center to help the UAVs simulate the results of each decision. We set the speed of UAV as $V = 10dB$, the constant $c_1 = 9.26 \times 10^{-4}$ and $c_2 = 2250$. The learning step is set as 0.5. The link transmission peak rate of the master and the leader UAV is calculating by the Shannon formula $R = B\log_2(1 + P/(B * \sigma^2))$.

The simulation results mainly include the following two parts. The first part is the convergence of the simulation algorithm. In particular, for any selected user, we study the change of the network access probability with the iteration number. In addition, in order to reflect the overall convergence of the system, we also study the change of the number of users in different networks and give the convergence network topology. The second part gives the performance evaluation of the algorithm and compares the utility function of the four methods: (i) The dynamic network access algorithm based on SLA, (ii) The centralized algorithm, (iii) Random access and (iv) The closet network access algorithm. In the centralized algorithm, we assume that each user knows all the message of the system. They know the rewards of access any network and all choose the best one to access. As the users only know the location of the network, the random access algorithm choose the network as the same probability and the closet network access algorithm choose the closet network to access are all feasible.

## 4.1 Convergence Behavior

Firstly, we study the variation of network access probability with iteration number. Simulation of a dynamic network access system with twenty-five dynamic loads, twenty dynamic users and three networks. And the bandwidth between this three networks is 2:2:1 which represents the size of the communication coverage. The UAV's flight loss is several orders of magnitude larger compared with the throughput. The goal of this paper is to ensure the quality of communication, so we set the normalized coefficient $\beta$ as 0.015.

The Fig. 2 gives the convergence of network access probability of any selected user. We can see that this user's network access probability vector is approximately running 140 iterations from $\{1/3, 1/3, 1/3\}$ to $\{0, 1, 0\}$. That is to see, this small UAV finally choose the master UAV $N_2$ to access. The Fig. 4 shows the network topology after the algorithm is convergence. Each users have network to get service. Some users originally in the $N_1$ may move to $N_2$ and $N_3$ to find

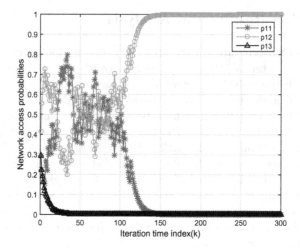

**Fig. 2.** The convergence process of arbitrary user network access probability.

better service, some users do not change their location. The number of the users in each network is related to the network capacity.

## 4.2 Performance Analysis

In this section, we study how the different parameters influence the algorithms. Figure 3 represents the relationship between the number of the dynamic users with the social welfare. All these four algorithm, we do 500 independent simulations and then take the average. As can be seen form the figure, the algorithm we proposed is far more efficient than the random access algorithm and the closet network access algorithm no matter how many dynamic users in this system. The algorithm we proposed also get the same social welfare as the centralized algorithm at any time. The reasons are as follows: (i) The proposed algorithm can converge to the optimal solution, and the users will be scattered on different networks. (ii) In the random access algorithm, as the number of dynamic users increases, it is possible to make unreasonable decisions. So this situation may make low throughput and high flight loss. (iii) In the closet network access algorithm, as the number of dynamic users increases, some networks may be accessed by multiple users which make the congestion of the network.

In Fig. 4, we change the normalized coefficient $\beta$ of the flight loss. This change only has a little effect on our algorithm. The dynamic network access algorithm based on SLA can also get high social welfare like the centralized algorithm. With the low level of the normalized coefficient $\beta$, the random access algorithm and the closet network access algorithm may get the social welfare close to the algorithm we proposed. But effected by the improve of the normalized coefficient $\beta$, the social welfare get by the random access algorithm and the closet network access algorithm all drop faster. It can be seen, the algorithm we proposed has strong robustness and can get good utility regardless of the environment change.

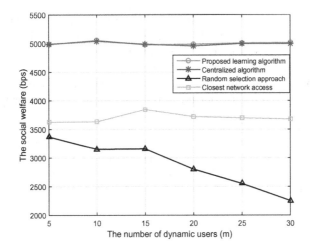

**Fig. 3.** The utility comparison of the four algorithms with different user numbers.

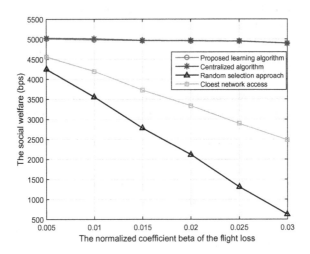

**Fig. 4.** The utility comparison of the four algorithms with different normalized coefficient $\beta$ of the flight loss.

## 5    Conclusion

This paper put forward the network scenario of the master UAVs serving the small UAVs for communication. We transformed the UAV group communication problem into the optimization problem of the network access. We consider the characteristic of UAV's mobility and make it possible for each UAV to move to any master UAV for better service. We combine the traditional network access throughput optimization with the flight loss of UAV which becomes a joint optimization for the throughput and flight loss. We proposed a dynamic network access algorithm based on SLA to get the Nash equilibrium. Due to the limitation of flight loss, the UAVs can not fly to different networks many times for learning. We set up a load aggregator cloud to help the UAVs simulate the results of each decision. The simulation shows that the algorithm we proposed can get good utility than other algorithms regardless of how the environment changes. The algorithm realizes the robust optimization in dynamic unknown environment.

**Acknowledgment.** This work was supported by the National Science Foundation of China under Grant No. 61771488, No. 61671473, No. 61631020 and No. 61401508, the in part by Natural Science Foundation for Distinguished Young Scholars of Jiangsu Province under Grant No. BK20160034, and in part by the Open Research Foundation of Science and Technology on Communication Networks Laboratory.

# References

1. Zeng, Y., Zhang, R., Lim, T.J.: Wireless communications with unmanned aerial vehicles: opportunities and challenges. IEEE Commun. Mag. **54**(5), 36–42 (2016)
2. Kuriki, Y., Namerikawa, T.: Formation control with collision avoidance for a multi-UAV system using decentralized MPC and consensus-based control. In: European Control Conference (ECC), Linz, pp. 3079–3084 (2015)
3. Mozaffari, M., Saad, W., Bennis, M., Debbah, M.: Drone small cells in the clouds: design, deployment and performance analysis. In: IEEE Global Communications Conference (GLOBECOM), San Diego, CA, pp. 1–6 (2015)
4. Mozaffari, M., Saad, W., Bennis, M., Debbah, M.: Efficient deployment of multiple unmanned aerial vehicles for optimal wireless coverage. IEEE Commun. Lett. **20**(8), 1647–1650 (2016)
5. Al-Hourani, A., Kandeepan, S., Lardner, S.: Optimal LAP altitude for maximum coverage. IEEE Wirel. Commun. Lett. **3**(6), 569–572 (2014)
6. Lyu, J., Zeng, Y., Zhang, R., Lim, T.J.: Placement optimization of UAV-mounted mobile base stations. IEEE Commun. Lett. **21**(3), 604–607 (2017)
7. Bor-Yaliniz, R.I., El-Keyi, A., Yanikomeroglu, H.: Efficient 3-D placement of an aerial base station in next generation cellular networks. In: 2016 IEEE International Conference on Communications (ICC), Kuala Lumpur, pp. 1–5 (2016)
8. Sharma, V., Bennis, M., Kumar, R.: UAV-assisted heterogeneous networks for capacity enhancement. IEEE Commun. Lett. **20**(6), 1207–1210 (2016)
9. Mozaffari, M., Saad, W., Bennis, M., Debbah, M.: Optimal transport theory for power-efficient deployment of unmanned aerial vehicles. In: 2016 IEEE International Conference on Communications (ICC), Kuala Lumpur, pp. 1–6 (2016)
10. Wu, Q., Zeng, Y., Zhang, R.: Joint trajectory and communication design for UAV-enabled multiple access. In: 2017 IEEE Global Communications Conference, GLOBECOM 2017, Singapore, pp. 1–6 (2017)
11. Wu, Q., Zeng, Y., Zhang, R.: Joint trajectory and communication design for multi-UAV enabled wireless networks. IEEE Trans. Wirel. Commun. **PP**(99), 1
12. Han, Z., Swindlehurst, A.L., Liu, K.J.R.: Optimization of MANET connectivity via smart deployment/movement of unmanned air vehicles. IEEE Trans. Veh. Technol. **58**(7), 3533–3546 (2009)
13. Kim, S., Oh, H., Suk, J., Tsourdos, A.: Coordinated trajectory planning for efficient communication relay using multiple UAVs. Control Eng. Pract. **29**, 42–49 (2014)

14. Du, Z., Wu, Q., Yang, P.: Dynamic user demand driven online network selection. IEEE Commun. Lett. **18**(3), 419–422 (2014)
15. Kandeepan, S., Gomez, K., Reynaud, L., Rasheed, T.: Aerial-terrestrial communications: terrestrial cooperation and energy-efficient transmissions to aerial base stations. IEEE Trans. Aerosp. Electron. Syst. **50**(4), 2715–2735 (2014)
16. Mozaffari, M., Saad, W., Bennis, M., Debbah, M.: Optimal transport theory for power-efficient deployment of unmanned aerial vehicles. In: 2016 IEEE International Conference on Communications (ICC), Kuala Lumpur, pp. 1–6 (2016)
17. Li, K., Ni, W., Wang, X., Liu, R.P., Kanhere, S.S., Jha, S.: Energy-efficient cooperative relaying for unmanned aerial vehicles. IEEE Trans. Mobile Comput. **15**(6), 1377–1386 (2016)
18. Zeng, Y., Zhang, R.: Energy-efficient UAV communication with trajectory optimization. IEEE Trans. Wirel. Commun. **16**(6), 3747–3760 (2017)
19. Xu, Y., Xu, Y., Anpalagan, A.: Database-assisted spectrum access in dynamic networks: a distributed learning solution. IEEE Access **3**, 1071–1078 (2015)
20. Kaelbing, L.P., Littman, M.L., Moore, A.W.: Reinforcement learning: a survey. J. Artif. Intell. Res. **4**(1), 237–285 (1996)
21. Xue, P., Gong, P., Park, J.H., Park, D., Kim, D.K.: Radio resource management with proportional rate constraint in the heterogeneous networks. IEEE Trans. Wirel. Commun. **11**(3), 1066–1075 (2012)

# Probability-Based Routing Symmetry Metrics

Qin Wang[1], Fang Dong[2(✉)], Xin-Li Yang[3], and Rui Yin[2]

[1] China University Program, Texas Instruments Semiconductor Technologies
(Shanghai), Shanghai, China
qin-wang@ti.com
[2] College of Information and Electronic Engineering,
Zhejiang University City College, Hangzhou, China
{dongf,yinrui}@zucc.edu.cn
[3] Port Management Office of Haiyan County, Jiaxing, Zhejiang Province, China
hyhangyun@163.com

**Abstract.** In communication networks, if streams between two endpoints follow the same physical paths for both forward and reverse direction, they are symmetric. Routing asymmetry affects several protocols, and impacts part of traffic analysis techniques. We propose two routing symmetry metrics to express different meanings when talking about routing symmetry, namely, (1) the forward and reverse flows coming from one node to another are exactly the same, and (2) one single node is visited by both flows. The two metrics are termed as identity symmetry and cross symmetry, respectively. Then, we build a model to link the macroscopic symmetry with the microscopic routing behavior, and present some analysis results, thus make it possible to design a routing algorithm with some desired symmetry. The simulation and dataset study show that routing algorithms that generate next hop randomly will lead to a symmetric network, but it is not the case for Internet. Because the paths of Internet are heavily dominated by a small number of prevalent routes, Internet is highly asymmetry.

**Keywords:** Routing symmetry · Routing behavior model · Statistical process

## 1 Introduction

In communication networks, if streams between two endpoints follow the same physical paths for both forward and reverse direction, they are symmetric [1]. Routing asymmetry affects several protocols and impacts traffic analysis techniques. Knowing to which degree the routings are symmetric is helpful in protocol design and traffic analysis.

In practice, the one-way propagation time is commonly estimated to be half of the round-trip time (RTT) between nodes, e.g., the NTP (Network Time Protocol) of Internet [2, 3]. However, this estimate will be inappropriate if routes are asymmetric.

The paper is supported by Basic Public Welfare Research Projects (No. LGF18F010007) of Zhejiang Province and National Natural Science Foundation Program of China (No. 61771429).

© ICST Institute for Computer Sciences, Social Informatics and Telecommunications Engineering 2018
L. Meng and Y. Zhang (Eds.): MLICOM 2018, LNICST 251, pp. 370–380, 2018.
https://doi.org/10.1007/978-3-030-00557-3_37

Today's communication protocols rely heavily on the estimate of link condition to exploit available communication resources effectively, which is especially the case in wireless communications. The estimate is usually based on measurement of the statistical parameters of incoming packet, which will not infer the real condition of the outgoing link in situations of routing asymmetry.

Some traffic analysis techniques [4–6] are embedded in an assumption that routings are symmetric, i.e., all the packets of a session on both directions can be monitored by a sniffer located on a specific link. But it is not the case in practice [7, 8]. Routing asymmetry has a significant impact of these techniques [9, 10].

A common cause of routing asymmetry is that routing is selected independently for each flow, and at each node, taking many factors into account, including load-balancing and congestion controlling, which varied among nodes. This cause is especially prominent in the case of multipath routing. Another commonly mentioned cause is the "hot-potato routing", which is a business practice of passing traffic off to another autonomous system (AS) as soon as possible. By autonomous system, we mean a domain in which the routers and hosts are unified by a single administrative authority, and a set of interior gateway protocols [11].

## 2   Related Works

Literatures contain many studies of routing protocols, but considerably few studies of routing behavior [2, 3]. But recently there is a growing research of macroscopic properties of the network routing, including routing asymmetry, by studying datasets or modeling network behavior.

It is more than ten years since Paxson revealed that about 50% of the time an Internet path includes a major asymmetry [12]. In the past few years, it became clearer that this phenomenon has a significant impact on network measuring, modeling, and managing. [9] studied impact that asymmetric routing can have on statistical traffic classifiers. [8] pointed out that over 60% of AS-level paths are asymmetric, and path asymmetry will increasingly spread in the future. [12] studied the path stability and symmetry in 6 levels of granularity: router, point of presence (PoP), address prefix (AP), autonomous systems (AS), city and country. [1] used passively captured network data to estimate the amount of routing symmetry on a specific link, and [5, 13, 14] made an impractical assumption of traffic symmetry in tools and analysis.

Most work quantified the asymmetry with the number of different nodes between the forward and reverse paths, or classified a path as either asymmetric or symmetric, without considering quantifying the degree of symmetry [2, 3]. [7] proposed an approach to quantify the magnitude of routing asymmetry, measuring the dissimilarity between a pair of routes by aligning the two routes together and counting the minimal total cost incurred in aligning them. [15] defined the similarity coefficient as the number of similar nodes divided by the total number of distinct nodes in the two paths. [12, 16] quantified the difference between two routes (at any level) by calculating their Edit Distance [17] value. The metric defined in [16, 17] are different because the only operation considered in the former was aligning, while the latter considered inserting, deleting, and modifying.

These metrics of symmetry/asymmetry are not suited for modeling the behavior of routing theoretically, since they can only be calculated by algorithm or program. Some metrics [15, 16] does not meet the reality, because routing symmetry means different things under different contexts: (1) when estimating path condition, it means whether or not the forward and reverse path coming from a specific node to another specific node are exactly the same; (2) when talking a sniffer can or cannot monitor flows from both directions, it means whether or not a specific node is visited by both flows. So, accordingly, we will define 2 metrics, which will be called identity routing symmetry and cross routing symmetry.

## 3  Modeling and Statistical Analysis

### 3.1  Routing Symmetry Metrics

In this paper, when $A$ and $B$ be $m \times n$ matrices, the element-wise product of $A$ and $B$ is defined by $[A \circ B]_{i,j} = [A]_{i,j}[B]_{i,j}$, for all $1 \leq i \leq m, 1 \leq j \leq n$.

In a connected network, there are an infinite number of paths from any node $s$ to any other node $d$, i.e. $path_1, path_2, path_3, \ldots$ when counting circles. Suppose the frequency that the source node $s$ selects these paths to route packets to be $p_1, p_2, p_3, \ldots$. Similarly, there are also an infinite number of paths from node $d$ to $s$, $path_1^{-1}$, $path_2^{-1}, path_3^{-1}, \ldots$, with $path_i^{-1}$ we mean the reverse path of $path_i$, and the corresponding selecting frequency $q_1, q_2, q_3, \ldots$. Informally, we will use $p$ to denote the vector $[p_1, p_2, p_3, \ldots]$ and $q$ to denote $[q_1, q_2, q_3, \ldots]$.

A. Identity routing symmetry
We use the normalized inner product of $p$ and $q$ to define identity routing symmetry:

$$\rho^{id}(s, d) = \frac{(p, q)}{\sqrt{(p, p)}\sqrt{(q, q)}}. \tag{1}$$

In algebra, $\rho^{id}$ is also viewed as the cosine of the angle between $p$ and $q$. It is varied in the range [0, 1]. When $\rho^{id}$ is close to 0, $p$ and $q$ are orthogonal to each other. So, if for some $path_i$, the frequency that it is selected as the forward path, namely $p_i$, is large, then the frequency that $path_i^{-1}$ is selected as the reverse path, $q_i$, must be small, otherwise $\rho^{id}$ will not be close to 0. Conversely, when $\rho^{id}$ is close to 1, $p$ and $q$ are parallel to one another, so for each $i, p_i$ and $q_i$ are both large or both small. This makes $\rho^{id}$ a good choice for defining our identity routing symmetry. Note that the defined $\rho^{id}$ is not a linear function of the angle between $p$ and $q$, so we may use $1 - arccos(\rho^{id})$ to calculate the identity symmetry. As this is an increasing function of $\rho^{id}$, they are essentially the same metric.

In practical networks, usually a small number of paths are used to transfer packet stream. In such cases, $p$ and $q$ are sparse vectors.

**B. Cross routing symmetry**

Cross routing symmetry is defined by the probability that a specific node is visited by the forward flow and the reverse flow:

$$\rho^{cross}(v, s, d) = P\{v \in path_i \text{ and } v \in path_j^{-1}, \text{for any } i, j\}, \tag{2}$$

where $v$ is different from $s$ and $d$.

### 3.2    Modeling

The model links the macroscopic symmetry with the microscopic routing behavior, thus make it possible to design a routing algorithm with a desired symmetry.

The routing selection is modeled as a Markov Chain. The *routing probability* from node $i$ to $j$ is the probability that node $i$ select a neighboring node $j$ as the next hop to route data packets. Figure 1 gives a further demonstration of routing probability. The probability of data packet routed from node $i$ to $j$ in one hop is denoted by $p_{ij}$. The routing probability matrix, or *routing matrix* for short, is given by using $p_{ij}$ as the $i$-th row and $j$-th column element. The assumptions are:

(a)  Routing probability is time-invariant;
(b)  Routing probability is independent of the source node, but depends on the destination node.

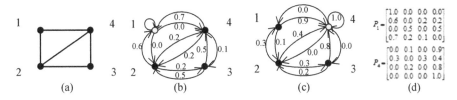

**Fig. 1.** Explanation of routing matrix (a) A network with 4 nodes; (b) Packets are destined to node 1. Each routing probability is labeled on a directed link from a source node to a destination node; (c) When data packets are destined to node 4, the routing probabilities are different from (b); (d) The routing matrices of (b) and (c).

Without the second assumption, the model is identical to the *random walk* model, which is a well-known routing behavior model. Actually, this model is an extension of random walk, so assumption (2) is not a restriction but rather a generalization. The introduction of assumption (2) make the model more realistic, as in communication networks, many routing protocols are designed to behave destination dependent. Thus the subscript to specify the destination node is used as $P_1$ and $P_4$ in Fig. 1(d). Some notes of $P_d$ are:

(a) Node $d$ is a destination node, and thus $d$ is an absorbing state in Markov Chain, so $[P_d]_{d,d} = 1$, and $[P_d]_{d,j} = 0, j \neq d$;

(b) For any $i$, $\sum_j [P_d]_{i,j} = 1$.

## A. Identity routing symmetry

Let nodes $s$ and $d$ be any two different nodes of a connected network. There is only one possible path from $s$ to $d$ in the network with length 1, which is $s,d$. This path will be chosen to transfer packets with probability $[P_d]_{s,d}$ (if path $s,d$ does not exist, $[P_d]_{s,d}$ will be zero). There are $(N\text{-}2)$ possible paths in the network with length 2, chosen with probability $[P_d]_{s,h_1}[P_d]_{h_1,d}$, $h_1 = 1,2,\ldots,N$ and $h_1 \neq s,d$. There are $(N\text{-}2)^2$ paths in the network with length 2, chosen with probability $[P_d]_{s,h_1}[P_d]_{h_1,h_2}[P_d]_{h_2,d}$, $h_1,h_2 = 1,2,\ldots,N$ and $h_1, h_2 \neq s,d$. And the rest can be deduced by analogy. So the inner product of previously mentioned vectors $p$ and $q$ is

$$
(p,q) = [P_d]_{s,d} \cdot [P_s]_{d,s} + \sum_{h_1 \neq s,d} [P_d]_{s,h_1}[P_d]_{h_1,d} \cdot [P_s]_{d,h_1}[P_s]_{h_1,s} + \\
\sum_{h_1,h_2 \neq s,d} [P_d]_{s,h_1}[P_d]_{h_1,h_2}[P_d]_{h_2,d} \cdot [P_s]_{d,h_2}[P_s]_{h_2,h_1}[P_s]_{h_1,s} + \cdots . \tag{3}
$$

All $p_i$'s are not larger than 1 and the sum of all $q_i$'s is 1, so the partial sum of the RHS (right-hand side) of (3) is less than 1, and the sequence of partial sums are incremental. So the RHS of (3) is convergence.

Use the definition of element-wise product operator 'o', Eq. (3) can be written in another form:

$$
(p,q) = [\sum_{i=1}^{\infty} (P_d^{(s)} \circ (P_s^{(d)})^T)^i]_{s,d}. \tag{4}
$$

Matrix $P_d^{(s)}$ is $P_d$ with $s$-th column replaced by a zero vector, and similarly, $P_s^{(d)}$ is $P_s$ with $d$-th column replaced by zero vector.

[10] in appendix makes it possible to write (4) with a closed form. The only requirement is $I - P_d^{(s)} \circ P_s^{(d)}$ to be invertible. Suppose this requirement is satisfied, then

$$
(p,q) = [\lim_{n \to \infty} ((I - P_d^{(s)} \circ (P_s^{(d)})^T)^{-1}(P_d^{(s)} \circ (P_s^{(d)})^T - (P_d^{(s)} \circ (P_s^{(d)})^T)^{n+1}))]_{s,d}. \tag{5}
$$

Because the $d$-th column and $d$-th row of $(P_d^{(s)} \circ (P_s^{(d)})^T)$ are all zeros, so for any $n$, the term $(P_d^{(s)} \circ (P_s^{(d)})^T)^{n+1}$ will have $d$-th column be zeros. So,

$$
(p,q) = [(I - P_d^{(s)} \circ (P_s^{(d)})^T)^{-1}(P_d^{(s)} \circ (P_s^{(d)})^T)]_{s,d}. \tag{6}
$$

With some similar but simpler steps, we get

$$(\boldsymbol{p},\boldsymbol{p}) = [\sum_{n=0}^{\infty} (\boldsymbol{P}_d^{(d)} \circ \boldsymbol{P}_d^{(d)})^n (\boldsymbol{P}_d \circ \boldsymbol{P}_d)]_{s,d} = [(\boldsymbol{I} - \boldsymbol{P}_d^{(d)} \circ \boldsymbol{P}_d^{(d)})^{-1} (\boldsymbol{P}_d \circ \boldsymbol{P}_d)]_{s,d}, \qquad (7)$$

$$(\boldsymbol{q},\boldsymbol{q}) = [\sum_{n=0}^{\infty} (\boldsymbol{P}_s^{(s)} \circ \boldsymbol{P}_s^{(s)})^n (\boldsymbol{P}_s \circ \boldsymbol{P}_s)]_{d,s} = [(\boldsymbol{I} - \boldsymbol{P}_s^{(s)} \circ \boldsymbol{P}_s^{(s)})^{-1} (\boldsymbol{P}_s \circ \boldsymbol{P}_s)]_{d,s}. \qquad (8)$$

Finally,

$$\rho^{id} = \frac{[(\boldsymbol{I} - \boldsymbol{P}_d^{(s)} \circ (\boldsymbol{P}_s^{(d)})^T)^{-1} (\boldsymbol{P}_d^{(s)} \circ (\boldsymbol{P}_s^{(d)})^T)]_{s,d}}{\sqrt{[(\boldsymbol{I} - \boldsymbol{P}_d^{(d)} \circ \boldsymbol{P}_d^{(d)})^{-1} (\boldsymbol{P}_d \circ \boldsymbol{P}_d)]_{s,d}} \sqrt{[(\boldsymbol{I} - \boldsymbol{P}_s^{(s)} \circ \boldsymbol{P}_s^{(s)})^{-1} (\boldsymbol{P}_s \circ \boldsymbol{P}_s)]_{d,s}}}. \qquad (9)$$

### B. Cross routing symmetry

With the aforementioned assumptions, the forward routing process is independent of the reverse routing process. So, the cross routing symmetry is

$$\rho^{cross}(v, s, d) = P\{v \in path_i, \text{for any } i\} P\{v \in path_j^{-1}, \text{for any } j\}$$
$$= (1 - P\{v \notin path_i, \text{for all } i\})(1 - P\{v \notin path_j^{-1}, \text{for all } j\}). \qquad (10)$$

Similar to the derivation of previous section, there is only one possible path in the network with length 1, which is $s,d$, chosen with probability $[\boldsymbol{P}_d]_{s,d}$ (if path $s,d$ does not exist, $[\boldsymbol{P}_d]_{s,d}$ will be zero). Flow that follows this path definitely will not visit node $v$ (which will be called "miss $v$" in the following). There are $N$-2 possible paths in the network with length 2. Flow that follows these paths will miss node $v$ with a probability $[\boldsymbol{P}_d]_{s,h_1}[\boldsymbol{P}_d]_{h_1,d}$ respectively, $h_1 = 1, 2, \ldots, N$ and $h_1 \neq s, v, d$. There are $(N\text{-}2)^2$ possible paths in the network with length 2. Flow that follows these paths will miss node $v$ with a probability $[\boldsymbol{P}_d]_{s,h_1}[\boldsymbol{P}_d]_{h_1,h_2}[\boldsymbol{P}_d]_{h_2,d}$ respectively, $h_1, h_2 = 1, 2, \ldots, N$ and $h_1, h_2 \neq s, v, d$. And the rest can be deduced by analogy. So $\rho^{cross}$ is

$$\rho^{cross}(v, s, d) = (1 - P\{v \notin path_i, \text{for all } i\})(1 - P\{v \notin path_j^{-1}, \text{for all } j\})$$
$$= (1 - [\boldsymbol{P}_d]_{s,d} - \sum_{h_1 \neq s,v,d} [\boldsymbol{P}_d]_{s,h_1}[\boldsymbol{P}_d]_{h_1,d} - \sum_{h_1,h_2 \neq s,v,d} [\boldsymbol{P}_d]_{s,h_1}[\boldsymbol{P}_d]_{h_1,h_2}[\boldsymbol{P}_d]_{h_2,d} - \cdots) \cdot$$
$$(1 - [\boldsymbol{P}_s]_{d,s} - \sum_{h_1 \neq s,v,d} [\boldsymbol{P}_s]_{d,h_1}[\boldsymbol{P}_s]_{h_1,s} - \sum_{h_1,h_2 \neq s,v,d} [\boldsymbol{P}_s]_{d,h_1}[\boldsymbol{P}_s]_{h_1,h_2}[\boldsymbol{P}_s]_{h_2,s} - \cdots)$$
$$= (1 - [\sum_{n=0}^{\infty} (\boldsymbol{P}_d^{(s,v,d)})^n \boldsymbol{P}_d]_{s,d})(1 - [\sum_{n=0}^{\infty} (\boldsymbol{P}_s^{(s,v,d)})^n \boldsymbol{P}_s]_{d,s}). \qquad (11)$$

Matrix $\boldsymbol{P}_d^{(s,v,d)}$ is $\boldsymbol{P}_d$ with $s$-th column, $v$-th column and $d$-th column replaced by zero vectors, while matrix $\boldsymbol{P}_s^{(s,v,d)}$ is $\boldsymbol{P}_s$ with $s$-th column, $v$-th column and $d$-th column replaced by zero vectors. Suppose matrix $\left(\boldsymbol{I} - \boldsymbol{P}_d^{(s,v,d)}\right)$ and $\left(\boldsymbol{I} - \boldsymbol{P}_s^{(s,v,d)}\right)$ to be invertible,

$$
\begin{aligned}
\rho^{cross}(v,s,d) = (1 - [\lim_{n\to\infty}(\boldsymbol{I} - \boldsymbol{P}_d^{(s,v,d)})^{-1}(\boldsymbol{I} - (\boldsymbol{P}_d^{(s,v,d)})^n)\boldsymbol{P}_d]_{s,d}) \cdot \\
(1 - [\lim_{n\to\infty}(\boldsymbol{I} - \boldsymbol{P}_s^{(s,v,d)})^{-1}(\boldsymbol{I} - (\boldsymbol{P}_s^{(s,v,d)})^n)\boldsymbol{P}_s]_{d,s})
\end{aligned} \tag{12}
$$

Finally, we get

$$
\rho^{cross}(v,s,d) = (1 - [(\boldsymbol{I} - \boldsymbol{P}_d^{(s,v,d)})^{-1}\boldsymbol{P}_d]_{s,d})(1 - [(\boldsymbol{I} - \boldsymbol{P}_s^{(s,v,d)})^{-1}\boldsymbol{P}_s]_{d,s}). \tag{13}
$$

## 4 Evaluation and Analysis

### 4.1 Evaluation of Random Walk Based Routing

According to their topology, networks are usually classified into random networks, regular networks, small world networks and scale free networks. To avoid bias introduced by topology, three typical networks (random network, WS [18] network and BA [19] network) are considered. In the simulation, each of these 3 networks is composed of 128 nodes, thus there will be $(128 \times 127)/2 = 8128$ different pairs of nodes to be considered when evaluating identity symmetry. Cross symmetry of all intermediate nodes of two fixed nodes is also evaluated. Three different random walk-based routing algorithms are evaluated. There are some literatures focusing on random walk-based routings in practical networks [20, 21].

The routing probability from node $i$ to $j$ of these routing algorithms is

$$
p_{ij} = \frac{d_j^{\alpha}}{\sum_{k \in N(i)} d_k^{\alpha}}, \tag{14}
$$

but taking different values of parameter $\alpha$, namely, $-1$, $0$, and $1$, respectively. Notation $d_j$ is the degree of node $j$, and $N(i)$ the set of all neighboring nodes of node $i$.

Results are shown in Figs. 2 and 3.

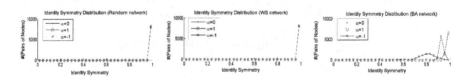

**Fig. 2.** Identity symmetry distribution

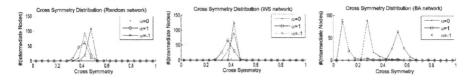

**Fig. 3.** Cross symmetry distribution

In Fig. 2, most node pairs' identity symmetry metrics are close to 1 in random network and WS network, regardless of which routing algorithm is applied. This result is consistent with assumptions that networks are symmetric. The reason for the first two routings are symmetric is explained by an example. Consider a path $s, i, j, d$, the probability that it is selected as a forward route is

$$p_f = \frac{d_i^\alpha}{\sum\limits_{k\in N(s)} d_k^\alpha} \frac{d_j^\alpha}{\sum\limits_{k\in N(i)} d_k^\alpha} \frac{d_d^\alpha}{\sum\limits_{k\in N(j)} d_k^\alpha}, \tag{15}$$

and correspondingly, the probability that path $d, j, i, s$ is selected as a reverse route is

$$p_r = \frac{d_j^\alpha}{\sum\limits_{k\in N(d)} d_k^\alpha} \frac{d_i^\alpha}{\sum\limits_{k\in N(j)} d_k^\alpha} \frac{d_s^\alpha}{\sum\limits_{k\in N(i)} d_k^\alpha}. \tag{16}$$

With a little more effort we can calculate the ratio of $p_f$ to $p_r$. In random networks or small world networks, nodes are of similar degrees, so the ratio will be approximately 1. Thus, we can see the angle between vectors $p$ and $q$ will be very small, thus the identity symmetry is close to 1. But in scale-free network, degrees of nodes are varied significantly, thus the identity symmetry metrics are scattered.

Figure 3 shows that no matter which topology is, the routing algorithm with $\alpha = 1$ will be of lowest cross symmetry, the difference of the three routing algorithms is especially significant in scale free networks. According to the motivation that this metric is present, a conclusion can be drawn that routing algorithm with $\alpha = 1$ will be the safest of the three, especially in a scale-free network.

Many researchers have found that a large number of networks, including Internet, have scale free property [22]. Figures 2 and 3 shows that scale free networks are not symmetric under either definition of symmetry.

## 4.2   Dataset Evaluation

We do not have sufficient evidence to conclude that some networks are asymmetric without studying some widely deployed networks. In the rest of this section, a dataset study of Internet is presented. The data is measured by [2, 3] (only the second set of measurements, which is termed D2 there, is suitable and thus used in this paper for symmetry analysis), using a computer program called *trace route*, which can display the route path. The measurement is conducted on Internet, including nodes (computers) from one hundred or so cities of different countries. To reduce complexity and make it tractable for symmetry metric calculation, we choose the method used by [2, 3], abstracting computers from the same city with a single node, thus constructing a new network with a relatively small number of nodes. The constructed network contains 101 nodes, with 27 nodes have route to them. The identity symmetry metrics are evaluated of any possible pairs of these 27 nodes.

To show the difference of the measured data and the data generated by random walk, we use an algorithm, similar to the algorithm of random redistribution of link weights [22], to randomize the originally data. First, for each destination $d$, by analyzing the data, we get the routing probability matrix $P_d$. Then, for each row of $P_d$, the non-zero entries are divided into a smaller unit $\varDelta$. Each unit is extracted randomly with probability $p$, unless it is the last unit of this entry. Lastly, we equiprobably lay back each extracted unit to all non-zero entries in the same row. The parameter $p$ controls the degree to which the routing probability is randomized, without changing the topology of the network.

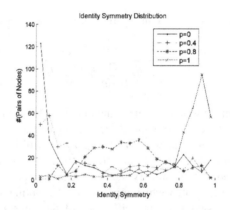

**Fig. 4.** Identity symmetry distribution of internet

The result is shown in Fig. 4. The curve corresponds to the original data ($p = 0$) shows that routing in Internet is highly asymmetric, with almost all the pairs' identity symmetry metrics centered in the range (0, 0.2). While $p$ increases, the metrics are gradually moves to 1. When $p = 1$, similar to the result of the previous simulation (Fig. 2), most node pairs' identity symmetry metrics are close to 1. This implies that routing algorithms that generate next hop randomly will lead to a symmetric network, and that Internet does not work in this way. The routing is not random but rather specialized, consistent with [2], which shows that Internet paths are heavily dominated by a small number of prevalent routes.

## 5   Conclusions

In this work, we propose two routing symmetry metrics to express different meanings when talking about routing symmetry, namely, (1) the forward and reverse flows coming from one node to another are exactly the same, and (2) one node is visited by both flows. Then, we build a model to link the macroscopic symmetry with the microscopic routing behavior, thus make it possible to design a routing algorithm with a desired symmetry. The simulation and dataset study shows that routing algorithms that generate next hop randomly will lead to a symmetric network, but Internet does not work in this way, because the paths of which are heavily dominated by a small number of prevalent routes, it is highly asymmetry.

## References

1. John, W., Dusi, M., Claffy, K.: Estimating routing symmetry on single links by passive flow measurements, pp. 473–478. ACM (2010)
2. Paxson, V.: End-to-end routing behavior in the internet. IEEE/ACM Trans. Netw. 5(5), 601–615 (1997). https://doi.org/10.1109/90.649563
3. Alderson, D., Chang, H., Roughan, M., Uhlig, S., Willinger, W.: The many facets of internet topology and traffic. Netw. Heterog. Media 1(4), 569–600 (2017)
4. Nguyen, T., Armitage, G.: A survey of techniques for internet traffic classification using machine learning. IEEE Commun. Surv. Tutor. 10(4), 56–76 (2009)
5. McGregor, A., Hall, M., Lorier, P., Brunskill, J.: Flow clustering using machine learning techniques. In: Barakat, C., Pratt, I. (eds.) PAM 2004. LNCS, vol. 3015, pp. 205–214. Springer, Heidelberg (2004). https://doi.org/10.1007/978-3-540-24668-8_21
6. Fahad, A., Alshatri, N., Tari, Z., Alamri, A.: A survey of clustering algorithms for big data: taxonomy and empirical analysis. IEEE Trans. Emerg. Top. Comput. 2(3), 267–279 (2014)
7. He, Y., Faloutsos, M., Krishnamurthy, S.: Quantifying routing asymmetry in the internet at the as level, pp. 1474–1479. IEEE(2004)
8. Mao, Z.M., Qiu, L., Wang, J., Zhang, Y.: On as-level path inference, pp. 339–349. ACM (2005)
9. Crotti, M., Gringoli, F., Salgarelli, L.: Impact of asymmetric routing on statistical traffic classification, pp. 1–8. IEEE (2009)
10. Dong, F., Liu, J., Dai, S.: Identity routing symmetry metrics for routing behavior. In: Atlantis Conference, pp. 1853–1856 (2016)
11. Tozal, M.: Autonomous system ranking by topological characteristics: a comparative study. In: Systems Conference, pp. 1–8 (2017)
12. Weinsberg, U., Shavitt, Y., Schwartz, Y.: Stability and symmetry of internet routing, pp. 1–2. IEEE (2009)
13. Keralapura, R., Mellia, M., Grimaudo, L.: Self-learning classifier for internet traffic. US 8694630 B1. IEEE (2014)
14. Zhang, J., Chen, X., Xiang, Y., Zhou, W., Wu, J.: Robust network traffic classification. IEEE/ACM Trans. Netw. 23(4), 1257–1270 (2015)
15. Pucha, H., Zhang, Y., Mao, Z.M., Hu, Y.C.: Understanding network delay changes caused by routing events, pp. 73–84. ACM (2007)
16. Schwartz, Y., Shavitt, Y., Weinsberg, U.: On the diversity, stability and symmetry of end-to-end internet routes, pp. 1–6. IEEE (2010)

17. Lcvenshtcin, V.: Binary coors capable or 'correcting deletions, insertions, and reversals (1966)
18. Watts, D.J., Strogatz, S.H.: Collective dynamics of 'small-world' networks. Nature **393** (6684), 440–442 (1998)
19. Barabási, A.L., Albert, R.: Emergence of scaling in random networks. Science **286**(5439), 509–512 (1999)
20. Servetto, S.D., Barrenechea, G.: Constrained random walks on random graphs: routing algorithms for large scale wireless sensor networks. In: Proceedings of the 1st ACM International Workshop on Wireless Sensor Networks and Applications, pp. 12–21. ACM (2002)
21. Blondel, O., Hilario, M.R., Santos, R.S.D., Sidoravicius, V., Teixeira, A.: Random walk on random walks: low densities. Mathematics (2017)
22. Li, M., et al.: Effects of weight on structure and dynamics in complex networks. arXiv preprint cond-mat/0601495 (2006)

# Dynamic Opportunistic Spectrum Access with Channel Bonding in Mesh Networks: A Game-Theoretic Approach

Chen Pan[1], Yunpeng Cheng[1(✉)], Zhengju Yang[2], and Yuli Zhang[1]

[1] College of Communication Engineering, Army Engineering University of PLA, Haifuxiang 1st, Nanjing 210007, China
panchenlgdx@163.com, ypcheng@yahoo.com, yulipkueecs08@126.com
[2] No. 92274 Troops of PLA, Kunming 650000, China
yangzhengju1001@126.com

**Abstract.** The opportunistic spectrum access with dynamic users and channel bonding technology in mesh networks is studied in this paper. Different from the traditional static and fixed transmitting model, nodes would change their states between active and silent, due to their traffic demand. Also, the channel bonding technology, which mitigates interference and improves throughput significantly, is employed in this paper. The interference mitigation problem with channel bonding is modeled as a distributed and non-cooperative game. We proved it to be an exact potential game. Based on the good property of the potential game, it guarantees the existence of at least one pure Nash equilibrium (NE). Due to the potential function is formulated as the aggregate interference of the network, the final optimal NE point also achieves the minimization of the system's total interference. A multiple-agent learning algorithm is designed to approach the NE points. Compared with other algorithms, simulation results show that the modified algorithm achieves a lower interference performance, and the channel bonding contributes to the throughput performance.

**Keywords:** Opportunistic spectrum access · Dynamic users
Channel bonding · Potential game

## 1 Introduction

With the wireless technologies fast developed, the wireless traffic data has shown an explosive improvement. The opportunistic spectrum access (OSA) has been regarded as a promising technology, to solve the spectrum shortage and improve the spectrum efficiency. Many excellent studies have been done about the OSA in many fields.

In the related researches, the users are always static and keep transmitting data all the time. However, users have different traffic demands and can change state between active and silent based on demand requirement. The static user

© ICST Institute for Computer Sciences, Social Informatics and Telecommunications Engineering 2018
L. Meng and Y. Zhang (Eds.): MLICOM 2018, LNICST 251, pp. 381–390, 2018.
https://doi.org/10.1007/978-3-030-00557-3_38

assumption does not describe the dynamic property in the practical wireless communication well. Furthermore, there are some new technologies can be used in spectrum assignment, such as partially overlapping channels and channel bonding. But the new technologies have not been considered and investigated with the OSA well.

The dynamics property makes user dynamic participating the channel access competition. In this way, it also make a influence to other users. To model the dynamic characteristics, we investigated the node's interference with channel bonding situation. The throughput performance is also formulated based on the interference. However, the throughput is too much complicated, and hard to analyze the formulation or design a proper game model to couple with. Hence, based on the correlative relationship between the interference and throughput, we model interference mitigation game to achieve a higher throughput. To summarize, the contributions of this paper are as follows:

- We considered an opportunistic spectrum access problem in canonical networks. The dynamic issue about node participation and channel bonding technology were jointly considered.
- The dynamic spectrum access problem with channel bonding was modeled as an interference mitigation game, and was proved to be an exact potential game, which has at least one pure Nash equilibrium. Based on the potential function design, the system total interference was also minimized with the NE points.
- The modified multiple-agent learning algorithm was modified to approach the Nash equilibrium. Nodes could update their channel selection strategies same time. The algorithm converged to a Nash equilibrium (NE) which optimize the total system's interference.

## 2   Related Works

Authors in [4] presented a comprehensive survey about the opportunistic access from methods and models, especially for the interaction among multiple users. The dynamics for opportunistic spectrum access has been studied in many studies. In a previous work [7], a dynamic player participation problem in channel allocation was studied. A binary interference model was employed instead of the physical interference. Authors in [9] extended the binary interference model to hyper-graph model and also considered the dynamic issues. A joint dynamic user and asymmetric interference model was investigated in [6]. The channel access problem was modeled into an ordinary potential game with ALOHA mechanism.

The channel bonding technology improves the channel capacity significantly. Authors in [3] investigated the average channel throughput at the medium access control layer. A comprehensive introduction about channel bonding for kinds of networks and discussed the channel bonding for cognitive radio networks, especially for sensing situations in [1]. A recently research [2] studied about a distributed and coordinated channel bonding selection method with only limited feedback under SINR and collision-protocol models.

In this paper, we studied the dynamic spectrum access problem with channel bonding technology. An interference mitigation game is modeled, and proved to be an exact potential game. A modified multiple-agent learning algorithm was designed to approach the Nash equilibrium.

# 3  System Model and Problem Formulation

## 3.1  System Model

In this paper, we consider a distributed mesh network, as shown in Fig. 1. The mesh network is a kind of canonical networks, where nodes are collections of entities. A classical example of canonical network is the 802.11-based WLAN, where nodes are collections of some users located in a relatively small region. In mesh networks, one communication node also represents a collections of nearby users. Nodes make the spectrum resource allocation strategies for their belonging users to achieve a high throughput performance.

We consider a mesh network with $N$ nodes and $M$ channels in this paper. Different from the traditional mesh networks, we assume that nodes might be dynamic due to their traffic demands. In other words, nodes may change states between silent and active based on their traffic. This dynamic transmitting behavior is more common and practical in wireless communication systems, but might bring about some differences in modeling and formulating the spectrum assignment problem. For example, the network interference topology is changing with varying node states.

Besides the dynamic node state, the channel bonding technology is also employed in this paper. As the bandwidth increases through bonding channels together, the throughput performance is also improved, with the total fixed power consumption. The channel bonding also influences the interference and throughput formulation.

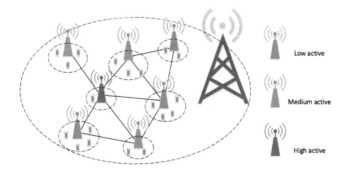

**Fig. 1.** The system model of mesh networks with dynamic nodes.

## 3.2   Problem Formulation

Denote the node set as $\mathcal{N} = \{1, 2, \ldots, N\}$ and channel set as $\mathcal{M} = \{1, 2, \ldots, M\}$. Denote the active probability of node $n$ as $0 < \theta_n \leq 1$, which means node $n$ is active with the probability $\theta_n$. Denote the distance between node $n$ and node $i$ is $d_{ni}$. Considering the node in canonical networks is a collection of communication entities, we regard the node as a combination of transmitter and receiver. Denote the communication range of one node is as $D_{range}$.

For the node $n$, denote its strategy as $a_n = \{c_{n1}, c_{n2}\}, c_{n1,n2} \in \mathcal{M}, c_{n2} = c_{n1} + 1$. In this paper, we only consider the 2-channel bonding situations. For the more than 2-channel situations, the problem formulation and the corresponding theoretic analysis are also similar. Therefore, we only consider the 2-channel situations in this paper. Assume the power consumption of node $n$ on each channel is equal and denote as $P_n$. For node $n$ with channel strategy $a_n$, denote the neighbor set $\mathcal{J}_n$ as follows:

$$\mathcal{J}_n = \{i : |c_{i1} - c_{n1}| \leq 1\}. \tag{1}$$

The neighbor set $\mathcal{J}_n$ means that the two nodes have at least one same channel selection. To distinguish neighbor set with the different channels, denote the $\mathcal{J}_{n1}$ and $\mathcal{J}_{n2}$ are the corresponding nodes set for channel $c_{n1}$ and $c_{n2}$.

Therefore, the expectation of node $n$' interference on channel $c_{n1}$ is as follows:

$$I_n^{c_{n1}}(a_n, a_{-n}) = \sum_{i \in \mathcal{J}_{n1}} \theta_n \theta_i P_i d_{in}^{\alpha} \tag{2}$$

where $\alpha$ is the fade loss factor.

Considering the dynamic state of nodes, the active state of node $n$ is as $\lambda_n = 0, 1, 1$ represents to be active. The total state of all nodes are $\Lambda = \{\lambda_1, \lambda_2, \ldots, \lambda_N\}$. Therefore, the state of node $n$ on channel $c_{n1}$ is $\Lambda(\mathcal{J}_{n1})$. Hence, the probability is as follows:

$$Pr[\Lambda(\mathcal{J}_{n1})] = \prod_{i \in \mathcal{J}_{n1}} \theta_i \lambda_i + (1 - \theta_i)(1 - \lambda_i). \tag{3}$$

The throughput of node $n$ on channel $c_{n1}$ is as follows:

$$r_n^{c_{n1}}(a_n, a_{-n}) = \sum_{\Lambda(\mathcal{J}_{n1})} \theta_n Pr[\Lambda(\mathcal{J}_{n1})] \log(1 + \frac{P_n D_{range}}{N_0 + I_n^{c_{n1}}(\Lambda(\mathcal{J}_{n1}))}). \tag{4}$$

Therefore, the throughput of node $n$ is as follows:

$$r_n(a_n, a_{-n}) = r_n^{c_{n1}} + r_n^{c_{n2}}, \tag{5}$$

Thus, the objectives in this paper is to achieve high throughput for each node. Formally,

$$P : \arg\max_{a_n} r_n(a_n, a_{-n}) \tag{6}$$

# 4    Potential Game with Interference Mitigation

## 4.1    Game Model

We formulate the interference mitigation problem with channel bonding as a distributed and non-cooperative game. The game is denoted as $\mathcal{G} = \{\mathcal{N}, \mathcal{A}, \mathcal{E}, u_n\}$, where $\mathcal{N}$ is the node set, $\mathcal{A}$ is the nodes strategy space, and $\mathcal{E}$ is the network topology. The utility function is denoted as $u_n(\mathbf{a}_n, \mathbf{a}_{-n})$. We define the utility function as follows:

$$u_n(a_n, a_{-n}) = I_n^{c_{n1}} + I_n^{c_{n2}}, \tag{7}$$

where the utility function is just the expectation of the total interference of node $n$. For low interference, the corresponding throughput is commonly high. Based on the relationship between interference and throughput, we focus on the interference mitigation problem instead of the complex throughput formulation. The proposed dynamic spectrum access with channel bonding is as follows:

$$\mathcal{G} : \min u_n(a_n, a_{-n}), \forall n \in \mathcal{N}. \tag{8}$$

## 4.2    Analysis of the Nash Equilibrium

**Definition 1 (NE):** The channel bonding and selection strategies of all users are $(\mathbf{a}_1^*, \mathbf{a}_1^*, \ldots, \mathbf{a}_1^*)$ is a pure strategy NE if and only if no user can improve its utility by deviating unilaterally, i.e.,

$$u(a_n^*, a_{-n}^*) \leq u(a_n', a_{-n}^*), \forall n \in \mathcal{N}, \forall a_n \in \mathcal{A}, a_n' \neq a_n^* \tag{9}$$

**Definition 2 (Exact Potential Game)** [5,11]**:** A game $\mathcal{G}$ is an exact potential game if there exists a function $\Phi$ such that

$$\Phi(a_n^*, a_{-n}^*) - \Phi(a_n', a_{-n}^*) = u_n(a_n^*, a_{-n}^*) - u_n(a_n', a_{-n}^*), \forall a_n^* \in \mathcal{A}_n, a_n' \neq a_n^* \tag{10}$$

The function $\Phi$ is the potential function for the game $\mathcal{G}$.

**Theorem 1:** The proposed opportunistic spectrum access game $\mathcal{G}$ is an exact potential game, which has at least one pure NE.

*Proof.* We design the potential function of the game is as:

$$\Phi(a_n, a_{-n}) = \frac{1}{2} \sum_{i \in \mathcal{N}} u_i(a_i, a_{-i}). \tag{11}$$

which is just the total interference of all nodes in the network.

when node $n$ changes its channel selection from $a_n$ to $a'n$, the changes in potential function is as follows.

$$
\begin{aligned}
&\Phi(a_n, a_{-n}) - \Phi(a'_n, a_{-n}) \\
&= \frac{1}{2} \sum_{i \in \mathcal{N}} u_i(a_i, a_{-i}) - \frac{1}{2} \sum_{i \in \mathcal{N}} u_i(a'_n, a_{-i}) \\
&= \frac{1}{2} \sum_{c \cup d \cup n} u_i(a_i, a_{-i}) - \frac{1}{2} \sum_{c \cup d \cup n} u_i(a'_i, a_{-i}) \\
&= \frac{1}{2} * 2 * [I_n(a_n, a_{-n}) - I_n(a'_n, a_{-n})] \\
&= u_n(a_n, a_{-n}) - u_n(a'_n, a_{-n})
\end{aligned}
\tag{12}
$$

The total node set except node $n$ can be divided into four parts due to the influence by the strategy change: (a) both in the neighbor set of $a_n$ and $a'_n$, (b) none in the two set, (c) with $a_n$ but not with $a'_n$ and (d) with $a'_n$ but not with $a_n$. For the part (a) and (b), the strategy change does not make any change for them. For the parts (c) and (d), due to the symmetric property of interference, the change is just the as the change in utility function. Therefore, the change in potential function is same as the change in utility function. Hence, the proposed interference mitigation game is an exact potential game. Based on the lemma, there exists at least one Nash equilibrium. Due to the potential function is formulated as the aggregate interference of the network, the final optimal NE point also achieves the minimization of the system's total interference.

**Remark:** Based on the proof in [8], for the two correlative metrics when one follows the potential game, they other one also keeps the trends. Then for interference and throughput, in most situations, a lower interference would bring about a higher throughput. Only some special situations this relation cannot be guaranteed. Therefore, it is reasonable that we can improve the throughput through mitigating the interference in this paper.

### 4.3   Dynamic Spectrum Access with Channel Bonding Algorithm

In this paper, we modify the multiple-agent learning algorithm [10,13] into the dynamic spectrum access game, to approach the NE points.

**Theorem 2.** The modified multiple-agent learning algorithm converges to the NE points.

*Proof.* Due to the proposed game have been proved to be an exact potential game, the finite improvement property (FIP) exists. With following the FIP, players can improve the utility step by step. Compared with the traditional better reply algorithm, the modified multiple-agent learning algorithm makes all users update their strategies same time. The convergence of the modified is guaranteed by the FIP in [12]. The proof is similar and we omit the process in this paper.

*Algorithm 1: Dynamic spectrum access with channel bonding algorithm*

**Initialization**   In $j = 0$ slot, every node makes the channel selection strategy $a_n$ randomly.

**Loop** $j = 1, 2, ...$

**Interference evaluation:** For all nodes in the network, keep its channel selection $a_n(j), n \in \mathcal{N}$ for a period time to evaluate its channel interference $I_n$.

**Channel selection:** For every nodes, randomly changes its changes its strategy to $a'_n(j)$. Achieve the new utility function $I'_n$.

**Update** : Every node updates its strategy through the following rule:

$$
\begin{aligned}
Pr[a_n(j + 1) = a_n(j)] &= \frac{\exp(\beta I_n)}{X} \\
Pr[a_n(j + 1) = a'_n(j)] &= \frac{\exp(\beta I'_n)}{X}
\end{aligned}
\tag{13}
$$

where $X = \exp(\beta I_n) + \exp(\beta I'_n)$ and $\beta$ is the learning parameter.

**End** Until all nodes keeps their strategies for a long time or the maximum iteration times is achieved.

# 5   Simulation Results and Discussions

In this section, we compared three algorithms: (i) the modified multi-agent learning algorithm, (ii) a random channel access algorithm, where users select channel randomly, and (iii) the modified multi-agent learning algorithm without channel bonding. The basic simulation parameters are set as follows: the number of channels $M = 4$, the number of users $N = 10$, the power on each channel $0.1\,\mathrm{W}$[1], the noise power $N_0 = -110\,\mathrm{dBm}$, the path fade loss $\alpha = -3$ and the communication range $D_{range} = 30\,\mathrm{m}$. We assume users are located in a $200\,\mathrm{m} \times 200\,\mathrm{m}$ area. The active probability is in the range $[0.3 - 0.9]$.

The total interference performance is compared in Fig. 2. From this figure, it is obviously that the random access algorithm achieves worst and largest interference. The multi-agent learning algorithm achieves better performance than the random access algorithm.

The total throughput performance is compared in Fig. 3. From the figure, we can find that the multi-agent learning algorithm achieves best throughput performance than the other two algorithms, especially for the non-channel bonding situations. It is indicated that the channel bonding technology improves the channel capacity significantly. The total throughput performance with different active probabilities is compared in Fig. 4. It is obviously that the throughput is decreasing with an increasing active probability.

---

[1] For the without channel bonding situations, to make the total power same with the channel bonding situations, the power on each channel is set as $0.2\,\mathrm{W}$.

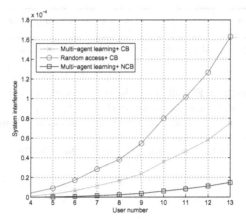

**Fig. 2.** The total interference of system with different algorithms.

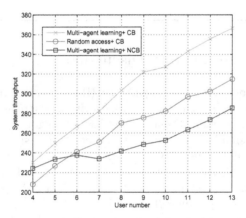

**Fig. 3.** The total throughput of system with different algorithms.

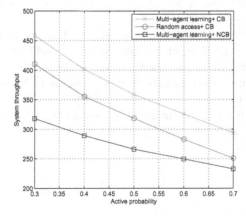

**Fig. 4.** The total throughput of system with different active probabilities.

# 6    Conclusion

The opportunistic spectrum access with dynamics users and channel bonding technology in mesh networks was studied in this paper. We investigated the interference of the dynamic users with channel bonding mechanism and formulated the throughput of users. The interference mitigation problem with channel bonding is modeled as a distributed and non-cooperative game. We proved it to be an exact potential game. Based on the good property of the potential game, it guarantees the existence of at least one pure Nash equilibrium (NE). Due to the potential function is formulated as the aggregate interference of the network, the final optimal NE point also achieves the minimization of the system's total interference. A multiple-agent learning algorithm is designed to approach the NE points. According to the correlative relationship between interference and throughput, a high throughput was guaranteed by a low interference. A multiple-agent learning algorithm is designed to approach the NE points. Simulation results show that the modified multiple-agent learning algorithm achieves better performance compared with other algorithms, and the channel bonding contributes to the throughput performance.

**Acknowledgment.** This work was supported in part by the Natural Science Foundation for Distinguished Young Scholars of Jiangsu Province under Grant BK20160034, in part by the National Science Foundation of China under Grant 61631020, Grant 61401508, and Grant 61671473, and in part by the Open Research Foundation of Science and Technology on Communication Networks Laboratory.

# References

1. Bukhari, S.H.R., Rehmani, M.H., Siraj, S.: A survey of channel bonding for wireless networks and guidelines of channel bonding for futuristic cognitive radio sensor networks. IEEE Commun. Surv. Tutor. **18**(2), 924–948 (2016)
2. Khan, Z., Lehtomaki, J., Scott, S., Han, Z., Krunz, M., Marshall, A.: Distributed and coordinated spectrum access methods for heterogeneous channel bonding. IEEE Trans. Cogn. Commun. Netw. **3**(3), 267–281 (2017)
3. Joshi, S., Pawelczak, P., Cabric, D., Villasenor, J.: When channel bonding is beneficial for opportunistic spectrum access networks. IEEE Trans. Wirel. Commun. **11**(11), 3942–3956 (2012)
4. Xu, Y., Anpalagan, A., Wu, Q., Shen, L., Gao, Z., Wang, J.: Decision-theoretic distributed channel selection for opportunistic spectrum access: strategies, challenges and solutions. IEEE Commun. Surv. Tutor. **15**(4), 1689–1713 (2013). Fourth Quarter
5. Xu, Y., Wang, J., Wu, Q., et al.: Opportunistic spectrum access in cognitive radio networks: global optimization using local interaction games. IEEE J. Sel. Top. Singal Process. **6**(2), 180–194 (2012)
6. Zhang, Y., Xu, Y., Wu, Q.: Opportunistic spectrum access with dynamic users: directional graphical game and stochastic learning. KSII Trans. Internet Inf. Syst. **11**(12–8), 5820–5824 (2017)

7. Zhang, Y., Zhao, Q.: Distributed opportunistic spectrum access with dynamic users: a game-theoretic learning approach. In: 2015 International Conference on Wireless Communications & Signal Processing (WCSP), Nanjing, pp. 1–5, October 2015
8. Yao, K., Wu, Q., Xu, Y., Jing, J.: Distributed ABS-slot access in dense heterogeneous networks: a potential game approach with generalized interference model. IEEE Access **5**, 94–104 (2017)
9. Zhu, X., Liu, X., Xu, Y., Zhang, Y., Ruan, L., Yang, Y.: Dynamic spectrum access for D2D networks: a hypergraph game approach. In: IEEE ICCT 2017, Chengdu, China (2017)
10. Xu, Y.: Load-aware dynamic spectrum access for small-cell networks: a graphical game approach. IEEE Trans. Veh. Technol. **65**(10), 8794–8800 (2016)
11. Monderer, D., Shapley, L.S.: Potential games. Game Econ. Behav. **14**, 124–143 (1996)
12. Mukherjee, A., Fakoorian, S.A.A., Huang, J., Swindlehurst, A.L.: A comprehensive survey of potential game approaches to wireless networks. IEEE Commun. Surv. Tutor. **16**(3), 1550–1573 (2014)
13. Zhang, Y., Xu, Y., Wu, Q., Yao, K., Anpalagan, A.: A game-theoretic approach for optimal distributed cooperative hybrid caching in D2D networks. IEEE Wirel. Commun. Lett. (2018, to appear)

# Secrecy Performance Analysis of SWIPT System Based on OFDM Assisted Interference

Mei Qin$^{(\boxtimes)}$, Weidang Lu, Hong Peng, and Zhijiang Xu

College of Information Engineering, Zhejiang University of Technology,
Hangzhou 310023, China
1819510836@qq.com

**Abstract.** In this paper, we consider the security communications in an OFDM - based SWIPT system by adding a full-duplex, friendly jammer with wireless powered equipment between a transmitter (Tx) and an information receiver (IR) and an energy receiver (ER) which called (regarded as) a potential eavesdropper. We propose a scheme that under friendly jammer protection TX sends source messages to IR and jammer, the jammer sends jammer signal to ER and IR while receiving information from Tx to confound potential eavesdroppers but can be eliminated at IR. Our goal is to maximize the sum secrecy information rate by jointly optimizing the power allocation at the Tx and jammers while satisfying the energy harvesting at the ER.

**Keywords:** OFDM · SWIPT · Cooperative jamming (CJ)
Resource allocation

## 1 Introduction

Wireless Information and Power Transmission (WIPT) is an energy harvesting technology that addresses energy supply issues in network communications by eliminating the need for frequent battery charging and replacement. But the channel is open, it may be subjected to information theft. This paper proposes that there are several notable features of confidential wireless messaging and SWIPT over traditional secure communications. First, there is a potential for eavesdropping of wireless power transmission because the potential eavesdropper's power receiver is usually shorter than the information receiver Visit distance. Second, a lot of data prove that SWIPT also can enhance the security and reliability of wireless communications [1–3].

A SWIPT system basically includes an access point (AP) with a constant power supply and broadcasted broadcast signals to a group of user terminals, some of which are mainly used to decode information called the information receiver (IR), While others collect energy from the surrounding radio signals, known as the energy receiver (ER). However, since the ER is closer to the AP, it may eavesdrop on the valid information sent to the IR. And this will pose a huge challenge to the wireless secure communication [4].

In recent years, the confidentiality of the physical layer has become a new method for improving the information security of wireless networks, attracting many scientists

© ICST Institute for Computer Sciences, Social Informatics and Telecommunications Engineering 2018
L. Meng and Y. Zhang (Eds.): MLICOM 2018, LNICST 251, pp. 391–399, 2018.
https://doi.org/10.1007/978-3-030-00557-3_39

began to study in this area. The physical layer of secure communication has two main types of interference: Cooperative jamming and adding artificial noise.

In [5, 6], the authors propose to confuse and reduce the eavesdropper's channel by adding artificial noise to ensure the confidential transmission of transmitter information. In the presence of one or more eavesdroppers, multiple relay collaborations are used to solve a secure communication from a source node to a destination node in [7]. and based on the RF-EH system, the authors propose that choose the best transmission station and ensure safe transmission in the presence of a source node and multiple eavesdroppers [8]. In [4, 9, 10], some researchers proposed adding artificial noise or Jammer so that ensure the security communication of the IR and maximize the secrecy rate of the IR while meeting the minimum energy receiving requirements of the ER.

The technique of creating interference on the eavesdropper's reception to reduce the associated links appears to be an effective method in practical applications in [11–13]. In [14], the author proposes a relay option to interrupt the security cooperation network to increase security against eavesdroppers. The first relay assists the source in transmitting the data to the destination by decoding the forwarding strategy. The second relay is used to send interference to the eavesdropper node to protect the destination node from interference and eavesdropping and prevent eavesdroppers from intercepting information.

In this article, we consider a secure communications transmission in an OFDM-based SWIPT system, which consists of an IR, a jammer, a Tx and an ER (potential eavesdropper), as shown in Fig. 1. We assume that Tx is a device with a constant energy supply and jammer does not have a constant energy supply and can only harvest energy from Tx. All devices are single antennas except that the jammer is a dual antenna and the jammer side receiving information from Tx while sending its own interference information to the ER and the IR, assuming equal power allocation above each subcarrier, the transmit power above each subcarrier at Tx and jammer is equal power allocated, with minimal energy acceptance, we optimize the system's security rate by jointly optimizing the power distribution factor of ER at Tx and jammer.

Although there are some similarities between our network settings and those used in [15] in terms of wirelessly powered dual-antenna jammers to confuse eavesdroppers. The research questions in our study are essentially different, especially when considering that the energy receiver ER is accepting data from the signals sent by Tx and Jammer are processed differently. The main innovations of our article can be summarized in several ways:

(1) Environmental Design: This article considers the case of eavesdropping using wireless CJ jamming machine to protect the communication between the source node and the destination node, we consider cooperative jamming (CJ) schemes, CJ adopts the full-duplex mode, it sends interference information to ER and IR while harvest energy from source information. The total power that CJ can transmit depends on the energy that it receives. Eavesdroppers eavesdrop on the information sent by the source node will also harvest the jammer to send the interference signal, we use the power distribution protocol, part of the eavesdropper used to intercept the information, part of the energy used to receive the source node and the jammer signal eavesdroppers have this configuration, however, the interference information received at the destination node can be ignored

by some mechanism [6]. With our network setup, you can maximize the transmission of your system's confidential information.

(2) Performance Evaluation: In order to see the proposed protocol confidentiality performance, we can see the impact on the system performance by changing the different parameters of the system, such as the distance between the jammer and the source node and the sending power of the source node.

## 2 System Model

We assume an OFDM-based secrecy communication scenario for SWIPT, as shown in Fig. 1, there are four-node system, consisting of one Tx, one jammer, one ER (potential eavesdropper) and one IR. The Tx, IR, and ER are set to single antenna while the jammer is dual antenna with one of them is used to receive energy and the other is used to transmit interference signal. When the Tx sends original information to the IR, the ER can harvest energy and eavesdrop information from the information source. At the same time, the jammer transmits interfering signals to IR and ER while receiving energy from original information, since it is a full-duplex mode of operation, we assume that the interference between the two antennas is negligible. It is noteworthy that the interference signal from the jammer is not only used to interfere with ER but also to ER as an energy source. We assume that the system has N subcarriers. The channel power gain of $Tx \rightarrow IR, Tx \rightarrow ER, Tx \rightarrow jammer$ are expressed as $h_{I,n}, h_{E,n}$, and $h_{J,n}$, also the channel power gain from jammer to IR and ER are expressed as $g_{I,n}, g_{J,n}$.

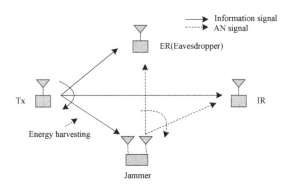

**Fig. 1.** System model of the wireless-powered secrecy SWIPT

In this paper we assume that the total transmit power of the transmitter is P, and the transmit power of Tx on the SC n is $p_n$ and the jammer on the SC n is $q_n$. We consider the constraint of peak power on $p_n$ and $q_n$, $0 < p_n \leq \bar{p}_n, 0 < q_n \leq \bar{q}_n$, for $n = 1, \ldots, N$. The total transmit power at the Tx is thus given by

$$\sum_{n=1}^{N} p_n \leq P \tag{1}$$

Since the jammer harvests energy at the original information sent by the Tx, the transmit power constraint at the jammer can be expressed as:

$$\sum_{n=1}^{N} q_n \leq \zeta \sum_{n=1}^{N} p_n h_{J,n} \tag{2}$$

where $\zeta$ is a constant that account for the energy conversion efficiency, in order to simplify the calculation of the next we assume that $\zeta = 1$.

Energy received by the energy receiver ER comes from two parts, one from Tx, and the other from jammer, the harvested power should reach the minimum energy requirement $\bar{Q}_n$:

$$\sum_{n=1}^{N} \left( (1-\alpha)p_n h_{E,n} + (1-\beta)q_n g_{E,n} \right) \geq \sum_{n=1}^{N} \bar{Q}_n \tag{3}$$

where $\bar{Q}_n$ is the minimum energy requirement that the ER should satisfy on SCn.

In this paper, we assume that the interfering signal sent by jammer can be removed at IR but can not at ER, so the rates of information obtained at classes IR and ER, respectively, can be expressed as:

$$r_n = \log\left(1 + \frac{p_n h_{I,n}}{\sigma^2}\right), r_n^e = \log\left(1 + \frac{\alpha p_n h_{E,n}}{\sigma^2 + \beta q_n g_{E,n}}\right) \tag{4}$$

The achievable information secrecy rate for $R_n$ on SCn can be expressed as:

$$R_n = \left[ r_n - r_n^e \right]^+ = \left[ \log\left(1 + \frac{p_n h_{I,n}}{\sigma^2}\right) - \log\left(1 + \frac{\alpha p_n h_{E,n}}{\sigma^2 + \beta q_n g_{E,n}}\right) \right]^+ \tag{5}$$

for all $n \in N$, where $[\bullet]^+ \triangleq \max(0, \bullet)$.

In such jammer and eavesdropper model, we aim to jointly optimize the power $p_n$ and $q_n$, and power distribution ratio $\alpha, \beta$, while ensuring that the constraints (1)–(3) condition is established. Our optimization problem can be expressed as:

$$(P1): \max_{\{\alpha,\beta,p_n,q_n\}} \sum_{n=1}^{N} R_n \tag{6}$$

$$s.t. \quad (1)-(3) \tag{6a}$$

$$0 \leq \alpha \leq 1, 0 \leq \beta \leq 1 \tag{6b}$$

$$0 \leq p_n \leq \bar{p}, 0 \leq q_n \leq \bar{q} \tag{6c}$$

## 3  The Problem Formulation and Solution

First, we need to find the optimal $\alpha^*, \beta^*$, in order to ensure $R_n > 0$ in (5) and satisfy the constraints of (3), the range of $\beta$ can be expressed as:

$$\beta_1 \leq \beta \leq \beta_2 \tag{7}$$

where

$$\beta_1 = \frac{\sigma^2 \left(\alpha h_{E,n} - h_{I,n}\right)}{h_{I,n} q_n g_{E,n}}, \beta_2 = \frac{(1-\alpha)p_n h_{E,n} + q_n g_{E,n} - \bar{Q}_n}{q_n g_{E,n}}$$

union (6c) and (7) we can get the value of $\alpha$ range is given by:

$$\alpha \geq \alpha_2, \alpha \geq \alpha_1, \alpha \leq \alpha_3$$

where

$$\alpha_1 = \frac{h_{I,n}}{h_{E,n}}, \alpha_2 = 1 - \frac{\bar{Q}}{p_n h_{E,n}}, \alpha_3 = \frac{h_{I,n}\left(p_n h_{E,n} + q_n g_{E,n} - \bar{Q} + \sigma^2\right)}{h_{E,n}\left(\sigma^2 + p_n h_{I,n}\right)}$$

On the other hand, we derive the partial derivative of $\alpha$ and $\beta$ in (5), we can get

$$\begin{cases} \dfrac{\partial R_n}{\partial \alpha} = \dfrac{-p_n h_{E,n}}{\left(\sigma^2 + \beta q_n g_{E,n} + \alpha p_n h_{E,n}\right)\ln 2} < 0 \\[3mm] \dfrac{\partial R_n}{\partial \beta} = \dfrac{\alpha p_n h_{E,n} q_n g_{E,n}}{\left(\sigma^2 + \beta q_n g_{E,n} + \alpha p_n h_{E,n}\right)\left(\sigma^2 + \beta q_n g_{E,n}\right)\ln 2} > 0 \end{cases}$$

Obviously, $R_n$ is monotonically decreasing with $\alpha$, and $R_n$ is monotonically increasing with $\beta$, therefore, there are two cases for the value of $\alpha$.

Case1. When $\alpha_1 > \alpha_2$, then we can obtain $\alpha_1 \leq \alpha \leq \alpha_3$, and the optimal $\alpha^*, \beta^*$ are given by

$$\alpha^* = \alpha_1, \beta^* = \beta_2 \tag{8}$$

Case2. When $\alpha_1 \leq \alpha_2$, we can get $\alpha_2 \leq \alpha \leq \alpha_3$, the optimal $\alpha^*, \beta^*$ are given by

$$\alpha^* = \alpha_2, \beta^* = 1 \tag{9}$$

## 4  Simulation Results

In this section, we use experimental data to verify the performance of our proposed CJ scheme system. we assuming equal power allocation at Tx and CJ on SCs, $p_{k,n} = P/N$, $q_{k,n} = p_{k,n}/h_{J,n}$, here we drop index n and k of $p_{k,n}, q_{k,n}$ for brevity, System parameters are set as $N = 32$, the noise power $\sigma^2 = -60$ dBm, and the pass-loss exponent is 2.

The jammer, IR and Tx are in the same straight line and the distance from Tx to IR is 6 m. The jammer moves between Tx and IR, and we denote the distance from Tx to jammer as $d1$, in addition, we assume that the distance from Tx to ER is 3 m with 30°.

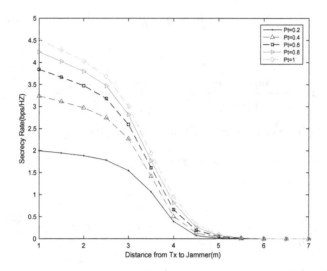

**Fig. 2.** Secrecy rate versus d1(m), with $\bar{Q} = -40$ dbm

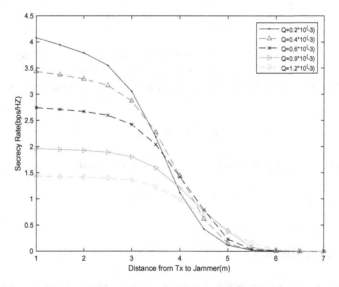

**Fig. 3.** Secrecy rate versus d1(m), with $P = 30$ dbm

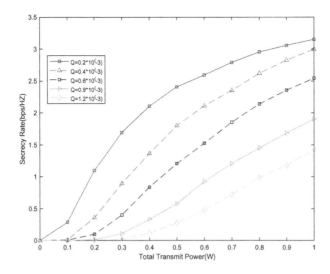

**Fig. 4.** Secrecy rate versus total power P(W), with $d1 = 3$ m

Figures 2 and 3 show the impact of minimum energy reception requirements $\bar{Q}$ and the total transmit power $P$ of the source node on the system's secrecy rate. The $\bar{Q}$ set as $\bar{Q} = -40$ dbm in Fig. 2, and the total transmit power set as $P = 30$ dbm, it can be seen from Fig. 2 that the confidentiality of the system decreases with the increase of the distance from the source node of the jammer. However, it can be seen from Fig. 3 that the confidentiality of the system does not increase with the increase of the minimum energy receiving requirement, In the case of short distances (d1 < 2 m), the confidentiality of the system will increase as the energy receiving requirements decrease.

Figure 4 demonstrate the effect of the fraction of the total power $P$ on the system's security rate, and it can be observed that the security rate of system can be improved by increasing $P$ or reduce the distance from jammer to Tx. We can see that when the distance is increased to 5 m, the system's secrecy rate is very small, and this result is consistent with the result in Figs. 2 and 3.

Figure 5 depict the optimal power distribution factor versus source node transmit power, and we can see the effect of transmit power and the harvested energy constraint on $\alpha^*, \beta^*$ with $d1 = 3$ m, from Fig. 4, we can see that when the transmission power is constant, the system's information security rate will decrease with the increase of the receiving energy constraint. Therefore, in combination with Fig. 3, we can obtain: by reducing the receiving energy constraint, increasing the transmission power and reducing the distance from Tx to jammer to improve the system's information security rate.

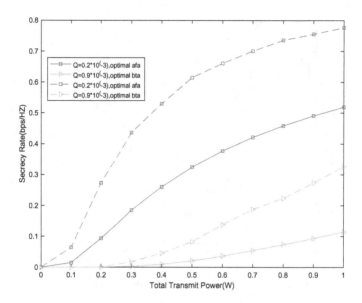

**Fig. 5.** Optimal versus total power P(W), with $d1 = 3$ m

## 5 Conclusion

We propose a scheme for OFDM-based SWIPT systems to maximize the security of system secrets with a friendly jammer. In addition, we describe the effect of certain parameters on the security rate of the system. According to our theoretical analysis, we can get the result that when the total transmit power increases or the short-distance distance decreases, the system security and confidentiality Better. Numerical analysis of the theory also shows that compared with the method without CJ, our scheme obviously improves the performance of the system. Our results also prove that optimized performance is better.

## References

1. Chen, X., Ng, D.W.K., Chen, H.H.: Secrecy wireless information and power transfer: challenges and opportunities[M]. IEEE Press (2016)
2. Varshney, L.R.: Transporting information and energy simultaneously. In: Proceedings of IEEE International Symposium on Information Theory (ISIT), pp. 1612–1616, Toronto, ON, CA, July 2008
3. Grover, P., Sahai, A.: Shannon meets Tesla: wireless information and power transfer. In: Proceedings of IEEE International Symposium on Information Theory (ISIT), Austin, TX, USA, pp. 2363–2367, June 2010
4. Xing, H., Wong, K.K., Chu, Z., et al.: To harvest and jam: a paradigm of self-sustaining friendly jammers for secure AF relaying. IEEE Trans. Signal Process. **63**(24), 6616–6631 (2015)

5. Goel, S., Negi, R.: Guaranteeing secrecy using artificial noise. IEEE Trans. Wirel. Commun. **7**(6), 2180–2189 (2008)
6. Zhang, M., Liu, Y., Zhang, R.: Artificial noise aided secrecy information and power transfer in OFDMA systems. IEEE Trans. Wirel. Commun. **15**(4), 3085–3096 (2016)
7. Dong, L., Han, Z., Petropulu, A.P., Poor, H.V.: Improving wireless physical layer security via cooperating relays. IEEE Trans. Signal Process. **58**(3), 1875–1888 (2010)
8. Vo, V.N., Nguyen, T.G., So-In, C., et al.: Secrecy performance analysis of energy harvesting wireless sensor networks with a friendly jammer. IEEE Access **PP**(99), 1 (2017)
9. Bi, Y., Chen, H.: Accumulate and jam: towards secure communication via a wireless-powered full-duplex jammer[J]. IEEE J. Sel. Top. Signal Process. **10**(8), 1538–1550 (2016)
10. Liu, W., Zhou, X., Durrani, S., et al.: Secure communication with a wireless-powered friendly jammer. IEEE Trans. Wirel. Commun. **15**(1), 401–415 (2016)
11. Simeone, O., Popovski, P.: Secure communications via cooperating base stations. IEEE Commun. Lett. **12**, 188–190 (2008)
12. Popovski, P., Simeone, O.: Wireless secrecy in cellular systems with infrastructure-aided cooperation. Trans. Inf. Forensics Secur. **4**, 242–256 (2009)
13. Tekin, E., Yener, A.: The general Gaussian multiple access and two-way wire-tap channels: achievable rates and cooperative jamming. IEEE Trans. Inf. Theory **54**, 2735–2751 (2008)
14. Krikidis, I., Thompson, J.S., Mclaughlin, S.: Relay selection for secure cooperative networks with jamming. IEEE Trans. Wirel. Commun. **8**(10), 5003–5011 (2009)
15. Liu, M., Liu, Y.: Power allocation for secure SWIPT systems with wireless-powered cooperative jamming. IEEE Commun. Lett. **PP**(99), 1 (2017)

# Contract Theory Based on Wireless Energy Harvesting with Transmission Performance Optimization

Chen Liu[(⊠)], Hong Peng, Weidang Lu, Zhijiang Xu, and Jingyu Hua

College of Information Engineering, Zhejiang University of Technology,
Hangzhou 310023, People's Republic of China
1078017312@qq.com, {ph,luweid,zyfxzj,eehjy}@zjut.edu.cn

**Abstract.** In this paper, we proposed a contract theory on optimization of wireless energy collection and transmission systems. Its purpose is to maximize the transmission rate of the source node to the destination node. Source node broadcasts signal to relay node. We assume that the quality of the link between the source node and the destination node link is poor, and the signal cannot be directly transmitted to the destination node. Relay node have no energy to forward the signal. At this time, the relay node needs energy from surrounding energy access points (EAPs) and the destination node will pay corresponding rewards. We designed the optimal contract theory in order to maximize the transmission performance of the source node. Finally, we use the optimal algorithm to get the best result.

**Keywords:** Contract theory · Wireless Energy Harvesting · Optimal algorithm
Performance optimization

## 1 Introduction

Wireless Energy Harvesting has been a lot of research. In the literature [1], An IOT system based on radio frequency energy collection is considered, which consists of a data access point (DAP) and multiple energy access points (EAP). Compare stackelberg game and optimal contract with symmetric and asymmetric information respectively. Contract Theory is also used in many scientific researches. A contract-theory based framework under asymmetric and symmetric channel information is proposed in [2], and introduced the cooperation between the primary user and the secondary user. And system performance can be improved by obtaining diversity gain in cooperative communication [3]. While there are several initial work designing the incentive mechanism [4–6] for the EAPs belonging to different operators, complete information was considered in these schemes. In [7, 8], Amplify-and-forward (AF) and decode-and-forward (DF) protocol transmission methods are also studied. In order to maximize throughput in wireless powered communication networks, which paper use convex optimization and get the optimal solution in [9, 10].

In this paper, we discuss that the relay node amplifies and forwards information to the destination node through the AF protocol.

© ICST Institute for Computer Sciences, Social Informatics and Telecommunications Engineering 2018
L. Meng and Y. Zhang (Eds.): MLICOM 2018, LNICST 251, pp. 400–408, 2018.
https://doi.org/10.1007/978-3-030-00557-3_40

We assume that the relay node has no energy and only one EAP around it provides energy to the relay node to help it forward information. The structure of this article is as follows. Section 2 introduces the system model and formulates the optimization problem of the model. Section 3 we give the optimal solution to the optimization problem. Computer simulation results are displayed in Sects. 4 and 5 we finally make conclusions for this paper.

## 2   System Model and Problem Formulation

### 2.1   System Model

We suppose source node to the destination node link experiences a poor link quality. Source node needs the relay node to help forward its information to the destination node using the AF protocol, but the destination node has no energy to forward signal. In this case, it needs to obtain energy from the EAP and forward the information with the acquired energy and EAP get the profit by the backhaul. The model is shown in Fig. 1.

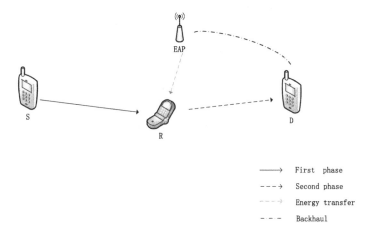

| | |
|---|---|
| ⟶ | First phase |
| - - -→ | Second phase |
| - - -→ | Energy transfer |
| - - - | Backhaul |

**Fig. 1.**  System model

In the first phase, source node sends signal to the relay node, and surrounding EAP send the energy to the relay node. The energy harvested by the relay node can be expressed as

$$E_R = \eta p_E G_{E,R} \tag{1}$$

Where $p_E$ denotes the charging power of the EAP and $G_{E,R}$ denotes the channel power gain between the EAP and the relay node.

The energy obtained by the relay is used to transmit information to the destination node in the second time slot. We assume that the relay node use all the energy to forward the message. The transmit power of the relay node is thus given by

$$E_R = P_R \tag{2}$$

The system uses AF protocol to forward information. The signal received by the relay node is denoted as

$$y_R = \sqrt{P_{SR}}h_{S,R}x_1 + n_1 \tag{3}$$

The relay node amplifies the signal and forwards it to the destination node, which is expressed as

$$y_D = \Phi y_R h_{R,D} + n_2 \tag{4}$$

Where $P_{SR}$ is the transmit power of source node, $h_{S,R}$ is the channel gain between the source node and the relay node, $\phi$ is a magnification factor, $X_1$ is the signal that sent by the source node, $n_1$ and $n_2$ is the noise power, $h_{R,D}$ is the channel gain from the relay node to the destination node.

Therefore, the SNR of destination node is expressed as:

$$
\begin{aligned}
SNR &= \frac{\frac{p_{SR}|h_{S,R}|^2}{\sigma^2} \cdot \frac{\eta p_E G_{E,R}|h_{R,D}|^2}{\sigma^2}}{1 + \frac{p_{SR}|h_{S,R}|^2}{\sigma^2} + \frac{\eta p_E G_{E,R}|h_{R,D}|^2}{\sigma^2}} \\
&= \frac{\eta p_{SR}|h_{S,R}|^2|h_{R,D}|^2 p_E G_{E,R}}{\sigma^4 + \sigma^2 p_{SR}|h_{S,R}|^2 + \eta\sigma^2|h_{R,D}|^2 p_E G_{E,R}}
\end{aligned}
\tag{5}
$$

Hence the achievable throughput (bps) from the relay node to the destination node can be expressed

$$
\begin{aligned}
R_{R,D} &= \frac{1}{2}\log_2(1 + SNR) \\
&= \frac{1}{2}\log_2(1 + \frac{\eta p_{SR}|h_{S,R}|^2|h_{R,D}|^2 p_E G_{E,R}}{\sigma^4 + \sigma^2 p_{SR}|h_{S,R}|^2 + \eta\sigma^2|h_{R,D}|^2 p_E G_{E,R}})
\end{aligned}
\tag{6}
$$

In order to facilitate the calculation, we make the following substitutions.

$$q_R = p_E G_{E,R} \tag{7}$$

$$a = \eta p_{SR}|h_{S,R}|^2|h_{R,D}|^2 \tag{8}$$

$$b = \sigma^4 + \sigma^2 p_{SR}|h_{S,R}|^2 \tag{9}$$

$$c = \eta \sigma^2 |h_{R,D}|^2 \tag{10}$$

Therefore,

$$R_{R,D} = \frac{1}{2} log_2 \left( 1 + \frac{aq_R}{b + cq_R} \right) \tag{11}$$

Where $q_R$ is the received signal power at the relay node from the EAP.

We assume that $\pi_E$ is the gain of EAP. The utility function of the destination node can be defined as

$$U_D(\pi_E, q_R) = R_{R,D} - \pi_E \tag{12}$$

The utility of EAP is defined as

$$U_E(\pi_E, q_R) = \pi_E - C_k(p_E) \tag{13}$$

Where $C_k(x)$ is used to model the energy cost of the EAP, given by

$$C_k(x) = a_E x^2 \tag{14}$$

Where $a_E$ is the energy cost coefficient. The utility function of the EAP becomes

$$U_E(\pi_E, q_R) = \pi_E - \frac{a_E}{G_{E,R}^2} q_R^2 \tag{15}$$

We define the type of the EAP as

$$\theta = \frac{G_{E,R}^2}{a_E} \tag{16}$$

$$U_E(\pi_E, q_R) = \pi_E - \frac{q_R^2}{\theta} \tag{17}$$

The utility of the destination node with EAP is given by

$$U_D(\pi_E, q_R) = \frac{1}{2} log_2 \left( 1 + \frac{aq_R}{b + cq_R} \right) - \pi_E \tag{18}$$

## 2.2  Problem Formulation

**Definition 1** (Individual Rationality, IR). The contract satisfies the IR constraint that the EAP obtains a nonnegative payoff when it provides power for the relay, i.e.

$$U_E(\pi_E, q_R) = \pi_E - \frac{q_R^2}{\theta} \geq 0 \tag{19}$$

Following the idea of contract theory, the goal of the source node is to maximize the use of IR constraints. Therefore, the optimization problem can be solved using the optimal contract.

$$\textbf{P1}: \quad \max\{U_D(\pi_E, q_R)\} \tag{20}$$

$$\text{s.t} \quad \pi_E - \frac{q_R^2}{\theta} \geq 0 \tag{21}$$

$$q_R \geq 0, \pi_E \geq 0, \theta \geq 0 \tag{22}$$

## 3   Optimal Solution

The optimal contract is designed to maximize transmission efficiency of the source node to the destination node utility. We first realize that the following necessary conditions can be derived from the IR constraints.

**Lemma 1.** In an optimal contract, the EAP obtains zero payoff by accepting the corresponding contract item, the optimal prices are given by

$$\pi_E^* = \frac{q_R^2}{\theta} \tag{23}$$

**Proof.** Since the optimization objective function is an increasing function of $q_R$ and a decreasing function of $\pi_E$. When they are equal, it can be achieved maximum utility of transmission efficiency of the source node to the destination node. So we completed the proof.

We substitute $\pi_E$ with $\pi_E^*$ and get

$$\textbf{P2}: \quad \max\{U_D(\pi_E^*, q_R)\} \tag{24}$$

$$\text{s.t} \quad q_R \geq 0, \pi_E \geq 0, \theta \geq 0 \tag{25}$$

Then put (18) and (23) into this formula, we get

$$U_D(\pi_E, q_R) = \frac{1}{2}\log_2\left(1 + \frac{aq_R}{b + cq_R}\right) - \frac{q_R^2}{\theta} \tag{26}$$

Take the first derivation of $U_D$ with regard to $q_R$, then, the optimal solution can be obtained when the first derivation of $U_D$ equals to zero. Thus, we can obtain:

$$\frac{1}{2} \frac{\left[\frac{a(b+cq_R)-aq_Rc}{(b+cq_R)^2}\right]}{\left(1+\frac{aq_R}{b+cq_R}\right)\ln 2} - \frac{2q_R}{\theta} = 0 \tag{27}$$

$$q_R = \frac{\sqrt{a^2b^2 \ln^2 2 + 2a^2bc\theta \ln 2 + 2abc^2\theta \ln 2} - ab \ln 2 - 2bc \ln 2}{2(ac \ln 2 + c^2 \ln 2)} \tag{28}$$

$$\pi_E^* = \frac{q_R^2}{\theta} \tag{29}$$

So we can get the optimal solution from the above.

## 4  Simulation Results

In this section, we draw the graph of the maximum utility function based on the optimal solution found above. Without loss of generality, we assume that the noise for all the links is white Gaussian noise. Considering a cooperative system which is composed one source node, one relay node and destination node and one EAP that provides energy. So, we set a few different parameters and compare them and see how the graph changes from the simulation. We can draw some conclusions through the simulation chart.

Figure 2 shows the distance from the relay node to the destination node influences the value of the utility function. We can observe that the further the distance from the relay node to the destination node, the smaller the value of the transmission utility will be. It is because of the distance increasing, the channel quality will become worse. In the upper right corner of the figure, $\eta$ stands for the energy harvesting efficiency. We can also see from the figure that the higher the energy harvesting efficiency, the more energy the relay node receives, therefore, the larger the value of the transmission utility function.

Figure 3 shows the relationship between the value of the utility function and the energy cost coefficient. As the energy cost coefficient gradually increases, the value of the utility function rises first to reach a peak and then begins to decline. Because of the contract theory that they have reached, EAP with the exchange of energy to get the benefits, when reaching a certain value, the utility function will be the best. After this point, the value of the utility function will begin to decrease as the energy cost coefficient decreases. Due to the higher the energy cost coefficient, the greater the payoff will be given by destination node. And it can also be observed that as the noise variance gradually increase, the value of the utility function decreases gradually, because the channel gain is getting worse.

From the Fig. 4, we can observe that accompanied by $p_{SR}$ gradual increase, $U_D$ first rises quickly then slowly, finally tends to be stable. We can observe that transmit power also affects the value of the utility function. From the figure, we can also see that if the energy cost coefficient becomes larger, the value of the utility function will also decrease. This is also because with the energy cost coefficient increases, EAP revenue will increase, lead to transmission utility will also be reduced.

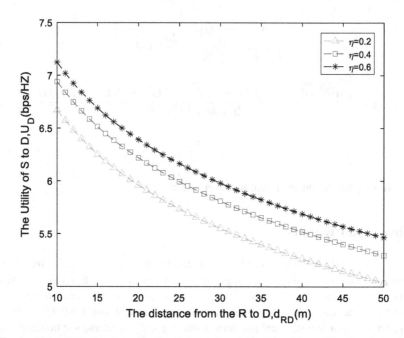

**Fig. 2.** The relationship between the distance from R to D and the utility function value

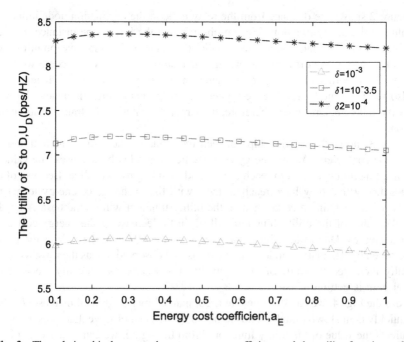

**Fig. 3.** The relationship between the energy cost coefficient and the utility function value

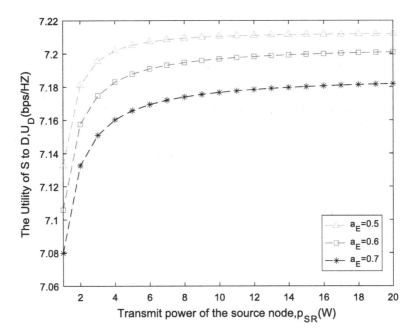

**Fig. 4.** The relationship between transmit power of the S node and the utility function value

## 5   Conclusion

In this paper, we proposed a contract theory based on Wireless Energy Harvesting in order to maximize the transfer efficiency of source node. We also use the IR constraint to simplify the target formula. Finally, we use the convex optimization algorithm to obtain the optimal solution. In the model, we use contract theory to hire surrounding EAPs to provide energy to help forward information. For convenience, we suppose only one EAP participate in the contract theory to provide energy. The final simulation shows that there are still many factors that affect transfer efficiency.

## References

1. Hou, Z., Chen, H., Li, Y., Vucetic, B.: Incentive mechanism design for wireless energy harvesting-based Internet of Things. IEEE Internet Things J. (2017). https://doi.org/10.1109/JIOT
2. Lu, W., He, C., Lin, Y.: Contract theory based cooperative spectrum sharing with joint power and bandwidth optimization. Project funded by China Postdoctoral Science Foundation under Grand No. 2017M612027
3. Liu, J., Ding, H., Cai, Y., Yue, H., Fang, Y., Chen, S.: An energy-efficient strategy for secondary users in cooperative cognitive radio networks for green communications. IEEE J. Sel. Areas Commun. **34**(12), 3195–3207 (2016)

4. Chen, H., Li, Y., Han, Z., Vucetic, B.: A stackelberg game-based energy trading scheme for power beacon-assisted wireless-powered communication. In: Proceedings of ICASSP, pp. 3177–3181, April 2015
5. Sarma, S., Kandhway, K., Kuri, J.: Robust energy harvesting based on a Stackelberg game. IEEE Wirel. Commun. Lett. **5**(3), 336–339 (2016)
6. Ma, Y., Chen, H., Lin, Z., Li, Y., Vucetic, B.: Distributed and optimal resource allocation for power beacon-assisted wireless-powered communications. IEEE Trans. Commun. **63**(10), 3569–3583 (2015)
7. Li, Y., Wang, W., Kong, J., Peng, M.: Subcarrier pairing for amplify-and-forward and decode-and-forward OFDM relay links. IEEE Commun. Lett. **13**(4), 209–211 (2009)
8. Zhong, C., Suraweera, H., Zheng, G., Krikidis, I., Zhang, Z.: Wireless information and power transfer with full duplex relaying. IEEE Trans. Commun. **62**(10), 3447–3461 (2014)
9. Ju, H., Zhang, R.: Throughput maximization in wireless powered communication networks. IEEE Trans. Wirel. Commun. **13**(1), 418–428 (2014)
10. Boyd, S., Vandenberghe, L.: Convex Optimization. Cambridge University Press, Cambridge (2004)

# Intelligent Signal Processing in Wireless and Optical Communications

# Probabilistic Sorting Memory Constrained Tree Search Algorithm for MIMO System

Xiaoping Jin[1], Zheng Guo[1(✉)], Ning Jin[1], and Zhengquan Li[2,3]

[1] Department of Information Engineering, China Jiliang University,
Hang Zhou 310018, China
{jxpl023,jinningl117}@cjlu.edu.cn,
Guozheng311@sina.com
[2] State Key Laboratory of Networking and Switching Technology,
Beijing University of Posts and Telecommunications, Beijing 100876, China
lzq722@sina.com
[3] National Mobile Communications Research Laboratory,
Southeast University, Nanjing 210096, China

**Abstract.** Considering the shortcomings of large storage space requirements and high complexity in multiple-symbol differential detection algorithm in current Multiple Input Multiple Output (MIMO) system, this paper proposes a probabilistic sorting memory constrained tree search algorithm (PSMCTS) by using performance advantage of sorting algorithm and storage advantage of memory constrained tree search (MCTS). Based on PSMCTS, a pruning PSMCTS named PPSMCTS is put forward. Simulation results show that the performance of PSMCTS is approach to that of ML algorithm under fixed memory situations, while the computational complexity is lower than that of MCTS algorithm in small storage capacity conditions under low signal noise ratio (SNR) region. PPSMCTS has more prominent advantages on reduction of computational complexity than PSMCTS algorithm. Theoretical analysis and simulation demonstrate that the two proposed algorithms can effectively inherit the good feature of MCTS algorithm, which are suitable for hardware implementation.

**Keywords:** MIMO · Probabilistic sorting · Memory constrained tree search
Pruning algorithm

## 1 Introduction

Recent years, the combination of Multiple Input Multiple Output (MIMO) technology and Orthogonal Frequency Division Multiplexing (OFDM) technology expands the application of MIMO system greatly, makes the system works more efficiently in frequency selective fading environment. However, under severe channel states, for example high-speed mobile condition, it is very difficult for the receiver to obtain the channel state information. Therefore, differential encoded signaling combined with low-complexity differential detection at the receiver becomes an attractive design alternative. But 3 dB performance loss would be paid compared with traditional correlation detection [1]. Then multiple-symbol differential detection (MSDD) which

© ICST Institute for Computer Sciences, Social Informatics and Telecommunications Engineering 2018
L. Meng and Y. Zhang (Eds.): MLICOM 2018, LNICST 251, pp. 411–425, 2018.
https://doi.org/10.1007/978-3-030-00557-3_41

using N + 1 received symbols to detect N symbols (N is regarded as observation window length or block length) is proposed as an effective solution to this problem. The increasing length of observation window can effectively shorten the performance gap of 3 dB [2].

At present, most multiple-symbol differential detection algorithms are based on tree-searching principle [1, 3]. Maximum likelihood (ML) detection [2] is the most representative algorithm of best performance. But the exhaustive search strategy makes its complexity increase in an exponential relationship with the block length and the number of antenna, which leads to a computationally intractable problem. Therefore, some detection algorithms with lower complexity were proposed [4–9]. Around these algorithms, there are three kinds of search strategies in general: depth-first [4, 5], breadth-first, and metric-first. Sphere detection (SD) is a typical depth-first searching detection algorithm. Due to its continuous backtracking, this algorithm has different throughput when in different channel environment, which does not lend itself to parallel and pipeline processing. Breadth-first search strategy [6, 10, 11], such as K-BEST algorithm, has high throughput and stable complexity, which is suitable for pipeline processing, but the K value constraint brings loss in performance. Stack algorithm [7] mainly based on metric-first strategy, as named as Dijkstra algorithm [8, 9], it always extends the node with the minimum metric value in measure list, so it has least visited node number among the three search strategies.

However, the hardware implementation of these algorithms usually has high computational complexity and requires large storage capacity. But in practice, the storage space is confining, which limits the algorithm performance. MCTS (Memory Constrained Tree Search) proposed in paper [12] gave a solution to this problem. It can approximate the performance of ML algorithm under any storage space situation. When the storage space is set as minimum value or maximum value, the performance of the MCTS algorithm approaches to that of the SD algorithm and stack algorithm respectively. Moreover, the average computational complexity reduces with the increasing of storage space. It possesses a good compromise between memory requirement and computational complexity. But, the complexity is still high when in small memory space because of approximating SD strategy.

DSPS (Dijkstra Search with Probabilistic Sorting) algorithm is a new tree search algorithm proposed by Chang [13, 14]. Compared with the Dijkstra algorithm of full search, DSPS greatly reduces the number of visited nodes and effectively enhances the bit error ratio (BER) performance by using mathematical statistical probability on the nodes. It has high research value in respect of saving storage space and reducing complexity.

In this context, we focus on using efficient methods to improve MCTS algorithm, which aiming to reduce the computational complexity of MSDD MIMO system, especially under memory constrained situation. We make the following contributions:

1. We propose a new memory constrained search algorithm - PSMCTS (probabilistic sorting memory constrained tree search), in which the DSPS merges into the MCTS algorithm to reduce the access node number and improve the decision accuracy of the MCTS algorithm.

2. To enhance the PSMCTS's advantage of low complexity under small memory size, a pruning algorithm is applied into PSMCTS. The improved scheme is called PPSMCTS. The key work here is how to decide the pruning threshold and use it to prune the searching tree layer by layer.

The rest of the paper is organized as follows. Section 2 presents the system model and signal construction. Section 3 introduces the PSMCTS algorithm applied in our MSDD MIMO system. In Sect. 4, PPMCTS algorithm is proposed. Section 5 provides system complexity and performance analysis, and Sect. 6 concludes the paper.

## 2   System Model

We consider a MIMO-OFDM system with $N_R$ receive and $N_T$ transmit antennas and communicating over a quasi-static, frequency-flat fading channel. The system diagram is shown in Fig. 1, in which the MSDD block is the focus of our research.

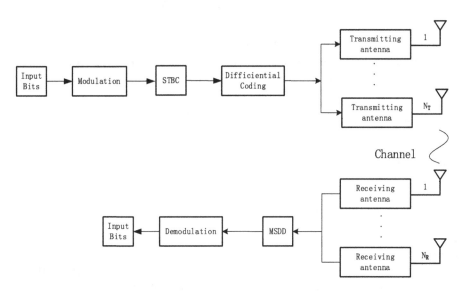

**Fig. 1.** Block diagram of MIMO system

In Fig. 1, the space-time block coding (STBC) module is constructed on Alamouti's transmit diversity scheme when $N_T = 2$. Other scheme can also be used, depending on the number of antennas. Define information matrix $S_t = \begin{bmatrix} s_{1,t} & s_{2,t} \\ -s_{2,t}^* & -s_{1,t}^* \end{bmatrix}$, where $S_{1,t}$ and $S_{2,t}$ belongs to a L-PSK modulation constellation collection $V$ and

$$V = \{e^{j2\pi(m-1)/L} | m = 1, 2 \cdots, L\} \tag{1}$$

$S_t$ satisfies $S_t S_t^H = I_2$, $(\cdot)^*$ means conjugate. For differential coding, setting reference matrix $C_0 = \begin{bmatrix} 1/\sqrt{2} & 1/\sqrt{2} \\ -1/\sqrt{2} & 1/\sqrt{2} \end{bmatrix}$, the coding rule is

$$C_t = S_t C_{t-1} \tag{2}$$

where $C_t$ denotes differential coding matrix. After differential coding, the data is transmitted through the space-time matrix using different multipath channel model. Now the receive signal at t time is

$$R_t = C_t H_t = W_t \tag{3}$$

where $R_t = \begin{bmatrix} r_{1,t} \\ r_{2,t} \end{bmatrix}$, $C_t = \begin{bmatrix} c_{1,t} & c_{2,t} \\ -c_{2,t}^* & -c_{1,t}^* \end{bmatrix}$, $H_t = \begin{bmatrix} h_{1,1} \\ h_{2,1} \end{bmatrix}$ is channel matrix, in which each element $h_{i,1}(i=1,2)$ follows Gauss distribution with 0 mean and variance $\sigma_H^2$, $W_t = \begin{bmatrix} w_{1,t} \\ w_{2,t} \end{bmatrix}$ is a noise matrix, in which each element follows Gauss distribution with mean 0 and variance $\sigma_W^2$.

Assuming the window length of multiple-symbol differential detection (MSDD) is N + 1, namely the receiver continuously receives N + 1 symbols to detect N symbols. The ML decision criterion is based on the following formula (proof see Appendix A)

$$\hat{V}_{ML} = \underset{V_{t+1},\dots,V_{t+N}}{\arg\min} \sum_{i=1}^{N} \sum_{l=i+1}^{N+1} \|R[l+t-1] - (\prod_{m=i+t}^{l+t-1} V[m]) \times R[i+t-1]\|_F^2 \tag{4}$$

where $t$ denotes the start time of detection.

## 3   PSMCTS Algorithm

In MCTS algorithm, (4) is used as metric decision, and the visiting node selection is restricted to the storage space and the metric value. It visits the node with minimum metric value per time. This feature can reduce the requirement of storage space. But in small storage space condition, MCTS tends to use a depth-first search strategy, like sphere detection (SD) algorithm, which still needs to backtrack to visit a large number of nodes and the computational complexity is still large.

To optimize formula (4), we use the cumulative distribution function of [10] as the decision metric

$$\hat{F} = \arg\min F(D;k) = \arg\min \frac{\gamma(k/2, D/\sigma^2)}{\Gamma(k/2)} \tag{5}$$

where $D = \sum_{i=1}^{N} \sum_{l=i+1}^{N+1} \|R[l+t-1] - (\prod_{m=i+t}^{l+t-1} V[m]) \times R[i+t-1]\|$ has k-dimensional chi-square distribution (proof see Appendix B).

Based on MCTS and (5), combined with Dijkstra algorithm characteristic, we propose a probabilistic sorting memory constrained tree search algorithm (PSMCTS), its search procedure is as follows:

1. According to the system requirements, modulation constellation size is $L$. Initialize the available storage space number with $M, M \geq (N-1)(L-1)+1$. Initialize multiple window length with $N$, and send the receiving signals with block size $N+1$ into PSMCTS decoder.

2. Set tree level $K = N$, which represents the search starts from the tree root. If $K \neq 2$, expend the root node to $L$ child nodes, save them into memory storage and delete the root node. Do search process of MCTS algorithm according to (5).

   (a) Start from $K = N$, namely from $V[t+N]$. According to PSMCTS, expand L child nodes, save them into memory storage and delete the node itself. Choose the best node from storage which satisfies (5), then expand it to next level. Save L expanding nodes into storage and delete the chosen best node.

   (b) Expand the best node from upper level, and save $L$ child nodes into memory storage. In condition of low storage space, due to the stored branch node number is small, choose the best branch node to expand directly. If $K = 1$, output the node with minimum value directly. If storage space is enough, retain multiple branch nodes. Expand the best node and add $L$ child nodes into memory storage. Do stack algorithm in the storage. Repeat the above steps until the best leaf node is found.

   (c) Repeat the above steps until the bottom of the tree is reached. Then output the best path.

3. If $K = 2$, find the best leaf node, and output the best path.

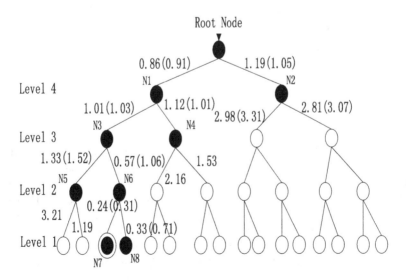

**Fig. 2.** Tree search analysis of PSMCTS

The search demos of PSMCTS and MCTS are shown as Figs. 2 and 3, respectively. In the figures, ○ denotes the branch nodes which are not visited. ● denotes the visited nodes. ◉ denotes the best path node. Figure 2 shows tree search analysis of PSMCTS. In this figure, numerical value is probabilistic metric value, which in parenthesis is traditional metric value. After the iterative computation runs to the step when $N3$ is selected, the node list contains four nodes $N2$, $N4$, $N5$, $N6$, which ordered as $N2$, $N6$, $N4$, $N5$ by traditional metric, and $N2$ will be selected as the best node to iterative computation for next round. But the four nodes will be ordered as $N6$, $N4$, $N5$, $N2$ by probabilistic metric, $N6$ will be chosen directly as the best node for next round iterative computation. Figure 3 is the chart of tree search analysis for MCTS. In this figure, numerical value is traditional metric value. It is intuitively show that the PSMCTS algorithm has the advantage of less visited nodes as compare to MCTS. In addition, in order to express the search process advantage more intuitively, Tables 1 and 2 show the specific search storage state of PSMCTS and MCTS respectively, where the bold number denotes visited node chosen for expanding.

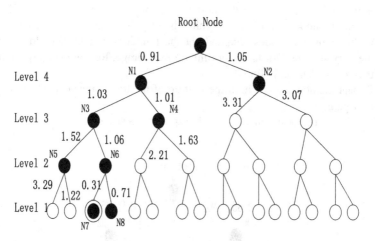

**Fig. 3.** Tree search analysis of MCTS

The two tables below show the use of storage of the two algorithms respectively. In PSMCTS, the storage space of each layer only needs to retain 3 branch nodes, while MCTS needs to retain 4 nodes at least. This reveals the PSMCTS algorithm has advantage in reducing storage space requirement, and this advantage will increase along with the number of constellation points. The tables also show the advantages of simplified steps in PSMCTS algorithm. Because it can accurately represent node metrics, the storage space is reduced, the number of visited nodes is reduced and the tree search process is accelerated, which makes the algorithm more effective and fast.

**Table 1.** PSMCTS search state

| Visited node | Memory nodes metric (level) | Visited level |
|---|---|---|
| (1) | **0.86(4)**, 1.19(4) | 4 |
| (2) | **1.01(3)**, 1.21(3), 1.19(4) | 3 |
| (3) | 1.33(2), **0.57(2)**, 1.21(3) | 2 |
| (4) | **0.24(1)**, 0.33(1) | 2 |
| (5) | **0.24(1)** | 1 |

**Table 2.** MCTS search state

| Visited node | Memory nodes metric (level) | Visited level |
|---|---|---|
| (1) | **0.91(4)**, 1.05(4) | 4 |
| (2) | **1.01(3)**, 1.03(3), 1.05(4) | 3 |
| (3) | 1.03(3), 1.63(2), 2.21(2), 1.05(4) | 2 |
| (4) | **1.06(2)**, 1.52(2), 2.21(2), 1.63(2) | 3 |
| (5) | **0.31(1)**, 0.71(1), 1.52(2) | 2 |
| (6) | **0.31(1)** | 1 |

# 4  PPSMCTS

As introduced in Sect. 3, the PSMCTS algorithm can adjust its search strategy dynamically according to the memory size. When the pre-specified memory size is very small, the computational complexity cannot but become large. As the pre-specified memory size increases, the average of the computational complexity will decrease. The key point is to find the best trade-off between memory requirement and computational complexity. Aiming at reducing the computational complexity further on the constraint of small memory, this part puts forward a pruning PSMCTS algorithm called PPSMCTS.

The PPSMCTS algorithm is proposed based on the PSMCTS algorithm. The difference is that, in PPSMCTS, we set a pre-specified pruning threshold and use it to prune the searching tree layer by layer, only those nodes whose metric are smaller than the pruning threshold are retained. The pruning process can reduce the total number of visited nodes throughout detecting and it is especially effective in low SNR region with small memory constraint. When SNR is high, the number of visited nodes can reach to only N nodes.

The pruning threshold is a key fact. If the value is too large, the memory will contain lots of useless nodes and will not be able to reduce the complexity. And if the value is too small, the probability of removing the maximum likelihood solution will be increased. It will affect the performance of detection.

In PPSMCTS algorithm, from formula (A.3 in Appendix A), the metric (i.e., weight) of the node $S(n)$ atn $(1 \leq n \leq N)$ level of weighted L-ray tree is

$$d_n = \sum_{n_R}^{N_R} \mathbf{R}_{n_R}^H(n) \Lambda_n^{-1} \mathbf{R}_{n_R}(n) \tag{6}$$

where $\Lambda_n = S(n)(\mathbf{C}_{R,n} \otimes \mathbf{I}_{N_T}) S^H(n)$. For the root node, $d_0 = 0$. $Th_n$ denotes the corresponding pruning threshold of the n-level. The retained probability of node $S(n)$ after pruning operation is taken as $\Pr\{d_n \leq Th_n\} = 1 - \varepsilon$. In order to ensure the BER performance, the pre-specified probability can be set as $P_0 = 1 - \varepsilon$. Then the pruning threshold $Th_n$ should satisfy

$$\Pr\left\{ d_n = \sum_{n_R}^{N_R} R_{n_R}^H(n) \Lambda_n^{-1} R_{n_R}(n) \leq Th_n \right\} = P_0 = 1 - \varepsilon \tag{7}$$

where $R_{n_R}(n)$ meets $CN(0, \Lambda_n)$ distribution, and its quadratic form $2R_{n_R}^H(n) \Lambda_n^{-1} R_{n_R}(n)$ meets $\chi^2_{2(n+1)N_T}$ distribution of $2(n+1)N_T$ degree of freedom. Owing to the statistical independence of $R_{n_R}(n), n_R = 1, 2, \ldots, N_R, 2d_n = 2\sum_{n_R}^{N_R} R_{n_R}^H(n) \Lambda_n^{-1} R_{n_R}(n)$ meets $\chi^2_{2(n+1)N_T N_R}$ distribution of $2(n+1)N_T N_R$ degree of freedom. Substitute these data into (7), we get

$$Th_n = \frac{\left(\chi^2_{2(n+1)N_T N_R}(P_0)\right)^{-1}}{2} \tag{8}$$

Here, the superscript '−1' represents the inverse of Chi square distribution. (9) is then obtained according to the Chi square distribution of $2(n+1)N_T N_R$ degree of freedom.

$$\int_0^\alpha \frac{1}{2^{(n+1)N_T N_R} \Gamma((n+1)N_T N_R)} x^{(n+1)N_T N_R - 1} e^{-\frac{x}{2}} dx = P_0 = 1 - \varepsilon \tag{9}$$

Here, $\varepsilon$ is very small, such as 0.1, 0.01, etc. $\alpha$ can be obtained from (9), which is equivalent to $\left(\chi^2_{2(n+1)N_T N_R}(P_0)\right)^{-1}$. In order to find ML solution, all children of the root node will remain without being pruned. We adopt the pruning threshold which is expressed as

$$Th_n = \frac{n}{2}\alpha, n = 1, 2 \ldots, N \tag{10}$$

Where $\alpha$ can be obtained from (9), and $n$ is an empirical value related to the tree level which is set to increase the threshold value [16].

## 5   Complexity and Performance Analysis

In order to verify the effectiveness of PSMCTS, we analyze the complexity and the bit error ratio (BER) performance in this section, where the noise is a Gaussian white noise with a mean 0 and a variance of 1, the channel is quasi-static frequency flat fading channel and it remains constant within an observation window.

### 5.1   Complexity Analysis

In MCTS algorithm, $M$ must has a minimum bound to ensure the MCTS algorithm can be achieved. According to the proof about $M$ minimum bound in [12], set $M$ value as $(N - 1)(L - 1) + 1$ in multi-symbol differential system, where $L$ is the number of constellation. Here, window length $N = 4$, with QPSK modulation $L = 4$, and $M \geq (N - 1)(L - 1) + 1$. For ML algorithm, the visited node number is $L^0 + \ldots + L^{N-1} = (L^N - 1)/(L - 1)$. The visited node number of MCTS and PSMCTS are shown in Figs. 4 and 5 respectively.

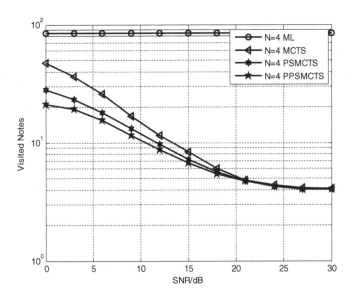

**Fig. 4.**  Complexity analysis comparison chart

In Fig. 4, all kinds of comparisons are discussed in the condition that the window length is 4. The horizontal and vertical coordinates denotes signal-to-noise ratio and visited nodes number respectively. The result shows that under the same window length and storage space, for the same kind of modulation, PSMCTS shows more advantages compared with MCTS, especially in low SNR, which is conductive to a lower average complexity. Furthermore, based on pruning algorithm, PPSMCTS has the lowest calculate complexity among the four mentioned algorithms.

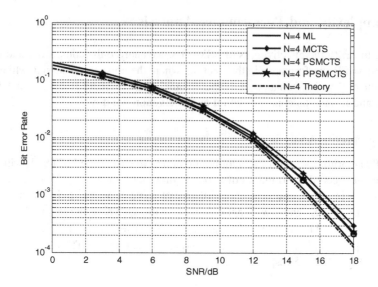

**Fig. 5.** Performance analysis diagram

## 5.2    Performance Analysis

This part mainly conducts performance simulation and analysis on algorithms in the test environment. In Alamouti STBC system, the binary bits is modulated to signal set $S = \{\exp[2\pi j(i-1)/M]\}$ after MPSK mapping, where $i = 1,\dots,M$. After differential coding and $2 \times 2$ matrix transformation, each group symbol denotes as $S_t$, and 2 pair symbols $[s_{1,t} - s_{2,t}]$ and $\left[-s_{2,t}^*, s_{1,t}^*\right]$ are sent through two different antennas. Assuming the MPSK signal amplitude is A, single antenna transmit power $P = A^2$. Total transmit power is $P_T = A^2$. If Rayleigh channel h1 and h2 keep unchanged in the two symbol times, the received signals are:

$$r_1 = h_1 s_1 + h_2 s_2 + n_1$$
$$r_2 = -h_1 s_2^* + h_2 s_1^* + n_2 \tag{11}$$

where $n_1, n_2$ is AWGN channel with zero mean, and $r_1, r_2$ is received signals at two time slots.

$$s_1' = h_1^* r_1 + h_2 r_2^* = \alpha s_1 + h_1^* n_1 + h_2 n_2^* \tag{12}$$

$$s_2' = h_2^* r_1 - h_1 r_2^* = \alpha s_2 + h_2^* n_1 - h_1 n_2^* \tag{13}$$

where $\alpha = |h_1|^2 + |h_2|^2$. Refer to MPSK theoretical bit error rate formula in Ref. [17], we have

$$SER = \frac{M-1}{M} - \left( \frac{2a(2a^2+3)\tan^{-1}\left(\sqrt{\frac{\bar{\gamma}_s-2a^2}{2a^2+2}}\right)}{4\pi(a^2+1)^{3/2}} + \frac{a\,\sin\left(2\,\tan^{-1}\left(\sqrt{\frac{\bar{\gamma}_s-2a^2}{2a^2+2}}\right)\right)}{4\pi(a^2+1)^{3/2}} + \frac{a(2a^2+3)}{4(a^2+1)^{3/2}} \right)$$

$$(14)$$

where $a = \sqrt{\bar{\gamma}_s/2}\sin(\pi/M), \bar{\gamma}_s = 2A^2/N_0$ is average SNR.

The simulation results are shown in Fig. 5. Using theoretical BER for comparison, ML algorithm which has best performance is most close to theoretical BER. Under the same storage space, both PSMCTS and PPSMCTS have certain performance improvement compared with MCTS and are more approximate to ML, this is due to the use of probabilistic sorting algorithm effectively.

# 6  Summary

Considering the large computational complexity problem under the condition of the hardware storage space constraints and the small storage space, this paper proposed PSMCTS algorithm, which effectively provides better performance by using the advantage of DSPS algorithm and MCTS algorithm. Overall, PSMCTS algorithm not only has low storage space demand and easy hardware implementation, but also reduces the computational complexity in the low SNR region, which reduces the average system complexity. With using pruning algorithm, PPSMCTS has more obvious advantage in reducing complexity. At the same time, the detection performance of the two algorithms this paper proposed approach ML algorithm. Therefore, PSMCTS and PPSMCTS both are good detection algorithms.

**Acknowledgement.** This work was supported by Zhejiang Provincial Natural Science Foundation of China (no. LY17F010012), the Natural Science Foundation of China (no. 61571108), the open Foundation of State key Laboratory Of Networking and Switching Technology (Beijing University of Posts and Telecommunication no. SKLNST-2016-2-14).

**Authors' Contributions.** Xiaoping Jin conceived the idea of the system model and designed the proposed schemes. Zheng Guo has done a part of basic work in this article. Ning Jin performed simulations of the proposed schemes. Zhengquan Li provided substantial comments on the work and supported and supervised the research. All of the authors participated in the project, and they read and approved the final manuscript.

**Competing Interests.** The authors declare that they have no competing interests.

# Appendix A

On the basis of the signal model given in Sect. 2, we define an additional $2(N+1) \times 2(N+1)$ information matrix as $\mathbf{S} = diag\{S_k, S_{k-1}, \ldots, S_{k-N}\}$. Within one observation window, the received matrix R conditioned on the message matrix S has a multivariate Gaussian conditional Probability Density Function (PDF)

$$p(\mathbf{R}|\mathbf{S}) = \frac{1}{\pi^{4(N+1)} \det \Lambda} \exp\{-tr(\mathbf{R}^H \Lambda^{-1} \mathbf{R})\} \tag{A.1}$$

where $\Lambda = \mathbf{S}(\mathbf{C}_R \otimes \mathbf{I}_{N_T})\mathbf{S}^H$. Here, $\mathbf{C}_R = \sigma_n^2 \mathbf{I}_{N+1} + \mathbf{C}_h$ is the covariance matrix of R [18], $\otimes$ denotes the Kronecker product of two matrices or vectors and $\mathbf{C}_h$ denotes the autocorrelation matrix of the channel which can be expressed as

$$\mathbf{C}_h = \begin{bmatrix} C_h(0) & \cdots & C_h(N) \\ \vdots & \ddots & \vdots \\ C_h(-N) & \cdots & C_h(0) \end{bmatrix}.$$

Thus, the ML decision metric within the observation window can be written as

$$S_{ML} = \arg\min\{tr(\mathbf{R}^H \Lambda^{-1} \mathbf{R}) + \ln \det(\Lambda)\} \tag{A.2}$$

Considering that $\det(\Lambda)$ can be ignored because it is independence with the transmitted information, (A.2) becomes

$$S_{ML} = \arg\min\{tr(\mathbf{R}^H \Lambda^{-1} \mathbf{R})\} \tag{A.3}$$

Using the results of the literature [19], (A.3) can be simplified to (A.4).

$$\begin{aligned} \hat{V}_{ML} &= \arg\min_{V_{t+1},\ldots,V_{t+N}} \sum_{i=1}^{N} \sum_{l=i+1}^{N+1} -\tilde{c}_{i,l} ||R[i+t-1]( \prod_{m=i+t}^{l+t-1} V[m])^H \times R[l+t-1]||_F^2 \\ &= \arg\min_{V_{t+1},\ldots,V_{t+N}} \sum_{i=1}^{N} \sum_{l=i+1}^{N+1} ||R[l+t-1] - \tilde{c}_{i,l}( \prod_{m=i+t}^{l+t-1} V[m]) \times R[i+t-1]||_F^2 \end{aligned} \tag{A.4}$$

In formula (A.4), $c_{i,l}$ is the entity element of $\Lambda$ [15]. Normalize $c_{i,l}$ as follows, $c_m = \max|c_{k,k+1}|, k = 1,\ldots,N$ or $c_m = c_{\lfloor N/2 \rfloor,\lfloor N/2 \rfloor+1}$, $\tilde{c}_{i,l} = c_{i,l}/c_m$, where $\lfloor \cdot \rfloor$ denotes the floor operation, $|\bullet|$ denotes the absolute value. When the channel condition remains within an observation window, $C_h(n) = 1$. Therefore $\tilde{c}_{i,l} = 1(i = 1,2,\ldots,N, l = 2,\ldots,N+1$ and $i \neq l)$. So (A.4) can be simplified to (A.5).

$$\hat{V}_{ML} = \arg\min_{V_{t+1},\ldots,V_{t+N}} \sum_{i=1}^{N} \sum_{l=i+1}^{N+1} ||R[l+t-1] - ( \prod_{m=i+t}^{l+t-1} V[m]) \times R[i+t-1]||_F^2 \tag{A.5}$$

When N = 1, (A.5) can be simplified to (A.6)

$$\hat{V} = \arg\min_{V_{t+1},\ldots,V_{t+N}} ||R[t+1] - V[t+1] \times R[t]||_F^2 \tag{A.6}$$

## Appendix B

When observation window N = 1, from formula (A.6), we obtain

$$
\begin{aligned}
D &= ||R[t+1] - V[t+1]R[t]||_F^2 \\
&= ||C[t+1]H[t+1] + W[t+1] - V[t+1](C[k]H[t] + W[t])||_F^2 \\
&= ||C[t+1]H[t+1] + W[t+1] - C[k+1]H[t] - V[t+1]W[t]||_F^2
\end{aligned}
\tag{B.1}
$$

Since it is assumed that the channel remains unchanged at an adjacent interval, i.e. $H[t+1] = H[t]$, so

$$
D = ||W[t+1] - V[t+1]W[t]||_F^2
\tag{B.2}
$$

In this paper, the $W[n], n = t, t+1, \ldots, t+N$ is a matrix with NT rows and NR columns, each element follows Gauss distribution with 0 mean and variance $\sigma_W^2$. It can be seen that $D/2\sigma_w^2$ is a chi-square random variable with a degree of freedom of $N_R N_T$. Thus, from formula (A.5), it can be deduced to (B.3) and (B.4) when the length of the observation window is N + 1 in the multi-symbol differential detection system.

$$
\begin{aligned}
D &= ||C[t+N]H[t+N] + W[t+N] - V[t+N]C[t+N-1]H[t+N-1] - V[t+N]W[t+N-1]||_F^2 \\
&\quad + \ldots + ||C[t+N]H[t+N] + W[t+N] - V[t+N-1]V[t+N]C[t+N-2]H[t+N-2] \\
&\quad - V[t+N-1]V[t+N]W[t+N-2]||_F^2 + \ldots + ||C[t+N]H[t+N] + W[t+N] \\
&\quad - V[t+1]\ldots V[t+N-1]V[t+N]C[t]H[t] - V[t+1]\ldots V[t+N-1]V[t+N]W[t]||_F^2 \\
&= ||C[t+N]H[t+N] + W[t+N] - C[t+N]H[t+N-1] - V[t+N]W[t+N-1]||_F^2 \\
&\quad + \ldots + ||C[t+N]H[t+N] + W[t+N] - C[t+N-1]H[t+N-2] - V[t+N-1]V[t+N]W[t+N-2]||_F^2 \\
&\quad + \ldots + ||C[t+N]H[t+N] + W[t+N] - C[t+1]H[t] - V[t+1]\ldots V[t+N-1]V[t+N]W[t]||_F^2 \\
&= ||W[t+N] - V[t+N]W[t+N-1]||_F^2 + \ldots + ||W[t+N] - V[t+N-1]V[t+N]W[t+N-2]||_F^2 \\
&\quad + \ldots + ||W[t+N] - V[t+1]\ldots V[t+N-1]V[t+N]W[t]||_F^2
\end{aligned}
\tag{B.3}
$$

In the derivation of (B.3), the third equal sign assumes that the channel remains constant within an observation interval, resulting in the formula (B.4)

$$
D = \sum_{i=1}^{N} \sum_{l=i+1}^{N+1} ||W[l+t-1] - (\prod_{m=i+t}^{l+t-1} V[m]) \times W[i+t-1]||_F^2
\tag{B.4}
$$

At this point, according to the chi-square random variable degrees of freedom of the nature of the cumulative, $D/2\sigma_w^2$ is a chi-square random variable with a degree of freedom of $N(N+1)N_R N_T$. So, the decision metrics distributed according to the chi-square distribution with $k = 2N(N+1)N_R N_T \sigma_w^2$ degrees of freedom [13]. Its cumulative distribution function (cdf) is given by

$$F(D; k) = \frac{\gamma(k/2, D/\sigma^2)}{\Gamma(k/2)} \tag{B.5}$$

where $\sigma^2$ is variance of $W[l + t - 1] - (\prod\limits_{m=i+t}^{l+t-1} V[m]) \times W[i + t - 1]$ in formula (B.4).
According to formulas (2) and (3), and the distribution character of channel and noise, $\sigma^2$ is equal to $2\sigma_W^2$. Both $\gamma(.)$ and $\Gamma(.)$ are Gamma functions and show as

$$\gamma(s, x) = \int_0^x t^{s-1} e^{-t} dt \tag{B.6}$$

$$\Gamma(x) = \int_0^{+\infty} t^{x-1} e^{-1} dt \tag{B.7}$$

# References

1. Wei, R.Y.: Differential encoding by a look-up table for quadrature-amplitude modulation. IEEE Trans. Commun. **59**(1), 84–94 (2011)
2. Kim, J.-S., Moon, S.-H., Lee, I.: A new reduced complexity ML detection scheme for MIMO systems. IEEE Trans. Commun. **58**(4), 1302–1310 (2010)
3. Bello, I.A., Halak, B., El-Hajjar, M., Zwolinski, M.: A survey of VLSI implementations of tree search algorithms for MIMO detection. Circ. Syst. Signal Process. **35**(10), 3644–3674 (2016)
4. Schenk, A., Fischer, R.F.H.: A stopping radius for the sphere decoder: complexity reduction in multiple-symbol differential detection. In: International ITG Conference on Source and Channel Coding, pp. 1–6. IEEE (2010)
5. Takahashi, T., Fukuda, T., Sun, C.: An appropriate radius for reduced-complexity sphere decoding. In: International Conference on Communications, Circuits and Systems (ICCCAS), 28–30 July 2010, Chengdu, China, pp. 41–44 (2010)
6. Jin, N., Jin, X.P., Ying, Y.G., Wang, S., Lou, X.Z.: Research on low-complexity breadth-first detection for multiple-symbol differential unitary space-time modulation systems. IET Commun. **5**(13), 1868–1878 (2011)
7. Mao, X., Ren, S.: Adjustable reduced metric-first tree search. In: International Conference on Wireless Communications, Networking and Mobile Computing (WiCOM), 23–25 September 2011, Wuhan, China, pp. 1–4 (2011)
8. Kim, T., Park, I.: High-throughput and area efficient MIMO symbol detection based on modified Dijkstra search. IEEE Trans. Circuits Syst. I Regul. Pap. **57**(7), 1756–1766 (2010)
9. Jasika, N., Alispahic, N., Elma, A.: Dijkstra's shortest path algorithm serial and parallel execution performance analysis. In: MIPRO 2012 Proceedings of the 35th International Convention, 21–25 May 2012, Opatija, pp. 1811–1815 (2012)
10. Suh, S., Barry, J.R.: Reduced-complexity MIMO detection via a slicing breadth-first tree search. IEEE Trans. Wirel. Commun. **16**(3), 1782–1790 (2017)
11. Sah, A.K., Chaturvedi, A.K.: Stopping rule-based iterative tree search for low-complexity detection in MIMO systems. IEEE Trans. Wirel. Commun. **16**(1), 169–179 (2017)

12. Dai, Y., Yan, Z.: Memery constrained tree search detection and new ordering schemes. IEEE J. Sel. Top. Signal Process. **3**(6), 1026–1037 (2009)
13. Chang, R.Y., Chung, W.-H.: Efficient tree-search MIMO detection with probabilistic node ordering. In: IEEE International Conference on Communications, 5–9 June, 2011, Kyoto, pp. 1–5 (2011)
14. Chang, R.Y., Chung, W.-H.: Best-first tree search with probabilistic node ordering for MIMO detection: generalization and performance-complexity tradeoff. IEEE Trans. Wirel. Commun. **11**(2), 780–789 (2012)
15. Cui, T., Tellambura, C.: Bound-intersection detection for multiple-symbol differential unitary space–time modulation. IEEE Trans. Commun. **53**(12), 2114–2123 (2005)
16. Li, Y., Wei, J.B.: Multiple symbol differential detection algorithm based on the sphere decoding in unitary space time modulation system. Sci. China Ser. F-Inf. Sci. **39**(5), 569–578 (2009)
17. Hu, X., Gao, Y., Pan, Y.: Error rates calculation and performance analysis of (2,1) STBC systems. In: 7th International Conference on Signal Processing Proceedings ICSP, 31 August–4 September 2004, Beijing, pp. 1902–1905 (2004)
18. Cui, T., Tellambura, C.: On multiple symbol detection for diagonal DUSTM over ricean channels. IEEE Trans. Wirel. Commun. **7**(4), 1146–1151 (2008)
19. Bhukania, B., Schniter, P.: On the robustness of decision-feedback detection of DPSK and differential unitary space-time modulation in Rayleigh-fading channels. IEEE Trans. Wirel. Commun. **3**(5), 1481–1489 (2004)

# Intelligent Cooperative Communications and Networking

# Uplink Transmission Scheme Based on Rateless Coding in Cloud-RAN

Lingjie Xie, Yu Zhang$^{(\boxtimes)}$, Yefan Zhang, Jingyu Hua,
and Limin Meng

College of Information Engineering,
Zhejiang University of Technology, Hangzhou, China
xielingjie@hotmail.com,
{yzhang,eehjy,mlm}@zjut.edu.cn, 373679192@qq.com

**Abstract.** We consider a Cloud Radio Access Network (C-RAN) uplink system composed of single user, multiple remote radio heads (RRH) and baseband unit (BBU) pool. The user encodes the messages with rateless code which are then modulated and sent. Each RRH which covers the user quantizes the received signals and transfers them to the BBU pool through the high rate fronthaul link. The BBU pool applies belief propagation (BP) algorithm for joint decompression and decoding for the user information. In order to further improve the performance of the system, we resort to the extrinsic mutual information transfer (EXIT) analysis to optimize the degree profile of the rateless code. The numerical simulation shows that the BER performance of the proposed rateless coded scheme is close to the theoretical upper bound.

**Keywords:** Cloud Radio Access Network (C-RAN) · Rateless code
Extrinsic mutual information transfer (EXIT)

## 1 Introduction

With the rapid growth of mobile Internet, the next generation communication system will face a huge number of users and a huge amount of data transmission [1]. Under this situation, current Radio Access Network (RAN) has potential problems such as low quality of wireless coverage and a large number of sites leading to high energy consumption. For these problems, IBM and China mobile have proposed a new type of access network architecture: Cloud Radio Access Network (C-RAN) [2]. Compared with the traditional cellular networks, C-RAN network status and channel condition are more complex and changeable, and each user may access through multiple remote radio head (RRH) and interfere each other. During transmission, the RRHs via which the user accesses may also change. These characteristics bring challenge to the application of traditional fixed-rate channel coding (such as LDPC code, turbo code) in C-RAN. However, with rateless code [3] (such as LT code, Raptor code), the rate changes adaptively with the experienced channel. Moreover, the optimized rateless code can still approach the channel capacity even when the channel information is unknown to the transmitter [4]. In addition, the rateless code does not need to use hybrid automatic repeat request (HARQ) mechanism in the case of decoding failure. It

© ICST Institute for Computer Sciences, Social Informatics and Telecommunications Engineering 2018
L. Meng and Y. Zhang (Eds.): MLICOM 2018, LNICST 251, pp. 429–437, 2018.
https://doi.org/10.1007/978-3-030-00557-3_42

can effectively alleviate the system loss caused by ACK\NACK signal feedback which is a severe problem in C-RAN due to the long fronthaul. Therefore, rateless code is suitable for C-RAN architecture naturally.

When each RRH is regarded as a relay, the C-RAN network has an internal relation with the relay systems. In [5], rateless coded transmission was considered and optimized for the three-node decode-and-forward relay system and the compress-and-forward relay system respectively. References [6–8] focused on the problem of resource allocation for the C-RAN network. The authors in [9, 10] studied the rateless coding in a two-way and multiple access relay network. The above works mainly focus on the rateless network coding design for multi-point coordination. Note that in these works, the relay has a complete set of baseband signal processing and decoding functions. It is not the case for the C-RAN system because the RRH in C-RAN does not have or has limited signal processing capability so that it is unable to implement complex signal processing and decoding. Besides, rateless codes with optimized degree profiles can also approach the channel capacity like the fixed rate channel code. Rateless coded transmission have been studied for various communication systems including wireless broadcast systems, relay systems and distributed antenna systems [11, 12].

This paper proposes a rateless coded uplink transmission scheme for the single user scenario in C-RAN. The user encodes the messages with rateless code which are then BPSK modulated and sent. Each RRH that covers the user preprocesses the received signal to obtain baseband signals. Then the RRH quantizes the baseband signals and transfers them to the BBU pool through the high rate link. The BBU pool applies belief propagation (BP) algorithm for joint decompression and decoding for the user information. In addition, we resort to the extrinsic mutual information transfer (EXIT) analysis to optimize the degree profile of the rateless code.

The remaining of this paper is organized as follows. In Sect. 2, we introduce the system model. In Sect. 3, we present the C-RAN uplink rateless coded transmission strategy. In Sect. 4, we optimize the output degree of the rateless code used at the user to improve the system performance and gives the numerical simulation. We conclude in Sect. 5.

## 2  System Model

As shown in Fig. 1, the C-RAN system consists of single user $S$, remote single-antenna radio frequency unit $RRH_j$, $j = 1, 2, \ldots, L$ and BBU pool. The channel gain of the link between user $S$ and $RRH_j$ is defined as $h_j, j = 1, 2, \ldots, L$ which is randomly distributed. The variance of Gaussian noise at each RRH is $\sigma_0^2$. The link SNR from user $S$ to $RRH_j$ is expressed as: $\gamma_j = |h_j|^2 P / \sigma_0^2$, where $P$ is the transmit power of the user, and for simplicity we normalize it as $P = 1$.

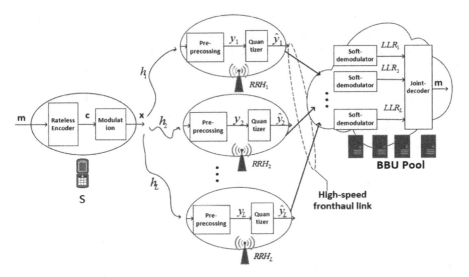

**Fig. 1.** The C-RAN single user uplink transmission system.

The Firstly, the user $S$ encodes $k$ bit message $m$ to obtain rateless codeword $c[i], i = 1, \ldots, k$. Then it do modulation and send the modulated symbol $x[i], i = 1, \ldots, N$ to each RRH that covers the user. Each RRH pre-processes the received signal to obtain the baseband signal:

$$y_j[i] = h_j x[i] + n_j[i], j = 1, 2, \ldots, L \tag{1}$$

where $n_j[i]$ is Gaussian white noise at $RRH_j$. Next, the RRH quantizes the signal $y_j[i]$, and the quantized signal $\hat{y}_j[i]$ is transmitted to the BBU pool through the high rate fronthaul link. Then BBU performs joint decompression and demodulation on the receives signals from all the RRHs. Finally, the joint decoder applies belief propagation (BP) algorithm for joint decoding the user information. After successful decoding, the ACK signal is fed back by the RRH through the downlink to inform the user to stop sending the information.

## 3 Rateless Codes Uplink Transmission Scheme

### 3.1 Rateless Coding at User

The user encodes the information by Raptor code [3] and use LDPC code as its precoding. The message $m$ passes through the LDPC encoder and LT encoder. The output of the LT encoder is derived by:

$$\Omega(x) = \sum_{d=1}^{d_c} \Omega_d x^d \tag{2}$$

where $\Omega_d$ denotes the probability that the output node with degree $d$ appears in the output node, $d_c$ denotes the maximum degree of the output node. For the output node with degree $d$, $d$ bits are randomly and equally probabilistically selected from the input node for XOR operation, and the result of the operation is taken as the corresponding output bit value. Through the above encoding process, a steady stream of rateless codes $c$ is generated. Next, rateless code adopts binary phase shift keying (BPSK) modulation, where bits 0 and 1 are mapped to $+1$ and $-1$ respectively. The user continuously sends the modulated signal $x$ until the BBU pool recovers the user information correctly and feeds back the ACK signal.

## 3.2 Signal Quantization Scheme at RRH

The quantizer of RRH compresses the received signal to satisfy the forward link capacity requirement. In order to reduce the complexity, we use a scalar quantization compression algorithm. In addition, the quantization interval and threshold of quantizer at RRH are fixed and do not change during the transmissoin. This will further reduce RRH complexity. The RRH receives the signals sent by the user which are given by (for simplicity, we omitted the time subscript):

$$y = hx + n \tag{3}$$

The expectation of $y$ (for the probability density space of channel gain $h$, signal $x$ and noise $n$) is derived by:

$$E(y) = E(hx + n) = E(h) \cdot E(x) + E(n) = 0 \tag{4}$$

The variance of $y$ is derived as:

$$D(y) = E(y^2) - (E(y))^2 = E(h^2 x^2) + 2E(hx) + E(n^2) = 2\sigma_h^2 + \sigma_0^2 \tag{5}$$

where $\sigma_h^2$ is the variance of the channel gain coefficient. According to the $"3\sigma"$ criterion [13], it can be considered that almost all the values of $y$ are distributed in the interval $(-3\sqrt{D(y)}, +3\sqrt{D(y)})$. Let the quantizer uses b-bit quantization, then the number of quantization levels satisfies $2M = 2^b$. We use the uniform quantization, through the following rules:

$$\hat{y} = Q(y) = \begin{cases} q_{-M} & -\infty < y < (-M+1)\Delta \\ q_k & k < 0时k\Delta < y < (k+1)\Delta, k > 0时 \ (k-1) \ \Delta \le y < k\Delta \\ q_M & (M-1)\Delta \le y < \infty \end{cases} \tag{6}$$

to quantify $y$ into a quantized signal $\hat{y}$. Where $\Delta = \frac{3\sqrt{D(y)}}{M}$ is the quantization interval and $q_k = \left(j - \frac{\mathrm{sgn}(j)}{2}\right)\Delta$, $k = \pm 1, \pm 2, \ldots, \pm M$ is the quantized value.

### 3.3 Iterative Decoding at BBU Pool

The BBU pool first performs soft decompression and demodulation on the quantized signals sent by the RRH before iterative decoding. For the rateless code, the $i$th coding bit $c[i]$ is made of 0 or 1 equiprobably. Assuming that the quantized signal which the $j$th RRH uploads to the BBU pool is $\hat{y}_j[i] = q_k$, then the corresponding Log Likelihood Ratio (LLR) is:

$$LLR_j[i] = \ln \frac{\Pr(\hat{y}_j[i] = q_k | c[i] = 0)}{\Pr(\hat{y}_j[i] = q_k | c[i] = 1)}, j = 1, 2, \ldots, L \tag{7}$$

The LLR of the $i$ th bits when considering the compressed signals from all RRHs is given by:

$$LLR[i] = \ln \frac{\Pr(\hat{y}_1[i], \hat{y}_2[i], .., \hat{y}_L[i] | c[i] = 0)}{\Pr(\hat{y}_1[i], \hat{y}_2[i], .., \hat{y}_L[i] | c[i] = 1)} = \sum_{j=1}^{L} \ln \frac{\frac{1}{2} \int_{\Delta_k} \frac{1}{\sqrt{2\pi\sigma_0^2}} e^{-\frac{(x-h_j)^2}{2\sigma_0^2}} dx}{\frac{1}{2} \int_{\Delta_k} \frac{1}{\sqrt{2\pi\sigma_0^2}} e^{-\frac{(x+h_j)^2}{2\sigma_0^2}} dx},$$

$$k \in \{-M, \ldots, M\} = \sum_{j=1}^{L} LLR_j[i] \tag{8}$$

where $\Delta_k$ is the quantization interval corresponding to the quantization level $q_k$, $\sigma_0^2$ is the Gaussian noise variance at each RRH, and $h_j$ is the link channel gain.

Next, the BBU performs iterative decoding using the LLRs given in (8). Using BP decoding algorithm [14] based on Factor diagram, the decoding process is divided into two steps. The first step, as shown in Fig. 2, is to perform decoding iterations over the entire graph. The message updates sequence between input nodes and output nodes are: from the input node to the LDPC check node, then the LDPC check node returns the input node, then from the input node to the output node, and finally returns the input node. In details, the message passing process is as follows (in the $l$th iteration): The message sent from input node $i$ to LDPC check node $c$ is:

$$m_{ic}^{(l)} = \sum_{o} m_{oi}^{(l-1)} \tag{9}$$

where $m_{oi}^{(l-1)}$ is the input node $i$ connected to the output node $o$ in the previous round of transmission to the input node message. LDPC check node $c$ back to the input node messages is:

$$\tanh\left(\frac{m_{ci}^{(l)}}{2}\right) = \prod_{i' \neq i} \tanh\left(\frac{m_{i'c}^{(l)}}{2}\right) \tag{10}$$

where $i'c$ is the input node connected to the LDPC check node $c$ (except $i$). Then, the message from input node $i$ to output node $o$ is:

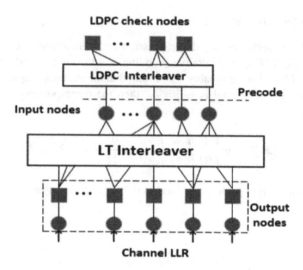

**Fig. 2.** The Raptor code decoding Factor graph.

$$m_{io}^{(l)} = \sum_{o' \neq o} m_{o'i}^{(l-1)} + \sum_{c} m_{ci}^{(l)} \tag{11}$$

where $m_{o'i}^{(l-1)}$ is the message that the output node (except $o$) connected to input node $i$ transmitted to the input node in the previous round, $m_{ci}^{(l)}$ is the message transmitted from LDPC check node $c$ to input node $i$. Finally, the message which the output node $o$ return back to the input node $i$ can be expressed as:

$$\tanh\left(\frac{m_{oi}^{(l)}}{2}\right) = \tanh\left(\frac{Z_o}{2}\right) \prod_{i' \neq i} \tanh\left(\frac{m_{i'o}^{(l)}}{2}\right) \tag{12}$$

where $m_{oi}^{(l)}$ is the message transmitted by the output node $o$ to the input node $i$ in the iteration $l$, $m_{i'o}^{(l)}$ is the message sent by input node $i$ to output node $o$ in iteration $l$, $Z_o$ is the channel LLR calculated by Eq. (7) based on the quantized value of the corresponding bit at the output node. After each round of iteration, the LLR of the input node is updated as:

$$m_i^{(l)} = \sum_{o} m_{oi}^{(l)} \tag{13}$$

When the mean value of the input node LLR (or equivalently, the corresponding amount of external information) exceeds a certain threshold, the second step of joint coding is performed.

### 3.4 Degree Profile Optimization

To further improve the performance of the rateless coded scheme, the degree profile in Eq. (2) deployed at the user is optimized. We resort to extrinsic information transfer (EXIT) analysis to do the optimization. Explicitly, we maximize the achievable rate under the constraint that the average extrinsic information transferred from the input nodes to the output nodes increases for each iteration until it reaches a threshold during the decoding. The detailed degree profile optimization procedure is not given here due to the limited space, for which the readers can refer to [9].

## 4 Numerical Simulation

### 4.1 Theoretically Achievable Rates

We use the case that the RRH does not quantify the signal, and directly transmitting the baseband signal (3) to the BBU pool as theoretical upper bound. It is easy to prove that when the quantization interval of RRH tends to 0 and the quantization threshold tends to be infinite, the LLR combination (8) of the BBU pool is equivalent to the maximum ratio combination. Therefore, the BBU pool receives the SNR as:

$$\gamma_{MRC} = \frac{P(\sum_{j=1}^{L} |h_j|^2 / \sigma_0^2)^2}{E\left[\left|\sum_{j=1}^{L} (h_j^* / \sigma_0^2) n_j\right|^2\right]} = \frac{P(\sum_{j=1}^{L} |h_j|^2 / \sigma_0^2)^2}{\sum_{j=1}^{L} |h_j|^2 / \sigma_0^2} = \sum_{j=1}^{L} \gamma_j \tag{14}$$

When the RRH is not quantized, the theoretical channel capacity of C-RAN single-user uplink system is $C$. Due to BPSK modulation, the theoretical capacity of binary input symmetric Gaussian channel with a SNR of $\gamma_{MRC}$ [15] can be derived as follows:

$$C(\gamma_{MRC}) = 1 - \frac{1}{2\sqrt{2\pi\gamma_{MRC}}} \int_{-\infty}^{\infty} \log_2(1 + e^{-x}) \cdot e^{-\frac{(x - 2\gamma_{MRC})^2}{8\gamma_{MRC}}} dx \tag{15}$$

which is the theoretical upper bound of the studied C-RAN system.

### 4.2 BER Performance of the System

We consider a scenario with single user and two RRHs. The user uses the LDPC code with a rate of 0.95 and a length of 10000 as a pre-coding of the rateless code. The correct decoding threshold of LDPC code is $x_u^{th} = 0.9818$. Let the noise variance at each RRH be $\sigma_0^2 = 1.4^2$. The channel fading coefficients of the users $S$ to $RRH_1$ and $RRH_2$ are respectively $h_1 = 0.7$ and $h_2 = 1.1$. The decoding overhead is defined as:

$$overhead = \frac{C \cdot N}{k} - 1 \tag{16}$$

where $C$ is the theoretical channel capacity of the uplink system given by Eq. (15), $N$ is the actual transmitted code length when decoding is successful, and $k$ is the user original information length. According to the EXIT analysis in article [9], we optimize the user's rateless code degree profile $\Omega(x)$ in Gaussian channels. The optimized degree profile $\Omega_{opt}(x)$ is given in the following:

$$\Omega_1 = 0.004715, \Omega_2 = 0.436706, \Omega_3 = 0.272642, \Omega_6 = 0.127585, \Omega_7 = 0.085293,$$
$$\Omega_{19} = 0.055493, \Omega_{20} = 0.011292, \Omega_{60} = 0.006274;$$

As a benchmark, we use the optimized degree profile for BEC given in [15]. Under different overhead, we compare the system BER achieved by degree profile $\Omega_{BEC}(x)$ and degree profile $\Omega_{opt}(x)$ respectively. Simulation results are shown in Fig. 3. It can be seen from that when the RRH applies 4-bit quantization, the degree profile $\Omega_{opt}(x)$ is about 5% better than the degree profile $\Omega_{BEC}(x)$. With 8-bit quantization, the degree profile $\Omega_{opt}(x)$ is about 3% better than the degree profile $\Omega_{BEC}(x)$ and about 4% better than the degree profile $\Omega_{opt}(x)$ with 4-bit quantization. When the RRH is quantized with 10-bits, the performance of the degree profile $\Omega_{opt}(x)$ tends to be the same as when using the 8-bit quantization, and the overhead is only about 11% more than the theoretical limit under the assumption of no signal compression at the RRH.

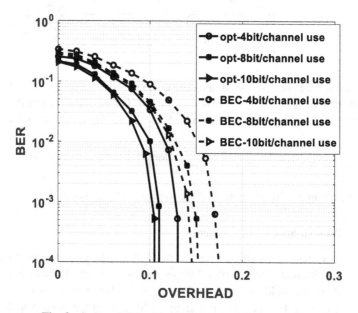

**Fig. 3.** System BER with different output degree profiles.

# 5   Conclusion

This paper mainly studies the transmission scheme based on rateless code in single-user uplink access scenario in C-RAN. A scalar quantization algorithm with lower complexity at RRH and a joint decompression, demodulation and decoding algorithm at BBU pool are designed. In order to further improve the performance, we optimized the degree profile based on the EXIT analysis for the rateless code. The simulation results show that the optimized is better than the BEC degree profile in bit error rate and its performance is close to the theoretical limit.

**Acknowledgement.** This work was supported by Zhejiang Provincial Natural Science Foundation of China under Grant No. LY17F010014.

# References

1. Cisco: Cisco visual networking index: global mobile data traffic forecast update, 2015–2020. White paper, pp. 1–39 (2016)
2. China Mobile: C-RAN: the road towards green RAN. White Paper (2011)
3. Shokrollahi, A.: Raptor codes. IEEE Trans. Inf. Theory **52**(6), 2551–2567 (2006)
4. Castura, J., Mao, Y.: Rateless coding over fading channels. IEEE Commun. Lett. **10**(1), 46–48 (2006)
5. Uppal, M., Yue, G., Wang, X., et al.: A rateless coded protocol for half-duplex wireless relay channels. IEEE Trans. Signal Process. **59**(1), 209–222 (2011)
6. Wu, Y., Qian, L., Maom H., et al.: Optimal power allocation and scheduling for non-orthogonal multiple access relay-assisted networks. IEEE Trans. Mob. Comput. (2018)
7. Wu, Y., Chen, J., Qian, L., et al.: Energy-aware cooperative traffic offloading via device-to-device cooperations: an analytical approach. IEEE Trans. Mob. Comput. **16**(1), 97–114 (2017)
8. Lu, W., Gong, Y., Liu, X., et al.: Collaborative energy and information transfer in green wireless sensor networks for smart cities. IEEE Trans. Industr. Inf. **14**(4), 1585–1593 (2018)
9. Zhang, Y., Zhang, Z.: Joint network-channel coding with rateless code over multiple access rely system. IEEE Trans. Wireless Commun. **12**(1), 320–332 (2013)
10. Zhang, Y., Zhang, Z., Yin, R., et al.: Joint network channel coding with rateless code in two-way relay systems. IEEE Trans. Wirel. Commun. **12**(7), 3158–3169 (2013)
11. Chen, X., Zhang, Z., Chen, S., et al.: Adaptive mode selection for multiuser MIMO downlink employing rateless codes with QoS provisioning. IEEE Trans. Wirel. Commun. **11**(2), 790–799 (2012)
12. Chen, X., Yuan, C.: Efficient resource allocation in rateless coded MU-MIMO cognitive radio network with QoS provisioning and limited feedback. IEEE Trans. Veh. Technol. **62**(1), 395–399 (2013)
13. Pukelsheim, F.: The three sigma rule. Am. Stat. **48**(2), 88–91 (1994)
14. Venkiah, A., Poulliat, C., Declercq, D.: Analysis and design of raptor codes for joint decoding using information content evolution. In: 2007 IEEE International Symposium on Information Theory, ISIT 2007, pp. 421–425. IEEE (2007)
15. Venkiah, A., Poulliat, C., Declercq, D.: Jointly decoded raptor codes: analysis and design for the biawgn channel. EURASIP J. Wirel. Commun. Netw. **2009**(1), 657970 (2009)

# Rateless Coded Downlink Transmission in Cloud Radio Access Network

Hong Peng, Yefan Zhang, Yu Zhang$^{(\boxtimes)}$, Lingjie Xie,
and Limin Meng

College of Information Engineering,
Zhejiang University of Technology, Hangzhou, China
{ph,yzhang,mlm}@zjut.edu.cn, 373679192@qq.com,
xielingjie@hotmail.como

**Abstract.** In this paper, we consider the downlink in cloud radio access networks (C-RAN). In the network, multiple users are served by a cluster of remote radio heads (RRHs), which are connected to the building baseband units (BBU) pool through the fronthaul links with limited capacity. We propose a rateless coded transmission scheme which the rateless coding, precoding, signal compression are jointly designed for the C-RAN downlink. In order to approach the theoretical limit, we further optimize the degree profiles of rateless code based on extrinsic information transfer (EXIT) function analysis.

**Keywords:** Cloud radio access networks · Rateless code
Degree profile optimization

## 1 Introduction

Nowadays mobile networks are becoming smaller while introducing the problems of inter-cell interference and cell association [1]. C-RAN is a new type mobile network architecture which has the potential to solve the above challenges [2]. In C-RAN, the baseband processing units are migrated from the base stations to the BBU Pool where the signals from/to multiple cells are jointly processed. Moreover, the C-RAN is able to adapt to non-uniform traffic and make a rational use of resources [3]. However, one of the main impairments to the implementation of C-RAN is given by the capacity limitations of the fronthaul links [4].

In this work, we consider the multi-user downlink scenario in C-RAN. The BBU pool performs multi-antenna precoding on the messages intended for the users which are then compressed and delivered to each RRH via capacity-limited fronthaul links. The C-RAN downlink has been widely studied, e.g., [5–10]. Authors in [5] investigated the criterion for the optimization of the precoding matrix which assume the knowledge of global channel states information (CSI). The authors in [6, 7] studied the compression scheme with the aim at lowering the effect of the compression noise which exploits the correlations of signals for RRHs. References [8–10] focused on the problem of resource allocation for the C-RAN network.

As for the coded transmission in the downlink of C-RAN, the design and practical implementations with fixed-rate channel codes can be found in [11]. Note that in

© ICST Institute for Computer Sciences, Social Informatics and Telecommunications Engineering 2018
L. Meng and Y. Zhang (Eds.): MLICOM 2018, LNICST 251, pp. 438–448, 2018.
https://doi.org/10.1007/978-3-030-00557-3_43

C-RAN, the fronthaul links with considerable lengths will cause additional signaling delay, which imposes stringent requirements on the decoding time at the BBU pool and users to insure hybrid automatic repeat request (HARQ) work properly [12]. Besides, rateless codes with optimized degree profiles can also approach the channel capacity like the fixed rate channel code [13]. Rateless coded transmission have been studied for various communication systems including relay systems and distributed antenna systems [14–16].

We consider the multi-user downlink of C-RAN network in which the RRHs and users are all equipped with single antenna and each RRH has an individual peak transmit power constraint. Explicitly, we deploys zero-forcing precoding at the BBU pool and a scalar quantizer based on automatic gain control (AGC) is used in this work. To further approach the theoretical limit, we optimize the degree profiles for the rateless code applied at the BBU based on the extrinsic information transfer (EXIT) function [17]. The optimization problem is non-convex, and we provide an approximation approach which the problem can be transformed to a tractable integer linear programming (ILP) problem. Simulations show that the proposed strategy with the optimized profile achieves a lower bit error rate (BER) as well as a higher throughput.

The remainder of this paper is organized as follows. In Sect. 2, we introduce the system model. The rateless downlink transmission strategy is described in Sect. 3. Section 4 gives the optimization method for degree profile. Simulation results are presented in Sect. 5 and Sect. 6 concludes the paper.

## 2  System Model

The downlink of C-RAN is illustrated in Fig. 1. We assume there are $M$ RRHs and $K$ users in the network. Each fronthaul links is restricted by an individual rate.

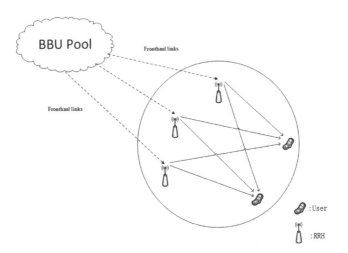

**Fig. 1.** System model of C-RAN downlink

The BBU pool first encodes the message $M_k$ intended for kth user using rateless code, which is then BPSK modulated. Figure 2 shows the operations in the BBU pool.

We use the zero-forcing precoding method, where the precoding matrix $w = GH^H(HH^H)^{-1}$, $H = [H_1, H_2, \ldots, H_K]^T$ represents the channel matrix, where $H_k$ is the channel parameters of kth user. The signals after precoding are

$$\tilde{x} = wS \tag{1}$$

where G is the diagonal AGC gain matrix and S is the modulated signals. We assume $q_m$ is the quantization noise received by mth RRH, therefore the message sent by the mth RRH

$$x_m = \tilde{x}_m + q_m \tag{2}$$

Specially, we assume that all RRHs have got information about G. Before the data streams sent out, $x = [x_1, \ldots, x_M]$ needs to be multiplied by $G^{-1}$ to recover the precoded signals. Assuming flat-fading channels, the received signal at the users can be written as

$$Y = HG^{-1}x + z \tag{3}$$

The noise at each user is assumed to be white Gaussian with a variance of $\sigma^2$. According to the ZF precoding principle, Eq. (3) also can be written as

$$Y = S + HG^{-1}q + z \tag{4}$$

where $HG^{-1}q = [Q_1, \ldots, Q_K]^T$ represents the quantization noise, and the signal power can be written as

$$E\left[|y_k|^2\right] = 1, k = 1, \ldots, K \tag{5}$$

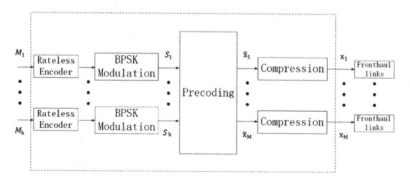

**Fig. 2.** The operations in the BBU pool

## 3 Rateless Codes Downlink Transmission Scheme

We employ Raptor codes in the BBU pool. The Low Density Parity Check (LDPC) code is used as the precoder of Raptor code in this paper.

### 3.1 Rateless Coding Scheme in the BBU Pool

Raptor code is parameterized by $(v, C, \Omega(x))$, where $\Omega(x)$ is the output-symbol degree distribution on $v$ source symbols which are the coordinates of codewords $C$. Specifically, $\Omega(x) = \sum_{d=1}^{D} \Omega_d x^d$ with $\Omega_d$ is the fraction of output symbols with degree $d$. A related notion of output degree distribution is $w(x) = \sum_{d=1}^{D} w_d x^{d-1}$, where $w_d$ is the fraction of edges in the LT part of the Raptor code connecting to a degree $d$ output symbol.

In the LDPC pre-code, a $v$ − bit information vector is first mapped to a $v'$ − bit codeword of $C$, where the codeword bits are usually referred to as the input symbols. Then via the LT code, a randomly selected fraction of input symbols are used to generate a new bit via the XOR operation based on $\Omega(x)$ and as this process repeats, a potentially infinite stream of bits — usually referred to as the output symbols — are generated and transmitted.

### 3.2 The Design of Quantizer Based on AGC

In this paper, we design a uniform symmetric scalar quantizer. The quantizer input thresholds are given by

$$
u_\ell = \begin{cases} -L_{max}, l = 1 \\ \left(\frac{-L}{2} - \frac{1}{2} + \ell\right)\Delta, l = 2, 3, \ldots, L \\ L_{max}, l = L+1 \end{cases} \tag{6}
$$

where $\Delta = (2/L)$ is the quantizer step-size, and $L = 2^b$ is the number of quantizer levels for $b$ quantizer bits. All of the received-constellation points at the quantizer output are within the normalized range $[-1, 1]$, which is achieved by setting

$$
G_{mm} = 1/\left(max\left\|\sum_{k=1}^{K} e_m^T w_k\right\|\right) \tag{7}
$$

Besides, the transmit power at mth RRH can be calculate as

$$
P_m = \sum_{k=1}^{K} \left|e_m^T w_k\right|^2 \tag{8}
$$

where $G_{mm}$ is the AGC gain for the mth RRH and $e^m$ is a standard basis vector which has 1 for its mth component and 0 for every other component. Besides, $w_k$ denotes the kth column of w.

### 3.3 Iterative Decoding Algorithm at the Users

The received signals are soft-demodulated before being decoded by the users. The bit $c$ takes 0 and 1 randomly, and the quantized bit $\tilde{c}_k = Q_k$ received by kth user with a corresponding Log Likelihood Ratio (LLR) of

$$LLR_i = \ln \frac{\Pr(\tilde{c}_k = Q_k | c = 0)}{\Pr(\tilde{c}_k = Q_k | c = 1)} \tag{9}$$

The BP algorithm operates in an iterative way where messages are passed along each edge between the neighboring nodes. The decoding algorithm takes two steps. First, messages follow the schedule on the global factor graph involving both the LT part and the LDPC part which is shown in Fig. 3. When the average LLR of the input symbols exceeds a certain threshold $x_u^{th}$, the decoding iteration is performed independently on the LDPC part to eliminate the residual error. The message passing rules in round $l$ can be written as

(i) The message from input symbol i to LDPC check node c

$$m_{ic}^{(l)} = \sum_o m_{oi}^{(l-1)} \tag{10}$$

(ii) The message from LDPC check node c to input symbol i

$$\tanh\left(\frac{m_{ci}^{(l)}}{2}\right) = \prod_{i' \neq i} \tanh\left(\frac{m_{i'c}^{(l)}}{2}\right) \tag{11}$$

where the product is over all input symbols adjacent to c other than $i$.

(iii) The message from input symbol i to output symbol o

$$m_{io}^{(l)} = \sum_{o' \neq o} m_{o'i}^{(l-1)} + \sum_c m_{ci}^{(l)} \tag{12}$$

where the first part is over all output symbols adjacent to $i$ other than $o$.

(iv) The message from output symbol o to input symbol i

$$\tanh\left(\frac{m_{oi}^{(l)}}{2}\right) = \tanh\left(\frac{Z_o}{2}\right) \prod_{i' \neq i} \tanh\left(\frac{m_{i'o}^{(l)}}{2}\right) \tag{13}$$

where $Z_o$ is the LLR of output symbol o calculated from (9) according to the corresponding received bits and the product is over all input symbols adjacent to o other than $i$.

(v) The LLR updates at input symbol i

$$m_i^{(l)} = \sum_o m_{oi}^{(l)} \tag{14}$$

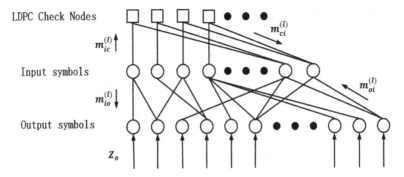

**Fig. 3.** BP decoding on the factor graph

We then gather these LLRs and run a decoding algorithm for the decoding on the LDPC part.

## 4  Degree Profile Design

We assume that the quantization noise is Gaussian distributed where $Q_k \sim (0, \sigma_k^2)$. Considering Eq. (4), the system model is similar to AWGN channel. In [17], the extrinsic information transfer function is used to analyze the joint decoding process and obtains the convergence condition that guarantees the successful decoding.

### 4.1  Information Content Evolution

We assume the sum of noise at users is Gaussian distributed. According to Eq. (9), the average LLR received by $k$th user from the channel is

$$\tau = \ln \frac{\frac{1}{\sqrt{2\pi(\sigma^2 + \sigma_k^2)}} e^{-\frac{(x-1)^2}{2(\sigma^2 + \sigma_k^2)}}}{\frac{1}{\sqrt{2\pi(\sigma^2 + \sigma_k^2)}} e^{-\frac{(x+1)^2}{2(\sigma^2 + \sigma_k^2)}}} = \frac{2}{\sigma^2 + \sigma_k^2} \tag{15}$$

The messages (i.e., LLRs) passed between nodes during iterative decoding can be seen as a random variable that satisfies a symmetric Gaussian distribution with mean $\tau$ and variance $2\tau$, the extrinsic information (EI) corresponding to such a message can be derived as follows [17]

$$J(\tau) = 1 - \frac{1}{\sqrt{4\pi\tau}} \int_{-\infty}^{+\infty} \log_2(1 + e^{-\nu}) \exp\left(-\frac{(\nu - \tau)^2}{4\tau}\right) d\nu \tag{16}$$

We consider that the EI is passed between the LDPC part and the LT part in each round. The specific process at round $l$ is as follows

(i)  EI from input symbols to output symbols

$$x_v^{(l)} = \sum_{i=1}^{d_v} l_i J\left((i-1)J^{-1}(x_u^{l-1}) + J^{-1}\left(T\left(x_{ext}^{(l-1)}\right)\right)\right) \qquad (17)$$

where $l_i$ is the probability that a randomly chosen edge in the LT decoding graph of the Raptor code is connected to an input node of degree i.

(ii)  EI from output symbols to input symbols

$$x_u^{(l)} = 1 - \sum_{d=1}^{d_c} w_d J\left((d-1)J^{-1}\left(1 - x_v^{(l)}\right)J^{-1}\left(1 - J\left(\frac{2}{\sigma^2 + \sigma_k^2}\right)\right)\right) \qquad (18)$$

where $w_d$ is the fraction of edges in the LT part of the Raptor code connecting to a degree $d$ output symbol.

(iii)  EI from input symbols to LDPC check nodes

$$x_{ext}^{(l-1)} = \sum_i I_i J\left(iJ^{-1}\left(x_u^{(l-1)}\right)\right) \qquad (19)$$

where $I_i$ denotes the probability that a randomly chosen input node is of degree i.

(iv)  EI from LDPC check nodes to input symbols

$$T\left(x_{ext}^{(l-1)}\right) = \sum_{i=2}^{d_v} \Lambda_i J\left(iJ^{-1}\left(1 - \sum_{j=2}^{d_c} p_j J\left((j-1)J^{-1}\left(1 - x_{ext}^{(l-1)}\right)\right)\right)\right) \qquad (20)$$

where $\Lambda_i$ denotes the input symbols edge degree distribution and $p_j$ denotes the check nodes edge distribution in the LDPC part of Raptor code.

Considering the Eqs. (17)–(20), we give the recursive equation $x_u^{(l)} = \Phi\left(x_u^{(l-1)}, \sigma^2 + \sigma_k^2, w_d, T\left(x_{ext}^{(l-1)}\right)\right)$ that describes the evolution through joint decoding iteration of the EI at input symbols:

$$x_u^{(l)} = \Phi\left(x_u^{(l-1)}, \sigma^2 + \sigma_k^2, w_d, T\left(x_{ext}^{(l-1)}\right)\right)$$

$$= 1 - \sum_{d=1}^{d_v} w_d J\left((d-1)J^{-1}\left(1 - \sum_{i=1}^{d_c} l_i J\left((i-1)J^{-1}(x_u^{l-1}) + J^{-1}\left(T\left(x_{ext}^{(l-1)}\right)\right)\right)\right)\right)$$

$$+ J^{-1}\left(1 - J\left(\frac{2}{\sigma^2 + \sigma_k^2}\right)\right)\right) \qquad (21)$$

After the decoding is completed, we run a decoding algorithm on the LDPC part. The extrinsic information passing is no long analyzed on the LDPC part.

Obviously Eq. (21) has a linear relationship with the degree profile $w_d$. To guarantee a successful decoding, the following conditions should be satisfied: (1) $x_u^{(l+1)} > \Phi\left(x_u^{(l-1)}, \sigma^2 + \sigma_k^2, w_d, T\left(x_{ext}^{(l-1)}\right)\right)$; (2) $x_u^{(l_{max})} > x_u^{th}$, where $l_{max}$ is decoding iterations.

### 4.2  Optimization of Degree Profile

The intention is to maximize the rate $R = 1/\left(\beta \sum_{d=1}^{D} (w_d/d)\right)$, which is equivalent to minimize $\beta \sum_{d=1}^{D} (w_d/d)$ [18]. It is necessary to fix a choice of average input-symbol degree $\beta$, maximal output-symbol degree $D$, and targeted threshold $x_u^{th}$, and the following problem by linear programming

$$
\begin{aligned}
\min \quad & \beta \sum_{d=1}^{D} (w_d/d) \\
\text{s.t.} \quad & \forall d = 1, \ldots, D : w_d \geq 0 \\
& \sum_{d=1}^{D} w_d = 1
\end{aligned}
\tag{22}
$$

$$
\forall l = 1, \ldots, l_{max} : x_u^{(l+1)} > \Phi\left(x_u^{(l-1)}, \sigma^2 + \sigma_k^2, w_d, T\left(x_{ext}^{(l-1)}\right)\right)
$$

where $\left\{x_u^{(l)} : l = 1, \ldots, l_{max}\right\}$ is a set of spaced values in range $\left(0, x_u^{th}\right]$.

## 5  Simulation Results

In this section, we simulate the BER and throughout performance of the proposed downlink rateless coded transmission scheme with the optimized degree profile.

### 5.1  Theoretically Achievable Rates

We consider the theoretically achievable rate under the assumption that the quantization is not performed at the BBU pool and Eq. (4) is considered as

$$
Y = S + z \tag{23}
$$

Since BPSK modulation is utilized in the BBU pool, the capacity for a binary input additive Gaussian noise channel can be calculated as [18]

$$
C(\gamma_k) = 1 - \frac{1}{2\sqrt{2\pi\gamma_k}} \int_{-\infty}^{\infty} \log_2(1 + e^{-x}) \cdot e^{\frac{(x - 2\gamma_k)^2}{8\gamma_k}} dx \tag{24}
$$

where $\gamma_k = \frac{2}{\sigma^2}$ is the signal to noise ratio at kth user.

## 5.2  Performance of the Optimized Degree Profile for C-RAN Downlink

In the simulation, we consider the scenario where there are 2 users and 2 RRHs. Besides, we consider the channel matrix $H = \begin{vmatrix} 1.395 & 1.731 \\ 1.412 & 0.362 \end{vmatrix}$. We set $\sigma^2 = 4$. Moreover, the capacity of each fronthaul link is the same.

A rate-0.95 LDPC code is implemented as the pre-code of Raptor codes. The threshold $x_u^{th}$ is 0.9815 and the maximal output node degree $D$ is set to be 60.

### (1)  BER performance of the optimized degree profile.

We examine the BER performance of user 1. We first consider quantizer bit $b = 5$, and the variance of quantization noise $\sigma_1^2 = 0.0696^2$. The optimized degree profile $\Omega_{opt,user1,5bit}(x)$ :

$$\Omega_1 = 0.0051, \Omega_2 = 0.3846, \Omega_3 = 0.3089, \Omega_6 = 0.0707$$
$$\Omega_7 = 0.1458, \Omega_{18} = 0.0128, \Omega_{19} = 0.0626, \Omega_{60} = 0.0095$$

Then consider quantizer bit $b = 10$, and the variance of quantization noise $\sigma_1^2 = 0.0023^2$. The optimized degree profile $\Omega_{opt,user1,10bit}(x)$ :

$$\Omega_1 = 0.0051, \Omega_2 = 0.3843, \Omega_3 = 0.3098, \Omega_6 = 0.0634$$
$$\Omega_7 = 0.1539, \Omega_{19} = 0.0587, \Omega_{20} = 0.0157, \Omega_{60} = 0.0090$$

We simulate the BER for the optimized degree as well as the optimized degree profile without considering the quantization noise (when $\tau = \frac{2}{\sigma^2}$) and degree profile of BEC, under various overhead.

As shown in Fig. 4, the optimized profiles achieves a BER under $10^{-5}$ at a smaller overhead comparing with other two profiles. Moreover, it is observed that as the quantization bit $b$ becomes larger, the optimized profile achieves a lower BER.

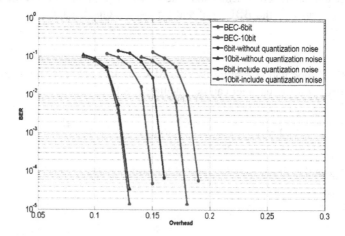

**Fig. 4.** BER curves of the optimized profile and other two profiles

(2) **Throughout performance of the optimized degree profile.**

We examine the throughout performance of user 1. The quantization bit $b = 10$, and the degree profile is $\Omega_{opt,user1,10bit}(x)$. The length of information blocks $k$ is set to be 9500.

As shown in Fig. 5, comparing with other two profiles, the optimized profile achieves a higher throughput which is within 0.13 away from the theoretical limit.

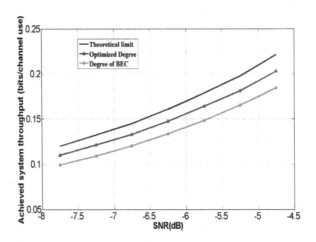

**Fig. 5.** Throughput performance of the optimized profile and other two profiles

## 6 Conclusion

In this paper, we proposed the downlink rateless coded transmission scheme in C-RAN. We fully investigated the design of quantizer based on AGC and degree profile optimization using EXIT analysis. The simulation results show that the optimized profile has better performance in the metrics of BER and throughput.

**Acknowledgement.** This work was supported by Zhejiang Provincial Natural Science Foundation of China under Grant No. LY17F010014.

## References

1. Andrews, J.: Seven ways that hetnets are a cellular paradigm shift. IEEE Commun. Mag. **51** (3), 136–144 (2013)
2. Lin, Y., Shao, L., Zhu, Z., Wang, Q., Sabhikhi, R.K.: Wireless network cloud: Architecture and system requirements. IBM J. Res. Dev. **54**(1), 4:1–4:12 (2010)
3. Marsch, P., et al.: Future mobile communication networks: challenges in the design and operation. IEEE Veh. Technol. Mag. **7**(1), 16–23 (2012)
4. Chandrasekhar, V., Andrews, J.G., Gatherer, A.: Femtocell networks: a survey. IEEE Commun. Mag. **46**(9), 59–67 (2008)

5. Simeone, O., Kang, J., Kang, J., et al.: Cloud Radio Access Networks: Uplink Channel Estimation and Downlink Precoding. arXiv pre-print (2016)

6. Lee, W., Simeone, O., Kang, J., et al.: Multivariate fronthaul quantization for downlink C-RAN. IEEE Trans. Signal Process. **64**(19), 5025–5037 (2016)

7. Park, S.H., Simeone, O., Sahin, O., Shamai, S.: Joint precoding and multivariate backhaul compression for the downlink of cloud radio access networks. IEEE Trans. Signal Process. **61**(22), 5646–5658 (2013)

8. Wu, Y., Qian, L., Mao, H., Yang, Y., Shen, X.: Optimal power allocation and scheduling for non-orthogonal multiple access relay-assisted networks. IEEE Trans. Mob. Comput. (2018). https://doi.org/10.1109/tmc.2018.2812722

9. Wu, Y., Chen, J., Qian, L., Huang, J., Shen, X.: Energy-aware cooperative traffic offloading via device-to-device cooperations: an analytical approach. IEEE Trans. Mob. Comput. **16**(1), 97–114 (2017)

10. Lu, W., Gong, Y., Liu, X., Wu, J., Peng, H.: Collaborative energy and information transfer in green wireless sensor networks for smart cities. IEEE Trans. Ind. Inform. **14**(4), 1585–1593 (2018)

11. Wübben, D., et al.: Decoder implementation for cloud based architectures. In: Proceedings of European Conference on Networks and Communications (2014)

12. Han, Q., et al.: On the Effect of Fronthaul Latency on ARQ in C-RAN Systems, pp: 1–12. ArXiv preprint (2015)

13. Castura, J., et al.: Rateless coding over fading channels. IEEE Commun. Lett. **10**(1), 46–48 (2006)

14. Zhang, Y., Zhang, Z.Y.: Joint network-channel coding with rateless code over multiple access relay system. IEEE Trans. Wirel. Commun. **12**(1), 320–332 (2013)

15. Zhang, Y., Zhang, Z.Y.: Joint network-channel coding with rateless in two-way relay system. IEEE Trans. Wirel. Commun. **12**(7), 3158–3169 (2013)

16. Chen, X.M., Zhang, Z.Y., Chen, S.L., Wang, C.: Adaptive mode selection for multiuser MIMO downlink employing rateless codes with QoS provisioning. IEEE Trans. Wirel. Commun. **11**(2), 790–799 (2012)

17. Venkiah, A., Poulliat, C., Declercq, D.: Jointly decoded raptor codes: analysis and design for the biawgn channel. EURASIP J. Wirel. Commun. Netw. **2009**(16), 657970 (2009)

18. Etesami, O., Shokrollahi, A.: Raptor codes on binary memoryless symmetric channels. IEEE Trans. Inf. Theory **52**(5), 2033–2051 (2006)

# The Second Round

# WiFi/PDR Integrated System for 3D Indoor Localization

Mu Zhou$^{(\boxtimes)}$, Maxim Dolgov, Yiyao Liu, and Yanmeng Wang

Chongqing Key Lab of Mobile Communications Technology,
Chongqing University of Posts and Telecommunications, Chongqing 400065, China
zhoumu@cqupt.edu.cn, maxsnezh@icloud.com, wonderful_yao@foxmail.com,
hiwangym@gmail.com

**Abstract.** In recent years, location-based services LBS have received extensive attention from scholars at home and abroad, and how to obtain location information is a very important issue. The creation of systems for solving problems of positioning and navigation inside buildings is a very perspective, actual and complicated task, especially in a multi-floor environment. To improve the indoor localization performance, we proposed a three-dimensional (3D) indoor localization system integrating WiFi/Pedestrian Dead Reckoning (PDR), where extended Kalman filter (EKF) is used to estimate target location. The algorithm first relies on MEMS in our mobile phones to evaluate the speed and heading angle of the test nodes. Second, for two-dimensional (2D) localization, the speed and heading angle as with as the results of the WiFi Fingerprint-based localization are utilized as the inputs to the EKF. Third, the proposed algorithm works out the height of the test nodes by utilize a barometer and geographical data which have been recorded in real time. Our experimental results in a real multi-layer environment indicate that the proposed WiFi/PDR integrated system algorithm means that the localization accuracy error is at least 1 m lower than WiFi and PDR itself.

**Keywords:** Wi-Fi fingerprinting · PDR · Extended Kalman Filter
Multi-floor positioning

## 1 Introduction

Indoor localization technology is widely used in shopping mall navigation, smart home, personnel search and rescue and other fields, with great commercial value and broad application prospects. High-precision indoor localization technology can bring immeasurable value to the enterprise. GPS [1] can provide good positioning accuracy for outdoor localization, but the satellite signal is seriously attenuated indoors [2], which is difficult to meet indoor localization needs and makes indoor localization technology a major challenge. Many indoor localization technologies utilize integrated sensors to assist in indoor localization systems to improve localization accuracy. Among them, Kalman filter is one of the widely used data fusion methods, but due to indoor multipath effect and

© ICST Institute for Computer Sciences, Social Informatics and Telecommunications Engineering 2018
L. Meng and Y. Zhang (Eds.): MLICOM 2018, LNICST 251, pp. 451–459, 2018.
https://doi.org/10.1007/978-3-030-00557-3_44

wall attenuation, Kalman filter is difficult to accurately describe indoor signals. Compared with outdoor scenario, indoor localization and navigation methods usually require higher accuracy and better environmental adaptability. In this situation, many localization technologies have been studied and even utilized in many special scenarios, such as WiFi fingerprinting, RFID (Bluetooth RFID) and other technologies [3–5].

It is well known that due to the low cost of equipment, extensive infrastructure deployment and high positioning accuracy, WiFi fingerprint based localization technology is very popular in indoor and underground environments [6–10]. However, complex indoor environments can cause blocking, attenuation, and multipath effects on Received Signal Strength Indication (RSSI) measurements. And RSSI is difficult to reflect accurate location information, which degrades the accuracy of fingerprint-based positioning. In order to solve this problem, some positioning technologies integrating WiFi fingerprint recognition and MEMS sensors are proposed in [11–15].

MEMS sensor based positioning techniques have been widely adopted for most mobile terminals currently integrate different types of sensors, such as accelerometers, magnetometers and barometers. In most cases, MEMS sensor-based positioning has low infrastructure costs and satisfactory positioning [16–19]. However, cumulative errors associated with MEMS sensor based positioning have long been considered one of the most important issues.

The main contributions of this paper are as follows. First, we use gait detection to optimize the speed calculation. In addition, we use the quaternion algorithm to improve the accuracy of the heading angle calculation. Second, we designed an extended Kalman filter (EKF) to reduce the cumulative error based on MEMS sensor positioning and large errors based on WiFi fingerprint recognition. Finally, in order to achieve 3D positioning in multi-layer scenes, a calculation algorithm based on floor height is proposed.

The rest of this paper is organized as follows. The second part introduces the integrated WiFi/PDR positioning algorithm and the high degree of calculation method. In the third part we integrated the data from wifi fingerprinting and MEMS sensors to verify our algorithm in a multi-layer scenario. In the fourth part, the experimental conclusions are utilized in the 3D indoor localization WiFi/PDR integrated system.

## 2   System Description

As shown in Fig. 1, the WiFi/PDR fusion multi-floor 3D positioning algorithm mainly includes four parts: the WiFi fingerprinting positioning, the PDR part, where speed and heading where determined, the EKF part, and the height calculation part. Firstly, we obtained WiFi fingerprinting based positioning, then the speed and heading information of the pedestrian were calculated through the measurement information obtained by the MEMS sensors, and then the combined data was used as the input of the Extended Kalman Filter (EKF). In the fourth step, the height information measured by the barometer. Finally, we got the 3D positioning result of the pedestrian.

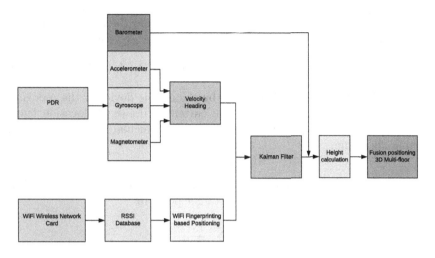

**Fig. 1.** System scheme.

## 2.1 WiFi Fingerprinting-Based Positioning

The indoor fingerprinting technology based on location fingerprint mainly includes two stages: offline phase and online phase. In offline phase, the location information and corresponding signals, such as RSSI, AOA, TOA, etc., are collected at the reference point (RP) of the target area. Then we calculate the distribution corresponding to the signals received by different RPs, and then construct an offline location fingerprint database. In online phase, the signals are collected in real time in the target area and the distribution of real-time signals is calculated, and then we compare it with the fingerprint database to find the target location. The best match RP is regarded as the estimated target position.

This paper uses the k-nearest neighbor (KNN) algorithm for localization. The KNN algorithm is a basic classification and regression method. For a training set, input new data, and find k data nearest to the data in the training set. If most of the k data belong to a certain class, the data belongs to this class.

The signal information received by the $i$th RP can be denoted as [20]

$$\mathbf{T}_i = \begin{bmatrix} \Pr(A_1O_1|\ Pt_i)\ \Pr(A_2O_1|\ Pt_i)\ \cdots\ \Pr(A_nO_1|\ Pt_i) \\ \Pr(A_1O_2|\ Pt_i)\ \Pr(A_2O_2|\ Pt_i)\ \cdots\ \Pr(A_nO_2|\ Pt_i) \\ \vdots\qquad\qquad \vdots\qquad\quad \ddots\qquad \vdots \\ \Pr(A_1O_v|\ Pt_i)\ \Pr(A_2O_v|\ Pt_i)\ \cdots\ \Pr(A_nO_v|\ Pt_i) \end{bmatrix} \quad (1)$$

Where A represents AP information, O represents the value obtained by the RSSI experiment, and Pt represents the position information of the RP. The mathematical expectation of the signal strength from each AP is calculated in the RP. The experimental results were utilized to build the required fingerprint database. The fingerprint for the $i$th RP can be expressed as:

$$\mathbf{T}_i = [\bar{\mathbf{S}}_i | Pt_i] = [\Pr(A_1\bar{O})\,\Pr(A_2\bar{O})\cdots\Pr(A_n\bar{O})|Pt_i] \tag{2}$$

If the WiFi signal strength detected by the mobile device of the user under test is $\mathbf{S}$, hen the distance between the current WiFi signal location feature parameters and the fingerprint database can be calculated by the following matching algorithm.

$$d_i = \left\| \mathbf{S} - \bar{\mathbf{S}}_i \right\| \tag{3}$$

Using the $K$-nearest neighbors algorithm, the $K$ smallest values of $d_i$ are used to compute the coordinates of the target point by

$$\bar{L} = \sum_{i \in \mathbf{C}} \frac{L_i}{d_i} \tag{4}$$

where $\mathbf{C}$ is the set made up by the $K$ smallest values of $d_i$ and $L_i$ means the coordinates of RP.

## 2.2   PDR (Pedestrian Dead Reckoning)

PDR (Pedestrian Dead Reckoning) positioning algorithm is a relative positioning algorithm. The basic principle of the PDR positioning algorithm is to use inertial sensors and magnetometers to measure the acceleration, angular velocity, and other information of pedestrian movement, so as to calculate the direction and distance of the pedestrian movement, and together with the known pedestrian position information from the previous moment, to calculate the present moment pedestrians location information. Therefore, when the pedestrian's initial position is known, the pedestrian's position information can be calculated continuously in real time. The basic principle is shown in the Fig. 2.

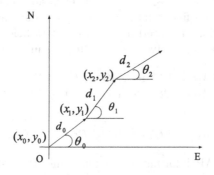

**Fig. 2.** Illustration of walking path.

If the position of the pedestrian at the initial time t1 is known $(x_0, y_0)$, the initial heading angle $\theta_0$ is the distance measured by the inertial sensor $d_0$, and the position of the pedestrian at the moment $(x_1, y_1)$ can be calculated as

$$\begin{cases} x_1 = x_0 + d_0 \cos \theta_0 \\ y_1 = y_0 + d_0 \sin \theta_0 \end{cases} \tag{5}$$

In the same way, the position of the pedestrian $(x_1, y_1)$ at the moment $t_1$ can be calculated by using the heading angle and the position $(x_2, y_2)$ of the moment $t_2$ as

$$\begin{cases} x_2 = x_1 + d_1 \cos \theta_1 = x_0 + d_0 \cos \theta_0 + d_1 \cos \theta_1 \\ y_2 = y_1 + d_1 \sin \theta_1 = y_0 + d_0 \sin \theta_0 + d_1 \sin \theta_1 \end{cases} \tag{6}$$

According to this calculation, we can calculate the position $(x_k, y_k)$ at the moment $t_k$ by

$$x_k = x_0 + \sum_{i=0}^{k-1} d_i \cos \theta_i$$
$$y_k = y_0 + \sum_{i=0}^{k-1} d_i \sin \theta_i \tag{7}$$

In the formula, $d_i$ it is the time $t_{i-1}$ to $t_i$ forward displacement, which is the heading $\theta_i$ of the pedestrian position at the time of $i$.

### 2.3   Extended Kalman Filter

When the WiFi signal is in an available state, the time update and the observation update are generally performed in the WiFi/PDR integrated system by using a Kalman filter to complete the state parameter, thereby reducing the estimation error. The time update process is expressed as

$$\begin{aligned} \bar{\mathbf{X}}_i &= \mathbf{F}_{k,k-1} \hat{\mathbf{X}}_{k-1} \\ \bar{\mathbf{P}}_k &= \mathbf{F}_{k,k-1} \mathbf{P}_{k-1} \mathbf{F}_{k,k-1}^T + \mathbf{Q}_{k-1} \end{aligned} \tag{8}$$

In addition, the Kalman filter observation update equation is written by

$$\begin{aligned} \bar{\mathbf{V}}_k &= \mathbf{Z}_k - \mathbf{H}_k \bar{\mathbf{X}}_k \\ \mathbf{P}_{\bar{V}_k} &= \mathbf{H}_k \bar{\mathbf{P}}_k \mathbf{H}_k^T + \mathbf{R}_k \\ \mathbf{G}_k &= \bar{\mathbf{P}}_k \mathbf{H}_k^T \mathbf{P}_{\bar{V}_k}^{-1} \\ \hat{\mathbf{X}}_k &= \bar{\mathbf{X}}_k + \mathbf{G}_k \bar{\mathbf{V}}_k \\ \mathbf{P}_k &= (\mathbf{I} - \mathbf{G}_k \mathbf{H}_k) \bar{\mathbf{P}}_k \end{aligned} \tag{9}$$

where $\bar{\mathbf{X}}_k$ is the prior probability estimate, $\hat{\mathbf{X}}_k$ is the posterior information estimate, $\mathbf{G}_k$ is the gain matrix of the Kalman filter, $\bar{\mathbf{P}}_k$ is the covariance matrix of prior probability State vector, $\mathbf{P}_k$ is the posterior probability covariance matrix of the state vector, $\mathbf{R}_k$ is the covariance matrix of the observation noise vector, and $\mathbf{Q}_{k-1}$ is the covariance matrix of the process noise. The subscript $k$ denotes the time, and the subscript $k$, $k-1$ represents the forward positional feature or covariate interference estimate from $k-1$ to $k$.

## 2.4   Altitude Calculation

Under normal circumstances, pedestrians are divided into three types: walking on flat roads, climbing stairs and descending the stairs. In these three cases, the method of solving two-dimensional positions is the same. Only a small difference in the size of the specified step, i.e., the step length should be set to the width of the stair step.

This article uses only the altitude value measured by the barometer to judge the upper and lower levels, and the actual height information is calculated by estimating the height from the floor. Pedestrians can be divided into two types of situations: (1) walking on the floor; (2) climbing the stairs or going down the stairs.

## 3   Experimental Results

The tests were carried on the first and second floors in a building of a university. The floors plan is described in Fig. 3, the first floor dimensions are $64.6 \times 18.5\,\mathrm{m}^2$ and second floor are $81.2 \times 18.5\,\mathrm{m}^2$. 10 D-Link DAP 2310 APs (marked in red) are disposed in this scenario, named $AP_1$, $AP_2$, $AP_3$, $AP_4$, $AP_5$, $AP_6$, $AP_7$, $AP_8$, $AP_9$, and $AP_{10}$. The RPs are evenly regulated with an spacing of 0.6 m.

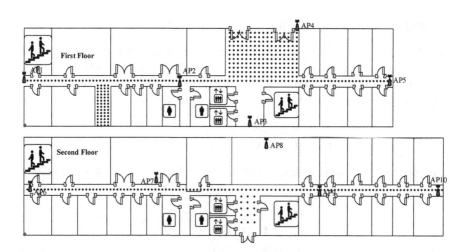

**Fig. 3.** Floor plan. (Color figure online)

In our experiment, the smartphone Samsung Galaxy S3 was selected as the receiver, which integrates an accelerometer, gyroscope, magnetometer, barometer, and WiFi module. We used two applications, Wifi sensors and Wifi localization for MEMS sensors and WiFi RSSI measurements. Measured data is stored on a Secure Digital (SD) card and the recording frequency is equivalent to 50 Hz. Figure 4 shows the WiFi AP and the mobile phone for test.

**Fig. 4.** WiFi AP and mobile phone for test.

Figure 5 shows the real path and positioning results of the test node. In the 3D plan, the estimated path is displayed utilizing PDR (traditional MEMS sensor-based localization method [16] and WiFi fingerprint-based localization method [4]) and the proposed integrated WiFi/PDR positioning method. The measurements indicate that the proposed method effectively reduces the errors which accumulated in the PDR, thus significantly improves the 3D positioning work in a multi-tier scenario compared to a separate WiFi and PDR system.

By adopting the proposed height work-out method, the traditional height calculation method based on barometer [21], the height work-out method based on K-means [22], the height estimation error cumulative distribution function (CDF)/PDR against PDR and WiFi, respectively Compare in Fig. 6. As can be seen from Figs. 5 and 6, the result of the calculation method based on the barometer height is not stable, and when the test node is located in the stairway, the efficiency of the height work-out method based on the K value is seriously deteriorated.

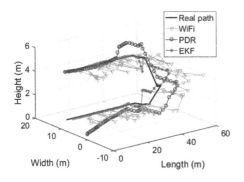

**Fig. 5.** Localization results.

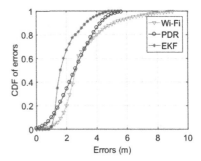

**Fig. 6.** CDF of localization error.

Errors of CDFs for 3D localization using PDR and WiFi/PDR integrated systems using WiFi with Kalman filter method is also included in Table 1. As depected in Table 1, we can see that the proposed method gets an average positioning error of 1.6 m and a 90% error is less than 3.4 m, which is much more precise than the performance of traditional Wi-Fi-based and PDR-based methods.

**Table 1.** Comparison of algorithm performance

|        | Largest positioning error (m) | Mean positioning error (m) | 67% positioning error (m) | 90% positioning error (m) |
| ------ | ----------------------------- | -------------------------- | ------------------------- | ------------------------- |
| Wi-Fi  | 9                             | 2.6                        | 2                         | 5.2                       |
| PDR    | 5.6                           | 2.6                        | 3.2                       | 4.2                       |
| EKF    | 5.4                           | 1.6                        | 2                         | 3.4                       |

## 4  Conclusion

In this paper, we propose a innovative smartphone-based indoor WiFi/PDR multi-layer location algorithm to locate a multi-layer environment in 3D. Experimental results indicate that our method can reduce the errors accumulated by the localization based on PDR sensors and the significant errors of WiFi Fingerprint-based localization. Compared with traditional PDR sensor-based localization and WiFi fingerprint-based localization methods, our method achieves higher accuracy measurements with an average localization error of 1.6 m and a 90% 3D positioning error of less than 3.4 m. In addition, for our future work we can adapt our system to different users by changing the step size.

**Acknowledgments.** This work is supported in part by Program for Changjiang Scholars and Innovative Research Team in University (IRT1299), Special Fund of Chongqing Key Laboratory (CSTC), Fundamental and Frontier Research Project of Chongqing (cstc2017jcyjAX0380), Scientific and Technological Research Foundation of Chongqing Municipal Education Commission (KJ1704083).

## References

1. Gao, Z., Yu, Y.: Interacting multiple model for improving the precision of vehicle-mounted global position system. Comput. Electr. Eng. **51**, 370–375 (2016)
2. Chowdhury, T., Elkin, C., Devabhaktuni, V., Rawat, D., Oluoch, J.: Advances on localization techniques for wireless sensor networks: a survey. Comput. Netw. **110**, 284–305 (2016)
3. Zhou, J., Shi, J.: RFID localization algorithms and applications-a review. J. Intell. Manuf. **20**, 695 (2009)

4. Tsukuda, D., Fujimoto, M., Oda, Y., Wada, T., Okada, H., Mutsuura, K.: A new indoor position estimation method of RFID tags for continuous moving navigation systems. In: IEEE International Conference on Indoor Positioning and Indoor Navigation, pp. 1–8 (2012)
5. Bahl, P., Padmanabhan, V.N.: RADAR: an in-building RF-based user location and tracking system. In: Annual Joint Conference of the IEEE Computer and Communications Societies, pp. 775–784 (2000)
6. Kim, H., Li, B., Wan, S.: Spatiotemporal location fingerprint generation using extended signal propagation model. J. Electr. Eng. Technol. **7**, 789–796 (2012)
7. Wu, C., Yang, Z., Liu, Y., et al.: WILL: wireless indoor localization without site survey. In: Proceedings of IEEE INFOCOM, pp. 64–72. IEEE Press (2012)
8. Yang, Z., Wu, C., Liu, Y.: Locating in fingerprint space: wireless indoor localization with little human intervention. In: International Conference on Mobile Computing and Networking, pp. 269–280. ACM (2012)
9. Jin, Y., Soh, W.S., Wong, W.C.: Indoor localization with channel impulse response based fingerprint and nonparametric regression. IEEE Trans. Wirel. Commun. **9**, 1120–1127 (2010)
10. Swangmuang, N., Krishnamurthy, P.: An effective location fingerprint model for wireless indoor localization. Pervasive Mob. Comput. **4**, 836–850 (2008)
11. Chen, L., Yang, K., Wang, X.: Robust cooperative Wi-Fi fingerprint-based indoor localization. IEEE Internet Things J. **3**, 1406–1417 (2016)
12. Malyavej, V., Kumkeaw, W., Aprpimai, M.: Indoor robot localization by RSSI/IMU sensor fusion. In: 10th IEEE International Conference on Computer, Telecommunications and Information Technology, Krabi, Thailand (2013)
13. Liu, X., Zhang, S., Lin, X.: WLAN/MARG integrated positioning system using data fusion. Syst. Eng. Electron. **34**, 2361–2365 (2012)
14. Wang, H., Lenz, H., Szabo, A., Bamberger J., Hanebeck, U.D.: WLAN-based pedestrian tracking using particle filters and low-cost MEMS sensors. In: 4th IEEE Workshop on Positioning, Navigation and Communication (2007)
15. Atia, M.M., Korenberg, M., Noureldin, A.A.: WiFi-aided reduced inertial sensors-based navigation system with fast embedded implementation of particle filtering. In: IEEE International Symposium on Mechatronics and its Applications (2012)
16. Tian, Z., Zhang, Y., Zhou, M.: Pedestrian dead reckoning for MARG navigation using a smartphone. EURASIP J. Adv. Signal Process. **2014**, 65 (2014)
17. Zhang, R., Bannoura, A., Hoflinger, F., Reindl, L.M., Schindelhauer, C.: Indoor Localization Using a Smart Phone. In: IEEE Sensors Applications Symposium (SAS), pp. 38–42 (2013)
18. Galvntejada, C.E., Galvntejada, J.I., Delgadocontreras, J.R.: Infrastructure-less indoor localization using the microphone, magnetometer and light sensor of a smartphone. Sensors **15**, 20355–20372 (2015)
19. Kim, B., Kong, S.H.: Indoor positioning based on Bayesian filter using magnetometer measurement difference. In: Vehicular Technology Conference, pp. 1–5. IEEE (2015)
20. Li, Z., Wang, J., Gao, J.: An enhanced GPS/INS integrated navigation system with GPS observation expansion. J. Navig. **69**, 1041–1060 (2016)
21. Ye, H., Gu, T., Tao, X.: Scalable floor localization using barometer on smartphone. Wirel. Commun. Mob. Comput. **16**, 2557–2571 (2016)
22. Wei, L.: Localization Algorithm Analysis Based on K-means Clustering. J. Guangxi Univ. Technol. PP. 2696–2704 (2012)

# Highly-Available Localization Techniques in Indoor Wi-Fi Environment: A Comprehensive Survey

Mu Zhou, Oyungerel Bulgantamir[✉], and Yanmeng Wang

Chongqing Key Lab of Mobile Communications Technology,
Chongqing University of Posts and Telecommunications, Chongqing 400065, China
zhoumu@cqupt.edu.cn,oyukagerele@gmail.com,hiwangym@gmail.com

**Abstract.** With the increasing interests on received signal strength (RSS) fingerprint-based Wi-Fi localization, the requirement of recording reliable and accurate RSS fingerprints for radio map construction becomes a significant concern. The neighbor matching and Bayesian estimation is recognized as the two most representative algorithms for RSS fingerprint-based indoor Wi-Fi localization. To guarantee the accuracy performance of neighbor matching and Bayesian estimation algorithms, we introduce several method to eliminate RSS sample noise for the sake of improving the distance dependency of Wi-Fi RSS fingerprints.

**Keywords:** Wi-Fi localization · RSS correlation · Smooth filtering
Neighbor matching · Bayesian estimation

## 1 Introduction

A large amount of attention has been paid to the design of indoor highly-accurate and reliable localization systems in recent ten years with the significant growth of interests on the ubiquitous context-awareness and mobile computing [1–3]. Due to the requirements of special infrastructures and devices by ultrasonic wave (UW) [4], ultra-wideband (UWB) [5], infrared ray (IR) [6], radio frequency identification (RFID) [7], Bluetooth [8], and inertial navigation system (INS) [9] based localization systems, the received signal strength (RSS) fingerprint-based Wi-Fi localization system is more preferable owing to the advantages of sufficient accuracy in indoor localization, widely-deployed Wi-Fi infrastructures, and free 2.4 GHz Industrial, Scientific and Medical (ISM) band [10–12]. Another good reason to the popularization of indoor Wi-Fi localization is that the Global Navigation Satellite System (GNSS) (e.g., GPS in USA [13], Global Navigation Satellite System (GLONASS) in Russia [14], BD in China [15], and Galileo Positioning System in Europe [16]) cannot work well in urban and indoor environments due to the poor quality of RSS received from satellites. On this basis, we compare several typical indoor location systems in Table 1.

© ICST Institute for Computer Sciences, Social Informatics and Telecommunications Engineering 2018
L. Meng and Y. Zhang (Eds.): MLICOM 2018, LNICST 251, pp. 460–469, 2018.
https://doi.org/10.1007/978-3-030-00557-3_45

**Table 1.** Comparison of several indoor location systems

| Systems | Accuracy | Cost | Infrastructures and devices |
|---|---|---|---|
| UW [4] | Cm-level accuracy but limited within a room and easily interfered by sound sources | Extra infrastructures and devices | Multiple UW emitters and receivers |
| UWB [5] | Cm-level accuracy but strict time synchronization required | Extra infrastructures and devices | Multiple UWB emitters and receivers |
| IR [6] | Cm-level accuracy but limited within a room and easily interfered by light sources | Extra infrastructures and devices | Multiple IR emitters and receivers |
| RFID [7] | With errors less than 1 m in passive mode and with errors between 3 m and 5 m in active mode | Extra infrastructures and devices but easily built in | Single RFID tag without battery power in passive mode and multiple RFID tag with battery power lasting for several years in active mode |
| Bluetooth [8] | With errors between 1 m and 5 m | Extra infrastructures and devices but easily built in | Single Bluetooth beacon for 2D localization and multiple Bluetooth beacons for 3D localization with battery power lasting for several years |
| INS [9] | With errors less than 1 m but easily interfered by drift | Existing function and easily accessed | Micro-Electro-Mechanical Systems with wide operating temperature range |
| Wi-Fi [10] | M-level accuracy but easily interfered by environmental factors | Existing infrastructures and devices | Single access point for proximity localization and multiple access points for fingerprintbased and propagation model-based localization |

Up to now, there are three typical categories of Wi-Fi localization algorithms: RSS fingerprint-based, time of arrival (TOA) and angle of arrival (AOA)-based, and propagation model-based localization. Based on the consideration of localization accuracy and computation and maintenance cost, RSS fingerprint-based localization algorithm is preferred [17–19]. However, the existence of burst noise, e.g., the adjacent-channel interference from cordless phones, Bluetooth devices, and near field communication devices and the human body and indoor infrastructure shadowing, is recognized as one of the most significant drawbacks of Wi-Fi RSS fingerprint-based localization [20,21]. In response to this compelling drawback, we propose as a new approach to eliminate the RSS samples which are interfered by burst noise for the sake of improving the accuracy of neighbor matching and Bayesian estimation algorithms in Wi-Fi localization. Much different from many of the existing fingerprint filtering approaches, there is no need to record RSS statistics (e.g., RSS mean, median, maximum, and minimum) and RSS distributions (e.g., Gaussian fitting curves) at each reference point (RP). The localization accuracy is examined in a typical indoor scenario, a straight corridor, which is also used in [17,35,37,38]. The location target is moving in a normal course and only two RSS samples are recorded at each location for the testing. The rest of this paper is organized as follows. Section 2 shows using Wi-Fi technique on Wi-Fi localization. Section 3 shows that Network Deployment and Fingerprint-based Wi-Fi localization system, TOA and AOA-based Localization, Propagation Model-based Localization respectively. Experimental result is discussed In Sect. 3. Finally, we conclude this paper in Sect. 4.

## 2    Using Wi-Fi Technique

With the remarkable growth of location-based services (LBSs), the work on indoor localization has attracted significant attention in recent decade. The LBSs have ranged from the military to public uses, like the emergency rescue, guidance in airports and unfamiliar buildings, and entity management inside modern buildings, libraries, and warehouses [22,23]. To achieve these goals, the Wi-Fi technique is suggested as a reliable and cost-efficient way to provide the highly-accurate, cost-efficient, and real-time indoor LBSs due to the two main reasons below.

The first main reason is that in many indoor and underground environments, GPS signals cannot be received due to the serious shadowing effect by the buildings and ground. Although the cellular network (e.g., WCDMA) can help to improve accuracy and reduce acquisition time of GPS receiver, the requirement of the additional radio frequency (RF) transceiver modules designed for cellular network significantly increases the device cost and power consumption of GPS receiver. As an alternative to indoor localization, the INS relies on accelerometer, gravimeter, compass, and many other sensors to infer the targets speed, height, orientation, and other actions [9]. The accuracy and scalability of INS are suffered from the error accumulation which is caused by sensor noise and the limited availability of motion sensors. Since the Wi-Fi networks are widely deployed in public hotspots and enterprise locations, the Wi-Fi fingerprint-based localization and tracking become more popular. The average errors by Wi-Fi fingerprint-based localization generally fall into the range between 2 m and 10 m with the response time in a few seconds.

The second main reason of using Wi-Fi technique to conduct indoor localization is that the target can calculate its own locations by itself, namely the mobile-based localization mode, or rely on the network to obtain its locations, namely the network-based localization mode. In network-based localization mode, the access points (APs) relay the received signals to a central location server to do location calculation and then send the localization results back to the target. Since the target is not involved in signal processing and location calculation process, there is no need to modify the conventional Wi-Fi network interface card (NIC) which can be easily designed and embedded into the existing mobile devices.

# 3    Network Deployment

Since the indoor Wi-Fi localization is normally based on the 802.11a/b/g infrastructures and devices, the deployment and maintenance are cost-efficient for the widespread use [24,25]. Although the targets location can be well-estimated based on three APs in the open environment by using triangulation algorithm, there are always more than three APs required for indoor localization due to the RSS refraction, reflection, scattering, and adjacent-channel and multi-path interference [26]. The network deployment including the deployment of APs and calibration of RPs should also be seriously considered for indoor Wi-Fi localization.

Up to now, there are mainly three representative methods for network deployment: (1) uniform deployment by which the RPs are uniformly calibrated in target environment [27]; (2) non-uniform deployment by which the locations of RPs and APs are optimized based on the criterion of coverage requirement [28]. For instance, the area with high priority of coverage requirement is more likely to be calibrated with more RPs; and (3) Zigzag deployment by which the average RSS difference between different RPs are maximized to improve the location resolution of RSS [29]. The detailed discussion on indoor Wi-Fi network deployment is beyond the scope of this paper. In our experiments, the RPs are uniformly calibrated and the three APs are fixed at the left and right ends of a straight corridor.

## 3.1    Fingerprint-Based Wi-Fi Localization System

Fingerprint-based localization is based on the calculation of the similarity between the off-line pre-stored fingerprints and the on-line newly recorded samples [17,18]. As the first fingerprint-based Wi-Fi localization system, RADAR defines the Euclidean distances between the fingerprints and the new samples as the similarities and selects the RP with the smallest distance, namely the nearest neighbor (NN), as the estimated position [17]. This process is named as the neighbor matching. If there are RPs to be selected as the NNs, namely the K nearest neighbors (KNN), the targets position can be estimated at the geometrical center of the KNN [17,30], [47]. The accuracy of the original RADAR system is about 4 m with probability [17], while the enhanced RADAR system by using the Viterbi-like algorithm [31] achieves the accuracy around 2.37 m to 2.65 m over 50 percentile and 5.93 m to 5.97 m over 90 percentile. In RADAR system, the response time is mainly determined by the time cost for the traversal of radio map to search for the NN(s). This cost increases dramatically with the dimensions of radio map. For instance, if there are RPs calibrated in target area and sample (of dimensions) recorded at each RP, the number of sample values stored in radio map equals to $(Ns * M) * Nr$.

Another representative fingerprint-based Wi-Fi localization algorithm to be discussed in this paper is the Bayesian estimation. Marylands Horus [18] is recognized as the most prominent Bayesian estimation based localization system which is featured with high accuracy and low computation cost. Horus mainly focuses on the issues including the relationship between the mean of RSS and the sample number, compensation for small-scale RSS fading, and RSS variations with respect to spatial characteristics. In Horus system, the target is estimated at the RP with the highest likelihood by Bayesian estimation. The experimental results in [32] show that the Horus system can achieve the accuracy of more than 90 percentile within 2.1 m. The increase of the number of samples at each RP improves localization accuracy due to the better estimation of the mean and standard deviation of the Gaussian RSS distribution at each RP. The drawback of Horus system is that a large amount of computation cost is required to calculate the small-scale compensation. For instance, to achieve small-scale compensation, we need to try combinations to perturb samples in our experimental environment which is covered by 9 APs.

Similarly, Castro in [33] developed another Bayesian estimation based localization system, Nibble, to infer the targets locations by using signal quality measurements. Nibble uses a different concept of localization accuracy which is defined as the proportion of correct readings in reading set. A correct reading is counted when the targets actual location is located in its most likely referred area. In [33], by consulting all the APs for each location request, the Nibble system can achieve 97% accuracy. To save computation cost, the Nibble system only consults three most neighboring APs to achieve 96% accuracy. Compared to RADAR and Horus, although the computation cost for coordinate calculation is not considered by Nibble, the recording of location frequency and frequency updating are required. The accuracy of Nibble heavily relies on the deployment of RPs. For instance, if the target is far away from its nearest RP, the localization accuracy cannot be guaranteed. The major difference between Horus and Nibble is the approach to record RSS distributions. The former one fits each RSS distribution as a Gaussian curve and stores the parameters of the fitted Gaussian curves into a database, while the latter one records the frequency of each RSS value and constructs a RSS distribution histogram. In [20], Kaemarungsi studied the variations of RSS distributions with respect to the interference of device orientation and body and infrastructure shadowing. The results in [20] can help to examine the properties of RSS fingerprints.

Besides neighbor matching and Bayesian estimation algorithms, pattern matching algorithm can also be used for fingerprint-based Wi-Fi localization. With the help of topological counter propagation network (CPN) and k-nearest neighborhood vector mapping, LENSR [34] can not only improve location speed, but also reduce computation cost. Similar work can be found in [35–37]. In [35], Outemzabet used particle filtering to enhance the accuracy of artificial neural network (ANN) based location system which is mounted with a digital compass. A compass and particle filtering approach are applied to avoid trajectory discontinuity and modify motion orientation respectively. In [36], the targets location is estimated by using a modular multi-layer perceptron (MMLP) which contains five key steps: RSS recording and outlier filtering, data normalization, neural network training, data post processing, and regression analysis to conduct location estimation. Different from LENSR and MMLP, a discriminant-adaptive neural network (DANN) is introduced in [37] to extract the most useful information into discriminative components for neural network training. In DANN, since most of the redundant information is discarded before neural network training, the localization accuracy and real-time capability are improved. In all, the training process is recognized as one of the most challenging parts for the better design of pattern matching based localization algorithm.

### 3.2   TOA and AOA-Based Localization

TOA and AOA-based localization are with the ideas of trilateration and triangulation algorithms. To enable the localization in 2-dimensional domain, the propagation time and arrival angles from 3 and 2 APs to the target are used for TOA and AOA-based localization respectively [38–40].

In TOA-based localization [38], by assuming that the propagation time is directly proportional to the distance, we apply trilateration algorithm to estimate the targets locations based on the distances from 3 APs to the target. These distances are calculated from the measured propagation time.

We should not only guarantee the precise time synchronization between APs and receiver, but also label the transmitting signal by the exact timestamps for the sake of precisely calculating the distances the signal has traveled. In concrete terms, the estimated location is determined by the hyperbolic curve which has the constant difference in signal arrival time from each pair of APs [39].

The two key advantages of AOA-based localization are that there are as few as 2 APs for 2-dimensional localization, and meanwhile the time synchronization is not required [40]. The localization accuracy could be seriously deteriorated when the signal is blocked by the walls or the target is significantly far away from APs. In all, TOA and AOA-based location systems involve substantial changes of both APs and receivers.

### 3.3   Propagation Model-Based Localization

As discussed in [41], the mean of RSS decreases logarithmically with the increase of the distance between AP and receiver in ideal space. If the small-scale fading dominants over the large-scale fading or the propagation models are not predicted precisely, the accuracy of propagation model-based localization could be degraded. Ahn [42] studied the integration of Wi-Fi, UWB, and ZigBee technologies for indoor localization and introduced a new way to the prediction of finer propagation model corresponding to the target domain by using an iterative model modification process.

Narzullaev [43] compared the performance of three representative propagation models: (1) log-distance model which is based on the assumption that the mean of RSS varies logarithmically with respect to the propagation distance; (2) multi-slope model which gives better estimation of RSS distributions and saves the effort for RSS recording; and (3) multi-wall model which provides the finest prediction of RSS in indoor environments. More studies on propagation model-based Wi-Fi localization can be found in [44,45]. Finally, Table 2 briefly

**Table 2.** Comparison of several indoor location solutions

| Solutions | Algorithms | Accuracy | Main cost | Availability |
|---|---|---|---|---|
| RADAR [17] | KNN and Viterbi-like enhanced KNN | 4 m within 50% by KNN; 2.37 m–2.65 m within 50% and 5.93 m–5.97 m within 90% by Viterbi-like enhanced KNN | Traversal of radio map to find the nearest neighbor(s) | On the same floor in a 3-storey building with dimensions of 43.5 m by 22.5 m and all the 70 RPs calibrated in linear corridors |
| Horus [32] | Bayesian estimation | 2.1 m within more than 90% | Small-scale compensation | On the fourth floor in a building with dimensions of 68.2 m by 25.9 m and 110 RPs and 62 RPs calibrated in linear corridors and rooms |
| Nibble [33] | Bayesian estimation | 97% accuracy by using all APs and 96% accuracy by using 3 neighboring APs | Recording of the frequency the target is at a certain location and the updating of frequency | On the second floor in a building with dimensions of 224 by 9 feet including 40 offices, three clusters of cubicles, and several conference rooms |
| LENSR [34] | CPN with KNN | 1 m within 90.6% and 1.5 m within 96.4% | Creation of the theoretical propagation model | Simulation environment with dimensions of 20 m by 20 m and all the RPs calibrated with the interval of 1 m |
| Outemz abet [35] | Enhanced ANN | 39% and 50% accuracy improvement by using nonlinear and linearized filtering compared to Kalman filtering | Particle filtering | On the fifth floor in a building which has a trapezoidal shape with dimensions of 95 m, 70 m, and 40 m and all the 555 RPs calibrated in linear corridors |
| MMLP [36] | MMLP | 0.1258 m error in average and the maximum error of 2.1667 m | Filtering of the timely nonregular patterns for neural network training | On the third floor in a building covering an area of 286 m² and 24 RPs and 39 RPs calibrated in linear corridors and rooms |
| DANN [37] | DANN | 4 m within 88.6% and 2.5 m within 70.48% | Extraction of the most useful information into discriminative components for neural network training | On the same floor in a building with dimensions of 24.6 m by 17.6 m and all the 45 RPs calibrated in linear corridors with the interval of about 2 m |
| TOA [38] | Trilateration | Average root-mean-square error (RMSE) of 1.1 m | Precise time synchronization between APs and receiver | In a linear corridor with an AP mounted on one end of the corridor and the RPs calibrated at 2 m increments |
| Ahn [42] | Propagation model | Most of the errors falling into the range of [2 m, 4 m] | Integration of Wi-Fi, UWB, and ZigBee technologies | In an office with 5 reference transmitters and mobile reference tags fixed 3 m height |
| Narzullaev [43] | Propagation model | Average error of 5.9 m, 5.3 m within 50%, 7.3 m within 67%, and 9.6 m within 90% | Optimization of calibration procedure | In an office with dimensions of 18 m by 12 m and 51 RPs calibrated in a 2 m-grid |

compares the previously mentioned location solutions in terms of algorithms, accuracy, main cost, and availability.

## 4 Conclusion

In this paper, we have reviewed and studied several comparisons of the computations to improve the distance dependency of Wi-Fi RSS fingerprints and enhance the location accuracy of neighbor matching and Bayesian estimation for Wi-Fi localization. Because it is cannot work well in urban and indoor environment due to the poor quality of RSS received from satellites. There are three typical categories of Wi-Fi localization algorithms: RSS fingerprint-based, time of arrival (TOA) and angle of arrival (AOA)-based, and propagation model-based localization. In this paper can be considered of localization accuracy and computation and maintenance cost, RSS fingerprint-based indoor Wi-Fi localization algorithm is preferred. The major contribution of this paper is that based on autocorrelation property of the real Wi-Fi RSS sequences, we present to eliminate the unstable RSS samples which are much likely to be interfered by burst noise. A reliable approach to be used to detect the existence of burst noise in each RSS sequence forms another interesting direction.

**Acknowledgments.** The authors wish to thank the reviewers for the careful review and valuable suggestions. This work is supported in part by the National Natural Science Foundation of China (61771083,61704015), Program for Changjiang Scholars and Innovative Research Team in University (IRT1299), Special Fund of Chongqing Key Laboratory (CSTC), Fundamental and Frontier Research Project of Chongqing (cstc2017jcyjAX0380, cstc2015jcyjBX0065), Scientific and Technological Research Foundation of Chongqing Municipal Education Commission (KJ1704083), University Outstanding Achievement Transformation Project of Chongqing (KJZH17117), and Postgraduate Scientific Research and Innovation Project of Chongqing (CYS17221).

## References

1. Jin, Y., Soh, W., Wong, W.: Indoor localization with channel impulse response based fingerprint and fonparametric regression. IEEE Trans. Wirel. Commun. **9**, 1120–1127 (2010)
2. Zhou, M., Tian, Z., Xu, K., Yu, X., Wu, H.: Error analysis for RADAR neighbor matching localization in linear logarithmic strength varying Wi-Fi environment. Sci. World J. 15 p. Article ID 647370 (2014)
3. Casas, A.R., Falco, J., Gracia, H., Artigas, J.I., Roy, A.: Location-based services for elderly and disabled people. Comput. Commun. **31**, 1055–1066 (2008)
4. Hazas, M., Hopper, A.: Broadband ultrasonic location systems for improved indoor positioning. IEEE Trans. Mob. Comput. **5**, 536–547 (2006)
5. Steiner, C., Wittneben, A.: Low complexity location fingerprinting with generalized UWB energy detection receivers. IEEE Trans. Signal Process. **58**, 1756–1767 (2010)
6. Hernandez, A., Badorrey, R., Choliz, J., Alastruey, I.: Accurate indoor wireless location with IR UWB systems a performance evaluation of joint receiver structures and TOA based mechanism. IEEE Trans. Consum. Electron. **54**, 381–389 (2008)

7. Silva, R.D.A., Goncalves, P.A.D.S.: Enhancing the efficiency of active RFID-based indoor location systems. In: IEEE Wireless Communications and Networking Conference, pp. 1–6 (2009)
8. Aparicio, S., Perez, J., Bernardos, A.M., Casar, J.R.: A fusion method based on Bluetooth and WLAN technologies for indoor location. In: IEEE Multi-Sensor Fusion and Integration for Intelligent Systems Conference, pp. 487–491 (2008)
9. Pan, J.J., Pan, S.J., Yin, J., Ni, L.M., Yang, Q.: Tracking mobile users in wireless networks via semi-supervised colocalization. IEEE Trans. Pattern Anal. Mach. Intell. **34**, 587–600 (2012)
10. Kaemarungsi, K., Krishnamurthy, P.: Modeling of indoor positioning systems based on location fingerprinting. In: IEEE INFOCOM, pp. 1012–1022 (2004)
11. Zhou, M., Wong, A.K., Tian, Z., Zhang, V.Y., Yu, X., Luo, X.: Adaptive mobility mapping for people tracking using unlabelled Wi-Fi shotgun reads. IEEE Commun. Lett. **17**, 87–90 (2013)
12. Zhou, M., Tian, Z., Xu, K., Yu, X., Wu, H.: Theoretical entropy assessment of fingerprint-based Wi-Fi localization accuracy. Expert Syst. Appl. **40**, 6136–6149 (2013)
13. Kayton, M.: Global positioning system: signals, measurements, and performance. IEEE Aerosp. Electron. Syst. Mag. **17**, 36–37 (2002)
14. Broumandan, A., Nielsen, J., Lachapelle, G.: Indoor GNSS signal acquisition performance using a synthetic antenna array. IEEE Trans. Aerosp. Electron. Syst. Mag. **47**, 1337–1350 (2011)
15. Chen, C., Zhang, X.: Simulation analysis of positioning performance of BeiDou-2 and integrated BeiDou-2/GPS. In: IEEE Communications and Mobile Computing Conference, vol. 2, pp. 505–509 (2010)
16. Hu, H., Yuan, C.: Performance analysis of Galileo global position system. In: IEEE Power Electronics and Intelligent Transportation System Conference, pp. 396–399 (2009)
17. Bahl, P., Padmanabhan, V.N.: RADAR: an in-building RF-based user location and tracking system. In: IEEE INFOCOM, pp. 775–784 (2000)
18. Youssef, M., Agrawala, A.: The horus location determination system. Wirel. Netw. **14**, 357–374 (2008)
19. Figuera, C., Alvarez, J.L.R., Jimenez, I.M., Curieses, A.G.: Time-space sampling and mobile device calibration for WiFi indoor location systems. IEEE Trans. Mob. Comput. **10**, 913–926 (2011)
20. Kaemarungsi, K., Krishnamurthy, P.: Properties of indoor received signal strength for WLAN location fingerprinting. In: IEEE MOBIQUITOUS, pp. 14–23 (2004)
21. Alasti, H., Xu, K., Dang, Z.: Efficient experimental path loss exponent measurement for uniformly attenuated indoor radio channels. In: IEEE Southeast Conference, pp. 255–260 (2009)
22. Cura, T.: A parallel local search approach to solving the uncapacitated warehouse location problem. Comput. Ind. Eng. **59**, 1000–1009 (2010)
23. Hansen, T.R., Bardram, J.E., Soegaard, M.: Moving out of the lab: deploying pervasive technologies in a hospital. IEEE Pervasive Comput. **5**, 24–31 (2006)
24. Swangmuang, N., Krishnamurthy, P.: An effective location fingerprint model for wireless indoor localization. Pervasive Mob. Comput. **4**, 836–850 (2008)
25. Zhou, M., Xu, Y., Ma, L., Tian, S.: On the statistical errors of radar location sensor networks with built-in Wi-Fi gaussian linear fingerprints. Sensors **12**, 3605–3626 (2012)
26. Zhou, M., Xu, Y., Tang, L.: Multilayer ANN indoor location system with area division in WLAN environment. J. Syst. Eng. Electron. **21**, 914–926 (2010)

27. Ouyang, R.W., Wong, A.K., Lea, C.T., Chiang, M.: Indoor location estimation with reduced calibration exploiting unlabeled data via hybrid generative/discriminative learning. IEEE Trans. Mob. Comput. **11**, 1613–1626 (2012)

28. Fang, S., Lin, T.: A dynamic system approach for radio location fingerprinting in wireless local area networks. IEEE Trans. Commun. **58**, 1020–1025 (2010)

29. Zhao, Y., Zhou, H., Li, M.: Indoor access points location optimization using differential evolution. In: IEEE CSSE, pp. 382–385 (2008)

30. Xu, Y., Zhou, M., Meng, W., Ma, L.: Optimal KNN positioning algorithm via theoretical accuracy criterion in WLAN indoor environment. In: IEEE GLOBECOM, pp. 1–5 (2010)

31. Bahl, P., Padmanabhan, V. N.: Enhancements to the RADAR user location and tracking system, Microsoft Corpration, Technical report, MSR-TR-2000-12

32. Youssef, M., Agrawala, A., Shankar, A.U.: WLAN location determination via clustering and probability distributions. In: IEEE Pervasive Computing and Communications Conference, pp. 143–151 (2003)

33. Castro, P., Chiu, P., Kremenek, T., Muntz, R.: A probabilistic room location service for wireless networked environments. In: Abowd, G.D., Brumitt, B., Shafer, S. (eds.) UbiComp 2001. LNCS, vol. 2201, pp. 18–34. Springer, Heidelberg (2001). https://doi.org/10.1007/3-540-45427-6_3

34. Kurt, D., Milos, M.: Wireless based object tracking based on neural networks. In: IEEE ICIEA, pp. 308–313 (2008)

35. Outemzabet, S., Nerguizian, C.: Accuracy enhancement of an indoor ANN-based fingerprinting location system using particle filtering and a low-cost sensor. In: IEEE VTC Spring, pp. 2750–2754 (2008)

36. Ahmad, U., Gavrilov, A., Lee, S., Lee, Y.: Modular multilayer perceptron for WLAN based localization. In: IEEE IJCNN, pp. 3465–3471 (2006)

37. Fang, S., Lin, T.: Indoor location system based on discriminant-adaptive neural network in IEEE 802.11 environments. IEEE Trans. Neural Netw. **19**, 1973–1978 (2008)

38. Golden, S.A., Bateman, S.S.: Sensor measurements for Wi-Fi location with emphasis on time-of-arrival ranging. IEEE Trans. Mob. Comput. **6**, 1185–1198 (2007)

39. Schwalowsky, S., Trsek, H., Exel, R., Kero, N.: System integration of an IEEE 802.11 based TDOA localization system. In: IEEE Precision Clock Synchronization for Measurement Control and Communication Conference, pp. 55–60 (2010)

40. Nasipuri, A., Li, K.: A directionality based location discovery scheme for wireless sensor networks. In: ACM Wireless Sensor Networks and Applications Conference, vol. 6, pp. 1185–1198 (2002)

41. Emery, M., Denko, M.K.: IEEE 802.11 WLAN based real-time location tracking in indoor and outdoor environments. In: IEEE CCECE, pp. 1062–1065 (2007)

42. Ahn, H.S., Yu, W.: Wireless localization networks for indoor service robots. In: IEEE/ASME MESA, pp. 65–70 (2008)

43. Narzullaev, A., Park, Y.W., Jung, H.Y.: Accurate signal strength prediction based positioning for indoor WLAN systems. In: IEEE/ION PLANS, pp. 685–688 (2008)

44. Widyawan, Klepal, M., Pesch, D.: Influence of predicted and measured fingerprint on the accuracy of RSSI-based indoor location systems. In: IEEE WPNC, pp. 145–151 (2007)

45. Borrelli, A., Monti, C., Vari, M., Mazzenga, F.: Channel models for IEEE 802.11b indoor system design. In: IEEE ICC, pp. 3701–3705 (2004)

# Detecting Phishing Websites with Random Forest

Shinelle Hutchinson[(⊠)], Zhaohe Zhang[(⊠)], and Qingzhong Liu[(⊠)]

Sam Houston State University, Huntsville, TX, USA
{sdh053,zxz003,liu}@shsu.edu

**Abstract.** Phishing has been a widespread issue for many years, claiming countless victims, some of which have not even realized that they fell prey. The sole purpose of phishing is to obtain sensitive information from its victims. There have yet to be a consensus on the best way to detect phishing. In this paper, we analyze web-based phishing detection by using Random Forest. Some important URL features are identified and our study shows that the detection performance with feature selection is improved.

**Keywords:** Phishing · Random forest · Classification · Website Detection

## 1 Introduction

Phishing is a cyberattack rooted in scare tactics, with the sole purpose of eliciting personally identifiable information (PII) from its victims. An attacker disseminates a fraudulent version of a legitimate website, usually via email, telephone or text messages [1], in the hope that the victim would believe the claims made in the email. A successful phishing attack can result in an attacker obtaining credit card details and login information.

With the ever-increasing number of Internet users, comes even more data that needs to be protected. This data includes login information and credit card information, both of which are priceless to cyber criminals. These cybercriminals would try anything to gain this information. One such way that has been overutilized is via phishing websites.

Phishing can occur in three forms: web-based phishing where a website is duplicated to resemble a trusted website and tricks users into submitting sensitive information [2]. Email-based phishing, where an attacker sends email to countless users claiming some account issue, in hope some of them fall for it. Email phishing usually involves web-based phishing as well [2]. Malware-based phishing where malicious code is injected into a legitimate website and when the user visits that site, the malicious soft-ware is installed on the user's system [2].

Our paper focuses on web-based phishing detection and aims to identify the most relevant subset of features that can accurately identify phishing URLs, using the Random Forests classifier.

---

S. Hutchinson and Z. Zhang—equal contribution.

© ICST Institute for Computer Sciences, Social Informatics and Telecommunications Engineering 2018
L. Meng and Y. Zhang (Eds.): MLICOM 2018, LNICST 251, pp. 470–479, 2018.
https://doi.org/10.1007/978-3-030-00557-3_46

## 2   Related Work

Recent research in phishing detection saw the use of sophisticated approaches that all prove worthwhile. We've studied four such approaches in an attempt to better the current detection rate of phishing URLs.

One method proposed for the detection of phishing websites was the use of Public Key Certificates. In an article by Dong et al. [2], they highlighted a method of using the structure of the X.509 certificates to confirm phishing websites. Their method used machine-learning to build a phishing detection system. This system contained a Certificate Downloader, Feature Extractor, Classification Executor and a Decision Maker. A total of 42 features were selected based on the structure and content of the X.509 certificate. Decisions were made based on the output of six classification algorithms including Naïve Bayes Tree and Random Forests. This model was an improved alternative to traditional detection approaches, like blacklisting, as it could be run by end users in real time. It also did not require frequent updates from a central server, which eliminated any vulnerabilities users may have faced if they were using blacklists. However, this model was susceptible to sophisticated learning attacks such as evasion and poisoning.

Rao and Ali [3], developed a desktop application called PhishShield, which was able to detect phishing URLs based on heuristics and whitelists. Decisions are made based on Footer links with NULL values, Zero links in the body of the HTML, Copyright Content, Title Content and Website Identity. PhishShield prides itself on being able to detect phishing sites that employ Image Based Phishing Attacks. Rao and Ali also claim that a heuristic approach resulted in fewer false positives and false negatives. Unfortunately, PhishShield fails when its parse, JSoup, fails and also when all the filters are bypassed.

Rao and Pais [4] proposed a phishing detection approach that used automation of human behavior. Their model would submit fake credentials to the suspected phishing website in an attempt to determine if the site was indeed phishing. This approach was able to detect phishing websites that used captcha verification on its login page and those that contained embedded HTML text. One advantage over the other approaches discussed so far is that this method does not require any data to be trained. However, this approach can only detect phishing websites that use login pages.

Kumar et al. [5] proposed a datamining approach to extract URL links from emails. The proposed algorithm had two phases to detect the phishing website: phase one extracted all URLs from an email, the application (DC scanner) was used to verify the domain authority and other information that might be hidden under the HTML code; phase two checked that the web page sent the contents of a form to a web server. The application verified that the URL links in the web page was the same as in the domain. If the URLs pass all the checks in phases one and two, the email/link was deemed as non-phishing website. Unfortunately, this design was unable to detect malware-based phishing attacks.

Our approach would aim to improve on a machine learning take on phishing detection in hopes of achieving higher accuracy than previously attainable.

## 3 Methodology

The aim of phishing websites is to trick users into submitting their private information like login credentials or credit card information. Some of these websites are easily recognizable as illegitimate but others require deeper analysis. One method of conducting a deeper analysis of websites is to look at their URLs.

In order to detect phishing websites with high precision and recall, we carefully select specific features that represent each URL. These features are used in training and testing inputs. We divide this input into four different arrays: training input, training output, testing input and testing output. We then use the training input array to train our Random Forest classifier. Once the classifier is trained to accept the specific features and make the appropriate decision, we used the testing input to test the classifier. This process [9] is summarized in Fig. 1. These predictions are then evaluated based on accuracy, precision, recall and F-score.

We've recorded these four scores for five different subsets of features and compared them. Our goal was to find the subset of features that give the highest precision and recall rates.

### 3.1 Data

We collected our training and test data from the UCI phishing dataset [6] that is publicly available. This dataset contained 2456 unique URL instances and a total of 11,055 URLs of which 6,157 are phishing and 4,898 are legitimate sites. Each row represented a URL and each URL was previously parsed and represented according to 30 features which could determine whether or not the URL is used for phishing or just identify a specific feature as suspicious for a particular URL. The features considered include whether or not an IP Address is used instead of a URL, the length of the URL, the presence of link tags to the same domain as the webpage and whether or not the webpage uses IFrames. At the end of each row, there is a result which identifies the true nature of the URL, 1 if it is a phishing site and −1 if it a legitimate site.

### 3.2 Feature Selection

In any classification scheme, there are features which seem more prominent than others in achieving a correct classification. These features, combined with other salient features or even less salient features, can perform outstandingly. The difficulty arises when we must determine what are the most relevant features from a set and what combination of features give us near perfect classification accuracies. From the 30 features, we identified five subsets. These were grouped as shown below.

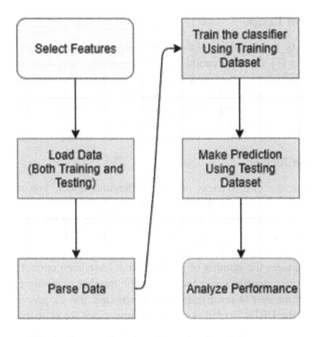

**Fig. 1.** Process flowchart for each selected feature set.

Set A: Web-presence related features. We chose these four features to determine if it is practical to determine the nature of a URL simply by looking at its presence on the internet, and not by any structural features of the URL itself. These features included: Domain age, Website traffic, Page Rank, Google Index.

Set B: Features with only two (2) possible outcomes {−1,1}. This makes the data more binary and eliminates the possibility of uncertain URLs. These features included: having_IP_Address, Shortining_Service, having_At_Symbol, double_slash_redirecting, Domain_registeration_length, Favicon, port, Prefix_Suffix, HTTPS_token, Request_URL, Submitting_to_email, Abnormal_URL, Redirect, on_mouseover, RightClick, popUpWidnow, Iframe, age_of_domain, DNSRecord, Page_Rank, Google_Index, Statistical_report.

Set C: Features with three (3) possible outcomes {−1,0,1}. These features allow for uncertainty in their output and includes: URL_Length, having_Sub_Domain, SSLfinal_State, URL_of_Anchor, Links_in_tags, SFH, web_traffic, Links_pointing_to_page.

Set D: Combination of Sets B and C. This set contains all 30 features.

Set E: The most important features (those rated 0.01 and up) according to Ran-dom Forest's feature_importances_ attribute. These include: having_IP_Address, URL_Length, Prefix_Suffix, having_Sub_Domain, SSLfinal_State, Do-main_registeration_length, HTTPS_token, Request_URL, URL_of_Anchor, Links_in_tags, SFH, age_of_domain, DNSRecord, web_traffic, Page_Rank, Google_Index, Links_pointing_to_page.

## 3.3    Experiment Design

Random Forest is a supervised classification algorithm that makes use of several classification trees [7]. A classification is made by passing each input vector down each tree, randomly. Each tree gives a classification, or vote, and the forest chooses the classification with the most instances, or votes [8]. We decided to use this algorithm because it is unexcelled in accuracy among its counterparts [8], it runs efficiently on large datasets and it can handle missing values [7].

## 3.4    Evaluation Methods

To fully evaluate the effectiveness of a classification model, you must include its precision and recall scores. In order to evaluate the performance of our classifications, we've calculated the Accuracy, Precision, Recall and F1 Scores for each set tested. Each metric is calculated based on True Positive (TP), True Negative (TN), False Positive (FP) and False Negative (FN) scores.

Precision measures the number of instances that have been correctly classified and is a measure of the classifier's exactness. It is the number of positive predictions divided by the total number of positive instances predicted. For us, precision answers the question, "Of all the URLs labeled as phishing, how many are actually phishing?" The formula to calculate precision is given by Eq. 1 below.

$$Precision = \frac{TP}{TP + FP} \qquad (1)$$

Recall measures the number of positive instances that the classifier correctly identified from the set of all positive instances. In other words, recall measures the number of instances that were missed [1]. Recall is a measure of the classifier's completeness. For us, recall answers the question, "Of all the URLs that are truly phishing, how many did we identify as phishing?" The formula to calculate recall is given by Eq. 2 below.

$$Recall = \frac{TP}{TP + FN} \qquad (2)$$

Simply looking at a classifier's precision and recall scores would not constitute a substantial evaluation. As such, we include the F1 score, which is the weighted average of precision and recall scores. The formula to calculate F1 Score is given by Eq. 3 below.

$$F1Score = \frac{2TP}{2TP + FP + FN} \qquad (3)$$

Accuracy, simply put, is the number of correct classifications made out of all instances in the test data. The formula to calculate accuracy is given by Eq. 4 below.

$$Accuracy = \frac{TP + TN}{TP + TN + FP + FN} \tag{4}$$

The Receiver Operating Characteristic (ROC) curve is ideal for representing binary classifications like this one. The curve is plotted with the False Positive Rate (FPR) on the x-axis and the True Positive Rate (TPR) on the y-axis. The Area Under the ROC Curve (AUC) shows how well the classifier is able to discriminate between phishing and legitimate URLs. The formulas to calculate FPR and TPR are given by Eqs. 5 and 6 below.

$$FPR = \frac{FP}{FP + TN} \tag{5}$$

$$TPR = \frac{TP}{TP + FN} \tag{6}$$

### 3.5 Results

In this section we provide details on the performance of our classification model. As previously mentioned, thirty (30) initial features were broken down into five subsets and investigated. The overall performance of these subsets is reported in Table 1.

**Table 1.** Classifier performance

|       | Precision | Recall | F1 Score | Accuracy | FPR    | TPR    | AUC    |
|-------|-----------|--------|----------|----------|--------|--------|--------|
| Set A | 0.4283    | 0.5119 | 0.4664   | 48.8%    | 0.488  | 0.4669 | 0.4908 |
| Set B | 0.7148    | 0.783  | 0.7474   | 76.9%    | 0.2169 | 0.7575 | 0.7703 |
| Set C | 0.9213    | 0.9154 | 0.9183   | 92.9%    | 0.0845 | 0.9393 | 0.9273 |
| Set D | 0.9559    | 0.9414 | 0.9486   | 95.5%    | 0.0585 | 0.9663 | 0.9538 |
| Set E | 0.9711    | 0.9479 | 0.9593   | 96.5%    | 0.052  | 0.9781 | 0.963  |

Sets C, D and E were able to achieve great precision and recall rates, above 91.5%. Set E outperformed the other sets, achieving 97.1% precision and 94.8% recall. This set produced results that surpass some previous research [1] and closely follow others [3]. High precision and recall rates are directly related to high quality feature selection. Set A underperformed with 48.8% accuracy and 51.2% precision, while Set B produced average results, obtaining 76.9% accuracy and 71.5% precision. The increasing performance of each set can be easily seen in Fig. 2.

Each set contained varying amounts of features. The relation between feature count and performance is shown in Fig. 3. We can observe one profound characteristic: the number of features is not as important as the importance of the features within the set. Set B contained 21 features to obtain 76.9% accuracy while Sets C and E used 8 and 16 features respectively and achieved over 92% accuracy.

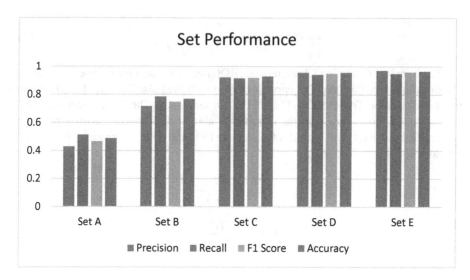

**Fig. 2.** Overall performance of each set.

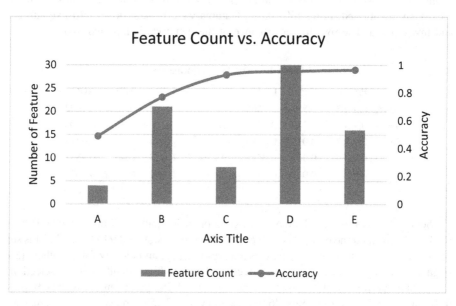

**Fig. 3.** Accuracy of using different numbers of features.

The ROC Curve is useful in showing the relationship between False Positive Rate and True Positive Rate. The ideal case occurs when the curve has the shortest distance to the upper left corner of the graph. The AUC is an important indicator of classifier performance. We see the Random Forest classifier achieves the best AUC for Set E, with 0.963. This is depicted in Fig. 4.

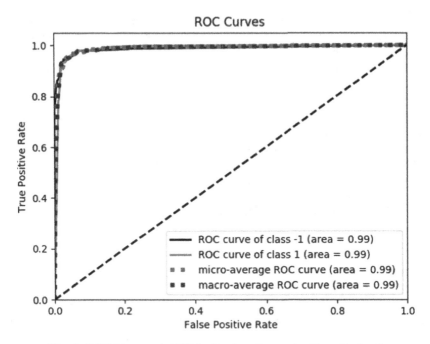

**Fig. 4.** ROC Curve and AUC for Random Forest classifier with Set E.

## 4  Discussion

In this section we further analyze the performance of Random Forest classifier with our five Sets and identify some limitations of our model.

Intuitively, increasing the number of features tend to yield better results on the performance. However, when we focused on selecting the features that were relatively important, we reduced the feature count by over half compared to the total number of features and were able to achieve better accuracy. This result indicates that adding more features does not necessarily result in better accuracy and may introduce more complexity that could downgrade the efficiency and performance of the classifier.

Our feature importance ranking was done using Random Forest's feature_importances_ attribute. This resulted in 16 features with a rating 0.01 or greater. These 16 features held the most weight and so was expected to perform extremely well. As evident by Set E's performance, using only the most important features are enough to increase the accuracy, precision and recall.

It was hoped that having binary input would make classification simpler for Random Forest. However, Set B's precision and recall scores, although good, were not desirable. In contrast, Set C obtained surprisingly better results although only containing features that could take on 3 possible outcomes. This means that some features had a value of zero, meaning that feature was suspicious, and not definitely phishing or legitimate.

Set A was chosen based on the URL's online presence rather than its structure. The performance of this set simply reiterates that we cannot determine, without a doubt, whether or not a website is phishing based solely on how long the site has been online, how many people visit the site and whether or not a user can visit the site from doing a Google search. These features are not substantial on their own.

We were restricted in the number and type of features under consideration. Had we been able to alter these parameters, we could have included current phishing URLs as reported by PhishTank. Another limitation of our method is that some of our subsets were built based on our judgement of feature importance, including Sets A, B and C.

When we divide the dataset into training and testing sets, one technique we could apply is k-fold cross validation. By partition our dataset into k-parts same sized sets, then running separate testing and training evaluations on those sets, we are confident that k-fold cross validation could significantly improve our assessment of the trained classifier.

## 5    Conclusion

We were able to improve the accuracy, precision and recall of the Random Forest classifier by using select features from all 30 features. This highlights the significance of first determining which features are most useful in determining whether a URL is phishing. Our findings give several possibilities for improvement. As a further step, we would include more features, find more important features, and combine all important features in hopes of achieving near perfect accuracy, precision and recall. We would also design our own URL parser, so as to be able to include more current phishing URLs. In order to improve the method of selecting important features for testing, we would employ forward feature selection and backward feature elimination methods.

## References

1. Phishing—What Is Phishing?. Phishing.org (2018). http://www.phishing.org/what-is-phishing.)
2. Dong, Z., Kapadia, A., Blythe, J., Camp, L.J.: Beyond the lock icon: real-time detection of phishing websites using public key certificates. In: 2015 APWG Symposium on Electronic Crime Research (eCrime). IEEE (2015)
3. Rao, R., Ali, S.: PhishShield: a desktop application to detect phishing webpages through heuristic approach. Procedia Comput. Sci. **54**, 147–156 (2015)
4. Rao, R.S., Pais, A.R.: Detecting phishing websites using automation of human behavior. In: Proceedings of the 3rd ACM Workshop on Cyber-Physical System Security - CPSS 17 (2017). https://doi.org/10.1145/3055186.3055188
5. Kumar, B., Kumar, P., Mundra, A., Kabra, S.: DC scanner: detecting phishing attack. In: 2015 Third International Conference on Image Information Processing (ICIIP) (2015). https://doi.org/10.1109/iciip.2015.7414779
6. Mohammad, R., McCluskey, L., Thabtah, F.: UCI machine learning repository: phishing websites data set. Archive.ics.uci.edu (2015). https://archive.ics.uci.edu/ml/datasets/phishing+websites

7. Gu, S., Wu, Q.: How Random Forest Algorithm Works in Machine Learning. Medium (2017). https://medium.com/@Synced/how-random-forest-algorithm-works-in-machine-learning-3c0 fe15b6674
8. Breiman, L., Cutler, A.: Random forests - classification description. Stat.berkeley.edu (2004). https://www.stat.berkeley.edu/~breiman/RandomForests/cc_home.htm
9. Papernot, N.: npapernot/phishing-detection. GitHub (2016). https://github.com/npapernot/phishing-detection

# Detecting Digital Photo Tampering
# with Deep Learning

Mitchell B. Singleton and Qingzhong Liu[✉]

Department of Computer Science, Sam Houston State University,
Huntsville, TX 77341, USA
{mitchellsingleton,liu}@shsu.edu

**Abstract.** The tools to tamper with digital photographs have become easier to use by the lay person and techniques have evolved that make detection of tampering more difficult, there is a clear need to not only discover novel ways to distinguish the difference between real and fake, but also to make the detection quicker and easier. Using content-aware resizing, which is also known as image retargeting, seam carving, content-aware rescaling, liquid rescaling, or liquid resizing, allows for changing the resolution of an image while keeping the content unchanged in the image. In this paper, the retraining of Inception ResNet v2, one of the best object detection deep learning classifiers, is undertaken to look at classifications of untampered versus tampered photos via seam removal.

**Keywords:** Photography · Detection of tampering · Detection of modification
Detection of falsification · Deep learning

## 1 Introduction

The ease of manipulating an image hasn't caused people to rely less on images as a source of truth. The reasons for the manipulation span the spectrum from what can seem benign (removing pimples, whitening teeth, or removing wrinkles in a school photo) all the way to intentionally malicious (falsified images passed as real, fear mongering, or deception).

Image manipulation tools have become widely available that allow anyone to perform robust image manipulation to the point where it is difficult to determine if an image has been falsified. Coupling that with an issue of the public becoming desensitized to the importance of image manipulation. The task for an average person to determine if an image has been tampered becomes herculean.

Previous investigations into manipulation of images have taken place looking at artifacts of specific file formats that occur after editing is done on an image. A very common standard to store digital images was created by the Joint Photographic Experts Group and the format became the known by the acronym JPEG and due to the popularity is an important file format to focus on for detection of tampering. To manipulate an image stored using the JPEG format there are a few basics operations; image scaling, rotation, copy and pasting, and double compression artifacts, are used and the detection of each have been well studied [1–7].

© ICST Institute for Computer Sciences, Social Informatics and Telecommunications Engineering 2018
L. Meng and Y. Zhang (Eds.): MLICOM 2018, LNICST 251, pp. 480–489, 2018.
https://doi.org/10.1007/978-3-030-00557-3_47

The need to be able to show image content over a range of resolutions has led to the creation of and current use of content-aware scaling. Shai Avidan of Mitsubishi Electric Research Labs (MERL) and Ariel Shamir of the Interdisciplinary Center and MERL, designed what they termed "seam-carving". This is a method that allows changing the size of an image by "carving-out or inserting pixels in different parts of the image." Seams are connected pixels from the top to the bottom or from the side to side of an image. Seam carving is done with the help of an energy function that is then used to identify the order of seams from lowest energy to highest energy [8]. The type of energy function used and the order that seams are removed can influence the resulting picture. Additionally, certain areas of the image can be artificially marked higher or lower in the energy function to protect from or ensure that certain areas are removed. An example of directed removal can be seen in Figs. 1, 2, and 3. Figure 1 is the original image. Figure 2 is the image with the marked pixels that will be protected (the man is highlighted in green) and removed (the man is highlighted in red). Figure 3 is the result of the seam carving.

**Fig. 1.** Original image

**Fig. 2.** An example image with overlays marking pixels in red and green. (Color figure online)

**Fig. 3.** An example of using seam carving to remove the red marked pixels while protecting the green marked pixels. (Color figure online)

## 2 Deep Learning

Deep learning is a specific type of machine learning that uses multiple layers of processing to find features of a data set and that categorizes the data into certain groupings based on the features. Most current deep learning models are based on an artificial neural network.

A new convolutional neural network (CNN) was released in 2017 named Inception-ResNet v2 by Christian Szegedy, Sergey Ioffe, Vincent Vanhoucke, and Alexander Alemi from Google Incorporated [9]. The new CNN builds upon the previous version of inception v1 [10], v2 [11] and v3 [12] along with the use of optimized residual connections based on residual connections presented by He, Zhang, Ren, and Sun [13]. The diagram for this network can be seen in Fig. 2.

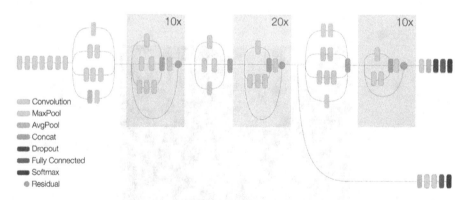

**Fig. 4.** Diagram of Inception ResNet v2 [14]

The layers that make up Inception ResNet v2 are convolution, pooling (max and average), concatenation, dropout, fully connected, softmax and residual. The convolution layer is where the tensor input is changed using a filter of a certain size. This filter then outputs the resulting tensor. The convolution process allows for extraction of features. Pooling allow shrinking the dimension of an input by looking at specific bundles of pixels and then using max or average on the bundle to determine a representative amount that then becomes the new value moving towards the input of the next layer. This is used to shrink the number of features from a convolution. A concatenation layer combines the tensors along a specified axis into a larger tensor. A dropout layer randomly drops data from a tensor into an output tensor that is the same size based on an entered probability. A fully connected layer does the classification on the features and every node in the layer is connected to a node in the preceding layer. Lastly a residual layer allows the skipping of certain layers to re-enforce the learning by addition of the tensor that skipped the layers with the output tensor that when through the layers.

In this paper, the Inception ResNet v2 network is fine-tuned to classify JPEG images that have been tampered, using seam carving, versus untampered. This paper seeks to study if Inception ResNet v2 can reliably determine if an image has been tampered via seam carving.

Recent research into using deep learning to detect and localize image tampering by way of resampling was shown by Bunk et al. [15] to be successful for copy-clone, removal, and splicing that was in the NIST Nimble 2016 dataset. This dataset contains images that were tampered in an advanced way to beat current state of the art detection techniques. Two methods of deep learning (CNN and LSTM) were used on Radon transformed data.

The application of external metadata allowed detection of tampering of images by Chen et al. [16]. They viewed images containing weather clues and compared them to the weather service for the same date and time. The correlation of the information was used to identify anomalies. The process could be further applied to also aid in detecting manipulations by comparing if clothing in images was weather appropriate for the date and location.

Deep learning was used by Shan [17] to learn from pathology patches to identify micro aneurysm in fundal images. They fine-tuned the training through a final iteration that allowed the accuracy results to move from high 80 s to low 90 s. The fine tuning used a stacked sparse autoencoder to do the deep learning. Autoencoders were part of early machine learning.

Deep learning was shown in research by Kalpana and Amritha to be able to identify "manipulations like median filtering, Gaussian blurring, resizing and cut and paste forgery..with... an average accuracy of 97%." [18] Their approach used the addition of a prediction error filter to get at the relationship of the pixels and not the content of the picture.

This paper uses the novel approach of re-tuning an object recognition model, Inception ResNet v2, to detect JPEG image tampering by vertical seam carving. The hypothesis is that the object detection training will allow the model to re-train to be able to learn to find images that have been tampered via vertical seam carving. Maybe through identification of objects that don't appear as they should or finding discrepancies in the colors or energy.

## 3 Methodology

A dataset was constructed from the 2017 ImageNet challenge test dataset containing 5500 images [19]. The first step cropped out a random selection from the original image with a size of 358 × 299. The untampered image is produced by cropping out a 299 × 299 selection randomly within the x axis of the original selection. Figure 3 shows an example untampered image.

**Fig. 5.** Untampered image

The original selection is then evaluated for the seams that will be removed. Figure 4 shows the original selection with green lines showing the seams that will be removed from the image.

**Fig. 6.** Expanded selection with seams indicated in green (Color figure online)

The last step creates the tampered image using the seam removal process, removing 59 vertical seams, which are marked in green in Fig. 4, from the width of the image, resulting in a 299 × 299 image. Figure 5 shows what an example tampered image looks like with the seams removed. Notice that the tail, all four legs, and the ear can be seen and that there is no noticeable change to the pattern of the fur.

**Fig. 7.** Tampered image with seams removed

This process led to a dataset with 5500 tampered and 5500 untampered images of size 299 by 299. The Python function, imwrite, writes the JPEG files at a quality of 95 (https://docs.opencv.org/3.0-beta/modules/imgcodecs/doc/reading_and_writing_images.html#imwrite). This size was chosen to match the input size of the Inception ResNet v2 classifier. The image classifier will be retrained into a binary classification of tampered or untampered using TensorFlow (Fig. 7).

To convert the tampered and untampered images from JPEG format into tfrecords, required for the retraining method, the download_and_convert_data.py script was used from https://github.com/tensorflow/models/tree/master/research/slim. Through this process 1,000 images were reserved in a validation set and the other 10,000 images were placed into a training set.

The TensorFlow library was used to create a convolutional neural network (CNN) allowing training on the data set for identification of tampered images and identification of the method used. TensorFlow is an open source library that was created by Google for numerical manipulation within data flow graphs where the nodes are mathematical operations and the edges are where the multidimensional data arrays (tensors) are transferred between. TensorFlow allows building deep neural networks easier than coding them from scratch for every use case. TensorFlow can be included in many different programing languages and for the purposes of this proposal will be used is in Python.

The retraining script and evaluation script were used from here, https://github.com/kwotsin/transfer_learning_tutorial. These scripts output the streaming accuracy metric into a summary scalar (accuracy and validation_accuracy) which allows easy tracking throughout in TensorBoard.

## 4   Results

The training accuracy is charted in Fig. 8 with the y axis the accuracy percentage and the x axis the number of global steps in the training and Fig. 9 shows the text of the x and y coordinates of the point at the rightmost position. Once the retraining ended at 10 epochs, the accuracy percentage had grown to 68%.

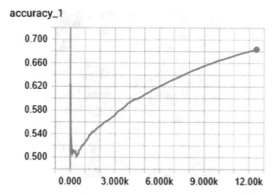

**Fig. 8.** Plot of training accuracy during training. 10 epochs and 1 day and 7 h later

| Name | Smoothed | Value | Step | Time | Relative |
|---|---|---|---|---|---|
| ◯ | 0.6837 | 0.6839 | 12.48k | Sat Apr 21, 14:35:32 | 1d 7h 1m 34s |

**Fig. 9.** Details for the right-most point of the right-most point in Fig. 8 - 68%

The validation script accuracy is charted in Fig. 10 with the y axis the validation accuracy percentage and the x axis the number of global steps in the validation and Fig. 11 shows the textual information of the x and y coordinates of the point at the rightmost position. After 10 epochs, the validation accuracy stabilizes around 82%.

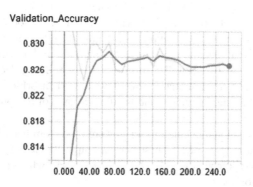

**Fig. 10.** Plot of validation accuracy against the number of steps in the validation. 1 epoch and 30 min later

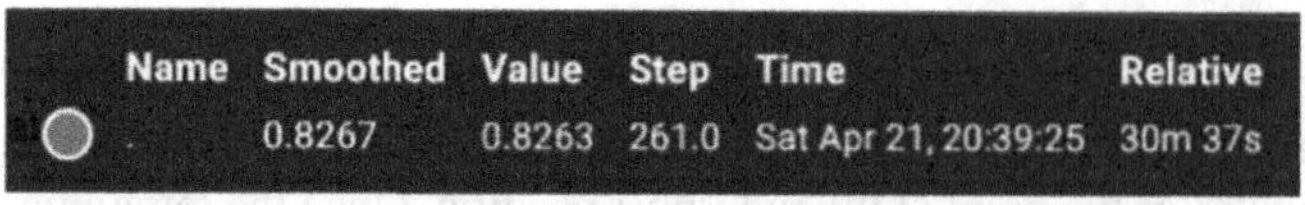

| Name | Smoothed | Value | Step | Time | Relative |
|---|---|---|---|---|---|
| ◯ | 0.8267 | 0.8263 | 261.0 | Sat Apr 21, 20:39:25 | 30m 37s |

**Fig. 11.** Details for the right-most point of the validation accuracy plot in Fig. 10 - 82%

There can be seen a discrepancy between the resulting training accuracy and the validation graphs and the numbers found. This can be explained due to the training not running until an equilibrium is reached. In Fig. 12, a longer running training can be seen – it ran for 3 days and 21 h compared to Fig. 6 which ran for 1 day and 7 h. The accuracy moved from 68% to 76% between the shorter run to the longer training session.

The y axis of Figs. 8, 10, and 12 is the accuracy percentage and the x axis shows the number of steps. Each step is a batch of images that have been processed. The number of steps directly correlates to the amount of time that was required and the number of images that was in each image set to do the training or validation in Figs. 6 (12.48k steps), 8 (261 steps), and 10 (37.49k steps) (Fig. 13).

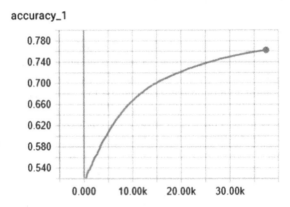

**Fig. 12.** A plot of training accuracy against the number of steps during training; 30 epochs and 3 days and 21 h later

| | Name | Smoothed | Value | Step | Time | | Relative |
|---|---|---|---|---|---|---|---|
| ◯ | | 0.7624 | 0.7625 | 37.49k | Thu Apr 26, 06:07:50 | | 3d 21h 32m 15s |

**Fig. 13.** Details for the right-most point of the plot in Fig. 12 - 76%

## 5   Conclusions

The Inception ResNet v2 model, the best at object detection across multiple classifications, does perform well when it is retrained for binary classification of tampered images. Figure 6 demonstrates that as training went on, the accuracy kept climbing and combined with Fig. 8, it is expected that an accuracy in the mid-80 percent isn't unreasonable if the training is left to continue or additional images were provided.

The validation percentage of around 80% confirms that the retraining of the model isn't overfitting to the data set. It also supports the idea that the training accuracy would continue to move higher until it was close or above the validation accuracy.

After reviewing the false images, there is a higher incidence of false negatives than false positives. This supports a suspicion that there may be image manipulation being done during the training that may have altered the truthfulness of the label and thus caused confusion with the model. For example, if the tampering in an image was localized and that area wasn't included in a crop distortion then the model would be given essentially an untampered photo but falsely labeled as tampered.

## 6   Future Work

This paper restricted the seam removal to only vertical seams and future work should confirm that expanding the seam removal to seams going in any number of directions has the ability detect image tampering. For example, image preparation with horizontal seams or diagonal seams would allow broadening the usefulness and applicability in the real world.

For future experimentation, a test to check if the model is looking at the image and not the format of the image. This may allow expanding the ability to detect seam carving in various file formats and even screen shots of tampered images where the artifacts of the file format and compression may be lost or hidden.

Reducing the image size for the training may allow a higher accuracy and a reduced amount of false predictions. This would ensure that any tampering that was done to the image would be included in the training and potentially help with the accuracy of false negatives where the tampered part of the image wasn't looked at during the training.

A real-world application of this model into a browser or email plugin or social media API would allow watermarking a suspected image to grab an end-user's attention to the possibility of image tampering. This may help to reduce false information being presented as pictures from making the leap from entertainment to fake news.

**Acknowledgments.** We highly appreciate the support for this study from the National Science Foundation under Award #1318688 and from the SHSU Office of Research and Sponsored Programs under an Enhanced Research Grant.

## References

1. Hsu, C.-M., Lee, J.-C., Chen, W.-K.: An efficient detection algorithm for copy-move forgery. Presented at the May (2015)
2. Chen, C., Shi, Y.Q., Su, W.: A machine learning based scheme for double JPEG compression detection. In: 2008 19th International Conference on Pattern Recognition. ICPR 2008, pp. 1–4. IEEE (2008)
3. Chen, Y.-L., Hsu, C.-T.: Detecting recompression of JPEG images via periodicity analysis of compression artifacts for tampering detection. IEEE Trans. Inf. Forensics Secur. **6**, 396–406 (2011). https://doi.org/10.1109/TIFS.2011.2106121
4. Dirik, A.E., Memon, N.: Image tamper detection based on demosaicing artifacts. Presented at the November (2009)

5. Farid, H.: Image forgery detection. IEEE Signal Process. Mag. **26**, 16–25 (2009). https://doi. org/10.1109/MSP.2008.931079

6. Liu, Q.: An approach to detecting JPEG down-recompression and seam carving forgery under recompression anti-forensics. Pattern Recogn. **65**, 35–46 (2017)

7. Liu, Q.: An improved approach to detecting JPEG seam carving under recompression. IEEE Trans. Circuits Syst. Video Technol. (in Press)

8. Avidan, S., Shamir, A.: Seam carving for content-aware image resizing. ACM Trans. Graph. **26**, 10 (2007). https://doi.org/10.1145/1239451.1239461

9. Szegedy, C., Ioffe, S., Vanhoucke, V., Alemi, A.: Inception-v4, inception-ResNet and the impact of residual connections on learning. arXiv:160207261 Cs. (2016)

10. Szegedy, C., et al.: Going deeper with convolutions. Presented at the June (2015)

11. Ioffe, S., Szegedy, C.: Batch normalization: accelerating deep network training by reducing internal covariate shift. arXiv:1502.03167 (2015)

12. Szegedy, C., Vanhoucke, V., Ioffe, S., Shlens, J., Wojna, Z.: Rethinking the inception architecture for computer vision. Presented at the June (2016)

13. He, K., Zhang, X., Ren, S., Sun, J.: Deep residual learning for image recognition. Presented at the June (2016)

14. Alemi, A.: Improving inception and image classification in TensorFlow, https://research. googleblog.com/2016/08/improving-inception-and-image.html

15. Bunk, J., et al.: Detection and localization of image forgeries using resampling features and deep learning. In: 2017 IEEE Conference on Computer Vision and Pattern Recognition Workshops (CVPRW), pp. 1881–1889. IEEE (2017)

16. Chen, B.-C., Ghosh, P., Morariu, V.I., Davis, L.S.: Detection of metadata tampering through discrepancy between image content and metadata using multi-task deep learning. In: 2017 IEEE Conference on Computer Vision and Pattern Recognition Workshops (CVPRW), pp. 1872–1880. IEEE (2017)

17. Shan, J., Li, L.: A deep learning method for microaneurysm detection in fundus images. Presented at the June (2016)

18. Kalpana, K., Amritha, P.P.: Image manipulation detection using deep learning in TensorFlow. Int. J. Control Theory Appl. **9**(40), 221–225 (2016)

19. Russakovsky, O., et al.: ImageNet large scale visual recognition challenge. arXiv 1409 (2014)

# Joint Time and Power Allocations for Uplink Nonorthogonal Multiple Access Networks

Yuan Wu[1,2(✉)], Cheng Zhang[1], Kejie Ni[1], Jiajun Shi[1], Liping Qian[1],
Liang Huang[1], Weidang Lu[1], and Limin Meng[1]

[1] College of Information Engineering, Zhejiang University of Technology,
Hangzhou 310023, Zhejiang, China
{iewuy,lpqian,lianghuang,luwd,mlm}@zjut.edu.cn, czhang_zjut@163.com,
kjni_zjut@163.com, jjshi_zjut@163.com
[2] State Key Laboratory of Integrated Services Networks, Xidian University,
Xian 710071, Shanxi, China

**Abstract.** The rapid development of mobile Internet services has yielded tremendous traffic pressure on cellular radio access networks. Exploiting nonorthogonal multiple access (NOMA) that enables a group of mobile users (MUs) to simultaneously share a same spectrum channel for radio access provides an efficient approach to achieve the goals of ultra-high throughput and massive connectivity in future 5G network. In this paper, we propose a joint time and power allocations for uplink NOMA. We aim at minimizing the delay for transmission and the total energy consumption of all MUs when the MUs send their data to the BS, while satisfying each MU's constrains on the transmission delay and energy consumption. Numerical results are provided to validate our proposed algorithm and the performance and advantage of our proposed joint optimization for time and power allocations for uplink NOMA.

**Keywords:** Nonorthogonal multiple access
Radio resource management · Optimization

## 1 Introduction

Nonorthogonal multiple access (NOMA), which enables a group of mobile users (MUs) to share the same time/frequency channel and utilizes the successive interference cancellation (SIC) to reduce the MUs' co-channel interference, has been introduced as one of the enabling technologies in the fifth-generation (5G) cellular networks [1–4]. Compared with in traditional orthogonal multiple access (OMA), NOMA is expected to realize massive connectivity for a large number of mobile terminals and significantly improve the spectrum-efficiency, which thus has attracted lots of research interests [5–13]. In [5], Wu *et al.* studied an optimal power allocation problem for downlink NOMA relay-transmission. In [6], Lei *et al.* studied the joint power and channel allocations for NOMA in a multi-cell

© ICST Institute for Computer Sciences, Social Informatics and Telecommunications Engineering 2018
L. Meng and Y. Zhang (Eds.): MLICOM 2018, LNICST 251, pp. 490–499, 2018.
https://doi.org/10.1007/978-3-030-00557-3_48

system. In [7], Qian *et al.* studied the joint optimization of cell association and power control. In [8], Elbamby *et al.* studied the resource allocation for the in-band full duplex-enabled NOMA networks. In [9], Qian *et al.* investigated the joint base station association and power control for uplink NOMA systems. In [10], Shirvanimoghaddam *et al.* investigated the application of NOMA for Internet of Things (IoT). Since traffic offloading has been considered as an promising approach to address the traffic congestion in future heterogeneous cellular system [11,12], an NOMA-enabled traffic offloading scheme has been proposed in [13], which shows the throughput advantage over the conventional orthogonal multiple access based offloading transmission.

In this paper, we consider a scenario in which a group of MUs send their respective data to the BS. To improve the spectrum efficiency, the MUs use NOMA to simultaneously transmit data to the BS over a same frequency channel. We jointly optimize the transmission time and the total energy consumption of all MUs. Despite the non-convexity of the formulated joint allocation problem, we introduce a variable-change and thus equivalently transform the original non-convex optimization problem into a convex optimization one, based on which we propose an efficient algorithm to solve it. Numerical results are provided to validate the effectiveness of our proposed algorithm and show the performance advantage of our proposed joint optimization of transmission time and power allocations for uplink NOMA.

The rest of this paper is organized as follows. Section 2 illustrates the system model and problem formulation. In Sect. 3, we propose an efficient algorithm to solve the formulated problem. Section 4 shows the numerical results. Finally, we conclude this work in Sect. 5.

## 2    System Model and Problem Formulation

As shown in Fig. 1, we consider the scenario where a group of MUs (denoted by mobile users) $\mathcal{I} = \{1, 2, \ldots, I\}$ are transmitting to a macro base station (BS). Each MU $i$ has a total data volume of size $s_i^{\text{req}}$ to be transmitted to the BS. We consider that the MUs form an NOMA-cluster to send the data volumes $\{s_i^{\text{req}}\}_{i \in \mathcal{I}}$ to the BS over a same frequency channel simultaneously.

### 2.1    MUs' NOMA Transmission to the BS

In the considered NOMA transmission, we use $t$ to denote the transmission delay of the MUs to send the data volumes $\{s_i^{\text{req}}\}_{i \in \mathcal{I}}$ to the BS. We use $p_i$ to denote MU $i$'s transmit-power to the BS. We assume that the MUs in $\mathcal{I}$ follow the following ascending-order of the channel power gains from the MUs to the BS. Furthermore, given a group of MUs, there are $I!$ different viable decoding-orders. For our future work, we will consider other ordering of the MUs.

$$g_{1B} > g_{2B} > g_{3B} > \ldots > g_{iB} > \ldots > g_{IB}, \tag{1}$$

where $g_{iB}$ denotes the channel power gain from MU $i$ to the BS.

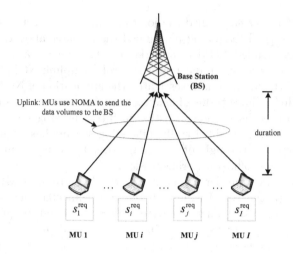

**Fig. 1.** Illustration of system model: uplink NOMA transmission.

Based on (1) and the SIC operation, the transmission rate from MU $i$ to the BS can be given by:

$$R_i = W \log_2 \left( 1 + \frac{p_i g_{iB}}{\sum_{j=1}^{i-1} p_j g_{jB} + W n_0} \right), \forall i \in \mathcal{I}, \tag{2}$$

where $W$ denotes the uplink channel-bandwidth, and $n_0$ denotes the spectral power density of the background noise.

For the sake of easy presentation, we introduce $\gamma_{iB}$ as the received signal to noise plus interference ratio (SINR) for MU $i$'s uplink NOMA transmission to the BS, i.e.,

$$\gamma_{iB} = \frac{p_i g_{iB}}{\sum_{j=1}^{i-1} p_j g_{jB} + W n_0}, \forall i \in \mathcal{I}. \tag{3}$$

Suppose that all MUs' $\{\gamma_{iB}\}_{i \in \mathcal{I}}$ are given in advance. Then, each MU $i$'s minimum transmit-power can be given by:

$$p_i^{\min}(\{\gamma_{jB}\}_{j \in \mathcal{I}, j \leq i}) = \frac{W n_0}{g_{iB}} \gamma_{iB} \prod_{j=1}^{i-1} (1 + \gamma_{jB}), \forall i \in \mathcal{I}. \tag{4}$$

Furthermore, given the MUs' data volumes $\{s_i^{\text{req}}\}_{i \in \mathcal{I}}$ to be transmitted and the transmission delay $t$, we have

$$R_i = \frac{s_i^{\text{req}}}{t} = W \log_2 \left( 1 + \gamma_{iB} \right), \forall i \in \mathcal{I},$$

which thus leads to:

$$\gamma_{iB} = 2^{\frac{s_i^{\text{req}}}{t} \frac{1}{W}} - 1, \forall i \in \mathcal{I}. \tag{5}$$

By substituting (5) into (4), we obtain each MU $i$'s minimum transmit-power, i.e.,

$$p_i^{\min}(t) = \frac{W n_0}{g_{iB}} \left( 2^{\frac{s_i^{\text{req}}}{t} \frac{1}{W}} - 1 \right) 2^{\frac{1}{t} \frac{1}{W} \sum_{j=1}^{i-1} s_j^{\text{req}}}, \forall i \in \mathcal{I}. \tag{6}$$

Notice that NOMA enables all MUs' simultaneously send their data to the BS. Thus, in this work, we aim at minimizing the delay for transmission and the total energy consumption of all MUs. The details are shown in the next subsection.

## 2.2  Problem Formulation

We formulate the following optimization problem that aims at minimizing the overall radio resource consumption of the uplink NOMA transmission which includes the transmission delay and the total energy consumption of all MUs (here "ORRCM" refers to "Overall Radio Resource Consumption Minimization"):

$$\text{(ORRCM):} \quad \min \alpha t + \beta t \sum_{i=1}^{I} p_i^{\min}$$

$$\text{subject to:} \quad t p_i^{\min}(t) \le E_i^{\max}, \forall i \in \mathcal{I}, \tag{7}$$

$$0 \le t \le T^{\max} \tag{8}$$

$$\text{variables:} \quad t.$$

In Problem (ORRCM), we use $\alpha$ and $\beta$ to denote the weight coefficients of the transmission delay and the total energy consumption of all MUs, respectively. Constraint (7) means that each MU $i$'s total energy consumption for transmission cannot exceed its maximum energy limit denoted by $E_i^{\max}$. We use $p_i^{\min}(t)$ (given in (6)) to denote MU $i$'s minimum transmit-power to the BS. Constraint (8) means that the transmission delay $t$ cannot exceed the maximum-delay $T^{\max}$.

Problem (ORRCM) is a typical non-convex optimization problem, and thus there exists no general algorithm that can efficiently solve Problem (ORRCM). We focus on proposing an efficient algorithm to solve Problem (ORRCM) in the following.

## 3  Proposed Algorithm to Solve Problem (ORRCM)

In this section, we propose an efficient algorithm to solve Problem (ORRCM). However, Problem (ORRCM) is a typical non-convex optimization problem. To efficiently solve this problem, we introduce a variable-change as:

$$x = \frac{1}{t} \tag{9}$$

Using (9) and making some equivalent manipulations, Problem (ORRCM) can be equivalently transformed into:

$$\text{(ORRCM-E):} \quad \min \alpha \frac{1}{x} + \beta \frac{1}{x} \sum_{i=1}^{I} p_i^{\min}$$

$$\text{subject to:} \quad p_i^{\min}(x) \leq x E_i^{\max}, \forall i \in \mathcal{I}, \tag{10}$$

$$x \geq \frac{1}{T^{\max}} \tag{11}$$

$$\text{variables:} \quad x.$$

For the sake of easy presentation, we define function $H_i(x)$ as:

$$H_i(x) = \frac{W n_0}{g_{iB}} \left( 2^{x \frac{s_i^{\text{req}}}{W}} - 1 \right) 2^{x \frac{1}{W} \sum_{j=1}^{i-1} s_j^{\text{req}}}, \forall i \in \mathcal{I}. \tag{12}$$

recall that $H_i(x)$ stems from (6).

The key idea to solve Porblem (ORRCM-E) is to introduce a new variable $\theta$. By using $\theta$, we can transform the Problem (ORRCM-E) into:

$$\text{(D1):} \quad \min \theta$$

$$\text{subject to:} \quad \frac{\theta x - \alpha}{\beta} - \sum_{i=1}^{I} H_i(x) \geq 0, \tag{13}$$

$$H_i(x) \leq x E_i^{\max}, \forall i \in \mathcal{I}, \tag{14}$$

$$x \geq \max\{\frac{1}{T^{\max}}, \frac{\alpha}{\theta}\}, \tag{15}$$

$$\text{variables:} \quad \theta.$$

A key observation is that Problem (D1) corresponds to finding the optimal value of $\theta$ (denoted by $\theta^*$) that can meet constraints (13), (14) and (15).

**(Procedures to Determine the Feasibility Under a Given $\theta$):** In order to determine the feasibility of Problem (D1) under a given $\theta$, we consider the Problem (D2) as follows:

$$\text{(D2):} \quad V_\theta = \min \sum_{i=1}^{I} H_i(x) - \frac{\theta x - \alpha}{\beta}$$

$$\text{subject to:} \quad H_i(x) \leq x E_i^{\max}, \forall i \in \mathcal{I}, \tag{16}$$

$$x \geq \max\{\frac{1}{T^{\max}}, \frac{\alpha}{\theta}\}, \tag{17}$$

$$\text{variables:} \quad x.$$

If $V_\theta \leq 0$, then the Problem (D1) is feasible. If $V_\theta > 0$, then the Problem (D1) is infeasible.

We then define the function $G(x)$ given by:

$$G(x) = \sum_{i=1}^{I} H_i(x) - \frac{\theta x - \alpha}{\beta}. \tag{18}$$

notice that $G(x)$ stems from the objective function of Problem (D2). We thus can derive the first order derivative of $G(x)$ as follows:

$$
\frac{\partial G(x)}{\partial x} = \frac{\partial \sum_{i=1}^{I} H_i(x)}{\partial x} - \frac{\theta}{\beta}
$$

$$
= \sum_{i=1}^{I} \{ \frac{W n_0}{g_{iB}} \left( 2^{x \frac{s_i^{req}}{W}} - 1 \right) 2^{x \frac{1}{W} \sum_{j=1}^{i-1} s_j^{req}} (\ln 2) \left( \frac{1}{W} \sum_{j=1}^{i-1} s_j^{req} \right)
$$

$$
+ \frac{W n_0}{g_{iB}} 2^{x \frac{1}{W} \sum_{j=1}^{i-1} s_j^{req}} 2^{x \frac{s_i^{req}}{W}} (\ln 2) \frac{s_i^{req}}{W} \} - \frac{\theta}{\beta} \tag{19}
$$

we observe that $\frac{\partial G(x)}{\partial x}$ is increasing in $x$. Then, we can conclude that the Problem (D2) is a convex optimization problem.

Exploiting the convexity of Problem (D2), we can use the interior point method to solve. In this paper, we use CVX (i.e., a commercial optimization package [14]) to solve Problem (D2) and compute the solution $V_\theta$.

(**Procedures to Determine** $\theta^*$): We then illustrate how to determine $\theta^*$. We exploit bisection-search method [15] to find $\theta^*$, which enables the Problem (D1) is feasible. The key rationale is as follows. Specifically, let us first suppose that the value of $\theta$ is given in advance. We then only need to check whether the Problem (D1) is feasible. If yes, then we can further reduce $\theta$ a little bit. Such a process continues, until we reach a threshold-value of $\theta$ which leads to that the Problem (D1) is infeasible. If no, then we need to increase the given value of $\theta$. We thus obtain $\theta^*$.

Based on the above rationale, we propose the following ORRCM-Algorithm to solve Problem (D1).

---

**ORRCM-Algorithm: to solve Problem (D1) and find $\theta^*$**

---

1: **Initialization:** The tolerable computation-error $\epsilon$ for the bisection-search method. Set $\theta^{uppbound}$ is a sufficiently large number and $\theta^{lowbound} = 0$.
2: **while** $|\theta^{uppbound} - \theta^{lowbound}| > \epsilon$ **do**
3:     Set $\theta^{cur} = \frac{\theta^{uppbound} + \theta^{lowbound}}{2}$.
4:     Solve Problem (D2) to obtain $V_\theta$ by using CVX.
5:     **if** $V_\theta \leq 0$ **then**
6:         Set $\theta^{uppbound} = \theta^{cur}$.
7:     **else**
8:         Set $\theta^{lowbound} = \theta^{cur}$.
9:     **end if**
10: **end while**
11: **Output:** $\theta^* = \theta^{cur}$.

---

## 4   Numerical Results

We provide the numerical results to evaluate the accuracy of our proposed ORRCM-Algorithm and demonstrate the performance of our proposed NOMA-enabled uplink transmission scheme. Specifically, we setup the scenario as follows. The BS is located at $(0\,\mathrm{m},\ 0\,\mathrm{m})$. The group of MUs are uniformly distributed within a plane whose central is the BS and the radius is $100\,\mathrm{m}$. We use the similar method as [16] to model the channel power gains from the MUs to the BS. For instance, the channel power gain from the MU $i$ to BS is given by $g_{i\mathrm{B}} = \frac{\varrho_{i\mathrm{B}}}{\ell_{i\mathrm{B}}^{\kappa}}$, where $\varrho_{i\mathrm{B}}$ denotes the distance between MU $i \in \mathcal{I}$ and the BS, and $\kappa$ denotes the power-scaling factor for the path-loss (we set $\kappa = 3$). To capture the fading and shadowing effects, we assume that $\varrho_{i\mathrm{B}}$ follows an exponential distribution with a unit mean. We set each MUs' maximum energy-capacity as $E_i^{\max} = 4\mathrm{J}$, and set $T^{\max} = 1\,\mathrm{s}$, and set the weight coefficient $\alpha = 1$ of the transmission delay and the weight coefficient $\beta = 1$ of the total energy consumption of all MUs. Other parameters setting will be provided when needed.

### 4.1   Effectiveness of Our Proposed ORRCM-Algorithm

We firstly evaluate the accuracy of our proposed ORRCM-Algorithm, with the detailed results shown in Tables 1 and 2. For the purpose of comparison, we use Enumeration method to solve Problem (ORRCM-E) and obtain the overall radio resource consumption as a benchmark.

**Table 1.** 8-MUs and 10-MUs scenario: we fix $W = 8\,\mathrm{MHz}$, and we set the unit of $s_i^{\mathrm{req}}$ to Mbits

| $I = 8$ | $s_i^{\mathrm{req}} = 3.5$ | $s_i^{\mathrm{req}} = 4$ | $s_i^{\mathrm{req}} = 4.5$ | $s_i^{\mathrm{req}} = 5$ | $s_i^{\mathrm{req}} = 5.5$ | $s_i^{\mathrm{req}} = 6$ | $s_i^{\mathrm{req}} = 6.5$ | Ave. Error |
|---|---|---|---|---|---|---|---|---|
| Proposed | 0.7818 | 0.8935 | 1.0052 | 1.1169 | 1.2286 | 1.3440 | 1.5011 | 0.0024% |
| Enumeration | 0.7818 | 0.8935 | 1.0052 | 1.1168 | 1.2285 | 1.3440 | 1.5011 | |
| $I = 10$ | $s_i^{\mathrm{req}} = 3.5$ | $s_i^{\mathrm{req}} = 4$ | $s_i^{\mathrm{req}} = 4.5$ | $s_i^{\mathrm{req}} = 5$ | $s_i^{\mathrm{req}} = 5.5$ | $s_i^{\mathrm{req}} = 6$ | $s_i^{\mathrm{req}} = 6.5$ | Ave. Error |
| Proposed | 1.0389 | 1.1873 | 1.3372 | 1.5451 | 1.8750 | 2.3968 | 3.2198 | 0.0013% |
| Enumeration | 1.0388 | 1.1873 | 1.3372 | 1.5451 | 1.8750 | 2.3968 | 3.2198 | |

**Table 2.** 8-MUs and 10-MUs scenario: we fix $W = 12\,\mathrm{MHz}$, and we set the unit of $s_i^{\mathrm{req}}$ to Mbits

| $I = 8$ | $s_i^{\mathrm{req}} = 3.5$ | $s_i^{\mathrm{req}} = 4$ | $s_i^{\mathrm{req}} = 4.5$ | $s_i^{\mathrm{req}} = 5$ | $s_i^{\mathrm{req}} = 5.5$ | $s_i^{\mathrm{req}} = 6$ | $s_i^{\mathrm{req}} = 6.5$ | Ave. Error |
|---|---|---|---|---|---|---|---|---|
| Proposed | 0.5730 | 0.6549 | 0.7368 | 0.8186 | 0.9005 | 0.9824 | 1.0643 | 0.0042% |
| Enumeration | 0.5731 | 0.6549 | 0.7368 | 0.8187 | 0.9005 | 0.9824 | 1.0643 | |
| $I = 10$ | $s_i^{\mathrm{req}} = 3.5$ | $s_i^{\mathrm{req}} = 4$ | $s_i^{\mathrm{req}} = 4.5$ | $s_i^{\mathrm{req}} = 5$ | $s_i^{\mathrm{req}} = 5.5$ | $s_i^{\mathrm{req}} = 6$ | $s_i^{\mathrm{req}} = 6.5$ | Ave. Error |
| Proposed | 0.7638 | 0.8728 | 0.9819 | 1.0911 | 1.2002 | 1.3093 | 1.4301 | 0.0030% |
| Enumeration | 0.7638 | 0.8729 | 0.9820 | 1.0911 | 1.2002 | 1.3093 | 1.4301 | |

Table 1 shows the comparison for a 8-MUs scenario and a 10-MUs scenario, respectively. Specifically, the locations for both 8-MUs and 10-MUs are randomly generated as mentioned before. We test $I = 8$ and $I = 10$ while fix $W = 8\,\text{MHz}$, and for the two cases, we vary $s_i^{\text{req}}$ from 3.5 Mbits to 6.5 Mbits. In each cell, the value denotes the overall radio resource consumption obtained by our proposed ORRCM-Algorithm or by Enumeration method. Table 1 shows that the results obtained by the two method are very close to each other, with the average error no more than 0.01%, which thus verify the accuracy of our proposed ORRCM-Algorithm. We test $I = 8$ and $I = 10$ while fix $W = 12\,\text{MHz}$ in Table 2, which shows the similar results as the Table 1.

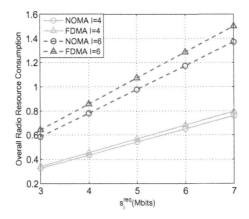

**Fig. 2.** Performance advantage of our proposed NOMA-enabled scheme compared with the FDMA-enabled scheme versus different $s_i^{\text{req}}$.

## 4.2 Performance Advantage of Our Proposed NOMA-Enabled Scheme Against FDMA-Enabled Scheme

We then compare our proposed NOMA-enabled uplink transmission scheme with the FDMA-enabled uplink transmission scheme. Specifically, Fig. 2 shows the performance comparison between our proposed NOMA-enabled scheme and the FDMA-enabled scheme versus different $s_i^{\text{req}}$ from 3 Mbits to 7 Mibts. We use two cases, i.e., $I = 4$ and $I = 6$ while we set $W = 8\,\text{MHz}$. It is reasonable to observe in Fig. 2 that when the total requirements increase, the overall radio resource consumption for both our proposed NOMA-enabled scheme and the FDMA-enabled scheme increase. However, our proposed NOMA-enabled scheme can efficiently reduce the overall radio resource consumption, compared with the FDMA-enabled scheme. Furthermore, with the increase in the number of MUs, it can be seen from Fig. 2 that our proposed NOMA-enabled scheme achieves a larger performance gain.

Figure 3 shows the performance comparison between our proposed NOMA-enabled scheme and the FDMA-enabled scheme versus different $W$ (i.e., the

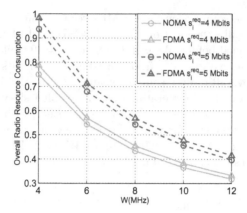

**Fig. 3.** Performance advantage of our proposed NOMA-enabled scheme compared with the FDMA-enabled scheme versus different channel bandwidths.

uplink channel bandwidth) from 4 MHz to 12 MHz. We set $I = 4$ and we use two cases, i.e., $s_i^{req} = 4$ Mbits and $s_i^{req} = 5$ Mbits. It is reasonable to observe in Fig. 3 that when the channel bandwidth increases, the overall radio resource consumption for both our proposed NOMA-enabled scheme and the FDMA-enabled scheme decrease. Meanwhile, our proposed NOMA-enabled scheme consumes a smaller total consumption than the FDMA-enabled scheme.

## 5    Conclusion

In this paper, we have studied the joint optimization of time and power allocations for uplink NOMA, with the objective of minimizing the overall radio resource consumption when the MUs send their data to the BS. We proposed an efficient algorithm to obtain the optimal solution. Moreover, we have validated our proposed algorithm and demonstrated the performance advantage of our proposed NOMA-enabled scheme via numerical results.

**Acknowledgements.** This work was supported in part by the National Natural Science Foundation of China under Grant 61572440, in part by the Zhejiang Provincial Natural Science Foundation of China under Grants LR17F010002 and LR16F010003, in part by the Young Talent Cultivation Project of Zhejiang Association for Science and Technology under Grant 2016YCGC011.

## References

1. Ding, Z.: Application of non-orthogonal multiple access in LTE and 5G networks. IEEE Commun. Mag. **55**(2), 185–191 (2017)
2. Islam, S., Avazov, N., Dobre, O., Kwak, K.: Power-domain non-orthogonal multiple access (NOMA) in 5G systems: potentials and challenges. IEEE Commun. Surv. Tutor. **19**(2), 721–742 (2017)

3. Liu, Y., Qin, Z., Elkashlan, M., Ding, Z., Nallanathan, A., Hanzo, L.: Non-orthogonal multiple access for 5G and beyond. Proc. IEEE **105**(12), 2347–2381 (2017)
4. Saito, Y., Kishiyama, Y., Benjebbour, A., Nakamura, T., Li, A., Higuchi, K.: Non-orthogonal multiple access (NOMA) for cellular future radio access. In: 2013 IEEE 77th Vehicular Technology Conference (VTC Spring), Dresden, pp. 1–5 (2013)
5. Wu, Y., Qian, L., Mao, H., Yang, X., Zhou, H., Shen, X.: Optimal power allocation and scheduling for non-orthogonal multiple access relay-assisted networks. IEEE Trans. Mob. Comput. (2018). https://doi.org/10.1109/TMC.2018.2812722
6. Lei, L., Yuan, D., Ho, C., Sun, S.: Joint optimization of power and channel allocation with non-orthogonal multiple access for 5G cellular systems. In: 2015 IEEE Global Communications Conference (GLOBECOM), San Diego, CA, pp. 1–6 (2015)
7. Qian, L., Wu, Y., Zhou, H., Shen, X.: Dynamic cell association for non-orthogonal multiple-access V2S networks. IEEE J. Sel. Areas Commun. **35**(10), 2342–2356 (2017)
8. Elbamby, M., Bennis, M., Saad, W., Debbah, M., Latva-aho, M.: Resource optimization and power allocation in in-band full duplex-enabled non-orthogonal multiple access networks. IEEE J. Sel. Areas Commun. **35**(12), 2860–2873 (2017)
9. Qian, L., Wu, Y., Zhou, H., Shen, X.: Joint uplink base station association and power control for small-cell networks with non-orthogonal multiple access. IEEE Trans. Wirel. Commun. **16**(9), 5567–5582 (2017)
10. Shirvanimoghaddam, M., Dohler, M., Johnson, S.: Massive non-orthogonal multiple access for cellular IoT: potentials and limitations. IEEE Commun. Mag. **55**(9), 55–61 (2017)
11. Wu, Y., Chen, J., Qian, L., Huang, J., Shen, X.: Energy-aware cooperative traffic offloading via device-to-device cooperations: an analytical approach. IEEE Trans. Mob. Comput. **16**(1), 97–114 (2017)
12. Wu, Y., Qian, L., Zheng, J., Zhou, H., Shen, X.: Green-oriented traffic offloading through dual connectivity in future heterogeneous small cell networks. IEEE Commun. Mag. **56**(5), 140–147 (2018)
13. Wu, Y., Qian, L.: Energy-efficient NOMA-enabled traffic offloading via dual-connectivity in small-cell networks. IEEE Commun. Lett. **21**(7), 1605–1608 (2017)
14. Grant, M., Boyd, S., Ye, Y.: CVX: matlab software for disciplined convex programming (2009). http://cvxr.com/cvx/
15. Weisstein, E.: "Bisection," from MathWorld - a wolfram web resource. http://mathworld.wolfram.com/Bisection.html
16. Zhang, R.: Optimal dynamic resource allocation for multi-antenna broadcasting with heterogeneous delay-constrained traffic. IEEE J. Sel. Top. Signal Process. **2**(2), 243–255 (2008)

# Performance Evaluation of Ad-hoc Routing Protocols in Hybrid MANET-Satellite Network

Xiaoye Xie[1,2], Jian Wang[1(✉)], Xiaobo Guo[2], and Xiaogang Wu[3]

[1] Nanjing University, Nanjing, China
1138369750@qq.com, wangjnju@nju.edu.cn
[2] Science and Technology on Information Transmission and Dissemination in
Communication Networks Laboratory, The 54th Institute of CETC,
Shijiazhuang, Hebei, China
guo_xiaobo@foxmail.com
[3] State Key Laboratory of Smart Grid Protection and Control,
NARI Group Corporation, 19 Chengxin Road, Nanjing, China

**Abstract.** Hybrid MANET-satellite network is a natural evolution in achieving ubiquitous communication. Their combination gives full play to respective advantages—autonomy and flexibility of MANET, wide coverage and resilience to natural disasters of satellite network. Although large quantities of researches have been conducted on hybrid MANET-satellite network, there are relatively few researches on its routing. In this paper, we construct a basic model of hybrid MANET-satellite network and explore the performance and applicability of ad-hoc routing protocols in hybrid network. Simulation results by NS3 demonstrate that the hybrid network working in ad hoc manner can acquire the performance that conforms to the standard of QoS.

**Keywords:** MANET · Satellite · Hybrid network · Ad-hoc · Routing

## 1 Introduction

Satellite network is a momentous pillar of global information infrastructure due to its wide coverage and resilience to natural disasters. Latest advancement in satellite commutation technology enables satellite network to provide 99.99% availability [1]. As a result, satellite based IoT [2,3] comes into sight as supplement and extension to terrestrial IoT network with limited coverage. Low earth orbit (LEO) satellite network whose altitude ranges from 500 km to 1500 km gains academic and commercial popularity for low propagation delay, low launch cost and small propagation loss [4]. OneWeb, Iridium and Globalstar, targeted to global communications and Internet service, are well-known LEO satellite constellations.

On the other hand, mobile ad-hoc network (MANET) meets with great favor among numerous terrestrial networks. MANET came into being for military

© ICST Institute for Computer Sciences, Social Informatics and Telecommunications Engineering 2018
L. Meng and Y. Zhang (Eds.): MLICOM 2018, LNICST 251, pp. 500–509, 2018.
https://doi.org/10.1007/978-3-030-00557-3_49

tactical network in the beginning. MANET is an autonomous, temporary and multihop wireless network consisting of mobile nodes. It can be deployed in infrastructure-less environment temporarily. Different from the single hop propagation of cellular network, packets in MANET are transmitted in a store-and-forward way from source to destination via intermediate nodes [5]. Due to its independence of Internet infrastructure and expeditiousness in deploying network, applications of MANET are expanded to desert, forests and coastal waters.

Hybrid MANET-satellite network is a natural evolution in achieving ubiquitous communication [6], which gives full play to respective merits of MANET and satellite network. Various projects about hybrid or integrated systems have been proposed for various purposes, such as SANSA [7], SALICE [8] and MONET [9]. However, these projects either focus on physical layer or discuss the methodology on network layer. A few of them study the performance of routing protocols in hybrid network in detail.

In this paper, we construct a basic model of hybrid MANET-satellite network and apply ad-hoc routing protocols to the hybrid network after obtaining snapshots of satellite network. Simulation results by NS3 verify that ad-hoc routing protocols are applicable to the hybrid network and the delay of hybrid network is up to the standard of QoS.

The remaining of this paper is organized as follows. Section 2 gives a brief review of background and related work. Section 3 depicts a basic model of hybrid MANET-satellite network and introduces the routing mechanism of the hybrid network. Section 4 provides simulation results and analysis. Finally, Sect. 5 concludes the paper.

## 2   Background and Related Works

### 2.1   Routing Protocols of MANET

In MANET, all the mobile nodes are equipped with a wireless transmitter and a receiver, which means every node can work as a transceiver or router of other nodes. Because mobile nodes move freely and arbitrarily, the topology of the MANET changes in a random and stochastic manner. The highly dynamic nature of MANET places severe restrictions on routing protocols designed for them [5].

MANET routing protocols are classified into two main categories, the proactive and the reactive. Proactive protocols update the routes within the network periodically, so that when source node needs forward a packet, the route already exists and can be used immediately [10]. Destination-Sequenced Distance-Vector (DSDV) and Optimized Link State Routing (OLSR) are typical proactive protocols. On the other hand, reactive protocols invoke a route determination procedure only on demand [11]. Thus, when a route is needed, some sort of global search procedure is initiated. Examples of reactive protocols include Ad hoc on-demand Distance Vector (AODV) and Dynamic Source Routing (DSR).

## 2.2 Routing Strategies of Satellite Network

From the perspective of connection, there are two kinds of routing scheme for single-layered satellite network, the connectionless and the connection-oriented. The rapid development of Internet has promoted the application of connectionless scheme in IP-based satellite network. Ekici et al. [12] introduces a distributed routing algorithm (DRA) which selects the path for each packet independently. DRAW in [13] improves DRA's applicability to variable topology. Guo et al. [4] proposed a novel routing algorithm WSDRA whose has much less overhead and delay than DRA.

Virtual topology method is a significant component in the connection-oriented scheme. The Snapshot method is a milestone in the development of virtual topology based satellite routing scheme. Gounder et al. firstly proposed the concept of snapshot in [14]. They defined the snapshot as the topology of the satellite network at a particular instant of time. Song et al. [15] and Tan et al. [16] proposed snapshot integration routing (SIR) method and dynamic detection routing algorithm (DDRA) respectively to improve routing performance. Tang et al. [17] slightly optimized the snapshot based routing by reassigning inter-satellite link (ISL) when simultaneous switch of routing table happens in all satellites.

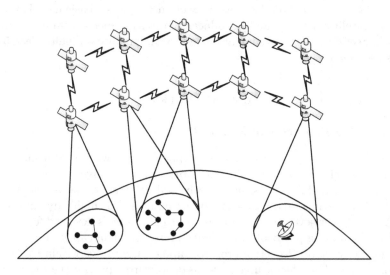

**Fig. 1.** Model of hybrid MANET-satellite network

## 3 Hybrid MANET-Satellite Network

### 3.1 Network Model of the Hybrid Network

Inspired by projects about hybrid networks mentioned above, we construct a model of hybrid MANET-satellite network, as is shown in Fig. 1. It consists of terrestrial MANET, satellite networks and satellite ground station. Terrestrial MANET contains mobile nodes equipped with antenna to communicate with satellites. As long as mobile nodes lie in the footprint of satellites, they can deliver messages to satellites or receive messages from satellites. The backbone of the satellite network comprises LEO constellation. It is responsible for transmitting messages to ground station. To simply our research, we assume that all the satellites transmit messages to a fixed ground station.

### 3.2    Routing Mechanism of the Hybrid Network

Conventional MANET routing protocols normally assume that nodes move in an entirely arbitrary manner and they can only connect temporarily with other nodes within a certain range. When nodes' random movement brings on link breaks, nodes have to reestablish connections based on network conditions before transmitting packets. Both nodes' movement and link breaks are unpredictable in MANET, while the satellite segment of the hybrid network owns predictable dynamic topology. For the efficiency of routing, we proposed a routing mechanism specified to the hybrid network, which takes regularity and predictability of satellites into account.

The routing mechanism consists of three steps. The first step is to acquire snapshots of satellite segment. By calculating the visibility among satellites in STK in advance, we obtain the data about predictable topology variation of satellite network. The dynamic topology of satellite network is converted into a sequence of static topology after we divide the simulation time $T$ into $N$ equal slots, $[t_1, t_2], [t_2, t_3], \ldots, [t_N, t_{N+1}]$. There are two critical criteria in acquiring snapshots: (1) The slot duration is short enough to guarantee the accuracy of snapshots. (2) We should control the complexity of space and time for the efficiency of routing. A practical approach is to make $\Delta t$ ($\Delta t = T/N$) no more than the minimum of all visibility durations.

$$\Delta t \leq min\{\tau_1, \tau_2, \ldots, \tau_N\} \tag{1}$$

Secondly, mathematical representations of snapshots are extracted from visibility data. The topology keeps static within a snapshot if no ISL is added or broken. During $[t_n, t_{n+1}](n = 1, 2, 3 \ldots, N)$, if a continuous direct line-of-sight exists between $i$ and $j$, then $i$ and $j$ are visible to each other. Snapshots $S_n$ are represented by an adjacency matrix $M_N$ whose element is $e_{i,j}(n)$. $e_{i,j}(n)$ represents the pairwise contacts between $i$ and $j$ during slot $[t_n, t_{n+1}]$.

$$e_{i,j}(n) = \begin{cases} 1 \text{ if } i \text{ is visible to } j \\ 0 \text{ else} \end{cases} \tag{2}$$

Thirdly, ad-hoc routing protocols are applied to the hybrid network, where MANET nodes move stochastically and satellite nodes move determinately. For satellite segment, a new snapshot, corresponding to the topology of satellite network during particular slot [14,18], is loaded at the beginning of each slot.

Table 1. Parameters of hybrid MANET-satellite network

| Parameter | Value |
|---|---|
| Mac type | IEEE 802.11 |
| Area acreage | $250\,\text{m} \times 250\,\text{m}$ |
| Size of packet | 64 bytes |
| Maximum velocity | $2\,\text{m/s}$ |
| Number of source nodes | 2, 4, 6, ..., 20 |
| Number of terrestrial nodes | 26 |
| Orbit altitude | 1000 km |
| Half cone angle | $10°$ |
| Number of planes | 6 |
| Satellites per plane | 4 |
| Simulation time | 200 s, 300 s, 400 s, 500 s, 600 s |

## 4   Simulation and Analysis

### 4.1   Simulation Settings

A communication scenario is constructed in AGI Systems Tool Kit (STK). The visibility dataset generated by STK is used to produce snapshots of satellite networks. We have established a hybrid MANET-satellite network in NS3, whose specific simulation parameters of hybrid MANET-satellite network are listed in Table 1. Routing mechanism demonstrated in Sect. 3 is adopted in extensive simulations to evaluate the performance and applicability of ad-hoc routing protocols in the hybrid network. We observe the performance by altering the simulation time and the number of source nodes separately.

### 4.2   Performance Metircs

The reliability and timeliness are significant in communication, so we assess the performance of four ad-hoc routing protocols in the hybrid network through average delay and packet delivery rate (PDR).

**Delay.** The overall time of a message travelling from the source node to the destination node is called delay.

$$AverageDelay = \frac{1}{N} \sum_{k=0}^{n-1} (rt_k - st_k) \tag{3}$$

$rt_k$: the moment when the kth packet arrives at the destination
$st_k$: the moment when the source generates the kth packet
N: number of packets successfully delivered

**PDR.** The ratio of packets delivered to the destination successfully to total number of packets sent by the source node is named PDR (Packet Delivery Rate).

$$PacketDeliveryRate = \frac{P_d}{P_s} \times 100\% \tag{4}$$

$P_d$: number of packets successfully delivered
$P_s$: number of packets the source node generates

### 4.3   Results and Analysis

In Fig. 2, the PDR of the hybrid network falls dramatically at 400 s. Snapshot transition is a probable explanation for this phenomenon. It is very likely that snapshots from 200 s to 400 s are quite different from each other. Routing strategies cannot respond to topology changes timely, especially proactive ones. For proactive routing protocols, when enormous differences exist among snapshots, routing tables based on the previous snapshot are useless for the routing of the next snapshot. In the hybrid network, PDRs of different protocols are close to each other when simulation time is less than 400 s. When simulation time is more than 500 s, the growth rate of PDR slows down and value of PDR tends to be stable, which means that the maximum PDR of the hybrid network is around 70%, 20% less than that of MANET. It is because link breaks in satellite segment are more frequent. The PDRs of reactive protocols exceed those of proactive ones for the first time at 500 s, which indicates reactive protocols are more flexible in the case of great topology changes.

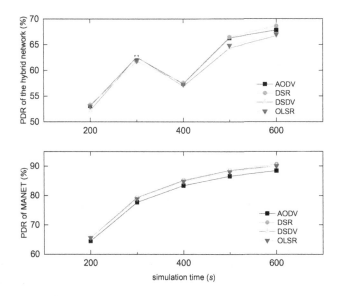

**Fig. 2.** PDR vs. simulation time

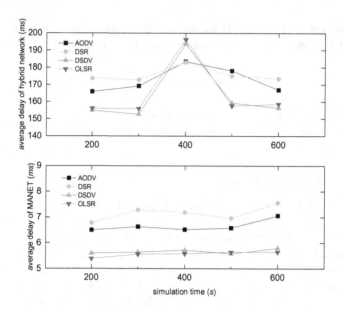

**Fig. 3.** Average delay vs. simulation time

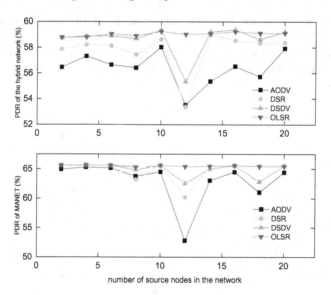

**Fig. 4.** PDR vs. number of source nodes

In Fig. 3, for hybrid network at 400 s, the delay of OLSR and DSDV rise by 27% suddenly and delay of AODV and DSR rise by 6%. By contrast, the delay of MANET keeps stable. The upsurge is mainly ascribed to snapshot transition where topology changes dramatically. Most nodes in the network have to

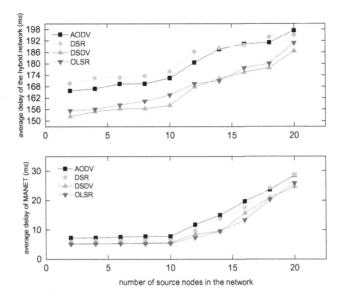

**Fig. 5.** Average delay vs. number of source nodes

re-establish routes in this case, which adds to the end-to-end delay. The sharp increase of delay corresponds to the sudden decrease of PDR in Fig. 2 at 400 s. The minimum and maximum of the delay in hybrid network are 152 ms and 196 ms respectively, both of them meeting the requirement of QoS class1 [20]. The upper subgraph shows that although the delay of reactive protocols is around 20 ms more than that of proactive ones under normal circumstances, the reactive protocols are more robust in dynamic environment, for the delay of AODV and DSR raises slightly, while that of DSDV and OLSR raises dramatically. Thus, AODV or DSR may be adequate for networks that are sensitive to delay jitter.

It is obvious in Fig. 4 that the trend of PDR in hybrid networks is the same as that in MANET on the whole. Except a few extremes, the PDR of hybrid network fluctuates around 58%, 7% less than that of MANET. The PDRs of AODV, DSR and DSDV all drop to the lowest when number of source nodes increases to 12. On the contrary, the PDR of OLSR remains stable, almost unaffected by the number of source nodes, which is attributed to the periodic maintenances and update of routing information of OLSR. When the number of source nodes equals 12, the PDR of the hybrid network and MANET slump to the minimum. Possible reason is that severe congestion makes packets at queue tail discarded. PDR of both networks rises to average again when number of source nodes exceeds 12. This phenomenon deserves further research.

In Fig. 5, the delay of both networks start to grow when number of source nodes exceeds 10 and the delay of hybrid network varies from 150 ms to 200 ms. This result is reasonable because the scale of satellite network is much larger than that of MANET. Furthermore, the typical value of end-to-end delay for

LEO satellites from [19] is 80–120 ms. Thus, it is meaningless to compare the delay of hybrid network with that of MANET. The delay of OLSR is the lowest in the hybrid network, which is attributed to the mechanism of OLSR. OLSR requires each node to maintain at least one table to store routing information about every other node in the network. Whenever a route is needed, there is negligible delay in determining the route. Consequently, OLSR is preferred for real-time communication. DSR and AODV perform worse than OLSR and DSDV in average delay. It is because route information may be unavailable when a packet is to be transmitted. Nodes have to wait until a route has been determined.

## 5   Conclusions

In this paper, we construct a basic model of hybrid MANET-satellite network and study the performance and applicability of ad-hoc routing protocols in hybrid network with MANET as a reference. Based on simulations by NS3, we come to three conclusions. Firstly, the delay of ad-hoc routing protocols in hybrid network conforms to the standard of QoS class1 [20]. Secondly, OLSR applies to hybrid networks that place high requirement for reliability and real-time performance. Last but not least, reactive protocols are more suitable for hybrid networks that are sensitive to delay jitter due to their robustness to topology changes.

**Acknowledgements.** This work was supported by State Key Laboratory of Smart Grid Protection and Control of NARI Group Corporation.

## References

1. Sanctis, M.D., Cianca, E., Araniti, G., et al.: Satellite communications supporting internet of remote things. IEEE Internet Things J. **3**(1), 113–123 (2016)
2. Qu, Z., Zhang, G., Cao, H., et al.: LEO satellite constellation for internet of things. IEEE Access **5**(99), 18391–18401 (2017)
3. Kawamoto, Y., Nishiyama, H., Kato, N., et al.: Internet of things (IoT): present state and future prospects. IEICE Trans. Inf. Syst. **97**, 2568–2575 (2014)
4. Guo, Z., Yan, Z.: A Weighted Semi-Distributed Routing Algorithm for LEO Satellite Networks. Academic Press Ltd., Cambridge (2015)
5. Grawal, D.P., Zeng, Q.A.: Introduction to Wireless and Mobile Systems. Publishing House of Electionics Industry, Beijing (2016)
6. Miao, Y., Sun, Z., Yao, F., Wang, N., Cruickshank, H.S.: Study on research challenges and optimization for internetworking of hybrid MANET and satellite networks. In: Dhaou, R., Beylot, A.-L., Montpetit, M.-J., Lucani, D., Mucchi, L. (eds.) PSATS 2013. LNICST, vol. 123, pp. 90–101. Springer, Cham (2013). https://doi.org/10.1007/978-3-319-02762-3_8
7. SANSA-Horizon 2020 Project site. http://www.sansa-h2020.eu
8. Del Re, E., Jayousi, S., Morosi, S., et al.: SALICE project: satellite-assisted localization and communication systems for emergency services. In: International Conference on Wireless Communication, Vehicular Technology, Information Theory and Aerospace & Electronic Systems Technology (2009) Wireless Vitae, pp. 544–548 (2013)

9. Oliveira, A., Sun, Z., Monier, M., et al.: On optimizing hybrid ad-hoc and satellite networks—the MONET approach. In: Future Network and Mobile Summit, pp. 1–8 (2011)
10. Al-khatib, A.A., Hassan, R.: Performance evaluation of AODV, DSDV, and DSR routing protocols in MANET using NS-2 simulator. In: Saeed, F., Gazem, N., Patnaik, S., Saed Balaid, A.S., Mohammed, F. (eds.) IRICT 2017. LNDECT, vol. 5, pp. 276–284. Springer, Cham (2018). https://doi.org/10.1007/978-3-319-59427-9_30
11. Thapar, S., Kalla, A.: A review on performance evaluation of routing protocols in MANET. In: Afzalpulkar, N., Srivastava, V., Singh, G., Bhatnagar, D. (eds.) Proceedings of the International Conference on Recent Cognizance in Wireless Communication & Image Processing, pp. 59–68. Springer, New Delhi (2016). https://doi.org/10.1007/978-81-322-2638-3_7
12. Ekici, E., Akyildiz, I.F., Bender, M.D.: A distributed routing algorithm for datagram traffic in LEO satellite networks. IEEE/ACM Trans. Netw. 9, 137–147 (2001)
13. Liu, H., Sun, F., Yang, Z., et al.: A novel distributed routing algorithm for LEO satellite network. In: International Conference on Industrial Control and Electronics Engineering. IEEE, pp. 37–40 (2012)
14. Gounder, V.V., Prakash, R., Abu-Amara, H.: Routing in LEO-based satellite networks. in: Wireless Communications and Systems (2000), 1999 Emerging Technologies Symposium IEEE, pp. 22.1–22.6 (1999)
15. Song, P., Wu, J., Jiang, H., et al.: Snapshot integration routing for high-resolution satellite sensor networks based on delay-tolerent network. In: IEEE International Conference on Computer and Information Technology; Ubiquitous Computing and Communications; Dependable, Autonomic and Secure Computing; Pervasive Intelligence and Computing. IEEE, pp. 2400–2406 (2016)
16. Tan, H., Zhu, L.: A novel routing algorithm based on virtual topology snapshot in LEO satellite networks. In: IEEE International Conference on Computational Science and Engineering, pp. 357–361 (2014)
17. Tang, Z., Feng, Z., Han, W., et al.: ISL reassignment based snapshot routing optimization for polar-orbit LEO satellite networks. IEICE Trans. Commun. 98, 1896–1905 (2015)
18. Fischer, D., Basin, D., Eckstein, K., et al.: Predictable mobile routing for spacecraft networks. IEEE Trans. Mob. Comput. 12(6), 1174–1187 (2013)
19. ITU-R: M.1636 : Basic reference models and performance parameters of internet protocol packet network transmission in the mobile-satellite service (2010)
20. Network performance objectives for IP-based services, ITU-T Y.1541 (2011). http://www.itu.int/rec/T-REC-Y.1541-201112-I/en

# An Improved Quadratic Programming LLOP Algorithm for Wireless Localization

Guangzhe Liu, Jingyu Hua$^{(\boxtimes)}$, Feng Li, Weidang Lu,
and Zhijiang Xu

College of Information Engineering, Zhejiang University of Technology,
Hangzhou 310023, China
eehjy@163.com

**Abstract.** With the rapid increasing of smart devices, wireless positioning technology has become a hot research area. Accordingly, this paper puts forward an optimization-based localization in the wireless network, in which both the quadratic programming (QP) and the principle of linear line of position (LLOP) are taken into account. Moreover, a two-step improvement is proposed to enhance the constrained optimization model, and the simulations demonstrate its effectiveness. Among the tested localization methods, the proposed algorithm performs the best in the non-line-of-sight (NLOS) propagating environment, and its estimating stability over original LLOP algorithm is also obviously observed.

**Keywords:** Wireless localization · Linear line of position (LLOP)
Quadratic programming · Non-line-of-sight error

## 1 Introduction

As early as 1996, the Federal Communications Commission (FCC) of the United States proposed the E-911 location service requirement [1], requiring network operators to provide location services for dialing 911 emergency phone users and ensure certain positioning accuracy. Moreover, with the development of mobile communications and the popularity of smart phones, wireless location technology has become an important research direction in the field of communications [2].

The existing location technology mainly uses time of arrival (TOA) [3, 4], angle of arrival (AOA) [5, 6], and time difference of arrival (TDOA) [7, 8]. In addition, there are also methods based on the received signal strength (RSS) [9, 10] and channel state information (CSI) [11, 12]. However in practical mobile communication systems, any positioning algorithm will suffer from various errors, such as NLOS error, measurement error, multi-path propagation and near-far effect, among which the NLOS error affects the localization performance most significantly [13]. Nokia conducted field tests on the GSM network and found that the NLOS error was up to 1,300 m [14].

In the existing positioning technology, the influence of NLOS error could be reduced by two kinds of methods, i.e., the direct reduction and the indirect reduction. The former identified the NLOS propagation, and then estimated position using line-of-sight (LOS) measurements only, such as the residual method of Wylie [15] and the hypothesis text of [16, 17]. On the other hand, the second kind of methods might

© ICST Institute for Computer Sciences, Social Informatics and Telecommunications Engineering 2018
L. Meng and Y. Zhang (Eds.): MLICOM 2018, LNICST 251, pp. 510–518, 2018.
https://doi.org/10.1007/978-3-030-00557-3_50

include the weighted algorithms [18], the optimized solution algorithms [19], the residual weight method [20].

This paper expands and improves the optimization based LLOP algorithm in [21]. On the basis of quadratic programming optimization, a new distance constraint is introduced according to a two-step processing. First, the proposed algorithm operates the original LLOP method to obtain coarse position estimation, and determine which region the target belongs to. Second, a tighter distance constraint is proposed according to the target region. Finally, the model is solved to obtain the optimal solution. Simulation results show that the improved algorithm has higher accuracy than the original algorithm and is also superior to other NLOS algorithms.

## 2   The Distance Measurement Model for Localization

Generally, we can calculate the distance $(R_i)$ between the mobile station (MS) and the base station (BS) as:

$$R_i = c\tau_i \tag{1}$$

where $c$ and $\tau_i$ represent the light speed and the TOA of $i$-th BS and MS.

Denoting $(X_m, Y_m)$ and $(x_i, y_i)$ as the MS position and the known coordinates of $i$-th base station, we have the distance equation according to Fig. 1

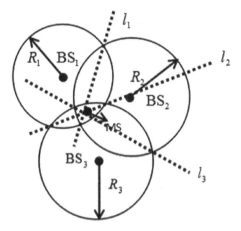

**Fig. 1.** Two-dimensional space model of LLOP positioning algorithm

$$R_i = \sqrt{(X_m - x_i)^2 + (Y_m - y_i)^2} \tag{2}$$

In Fig. 1, if there are three BSs, the MS position can be estimated by the intersection of lines $\{l_1, l_2, l_3\}$. When the number of BS is greater than three, the MS location can be obtained by the least squares estimation. Such an estimate is usually called as the LLOP estimation. Moreover, Zheng et al. had extended the LLOP algorithm to an optimization method, where the scaled range measurement was expressed as

$$r_i = \alpha_i R_i \tag{3}$$

where $r_i$ and $\alpha_i$ represent the scaled range and the scaling factor. In an actual cellular network, the measurement distance between the BS and MS must be greater than the actual distance due to the influence of NLOS error, i.e., $\alpha_i \leq 1$.

It is clear that MS is located within the intersecting region of circles in Fig. 1, then combining Eqs. (2) and (3), we have

$$\alpha_i^2 R_i^2 = (X_m - x_i)^2 + (Y_m - y_i)^2, i = 1, 2, \ldots, n \tag{4}$$

Let $\mathbf{v} = [v_1, v_2, \cdots, v_n]^{\mathrm{T}} = \left[\alpha_1^2, \alpha_2^2, \cdots, \alpha_n^2\right]^{\mathrm{T}}$, then if we can get the true value or accurate estimation of $\mathbf{v}$, we can solve (4) to accurately estimate the MS position, which has been explained in [21]. Next, we will use the abbreviation LLOP to denote the algorithm of [21].

## 3 The Two-Step Optimization Based LLOP Method

### 3.1 The New and Tighter Distance Constraint

For a wireless network consisting of $n$ BSs, the lower limit of the vector $\mathbf{v}$ should satisfy the following conditions [22],

$$\begin{cases} \alpha_{1,\min} = \max\left\{\frac{D_{1,2} - R_2}{R_1}, \frac{D_{1,3} - R_3}{R_1}, \cdots, \frac{D_{1,n} - R_n}{R_1}\right\} \\ \quad\quad\quad\quad \vdots \\ \alpha_{n,\min} = \max\left\{\frac{D_{1,n} - R_1}{R_n}, \frac{D_{1,3} - R_2}{R_n}, \cdots, \frac{D_{1,n} - R_{n-1}}{R_n}\right\} \end{cases} \tag{5}$$

where $\max(\bullet)$ and $D_{i,j}$ represent the maximum operation and the distance between the $i$-th and $j$-th BSs.

In general, the value of $v_i$ will not exceed one, i.e., $\mathbf{v_{max}} = [1, 1, \cdots, 1]$. Then we can get the constraint of $\mathbf{v}$

$$\mathbf{v_{min}} \leq \mathbf{v} \leq \mathbf{v_{max}} \tag{6}$$

However, the above constraint is loose, which makes the methods in [21] and [22] insufficiently suppress the NLOS error.

In order to tackle above issue, we take into consideration the classic seven-BS topology, where the MS is within a regular hexagon as shown in Fig. 2. Since the regular hexagon is symmetric and without loss of generality, we assume that MS is located in the triangle constructed by $\{BS_1, BS_2, BS_3\}$, and denoting $R$ as distance between neighboring BSs, we have

$$r_i \leq R, i = 1, 2, 3 \tag{7}$$

Besides, the distance measurements of other BSs must obey

$$r_i \leq 2R, i = 4, 5, 6, 7 \tag{8}$$

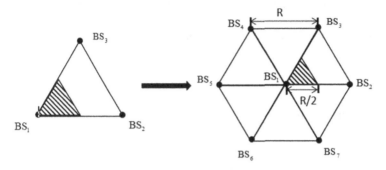

**Fig. 2.** The seven-BS topology

In particular, when the MS is located in the shaded area of Fig. 2, we have

$$r_i \leq \frac{3}{2}R \tag{9}$$

In fact, formula (9) means that the MS is located in the cell centered at $BS_1$. Moreover, the MS must belong to a certain cell in the cellular network, and therefore formula (9) is always correct for the cellular network, so long as we choose the MS-belonged BS as the $BS_1$.

According to the above discussions, so long as the MS region is known, we can construct tighter distance constraint for the optimizations. Then, how to obtain the knowledge of MS region will be explained next.

### 3.2 The Improved Two-Step LLOP Algorithm

Since we need know the coarse MS region, we propose a two-step processing in our study. In the phase I, after the $BS_1$ is determined, we operate the original LLOP algorithm of [21] to obtain the coarse estimation of MS position. Then, we can judge which region the MS belongs to. In the phase II, we can construct the constraint according to the MS region knowledge and formula (7)–(9). However, we also observe a small number of failure region decision, thus we will construct the proposed distance constraint in a robust manner. Then, the simulations demonstrate the above failure does not result in obvious performance degradation.

We have the following optimization cost

$$F(\mathbf{v}) = \sum_{i=1}^{n} \left| (x - x_i)^2 + (y - y_i)^2 - \alpha_i^2 R_i^2 \right| = \sum_{i=1}^{n} \left| (x - x_i)^2 + (y - y_i)^2 - v_i R_i^2 \right| \quad (10)$$

where $(x, y)$ represents the estimated coordinates of MS. Note that the objective function is defined as the cumulative sum of difference between two distances, i.e., the scaled range measurement and the computed distance from the MS position estimate to the BS.

According to Fig. 2 and (9), we revise the new constraint as

$$\begin{cases} \alpha_1 R_1 \leq \frac{1}{2} R \\ \alpha_i R_i \leq \frac{3}{2} R, i \neq 1 \end{cases} \quad (11)$$

Now the optimization model can derived as

$$\begin{aligned} & \underset{\mathbf{v}}{\text{Minimize}} \quad F(\mathbf{v}) \\ & \text{s.t.} \begin{cases} \mathbf{v}_{\min} \leq \mathbf{v} \leq \mathbf{v}_{\max} \\ \alpha_1 R_1 \leq \frac{1}{2} R \\ \alpha_i R_i \leq \frac{3}{2} R, i \neq 1 \end{cases} \end{aligned} \quad (12)$$

The model (12) can be solved by the QP tool, then the optimized vector $\mathbf{v}$ can be found, and therefore the optimized $r_i$ and position estimation.

Formula (4) can be expanded as

$$\begin{cases} v_2 R_2^2 - v_1 R_1^2 + x_1^2 + y_1^2 - x_2^2 - y_2^2 = -2(x_2 - x_1)x - 2(y_2 - y_1)y \\ v_3 R_3^2 - v_1 R_1^2 + x_1^2 + y_1^2 - x_3^2 - y_3^2 = -2(x_3 - x_1)x - 2(y_3 - y_1)y \\ \vdots \\ v_n R_n^2 - v_1 R_1^2 + x_1^2 + y_1^2 - x_n^2 - y_n^2 = -2(x_n - x_1)x - 2(y_n - y_1)y \end{cases} \quad (13)$$

and the matrix form is

$$\mathbf{Y} = \mathbf{AX} \quad (14)$$

where $\mathbf{X} = [x \ y]^{T}$, $\mathbf{A} = \begin{bmatrix} x_1 - x_2, y_1 - y_2 \\ \vdots \\ x_1 - x_n, y_1 - y_n \end{bmatrix}$.

To facilitate the constraint on $\mathbf{v}$, we denote $\mathbf{Y}$ as $\mathbf{Y} = \mathbf{Y}_1 \bullet \mathbf{v} + \mathbf{Y}_2$, where

$$\mathbf{Y}_1 = \begin{bmatrix} -R_1^2, R_2^2, 0, 0, \ldots, 0 \\ -R_1^2, 0, R_3^2, 0, \ldots, 0, \\ \vdots \\ -R_1^2, 0, 0, \ldots, 0, R_n^2 \end{bmatrix}, \mathbf{Y}_2 = \begin{bmatrix} x_2^2 + y_2^2 - x_1^2 - y_1^2 \\ x_3^2 + y_3^2 - x_1^2 - y_1^2 \\ \vdots \\ x_n^2 + y_n^2 - x_1^2 - y_1^2 \end{bmatrix}.$$

Then, we can use the least squares method to estimate the MS position:

$$\hat{\mathbf{X}} = \left(\mathbf{A}^{\mathrm{T}}\mathbf{A}\right)^{-1}\mathbf{A}^{\mathrm{T}}(\mathbf{Y}_1 \bullet \mathbf{v} + \mathbf{Y}_2) \tag{15}$$

which leads to the cost function

$$F(\mathbf{v}) = \sum_{i=1}^{n} \left| norm\left(\hat{\mathbf{X}} - BS_i\right) - v_i R_i^2 \right| \tag{16}$$

where norm $(x)$ means the norm of vector $x$. Now, by using (12), (13) and (16), we can find the optimal solution for $\mathbf{v}$ and therefore the optimal MS position estimation of (16).

## 4   Simulation and Analysis

Assume that there are five BSs located at $(0, R)$, $(\frac{R}{2}, \frac{\sqrt{3}}{2}R)$, $(-\frac{R}{2}, \frac{\sqrt{3}}{2}R)$, $(-R, 0)$, $(-\frac{R}{2}, -\frac{\sqrt{3}}{2}R)$, and $R$ represents the distance between adjacent BSs, i.e., $R = 1000\,\mathrm{m}$ in our study. Moreover, we address two main sources of errors: the NLOS $(d_{NLOS})$ and measurement error $(m_{ERROR})$, thus we have

$$R_i = r_i + d_{NLOS} + m_{ERROR} \tag{17}$$

where $d_{NLOS}$ is uniformly distributed between 100 m and MAX, while $m_{ERROR}$ is a zero-mean Gaussian with a standard deviation of 10 m. In addition, MS is uniformly distributed in the shaded area shown in Fig. 2.

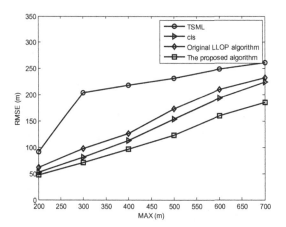

**Fig. 3.** RMSE variations versus different MAXs

In order to demonstrate the superiority of the proposed algorithm, we compare it with the original LLOP algorithm [21], TDOA two-step maximum likelihood algorithm (TSML) [23] and CLS algorithm [24]. We independently operate each simulation for 1000 times.

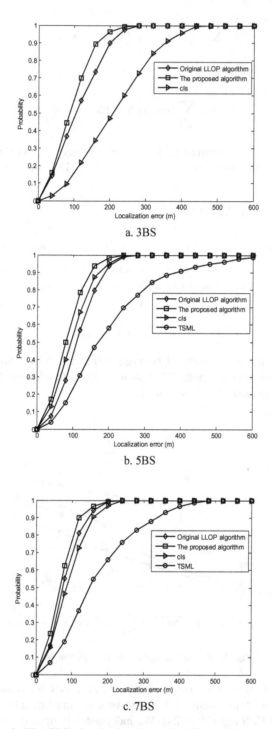

a. 3BS

b. 5BS

c. 7BS

**Fig. 4.** The CDF of each algorithm with different BS numbers

*(A) Influence of NLOS Error*
The minimum value of NLOS error equals 100 m, and we study the effect of MAX on the localization performance in Fig. 3.

Figure 3 shows the root mean square error (RMSE) of each algorithm. It can be clearly seen that the positioning accuracy of the proposed algorithm is improved by about 20% compared with the original algorithm. Meanwhile, it is superior to the other two algorithms. In addition, the larger the value of MAX, the more obvious the performance advantages of the proposed algorithm. Finally, with the increase of NLOS error, the performance of all algorithms will continue to degrade.

*(B) Effect of BS Number*
Here the value of MAX is 400 m and the comparison is shown by cumulative distribution function (CDF). Note that the TSML algorithm is only applicable to the case with more than three BSs, thus it is not used for performance comparison in the case of three BSs.

Figure 4 shows the influence of BS number. From it, we can explicitly see that the proposed algorithm yields obvious performance advantages for all tested BS numbers. In detail, the proposed algorithm outperforms other three conventional algorithms, whose CDF of 150 m error approximately equals 0.85 (3BS), 0.91 (5BS) and 0.96 (7BS).

## 5   Conclusion

Suppression of NLOS errors is a key and difficult issue in wireless localization. The proposed algorithm transforms the NLOS error suppression into a quadratic programming problem with new distance constraints. Simulations demonstrate that the proposed algorithm can reduce the impact of NLOS errors effectively and produce higher positioning accuracy than other conventional algorithms.

**Acknowledgement.** This paper was sponsored by the National Natural Science Foundation of China under grant No. 61471322.

## References

1. Reed, J., Rappaport, T.: An overview of the challenges and progress in meeting the E-911 requirement for location service. IEEE Commun. Mag. **36**(4), 30–37 (1998)
2. Konings, D., Faulkner, N., Alam, F., et al.: Do RSSI values reliably map to RSS in a localization system. In: Proceedings of the IEEE Recent Trends in Telecommunications Research, pp. 1–5 (2017)
3. Yang, C.Y., Chen, B.S., Liao, F.K.: Mobile location estimation using fuzzy-based IMM and data fusion. IEEE Trans. Mobile Comput. **9**(10), 1424–1436 (2010)
4. Liu, D., Wang, Y., He, P., et al.: TOA localization for multipath and NLOS environment with virtual stations. EURASIP J. Wirel. Commun. Netw. (2017). https://doi.org/10.1186/s13638-017-0896-1
5. Bnilam, N., Ergeerts, G., Subotic, D., et al.: Adaptive probabilistic model using angle of arrival estimation for IoT indoor localization. In: Proceedings of the IEEE International Conference on Indoor Positioning and Indoor Navigation, pp. 1–7 (2017)

6. Tomic, S., Beko, M., Rui, D., et al.: A closed-form solution for RSS/AoA target localization by spherical coordinates conversion. IEEE Wirel. Commun. Lett. **5**(6), 680–683 (2016)

7. Huang, B., Xie, L., Yang, Z.: TDOA-based source localization with distance-dependent noises. IEEE Trans. Wirel. Commun. **14**(1), 468–480 (2015)

8. Gholami, M.R., Gezici, S., Strom, E.G.: TDOA based positioning in the presence of unknown clock skew. IEEE Trans. Commun. **61**(6), 2522–2534 (2013)

9. Khalajmehrabadi, A., Gatsis, N., Pack, D., et al.: A joint indoor WLAN localization and outlier detection scheme using LASSO and elastic-net optimization techniques. IEEE Trans. Mobile Comput. **16**(8), 2079–2092 (2017)

10. Narzullaev, A., Park, Y., Yoo, K., et al.: A fast and accurate calibration algorithm for real-time locating systems based on the received signal strength indication. AEU-Int. J. Electron. Commun. **65**(4), 305–311 (2011)

11. Demeechai, T., Kukieattikool, P., Ngo, T., et al.: Localization based on standard wireless LAN infrastructure using MIMO-OFDM channel state information. EURASIP J. Wirel. Commun. Netw. **146**, 1–16 (2016)

12. Pecoraro, G., Domenico, S.D., Cianca, E., et al.: LTE signal fingerprinting localization based on CSI. In: Proceedings of the IEEE International Conference on Wireless and Mobile Computing, Networking and Communications, pp. 1–8 (2017)

13. Lo, Y.C., Chiu, C.C., Huang, C.H.: Mitigating NLOS error for UWB positioning system. In: Proceedings of the IET International Conference on Wireless, Mobile and Multimedia Networks, pp. 1–3 (2006)

14. Silventoinen, M.I., Rantalainen, T.: Mobile station emergency locating in GSM. In: Proceedings of the IEEE International Conference on Personal Wireless Communications, pp. 232–238 (1996)

15. Wylie, M.P., Holtzman, J.: The non-line of sight problem in mobile location estimation. In: Proceedings of the IEEE International Conference on Universal Personal Communications, pp. 827–831 (1996)

16. Muqaibel, A.H., Landolsi, M.A., Mahmood, M.N.: Practical evaluation of NLOS/LOS parametric classification in UWB channels. In: Proceedings of the International Conference on Communications, Signal Processing, and Their Applications, pp. 1–6 (2013)

17. Almazrouei, E., Sindi, N.A., Al-Araji, S.R., et al.: Measurement and analysis of NLOS identification metrics for WLAN systems. In: Proceedings of the IEEE International Symposium on Personal, Indoor, and Mobile Radio Communication, pp. 280–284 (2015)

18. Chan, Y.W.E., Soong, B.H.: Discrete weighted centroid localization (dWCL): performance analysis and optimization. IEEE Access **4**, 6283–6294 (2016)

19. Yang, K., An, J., Bu, X., et al.: A TOA-based location algorithm for NLOS environments using quadratic programming. In: Proceedings of the IEEE Wireless Communications and Networking Conference, pp. 1–5 (2010)

20. Al-Qahtani, K.M., Al-Ahmari, A.S., Muqaibel, A.H., et al.: Improved residual weighting for NLOS mitigation in TDOA-based UWB positioning systems. In: Proceedings of the International Conference on Telecommunications, pp. 211–215 (2014)

21. Zheng, X., Hua, J., Zheng, Z., et al.: LLOP localization algorithm with optimal scaling in NLOS wireless propagations. In: Proceedings of the IEEE International Conference on Electronics Information and Emergency Communication, pp. 45–48 (2013)

22. Venkatraman, S., Caffery, J.J., You, H.R.: A novel TOA location algorithm using LOS range estimation for NLOS environments. IEEE Trans. Veh. Technol. **53**(5), 1515–1524 (2004)

23. Chan, Y.T., Ho, K.C.: A simple and efficient estimator for hyperbolic location. IEEE Trans. Signal Process. **42**(8), 1905–1915 (1994)

24. Wang, X., Wang, Z., O'Dea, B.: A TOA-based location algorithm reducing the errors due to non-line-of-sight (NLOS) propagation. IEEE Trans. Veh. Technol. **52**(1), 112–116 (2003)

# Optimize Bundle Size in Satellite DTN Links with Markov Method

Peiyuan Si, Weidang Lu$^{(\boxtimes)}$, Zhijiang Xu, and Jingyu Hua

School of Information, Zhejiang University of Technology, Hangzhou,
People's Republic of China
490854591@qq.com, {luweid,zyfxzj,eehjy}@zjut.edu.cn

**Abstract.** Disruption-tolerant networks (DTN) are very useful in situations that links are unstable and bandwidth is precious, i.e. inter satellite links. Both distance and the size of transmitted bundles can affect the performance of network. As the distance of two satellites is predictable, we can optimize the size of bundle to achieve shorter delivery time. In this paper, we proposed a Markov method to optimize bundle size and tried to simplify the algorithm and improve its performance.

**Keywords:** Disruption-tolerant networks · Bundle size optimization
Markov decision · Inter-satellite-link

## 1  Introduction

In a inter satellite link (ISL), there many restrictions, i.e. limited resource of nodes, intermittent connection, long latency due to distance. Traditional TCP/IP protocol no longer works in such situation and delay tolerant network (DTN) was proposed to solve this kind of problems [1] and it has lots of advantages in space communication [2]. DTN networks use a custody transfer mechanism (intermediate node keeps a copy of received bundle until it was forwarded to next hop successfully) so that bundles can be delivered under terrible transmission conditions. Bundle protocol can be compatible with other underlying protocols and applied to many fields as an overlay layer protocol, which makes DTN more suitable for inter satellite links.

The Protocol Data Unit of bundle protocol is called bundle, which is sent to the convergence layer and fragmented into smaller segments. Bundle protocol provides reliable delivering service of bundles and the convergence layer, which works below bundle layer, provides fast and reliable data transmission. Bundle size and segment size are different in different protocols, which have significant impact on the performance of DTN as shown in recent studies. Sending messages with large bundles can reduce the transfer time of a file but on the other hand, if bundle is too large, it may even not be delivered due to the long latency of inter satellite link and lead to zero throughput. Sending with smaller bundles can improve the probability of a bundle is delivered successfully but also leads to longer transfer time. We can improve the performance of DTN by optimizing the size of bundles.

© ICST Institute for Computer Sciences, Social Informatics and Telecommunications Engineering 2018
L. Meng and Y. Zhang (Eds.): MLICOM 2018, LNICST 251, pp. 519–530, 2018.
https://doi.org/10.1007/978-3-030-00557-3_51

## 2 Related Work

Recently, a lot of studies focus on bundle size optimization in DTN links. In [3], a method is proposed to calculate the delivery time of bundle in space communication. Works has been done on message fragmentation in single links, such as solving the problem of in-time transmission of fragmented messages in single link disrupted networks [4] and the impact of fragmentation on message forwarding over a single link is investigated in [5]. In [6], the relationship between packet size and the performance such as delay and goodput at the convergence layer and the bundle layer is analyzed and formulated. The work in [7] evaluated the impact of transport segmentation policy on DTN performance and proposed a generic method to determine packet size in DTNs. The work in [8] proposed a fragmentation algorithm which divides the original packets into smaller ones whose size is bounded by the kth largest value among the last k + m channel availability periods. In [9], a bundle fragmentation policy for vehicle networks is presented and tested in a laboratory environment.

## 3 System Model

### 3.1 DTN Structure and Bundle Size Selection

In a satellite DTN network, BP layer receives message from application and encapsulate them into bundles, then LTP agent receives bundles from BP layer, encapsulate them into blocks and slice them into segments. Figure 1 shows the message transfer procedure in a DTN over two-hop ISL in which segment is considered as a basic data unit. The source node is only responsible for sending message and the intermediate node is only responsible for forwarding. The dotted lines represent path of acknowledgement character (ACK) while the solid lines represent path of bundle custody transfer. In the custody transfer mechanism, intermediate node keeps a copy of the received bundle and deletes it when the bundle is transferred successfully to the next hop.

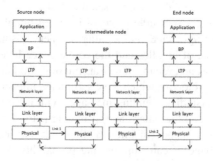

**Fig. 1.** DTN protocol model

To find a series of optimal bundle size, our Markov algorithm operates in BP layer and will return an optimal size of bundle at each moment (according to time-varying channel parameters). As the relative position of two satellites changes very fast over time and distance of two nodes has direct impact on propagation delay, we consider that other parameters of two links are stable and simplify the problem as optimizing the bundle size under time-varying distance. Link I and link II are two independent channels and have different channel parameters, so we should optimize the bundle size of two links jointly.

The optimal bundle size is selected from a set of optional bundle sizes which is related to the size of message. It can be integer times of the minimal bundle size and the algorithm decide the optimal bundle size according to the current state of transmission (Fig. 2).

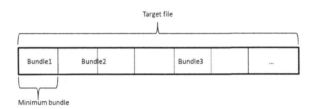

**Fig. 2.** Bundle size selection

## 3.2 Delivery Time Calculation

In this paper we intend to minimize the total delivery time of a file by optimizing the bundle size, so we need to calculate the round trip time (RTT) of one bundle. RTT consists of bundle and ACKs transmission delay and propagation delay, which is calculated as follows

$$\text{RTT}(t) = 2 \cdot T_p(t) + T_{ca} + T_b(t) \tag{1}$$

If a bundle is lost during transmission, retransmission will start after custody-confirm timer (CTRT) is timeout

$$\text{CTRT}(t) = 2 \cdot T_p(t) + T_{ca} \tag{2}$$

Propagation delay (Tp) can be calculated through distance D(t) and propagation speed c (speed of electromagnetic wave)

$$T_p(t) = D(t)/c \tag{3}$$

ACK transmission delay $T_{ca}$ and bundle transmission delay $T_b$ is calculated as follows

$$T_{ca} = L_{ca}/R_{ca} \tag{4}$$

$$T_b = L_{bundle}/R_{data} \tag{5}$$

As a result, taking bundle loss probability $P_{ef}(t)$ into consideration, round-trip time of one bundle should be calculated as follows

$$RTT_{ev}(t) = \left(1 - P_{ef}(t)\right) \cdot RTT(t) + P_{ef}(t) \cdot CTRT(t) \tag{6}$$

Bundle loss probability $P_{ef}$ is related to bundle size and bit error rate Pe(t).

$$P_{ef}(t) = 1 - (1 - P_e(t))^{8 \cdot Lbundle} \tag{7}$$

In which

$$P_e(t) = 1/2 \cdot erfc\left(\sqrt{SNR(t)}\right) \tag{8}$$

The function 'erfc' is complementary error function. Signal to noise ratio (SNR) is calculated by a series of channel parameters such as free space path loss ($L_{space}$) and other constant variables. SNR is calculate as follows

$$SNR(t) = E_0 - 10lgL_{space}(t) \tag{9}$$

In which

$$10lgL_{space}(t) = cons + 20lgD(t) + 20lgf \tag{10}$$

(Frequency is expressed as f) Thus, $P_e(t)$ can be represented as

$$P_e(t) = 1/2 \cdot erfc\left(\sqrt{E0 - (cons + 20lgD(t) + 20lgf)}\right) \tag{11}$$

Let

$$C_0 = E0 - (cons + +20lgf) \tag{12}$$

(The constant 'cons' equals to 92.45 dB) In conclusion, RTT can be represented as

$$RTT_{ev}(t) = \left(1 - 1/2 \cdot erfc\left(\sqrt{C_0 - 20lgD(t)}\right)\right)^{Lbundle} \times \left(2 \cdot T_p(t) + T_{ca} + T_b(t)\right)$$
$$+ \left(1 - \left(1 - 1/2 \cdot erfc\left(\sqrt{C_0 - 20lgD(t)}\right)\right)^{Lbundle}\right) \times CTRT(t) \tag{13}$$

Actually, some parameters including interference noise and transmit power are not considered, the only time-varying parameter left is distance between two nodes.

# 4  Markov Decision Based Algorithm

In most cases, a fixed optimal bundle size can achieve best network performance because channel parameters don't change rapidly. But in inter satellite links, the relative position of each satellite is always changing and the distance between two satellite changes rapidly and a fixed optimal bundle size is not able to cope with different situations. Thus we propose a Markov decision based method which could continuously update the optimal bundle size under time-varying channels such as two-hop ISL.

## 4.1  Problem Formulation

As shown in Fig. 3, the source node determines the optimal bundle size of current period and forwards the bundle to intermediate node. Intermediate node does not change the bundle size and just forward the received bundle to destination node. For convenience of analysis, we assume that the intermediate node can only restore one bundle, which means another bundle will not be received until the former bundle is forwarded successfully. First, we set a sampling period of channel parameters and in each sampling period we will find an optimal bundle size. Then at the beginning of a period, source node select a bundle size with shortest total round-trip-time from the action set as optimal bundle size of current period. The total RTT includes both RTT of link1 and RTT of link2. Once an optimal bundle size is found, the algorithm output the bundle size into the strategy set and messages will be transmitted with current bundle size until next period.

A relatively small bundle can easily be transmitted and leads to faster transfer of bundle but leads to longer total time of delivering a file. Meanwhile, a relatively big bundle size needs longer continuous connecting time which will cause difficulty in bundle transfer and even zero throughputs. It is very difficult to find a function relationship between the optimal bundle size and distance in the iteration algorithm (which will be stated later), so we choose to traverse all the optional bundle size and find the optimal bundle size the shortest total RTT.

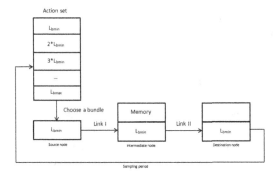

**Fig. 3.** Decision process in two-hop-DTN

## 4.2    Markov Decision Strategy

A standard Markov model consist of five sets: state set, action set, strategy set, transition probability and reword function. In this paper these five set are defined as follows.

**State Set**

The state set is defined as S: {S0, S1}. In state S0, memory of intermediate node is empty and source node is forwarding a bundle to the intermediate node. In state S1, intermediate node has already restored a bundle and the memory is occupied, the intermediate node is forwarding a bundle to the destination node. In other words, S0 represents the procedure of transferring bundles from source node to intermediate node while S1 represents the procedure of transferring bundles from intermediate node to destination node.

S0 and S1 are further divided into a number of child states, each of which contains $Max_r + 1$ grandchild states. The number of child state determined by minimum bundle size and file size. The remaining file size can be expressed as follows

$$R_{file} = L_{file} - i \cdot Lb_{min}$$

And the total number of divided states is

$$N_s = \frac{L_{file}}{Lb_{min}} \times (Max_r + 1)$$

**Action Set**

The action set A contains all the optional bundle sizes. Optional bundled size can be integer times of the minimum bundled size $Lb_{min}$ which is defined as a basic data unit. Optional bundle size varies from $Lb_{min}$ to $n \times Lb_{min}$ ($n \times Lb_{min}$ is the maximum acceptable bundle size).

**Strategy Set**

The strategy set is all the bundle sizes outputted by Markov decision algorithm.

**Transition Probability**

Transition probability is related to the grandchild state and bundle loss probability. It is expressed as follows

$$P_{nr} = \left(1 - P_{ef}\right) \cdot P_{ef}^{nr-1}$$

In which $nr$ represents sequence number of grandchild state, which also means how many times retransmission occurs. For example, if next state is the $3^{rd}$ grandchild state of the first child state of $S_0$, it means this bundle is retransmitted twice. In addition, the $(Max_r + 1)_{th}$ grandchild state means the bundle is abandoned.

In particular, state $S_0$ and $S_1$ occurs alternatively. If the current state is $S_{0,i,j}$, the next state must be a child state of $S_1$ whose remaining file size is the same as $S_{0,i,j}$, if the current state is $S_{1,i,j}$ and the selected bundle size is $a_i$, the next state must be a child state of $S_0$ whose remaining file size is $R_{file} - a_i$.

**Reward Function**

The reward function is the required time of a bundle to be successfully delivered from the source node to the destination node (Fig. 4).

$$r = RTT(a) + (n_r - 1) \times CTRT(a)$$

RTT and CTRT can be calculated by (1) and (2).

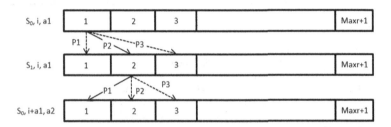

**Fig. 4.** State transition process

### 4.3 Iteration Algorithm

Our goal is to find an optimal bundle size 'a' that minimizes the reward function 'r'. With a set of optional bundle sizes and transition probability, we can infer the whole transition procedure by an iteration algorithm and calculate the corresponding reward function. By comparing all the reward functions produced by different bundle size, we can find the optimal bundle size that minimizes the reward function.

If the current state is $S_0$

$$v0(s_{current}) = \sum_{s\_next} P_{nr}(a) \cdot [r(a) + v1(s\_next)]$$

If the current state is $S_1$

$$v1(s_{current}) = \sum_{s\_next} P_{nr}(a) \cdot [r(a) + v0(s\_next)]$$

The iteration algorithm start from $S_0$ and ends when remaining file size is zero. After calculating the sum of all these terms, the reward function is equal to v0 and bundle size 'a' which produces smallest 'r' is selected as the optimal bundle size. As the distance parameter keeps changing, we update the optimal bundle size using iteration algorithm every sampling period.

The complexity of this algorithm is related to variables such as file size, $Max_r$, minimum bundle size $Lb_{min}$. One of the most important variables is $Max_r$ and number of child states sc because the complexity has an exponential relationship with $Max_r$ and sc.

## 4.4 Algorithm Simplification

The algorithm in Sect. 4.3 is written according to the Markov method directly. In fact its complexity has an exponential relationship with Maxr and sc which can cause huge number of calculations. As Maxr and sc increase, the complexity of former algorithm will become terrible, so we must find a way to reduce the complexity (Table 1).

**Table 1.** Iterative algorithm

```
Input S0,S1,A
While (res_file>0)
        For each s ∈ sum {
                (p_trans1,trans_round1)←(link_state1,a);
                (p_trans2,trans_round2)←(link_state2,a);
        If (trans_round1≤max_trans_round)&( trans_round2≤max_trans_round);
        v0(s) = minₐ Σₙ_next p_trans1 × (r(trans_round1, a) + v1(s_next))
        v1(s) = minₐ Σₙ_next p_trans2 × (r(trans_round2, a) + v0(s_next));
        output(s)←a;
        link_state1←new_state1;
        link_state2←new_state2;
        time_current←new_time;
        res_file←res_file_new;
        End if
    End for
End while
```

We found that the transition probability and bundle size are fixed in each attempt to find the optimal bundle size of each period of the algorithm. Thus, the number of child states can be calculated by $sc = res\_file/a$. The transition probability of $i_{th}$ grandchild state of $j_{th}$ child state is the same as the transition probability of $i_{th}$ grandchild state of $(j + n)_{th}$ child state. So the problem can be simplified as the expected value of sc independent events and the reward function can be calculated as follows

$$r = sc \times \sum_{1}^{maxr} P_{nr1}(a) \times r_1(a) + sc \times \sum_{1}^{maxr} P_{nr2}(a) \times r_2(a)$$

In this way, the complexity of algorithm is reduced to a linear relationship of Maxr and sc.

## 5   Simulation and Numerical Results

We make comparison of performance between Markov method and traditional method, and studied the impact of some parameters in the Markov algorithm. In particular, Lca = 100 Byte, Rca = 8000 bps and C0 = 104.22. We consider the bundle is delivered successfully if the bundle loss probability is less than 0.01. In this paper, Markov method is applied to two-hop LEO-GEO-LEO inter-satellite-link.

In Fig. 5, minimum bundle size of Markov method is 1 Mb and maximum bundle size is 10 Mb. Traditional method take more time to deliver because a bigger bundle size may cause much more delivery time in long distance, and Markov method chooses 1 Mb as optimal bundle size when the distance is longer. The relationship between optimal bundle size and distance is shown in Fig. 6

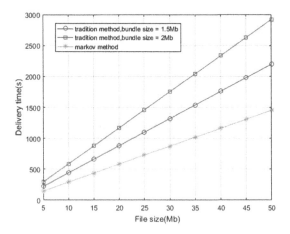

**Fig. 5.** Delivery time comparison

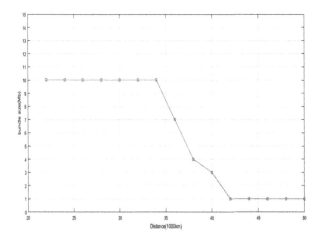

**Fig. 6.** Relationship between optimal bundle size and distance

As the distance gets longer, throughput of both Markov method and traditional decrease to zero, but throughput of Markov method has better resistance of it, as shown in Fig. 7. The performance of Markov method is influenced by $Lb_{max}$ and $Lb_{min}$, and Fig. 8 shows that when the distance reaches 40000 km, the difference of $Lb_{max}$ can be ignored. Figure 9 shows that decreasing $Lb_{min}$ can slightly reduce the delivery time, but if we increase $Lb_{min}$, as shown in Fig. 5, delivery time will increase rapidly.

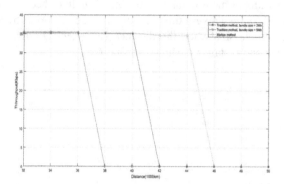

**Fig. 7.** The impact of distance on throughput

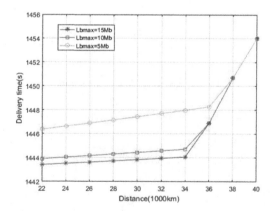

**Fig. 8.** Impact of maximum bundle size

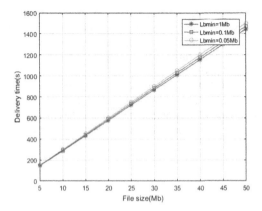

**Fig. 9.** Impact of minimum bundle size

# 6 Conclusions

In this paper, we proposed a bundle optimizing method based on Markov algorithm for two-hop inter-satellite-links and solved the problem of complexity. A dynamic optimal bundle size can adapt to continuously changing channel conditions and make up for the disadvantage of fixed bundle size. The performance of this algorithm can be improved by optimizing some parameters which need further study.

# References

1. Nichols, K., Holbrook, M., Pitts, R., Gifford, K., Jenkins, A., Kuzminsky, S.: DTN implementation and utilization options on the international space station. In: Oral/Visual Presentation of SpaceOps 2010 Conference, 25–30 April, Huntsville, AL, United States (2010). Introduce DTN implementation and operation and its development
2. Davis, F.A., Marquart, J.K., Menke, G.: Benefits of delay tolerant networking for earth science missions. In: Proceedings of IEEE Aerospace Conference, pp. 1–10, March 2012
3. Bezirgiannidis, N., Burleigh, S., Tsaoussidis, V.: Delivery time estimation for space bundles. IEEE Trans. Aerosp. Electron. Syst. **49**(3), 1897–1910 (2013). We present a method for predicting delivery time of bundles in space internetworks
4. Ginzboorg, P., Niemi, V., Ott, J.: Fragmentation algorithms for DTN links. Comput. Commun. **36**, 279–290 (2013). In this paper we show how the problem of in-time transmission of fragmented messages in disrupted networks can be solved in the simplest case of transmission over a single disrupted link
5. Ginzboorg, P., Niemi, V., Ott, J.: Message fragmentation in disruptive networks. NRC-TR-2009-003 (2009). In this paper, we formalize message fragmentation in such networks, investigate the impact of fragmentation on message forwarding over a single link
6. Jiang, F., Lu, H.: Packet size optimization in delay tolerant networks. In: 2014 IEEE 11th Consumer Communications and Networking Conference (CCNC), pp. 392–397. IEEE (2014). Our work focuses on the theoretic analysis and formulates the relationship between packet size at two layers

7. Samaras, C.V., Tsaoussidis, V.: Adjusting transport segmentation policy of DTN Bundle Protocol under synergy with lower layers. J. Syst. Softw. **84**(2), 226–237 (2011)
8. Jelenković, P.R., Tan, J.: Dynamic packet fragmentation for wireless channels with failures. In: Proceedings of the 9th ACM International Symposium on Mobile Ad Hoc Networking and Computing, pp. 73–82 (2008)
9. Magaia, N., Casaca, A., et al.: Bundles fragmentation in vehicular delay-tolerant networks. In: The 7th EURO-NGI Conference on Next Generation Internet (NGI), pp. 1–6 (2011). This paper presents data fragmentation techniques to optimize the efficiency of data delivery for the case of the short node contacts that characterize vehicle networks

# An Efficient Method for Estimating Time Series Motif Length Using Sequitur Algorithm

Nguyen Ngoc Phien[1,2]($\boxtimes$)

[1] Center for Applied Information Technology,
Ton Duc Thang University, Ho Chi Minh City, Vietnam
nguyenngocphien@tdtu.edu.vn
[2] Faculty of Information Technology, Ton Duc Thang University,
Ho Chi Minh City, Vietnam

**Abstract.** Motifs in time series are approximately repeated subsequence found within a long time series data. There are some popular and effective algorithms for finding motif in time series. However, these algorithms still have one major weakness: users of these algorithms are required to select an appropriate value of the motif length which is unknown in advance. In this paper, we propose a novel method to estimate the length of 1-motif in a time series. This method is based on GrammarViz, a variable-length motif detection approach which has Sequitur at its core. Sequitur is known as a grammar compression algorithm that is able to have enough identification not just common subsequences but also identify the hierarchical structure in data. As GrammarViz, our method is also based on the Sequitur algorithm, but for another purpose: a preprocessing step for finding motif in time series. The experimental results prove that our method can help to estimate very fast the length of 1-motif for some TSMD algorithms, such as Random Projection.

**Keywords:** Motif detection · Sequitur algorithm · Grammar inference
Motif length · Time series

## 1 Introduction

Time series (TS) data plays an important role in many fields of life, such as securities, health, communications, financial data, astronomical data, weather, and environmental pollution levels. People have paid great attention to the problem of discovering motif subsequences. Motifs are usually seen but with unidentical arrangements of a longer TS. Motif which is extracted from a TS represented as one of the most remarkable patterns [5, 15].

Since the first work on time series motif discovery (TSMD) was given by Lin et al., 2002 [10], many researchers have proposed expressive algorithms for finding motifs. Some typical algorithms for TSMD can be listed as follow. Chiu et al. in 2003 [4] proposed Random Projection algorithm which utilizes locality-preserving-hashing in TSMD. Tanaka et al. in 2005 [16] proposed EMD algorithm which applies MDL principle. Gruber et al. in 2006 [6] proposed an algorithm by dynamic RBF network. Mueen et al. in 2009 [13] proposed MK algorithm, is an exact algorithm for TSMD.

© ICST Institute for Computer Sciences, Social Informatics and Telecommunications Engineering 2018
L. Meng and Y. Zhang (Eds.): MLICOM 2018, LNICST 251, pp. 531–538, 2018.
https://doi.org/10.1007/978-3-030-00557-3_52

Castro and Azevedo in 2010 proposed a mutiresolution algorithm for TMMD [2]. However, many of them are limited: the requirement the length acknowledgement of the motifs in advance. However, there is an unavailability of those.

Recently in 2012, Li et al., proposed an approximate variable length TSMD algorithm, called GrammarViz [9], which is based on Sequitur algorithm [14]. Sequitur is known as a grammar compression algorithm that is able to have enough identify not just common subsequence but also identify the hierarchical structure in data. GrammarViz does not require users to provide the value of motif length. However, since Sequitur is an online and greedy algorithm, discovering motifs by GrammarViz are not optimal and most of them are relatively short. Therefore, GrammarViz still needs further enhancements to improve its performance.

In this paper, we propose a novel method to estimate the length of 1-motif in a TS. Similar to GrammarViz, our method is also based on the Sequitur algorithm, but for another purpose: a preprocessing step for TSMD. Our method is effective and efficient. The experimental results on six datasets show that our proposed method can help to estimate very fast the length of 1-motif for some motif detection algorithms, such as Random Projection or MK algorithm.

The rest of the paper is organized as follow. Section 2 presents some background and related works. Section 3 presents our proposed method for estimating the length of 1-motif in a time series. Section 4 describes experimental results. Section 5 gives some conclusions.

## 2    Background and Related Works

### 2.1    SAX and ESAX

TS are very high dimensionality and large noises. So we have to reduce time executing and space. The popular approach is to use Symbolic Aggregate Approximation (SAX) [11]. For a TS, it is divided into equal-sized segments by the PAA representation [7]. Next, for each value $\bar{C}_i$ in PAA, SAX maps it to a symbol based on a set of "breakpoints" which are the list of number under $N(0,1)$ Gaussian curve.

Lkhagva et al. in 2006 [12] proposed another discretization method, called ESAX (Extended SAX), which is an extended variant of SAX. Since the SAX method is based on the PAA to reduce the number of dimensionality, resulting in the loss of some important data, and in financial-economic data, these losses are sometimes important data. So the ESAX representation adds two special points to complete the SAX, the smallest and largest points of each segment. Thus, each segment represented by a triple <mean, min, max> which is mapped to three symbols rather than one symbol as in SAX. Experimental results revealed that ESAX can work with higher accuracy than SAX.

### 2.2    Sequitur Algorithm

Sequitur, the algorithm proposed by Nevill-Manning and Witten in 1997 [15], is known as a grammar compression algorithm that is able to have enough identify common subsequence and the hierarchical structure in data. Sequitur has applied in several areas, for example, looking for repetitive DNA sequences [3]. Sequitur generates grammar rules from a string based on repeated substring. Each repeated substring was replaced by a grammatical rule that produces a shorter original string. The Sequitur algorithm reads the input string and restructures the grammar rules to maintain the two following properties:

(i) Digram uniqueness: There is no pair of adjacent symbols appearing more than once in grammar.
(ii) Rule utility: All grammar rules (except the start rule) are used more than once.

Sequitur is an online algorithm, effective in terms of memory space and execution time, requiring $O(m)$ complexity to compress a string of size $m$ [9].

For example, string $S1$ = "$abcabdabcabd$" can be generated from the grammar rules shown in the Table 1.

**Table 1.** An example of Sequitur algorithm

| Grammar rule | The string |
|---|---|
| S1-> BB | abcabdabcabd |
| A-> ab | ab |
| B-> AcAd | abcabd |

The main advantages of Sequitur are three-fold: (i) it automatically detect repeated patterns, for example "$abcabd$" in the above example, and hierarchical structure; (ii) the grammar rules found may be any lengths and (iii) it is appropriate for streaming data.

# 3  Our Proposed Method for Estimating the Length of 1-Motif

Our proposed method for estimating the length of 1-Motif employs the GrammarViz approach for discovering TS motifs of variable lengths. But in our method, we use ESAX rather than SAX for discretization. Our method consists of four phases:

**Phase 1: [Discretization]** In this step, the original TS is discretized into a symbolic string by using ESAX transformation.

**Phase 2: [Applying Sequitur algorithm on ESAX strings]** After having transformed the TS into ESAX strings, we apply Sequitur on the ESAX strings to obtain the grammar rules.

**Phase 3: [Post-processing]** Since the original TS has been discretized before running the algorithm, we have to map the frequent subsequence back to the original TS. The amount of generated rules may be large and similar to association rule mining [1], so we do some refinements on the grammar obtained:

1. Eliminate trivial matches for a motif. The trivial match of a subsequence $M$ is any sequence that overlaps $M$.
2. Arrange the rules according to "interestingness" such as the frequency of occurrence, and the length of the motif.

**Phase 4: [Estimating the length of 1-motif]** Based on the table storing all the induced grammar rules and the plots of all motifs, we can identify the region with the highest density of motif instances. Since this region contains the most significant motif (1-motif) in the TS, we will use it to estimate the length of the 1-motif. This phase consists of 3 steps:

1. Based on the plots of all motifs (one motif for each grammar rule) we can identify the region with the highest density of motif instances. And from our inspection on this region, we can determine the length $n$ of the instances of the 1-motif. This length can be converted to $w$, the corresponding number of ESAX symbols.
2. Looking up at the table which stores all the grammar rules, we can find all the rules (motifs) which have the length approximately equal to $w$. We can also know the frequency of each such rule (motif).
3. In Step 1 we've already known the length $n$ of the 1-motif. We can use this value as the length of 1-motif for the Random Projection algorithm.

To visualize all the motifs found by Sequitur, in Phase 3, for each found grammar rules found we need to record the length of the rule and its start position.

The proposed algorithm can estimate the length of 1-motif with high efficiency. The algorithm requires $O(n)$ to convert the TS into ESAX string, and then requires $O(n)$ to perform Sequitur algorithm.

## 4    Experimental Results

We tested the Sequitur-based method for estimating the length of 1-motif and the TSMD algorithm, Random Projection, MK. Random Projection is chosen in this experiment due to its popularity. It is the most cited time series discovery method up to date and is the basis of many current approaches that handle this problem. We implemented the two algorithms with Microsoft Visual Studio C# 2017 and conducted the experiments on an Intel Core ™i5-525U, CPU@1.6Ghz, 8G RAM PC. We used six datasets from the UCR TS Data Mining Archive [8] for the experiments. The datasets are from different areas. Their names are: ECG, EEG, MEMORY, POWER, STOCK and ERP. We use SAX as discretization method in Random Projection and ESAX in our proposed method.

We set the alphabet size $a$ for SAX and ESAX to 6 and the size of PAA-segment to 10 and the size of *EPAA-segment* to 10.

### 4.1    Accuracy

In this section, we deduce the feasible of using Sequitur to estimate the length of 1-motif in TS. To prove that Sequitur induction can use to identify variable-length motifs, we show an example from the ECG dataset (3500 data points). A part of the grammar rules generated by Phase 2 in our proposed method is shown in the Table 2. Each found grammar rule represents a motif, column 1 and column 3 in Table 2 records the frequency and the length of each rule, respectively.

**Table 2.** An example of grammar rules found.

| Frequency | Rule | Length of motifs |
|---|---|---|
| 0 | R0 -> R1 R1 R2 R3 R4 R5 R6 R7 R6 R8 R9 R10 R11 R12 R13 R13 R14 R7 R14 R14 R14 R15 R16 R17 R17 R17 R18 R18 R19 R20 R21 | 1050 |
| 5 | R1 -> e e | 2 |
| 4 | R2 -> R1 e | 3 |
| 3 | R3 -> R22 R22 | 4 |
| 5 | R4 -> R23 R24 | 14 |
| 4 | R5 -> R8 R8 | 32 |
| 2 | R6 -> R5 R25 | 34 |
| 3 | R7 -> R26 b R27 R28 b R29 R2 R30 R23 R4 R31 | 43 |
| 3 | R8 -> R9 R9 | 16 |
| 6 | R12 -> R21 R30 R1 R23 R3 R24 | 36 |
| 2 | R13 -> R32 R32 | 24 |
| 7 | R14 -> R32 R15 | 18 |
| 2 | R16 -> R20 R12 | 41 |
| 3 | R17 -> R33 R33 | 20 |
| 2 | R18 -> R19 R16 R34 R35 | 210 |
| 2 | R19 -> R36 R7 R35 R34 | 109 |
| ... | ... | ... |

Figure 1 shows the plot of the ECG dataset. Figure 2 shows the plots of 37 motifs which correspond to 37 grammar rules found by Phase 2 in our proposed method on the ECG dataset. From the plots in Fig. 2, we can see that the region with the highest density of motif instances is around the starting part of the figure, and the span of this region is about 100-time points. Based on this observation, we determine the length of 1-motif as 100. Since the size of PAA-segment is 10, we can estimate the length $w$ of 1-motif in ESAX symbols as about 10.

After determining the motif length $w$, we can execute Random Projection or MK to find the 1-motif in the ECG dataset with this parameter value. Random Projection discovered the 1-motif with 9 instances as illustrated in Fig. 3. By inspection, we can see that the shape of the motifs found in the starting part of Fig. 2 in the span of 100 time points is exactly the same as the shape of the 1-motif found by Random Projection shown in Fig. 3.

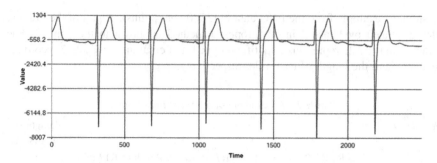

**Fig. 1.** The plot of the ECG time series

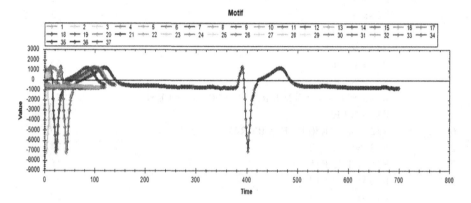

**Fig. 2.** All 37 motifs of different lengths found in ECG 3500 after Phase 2 in our method.

## 4.2 Efficiency

We measure the runtime of our proposed method for estimating the length of 1-motif and the runtime of Random Projection for discovering TS 1-motif. According to the Table 3 the runtime of our proposed method as a preprocessing step requires just a small percentage (about 4.6%) of the runtime for the Random Projection to find 1-motif in TS.

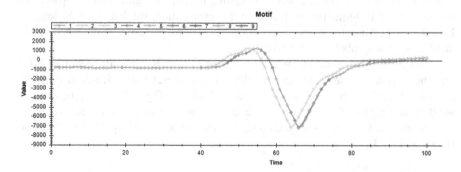

**Fig. 3.** Nine instances of the 1-motif found in ECG 3500 by Random Projection.

**Table 3.** Runtimes of our proposed method and Random Projection on 15 experiments.

| No | Dataset | Length | Our method | Random projection |
|----|---------|--------|------------|-------------------|
|    |         |        | Runtime (msecs) | |
| 1 | koski_ecg -3500 | 3500 | 13 | 240 |
| 2 | koski_ecg -7000 | 7000 | 22 | 893 |
| 3 | koski_ecg -10000 | 10000 | 43 | 1777 |
| 4 | koski_ecg -14000 | 14000 | 68 | 3369 |
| 5 | koski_ecg -20000 | 20000 | 98 | 4533 |
| 6 | Stock1 | 5056 | 45 | 506 |
| 7 | Stock2 | 5056 | 35 | 558 |
| 8 | Stock3 | 5508 | 52 | 579 |
| 9 | Stock4 | 5508 | 55 | 599 |
| 10 | ERP | 6622 | 62 | 803 |
| 11 | ERP2 | 10120 | 94 | 1846 |
| 12 | EEG | 12137 | 66 | 2616 |
| 13 | Memory1 | 13636 | 91 | 3342 |
| 14 | Memory2 | 12000 | 53 | 2766 |
| 15 | Power | 12000 | 51 | 2612 |

## 5 Conclusion and Future Works

We presented a method for estimating the length of 1-motif in a TS which is based on Sequitur algorithm. Our method can be used as a preprocessing step for any TSMD algorithms which requires the length of 1-motif as an input parameter. The results on six datasets prove that our method may use to estimate very fast the length of 1-motif for some motif discovery algorithms, such as Random Projection. As for future work, we plan to apply our method in some real world applications of TS motif discovery.

## References

1. Agrawal, R., Imielinski, T., Swami, A.: Mining association rules between sets of items in large databases. In: Proceedings of the 1993 ACM SIGMOD International Conference on Management of Data, Washington, D.C., pp. 207–216, 26–28 May 1993
2. Castro, N., Azevedo, P.: Multiresolution motif discovery in time series. In: Proceedings of SIAM International Conference on Data Mining, 29 April–1 May, Columbus, Ohio, USA, pp. 665–676 (2010)
3. Cherniavsky, N., Ladner, R.: Grammar-based Compression of DNA Sequences. UW CSE Technical Report 2007-05-02 (2007)
4. Chiu, B., Keogh, E. Lonardi, S.: Probabilistic discovery of time series motifs. In: Proceedings of the 9th International Conference on Knowledge Discovery and Data Mining (KDD 2003), pp. 493–498 (2003)
5. Fu, T.C.: A review on time series data mining. Eng. Appl. Artif. Intell. **24**(1), 164–181 (2011)

6. Gruber, C., Coduro, M., Sick, B.: Signature verification with dynamic RBF network and time series motifs. In: Proceedings of 10th International Workshop on Frontiers in Hand Writing Recognition (2006)
7. Keogh, E., Chakrabarti, K., Pazzani, M., Mehrotra, S.: Dimensionality reduction for fast similarity search in large time series databases. J. Knowl. Inf. Syst. **3**(3), 263–286 (2000)
8. Keogh, E.: The UCR Time Series Data Mining Archive (2018)
9. Li, Y., Lin, J., Oates, T.: Visualizing variable-length time series motifs. In: Proceedings of SDM (2012)
10. Lin, J., Keogh, E., Patel, P., Lonardi, S.: Finding motifs in time series. In: Proceedings of the 2nd Workshop on Temporal Data Mining, at the 8th ACM SIGKDD International Conference on Knowledge Discovery and Data Mining (2002)
11. Lin, J., Keogh, E., Lonardi, S., Chiu, B.: A symbolic representation of time series, with implications for streaming algorithms. In: Proceedings of the 8th ACM SIGMOD Workshop on Research Issues in Data Mining and Knowledge Discovery, San Diego, CA, 13 June 2003
12. Lkhagva, B., Suzuki, K., Kawagoe, K.: Extended SAX: extension of symbolic aggregate approximation for financial time series data representation. In: Proceedings of DEWS Data Engineering Workshop, DNEWS 2006, 4A-i8 (2006)
13. Mueen, A., Keogh, E., Zhu, Q., Cash, S., Westover, B.: Exact discovery of time series motif. In: Proceedings of 2009 SIAM International Conference on Data Mining. SIAM (2009)
14. Nevill-Manning, C.G., Witten, I.H.: Identifying hierarchical structure in sequences: a linear-time algorithm. J. Artif. Intell. Res. **7**, 67–82 (1997)
15. Ratanamahatana, C.A., Lin, J., Gunopulos, D., Keogh, E., Vlachos, M., Das, G.: Mining time series data. In: Maimon, O., Rokach, L. (eds.) Data Mining and Knowledge Discovery Handbook, 2nd edn, pp. 1049–1077. Springer, Heidelberg (2010)
16. Tanaka, Y., Iwamoto, K., Uehara, K.: Discovery of time series motif from multi-dimensional data based on MDL principle. Mach. Learn. **58**(2–3), 269–300 (2005)

# Optimal User Grouping and Resource Allocation for Downlink Non-Orthogonal Multiple Access Systems

Xiaoding Wang$^{(\boxtimes)}$, Kejie Ni, Xiangxu Chen, Yuan Wu, Liping Qian, and Liang Huang

College of Information Engineering, Zhejiang University of Technology, Hangzhou, China
wxd_zjut@163.com, kjni_zjut@163.com, xxchen_zjut@163.com, {iewuy,lpqian,lianghuang}@zjut.edu.cn

**Abstract.** Non-orthogonal multiple access (NOMA) with successive interference cancellation (SIC) has recently been considered as a key enabling technique for 5G cellular networks to satisfy future users' network needs, such as ultra-high transmission rate, ultra-high throughput, ultra-low latency and ultra-high density connections. A group of users is allowed to share the same spectrum and multiplex the power domain to transmit data. In this paper, we investigate the optimization of bandwidth allocation and user grouping under the conditions of transmission power limit, bandwidth allocation limit, and user traffic requirements, so that the total resource consumption is minimized. The key idea to solve the problem is to use the layer structure of the problem and divide the problem into the optimization grouping problem and the bandwidth allocation problem. We propose a simulated annealing algorithm to solve the optimization grouping problem.

**Keywords:** Bandwidth allocation · Power allocation
Non-orthogonal multiple access (NOMA)
Successive interference cancellation (SIC)

## 1 Introduction

Non-Orthogonal Multiple Access (NOMA) [1] is considered to be the most likely user access scheme for 5th generation cellular networks [2]. The key idea of NOMA is to actively introduce interference among users and use the same bandwidth resources to serve multiple users to improve spectrum utilization. Compared with conventional orthogonal multiple access (OMA), NOMA allows multiple message information of multiple users to be superimposed in the power domain. At the receiving end, SIC is used according to the size of the user's channel power gain to eliminate interference and decode each user's information signal, the users' throughput can be improved. Due to these advantages of NOMA, relevant researchers have developed a strong interest in this area.

ⓒ ICST Institute for Computer Sciences, Social Informatics and Telecommunications Engineering 2018
L. Meng and Y. Zhang (Eds.): MLICOM 2018, LNICST 251, pp. 539–548, 2018.
https://doi.org/10.1007/978-3-030-00557-3_53

In [3], Benjebbour *et al.* studied the obvious advantages of NOMA compared with traditional orthogonal access (OMA) in terms of power allocation and high mobility in practical application scenarios. In [4], Wu *et al.* proposed an optimal power allocation and scheduling for NOMA relay-assisted networks. In [5], Di *et al.* studied a joint sub-channel assignment and multi-user power allocation for downlink NOMA to keep balance between the number of served users and the total throughput maximization. In [6], Lei *et al.* proposed a joint channel and multi-user power allocation for downlink NOMA to maximizing the sum-rate utility. In [7], the authors proposed fixed and opportunistic two-user pairing schemes by statically power allocation for 5G NOMA downlink transmissions. In [8], the authors proposed power allocation on the fairness of downlink NOMA which considered perfect channel state information (CSI) feedback as well as average CSI feedback. In [9], an energy-efficient NOMA-enabled traffic offloading through small-cell networks has been proposed. In [10], the authors proposed a cooperative NOMA scheme to achieve the outage probability, diversity order and user pairing approach to reduce system complexity. In [11], the authors investigated the cooperative traffic offloading among mobiles devices, they are focus on receiving a common content from a cellular base station (BS). Considering the fast vehicle mobility and varying communication environment in vehicular communications, Qian *et al.* introduced the NOMA with SIC to the vehicle-to-small-cell networks to achieve dynamically allocate small-cell base stations and transmit power to vehicular users in [12].

Although there have been many studies on the performance of NOMA access solutions in the past, some papers have studied the allocation of channel bandwidth and power of users in a single cluster. Some papers have investigated the user clusters and power allocation (or bandwidth allocation) of multiple users under the condition of fixed bandwidth allocation (or power allocation). In this paper, based on our previous work [13], we consider the optimal multi-user grouping method, bandwidth allocation and power allocation in the downlink, and achieve the optimal total system resource consumption. Our main contributions are summarized below:

- In the downlink NOMA, we propose a method of joint bandwidth and power allocation within multi-user cluster so that the total bandwidth and power resource consumption in the cluster is minimized when the user traffic demand is satisfied.
- A feasible algorithm is provided to optimize the grouping of users to be served in the coverage of the base station (BS) to improve spectrum utilization.

## 2    System Model and Problem Formulation

### 2.1    System Model

We consider a cellular system with one Base Station (BS), and there exists $I$ mobile users (MUs) served by this BS. It is notable that the overall MUs are able to divide into $K$ ($1 \leq K \leq I$) user-cluster(s), which denoted by $\mathcal{K} =$

$\{1, .., k, .., K\}$. Figure 1 plots an illustrative model comprised of one BS, seven MUs and four user-clusters.

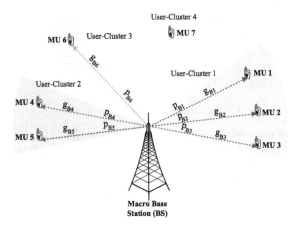

**Fig. 1.** System model comprised of one BS, 7 MUs and 4 user-clusters, with MU 1–3 are choose to access cluster 1 and MU 4–5 are in cluster 2, while cluster 3 only has one MU, which is MU 6. MU 7 is not served by BS.

In this scenario, the BS uses NOMA to send data to each user-cluster on different subchannels. Due to NOMA, the BS can use successive interference cancellation (SIC) to mitigate their intra-cluster co-channel interference when transmitting to the MU(s) in cluster $k$. Hence, the inter-cluster co-channel interference from other clusters (i.e., cluster $k'$, $k' \neq k$) can be neglected.

SIC requires an ordering of the MUs according to their channel power gains with respect to BS. Thus, we introduce the index-set $\mathcal{I}$, in which the group of MUs follow the following descending ordering, expressed as:

$$g_{B1} > g_{B2} > ... > g_{Bi} > ... > g_{BI}, \tag{1}$$

where $g_{Bi}$ denotes the channel power gain from the BS to MU $i, i \in \mathcal{I}$.

We use $a_{ki}$ to denote the $i$-th MU's access-selection to cluster $k$, namely, $a_{ki} = 1$ means that MU $i$ (i.e., the $i$-th MU in $\mathcal{I}$) chooses to access cluster $k$ (i.e., the $k$-th cluster in $\mathcal{K}$), otherwise, $a_{ki} = 0$. Hence, introducing index-set $I_k = \{a_{ki}\}_{k \in \mathcal{K}, i \in \mathcal{I}}$ to represent each cluster's access-selection.

It is reasonable to assume that each MU can only access one cluster, which corresponds to the following constraint:

$$\sum_{k \in \mathcal{K}} a_{ki} \leq 1, \forall i \in \mathcal{I}. \tag{2}$$

Besides, introducing $T_k$ to denote the number of MU(s) that choose to access cluster $k$, which means:

$$T_k = \sum_{i \in \mathcal{I}} a_{ki}, \forall k \in \mathcal{K}. \tag{3}$$

For the sake of easy presentation, we study arbitrary cluster $k$ firstly. We introducing the virtual index $\phi_k(i)$ for MUs in cluster $k$, which defined as follows:

$$\phi_k(i) < \phi_k(i'), \text{when } a_{ki}g_{Bi} > a_{ki'}g_{Bi'}, \forall k \in \mathcal{K}, \forall i, i' \in \mathcal{I}. \tag{4}$$

Similar with (1), in cluster $k$, the larger the channel power gain $g_{Bi}$ from BS to MU $i$, the smaller $\phi_k(i)$ will be. Moreover, we defined that $\phi_k(i) = 1$ when $i$ is the smallest ordering number according to (1) in cluster $k$, and $\phi_k(i) = T_k$ when $i$ is the biggest one.

Using $p_{Bki}$ to denote the transmit-power from BS to MU $i$ in cluster $k$, proposed the following constraint:

$$(1 - a_{ki})p_{Bki} = 0, \forall k \in \mathcal{K}, \forall i \in \mathcal{I}. \tag{5}$$

namely, $p_{Bki} > 0$ only when $a_{ki} = 1$, which means the MU $i$ chooses to access cluster $k$ and severed by BS. On the other side, $p_{Bki} = 0$ when $a_{ki} = 0$, which means the MU $i$ doesn't belong to cluster $k$.

While $a_{ki}g_{Bi} > 0$, according to virtual index $\phi_k(i)$, the MU $\phi_k(i)$ in the cluster $k$ and MU $i$ on the coverage of BS are the same one, then we use $g_{Bk\phi_k(i)}$ to represent $g_{Bi}$ in the following paper.

Based on NOMA, the BS broadcasts the superposition of signals to all the MU(s) within cluster $k$ via power domain division. For MU $\phi_k(i)$ (i.e., MU $i$), it decodes the message of MU $\phi_k(i')$ (i.e., MU $i'$, and $\phi_k(i') > \phi_k(i)$) and then removes the decoded message from the received signal. Meanwhile, for MU $\phi_k(i)$, it treats the message of MU $\phi_k(i')$ (with $\phi_k(i') < \phi_k(i)$) as noise. According to the above decoding scheme, the throughput from the BS to MU $\phi_k(i)$ (i.e., MU $i$) $R_{Bki}$ can be given by:

$$R_{Bki} = W_k \log_2(1 + \frac{g_{B\phi_k(i)}p_{Bki}}{g_{B\phi_k(i)}\sum_{\phi_k(i')<\phi_k(i)} p_{Bki'} + W_k n_0}), \forall i \in \mathcal{I}, \forall k \in \mathcal{K}. \tag{6}$$

where $W_k$ denotes the BS's bandwidth allocation for serving MUs in cluster $k$. Parameter $n_0$ denotes the background noise.

## 2.2    Problem Formulation

Our objective is to minimize the BS system-wise resource consumption cost comprised of the power consumption and the bandwidth usage, while it is necessary to satisfy all MUs' traffic demands. Above all, formulating the following Multi-Cluster Consumption Minimization (MCM) Problem:

$$\textbf{(MCM):} \ \min \ \alpha \sum_{k \in \mathcal{K}} \sum_{i \in \mathcal{I}} p_{Bki} + \beta \sum_{k \in \mathcal{K}} W_k$$

$$\text{Subject to:} \ \sum_{k \in \mathcal{K}} \sum_{i \in \mathcal{I}} p_{Bki} \leq P_B^{tot}, \tag{7}$$

$$\sum_{k \in \mathcal{K}} W_k \leq W_B^{tot}, \tag{8}$$

$$R_{Bki} \geq R_i^{req}, \tag{9}$$

Constraints (2) , (5) and (6),

Variables: $\{a_{ki} = \{1,0\}\}_{k \in \mathcal{K}, i \in \mathcal{I}}$, $\{p_{Bki}\}_{k \in \mathcal{K}, i \in \mathcal{I}}$ and $\{W_k\}_{k \in \mathcal{K}}$.

In Problem (MCM), in the objective function, $\alpha$ and $\beta$ denote the unit-prices announced by power and bandwidth, respectively. Constraint (7) means that the BS's total power consumption cannot exceed the capacity $P_B^{tot}$. (8) imposed to ensure that total bandwidth budget $W_B^{tot}$ will not be exceeded. Then we use parameter $R_i^{req}$ in (9) to denote MU's traffic demands which must be satisfied. Recalling that due to (2) and (5) only one element in $\{p_{Bki}\}_{k\in\mathcal{K}}$ is positive. (6) is the expression of throughput from BS to MU $i$.

# 3 Propose Algorithms to Solve Problem

## 3.1 Decomposed Structure of Problem (MCM)

Problem (MCM) is very difficult to solve, since it is a mixed binary non-convex optimization problem. To tackle with this difficulty, we separate the impact of binary variables $\{a_{ki} = \{1, 0\}\}$. Thus, we vertically decompose Problem (MCM) into top-problem and sub-problem.

The top-problem optimizes the access-selection of overall the MUs, which expressed as:

$$(\textbf{MCM-top}): \ \min V(\{a_{ki}\}_{k\in\mathcal{K}, i\in\mathcal{I}})$$
$$\text{Subject to: Constraints (2)},$$
$$\text{Variables: } \{a_{ki} = \{1, 0\}\}_{k\in\mathcal{K}, i\in\mathcal{I}}.$$

Specially, given $\{a_{ki}\}$ (i.e., $I_k$ is given), the value of $V(\{a_{ki}\})$ is given by the minimum objective function value of sub-problem, then the expression of sub-problem (MCM-sub) given by:

$$(\textbf{MCM-sub}): \ V(\{a_{ki}\}) =$$
$$\min \alpha \sum_{k\in\mathcal{K}} \sum_{i\in I_k} p_{Bki} + \beta \sum_{k\in\mathcal{K}} W_k$$
$$\text{Subject to: Constraints (6), (7), (8), and (9)},$$
$$\text{Variables: } \{p_{Bki}\}_{k\in\mathcal{K}, i\in I_k} \text{ and } \{W_k\}_{k\in\mathcal{K}}.$$

We then focus on solving sub-problem (MCM-sub) firstly and then solving top-problem (MCM-top).

## 3.2 Solving Problem (MCM-sub)

Although we have separated the impact of binary variables, it is difficult to solve Problem (MCM-sub) directly. Then we aim at minimizing the total resource consumption of all the MU(s) in cluster $k$, which means we take a single cluster into consideration:

$$\textbf{(MCM-sub-single)}: \quad F(\{a_{ki}\}_{i \in I_k}) =$$

$$\min \alpha \sum_{i \in I_k} p_{Bki} + \beta W_k$$

$$\text{Subject to: } W_k \leq W_B^{tot}, \tag{10}$$

$$\sum_{i \in I_k} p_{Bki} \leq P_B^{tot}, \tag{11}$$

Constraints (6) and (9),

Variables: $\{p_{Bki}\}_{i \in I_k}$ and $W_k$.

Where we imposing constraint (10) to ensure that total bandwidth $W_B^{tot}$ will not be exceed. Constraint (11) means that the BS's total power consumption cannot exceed the capacity $P_B^{tot}$.

After solving the Problem (MCM-sub-single) and driving $F(\{a_{ki}\}_{i \in I_k})$ according to the given $\{a_{ki}\}$, we are able to further solve the multi-clusters problem:

$$\textbf{(MCM-sub-multiple)}: \quad V(\{a_{ki}\}) = \sum_{k \in \mathcal{K}} F(\{a_{ki}\}_{i \in I_k})$$

Subject to: Constraints (7) and (8).

Problem (MCM-sub-single) has been resolved in [13], so we can derive the optimal bandwidth allocation $W_k^*$ of Problem (MCM-sub-single). Furthermore, we can recursively derive the optimal transmit-power allocation for the MU $i$ in given cluster $k$ as follows

$$p_{Bki}^* = (2^{x^* R_i^{req}} - 1)(\sum_{\phi_k(i') < \phi_k(i)} p_{Bki'}^* + \frac{n_0}{g_{B\phi_k(i)}} \frac{1}{x^*}). \tag{12}$$

Then, we finish solving the Problem (MCM-sub-single) and obtain the minimum total resource consumption cost $F^*(\{a_{ki}\}_{i \in I_k})$ of the cluster $k$.

After solving Problem (MCM-sub-single), we continue to solve Problem (MCM-sub-multiple). With the help of $F^*(\{a_{ki}\}_{i \in I_k})$, $W_k^*$ and $p_{Bki}^*$, transforming Problem (MCM-sub-multiple) as follows:

$$\textbf{(MCM-sub-multiple)}: \quad V(\{a_{ki}\}) = \sum_{k \in \mathcal{K}} F^*(\{a_{ki}\}_{i \in I_k})$$

$$\text{Subject to: } \sum_{k \in \mathcal{K}} \sum_{i \in I_k} p_{Bki}^* \leq P_B^{tot},$$

$$\sum_{k \in \mathcal{K}} W_k^* \leq W_B^{tot}.$$

The meaning of Problem (MCM-sub-multiple) is further optimizes the overall minimum total resource consumption cost under the given access-selection $\{a_{ki}\}$. Specially, we propose the following algorithm (i.e., Algorithm (sol-multiple)) to solve Problem (MCM-sub-multiple).

Then, we drive the solution of Problem (MCM-sub-multiple) under the given $\{a_{ki}\}$, i.e., $V(\{a_{ki}\})$. Thus, we finish solving the Problem (MCM-sub) completely.

---

**Algorithm (sol-multiple): to solve Problem (MCM-sub-multiple) and compute** $V(\{a_{ki}\})$

---

1: **Input:** $\{W_k^*\}_{k \in \mathcal{K}}$ and $\{p_{Bki}^*\}_{k \in \mathcal{K}, i \in I_k}$.
2: Initialize the feasibility status flag $s^{flag} = 1$ of the Problem (MCM-sub-multiple).
3: $W^* = \sum_{k \in \mathcal{K}} W_k^*$.
4: $p_B^* = \sum_{i \in \mathcal{I}} p_{Bki}^*$.
5: **if** $W^* \leq W_B^{tot}$ **and** $p^* \leq p_B^{tot}$ **then**
6:     $V(\{a_{ki}\}) = \sum_{k \in \mathcal{K}} F^*(\{a_{ki}\}_{i \in I_k})$.
7: **else**
8:     Output that Problem (MCM-sub-multiple) is infeasible and $s^{flag} = 0$.
9: **end if**
10: **Output:** $V(\{a_{ki}\})$ and $s^{flag}$ for Problem (MCM-sub-multiple).

---

### 3.3   Solving Problem (MCM-top)

Here, according to the previous section, under the each given $\{a_{ki}\}$, we are able to solve Problem (MCM-sub) completely and obtain the corresponding $V(\{a_{ki}\})$ which is the minimum total resource consumption cost for the given $\{a_{ki}\}$. We next continue to solve the Problem (MCM-top), which means finding the optimal MUs' access-selection $\{a_{ki}^*\}$ in this procedure to further minimize the total resource consumption cost globally. we exploit the Simulated Annealing (SA) algorithm to obtain the optimal solution, i.e., $V(\{a_{ki}^*\})$, since we propose the Total resource Consumption Simulated Annealing Algorithm (i.e., TCSA-Algorithm).

The output of TCSA-Algorithm, i.e., $\{a_{ki}^*\}$ and $V(\{a_{ki}^*\})$, are the optimal MUs' access-selection and the global total minimum resource consumption cost, namely, we finish solving the Problem (MCM-top). Finally, we solve the original Problem (MCM) completely.

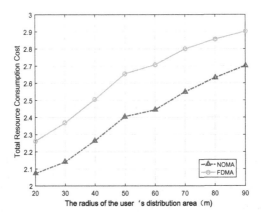

**Fig. 2.** Performance under different radius of the MUs.

---

**TCSA-Algorithm: solve Problem (MCM-top) to obtain $\{a_{ki}^*\}$ and $V(\{a_{ki}^*\})$**

---

1: Initialization: assign the MUs into $\{I_k\}_{k \in \mathcal{K}}$, set the iteration index $q = 1$, the initial temperature $T_{ini} = 97$, temperature decay function parameter d=0.99, the length of the Markov chain $L = I^2$ and the final temperature $T_{final} = 3$. The minimum value of resource consumption cost $V^{min}$ initial as infinite.

2: Given $\{I_k\}_{k \in \mathcal{K}}$, use the Algorithm (sol-multiple) to obtain $V(\{a_{ki}\})$. At time $t$, the system temperature is $T_t$.

3: **while** $(T_t \geq T_{final})$ **do**

4:     **while** $(q \leq L)$ **do**

5:         Randomly select two set $I_k$ and $I_k'$ with $I_k$ as a non-empty set. Randomly select one MU (let us say MU $r$) in $I_k$, and move MU $r$ from $I_k$ to $I_k'$. Denote the two updated sets as $\overline{I}_k$ and $\overline{I}_k'$, respectively, and denote the whole profile after updating as $\{\overline{a}_{ki}\}$.

6:         Given $\{\overline{I}_k\}$, use the Algorithm (sol-multiple) to obtain $V(\{\overline{a}_{ki}\})$.

7:         **if** $s^{flag} == 1$ **then**

8:             **if** $V(\{\overline{a}_{ki}\}) < V(\{a_{ki}\})$ **then**

9:                 Update $\{a_{ki}\} = \{\overline{a}_{ki}\}$.

10:                 **if** $V(\{\overline{a}_{ki}\}) < V^{min}$ **then**

11:                     Update $V^{min} = V(\{\overline{a}_{ki}\})$

12:                     Update $\{a_{ki}^*\} = \{\overline{a}_{ki}\}$

13:                 **end if**

14:             **else**

15:                 Set $\Delta = V(\{a_{ki}\}) - V(\{\overline{a}_{ki}\})$.

16:                 With probability equal to $\exp\{\frac{\Delta}{T_t}\}$. Update $\{a_{ki}\} = \{\overline{a}_{ki}\}$.

17:             **end if**

18:         **else**

19:             Update $q = q - 1$.

20:         **end if**

21:         Update $q = q + 1$.

22:     **end while**

23:     Update $T_t = T_t * d$

24: **end while**

25: Output $\{a_{ki}^*\}$ and $V(\{a_{ki}^*\}) = V^{min}, \forall i \in \mathcal{I}, k \in \mathcal{K}$.

---

## 4 Numerical Results

We use a scenario of five MUs are randomly distributed within the coverage of BS. Specially, the coverage of BS is a circle whose radius is $R_{MU}$, and we place the BS at the circle center. We model the channel power gain as $g_{Bi} = \frac{\varrho_{Bi}}{l_{Bi}^\kappa}$, where $l_{Bi}^\kappa$ denotes the distance between the BS and MU $i$, and $\kappa$ denotes the power-scaling factor for the path-loss (we set $\kappa$ as 2.5). Meanwhile, we set the BS's total bandwidth $W_B^{tot} = 15\,\text{MHz}$ and the power capacity $P_B^{tot} = 20\,\text{W}$.

Figure 2 shows the performance of proposed algorithms under different radius of the MUs compared with FDMA. Specifically, we randomly distribute MUs within the coverage of BS, vary radius $R_{MU}$ (i.e., coverage of BS is a plane) as $(20\,\text{m}, 30\,\text{m}, 40\,\text{m}, 50\,\text{m}, 60\,\text{m}, 70\,\text{m}, 80\,\text{m}, 90\,\text{m})$.

Figure 2 shows that the average total resource consumption cost of FDMA and the proposed algorithms increases when the radius $R_{MU}$ of circle moves away from the BS. This result is reasonable. With the expansion of $R_{MU}$, the MUs move away from the BS, which causes the resource-consuming long-distance transmission. Meanwhile, compared with FDMA scheme, Fig. 2 shows that our proposed algorithm can always save much more resource consumption.

We consider that 10 MUs are randomly distributed within the coverage of the BS, and the radius $R_{MU}$ is 50 m, 70 m, and 100 m respectively. With the number of given clusters increase, the changes of the optimal total resource consumption in the case of three user distributions are shown in Fig. 3. Figure 3 shows that the total resource consumption increases with the radius of distribution. When all users are in the same cluster, the total resource consumption is always the largest, which is because the weak co-channel interference in the cluster is too large. At the same time, as the number of given user clusters increases, the total resource consumption decreases first and then increases. This also explains why the FDMA scheme is not used in 5G networks, but NOMA's multi-user grouping scheme is chosen. The difference of the optimal resource consumption under the cluster number near the optimal cluster number and the optimal resource consumption under the optimal cluster number are very small.

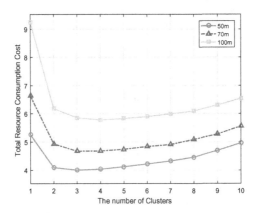

**Fig. 3.** The effect of the number of user clusters on total resource consumption.

## 5   Conclusion

In order to solve the problem of minimizing the total resource consumption of multi-user clusters formulated in this paper, we split it into the top-problem and the sub-problem. This split can make good use of the convexity of bandwidth allocation and simplify the process of the grouping optimization. From the final simulation results, our proposed algorithm can greatly reduce the system resource consumption.

**Acknowledgements.** This work was supported in part by the National Natural Science Foundation of China under Grant 61572440 and Grant 61502428, in part by the Zhejiang Provincial Natural Science Foundation of China under Grants LR17F010002 and LR16F010003, in part by the Young Talent Cultivation Project of Zhejiang Association for Science and Technology under Grant 2016YCGC011.

# References

1. Saito, Y., Kishiyama, Y., Benjebbour, A., Nakamura, T., Li, A., Higuchi, K.: Non-orthogonal multiple access (NOMA) for cellular future radio access. In: Proceedings of IEEE VTC Spring, pp. 1–5, June 2013
2. Dai, L., Wang, B., Yuan, Y., Han, S., I, C.-L., Wang, Z.: Non-orthogonal multiple access for 5G: solutions, challenges, opportunities, and future research trends. IEEE Commun. Mag. **53**(9), 74–81 (2015)
3. Benjebbour, A., Saito, Y., Kishiyama, Y., Li, A., Harada, A., Nakamura, T.: Concept and practical considerations of non-orthogonal multiple access (NOMA) for future radio access. In: Proceedings of International Symposium Intelligent Signal Processing and Communications Systems, pp. 770–774, November 2013
4. Wu, Y., Qian, L., Mao, H., Yang, X., Shen, X.: Optimal power allocation and scheduling for non-orthogonal multiple access relay-assisted networks. IEEE Trans. Mob. Comput. (2018). https://doi.org/10.1109/TMC.2018.2812722March
5. Di, B., Bayat, S., Song, L., Li, Y.: Radio resource allocation for downlink non-orthogonal multiple access (NOMA) networks using matching theory. In: Proceedings of IEEE GLOBECOM (2015)
6. Lei, L., Yuan, D., Ho, C.K., Sun, S.: Joint optimization of power and channel allocation with non-orthogonal multiple access for 5G cellular systems. In: Proceedings of IEEE GLOBECOM (2014)
7. Ding, Z., Fan, P., Poor, H.V.: Impact of user pairing on 5G nonorthogonal multiple-access downlink transmissions. IEEE Trans. Veh. Technol. **65**(8), 6010–6023 (2016)
8. Timotheou, S., Krikidis, I.: Fairness for non-orthogonal multiple access in 5G systems. IEEE Signal Process. Lett. **22**(10), 1647–1651 (2015)
9. Wu, Y., Qian, L.: Energy-efficient NOMA-enabled traffic offloading via dual-connectivity in small-cell networks. IEEE Commun. Lett. **21**(7), 1605–1608 (2017)
10. Ding, Z., Peng, M., Poor, H.V.: Cooperative non-orthogonal multiple access in 5G systems. IEEE Commun. Lett. **19**(8), 1462–1465 (2015)
11. Wu, Y., Chen, J., Qian, L., Huang, J., Shen, X.: Energy-aware cooperative traffic offloading via device-to-device cooperations: an analytical approach. IEEE Trans. Mob. Comput. **16**(1), 97–114 (2017)
12. Qian, L., Wu, Y., Zhou, H., Shen, X.: Dynamic cell association for Non-orthogonal Multiple-access V2S networks. IEEE J. Sel. Areas Commun. **35**(10), 2342–2356 (2017)
13. Wu, Y., Qian, L., Mao, H., Lu, W., Zhou, H., Yu, C.: Joint channel bandwidth and power allocations for downlink non-orthogonal multiple access systems. In: 2017 IEEE 86th Vehicular Technology Conference (VTC-Fall), Toronto, ON, pp. 1–5 (2017)

# Technologies and Applications of Narrowband Internet of Things

Jia Chen[✉], Jiajun Shi, Xiangxu Chen, Yuan Wu, Liping Qian, and Liang Huang

College of Information Engineering, Zhejiang University of Technology, Hangzhou 310023, China
{jiachen_zjut,jjshi_zjut,xxchen_zjut}@163.com, {iewuy,lpqian,lianghuang}@zjut.edu.cn

**Abstract.** Narrowband Internet of Things (NB-IoT) is one kind of Low Power Wide Area Network (LPWAN) technologies to achieve the aims of deep coverage penetration, low power consumption, low cost and massive connections. NB-IoT aims at supporting small data and low rate applications. In this paper, we first introduce the general background of NB-IoT. Then we overview several performances of NB-IoT and make comparison between NB-IoT with other wireless communication technologies, including WiFi, ZigBee and etc. Finally, we design an environmental monitoring system based on NB-IoT. In this proposed system, NB-IoT module transmits the data of the sensor nodes to cloud platform.

**Keywords:** NB-IoT · Internet of Things · LPWAN

## 1 Introduction

Over the past 20 years, Internet of Things (IoT) technologies have developed significantly, and they have been incorporated in various fields. From the perspective of transmission rate, the communication services of IoT can be classified into two categories: high-data-rate services (such as video service) and low-datarate services (such as meter reading service) [1]. Unlike traditional cellular communications, IoT applications have special requirements that support massive connections, low cost, low terminal power consumption and superior coverage capabilities. Low Power Wide Area Network (LPWAN) aims at addressing these requirements. The features of LPWAN are battery-powered, low-rate, ultra-low-power and maximum coverage up to 100 km. LPWAN are suitable for the IoT applications that only need to transmit tiny amounts of information in the long range [2, 3].

NB-IoT is a cellular network-based LPWAN solution. It supports large number connections, ultra-low power consumption and ultra-low cost [4]. In addition, it is well supported by cellular communication networks [5]. The NB-IoT can support coverage enhancement (20 dB coverage improvement), ultra-low power consumption (5W/h battery for 10 years), low latency (up to 10 s for uplink

© ICST Institute for Computer Sciences, Social Informatics and Telecommunications Engineering 2018
L. Meng and Y. Zhang (Eds.): MLICOM 2018, LNICST 251, pp. 549–558, 2018.
https://doi.org/10.1007/978-3-030-00557-3_54

delay) and a huge number of connections (a single sector can support more than 50000 connections) at transmission bandwidth of 180 kHz.

Lots of research efforts have been devoted to studying NB-IoT. In [2], Xu *et al.* studied NB-IoT's evolutions, technologies and issues, spanned from performance analysis, design optimization, to implementation and application. In [5], Chen *et al.* reviewed the background and state-of-the-art of the NB-IoT. In [6], Shi *et al.* proposed a smart parking system in order to mitigate problems such as high power consumption of sensor node and high deployment costs of wireless network. In [7], Miao *et al.* studied construction of NB-IoT model based on OPNET and verification of its characteristics. In [8], Ratasuk *et al.* provided an overview of NB-IoT design and also provided illustrative results with respect to performance objectives. In [9], Yang *et al.* investigated the small-cell assisted traffic offloading for NB-IoT systems. In [10], Adhikary *et al.* provided a detailed evaluation of the coverage performance of NB-IoT. Driven by the growing demand for improving energy-efficiency and greening wireless networks [11–13], many studies investigated the energy management for NB-IoT [14–17]. In [11], Wu *et al.* studied traffic offloading in future heterogeneous cellular networks. In [12], Wu *et al.* studied the NOMA downlink relay-transmission to accommodate tremendous traffic growth in future cellular networks. In [13], Wu *et al.* investigated the cooperative traffic offloading among mobiles devices. In [14], Malik *et al.* proposed an efficient resource allocation for NB-IoT with cooperative approaches. In [15], Liu *et al.* proposed a new resource allocation method, which includes a new definition of paging resource set and corresponding resource selection method. In [16], Zhuang *et al.* proposed a method for the uplink resource scheduling of power wireless private network based on NB-IoT and LTE hybrid transmission. In [17], Kroll *et al.* studied hardware implementation of the maximum likelihood crosscorrelation detection for energy savings in NB-IoT devices.

## 2   Overview of NB-IOT

### 2.1   NB-IOT in 3GPP

3GPP is promoting the related technology of Machine Type Communication (MTC), mainly in two directions. Because the challenges of non-3GPP technologies, the first direction carries out the further evolution of GSM and new access technologies to fulfill characteristics such as lower complexity, lower cost, lower power consumption, and stronger coverage [18]. And the second direction researches new technologies to replace 2G/3G IoT module. 3GPP defines the terminal types for many scenarios of different service requirements. R-8 has defined terminal types of cat 1–5 at different rates [19]. While newly defined terminal types supporting high-bandwidth, high-speed cat 6, cat 9, etc., it also newly defined cat 0 (R-12) terminal types that are lower in cost and support lower power consumption [18].

At present, 3GPP mainly focuses on NB-IoT, eMTC and EC-GSM. Among them, EC-GSM adds Power Saving Mode (PSM) and Enhanced Discontinuous Reception (eDRX) base on GSM. This is the technology that 3GPP researches in the first direction; And NB-IoT is a new radio access system built from existing LTE functionalities with essential simplifications and optimizations [7]. This is the technology that 3GPP researches in the second direction.

## 2.2   NB-IOT vs. Other Wireless Solutions

Nowadays common used wireless communication technologies are 4.0 Bluetooth, WiFi, ZigBee and etc. These solutions have their own advantages, disadvantages and applicable scenarios. The main differences are summarized as follows: transmission rate, transmission distance, terminal cost, terminal power consumption and signal penetration. For low-rate IoT applications, they have high requirements for low power consumption, large connections and wide coverage and not very sensitive to delay. NB-IoT has an excellent performance in terms of coverage, power consumption, cost and connection number. Comparison of wireless technologies as shown in Fig. 1 [5].

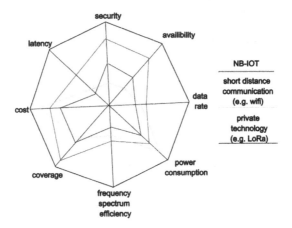

**Fig. 1.** Performance comparison of different wireless technologies

## 2.3   Features of NB-IOT

NB-IoT has lots of advantages. In this section, we briefly introduce the main advantages and features of NB-IoT.

Massive connection: By increasing the power spectral density and optimizing the base station and core network. The theoretical supported number of connection can reach 52547 per cell site sector.

Low power consumption: This feature is achieved mainly by two technologies: power saving mode (PSM) and extended discontinuous reception (eDRX) which provides 10 years battery life.

Super coverage: Due to NB-IoT's narrowband design and the increase in power spectral density and retransmission, the gain is increased by 20dB The transmission power of NB-IOT has increased by 100 times.

Low cost: NB-IOT's narrowband design and low complexity directly reduces the cost of the device unit.

# 3   Protocol of NB-IOT

The commonly used IoT application layer protocols include MQTT, XMPP, CoAP, LwM2M and so on. For IoT terminal nodes, simple protocols should be used as much as possible because of the limited resources they can use. And in NB-IOT, Lightweight protocols CoAP and LwM2M are used.

## 3.1   Coap Protocol

The Constrained Application Protocol (CoAP) is a lightweight protocol defined for resource-constrained conditions (power, storage space, etc.). CoAP is based on the REST architecture and adopts similar features as HTTP. It's core content is resource abstraction, RESTful interaction and extensible header options. In order to overcome the disadvantages of HTTP for constrained environments, CoAP considers both the optimization of the data length and reliable communications. Protocol stack of CoAP as shown in Fig. 2.

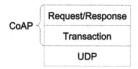

**Fig. 2.** Protocol stack of CoAP

CoAP is an application layer protocol and Based on the UDP protocol. CoAP complies with the UDP data packet format and transmits according to the CoAP format. With retransmission mechanism, protocol supports IP multicast, small protocol header only 4 bytes and low power consumption, CoAP is suitable for low-power IoT scenarios.

## 3.2   LwM2M Protocol

Lightweight Machine to Machine (LwM2M) is a lightweight IoT protocol, it can be applied to various scenarios such as NB-IoT. Because M2M devices are usually terminals with limited resources, the computing power and communication capabilities are limited. Therefore, OMA defines a lightweight protocol based on the traditional OMA-DM protocol for IoT devices, which are mainly used in devices with limited resources (including storage, power consumption, etc.). Protocol stack of LwM2M shown in Fig. 3.

LwM2M is an application layer protocol and above the CoAP protocol. LwM2M can do DTLS encryption processing and transmit it through UDP or SMS.

**Fig. 3.** Protocol stack of LwM2M

# 4 Cloud Platform OneNET

In this section, we introduce the cloud platform and the configuration of the cloud platform. In the environmental monitoring system, the cloud platform is used to store and process the data reported by the NB-IOT module. Using the cloud platform provided by the operator as the data receiving platform has multiple advantages: data security storage, rich API support, high concurrent availability and so on. Huawei's OceanConnect is an open ecosystem based on the IoT, cloud computing and big data. OceanConnect provides ecological API and serialized Agent software to achieve product connection, and supports the rapid access of various types of smart devices. OneNET is a PaaS IoT open platform created by China Mobile. The platform can implement device access and device connection, quickly complete product development and deployment. It provides comprehensive IoT solutions for smart hardware and smart home products. The NB-IOT based on the LwM2M protocol and the CoAP protocol implements communication between the UE and the OneNET platform. The transport layer protocol is CoAP and the application layer protocol is LwM2M. The architecture of the OneNET platform is shown in Fig. 4.

OneNET platform development process: North registration is required before the NB-IOT module interacts with the cloud platform. Each device needs to register through its International Mobile Equipment Identity (IMEI) and selects the appropriate transport protocol. After successful configuration, the device needs to report the data by using the encoded password. The password includes the IMEI numbers and the reported data. After the cloud platform receives the data, it will return a response. Configuration of Cloud platform as illustrated in Fig. 5.

# 5 Typical Application Scenario

NB-IOT's data rate is small and slow, high delay and poor real-time performance. And it is low data service frequency, poor mobility but the coverage is deep and wide. From these characteristics we consider deploying NB-IOT in the following application scenarios: Smart City [20]: NB-IOT can cope with the ever-growing information data and more and more IOT devices generated in smart cities. Smart Factory: The industry is moving toward intelligent, information-based production, resource-saving and high-efficiency. Smart factories require collect and transmit various data generated during plant operations. Smart agriculture: NB-IOT can effectively solve problems in the agricultural environment.

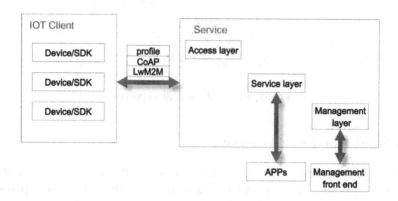

**Fig. 4.** Cloud platform communication framework

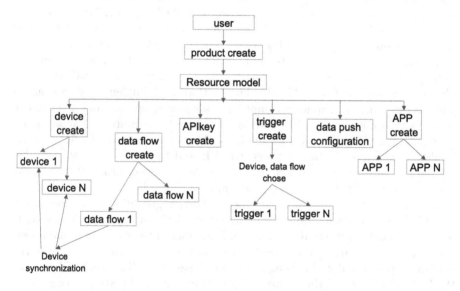

**Fig. 5.** Cloud platform configuration process

The cellular network basically achieves full coverage, and the power consumption of the terminal nodes is relatively ideal. Therefor, NB-IoT can resolve some pain points in smart agriculture.

## 6    Application System Test

In this section, we design an environmental monitoring system which includes NB-IoT devices, cloud platform and sensors. System as illustrated in Fig. 6. Through this system, we can monitor the environmental status in real time.

Specifically, the environmental monitoring system is mainly composed of data collection, data processing part, data transmission part and cloud platform part.

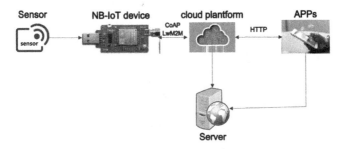

**Fig. 6.** System design

The first part is the sensors obtain environment data; the second part is the MCU processes data and the third part is the data transmitted by the NB-IOT module; the fourth part is configure the cloud platform. For the NB-IOT module, we chose Quectel's BC95-B8 and China Mobile's M5310. The operator is China Mobile. The IoT platform can use commercial platform, such as Huawei's OceanConnect and China Mobile's OneNet, and it can also use private platform. The system structure as illustrated in Fig. 7.

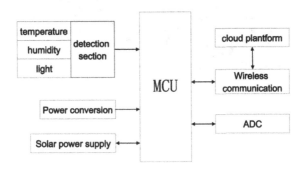

**Fig. 7.** System structure

The environmental monitoring system works as follow: system uses sensors to collect environmental data. The MCU processes data and uses the NB-IOT module to transmit data to the cloud platform. After the cloud platform is configured, it stores and displays data. The data flow as follows: (Fig. 8).

The environment of experiment were indoor and outdoor environments of laboratory and no cover on the test system. In this environment, the signal of the base station received by the NB-IOT module was stable, which ensured stable transmission. To ensure the accuracy of the data, we used more than one node at the same time. The test time was 10:00 and 21:00. The sensor sampling time was half a minute and the data stored in the cloud platform. The system board as shown in Fig. 9. The test results as shown in Fig. 10. And the different lines in Fig. 11 mean different nodes.

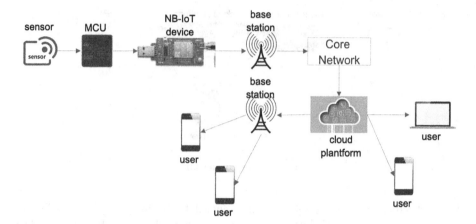

**Fig. 8.** Data transmission direction

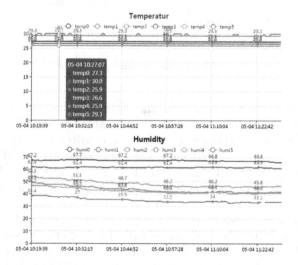

**Fig. 9.** System board

**Fig. 10.** Environmental parameter results

# 7    Conclusion

In this paper, we have introduced the general background of NB-IoT and gave a brief review of features. Then we have designed an environmental monitoring system that utilizes NB-IoT. The proposed system consists of three components: (1) the sensing part; (2) the transmission part; and (3) the cloud platform part. We have implemented this system by hardware and cloud platform. We have also shown some experiment results through this NB-IoT system.

**Acknowledgements.** This work was supported in part by the National Natural Science Foundation of China under Grant 61572440, in part by the Zhejiang Provincial Natural Science Foundation of China under Grants LR17F010002 and LR16F010003, in part by the Young Talent Cultivation Project of Zhejiang Association for Science and Technology under Grant 2016YCGC011.

# References

1. Raza, U., Kulkarni, P., Sooriyabandara, M.: Low power wide area networks: an overview. IEEE Commun. Surv. Tutor. **9**(2), 855–873 (2017). Secondquarter
2. Xu, J., Yao, J., Wang, L., Ming, Z., Wu, K., Chen, L.: Narrowband Internet of Things: evolutions, technologies and open issues. IEEE Internet Things J. https://doi.org/10.1109/JIOT.2017.2783374
3. 3GPP: Standardization of NB-IOT Completed (2016). http://www.3gpp.org/news-events/3gpp-news/1785
4. Ge, X., Li, Z., Li, S.: 5G software defined vehicular networks. IEEE Commun. Mag. **55**(7), 87–93 (2017)
5. Chen, M., Miao, Y., Hao, Y., Hwang, K.: Narrow band Internet of Things. IEEE Access **5**, 20557–20577 (2017)
6. Shi, J., Jin, L., Li, J., Fang, Z.: A smart parking system based on NB-IoT and third-party payment platform. In: 2017 17th International Symposium on Communications and Information Technologies (ISCIT), Cairns, QLD, pp. 1–5 (2017)
7. Miao, Y., Li, W., Tian, D., Hossain, M., Alhamid, M.: Narrow band Internet of Things: simulation and modelling. IEEE Internet Things J. https://doi.org/10.1109/JIOT.2017.2739181
8. Ratasuk, R., Mangalvedhe, N., Zhang, Y., Robert, M., Koskinen, J.: Overview of narrowband IoT in LTE Rel-13. In: 2016 IEEE Conference on Standards for Communications and Networking (CSCN), Berlin, pp. 1–7 (2016)
9. Yang, X., Wang, X., Wu, Y., Qian, L., Lu, W., Zhou, H.: Small-cell assisted secure traffic offloading for narrow-band Internet of Thing (NB-IoT) systems. IEEE Internet Things J. https://doi.org/10.1109/JIOT.2017.2779820
10. Adhikary, A., Lin, X., Wang, Y.: Performance evaluation of NB-IoT coverage. In: 2016 IEEE 84th Vehicular Technology Conference (VTC-Fall), Montreal, QC, pp. 1–5 (2016)
11. Wu, Y., Qian, L., Zheng, J., Zhou, H., Shen, X.: Green-oriented traffic offloading through dual connectivity in future heterogeneous small cell networks. IEEE Commun. Mag. **56**(5), 140–147 (2018)
12. Wu, Y., Qian, L., Mao, H., Yang, X., Zhou, H., Shen, X.: Optimal power allocation and scheduling for non-orthogonal multiple access relay-assisted networks. IEEE Trans. Mob. Comput. https://doi.org/10.1109/TMC.2018.2812722

13. Wu, Y., Chen, J., Qian, L., Huang, J., Shen, X.: Energy-aware cooperative traffic offloading via device-to-device cooperations: an analytical approach. IEEE Trans. Mob. Comput. **16**(1), 97–114 (2017)
14. Malik, H., Pervaiz, H., Alam, M., Moullec, Y., Kuusik, A., Imran, M.: Radio resource management scheme in NB-IoT systems. IEEE Access **6**, 15051–15064 (2018)
15. Liu, J., Mu, Q., Liu, L., Chen, L.: Investigation about the paging resource allocation in NB-IoT. In: 2017 20th International Symposium on Wireless Personal Multimedia Communications (WPMC), Bali, pp. 320–324 (2017)
16. Zhuang, Z., Feng, L., Yu, P., Li, W.: Uplink resource scheduling for power wireless private network based on NB-IoT and LTE hybrid transmission. In: 2017 IEEE International Conference on Computational Science and Engineering (CSE) and IEEE International Conference on Embedded and Ubiquitous Computing (EUC), Guangzhou, pp. 77–84 (2017)
17. Kroll, H., Korb, M., Weber, B., Willi, S., Huang, Q.: Maximum-likelihood detection for energy-efficient timing acquisition in NB-IoT. In: 2017 IEEE Wireless Communications and Networking Conference Workshops (WCNCW), San Francisco, CA, pp. 1–5 (2017)
18. TR 21.101: Technical Specifications and Technical Reports for a UTRAN-based 3GPP system. Technical report (2007). http://www.3gpp.org/ftp/Specs/archive/21_series/21.101/21101-5d0.zip
19. Duan, X., Zhao, C., He, S., Cheng, P., Zhang, J.: Distributed algorithms to compute walrasian equilibrium in mobile crowdsensing. IEEE Trans. Ind. Electron. **64**(5), 4048–4057 (2017)
20. Shah, S., Yaqoob, I.: A survey: Internet of Things (IOT) technologies, applications and challenges. In: 2016 IEEE Smart Energy Grid Engineering (SEGE), Oshawa, ON, pp. 381–385 (2016)

# A SAR Image Fast Stitching Algorithm Based on Machine Learning

Hongyuan Yao[✉], Haipeng Wang, and Xueyuan Lin

Naval Aviation University, Wuhan, China
506716109@qq.com

**Abstract.** Aiming at the splicing problem of Synthetic Aperture Radar (SAR) image, an improved algorithm for SURF is proposed to realize the fast splicing of SAR image. The SURF feature descriptor has scale invariance and rotation invariance, and has strong robustness to light intensity and affine transmission variation. The improved algorithm uses machine learning methods to build a binary classifier that identifies the key feature points in the SURF extracted feature points and eliminates the key feature points. In addition, the relief-F algorithm is used to reduce the dimensionality of the improved SURF descriptor to complete image registration. In the image fusion stage, a weighted fusion algorithm with a threshold is used to achieve seamless image mosaic. Experimental results show that the improved algorithm has strong real-time performance and robustness, and improves the efficiency of image registration. It can accurately mosaic multiple SAR images.

**Keywords:** SAR image · Fast image stitching · Machine learning
SURF · Image fusion

## 1 Introduction

The image splicing technology spatially aligns and aligns the image sequences with overlapping regions, and finally splices into a technique with a wide viewing angle panoramic image [1].

In recent years, it has been widely used in military, machine vision, virtual reality, medicine and other fields. Image mosaic technology as a hot issue of image processing has attracted many scholars at home and abroad to study it. Image splicing mainly includes image registration and image fusion. Among them, image registration is the core part of splicing.

Image fusion is another important step in image splicing. If the SAR images are directly and simply combined, there is a clear seam in the overlapped area of the stitched SAR images. In order to solve the above problems, this paper will study the fast splicing of SAR images based on machine learning, and propose a machine learning method to improve the SURF algorithm, identify key feature points, and

Foundation Items: The National Natural Science Fandation of China (61531020, 61471383).

© ICST Institute for Computer Sciences, Social Informatics and Telecommunications Engineering 2018
L. Meng and Y. Zhang (Eds.): MLICOM 2018, LNICST 251, pp. 559–564, 2018.
https://doi.org/10.1007/978-3-030-00557-3_55

eliminate the key feature points. In addition, the Relief-F algorithm [2] is used to simplify the improved SURF descriptor reduction and use it to train feature point classifiers. Finally, an improved weighted fusion algorithm [3] is used to fuse the images, which effectively solves the problems of blurring and ghosting and achieves seamless stitching of images.

## 2 The Basic Principle of SURF Algorithm

The SURF algorithm is an image splicing algorithm based on feature information proposed by Bay et al. [4]. It is proposed that the SIFT algorithm by Lowe [5] has large data volume high time complexity, and poor timeliness. SURF inherits the SIFT algorithm's advantages of strong anti-interference ability, high discrimination, and several times improvement in calculation speed [4].

The SURF algorithm is divided into two parts: feature point selection and feature point description.

(1) Feature point extraction: The SURF algorithm selects Hessian matrix-based detectors. For a point $(x, y)$ on the input image I, the Hessian matrix on the scale space $\sigma$ is expressed as shown in Eq. (1). Where, $L_{xx}$ represents the second-order partial derivative of the Gaussian function to $x$ and the convolution of the function image at the pixel point; likewise, $L_{yy}$ represents the second-order partial derivative of the Gaussian function to $y$ and the convolution of the function image at the pixel point.

$$H(x, \sigma) = \begin{bmatrix} L_{xx}(x, \sigma) & L_{xy}(x, \sigma) \\ L_{yx}(x, \sigma) & L_{yy}(x, \sigma) \end{bmatrix} \tag{1}$$

Then calculate the discriminant of the Hessian matrix, and determine whether the point is an extremum point according to whether the discriminant value is positive or negative. Because the discriminant formula of Hessian matrix is relatively high in computational complexity, the Hessian value of the candidate feature point and its surrounding points is calculated by using box filter approximation instead of the second-order Gaussian filter, and the approximate discriminant value $\det(H_{approx})$ is obtained, such as formula (2) as shown:

$$\det(H_{approx}) = D_{xx}D_{yy} - (\omega D_{xy})^2 \tag{2}$$

When the discriminant of the Hessian matrix has a local maximum, it is determined that the current point is a brighter or darker point than other points in the surrounding neighborhood, thereby locating the position of the key point. In a discrete digital image, the first derivative is the difference in gray levels of adjacent pixels. $D_{xx}, D_{yy}$ is the second derivative of the second derivative of its first derivative.

(2) Feature point description: The SURF algorithm feature point descriptor first constructs a window area centered on the feature point, divides this window into $4 \times 4$ sub-window areas, takes $5 \times 5$ sampling points in each sub-window, and calculates them separately. The Haar wavelet response of each sub-window region is horizontal and vertical, and the resulting wavelet coefficients are denoted as $d_x$ and $d_y$. The wavelet coefficients of each subarea are weighted by a Gaussian function to obtain $\sum d_x$, $\sum d_y$, $\sum |d_x|$, $\sum |d_y|$, which constitute the four dimensions of the descriptor. Each $4 \times 4$ sub-window has a four-dimensional vector, so a total of 64-dimensional vectors are obtained, which is the descriptor of the SURF algorithm.

SURF algorithm provides a similar replacement for SIFT, which greatly reduces the processing time of feature point detection and matching. However, to further improve the SURF-based image registration efficiency, it is necessary to study the influence of different feature points on the matching speed.

## 3   Improvement of SURF Algorithm Based on Machine Learning

The main idea of extracting feature points based on machine learning [6] is to classify the feature points extracted by the SURF algorithm into two categories: (1) key feature points, which is key areas of image feature recognition, in the two images to be stitched, these the correspondence between feature points is more important; (2) Non-critical feature points have little influence on feature point matching and can be excluded from the matching process. Before machine learning, it is necessary to remove redundant information from SURF extracted feature points and establish a binary classifier that can distinguish these two types of feature points. A set of feature points K is extracted in the image I using the SURF algorithm. Each of the feature points $k_i \in K$ can be described by a set of features F. The feature F is a feature image piece $Q_\omega^F(k_i)$ having width $\omega$ centered on $k_i$ extracted from. In addition, a classifier $Y\left(Q_\omega^F\right) \in L$, $L = \{-1, 1\}$ gives each feature point a label according to the feature patch, and when $Y\left(Q_\omega^F\right) = 1$, $k_i$ is considered as a key feature. Point; This feature point is discarded when $Y\left(Q_\omega^F\right) = -1$. Then, feature point matching is performed using the improved and simplified SURF descriptors, and the feature point classifier is trained with it to complete the image registration.

### 3.1   Remove Redundant Information

When the training data set is established, if the feature points extracted from the image are close in spatial position, the feature image piece may contain redundant information, thereby reducing the matching efficiency. In order to avoid redundancy, it is necessary to add a distance constraint between the extracted feature points. A set of feature points extracted from image $I$ is represented by $K_I$. For each pair of feature points $k_1 k_2 \in K_I$ of the same mark (all marked as 1 or $-1$), ensure that the distance between them is larger than the critical value d, that is $dist(k_1, k_2) > d$, $dist$ is a distance function, Euclidean distance is used here, d is set to 5 pixels.

### 3.2 Balanced Processing of Training Data Sets

The feature points extracted by the above method may lead to imbalance of the training data set, that is, in the data set, the number of non-key feature points far exceeds the number of key feature points, and an accurate classification result cannot be obtained based on the classification of unbalanced data sets.

To solve this problem, a uniform training data set is created by sampling the original data set, and a classifier is trained using no substitute random sampling [7]. This method creates a data set smaller than the original data set. No replacement sampling ensures that training is a real-world example and will make the classifier more accurate.

### 3.3 Balanced Processing of Training Data Sets

Before entering the learning phase, the characteristics of the training examples need to be described. The quality of the feature has a direct impact on the performance of the classifier. The SURF descriptor has 64 dimensions and is generated by calculating the response of the Harr wavelet in the $4 \times 4$ sub-area centered on the feature point. In this paper, SURF descriptors are used to describe feature points, and the following four attributes are added: (1) Intensity of feature points, positive values represent black points, and negative values represent white points; (2) Gaussian models of extracted feature points; (3) Used to Find the traces of the Gaussian matrix of the feature points; (4) The direction of the feature points. Then 68-dimensional feature vectors are obtained.

In order to further simplify calculations and remove redundancy, the above-mentioned 68-dimensional SURF descriptor reduction is reduced to 48-dimension using Relief-F algorithm [2]. The simplified SURF descriptor is used to describe the key feature points in the classification. The basic idea of the Relief-F algorithm is to randomly select instances from the training data set, calculate their neighborhood, adjust the feature weight vector to distinguish the instance from its different categories of neighboring elements, and use it to train the feature point classifier.

## 4  SAR Image Fusion

In the process of image collection, due to different shooting fields and errors in image registration, if the images are directly stitched together, there will be obvious mis-spellings, so a reasonable fusion strategy should be adopted. Although the traditional weighted average method can achieve a smooth transition at the image mosaic, the image overlap region may appear blurred and distorted [8].

The algorithm uses a weighted smoothing process with a threshold [9]. A threshold value N is introduced in the algorithm. The difference between the pixel value before the smoothing and the weighted average value is calculated for the stitched image and compared with the threshold value $N$. After taking the value. This method divides the image overlap area into three parts and fuses the three parts separately.

Let the overlapped parts of the two images to be stitched be $I_1$ and $I_2$, and the values of the corresponding pixel points are respectively $im_1$ and $im_2$, and the weighted average value is expressed as $Mean = d_1 \times im_1 + d_2 \times im_2 (0 \le d_1 \le 1, d_1 + d_2 = 1)$, $im_3$ represents the smoothed pixel value. The three sections divided from left to right in the overlapping area are denoted as $L_1$, $L_2$, $L_3$.

In $L_1$: when $|im_1 - Mean| < N, im_3 = Mean; otherwise, im_3 = im_1$.
In $L_2$: when $|max(im_1, im_2) - Mean| < N, im_3 = Mean; otherwise, im_3 = max(im_1, im_2)$.
In $L_3$: when $|im_2 - Mean| < N, im_3 = Mean; otherwise, im_3 = im_2$.

This smoothing method makes full use of the characteristics of SAR images in different regions. From the perspective of fusion effects, the resulting images are error-free stitching seams with good results and high speed.

## 5   Experimental Results and Analysis

The experimental platform personal computer was configured as an Intel Core i5-2450M 2.5GHZ with 4 GB of memory and the operating system was 32-bit Windows 7. The algorithm was based on OpenCV 2.4.8, programmed in C ++ and tested in Visual Studio 2010.

The experimental data is the SAR image captured by the first orbit of the satellite of No. 1 satellite of the environmental satellite. This experiment uses the Zhengzhou SAR image as the test image to show the mosaic effect of the proposed mosaic algorithm, and the algorithm is further analyzed by comparing the running time of the algorithm (Fig. 1 and Table 1).

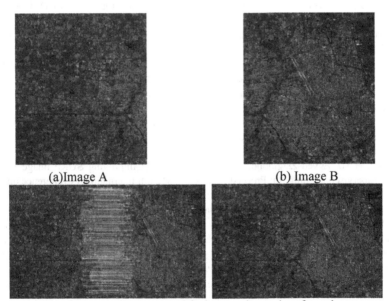

(a)Image A                    (b) Image B

(c) Key feature point maps and fusion result graphs of two images

**Fig. 1.**  Image mosaic experiment result chart

**Table 1.** The performance of the first set of images SURF and the improved algorithm.

| Algorithm | Feature point detection time/s | Logarithm of feature points | Registration time/s |
|---|---|---|---|
| SURF | 3.76 | 12472 | 3.58 |
| The improved algorithm | 4.83 | 6210 | 1.92 |

# 6 Conclusion

This paper presents a fast learning algorithm for SAR image mosaic based on machine learning. Using machine learning method, a binary classifier can be constructed to distinguish two types of feature points. Key feature points and non-critical feature points are identified to improve the original SURF. In addition, Relief-F algorithm is used to reduce the dimensionality of the improved SURF descriptors, and it is used to train feature point classifiers to complete SAR image feature point registration. In SAR image fusion, a threshold-based weighted fusion algorithm is used to achieve seamless image mosaic. The experimental results show that the proposed algorithm has good splicing effect, fast calculation speed, good robustness, and satisfies the practical application requirements of SAR image mosaic.

# References

1. Bai, Z., He, J., Yuan, Q.: Improving image stitching accuracy for double CCD. J. Appl. Opt. **31**(6), 918–921 (2010)
2. Liu, H., Motoda, H.: Computational Methods of Feature Selection, pp. 277–290. Chapman & Hall/CRC, Boca Raton (2007)
3. Zhang, Y.: Research on Image and Video Stitching Technology Based on SURF Features. Xi'an University of Science and Technology, Xi'an (2013)
4. Bay, H., Ess, A., Tuytelaars, T., et al.: SURF: speeded up robust features. Comput. Vis. Image Underst. **110**(3), 346–359 (2008)
5. Lowe, D.G.: Object recognition from local scale-invariant features. In: Proceedings of the 7th IEEE International Conference on Computer Vision, pp. 1150–1157. IEEE Press, Piscataway (1999)
6. Sergieh, H.M., Egyed-Zsigmond, E., Doller, M., et al.: Improving SURF image matching using supervised learning. In: Proceedings of the 2012 8th International Conference on Signal Image Technology and Internet Based Systems, pp. 230–237. IEEE Press, Piscataway (2012)
7. Provost, F.: Machine learning from imbalanced data sets 101. In: Proceedings of the AAAI 2000 Workshop on Imbalanced Data Sets, pp. 359–367. AAAI Press, Palo Alto (2000)
8. Zhou, D., He, M., Yang, Q.: A robust seamless image stitching algorithm based on feature points. Meas. Control. Technol. **28**(6), 32–36 (2009)
9. Guo, J.: A study on image-based cylinder panoramic image generation technology. Xi'an University of Science and Technology, Xi'an (2010)

# B2DASH: Bandwidth and Buffer-Based Dynamic Adaptive Streaming over HTTP

Peihan Du[1], Jian Wang[1(✉)], Xin Wang[2], and Zufeng Xu[3]

[1] Nanjing University, Nanjing, China
18523270951@163.com, wangjnju@nju.edu.cn
[2] 61428 unit of the Chinese People's Liberation Army, Beijing, China
xinwangwx@sina.com
[3] State Key Laboratory of Smart Grid Protection and Control,
NARI Group Corporation, 19 ChengxinRoad, Nanjing, jiangsu 211000, China

**Abstract.** Currently, video streaming technology is widely used for entertainment, advertising, social networking and so on. Dynamic adaptive streaming over HTTP (DASH) has largely replaced the previous release of streaming video using UDP. Many researchers have proposed algorithms to improve DASH performance. There are two types of methods: bandwidth-based and buffer-based. Both methods have pros and cons. In this article, we propose a DASH algorithm that takes both bandwidth and buffer into account. And we imitate the method of network congestion control to adjust bitrate of the video segment. The algorithm was implemented and tested, and compared with the state-of-the-art DASH algorithm–BOLA. The results showed that B2DASH outperformed BOLA for both the average bitrate and buffer rise time.

**Keywords:** Adaptive algorithm
MPEG dynamic adaptive streaming over HTTP (MPEG DASH)
Bandwidth and buffer-based algorithm · Congestion control

## 1 Introduction

With the popularization of the Internet and the rapid development of the computer communications industry, there is an increasing demand on multimedia data. The Cisco Technical Report [5] predicts that mobile data traffic will increase significantly in the next few years, reaching 24.3 EB per month by 2019, and nearly 72% of the it will be video traffic. Therefore, the design of an efficient video streaming algorithm is critical to provide a high quality experience (QoE) to meet the growing demand for video streaming over wireless networks.

The most popular content provider such as YouTube, Netflix uses adaptive HTTP streaming technology to transmit video [16]. Adaptive transmission technologies include HTTP Live Streaming (HLS) and HTTP Dynamic Adaptive Streaming (DASH) standards [11]. The video is encoded into multiple video representations that are segmented into k-second segments. At the end of each

© ICST Institute for Computer Sciences, Social Informatics and Telecommunications Engineering 2018
L. Meng and Y. Zhang (Eds.): MLICOM 2018, LNICST 251, pp. 565–574, 2018.
https://doi.org/10.1007/978-3-030-00557-3_56

segment, the client predicts the available bandwidth for the next k seconds and requests a video representation so that the segment bitrate matches the throughput.

According to past research, DASH's adaptive algorithm can be divided into two types of methods. First, the bandwidth-based method [1–4] is to select the video bitrate as close to the actual bandwidth as possible. However, it is difficult to predict instantaneous bandwidth because it depends on several factors such as delay, bandwidth change, buffer level or segment duration. Then, the buffer-based method [6,7] is to select the video bitrate based on the client's buffer level status. This method can reduce the number of interrupts, but it does not consider the bandwidth, and the video bitrate may be lower than it should be.

Since both methods have their own pros and cons, many studies have attempted to combine them in order to get better QoE. Jiang et al. [8] proposed an optimized bandwidth estimation algorithm based on the previous bandwidth average to improve the accuracy of bandwidth estimation and maintain the stability of the buffer length. Zhou et al. [9] proposed a buffer occupancy model to smooth short-term bandwidth changes. In order to maintain the smoothing of the video rate of the proportional-derivative (PD) controller, Zhou et al. [10] proposed a Markov decision model to estimate the bandwidth accurately, but it is difficult to obtain a good Markov transition matrix.

In this article, we proposed B2DASH, an adaptive algorithm combined buffer-based with bandwidth-based technique. The experimental results demonstrated the effectiveness of B2DASH adaptive algorithm in making users get higher bitrate and faster video startup speed than before.

We started this article by introducing the background of DASH. We described the algorithmic flow of the B2DASH algorithm in the third section, and then introduced our evaluation and data analysis in the fourth section. This article concluded with the fifth part of the conclusion.

## 2    Background and Related Work

Adaptive streaming media technology, especially DASH, can dynamically change video's quality to suit network conditions. Although DASH is gradually gaining popularity, there are still some issues that have led to inefficiencies. For example, Poor bandwidth prediction may causes bitrate fluctuations, especially in mobile networks; segmented transmission delays increase; video freezes, and may therefore have a negative effect on QoE.

Improvements in adaptive strategies can minimize the impact of changing networks on QoE. Recent work shows that client-side adaptive streaming algorithm uses two different methods: bandwidth-based and buffer-based. The representative of the bandwidth-based methods is PANDA [13] and Elastic [14]. The performance of the method may be affected by the accuracy of its bandwidth estimator. Bandwidth estimation and prediction are considered daunting tasks [15,16]. Buffer-based methods, such as the recent BOLA [17] and [18,19], avoid the inaccuracy of bandwidth estimation and use the system buffer as the main factor for bitrate switching. Most proposed buffer-based algorithms assume relatively large buffer sizes which are not suitable for short video. These work show that: one outstanding challenge was that under the two conditions of bandwidth stability and bandwidth fluctuation, the adaptive algorithm can play a relatively stable effect and achieve a higher bitrate.

This article is to develop an adaptive algorithm using both bandwidth and buffer-based algorithm to enhance the video's quality when the actual bandwidth is drastically changed, and the algorithm is combined with theory of congestion control. Furthermore, the loading speed of video playback has also been greatly optimized.

## 3   System Model

In this section, we proposed B2DASH, an adaptive algorithm which combines buffer-based with bandwidth-based optimization technique. B2DASH predicts the bandwidth according to the current bandwidth during the transmission of video, and will determine video bitrate by both bandwidth and buffer level. In addition, we imitate the TCP congestion control mechanism and divide the buffer into several levels. Different buffer level will lead to different adaptive method.

In this work, B2DASH consists of four parts: bandwidth prediction (Sect. 3.1), selection based on the bandwidth (Sect. 3.2), adjustment based on the congestion control (Sect. 3.3), algorithm overview (Sect. 3.4) The definitions of some variables are attached in Table 1.

**Table 1.** Main symbols and meaning

| Symbol | Meaning |
| --- | --- |
| $B(t)$ | The bandwidth at time t |
| $t_c$ | The current time |
| $S_c$ | The critical buffer size |
| $S_{adq}$ | The adequate buffer size |
| $S_{max}$ | The maximum buffer size |
| $S_{now}$ | The buffer size at now |
| QI | Quality index |
| $QI_n$ | QI of the $n-th$ transmission cycle |
| bufferLevel$_n$ | Buffer level at the start of n-th transmission cycle |

### 3.1   Bandwidth Prediction

In order to determine the benchmark value of the segment's bitrate, we first need to estimate the future bandwidth. Previous research [20] showed that simple prediction based on historical information has the best prediction accuracy.

Therefore, we use the measured bandwidth information of the previous segment to predict future bandwidth. Specifically, we extract the measurement information from the last transmission cycle and use the average as the future bandwidth. Assuming that the current time is $t_c$, the last round of transmission time we chose is $T_{max}$. During the period from $T_{max}$ to $t_c$, we selected x sample points, $T_{max} < t_{c-x} < ... < t_{c-1} < t_c$. Since the time is closer to $t_c$, the more referential for the next cycle of prediction, so we give it a higher weight. Select a function $w(t)$ monotonically increasing with t and normalize it from $T_{max}$ to $t_c$, i.e.:

$$\int_0^{T_{max}} w(t)dt = 1$$

Then, this transmission bandwidth can be predicted as:

$$B = \sum_{i=1}^{x} B(t_i) \int_{t_c - t_{i-1}}^{t_c - t_i} w(t_c - t_i)dt$$

## 3.2 Selection Based on the Bandwidth

After obtaining the prediction function $B(t)$ of the bandwidth for a period of time in the future, a basic bitrate b is assigned to the segment during this period of time;

The test set is assumed to have a total of k bitrates for selection. These bitrates $b$ are distributed from low to high in a set A=$\{b_1, b_2, ...b_k\}$. In the initial of playback, because the bandwidth is unstable and the buffer is limited, the minimum bitrate $b_1$ or $b_2$ is allocated. After that B2DASH allocate $b_i$ which is closest to bandwidth predicted to video segment. This is the initial allocation based on bandwidth.

Figure 1 shows the result of the initial allocation based on bandwidth. In the case of fixed bandwidth, this algorithm can always stabilize the bitrate between 1–2 $QIs$.

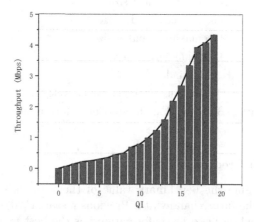

**Fig. 1.** Initial allocation based on bandwidth

With bandwidth stability, bandwidth prediction based on past experience can accurately and efficiently allocate bitrates to video segments without causing rebuffers. However, if the predicted bandwidth is much higher than the actual bandwidth, network congestion may occur. And for this reason, the buffer must be made to play a role in the selection of the bitrate.

## 3.3  Adjustment Based on the Congestion Control

The so-called congestion control is to avoid too much traffic into the network, to reduce the load of network communication links. At present, the Internet initiative standards have formulated four types of congestion control mechanisms: slow start, congestion avoidance, fast recover, and fast retransmission. We mainly use the method of slow start and congestion avoidance, and adjust bitrate according to length of buffer.

We assume that the maximum value of the buffer level is $S_{max}$. The goal of the algorithm is to keep the buffer within the interval $[S_c, S_{adq}]$. Then, B2DASH denote the current buffer level as $S_{now}$. When $S_{now}$ is close to 0, use the slow start algorithm to start. In this way, after establishing the network channel connection, the congestion window value is increased gradually. At the time of initial transmission, $QI=1$ is set. Whenever the transmitter receives feedback from the receiver, bitrate can be doubled. The idea of the congestion avoidance algorithm is to slowly increase the video bitrate. After a transmission cycle, linear increasing bitrate instead of doubling it.

## 3.4  Algorithm Overview

The total algorithm that combines the bandwidth estimation and buffer congestion control is as follows:

As shown in Algorithm 1, the client first determines the range of transmission cycle numbers. Then at the begin of each cycle, the client need to get the throughput predicted (*throughput*), the length of buffer (*bufferLevel$_n$*), the QI of last cycle($QI_{n-1}$). Then for each possible n, a suitable bitrate is selected via B2DASH. Function *estimate()* represent the process of selection based on the bandwidth. If the *bufferLevel$_n$* was within $[S_c, S_{adq}]$, B2DASH will simply use throughput to select bitrate. Otherwise slow start or congestion avoidance will adjust bitrate base on the result of *estimate(throughput)*. With such designs, the algorithm sketches the segment scheduling in a transmission cycle for B2DASH.

---

**Algorithm 1.** B2DASH

---
1: **for** $n = 1$ to $N$ **do**
2:     **if** $n = 1$ **then**
3:         $QI_n = 1$
4:     **else if** $bufferLevel_n < S_c$ **then**
5:         **if** $2 * QI_{n-1} < estimate(throughput)$ **then**
6:             $QI_n = 2 * QI_{n-1}$
7:         **else**
8:             $QI_n = estimate(throughput/2)$
9:         **end if**
10:     **else if** $bufferLevel_n < S_{adq}$ **then**
11:         $QI_n = estimate(throughput)$
12:     **end if**
13:     **if** $bufferLevel_n > S_{adq}$ **then**
14:         $QI_n = max[estimate(throughput) + 1, QI_{max}]$
15:     **end if**
16: **end for**

---

## 4 Evaluation

### 4.1 Experimental Environment

The system used in the experiment is Linux Ubuntu 14.04, equipped with a Linux kernel 3.13.0-66-generic; the server of the B2DASH system is deployed on a Jetty server. The B2DASH client uses the open source project dash.js[12] video player. This player is a DASH-compliant JavaScript player. In the network simulation, we used the Linux Traffic control (tc) to control and The bandwidth of the network was changed and the network structure was simulated using Linux netem. The data set used in the experiment was a distributed data set launched by the GPAC project.

We deployed the DASH standard dataset on the Jetty server and used tc to simulate the stable and variable network bandwidth. In order to compare with this proposed B2DASH, BOLA [17] was also simulated the same conditions, because BOLA showed good performance in other proposed works. The 20 bitrates for each video segment in the simulation are 47, 92, 135, 182, 226, 270, 353, 425, 538, 621, 808, 1.1M, 1.3M, 1.7M, 2.2M, 2.6M, 3.3 M, 3.8M, 4.2M and 4.7 Mbps. Video duration is 1 s. In this study, the performance indicator is the time of the buffer first rising to a safe level and the average bitrate.

(1) In general, the network conditions are most unstable at the beginning of video playback. Therefore, establishing a buffer as soon as possible can minimize video stuck in the initial transmission period.

(2) The average video bitrate is the average bitrate requested from the DASH server.

## 4.2    Buffer Rise Time Test

The test content in this section is: test the time that the video buffer reaches half of the buffer upper limit for the first time under different bandwidth conditions.

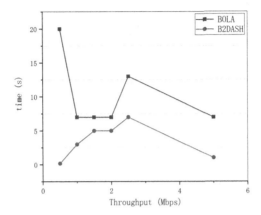

**Fig. 2.** Buffer rise time at different throughput

As can be seen from the Fig. 2, B2DASH benefits from its slow-start mechanism. It can quickly raise the buffer level to a very safe level at the beginning of the video's playback. B2DASH can deal with both high and low throughput. In contrast, BOLA's buffer is rise slowly and fluctuates at different throughputs. Especially when the link throughput is low, BOLA often takes a long time. Only then can the buffer be pulled up to half the maximum value.

## 4.3    Bitrate Comparison

There are test under stable throughput and test under variable throughput in this section.

The stable throughput test's content is: The throughput of the network is 1 Mbps in 0–100 s, then increase to 2 Mbps in 100–200 s, and then drop to 1 Mbps again in the following 100 s. The test content of variable throughput is that the throughput of the network is 1 Mbps within 0–100 s, then the code rate fluctuates between 1M and 2M every 10 s for 100 s, and then maintains a 2 Mbps for 100 s.

Table 2 shows the comparison of the two algorithms. Compared with BOLA, the average bitrate of B2DASH is higher, and the bitrate has increased by 15.72% and 7.36% respectively under the two different conditions of stable bandwidth and variable bandwidth. From the Figs. 3 and 4, it can be seen that, thanks to the slow start of B2DASH, when the network suddenly changes and the bitrate drops sharply, B2DASH can adapt to the change of the bitrate more quickly and quickly return to the appropriate bitrate. However, BOLA is not sensitive to bandwidth, and often finds the optimal bitrate after a long period of high throughput.

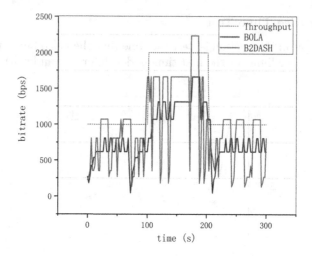

**Fig. 3.** Segment bitrate between BOLA and B2DASH in stable throughput

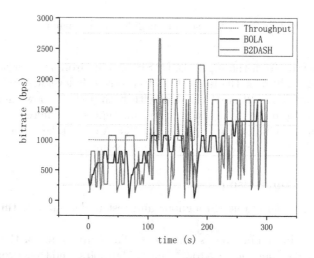

**Fig. 4.** Segment bitrate between BOLA and B2DASH in variable throughput

**Table 2.** Simulation results between BOLA and B2DASH

| Algorithm | Avg.video rate(kbps)/stable | Avg.video rate(kbps)/variable |
|---|---|---|
| BOLA | 833.23 | 914.25 |
| B2DASH | 967.21 | 981.58 |
| Improvement | 15.72% | 7.36% |

# 5    Conclusion

In this article, we propose the B2DASH algorithm combining the advantages of bandwidth and buffer-based methods to provide higher quality for video streams. And in the algorithm, the method of congestion control is applied to control the change of the bitrate. The proposed algorithm is implemented using the dash.js client, and compared with the advanced algorithm BOLA in dash.js, the performance metrics is the buffer rise time and the average transmission bitrate, both in the bandwidth stability and the bandwidth fast switching. The results show that B2DASH outperforms BOLA in both average bitrate and buffer rise time. Our future work will improve the performance of the B2DASH rate switching method.

**Acknowledgements.** This work was supported by State Key Laboratory of Smart Grid Protection and Control of NARI Group Corporation.

# References

1. Liu, C., Bouazizi, I., Gabbouj, M.: Rate adaptation for adaptive HTTP streaming. In: ACM Conference on Multimedia Systems, pp. 169–174. ACM (2011)
2. Zhou, B., Wang, J., Zou, Z., et al.: Bandwidth estimation and rate adaptation in HTTP streaming. In: International Conference on Computing, NETWORKING and Communications, pp. 734–738. IEEE (2012)
3. Zhao, M., Gong, X., Liang, J., et al.: QoE-driven cross-layer optimization for wireless dynamic adaptive streaming of scalable videos over HTTP. IEEE Trans. Circuits Syst. Video Technol. **25**(3), 451–465 (2014)
4. Fallah, Y.P., Mansour, H., Khan, S., et al.: A link adaptation scheme for efficient transmission of H.264 scalable video over multirate WLANs. IEEE Trans. Circuits Syst. Video Technol. **18**(7), 875–887 (2008)
5. White Paper: Cisco visual networking index: Global mobile data traffic- forecast update, 2014–2019. Technical report, Cisco, February 2015
6. Huang, T.Y., Johari, R., Mckeown, N.: Downton abbey without the hiccups: buffer-based rate adaptation for HTTP video streaming. In: ACM SIGCOMM Workshop on Future Human-Centric Multimedia NETWORKING, pp. 9–14. ACM (2013)
7. Huang, T.Y., Johari, R., Mckeown, N., et al.: A buffer-based approach to rate adaptation: evidence from a large video streaming service. In: ACM Conference on SIGCOMM, pp. 187–198. ACM (2014)
8. Jiang, J., Sekar, V., Zhang, H.: Improving fairness, efficiency, and stability in HTTP-based adaptive video streaming with FESTIVE. IEEE/ACM Trans. Netw. **22**(1), 326–340 (2014)
9. Zhou, C., Lin, C.W., Zhang, X., et al.: A control-theoretic approach to rate adaption for DASH over multiple content distribution servers. IEEE Trans. Circuits Syst. Video Technol. **24**(4), 681–694 (2014)
10. Zhou, C., Lin, C.W., Guo, Z.: mDASH: a markov decision-based rate adaptation approach for dynamic HTTP streaming. IEEE Trans. Multimed. **18**(4), 738–751 (2015)
11. ISO: Dynamic adaptive streaming over HTTP (DASH). Technical Report 23009, ISO/IEC (2012)

12. dash.js. https://github.com/Dash-Industry-Forum/dash.js/wiki
13. Li, Z.: Probe and adapt: rate adaptation for HTTP video streaming at scale. IEEE J. Sel. Areas Commun. **32**, 719–733 (2014)
14. De Cicco, L., Caldaralo, V., Palmisano, V., Mascolo, S.: ELASTIC: a client-side controller for dynamic adaptive streaming over HTTP (DASH). In: 2013 20th International Packet Video Workshop. IEEE (2013)
15. Yao, J., Kanhere, S.S., Hassan, M.: An empirical study of bandwidth predictability in mobile computing. In: Proceedings of the Third ACM International Workshop on Wireless Network Testbeds. ACM (2008)
16. Romirer-Maierhofer, P., Ricciato, F., D'Alconzo, A., Franzan, R., Karner, W.: Network-wide measurements of TCP RTT in 3G. In: Papadopouli, M., Owezarski, P., Pras, A. (eds.) TMA 2009. LNCS, vol. 5537, pp. 17–25. Springer, Heidelberg (2009). https://doi.org/10.1007/978-3-642-01645-5_3
17. Spiteri, K., Urgaonkar, R., Sitaraman, R.K.: BOLA: near-optimal bitrate adaptation for online videos (2016)
18. Huang, T.-Y., Johari, R., McKeown, N.: Downton abbey without the hiccups: buffer-based rate adaptation for http video streaming. In: Proceedings of the 2013 ACM SIGCOMM Workshop on Future Humancentric Multimedia Networking. ACM (2013)
19. Huang, T.-Y., Johari, R., McKeown, N., Trunnell, M., Watson, M.: A buffer-based approach to rate adaptation: evidence from a large video streaming service. ACM SIGCOMM Comput. Commun. Rev. **44**, 187–198 (2015)
20. Tian, G., Liu, Y.: Towards agile and smooth video adaptation in dynamic HTTP streaming. In: Proceedings of the 8th International Conference on Emerging Networking Experiments and Technologies, pp. 109–120. ACM (2012)

# ZigBee-Based Device-Free Wireless Localization in Internet of Things

Yongliang Sun[1,2], Xiaocheng Wang[2], Xuzhao Zhang[2(✉)], and Xinggan Zhang[1]

[1] School of Electronic Science and Engineering, Nanjing University, Nanjing, China
[2] School of Computer Science and Technology, Nanjing Tech University,
Nanjing, China
zxz_jsnj@qq.com

**Abstract.** In recent years, localization has been one of the research hot-spots in Internet of Things (IoT). Device-Free Wireless Localization (DFWL) that extends the application range of wireless localization has been considered as a promising technology. In this paper, we propose a ZigBee-based DFWL system using Artificial Neural Networks (ANNs) in IoT. The proposed system utilizes Received Signal Strength (RSS) variations, which is caused by the obstructing of the Line of Sight (LoS) links, to estimate the location of a target using an ANN model. A non-linear function is approximated between RSS difference information and location coordinates using the ANN model. With the ANN model, the location of the target can be estimated. The experimental results show that the proposed DFWL system is able to locate the target without any terminal device and offer a valuable reference for DFWL in IoT.

**Keywords:** Device-free wireless localization · Internet of Things
Artificial neural networks · ZigBee

## 1 Introduction

With the rapid development of information technology and Internet of Things (IoT), Location-Based Service (LBS) has drew more and more attentions [1,2], especially in some special application scenarios like museum, shopping mall, and airport, where users have an increasing demand for LBS. However, most of the existing developed localization systems need users to carry terminal devices like Wireless Local Area Networks (WLANs), Ultra Wideband (UWB), and Radio Frequency Identification (RFID) [3–5], which is not suitable for some special application scenarios such as life detection, the elder monitoring and so on. To solve this problem, Device-Free Wireless Localization (DFWL) system that utilizes Received Signal Strength (RSS) variations to estimate the location of a target has played an important role [6]. Therefore, in this paper, we propose a ZigBee-based DFWL system in IoT that is able to sense and locate a target in an Area of Interest (AoI) without any terminal device.

© ICST Institute for Computer Sciences, Social Informatics and Telecommunications Engineering 2018
L. Meng and Y. Zhang (Eds.): MLICOM 2018, LNICST 251, pp. 575–582, 2018.
https://doi.org/10.1007/978-3-030-00557-3_57

## 2  Related Works

Until now, many DFWL systems have been developed. One of the famous systems presented by Wilson and Patwariis was the DFWL based on Radio Tomographic Imaging (RTI) [6,7]. Due to the comparable localization performance of RTI-based DFWL, some other RTI-based DFWL systems were proposed as well [8,9]. Wang et al. applied saddle surface model, compressive sensing (CS), and Bayesian grid approach into DFWL and obtained significant achievements [10–12]. An energy-efficient framework for DFWL was proposed in [13]. The researchers also applied CS to guarantee high localization accuracy with less RSS measurements.

Referring to the fingerprinting localization method [4], Zhang et al. mounted some nodes on the ceiling and divided the tracking area into different triangle areas. They used Support Vector Regression (SVR) to estimate target locations in each area [14]. Youssef et al. first proposed a DFWL system based on radio-map. They computed localization results with probabilistic method [15]. Then they proposed a different DFWL system using particle filtering [16]. Xu et al. formulated the DFWL problem with probabilistic classification methods based on discriminant analysis and mitigated the errors caused by multipath effect [17]. Because the fingerprinting localization method has been proved that it performs well in multipath environments, we refer to this method and propose a DFWL system using Artificial Neural Networks (ANNs) in this paper.

## 3  Proposed Device-Free Wireless Localization System

### 3.1  System Overview

As shown in Fig. 1, the sensor nodes of the proposed DFWL system are deployed evenly in the edges of an AoI. When a target goes into the AoI, some wireless links between sensor nodes are obstructed. RSS variations caused by the target in the AoI are sensed and used for estimating the location of the target. If we take Fig. 1 as an example, the wireless links between sensor nodes 1 and 8, 2 and 10, 2 and 11, 3 and 13, 3 and 14 as well as 6 and 16 are obstructed, so the RSS variations of these wireless links are caused by the target. If we assume $L$ sensor nodes have been deployed in the AoI with known location coordinates, then there will be $H = \frac{L \times (L-1)}{2}$ wireless links. All the sensor nodes in the system send the measured RSS data to a sink node and then the sink node forwards these data to a localization server where the location coordinates of the target are computed. When the monitoring area is vacant, we collect the RSS data and compile them into RSS matrices. When a professional stands at a number of selected locations with known location coordinates in the AoI, some relative wireless links are obstructed and then RSS data are collected. We can also compile these RSS data into the RSS matrices and compute the RSS difference matrices. We take some RSS difference values and their matrix indices as the inputs of an ANN model, and also take the known location coordinates

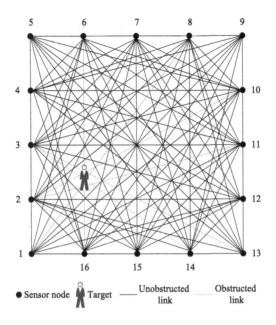

**Fig. 1.** The proposed DFWL system with ZigBee sensor nodes.

as the outputs of the model. A nonlinear function between the RSS difference information and location coordinates can be approximated with the ANN model, which is used for estimating the location coordinates of the target.

### 3.2   RSS Difference Matrix Calculation

When the localization server receives enough RSS data from a vacant AoI, these RSS data are compiled into an RSS matrix $\mathbf{R}$ with dimensions of $L \times L$ that can be denoted by (1). The row of the RSS matrix $\mathbf{R}$ represents the sensor node that receives the RSS data and the column of the RSS matrix $\mathbf{R}$ represents the sensor node that sends these data.

$$\mathbf{R} = \begin{bmatrix} 1 & R_{1,2} & \cdots & R_{1,L} \\ R_{2,1} & 2 & \cdots & R_{2,L} \\ \vdots & \vdots & \ddots & \vdots \\ R_{L,1} & R_{L,2} & \cdots & L \end{bmatrix}_{L \times L} \tag{1}$$

When a professional stands at $i$th location that is selected in the AoI, the RSS data can be collected and compiled into an RSS matrix $\mathbf{r}_i$ with the same dimensions denoted by:

$$\mathbf{r}_i = \begin{bmatrix} 1 & r_{1,2,i} & \cdots & r_{1,L,i} \\ r_{2,1,i} & 2 & \cdots & r_{2,L,i} \\ \vdots & \vdots & \ddots & \vdots \\ r_{L,1,i} & r_{L,2,i} & \cdots & L \end{bmatrix}_{L \times L} , i = 1, 2, \cdots, M \tag{2}$$

where, $M$ is the number of selected locations. So the RSS difference matrix $\Delta\mathbf{s}_i$ between $\mathbf{R}$ and $\mathbf{r}_i$ can be computed by:

$$\Delta\mathbf{s}_i = |\mathbf{R} - \mathbf{r}_i|, i = 1, 2, \cdots, M \tag{3}$$

Sometimes, the RSS data between the sensor nodes in the same edge may vary greatly due to some interference. If these data are used for localization, the localization errors might be significant. In order to eliminate the negative effect, we design a matrix $\mathbf{m}$ to set all the RSS difference values between the sensor nodes in the same edge of the AoI to be 0. So we calculate the final RSS difference matrix $\Delta\mathbf{s}'_i$ as follows:

$$\Delta\mathbf{s}'_i = \Delta\mathbf{s}_i\mathbf{m}, i = 1, 2, \cdots, M \tag{4}$$

When a target moves into the AoI, the real-time RSS data are sent to the localization server and then the RSS difference matrix can be computed in the same manner as mentioned above.

### 3.3    Proposed ANN Model for Localization

Because ANNs have a superior performance in nonlinear function approximation and data fusion, a three-layer perceptron network is applied as the proposed ANN model in this paper. As shown in Fig. 2, The proposed ANN model consists of one input layer, one hidden layer, and one output layer, and the numbers of the neurons in the three layers are $3K$, $N$, and 2, respectively. After obtaining the RSS difference matrix $\Delta\mathbf{s}'_i$, all the RSS difference values are sorted in a non-increasing order. Then the first $K$ maximum RSS difference values $\Delta s'_{i,j}, j = 1, 2, \cdots, K$ are selected and the indices of these values in matrix $\Delta\mathbf{s}'_i$ that are column $c_{i,j}$ and row $r_{i,j}, j = 1, 2, \cdots, K$, are determined. Then we fuse the RSS difference values and their indices as the input vector of the ANN model denoted by $\left(\Delta s'_{i,1}, c_{i,1}, r_{i,1}, \cdots, \Delta s'_{i,K}, c_{i,K}, r_{i,K}\right)$. At the same time, we take the location coordinates where the professional stands as the output vector denoted by $(x_i, y_i)$. Then the nonlinear function between the input vector and output vector can be approximated through training the ANN model. The nonlinear function $f$ can be denoted by:

$$(x_i, y_i) = f\left(\Delta s'_{i,1}, c_{i,1}, r_{i,1}, \cdots, \Delta s'_{i,K}, c_{i,K}, r_{i,K}\right), i = 1, 2, \cdots, M \tag{5}$$

After the training of the ANN model, when a target moves in and stands at a location in the AoI, the collected RSS data are processed in the same way and the RSS difference matrix $\Delta\hat{\mathbf{s}}'$ can be computed. The first $K$ maximum RSS difference values $\Delta\hat{s}'_j, j = 1, 2, \cdots, K$, as well as the indices of these values $\hat{c}_j$ and $\hat{r}_j, j = 1, 2, \cdots, K$, are fused as an input vector $(\Delta\hat{s}'_1, \hat{c}_1, \hat{r}_1, \cdots, \Delta\hat{s}'_K, \hat{c}_K, \hat{r}_K)$. Then the location coordinates $(\hat{x}, \hat{y})$ of the target are estimated with the nonlinear function $f$ by:

$$(\hat{x}, \hat{y}) = f\left(\Delta\hat{s}'_1, \hat{c}_1, \hat{r}_1, \cdots, \Delta\hat{s}'_K, \hat{c}_K, \hat{r}_K\right) \tag{6}$$

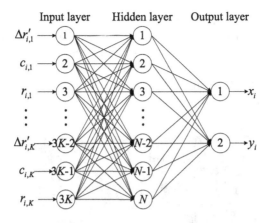

**Fig. 2.** The proposed three-layer ANN structure.

# 4    Experimental Setup, Results, and Analyses

## 4.1    Experimental Setup

In this paper, we adopt CC2530 ZigBee nodes as the experimental nodes. There are 16 sensor nodes and 1 sink node. The sensor nodes are deployed evenly in the edge of the experimental area with 1.8 m gaps and they are fixed on tripods with a height of 1.2 m. The plan of the experimental area is shown in Fig. 3. There are some chair and desks in the AoI and the sink node and localization server are not in the experimental area. A total of 52 locations are selected and their location coordinates are recorded. As shown in Fig. 3, the ZigBee sensor nodes are denoted by the black dots and the selected locations are denoted by the black crosses.

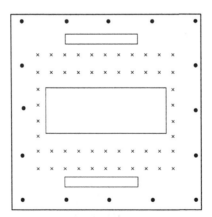

**Fig. 3.** Plan of the experimental area.

After the network startup, we collect enough RSS data and then compile them into 20 RSS matrices for each selected location. These data are divided into two data sets. One set that consists of 10 RSS matrices of each location is used for training the ANN model and the rest half of the data are used for testing the ANN model. The ANN model is trained with the famous back propagation algorithm. The experimental scenario is shown in Fig. 4.

**Fig. 4.** Photography of the experimental scenario.

## 4.2   Experimental Results and Analyses

In the experiment, we set parameter $K$ to be 5, which means the first 5 maximum RSS difference values are selected, and the number of neurons in the hidden layer to be 35. With the trained ANN model, localization results are computed. The mean error of the localization results is 0.98 m and the error standard deviation is

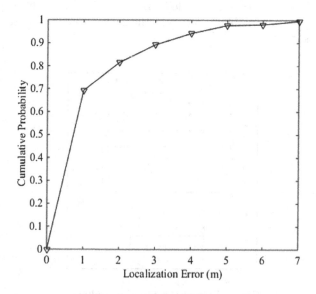

**Fig. 5.** Cumulative probability curve of the proposed DFWL system.

1.42 m. The cumulative probabilities within localization error of 1 m and 2 m are 69.2% and 81.5%, respectively. The cumulative probability curve of the proposed DFWL is shown in Fig. 5. Compared with the state of the art DFWL systems, the performance of the proposed DFWL system is not superior. The reasons may be the number of the training RSS data is not sufficient and the parameters of the proposed DFWL system are not optimal. So we may subsequently collect more RSS data for training the ANN model as well as optimize numbers of selected RSS difference values and neurons in the hidden layer to achieve a better localization performance.

## 5  Conclusions

In the paper, we propose a ZigBee-based DFWL system in IoT. This system utilizes RSS variations caused by a target in the AoI to locate the target without any terminal device. RSS data are collected and compiled into RSS matrices. Then the RSS difference values between the RSS matrices collected when the AoI is vacant and with a professional standing in it are computed. The first $K$ maximum RSS difference values and their matrix indices are determined and also used as inputs. Meanwhile, the location coordinates of the professional are used as outputs to train the ANN model. When a target enters into the AoI, the RSS difference values are computed in the same way, then the selected RSS difference values and their indices in the RSS difference matrix are input into the trained ANN model, so the location coordinates of the target can be calculated. The experimental results demonstrate that the proposed DFWL system is able to locate the target in the AoI without any terminal device and offer a valuable reference for the DFWL in IoT.

**Acknowledgment.** The authors gratefully thank the referees for the constructive and insightful comments. This work was supported by the Natural Science Foundation of the Jiangsu Higher Education Institutions of China under Grant No. 16KJB510014, the Natural Science Foundation of Jiangsu Province under Grant No. BK20171023, and the National Natural Science Foundation of China under Grant No. 61701223.

## References

1. Zanella, A., Bui, N., Castellani, A., Vangelista, L., Zorzi, M.: Internet of Things for smart cities. IEEE Internet Things J. **1**(1), 22–32 (2014)
2. Fantacci, R., Pecorella, T., Viti, R., Carlini, C.: A network architecture solution for efficient IOT WSN backhauling: challenges and opportunities. IEEE Wirel. Commun. **21**(4), 113–119 (2014)
3. Zhou, M., Tang, Y.X., Tian, Z.S., Xie, L.B., Geng, X.L.: Semi-supervised learning for indoor hybrid fingerprint database calibration with low effort. IEEE Access **5**(1), 4388–4400 (2017)
4. Sun, Y.L., Xu, Y.B.: Error estimation method for matrix correlation-based Wi-Fi indoor localization. KSII Trans. Internet Inf. Syst. **7**(11), 2657–2675 (2013)

5. Gu, Y.Y., Lo, A., Niemegeers, I.: A survey of indoor positioning systems for wireless personal networks. IEEE Commun. Surv. Tutor. **11**(1), 13–32 (2009)
6. Wilson, J., Patwari, N.: Radio tomographic imaging with wireless networks. IEEE Trans. Mobile Comput. **9**(5), 621–632 (2010)
7. Wilson, J., Patwari, N.: See through walls: motion tracking using variance-based radio tomography networks. IEEE Trans. Mobile Comput. **10**(5), 612–621 (2011)
8. Bocca, M., Kaltiokallio, O., Patwari, N., Venkatasubramanian, S.: Multiple target tracking with RF sensor networks. IEEE Trans. Mobile Comput. **13**(8), 1787–1800 (2014)
9. Alippi, C., Bocca, M., Boracchi, G., Patwari, N., Roveri, M.: RTI goes wild: radio tomographic imaging for outdoor people detection and localization. IEEE Trans. Mobile Comput. **15**(10), 2585–2598 (2016)
10. Wang, J., Gao, Q.H., Pan, M., Zhang, X., Yu, Y., Wang, H.Y.: Toward accurate device-free wireless localization with a saddle surface model. IEEE Trans. Veh. Technol. **65**(8), 6665–6677 (2016)
11. Wang, J., Gao, Q.H., Wang, H.Y., Cheng, P., Xin, K.F.: Device-free localization with multidimensional wireless link information. IEEE Trans. Veh. Technol. **64**(1), 356–366 (2015)
12. Wang, J., Gao, Q.H., Cheng, P., Wu, L., Xin, K.F., Wang, H.Y.: Lightweight robust device-free localization in wireless networks. IEEE Trans. Ind. Electron. **61**(10), 5681–5689 (2014)
13. Wang, J., Fang, D.Y., Yang, Z., et al.: E-HIPA: an energy-efficient framework for high-precision multi-target-adaptive device-free localization. IEEE Trans. Mobile Comput. **16**(3), 716–729 (2017)
14. Zhang, D., Liu, Y., Ni, L.M.: RASS: a real-time, accurate and scalable system for tracking transceiver-free objects. In: 2011 9th IEEE International Conference on Pervasive Computing and Communications, pp. 197–204 (2011)
15. Youssef, M., Mah, M., and Agrawala, A.: Challenges: device-free passive localization for wireless environments. In: 13th Annual ACM International Conference on Mobile Computing and Networking, pp. 222–229 (2007)
16. Saeed, A., Kosba, A.E., Youssef, M.: Ichnaea: a low-overhead robust WLAN device-free passive localization system. IEEE J. Sel. Topics Signal Process. **8**(1), 5–15 (2014)
17. Xu, C.R., Firner, B.Y., Zhang, Y., Howard, R.E.: The case for efficient and robust RF-based device-free localization. IEEE Trans. Mobile Comput. **15**(9), 2362–2375 (2016)

# Designing of Environmental Information Acquisition and Reconstruction System Based on Compressed Sensing

Qiuming Zhao, Bo Li, Hongjuan Yang[✉], Gongliang Liu, and Ruofei Ma

School of Information and Electrical Engineering,
Harbin Institute of Technology, Weihai 264209, China
qiumingzhaohit@163.com, {libol983,hjyang,liugl,
maruofei}@hit.edu.cn

**Abstract.** At present, the collection of environmental information is mostly accomplished by sensors. In order to reduce the redundancy of sensor data collection, reduce the energy consumption of nodes, improve the service life of sensors and reduce the cost of the system, a system that combines compressed sensing reconstruction with sensors is proposed in this paper to collect and reconstruct environmental information. The designed system collects the environment information with a limited number of nodes. Compressed sensing reconstructs all the data of the required area through the optimized OMP algorithm. The final information is displayed by the software based on C# designing. The final result shows that the verification system proposed in this paper can realize the accurate reconstruction of the original environmental information, and it is effective to the collection and processing of complex environmental information.

**Keywords:** Compressed sensing · Reconstruction
Environmental information collection · Visualization
Orthogonal matching pursuit algorithm

## 1 Introduction

The rapid development of wireless communication technologies and computer networks has promoted the development of wireless sensor networks. Current wireless sensor networks consist of a large number of regularly or randomly distributed sensor nodes and aggregation nodes with advanced data processing capabilities and advanced power supply reserves. This network is characterized by a large scale, strictly limited distributed network. The sensor node can be used to detect various environmental information such as temperature, humidity, light, and pressure. However, as information collection continues to increase, the lifespan of the sensor is greatly reduced, which resulting in high cost investment. In addition, according to the Shannon-Nyquist sampling theorem, the sampling frequency must be greater than or equal to twice the signal bandwidth to recover the original signal during the information collection process. The collected information does not play a role, resulting in low efficiency, and the

© ICST Institute for Computer Sciences, Social Informatics and Telecommunications Engineering 2018
L. Meng and Y. Zhang (Eds.): MLICOM 2018, LNICST 251, pp. 583–593, 2018.
https://doi.org/10.1007/978-3-030-00557-3_58

waste of resources. In addition, the cost of the equipment required for this sampling method is high. Aiming at the shortcomings of traditional sampling, Donoho, Candes and Tao et al. proposed compressed sensing [1]. Compressed sensing obtains signals directly through the transformation of space, collecting valid information in a large amount of data, which is performing certain compression while data is sampled. Then it obtains the required information through the sensing matrix. Finally some reconstruction algorithm will restore the original information. Therefore, when the amount of data is large, the number of sampling times required for compressed sensing is far lower than that of Nyquist's theory. In this paper, the design of the environment information processing system is designed by combining the sensor with the compression sensing technology, confirmation of the system is performed by adopting two information of temperature and humidity that have significant and sparse changes in environmental information, compression and transmission of information through the sensor, then the receiver reconstructs the original data through the optimized OMP algorithm. At the same time, the results are displayed on the PC side and error analysis is performed. The results show that the original data can be recovered accurately with a certain error, so the feasibility of the sensor and compressed sensing reconstruction technology cooperation system is verified.

## 2  Compressed Sensing

### 2.1  Basic Theory of Compressed Sensing

Compressive sensing technology is the combination of mathematics-based implementation and engineering applications. The premise of applying compressed sensing technology is that the information that needs to be collected must be sparse or compressible and irrelevant, so that it can realize simultaneous acquisition in information compression, so the sampling rate is lower than Nyquist sampling. Compared with traditional sampling techniques, compressed sensing technology has several differences. Compressed sensing technology is mainly applied to finite-dimensional vectors; When sampling, compressed sensing does not directly acquire information, but uses the inner product operation of the observation function and the acquired information as the value transmitted to the receiving end; The information reconstruction of the compressed sensing technology is not a simple reversible process, but a problem of mathematical optimization to find the optimal solution of the indefinite equation.

Assume that $X$ is a $N \times 1$ dimensional column vector of $R^N$ space, whose elements are $[n], n = 1, 2..., N$ and $\{\Psi_i\}_{i=1}^N$ is an orthogonal set of $R^{N \times N}$ spaces. Therefore $X$ can be expressed as $X = \Psi \Theta$: where $\Psi = [\Psi_1, \Psi_2, ..., \Psi_N]$, $\Theta = (\theta_i) = [\langle X, \Psi_i \rangle]$ is the expansion coefficient of $X$ on $\Psi$. If the number of non-zero coefficients is $K$ and $K \ll N$ is satisfied, $X$ is sparse or compressible. Therefore, we can get the compressed signal $Y = \Phi \Theta = \Psi^T X$, compressed sensing technology information reconstruction process show in Fig. 1.

**Fig. 1.** Compressed sensing information reconstruction process diagram

It mainly includes three main problems: determining the sparse matrix of the signal, determining the observation matrix, and signal reconstruction, which are described in detail in the following part of this chapter.

### 2.2 Compressed Sensing Reconstruction Process

(1) The problem of signal sparse representation is that an orthonormal basis $\Psi$ can be found, so that $X$ can be sparsely represented. The conditions for the sparseness of the coefficient vector are satisfied in $0 < p < 2$ and $R > 0$:

$$\|\Theta_p\| \equiv \left( \sum_i |\theta_i|^p \right)^{1/p} \leq R \tag{1}$$

The key is to find a suitable base $\Psi$, which is the first step in compressing perceptual reconstruction. Pevre integrates the orthogonal basis into an orthogonal base dictionary. For a certain signal, it can be found adaptively in the orthogonal base dictionary to find the optimal one, so that the most sparse representation can be achieved.

(2) The observation matrix $\Phi$ of size $M \times N$ is designed to ensure that it is not related to the transformation base $\Psi$ and has stability, so that the sparse vector $\Theta$ guarantees the integrity of important information in the dimension reduction process. According to the theory of compressed sensing, the observation matrix needs to meet the RIP, that is, for the signal $X$, $\varepsilon$ satisfies the following formula:

$$(1 - \varepsilon)\|X\|_2^2 \leq \|\Phi X\|_2^2 \leq (1 + \varepsilon)\|X\|_2^2 \tag{2}$$

In the literature [2, 3], it has been proved that most random matrices satisfy RIP, but the deficiency of this criterion is that the calculation is more difficult. Therefore, the rationality of the measurement matrix can generally be judged by the correlation discriminant theory, which is the measurement matrix and $\Psi$ is irrelevant, the literature [4] gives the calculation formula of the correlation coefficient to determine the correlation between the two:

$$\mu(\Phi, \Psi) = \max_{i \geq 1, j \leq N, i \neq j} \left| \langle \varphi_i \psi_j \rangle \right| \tag{3}$$

Therefore, the threshold of the correlation coefficient must be met when designing the measurement matrix.

(3) The signal reconstruction problem aims to solve the underdetermined equations sparsely by designing a fast and accurate reconstruction algorithm. Theoretically, the equations $Y = A^{CS}X$ have infinitely many solutions, but the equations are guaranteed due to the sparsity and compressibility of the original signal. The existence of a unique solution to the group means that the original signal can be accurately reconstructed from observational evidence. In [5] the problem was solved by $l_1$-norm optimization, as follows:

$$\min\left\|\Psi^T X\right\|_1 \quad s.t. A^{CS}X = \Phi\,\Psi^T = Y \tag{4}$$

Through this method, the linear solution is converted to a convex optimization problem. Based on this, a BP algorithm, a BPDN algorithm is proposed. However, these reconstruction algorithms have a large amount of computational deficiencies. Therefore, the matching quasi-tracking algorithm (MP) and orthogonal matching tracking algorithm (OMP) are proposed in the follow-up. The OMP algorithm has the characteristics of high computing speed and easy implementation. Therefore, in this paper the optimized OMP algorithm is used to complete the data reconstruction [6–8].

## 3 System Model, Reconstruction Algorithm and GUI Designing

### 3.1 Information Acquisition System Model

The design of environmental information acquisition and analysis system based on compressed sensing is shown in Fig. 2.

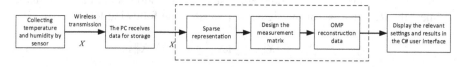

**Fig. 2.** Environmental information acquisition system block diagram

In the verification system designed in this paper, the temperature and humidity environment information collected by the temperature and humidity sensor has real-time and accuracy, and then the data is transmitted to the PC through the wireless serial port, which can reduce the delay and ensure the accuracy of the data in practical applications. On the PC side, through the joint design of MATLAB and C#, the user can manipulate the set parameters in the visual interface, and then use MATLAB to reconstruct the data, and finally feed the results back to the user interface.

## 3.2 Compressed Sensing Reconstruction Algorithm

In order to restore the original temperature and humidity accurately, the design of compressive sensing reconstruction algorithm is very important. The optimization algorithm based on the orthogonal matching pursuit algorithm adopted in this paper, because the OMP algorithm has the characteristics of high computing speed and easy to implement The strong anti-interference ability is very suitable for environmental information with complex features [9, 10]. The basic idea of the OMP algorithm is based on $K-$ sparse. The goal is to find $K$ larger components than the absolute values of other $N - K$ components. Therefore, the algorithm needs to find the column vectors involved in the original signal measurement from the observation matrix. The OMP algorithm process is:

---

step1 Initialization: residual $r^0 = y$, index set $\Gamma^0 = \varnothing$, number of iterations $l = 1$;

step2 Calculate the correlation between observational evidence and residuals, and take

the largest index value $i_{\max}$, that is $i_{\max} = \arg\max_i \left| \Theta_i^H r^{l-1} \right|$;

step3 Update: $\Gamma^l = \Gamma^{l-1} \cup i_{\max}$, $D^l = D^{l-1} \cup D_{i_{\max}}$;

step4 Using the Least Square Method to Solve $y = \Theta^l \theta^l$ Obtained $\hat{\theta}^l = \Theta_{\Gamma^l}^T y$;

step5 Update: $r_l = y - \Theta^l \hat{\theta}^l$;

step6 $l = l + 1$, If the judgment is satisfied or the residual is lower than the set threshold, iteratively enter step7; otherwise, return step2;

step7 $\hat{\theta}$ has non-zero elements at $\Gamma^l$, then the value is $\hat{\theta}^l$ for the last iteration.

---

## 3.3 GUI Designing

This article is mainly to develop the demonstration software based on the information reconstruction of compressed sensing environment, and complete the software design through the mixed programming of C# and MATLAB. The user interface design consists of four parts: start module, system parameter setting module, simulation analysis module, and information display module, as shown in Fig. 3.

**Fig. 3.** Software design block diagram

Part of the parameter setting module is set by user's menu, part of which is set according to the algorithm of reconstruction and the number of data collected randomly. In the data processing part, it is mainly to realize the call of the MATLAB program, and to complete the reconstruction processing and analysis of the collection data. In the user interface, the received data and the results of the processed data can be observed in real time. Specific design is such as Fig. 4.

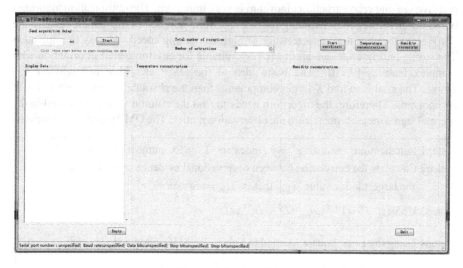

**Fig. 4.** User interface

## 4   Analysis of Results

Firstly, the influence of the sparsity and the number of measurement samples on the success probability of OMP algorithm reconstruction is verified by simulation. The original signal length is $N = 300$ and the sparsity is $s = 15$. The measurement matrix is the Gauss random measurement matrix of $M \times N$. The simulation results are shown in Figs. 5 and 6.

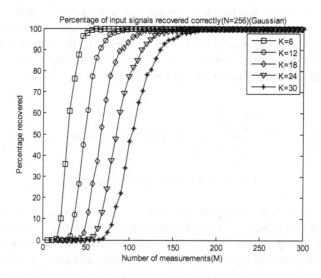

**Fig. 5.** Simulation diagram of the influence of sparsity on reconfiguration performance

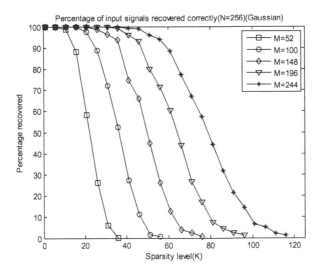

**Fig. 6.** Simulation diagram of the influence of observed quantity on reconfiguration performance

The simulation results show that on the one hand, with a certain degree of sparseness, the greater the number of measurement samples, the greater the probability of success of OMP reconstruction, and the probability of reconstruction success is 100% when a certain threshold is reached; on the other hand, when the measurement sample number is constant, the lower the sparseness is, the greater the probability of successful OMP reconstruction.

Secondly, we simulate the relationship between the measurement matrix and the reconstruction success probability. Let the length of the signal be $N = 256$, and the sparsity be taken as 16 and 30 respectively, for Gaussian random measurement matrix, Bernoulli random measurement matrix, partial Hadamard measurement matrix, Toplitz measurement matrix and cyclic measurement matrix have been verified, simulation results shown in Figs. 7 and 8.

Through the simulation results, we can find that in the case of low sparsity, the performance of the five measurement matrices is similar and data reconstruction can be achieved when the number of measurement samples reaches a certain value. In the case of high sparseness, the performance of some Hadamard measurement matrices outperforms the other four.

Based on the above simulation and verification of the performance of OMP algorithm, certain optimization is performed, reasonable parameters are set, the optimal situation is selected, and applied to the system designed in this paper. The collected temperature and humidity are reconstructed and verified. The results are shown in Figs. 9 and 10.

The results show that the temperature and humidity reconstruction errors are very small, and within a certain range of error, it can be demonstrated that the original temperature and humidity information is completely and accurately reconstructed

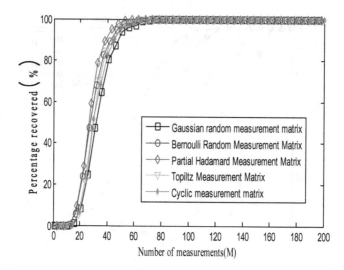

**Fig. 7.** Effect of five kinds of measurement matrices on the reconstruction performance when the sparsity is 16

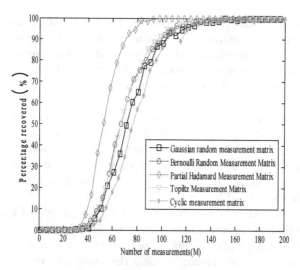

**Fig. 8.** Effect of five kinds of measurement matrices on the reconstruction performance when the sparsity is 30

through compressed sensing. That is compressed sensing theory is feasible in sensor data processing.

Finally, a complete design system operation test is performed. The test result is shown in Fig. 11.

The software operation interface mainly includes a user parameter setting section, which can set related parameters; the received temperature and humidity information

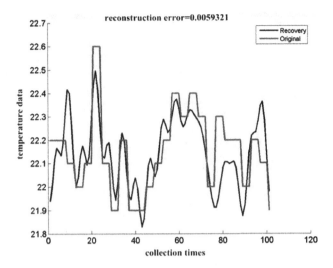

**Fig. 9.** Temperature reconstruction simulation based on compressed sensing

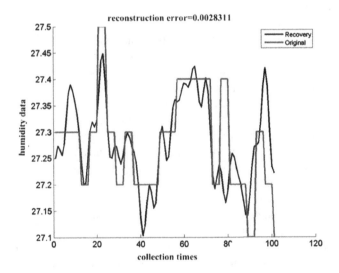

**Fig. 10.** Humidity reconstruction simulation based on compressed sensing

display part can be displayed in real time and stored; the other part is reconstructed based on a small number of temperature and humidity information. The reconstruction result of all the information is compared with the original data in order to verify the accuracy in this design, and the reconstruction error is calculated.

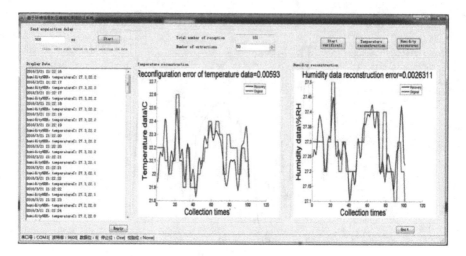

**Fig. 11.** Software running test interface

## 5 Conclusion

In the wireless sensor network of environment information collection, in order to collect data and transmit a large amount of data in real time, the energy consumption of the node is large and the service life is short. Compressed sensing technology provides a solution to this problem. This paper designs and develops an environment information reconstruction system based on compressed sensing technology, which can realize data collection in some unreachable environments, adopt compressed sensing technology to observe, then use the selected reconstruction algorithm to perform reconstruction and perform error and other performance analysis. In the process of this paper, we mainly use the random access compression sensing technology, C# and MATLAB mixed programming technology, as well as the optimization and improvement of the existing reconstruction algorithms. Finally, we verify the research results of the paper through the running test of the software.

The system designs in this paper has great significance. Firstly, Compressed Sensing technology is combined with sensors to verify the availability of compressed sensing theory in the acquisition of sensors, which can reduce the energy consumption, extend the life span, and reduce costs for the use of sensors; Secondly, through the verification of the system design, it can be found that compressed sensing technology can accurately reconstruct the original temperature and humidity data, and transmit data to the PC through wireless transmission. Therefore, for some environments where human beings cannot perform activities, such as underwater data collection and recovery can be performed through this system, then observations or analysis can be performed; In the software design of this article, a modular design is implemented through C#, and mixed programming is performed according to MATLAB's powerful data processing capabilities, so that it has a certain degree of scalability, portability, and application; Finally the design of the software has a good degree of display, simple operation, good interface, user-friendly and secondary development. Subsequent verification of changes to the software's test environment and real-time accuracy of the interface feedback have yet to be improved.

**Acknowledgments.** This work is supported in part by National Natural Science Foundation of China (No. 61401118, No. 61371100 and No. 61671184), Natural Science Foundation of Shandong Province (No. ZR2018PF001 and ZR2014FP016), the Fundamental Research Funds for the Central Universities (No. HIT.NSRIF.2016100 and 201720) and the Scientific Research Foundation of Harbin Institute of Technology at Weihai (No. HIT(WH)201409 and No. HIT (WH)201410).

# References

1. Donoho, D.L.: Compressive sensing. IEEE Trans. Inf. Theory **52**(4), 1289–1306 (2006)
2. Baraniuk, R., Davenpo, M., DeVore, R.: A simple proof of the restricted isometry property for random matrices. Constr. Approx. **28**(3), 253–263 (2007)
3. Tao, E., Near, T.: Optimal signal recovery from random projections: universal encoding strategies. IEEE Trans. Inf. Theory **52**, 5406–5425 (2006)
4. Candes, E., Tao, T.: Decoding by liner programming. IEEE Trans. Inf. Theory **51**(12), 4203–4215 (2005)
5. Chen, S., Saunders, M.: A atomic decomposition by basis pursuit. SIAM J. Sci. Compute. 33–61 (1998)
6. Ameha, T., Chung, G.K.: Compressive sensing-based random access with multiple-sequence spreading for MTC. In: 2015 IEEE Globecom Workshops (GC Wkshps), pp. 1–6. IEEE Press (2015)
7. Bockelmann, C., Schepker, H.F., Dekorsy, A.: Compressive sensing based multi-user detection for machine-to-machine communication. Trans. Emerg. Telecommun. Technol. **24**, 389–400 (2013)
8. Cui, J.: The challenges of building scalable mobile underwater wireless sensor networks for aquatic applications. IEEE Netw. **20**(3), 12–18 (2006)
9. Wang, W., Yang, W., Li, J.: An adaptive sampling method of compressed sensing based on texture feature. Optik-Int. J. Light Electron Opt. **127**(2), 648–654 (2016)
10. Cao, C., Gao, X.: Compressed sensing image restoration based on data-driven multi-scale tight frame. J. Comput. Appl. Math. **309**, 622–629 (2017)

# The Design of Inter-satellite Link Topology Based on Time-Slot Allocation Technology

Siqi Li, Bingbing Zhang, Wenjing Kang, Bo Li, Ruofei Ma, and Gongliang Liu[✉]

School of Information and Electrical Engineering,
Harbin Institute of Technology, Weihai 264209, China
liugl@hit.edu.cn

**Abstract.** Inter-satellite networking is the development trend of satellite navigation system through inter-satellite link technologies. How to schedule inter-satellite link resources is the key to whether the navigation satellite constellation network has the best performance in the time division multiple access system. To achieve this goal, this paper assumes a linking rule based on a multi-layer satellite constellation and constructs a corresponding mathematical model to describe the linking process of inter-satellite links. Based on the assumed linking rule and the proposed mathematical model, a time-division topology design scheme is proposed. The process of data transmission is simulated with the simulation software MATLAB and STK. The results show that the inter-satellite network topology generated under this scheme gets a very considerable promotion on inter-satellite measurement accuracy and transmission characteristics.

**Keywords:** TDMA · Inter-satellite link · Time-division topology
Simulation

## 1 Introduction

In the navigation satellite system, the topology of the inter-satellite network depends on factors such as constellation configuration, the shaped-beam and scanning range of on-board antenna, and network topology control strategy [1]. The interaction between satellites relies mainly on inter-satellite links for connecting satellite nodes. The inter-satellite link (ISL) plays an important role in satellite constellation communication networks. Especially in satellite navigation systems, it is mainly used for inter-satellite communications and inter-satellite ranging. At present, only GPS is used to apply the inter-satellite link technology more skillfully when other navigation systems are still at a preliminary stage of development in this technology [2].

The inter-satellite links work under the TDMA system in GPS, with the frame as the minimum period and the time slot as the minimum unit. The communication channel resources are used by all satellites in the constellation in the form of frame-timeslot. How to generate the topology of the inter-satellite link network in time-division multiplexing mode to minimize data transmission time is one of the most important issues in satellite network management.

© ICST Institute for Computer Sciences, Social Informatics and Telecommunications Engineering 2018
L. Meng and Y. Zhang (Eds.): MLICOM 2018, LNICST 251, pp. 594–603, 2018.
https://doi.org/10.1007/978-3-030-00557-3_59

The design of time-division topology in satellite networks is based on time-slot allocation of inter-satellite links. At present, the research results for the time-division inter-satellite link topology generation issues are as follows: Literature [3] proposed a slot seize-able TDMA mechanism under the definition of a new TDMA frame structure and preemptive mode, using the vertex coloring in graph theory to allocate time-slots. Although this method can reduce the communication time-delay, there is no guarantee that the inter-satellite links will work efficiently. In literature [4], the time-division inter-satellite link topology generation problem based on Walker constellation is studied, and the topology structure that minimizes the data transmission time while satisfying the transmission constraints is proposed. The literature [5] presented an inter-satellite links time-slot allocation and design based on STDMA.

Most previous works have focused on the inter-satellite topology design of a single-layer constellation, and there are few researches for time-division topology of multi-layer constellations. This paper adopts MEO + GEO/IGSO constellation model, inter-satellite links are divided into intra-layer ISLs and inter-layer ISLs by orbit altitudes of satellites [6]. Within the simulation analysis of the constellation, this paper proposes an inter-satellite link time-slot allocation scheme to obtain the time-division topology of satellite network, which provides a basis for further research.

## 2 Constellation Network Topological Characteristics Analysis

### 2.1 Double-Layer Satellite Network Structure

The spatial system studied in this paper consists of twenty four MEO satellites, three GEO satellites, three IGSO satellites and three ground stations. According to the altitude of orbits, it can be divided into the following two satellite layers:

1. Medium Earth Orbit Satellite

All MEO satellites in this layer are organized in the form of Walker constellation. The satellite orbits of Walker constellation use equal height and inclination. The satellites are evenly distributed across the orbits. The constellation configuration is $N/P/F$, where $N$ represents the number of satellites in the whole constellation, $P$ denotes the number of orbits, and F represents the phase of the eastern orbital over the western side [7]. The system in this paper adopts the configuration of Walker 24/3/1.

2. High Earth Orbit Satellite

GEO is located above the equator. It has the advantages of global coverage, less switching and simple control. IGSO have the same altitude as GEO and have the same inclination angle as MEO. They mainly provide coverage of polar regions in high latitudes [8].

## 2.2    Visibility Analysis

For running satellites, the necessary and sufficient condition for visibility is that the line that connects two satellites does not intersect the earth [9]. Figure 1 is a schematic diagram of the inter-satellite link. Assuming the earth is a sphere, then $O$ is the earth core, $R_e$ is the radius of the earth, $S_1$ and $S_2$ are two satellites on the orbit, respectively, and their orbital radiuses are respectively $r_1$ and $r_2$. Among them, the elevation angle of $S_1$ is $\varepsilon$, $\theta$ is geocentric separation angle, $d$ and $h$ are the instantaneous distance and vertical distance of the two satellites, respectively.

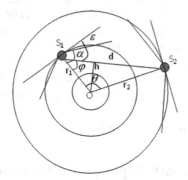

**Fig. 1.**    Inter-satellite link schematic diagram.

According to the sine theorem, the following formula can be obtained.

$$\frac{d}{\sin \theta} = \frac{r_2}{\sin \varphi}. \tag{1}$$

According to the cosine theorem, the following formula can be obtained.

$$d = \sqrt{r_1^2 + r_2^2 - 2r_1r_2 \cos \theta}. \tag{2}$$

According to the geometric relationship in Fig. 2, we get the following equation.

$$h = r_1 \cos \varepsilon = r_1r_2 \sin \theta/d. \tag{3}$$

The function that describes whether two satellites are visible to each other is defined as follows.

$$\Delta h = h - R_e. \tag{4}$$

On the other hand, the satellite will not be visible because of the antenna scanning range constraint ($\alpha$), so the satellite and link normal angle should satisfy the following relationship.

$$\varphi < \alpha. \tag{5}$$

So the inter-satellite visible satellite set is $\gamma_s = \{S|\Delta h > 0 \text{且} \varphi < \alpha\}$, and only the satellites that meet the visibility conditions can establish the inter-satellite links.

## 3  Time-Division Topology Design

### 3.1  Time Division Multiple Access Mode

The Ka-band is adopted to establish the links between satellites in this paper, and the satellite antenna is a kind of narrow-beam antenna. Thus, the ISL adopts the connection mode of point-to-point in the TDMA mode. Each satellite links with other satellites in turn according to the allocated time-slots in a frame. In order to reduce the interference among beams, it is assumed that there is only one antenna on each satellite for linking between satellites, that is, each satellite has only one inter-satellite link in each time-slot. A time slot reflects a linking of satellite networks, the topology of the inter-satellite link may change only when the time-slot changes.

The satellite-site link is not the main research content of this paper. In order to reduce its influence on the inter-satellite link, it is assumed that the satellites use the additional frequency band and antenna to transmit data with ground stations. The ground stations do not participate in the time-slot allocation.

### 3.2  Link Characteristics Analysis

Due to the large orbital radius, GEO satellites and IGSO satellites will have large time delays, it is sensible to consider using ISL within the MEO layer for information forwarding. Since the characteristics of the satellites in Walker constellation are consistent, taking MEO21 as an example to describe the characteristics of inter-satellite links. From the inter-satellite visibility analysis in Sect. 2.2, each MEO satellite has eight satellites that are continuously visible. These satellites can be used as the linking objects of complete links. Among them, four satellites are in the same orbit as MEO21, and the remaining four are evenly distributed on the other two orbits.

The system model can be established quickly by STK. Then let STK connect with MATLAB through STK/MATLAB interface. Establishing a connection between the objects and producing a report is achieved through the command 'stkAccReport' which can return the related information when there is a path between the two objects. Use the command 'stkFindData' to export the required data from the report, such as the visible time and distance of the two objects. It is known from STK that the average visible MEO satellite number of each MEO satellite is about sixteen.

### 3.3  Time-Division Topology Design

The inter-satellite link system designed in this paper is using the time-division transmission mode. Assuming that the slot-size is five seconds, the time for each MEO satellite to link with all visible satellites respectively is about 16 time-slots, then the frame-size is eighty seconds.

As the satellites keep moving, their inter-satellite visibility also changes. Through finite state thought, two satellites that are visible at any moment in each frame are defined as visible, and they are defined as invisible once they are not visible at a certain moment. After processing in this way, the distribution strategy of inter-satellite links is simplified.

**Mathematical Definition and Description.** 24 MEO satellites are numbered by 1–24. GEO satellites are numbered by 25–27, and IGSO satellites are numbered by 28–30. The definition and description of the symbols involved in the algorithm are as follows.

(1) There are three ground stations in the system. Define the matrix $V_1 = [v_{ij}]_{30 \times 3}$ to be a visibility matrix of satellite-site in a frame.

$$v_{ij} = \begin{cases} 1, & S_i \text{ and } P_j \text{ are visible} \\ 0, & S_i \text{ and } P_j \text{ are unvisible} \end{cases}. \tag{6}$$

The satellite with the number '$i$' is denoted by $S_i$ and the ground station with the number '$i$' is denoted by $P_i$. In this paper, a satellite that is not visible to all three ground stations is defined as an overseas satellite, and a satellite visible to at least one ground station is defined as a domestic satellite.

(2) Define the matrix $V_2 = [v_{ij}]_{30 \times 30}$ to be an inter-satellite visibility matrix in a frame.

$$v_{ij} = \begin{cases} 1, & S_i \text{ and } S_j \text{ are visible} \\ 0, & S_i \text{ and } S_j \text{ are unvisible} \end{cases}. \tag{7}$$

(3) Define the matrix $C = [c_{ip}]_{30 \times 16}$ as the time-slot allocation matrix of all the satellites within a frame, where the element $c_{ip}$ represents the linking satellite of $S_i$ in the $p-th$ time-slot. It should be noted that $C_M$ denotes the time-slot allocation matrix of MEO satellites. Because the links are bidirectional, the elements in $C$ must satisfy the following formula.

$$c_{c_{ip}p} = i. \tag{8}$$

(4) Define the matrix $T = [t_{ij}]_{30 \times 30}$ as the inter-satellite network topology matrix in a time-slot.

$$t_{ij} = \begin{cases} 1, & \text{ISL established between } S_i \text{ and } S_j \\ 0, & \text{No ISL established between } S_i \text{ and } S_j \end{cases}. \tag{9}$$

**Link Priority.** For the multi-layer satellite network designed in this paper, there are multiple types of inter-satellite links. In order to achieve the best performance of time-slot allocating, adopt the principle that the links with high quality link first. The priority analysis of inter-satellite links is performed below.

The inter-satellite link can be divided into inter-layer links and intra-layer links according to the different orbit altitudes of the satellites. Inter-layer links include GEO-MEO links and IGSO-MEO links. The inter-satellite distance is too large, resulting in poor link quality and lower priority than intra-layer links.

The intra-layer links include IGSO/GEO intra-layer links and MEO intra-layer links. For links in sub-constellations consisting of GEO satellites and IGSO satellites, since the high-orbit satellites are mainly used as relay satellites in the system, time-slots are not allocated for this type of links. The links in MEO layer can be divided into complete links and incomplete links according to whether the two satellites are continuously visible during a constellation period or not. Because the complete link can remain unblocked throughout the period, it can be used as the basis for link design, and its priority is higher than incomplete link. Complete links can be further subdivided into same-track links and off-track links. The same-track links have slow-changing inter-satellite distance and fixed topology attributes. Therefore, the priorities are greater than the complete links of the different tracks.

**Intra-ISL Design.** According to the inter-satellite visibility analysis, each MEO satellite has eight completely visible satellites and eight incompletely visible satellites during a constellation period. Taking MEO21 as an example, the design process of its links in a certain frame is as follows.

(1) Read the matrix $V_2$ to obtain all the satellite numbers that are permanently visible and intermittently visible with MEO21, and arrange the eight complete links into the first eight time-slots of the time-slot allocation matrix according to the link priority. The incomplete links are arranged into the last eight slots. Due to the instability of the topology of incomplete links, the time-slot arrangement changes with time and is represented by $s(t)$, and the matrix $C_M$ can be obtained as follows

$$C_M = \begin{bmatrix} \cdots & \cdots & \cdots & \cdots & \cdots & \cdots & \cdots & \cdots & \cdots \\ 1 & 6 & 11 & 12 & 14 & 15 & 17 & 20 & s(t) \\ \cdots & \cdots & \cdots & \cdots & \cdots & \cdots & \cdots & \cdots & \cdots \end{bmatrix}_{24 \times 16} . \tag{10}$$

(2) The eight complete links of the MEO satellite consist of four same-track links and four off-track links. In accordance with the link priority, the complete same-rack links are placed in the first half of the first eight slots, and the complete off-track links are put into the second half of the first eight slots. Then the matrix $C_M$ can be obtained as follows.

$$C_M = \begin{bmatrix} \cdots & \cdots & \cdots & \cdots & \cdots & \cdots & \cdots & \cdots & \cdots \\ 11 & 12 & 14 & 15 & 17 & 20 & 6 & 1 & s(t) \\ \cdots & \cdots & \cdots & \cdots & \cdots & \cdots & \cdots & \cdots & \cdots \end{bmatrix}_{24 \times 16} . \tag{11}$$

(3) Considering that the purpose of introducing the inter-satellite link technology is to enhance the communication of domestic and overseas satellites, for the two satellites within the borders at the same time, the existence of inter-satellite links reduces the data transmission efficiency on the contrary. Read the satellite-site visibility matrix $V_1$ to obtain the probability that other satellites will be visible to the ground stations when the MEO21 is out of the borders, and arrange them in descending order to obtain the following matrix $C_M$.

$$C_M = \begin{bmatrix} \cdots & \cdots & \cdots & \cdots & \cdots & \cdots & \cdots & \cdots & \cdots \\ 12 & 14 & 11 & 15 & 1 & 17 & 6 & 20 & s(t) \\ \cdots & \cdots & \cdots & \cdots & \cdots & \cdots & \cdots & \cdots & \cdots \end{bmatrix}_{24 \times 16} . \tag{12}$$

Since these links are always present, all the frames in the constellation period can be arranged in this way.

For incomplete links, the inter-satellite visibility changes with time, so the time-slot allocation also changes accordingly. Each MEO satellite in the frame has eight satellites that are intermittently visible. The longer the visible time is, the higher the quality of the incomplete link is. Similar to the method of allocating the complete links, the satellites are listed in the last eight time-slots in descending order of the visible time to the ground stations. The stability of the incomplete link is poor. On this basis, the matrix $V_2$ restrains the invisible satellites establishing a link. Therefore, the links that do not exist are set to zero in matrix $C_M$.

Other MEO satellites are arranged according to the above method on the premise of satisfying bidirectional linking, and a complete MEO intra-layer link allocating matrix $C_M$ can be obtained.

**Inter-ISL Design.** High Earth Orbit satellites are added on the basis of the links within the MEO layer. The HEO satellites have strong coverage. When the number of MEO satellites in the country is insufficient, they can be forwarded to satellites outside the borders through HEO satellites. The allocating method of HEO satellites is as follows: In the condition that two satellites are mutually visible, the satellites with a small number of inter-satellite links are preferentially selected for linking, and a complete time-slot allocation matrix $C$ for all satellites can be obtained.

In order to reduce the number of routes and improve the efficiency of relaying, the domestic and overseas links in $C$ are eliminated, and the corresponding positions of the original links are set to zero. Then connect the free domestic satellites to the overseas satellites and get the final time-slot allocation matrix in the frame as follows:

$$C = \begin{bmatrix} M_i & M_j & M_m & M_n & 0 & M_k & \cdots & G_p \\ \vdots & \vdots & \vdots & \vdots & I_q & M_l & \cdots & \vdots \end{bmatrix}_{30 \times 16}. \tag{13}$$

**Time-Division Topology Generation.** Every satellite is connected to another satellite and switches to another satellite in the new time-slot. It keeps the topology of the network unchanged in a time-slot, but will be regenerated following the time-slot allocating matrix when the next time-slot arrives. The topology matrix is continuously updated during a constellation period to generate the inter-satellite link network topology in TDMA mode.

The element $c_{ip}$ in the time-slot allocation matrix $C$ indicates that $S_i$ and $S_{c_{ip}}$ have an inter-satellite link in the $p-th$ slot of the frame. A complete topology matrix of the satellite network in the time-slot can be obtained from the slot matrix column vector.

$$t_{ij} = \begin{cases} 1, & j = c_{ip} \\ 0, & others \end{cases}. \tag{14}$$

Among them, '1' indicates that there is an inter-satellite link between $S_i$ and $S_j$ in the $p-th$ time-slot, '0' indicates that there is no inter-satellite link at this time.

## 4 Simulation Analysis

The performance of the designed mixed links and complete links is simulated from two aspects of inter-satellite transmission performance and inter-satellite orbit determination below. The transmission performance reflects in the domestic and overseas communication delays and the positioning accuracy is based on the position dilution of precision of the satellite.

1. Position dilution of precision

The effect of constellation geometry on the pointing accuracy of satellites is usually described by dilution of precision. This paper takes the position dilution of precision as the basis for measuring the link location accuracy. A small PDOP value means that the navigation constellation has a better geometric configuration. Taking the MEO21 satellite as the locating point, the PDOP values were calculated by MATLAB and STK under the complete link and mixed link. The simulation result is shown in Fig. 2.

From Fig. 2, it can be found that the PDOP values of the constellation are distributed between 1.3 and 1.4 in the time division topology scheme using the mixed links proposed in this paper, and that of the complete links are approximately 3 to 5. It can be seen that the inter-satellite link topology obtained by the method designed in this paper has higher accuracy in ranging and the positioning performance is superior to the complete link.

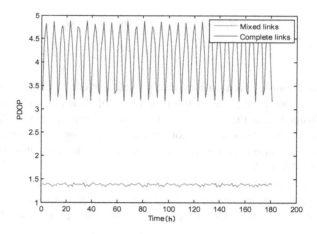

**Fig. 2.** The comparison of PDOP values.

## 2. Domestic and overseas communication delay

Figure 3 shows the average communication delay of a ground station to overseas satellites under two linking allocations.

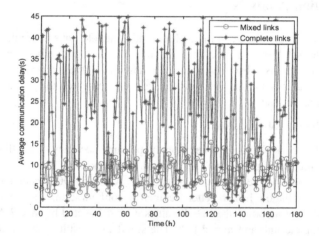

**Fig. 3.** Communication delay comparison diagram.

It can be seen from Fig. 3 that the average communication delay under the scheme of the mixed links is about 6 s, and that of complete links is about 20 s. It can be seen that the scheme of the mixed links greatly shortens the delay of domestic and overseas communications and improves communication performance.

# 5 Conclusion

Based on the analysis of the link characteristics and linking feasibility of the 24/3/1 Walker + GEO/IGSO multi-layer satellite constellation, a time-division topology generation scheme for the inter-satellite link network is proposed in this paper. The process of linking is described in detail based on the principle that high-quality links link first. The simulation and performance evaluation of the scheme has proved that the proposed scheme has good communication performance and positioning accuracy.

The topology generation scheme in this paper is only a preliminary result. The next step will continue to improve the proposed model in order to accommodate the more complex transmission requirements in inter-satellite link networks.

**Acknowledgments.** This work was supported by the National Natural Science Foundation of China (No. 61371100, No. 61501139, No. 61401118).

# References

1. He, J.F., Yong, J., Li, G.X.: Topology control technology based on dynamical inter-orbit ISL linkage in LEO satellite constellation communication system. In: Systems and Control in Aerospace and Astronautics, pp. 1–6. IEEE (2008)
2. Chen, J.Y., Wu, G.Y., Feng, X.Z, Liu, Y.: Analysis of the satellite constellation communication link topology. Chinese J. Sci. Instrum. **35**(12), 101–105 (2014). (in Chinese)
3. Shi, L.Y., Zhou, Y.: A preemptive time slot TDMA system suitable for inter-satellite links in satellite navigation systems. J. Wuhan Univ. **37**(6), 714–718 (2012). (in Chinese)
4. Chu, X.G., Chen, Y.: Time division inter-satellite link topology generation problem: Modeling and solution. Int. J. Satell. Commun. Netw. **1**, 74–88 (2017)
5. Wu, J.Y., Chen, J.Y.: Design and simulation evaluation of time allocation of inter-satellite link based on TDMA. Comput. Meas. Control **22**(12), 4087–4090 (2014). (in Chinese)
6. Akyildiz, I.F., Ekici, E., Bender, M.D.: MLSR: a novel routing algorithm for multilayered satellite IP networks. IEEE/ACM Trans. Netw. **10**(3), 411–424 (2002)
7. Shen, D.C., Wang, J.F., Liu, L.X.: Analysis of topology dynamics of walker constellation satellite networks. J. Commun. **27**(8), 45–51 (2006). (in Chinese)
8. Hu, M., Fan, L., Yang, X.R.: Study on the optimal distribution of IGSO satellite orbits for the optimal performance of MEO satellites. In: China Satellite Navigation Academic Annual Conference (2014). (in Chinese)
9. Yin, Z.Z., Zhang, L., Zhou, X.W.: LEO/HEO/GEO satellite network ISL performance analysis. Comput. Eng. Appl. **46**(12), 9–13 (2010). (in Chinese)

# MOPSO Optimized Radar CBMeMBer Forward-Backward Smoothing Filter

Jiazheng Pei, Yong Huang, Yunlong Dong, and Xiaolong Chen[✉]

Naval Aviation University, Ermalu Road 188, Yantai, Shandong, China
roycerover@163.com, huangyong_2003@163.com,
china_dyl@sina.com, cxlcxl1209@163.com

**Abstract.** For the tracking of multiple maneuvering targets under radar observations, the Cardinality-Balanced Multi-Bernoulli based Sequential Monte-Carlo Filter (SMC-CBMeMBer) tracking algorithm gets its shortcomings that the estimation of number is inaccurate and the state estimation accuracy is degraded. This paper presents an improved tracking algorithm based on SMC-CBMeMBer smoothing filter. In the prediction process, the algorithm uses Multi-objectIve Particle Swarm Optimization (MOPSO), combined with the measured values at the current moment, to move the particles to the location where the posterior probability density distribution takes a larger value; Besides the smooth recursive method is used to smooth the filter value with multi-target measurement data, and the estimation accuracy of the algorithm is improved on the basis of sacrificing certain operation efficiency. The simulation results show that compared with the traditional filter and smoothing methods, the proposed algorithm performs better in terms of the accuracy of the estimation of the number of maneuvering targets and the accuracy of the target state estimation.

**Keywords:** Particle swarm optimization · Particle filter · CBMeMBer filter Forward-backward smoothing

## 1 Introduction

Multi-target Multi-Bernoulli (MeMBer) filter [1] is another multi-target tracking method based on RFS proposed by Mahler after PHD [2] and CPHD [3] filter. For multi-objective nonlinear filtering, B-N Vo gives advantages of MeMBer [4] over the other two algorithms in terms of filtering accuracy and computational complexity, and on this basis, an improvement, i.e. Cardinality Balanced Multi-target Multi-Bernoulli (CBMeMBer) filter [5] was proposed to dispose the overestimation of the number of targets caused by MeMBer. The literature [6] proposed using Bernoulli random finite set to model the single-target motion state and complete forward-backward smoothing.

This work was supported in part by the National Science Foundation of China (U1633122, 61531020, 61501487), National Defense Science Foundation (2102024), the China Postdoctoral Science Foundation (2017M620862) and by the Special Funds of Taishan Scholars Construction Engineering, Young Elite Scientist Sponsorship Program of CAST.

© ICST Institute for Computer Sciences, Social Informatics and Telecommunications Engineering 2018
L. Meng and Y. Zhang (Eds.): MLICOM 2018, LNICST 251, pp. 604–616, 2018.
https://doi.org/10.1007/978-3-030-00557-3_60

Bernoulli forward-backward smoothing improves the recognition accuracy of the disappearance of the target and the accuracy of the state estimation. In addition, it validates the feasibility of the Bernoulli filtering forward-backward smoothing filter.

Based on the known background, this paper proposes an improved multi-target tracking method based on CBMeMBer smoothing, which consists of forward filtering and backward smoothing. Forward filtering uses CBMeMBer filtering. Multi-objective particle swarm optimization is added between prediction and updating step. Particles move in the direction of higher posterior probability density; backward smoothing still uses CBMeMBer probability density to approximate the multi-objective smooth states, and obtain the backward recursive formula of CBMeMBer probability density parameter, thereby achieving multi-targets Backward recursive calculation of smooth state probability density. Finally, the simulation experiments show that the tracking performance of the newly proposed algorithm is better than the previous algorithm in the multi-objective maneuvering scenario.

## 2   CBMeMBer Smoothing Filter

In contrast to MeMBer filtering, the probability generation functional of CBMeMBer is more accurate than that of MeMBer in the updating process, which averts a potential cardinality deviation. The implementation of CBMeMBer filtering needs to satisfy the following assumptions: (1) the RFS of the newborn target state is formed by a multi-Bernoulli random finite set; (2) the clutter obeys the multi-target Poisson process, and the clutter density is not too large; (3) The target has a higher detection probability.

The CBMeMBer forward-backward smoothing filter utilizes more measurement information, and can improve the estimation performance of the target number and the targets' state.

### 2.1   Forward Filtering Process

***Prediction.*** Suppose that Multi-objective posterior probability density at time $k - 1$ is a form of multiple Bernoulli RFS.

$$\pi_{k-1} = \left\{ \left( r_{k-1}^{(i)}, p_{k-1}^{(i)} \right) \right\}_{i=1}^{M_{k-1}} \tag{1}$$

So as to the Multi-objective predict probability density is of the same form,

$$\pi_{k|k-1} = \left\{ \left( r_{P,k|k-1}^{(i)}, p_{P,k|k-1}^{(i)} \right) \right\}_{i=1}^{M_{k-1}} \cup \left\{ \left( r_{\Gamma,k|k-1}^{(i)}, p_{\Gamma,k|k-1}^{(i)} \right) \right\}_{i=1}^{M_{\Gamma,k}} \tag{2}$$

where

$$r_{P,k|k-1}^{(i)} = r_{k-1}^{(i)} \left\langle p_{k-1}^{(i)}, p_{S,k} \right\rangle \tag{3}$$

$$p_{P,k|k-1}^{(i)} = \frac{\left\langle f_{k|k-1}(x|\cdot), p_{k-1}^{(i)} p_{S,k} \right\rangle}{\left\langle p_{k-1}^{(i)}, p_{S,k} \right\rangle} \tag{4}$$

$f_{k|k-1}(\cdot|\xi)$ denotes single-target transfer probability at time $k$, $p_{S,k}$ denotes the survival probability. $\left\{ \left( r_{\Gamma,k|k-1}^{(i)}, p_{\Gamma,k|k-1}^{(i)} \right) \right\}_{i=1}^{M_{\Gamma,k}}$ refers to Bernoulli RFS newborn parameters at time $k$.

**Update.** The predicted multi-target density at time $k$ is still in the form of multi Bernoulli $\pi_{k|k-1} = \left\{ \left( r_{k|k-1}^{(i)}, p_{k|k-1}^{(i)} \right) \right\}_{i=1}^{M_{k|k-1}}$, Then this posterior probability density can be represented by a multiple Bernoulli union.

$$\pi_k \approx \left\{ \left( r_{L,k}^{(i)}, p_{L,k}^{(i)} \right) \right\}_{i=1}^{M_{k|k-1}} \cup \left\{ \left( r_{U,k}(z), p_{U,k}(\cdot; z) \right) \right\}_{z \in Z_k} \tag{5}$$

Where

$$r_{L,k}^{(i)} = r_{k|k-1}^{(i)} \frac{1 - \left\langle p_{k|k-1}^{(i)}, p_{D,k} \right\rangle}{1 - r_{k|k-1}^{(i)} \left\langle p_{k|k-1}^{(i)}, p_{D,k} \right\rangle} \tag{6}$$

$$p_{L,k}^{(i)}(x) = p_{k|k-1}^{(i)}(x) \frac{1 - p_{D,k}(x)}{1 - \left\langle p_{k|k-1}^{(i)}, p_{D,k} \right\rangle} \tag{7}$$

$$r_{U,k}(z) = \frac{\sum_{i=1}^{M_{k|k-1}} \frac{r_{k|k-1}^{(i)} \left( 1 - r_{k|k-1}^{(i)} \right) \left\langle p_{k|k-1}^{(i)}, \psi_{k,z} \right\rangle}{\left( 1 - r_{k|k-1}^{(i)} \left\langle p_{k|k-1}^{(i)}, p_{D,k} \right\rangle \right)^2}}{\kappa_k(z) + \sum_{i=1}^{M_{k|k-1}} \frac{r_{k|k-1}^{(i)} \left\langle p_{k|k-1}^{(i)}, \psi_{k,z} \right\rangle}{1 - r_{k|k-1}^{(i)} \left\langle p_{k|k-1}^{(i)}, p_{D,k} \right\rangle}} \tag{8}$$

$$p_{U,k}(x; z) = \frac{\sum_{i=1}^{M_{k|k-1}} \frac{r_{k|k-1}^{(i)}}{1 - r_{k|k-1}^{(i)}} p_{k|k-1}^{(i)}(x) \psi_{k,z}(x)}{\sum_{i=1}^{M_{k|k-1}} \frac{r_{k|k-1}^{(i)}}{1 - r_{k|k-1}^{(i)}} \left\langle p_{k|k-1}^{(i)}, \psi_{k,z} \right\rangle} \tag{9}$$

$$\psi_{k,z}(x) = g_k(z|x) p_{D,k}(x) \tag{10}$$

$Z_k$ denotes observation set, $g_k(\cdot|x)$ and $p_{D,k}(x)$ respectively refer to single-target measurement likelihood function and target detection probability given the state at time $k$. $\kappa_k(\cdot)$ is Poisson clutter intensity parameter.

## 2.2  Backward Smoothing Process

The purpose of smoothing is to use the data at time $l$ to estimate the state value at time $k(l > k)$. Given the multi-Bernoulli smoothing density parameters $r_{k|l}$ and $p_{k|l}(\cdot)$, backward recursion is displayed as follow [7].

$$r_{k-1|l} = 1 - \left(1 - r_{k-1|l-1}\right)\left(\alpha_{B,k|l} + \beta_{B,k|l}\int \frac{p_{k|l}(\zeta)}{p_{k|k-1}(\zeta)}b_{k|k-1}(\zeta)d\zeta\right) \tag{11}$$

$$p_{k-1|l}(x) \propto p_{k-1|k-1}(x)\left(\alpha_{S,k|l}(x) + \beta_{S,k|l}(x)\int \frac{p_{k|l}(\zeta)}{p_{k|k-1}(\zeta)}f_{k|k-1}(\zeta|x)d\zeta\right) \tag{12}$$

where

$$\alpha_{B,k|l} = (1 - p_b)\frac{1 - r_{k|l}}{1 - r_{k|k-1}} \tag{13}$$

$$\beta_{B,k|l} = p_b\frac{r_{k|l}}{r_{k|k-1}} \tag{14}$$

$$\alpha_{S,k|l}(x) = \left(1 - p_{S,k|k-1}(x)\right)\frac{1 - r_{k|l}}{1 - r_{k|k-1}} \tag{15}$$

$$\beta_{S,k|l}(x) = p_{S,k|k-1}(x)\frac{r_{k|l}}{r_{k|k-1}} \tag{16}$$

## 2.3  Shortcomings of SMC-CBMeMBer Smoothing

Particle filter using Sequential Importance Sampling [8] (SIS) method, recursively sampling according to the weights of the particles to obtain an approximate distribution of posterior probabilities. An important flaw in resampling particles is the lack of particle diversity. When the observation information is so accurate that the peak of the likelihood function is narrow, the overlap space between the likelihood probability and the prior probability distribution is extremely limited. As an end, only a small fraction of overlapping particle weights will increase after the update. In addition, similar problems exist when the observation probability distributed at the tail of the prior distribution, since only a small part of the particles generated by the prior probability is located in the high likelihood region. It is very likely that the prediction result will lose important particles and miss good assumptions.

Another significant problem is that when faced with the actual initial state of the system is unknown, the state estimation of the system requires a large number of particles, which makes the calculation efficiency of particles greatly reduced.

## 3   MOPSO Optimized CBMeMBer Smoothing

In order to solve the problems described in Sect. 2.3 above, this chapter proposes an improved method that combines the particle swarm optimization algorithm with the CBMeMBer smoothing filter to improve the problem of the particle diversity.

### 3.1   Multi-objective Particle Swarm Optimization

Particle Swarm Optimization (PSO) is a cluster intelligent global optimization algorithm based on population search strategy jointly proposed by Kennedy and Eberhart [9].

In each iteration, the individual optimal solution is updated after one iteration of the particle $p_j$, and the global optimal solution in the entire particle swarm $g_j$ are used, where $j = 1, 2, \cdots, n$, $n$ is the maximum number of iterations.

Update each particle with the following speed update formula and position update formula, so that we can improve the position information carried by the particles,

$$v_i = wv_i + c_1 rand \left( p_j - x_i \right) + c_2 Rand \left( g_j - x_i \right) \tag{17}$$

$$x_{i+1} = x_i + rv_i \tag{18}$$

where $rand$ and $Rand$ are random numbers between 0 and 1, $w$ is the inertia coefficient, $c_1$ and $c_2$ are positive numbers, $x_i$ is the initial particle swarm state, $v_i$ is the updated speed, and $r$ is the constraint factor.

In the multi-objective optimization, this paper uses multi-objective particle swarm optimization (MOPSO). The MOPSO screens particles based on multiple objective functions by means of the NSGA-II algorithm [10]. The algorithm is an improvement over conventional genetic algorithms. The key steps are the following three processes.

(1)  Non-dominated sort.

The algorithm stratifies the population based on individual non-inferiority levels. The individuals are included in the 1st front $F_1$, and they are given the non-dominated order $i_{rank} = 1$; Then continue to identify non-dominated solutions and repeat this until the whole population is assigned.

(2)  Crowding distance calculation.

The individual crowding distances are calculated in order to be able to selectively rank individuals within the same non-dominant sequence $i_{rank}$. For different objective functions, we need to calculate repeatedly to obtain the individual's crowding distance.

(3)  Recombination and selection.

Firstly, the entire population is placed in new descendants in descending order of non-dominated sorting $i_{rank}$ until the population size exceeds the particle group $N$ when placed in a certain layer $F_j$; secondly, filling is continued in descending order of individual crowding distances of $F_j$ until the number of particle swarms reaches.

Besides, in order to avoid the problem of particle swarm optimization speeding up the convergence too quickly and causing a local optimal solution, this paper added a mutation mechanism to the algorithm to increase the diversity of particles.

## 3.2  Improved Smoothing Filter Optimized by PSO

The improved process is expressed as follow.

The whole algorithm can be illustrate by Fig. 1. Firstly, we need to initialize the essential parameters, such as existence probability $r$, particle state $x$ and particle weight $w$. Then the parameters will be used to describe the state of targets which is estimated by a series of work: prediction, PSO optimization, updating and smoothing. It should be noted that the raw observation data is utilized in the PSO optimization and updating process. Secondly, we will prune the tracks whose existence probability $r$ can not reach the threshold, merge the tracks which are adjacent to each other to one track. Finally, we resample the particles based in their weights. The existence probability $r$ can be used to get the targets' number. The particles' weights and state can be calculated to estimate the targets' state and can be used to join in the next filter iteration. The detailed description is stated as follows.

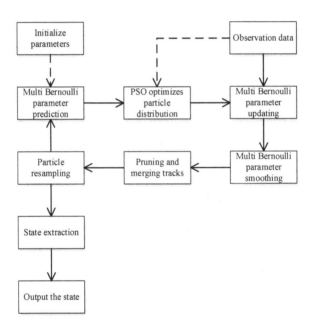

**Fig. 1.** The flow chart of PSO optimized CBMeMBer forward-backward smoothing

**Prediction.** Suppose that we have the posterior parameters at time $k - 1$ are given with $r_{k-1|k-1}$ and $p_{k-1|k-1}$ in the form of particle filter:

$$p_{k-1|k-1} \approx \sum_{i=1}^{N_{k-1}} w_{k-1}^{(i)} \delta_{x_{k-1}^{(i)}}(x) \tag{19}$$

Then the prediction parameters can be displayed as:

$$r_{k|k-1} \approx p_b\left(1 - r_{k-1|k-1}\right) + r_{k-1|k-1} \sum_{i=1}^{N_{k-1}} w_{k-1}^{(i)} p_{S,k|k-1}\left(x_{k-1}^{(i)}\right) \tag{20}$$

$$p_{k|k-1}(x) = \sum_{i=1}^{N_{k-1}+J_k} w_{k|k-1}^{(i)} \delta_{x_k^{(i)}}(x) \tag{21}$$

where the particles and weights are generated as [7]:

$$x_k^{(i)} \sim \begin{cases} q_k\left(\cdot|x_{k-1}^{(i)}, z_k\right), & i = 1 : N_{k-1} \\ s_k(\cdot|z_k), & i = N_{k-1}+1 : N_{k-1}+J_k \end{cases} \tag{22}$$

$$w_{k|k-1}^{(i)} = \begin{cases} \dfrac{r_{k-1|k-1}}{r_{k|k-1}} \dfrac{p_{S,k|k-1}\left(x_{k-1}^{(i)}\right) f_{k|k-1}\left(x_k^{(i)}|x_{k-1}^{(i)}\right) w_{k-1}^{(i)}}{q_k\left(x_k^{(i)}|x_{k-1}^{(i)}, z_k\right)}, & i = 1 : N_{k-1} \\ \dfrac{1-r_{k-1|k-1}}{r_{k|k-1}} \dfrac{p_b b_{k|k-1}\left(x_k^{(i)}\right)}{J_k s_k\left(x_k^{(i)}, z_k\right)}, & i = N_{k-1}+1 : N_{k-1}+J_k \end{cases} \tag{23}$$

and $p_b$ denotes probability of target newborn or reentry, $b_{k|k-1}\left(x_k^{(i)}\right)$ is spatial density of newborn process, $q_k$, $s_k$ respectively denotes the survival density and newborn density.

**Optimization.** The particle swarm optimization algorithm is applied after the prediction step of the multi-Bernoulli filtering, combining the current time measurement, taking into account the distance between the particles and the measurement points. For the $n$th measurement, the objective function value of the $i$th particle is as follows.

$$fit_i^n = \exp\left[-\frac{1}{\sigma^2}\left(par_n - meas_i\right)^2\right], i = 1, \cdots, length(meas), n = 1, \cdots, N \tag{24}$$

where $\sigma^2$ denotes observation noise variance, **meas** denotes observation set, **meas**$_i$ refers to the $i$th observation value, N is the total particle number. The particle swarm optimization algorithm motivates all particles to the Pareto optimal solution set by calculating the objective function value.

The optimized particle weights need to be redistributed by considering the particle's objective function values, and then normalized.

$$w_n = \sum_i fit_i^n, w_n = \frac{w_n}{\sum_{n=1}^{N} w_n} \tag{25}$$

The optimization process makes the particles far away from the real state move to the areas which have higher posterior probability and improves the effect of each particle. Even when the initial state is unknown, the problem of particle filtering that requires a large number of particles for accurate state estimation is also attenuated.

**Updating.** After the optimization, the particle state, weight, and probability of existence $r_{k|k-1}$ participate in the update [11].

$$r_{k|k} = \frac{r_{k|k-1} \sum_{i=1}^{N_k} \tilde{w}_k^{(i)}}{1 - r_{k|k-1} + r_{k|k-1} \sum_{i=1}^{N_k} \tilde{w}_k^{(i)}} \tag{26}$$

$$p_{k|k}(x) \approx \sum_{i=1}^{N_k} w_k^{(i)} \delta_{x_k^{(i)}}(x) \tag{27}$$

$$\tilde{w}_k^{(i)} \propto l_k\left(z_k | x_{k|k-1}^{(i)}\right) w_{k|k-1}^{(i)} \tag{28}$$

In order to maintain the diversity of particles in the next smoothing process, the resampling operation is not performed after the update is completed, and is performed after the smoothing is completed.

**Smoothing.** Given $r_{k|l}$ and $p_{k|l} = \sum_{i=1}^{N_{k|l}} w_{k|l}^{(i)} \delta_{x_{k|l}^{(i)}}(x)$, we

$$r_{k-1|l} \approx 1 - \left(1 - r_{k-1|k-1}\right) \times \left(\frac{1 - r_{k|l}}{1 - r_{k|k-1}}(1 - p_b) + \frac{r_{k|l}}{r_{k|k-1}} p_b \sum_{j=1}^{N_{k|l}} w_{k|j}^{(j)} \frac{b_{k|k-1}\left(x_{k|l}^{(j)}\right)}{p_{k|k-1}\left(x_{k|l}^{(j)}\right)}\right) \tag{29}$$

$$p_{k-1|l}(x) \approx \sum_{i=1}^{N_{k-1|k-1}} \tilde{w}_{k-1|l}^{(i)} \delta_{x_{k-1|k-1}^{(i)}}(x) \tag{30}$$

$$\tilde{w}_{k-1|l}^{(i)} \propto \frac{1 - r_{k|l}}{1 - r_{k|k-1}}\left(1 - p_{S,k|k-1} w_{k-1|k-1}^{(i)}\right) + \frac{r_{k|l}}{r_{k|k-1}} \sum_{j=1}^{N_{k|l}} p_{S,k|k-1} w_{k|l}^{(j)} \frac{f_{k|k-1}\left(x_{k|l}^{(j)} | x_{k-1|k-1}^{(i)}\right)}{p_{k|k-1}\left(x_{k|l}^{(j)}\right)} w_{k-1|k-1}^{(i)} \tag{31}$$

$$p_{k|k-1}\left(x_{k|l}^{(j)}\right) = \sum_{i=1}^{N_{k-1|k-1}} w_{k-1|k-1}^{(i)} f_{k|k-1}\left(x_{k|j}^{(j)} | x_{k-1|k-1}^{(i)}\right) \tag{32}$$

**Track Pruning and Resampling.** Only the track whose probability of existence gets greater than the threshold can be preserved. In the meanwhile, we need to select and reproduce particles with large weight values, i.e. resample the particle set.

$$\left\{ x_i^k, \frac{1}{N} \right\}_{i=1}^N = \left\{ x_i^k, w_i^k \right\}_{i=1}^N \tag{33}$$

## 4 Simulation

### 4.1 Maneuvering Target Cooperative Turning Model Establishment

In this CT model, the maneuvering target is a collaborative turn CT model. The state equation and measurement equation are as follows [12–14]:

$$X(k) = F(k)X(k-1) + \Gamma(k-1)v(k-1) \tag{34}$$

$$Z(k) = H(k)X(k) + W(k) \tag{35}$$

$$F(k) = \begin{bmatrix} 1 & \frac{\sin \omega T}{\omega} & 0 & \frac{\cos \omega T - 1}{\omega} & 0 \\ 0 & \cos \omega T & 0 & -\sin \omega T & 0 \\ 0 & \frac{1-\cos \omega T}{\omega} & 1 & \frac{\sin \omega T}{\omega} & 0 \\ 0 & \sin \omega T & 0 & \cos \omega T & 0 \\ 0 & 0 & 0 & 0 & 1 \end{bmatrix} \tag{36}$$

$$\Gamma(k-1) = \begin{bmatrix} T^2/2 & T & 0 & 0 & 0 \\ 0 & 0 & T^2/2 & T & 0 \\ 0 & 0 & 0 & 0 & 0 \end{bmatrix}' \tag{37}$$

$$H(k) = \begin{bmatrix} 1 & 0 & 0 & 0 & 0 \\ 0 & 0 & 1 & 0 & 0 \end{bmatrix} \tag{38}$$

### 4.2 Experimental Simulation

Suppose that the radar was located in the origin point; the detection area was defined as $[-2000\ \text{m},\ 2000\ \text{m}] \times [-500\ \text{m},\ 2000\ \text{m}]$; sampling interval $T = 1\,\text{s}$ and the total tracking time was set as 100 s. As for the CT model, the detection probability $p_{D,k} = 0.98$. Assume that there are multiple targets in the detection area for continuous motion within the detection area, and the $i$th target' state at time $k$ was $\mathbf{x}_{k,i} = \left[ x_{k,i}, y_{k,i}, \dot{x}_{k,i}, \dot{y}_{k,i}, \omega \right]^T$; the survival probability $p_{S,k} = 0.99$. Table 1 has set the initial state of each target and its starting and ending time, where the $w$ was positive for a clockwise turn and negative for a counterclockwise rotation [15]. Figure 2 has displayed the true tracks of the simulation.

**Table 1.** The initial state, start and end time of targets

| No | Start time (s) | End time (s) | Initial state |
|----|----------------|--------------|---------------|
| 1  | 1              | 100          | $[1000, -10, 1500, -10, \pi/36]$ |
| 2  | 10             | 100          | $[-250, 20, 1000, 3, -\pi/225]$ |
| 3  | 10             | 100          | $[-1300, 11, 300, 10, -\pi/90]$ |
| 4  | 10             | 70           | $[-1500, 43, 250, 0, 0]$ |
| 5  | 20             | 80           | $[-250, 11, 750, 5, \pi/180]$ |
| 6  | 40             | 100          | $[-500, -12, 1000, -12, -\pi/90]$ |

In the particle swarm optimization process, the number of iterations $gen = 10$ and the fitness function threshold $Th_{fit} = 0.01$ are counted at a time t. In the state extraction process, the track pruning threshold $Th_{prune} = 10^{-3}$ and the maximum track number $T_{max} = 100$ are set; the combined threshold $Th_{cap} = 10^{-5}$ of the track is set, the merging distance $D = 4\,\text{m}$; the maximum number of particles $J_{max} = 1000$, and the minimum $J_{min} = 300$.

Assume that the location of clutter points is uniformly distributed in the detection area at each time, and its number obeys a poisson distribution with an average value of 20. Under the condition of a clutter density of $\lambda_c = 2 \times 10^{-6}\text{m}^{-2}$.

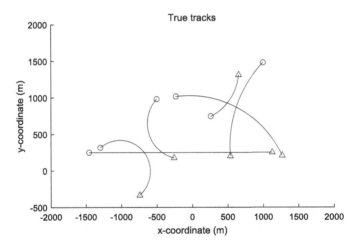

**Fig. 2.** Target actual movement status

After 100 times monte carlo experiments, the simulations found that all three can accurately estimate the number of targets, but the details can be seen at Fig. 3. when the number of targets changes, the new proposed algorithm is better than the general smoothing algorithm, both are better than the traditional filtering algorithm.

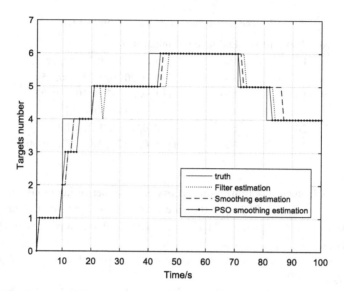

**Fig. 3.** Comparison of the number estimation of three tracking methods

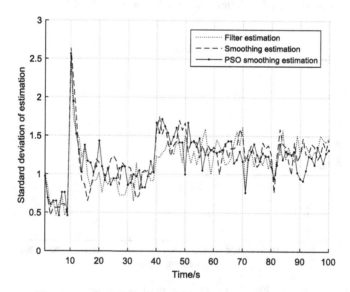

**Fig. 4.** Standard deviation of the three methods' estimation

From the Figs. 4 and 5, we can thoroughly analyze the standard deviation and OSPA error [16] of the three methods' estimation. In terms of specific estimation indicators, we can see that the two smoothing algorithms have better improvement effects than the traditional filtering methods in terms of estimation accuracy; while in the accuracy of the estimation number, the smoothing method has a certain degree of improvement over the filtering method. While the improved smoothing method again

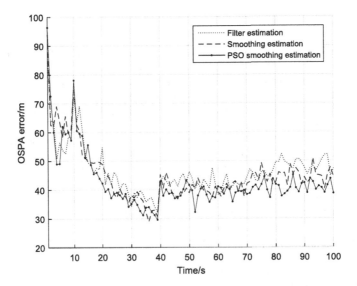

**Fig. 5.** OSPA error of the three methods' estimation

suppresses the standard deviation at the same level comparable to filtering. However, inevitably, the improved smoothing algorithm is longer in terms of running time than the former two kinds of algorithm. For more details, the numerical data was given in Table 2.

**Table 2.** The mean value of the standard deviation, OSPA error and running time

| Mean value | CBMeMBer filter | CBMeMBer smoothing | PSO-CBMeMBer smoothing |
|---|---|---|---|
| Standard deviation | 1.1606 | 1.2139 | 1.1882 |
| OSPA error(m) | 16.6089 | 15.0336 | 12.6689 |
| Running time(s) | 10.7 | 16.7 | 24.3 |

## 5 Summary

In order to deal with the tracking problem of multiple maneuvering targets, an SMC-CBMeMBer forward-backward smoothing filter with multi-objective particle swarm optimization was proposed. The simulation results show that the introduction of the particle swarm optimization algorithm improves the convergence performance of the CBMeMBer forward-backward smoothing filter algorithm for the maneuvering target, which improves the accuracy of the estimated number and position. In the next study, the predicted particles are selectively optimized, and the adaptive optimization is completed by setting the threshold of the objective function, focusing on improving the efficiency of the particle swarm optimization and saving the calculation cost.

# References

1. Mahler, R.: Statistical Multisource-Multitarget Information Fusion, pp. 5–11. Artech House, Boston (2007)
2. Mahler, R.: Multitarget Bayes filtering via first-order multitarget moments. IEEE Trans. Aerosp. Electron. Syst. **39**(4), 1152–1178 (2003)
3. Mahler, R.: PHD filters of higher order in target number. IEEE Trans. Aerosp. Electron. Syst. **43**(4), 1523–1543 (2007)
4. Vo, B.T., See, C.M., Ma, N., et al.: Multi-sensor joint detection and tracking with the Bernoulli filter. IEEE Trans. Aerosp. Electron. Syst. **48**(2), 1385–1402 (2012)
5. Vo, B.T., Vo, B.N., Cantoni, A.: The cardinality balanced multi-target multi-Bernoulli filter and its implementations. IEEE Trans. Sig. Process. **57**(2), 409–423 (2009)
6. Vo, B.T., Clark, D., Vo, B.N., et al.: Bernoulli forward-backward smoothing for joint target detection and tracking. IEEE Trans. Sig. Process. **59**(9), 4473–4477 (2011)
7. Wong, S., Vo, B.T., Papi, F.: Bernoilli forward-backward smoothing for track-before-detect. IEEE Sig. Process. Lett. **21**(6), 727–731 (2014)
8. Liu, J.S., Chen, R., Logvinenko, T.: A theoretical framework for sequential importance sampling with resampling. In: Doucet, A., de Freitas, N., Gordon, N. (eds.) Sequential Monte Carlo Methods in Practice, pp. 225–246. Springer, New York (2001). https://doi.org/10.1007/978-1-4757-3437-9_11
9. Kennedy, J., Eberhart, R.: Particle swarm optimization. In: Proceedings of the IEEE International Conference on Neural Networks, pp. 1941–1948. IEEE Service Center, Piscataway (1995)
10. Deb, K., Agrawal, S., Pratap, A., Meyarivan, T.: A fast elitist non-dominated sorting genetic algorithm for multi-objective optimization: NSGA-II. In: Schoenauer, M., et al. (eds.) PPSN 2000. LNCS, vol. 1917, pp. 849–858. Springer, Heidelberg (2000). https://doi.org/10.1007/3-540-45356-3_83
11. Ouyang, C., Ji, H., Li, C.: Improved multi-target multi-Bernoulli filter. IET Radar Sonar Navig. **6**(6), 458–464 (2012)
12. Zhou, G., Pelletier, M., Kirubarajan, T., et al.: Statically fused converted position and doppler measurement Kalman filters. IEEE Trans. Aerosp. Electron. Syst. **50**(1), 300–318 (2014)
13. Yoon, J.H., Kim, D.Y., Bae, S.H., et al.: Joint initialization and tracking of multiple moving objects using doppler information. IEEE Trans. Sig. Process. **59**(7), 3447–3452 (2011)
14. Vo, B.N., Ma, W.K.: The Gaussian mixture probability hypothesis density filter. IEEE Trans. Sig. Process. **54**(11), 4091–4104 (2006)
15. Vo, B.T., Vo, B.N., Cantoni, A.: Analytic implementations of the cardinalized probability hypothesis density filter. IEEE Trans. Sig. Process. **55**(7), 3553–3567 (2007)
16. Ristic, B., Vo, B.N., Clark, D., et al.: A metric for performance evaluation of multi-target tracking algorithms. IEEE Trans. Sig. Process. **59**(7), 3452–3457 (2011)

# Study of Radar Target Range Profile Recognition Algorithm Based on Optimized Neural Network

Xiaokang Guo, Tao Jian, Yunlong Dong, and Xiaolong Chen[✉]

Research Institute of Information Fusion, Naval Aviation University,
Yantai, Shandong, China
gxk157@163.com, work_jt@163.com,
cxlcxl1209@163.com, china_dyl@sina.com

**Abstract.** Neural network as an important aspect of artificial intelligence has received extensive research and long-term development. Radar target range profile recognition is a commonly used method in radar target recognition, in this paper, it is combined with neural network. The LVQ (Learning Vector Quantization) neural network has excellent classification and identification capabilities. This paper applies it to radar target one-dimensional range image recognition and achieves good results. This paper studies the problem of LVQ neural network sensitive to initial connection weights, and uses PSO (Particle Swarm Optimization) algorithm to optimize it of recognition classification. The experimental results show that the study of radar target range profile recognition algorithm based on optimized neural network can overcome the sensitivity of the LVQ neural network to the initial weight and improve its recognition ability.

**Keywords:** 1-D range profile recognition
LVQ (Learning Vector Quantization) · PSO (Particle Swarm Optimization)

## 1 Introduction

The radar target one-dimensional range image recognition uses the relevant information provided by the target echo of the high-resolution radar to make a corresponding decision on the class attribute of the target. The one-dimensional range image can reflect the geometric shape and structural information of the target, and can provide more required feature information than the low-resolution radar, and is easy to obtain and process. Therefore, target recognition based on one dimensional range profile of radar target has become a popular method [1, 2]. Some studies have proposed the application of subspace method, optimal clustering center method and BP neural

This work was supported by National Natural Science Foundation of China (61501487, 61471379, 61790551), National Defense science Foundation (2102024), Equipment Pre-research Project of Equipment Development Ministry (41413060101) and Taishan Scholar Project of Shandong Province, Young Elite Scientist Sponsorship Program of CAST.

© ICST Institute for Computer Sciences, Social Informatics and Telecommunications Engineering 2018
L. Meng and Y. Zhang (Eds.): MLICOM 2018, LNICST 251, pp. 617–622, 2018.
https://doi.org/10.1007/978-3-030-00557-3_61

network to radar target one-dimensional range image recognition [3–5], and achieved good results.

Neural network as an important aspect of artificial intelligence has received extensive research and long-term development. LVQ neural network has strong classification recognition ability and has been widely used [6]. In this paper, it is applied as a classifier to the radar target's one-dimensional range image recognition, which has achieved good results. The LVQ network algorithm is sensitive to the initial connection weights of the output layer and the competition layer. For this paper, the PSO algorithm is used to optimize and improve, and a PSO-LVQ radar target one-dimensional range image recognition algorithm is proposed. Experimentally verified that this method significantly improves the recognition effect.

## 2  LVQ Neural Network Model Analysis

The LVQ neural network is a supervised network for training the competition layer. And the algorithm is derived from the Kohonen [7] competition algorithm.

Figure 1 shows the structure of LVQ neural network [8]. LVQ neural network has three layers of neurons, input layer, competition layer and output layer. Set each distance image as a vector $X_i$, each input mode of the input layer is a distance image. The network input layer and the competition layer are fully connected, and the connection weights will change when the network is trained. The network training is the learning classification of the input vector based on the distance criterion. It is assumed that there are a total of M distance images from the K class targets, The input is $M = (x_1, x_2 \ldots, x_M)$, Then the number of input neurons is also M. Follow these steps to train:

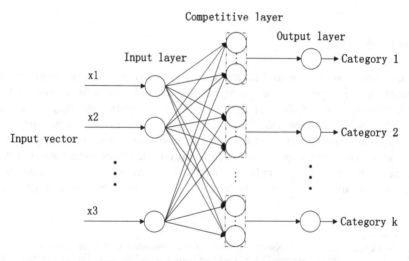

**Fig. 1.** The model of LVQ neural network

*Step 1:* Initialize the connection weight $\omega_{ij}$ between the input layer and the competition layer and learning rate $\eta(0)$. $i = 1, 2, \ldots, P$. $P$ is the number of neurons for the competition layer, $j = 1, 2, \ldots, M$

*Step 2:* Send the one-dimensional range image as input to the network and calculate the Euclidean distance between the input vector and the competitive layer neuron

$$d_i = \sqrt{\sum_{j=1}^{M} (x_j - \omega_{ij})^2} \tag{1}$$

*Step 3:* Establish the minimum Euclidean distance standard

*Step 4:* Determine if the classification is correct. Adjust the weight vector according to the following rules:

If $C_x = C_i$

$$w_{ij\_new} = w_{ij\_old} + \eta(x - w_{ij\_old}) \tag{2}$$

If $C_x \neq C_i$

$$w_{ij\_new} = w_{ij\_old} - \eta(x - w_{ij\_old}) \tag{3}$$

*Step 5:* Adjust the learning rate

*Step 6:* Determine whether the number of iterations exceeds, if it exceeds, the iteration ends, otherwise go to the second step.

Each neuron in the output layer corresponds to a radar target category.

The advantage of this training method is that there is no need to normalize and orthogonalize the input vector, only the distance between the input vector and the competitive layer neuron is calculated.

It was observed that the "winning" neurons were determined by calculating the minimum distance by (1). Using only information of "winning" neurons results in insufficient utilization of information resources between the input samples and the competition layer. Observing formula (1), it is easy to find that when the initial weight deviation is too large, the calculation error will be very large, which will affect the convergence speed and classification recognition effect of the LVQ network.

## 3  PSO-LVQ Radar Target One-Dimensional Range Recognition System

To solve the problem that the LVQ network mentioned above is sensitive to the initial connection weights of the output layer and the competition layer, this paper proposes a PSO-LVQ radar target one-dimensional range profile recognition system.

The particle swarm optimization algorithm is an optimization algorithm that was proposed by Kennedy and Eberhart [9] and others to simulate the swarm intelligence behavior of birds. In the particle swarm algorithm, a particle represents a bird. Each particle is represented by its own position and velocity, and is updated according to its own initial orientation, its own optimal direction of experience, and the empirical optimization direction of the surrounding particles. The performance of each particle is evaluated by defining a fitness function.

In this paper, particle swarm optimization algorithm is used to optimize the initial weights of LVQ neural network. The particle coding of the particle swarm is directly assigned to the weights and threshold matrix of the LVQ neural network. Then the predicted value is predicted by the LVQ neural network, and compared with the actual value of the training data to predict the error rate and the objective function to obtain the fitness of each particle.

The specific implementation steps of the PSO-LVQ radar target one-dimensional range profile recognition system are as follows:

**Step 1:** Create an LVQ network

An LVQ neural network is created, and each target selects a certain number of samples as input vectors for network training. Randomly generate n × m-dimensional matrices (n is the number of hidden layer neurons of the LVQ network, m is the dimension of the one-dimensional distance image) as the initial weight of the network. The number of neurons in the hidden layer affects the effect of the network. Too few will affect the recognition accuracy, and too many will affect the training speed. Determine the number based on the actual experiment.

**Step 2:** Initialization

Set the PSO algorithm parameters $c_1$, $c_2$, $r_1$ and $r_2$. Initialize the particle swarm, which defines parameters such as population size, number of iterations, and initializes the particle's velocity and position.

**Step 3:** Iterative optimization, adjusting the particle's velocity and position

Population iteration updates:
The speed of the particles is updated according to formula (4):

$$v_{ij}(t+1) = v_{ij}(t) + c_1 r_1 \left[ y_{ij}(t) - x_{ij}(t) \right] + c_2 r_2 \left[ \hat{y}_j(t) - x_{ij}(t) \right] \tag{4}$$

The position of the particle is updated according to formula (5):

$$x_{ij}(t+1) = x_{ij}(t) + v_{ij}(t+1) \tag{5}$$

$v_{ij}(t)$ is the velocity of particle $i$ in $j$ th dimension at $t$, $i = 1, 2, \ldots, m$, $m$ indicates the number of particles. $j = 1, 2, \ldots, J$, $J$ represents the dimension of the particle. $c_1, c_2$ express acceleration constant. $r_1, r_2$ are the random numbers between the intervals [0, 1]. $y_{ij}(t)$ indicates the past optimal position of the $i$ th particle while $\hat{y}_j(t)$ indicates the past optimal position of the entire particle swarm. $x_{ij}(t)$ is the position of particle $i$ in $j$ th dimension at $t$.

*Step 4:* Calculate the fitness value and update the individual extremum and population extremum

*Step 5:* Repeat (3) (4) two steps until the iteration is completed

*Step 6:* Assign an optimal value to the LVQ neural network and input samples for training.

# 4  Experiment

## 4.1  Data Preprocessing

One-dimensional range images have azimuthal sensitivity and amplitude sensitivity, which are one of the key issues in the identification of one-dimensional range images. In order to effectively identify the target, the data must be pre-processed. The fast Fourier transform (FFT) [10] method is used to divide the observation interval to solve the azimuth sensitivity. The HRRP sequence in the observation interval is defined as a frame distance image and represents a corresponding angle field. Normalize the range image amplitude spectrum to resolve amplitude sensitivity.

The experimental data is 260 distance images taken for each of the three types of aircraft. The data is processed as follows:

*Step 1:* Normalize, normalize each image with its total energy

*Step 2:* Distance alignment, using the Fourier invariant translation invariance, aligns a one-dimensional range image as a Fourier transform.

Each target selected 160 samples to form a training set, and the remaining 100 samples formed a test set. The number of neurons in the hidden layer is set to 20 and the number of output layer neurons is 3, the number of training is 100, the size of the population of particles is 50, and the number of iterations is 50.

## 4.2  Result Analysis

As shown in Table 1, the classification accuracy of LVQ algorithm and PSO-LVQ algorithm.

**Table 1.** Comparison of classification accuracy of LVQ and PSO-LVQ algorithms

| Target | Accuracy of LVQ (%) | Accuracy of PSO-LVQ (%) |
|---|---|---|
| Target 1 | 75.652 | 86.149 |
| Target 2 | 95.023 | 95.293 |
| Target 3 | 96.873 | 98.856 |
| Average recognition rate (%) | 89.183 | 93.433 |

Table 1 summarizes the performance of the two methods mentioned in the article applied to the radar target one-dimensional range image recognition. The LVQ algorithm can achieve a good classification effect, and after being optimized by the particle swarm optimization algorithm, the classification and recognition performance can be further improved. The classification accuracy of PSO-LVQ algorithm is much better than LVQ, and the average accuracy rate can reach 93.433%.

This shows that after optimizing the weights of the LVQ neural network through the PSO algorithm, the sensitivity of the LVQ neural network to the initial weight is overcome to a certain extent, and the classification effect of the network is better. Experiments prove the correctness of the algorithm.

## 5    Conclusion

In this paper, the LVQ neural network method is applied to the radar target's one-dimensional range image recognition to obtain a good recognition effect. And for the problem that the LVQ algorithm is sensitive to the initial weights, the particle swarm optimization algorithm is used to optimize the initial weights of the LVQ neural network. Through experimental tests, it is verified that this method can overcome the sensitivity of LVQ neural network to the initial weight to a certain extent and improve the classification effect of the classifier.

## References

1. Liu, H., Du, L., Yuan, L., Bao, Z.: Research progress in radar high resolution range image target recognition. J. Electron. Inf. Technol. **27**(8), 1328–1334 (2005)
2. Xu, B., Chen, W., Liu, H., et al.: High-resolution radar range image target recognition based on attentional circulate neural network model. J. Electron. Inf. Technol. **38**(12), 2988–2995 (2016)
3. Zhou, Y.: Research on radar target recognition based on high resolution range profile. University of Electronic Science and Technology (2016)
4. Zhao, F., Zhang, J., Liu, J.: Radar target recognition based on kernel optimal transformation and clustering center. Control Decis. **23**(7), 735–740 (2008)
5. Chen, W., Yang, P., Liu, C., et al.: Application of BP neural network in radar target recognition. Electron. Sci. Technol. **23**(12), 18–19 (2010)
6. Song, J., Zou, X., Yin, Y., et al.: Research on face orientation recognition based on neural network. Ind. Control Comput. **30**(4), 111–112 (2017)
7. Chen, Z., Feng, T.J., Houkes, Z.: Texture segmentation based on wavelet and Kohonen network for remotely sensed images. In: IEEE SMC 1999 Conference Proceedings IEEE International Conference on Systems, Man, and Cybernetics, vol. 6, pp. 816–821. IEEE (1999)
8. Xia, F., Luo, Z., Zhang, H., et al.: Application of hybrid neural network in transformer fault diagnosis. J. Electron. Meas. Instrum. **31**(1), 118–124 (2017)
9. Munlin, M., Anantathanavit, M.: Hybrid radius particle swarm optimization. In: Region 10 Conference, pp. 1–5. IEEE (2017)
10. Yuan, L., Liu, H., Bao, Z.: Radar HRRP automatic target recognition based on central moment feature. Chin. J. Electron. **32**(12), 2078–2081 (2004)

# Resource Allocation Based Simultaneous Wireless Information and Power Transfer for Multiuser OFDM Systems

Shanzhen Fang$^{(\boxtimes)}$, Weidang Lu, Hong Peng, Zhijiang Xu,
and Jingyu Hua

College of Information Engineering, Zhejiang University of Technology,
Hangzhou 310023, People's Republic of China
742430646@qq.com, {luweid,ph,zyfxzj,
eehjy}@zjut.edu.cn

**Abstract.** In this paper, we mainly study simultaneous wireless information and power transfer (SWIPT) for the multiuser resource allocation. All subcarriers are divided into two parts, part of which are for information decoding and another part are for energy harvesting. We optimize the subcarrier allocation and power allocation to maximize the energy that collected by all users under the target rate constraint. The original optimal problem is complicated, so it is hard to find the optimal solution directly. By transforming the primal problem, we finally solved the original problem by using the Lagrange dual method.

**Keywords:** Simultaneous Wireless Information and Power Transfer (SWIPT)
OFDM · Multiuser system · Energy harvesting

## 1 Introduction

Simultaneous Wireless Information and Power Transfer (SWIPT) is a new type of wireless communication that can transmit information and harvest energy simultaneously. More and more people are devoted to study this field [1–6]. Through this technology, it is expected to realize the power supply and control of equipment in harsh working environment. In addition, it has broad application prospects in the field of biomedicine. The traditional research is mainly for one user. There are a lot of literature on SWIPT in the aspect of single user performance analysis. [7] proposed two transmission protocols, namely power splitting (PS) protocol and the transmission mode adaptation (TMA) protocol. The authors studied amplify-and-forward (AF) and decode-and-forward (DF) protocol in [8, 9]. Different from the traditional single-user research, we studied the multiuser OFDM systems. There are also some scholars studying multiuser systems, a subcarrier separation (SS) strategy in multiuser OFDM systems was proposed in [10]. In [10], the authors put forward an optimization algorithm that maximizes the total transmission rate. Unlike [10], in this article, we provide a new optimization algorithm that maximizes the energy received by all users. The sum energy optimization problem is a complex multivariable problem. Although the

© ICST Institute for Computer Sciences, Social Informatics and Telecommunications Engineering 2018
L. Meng and Y. Zhang (Eds.): MLICOM 2018, LNICST 251, pp. 623–631, 2018.
https://doi.org/10.1007/978-3-030-00557-3_62

original problem is non-convex, after conversion, the original problem can be simplified. Then, we use the Lagrange dual method to get the optimal solution.

The rest of paper is organized as follows. In Sect. 2, we introduce the system model and provide optimization problem that maximizes the harvested energy. Section 3 solves this problem by the Lagrange dual method. The simulation results are presented and discussed in Sect. 4. Finally, we summarized this article in Sect. 5.

## 2 System Model and Problem Formulation

We consider a multiuser OFDM system, in this system, there are N subcarriers and K users. The set of subcarriers is represented as $S = \{1...N\}$, and all users are denoted as $K = \{1...K\}$, as shown in Fig. 1.

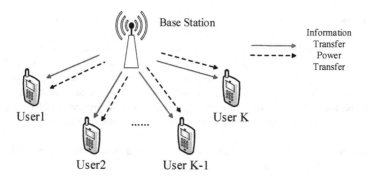

**Fig. 1.** System model

All subcarriers are divided into two parts, some subcarriers are used to harvest energy (denoted by $S_k^P$ for user k), while the others are used to decode information at the same time (denoted by $S_k^I$ for user k). The channel power gain on each subcarrier is assumed to be constant (expressed as $h_{k,n}$ for user k over subcarrier n), let $p_{k,n}$ denote power allocated on user k over subcarrier n. And each subcarrier is only allowed for one user to transmit information. We specify that each user has the minimum required target rate (denoted by $R_k$ for user k), and $B_k$ represent the minimum required energy for user k, if less than this minimum energy, it does not reach its sensitivity and does not receive it. The sum power constraint of the whole system is expressed as $P$. So the transmission rate $r_{k,n}$ achieved by user k on subcarrier n can be written as

$$\sum_{n \in S_k^I} \log(1 + \frac{h_{k,n}p_{k,n}}{\sigma^2}) \tag{1}$$

where $\sigma^2$ is denoted as noise power and the energy $Q_{k,n}$ harvested by user k on subcarrier n can be expressed as

$$\sum_{n \in s_k^P} (\varepsilon h_{k,n} p_{k,n} + \sigma^2) \tag{2}$$

Our target is to maximize the sum harvested energy, this optimization problem can be given as

$$\textbf{P1}: \max_{p_{k,n}, S_k^P} \sum_{k=1}^K \sum_{n \in s_k^P} (\varepsilon h_{k,n} p_{k,n} + \sigma^2)$$

$$s.t. \sum_{n \in s_k^I} \log(1 + \frac{h_{k,n} p_{k,n}}{\sigma^2}) \geq R_k, \forall k = 1, 2, \ldots K$$

$$\sum_{n \in s_k^P} (\varepsilon h_{k,n} p_{k,n} + \sigma^2) \geq B_k, \forall k = 1, 2, \ldots K \tag{3}$$

$$\sum_{k=1}^K \sum_{n \in N} p_{k,n} = P$$

$$S_{k1}^I \cap S_{k2}^I = \varnothing, \forall k_1, k_2 = 1, 2, \ldots K, k_1 \neq k_2$$

$$S_k^I \cap S_k^P = \varnothing$$

$$S_k^I \cup S_k^P = N$$

where $\varepsilon$ denote energy harvesting efficiency, in this article, we make it equal to 1 for the sake of convenience.

## 3   Optimal Solution

Solving (3) is a difficult task because it is an optimization problem with multiple variables. Our original idea was to get the optimal solution for each variable by the exhaustive method. Then, by comparing the energy in all cases, the optimal solution is selected and the optimal solution is determined. However, in practice this enumerative method is too complex. So we choose to solve the problem (3) with the following method.

In order to solve (3), first given $S_k^I$ and $S_k^P$, we only focus on the power for information decoding and energy harvesting $(p_{k,n}(n \in S_k^I), p_{k,n}(n \in S_k^P))$. So the (3) can be simplified as

$$\textbf{P2}: \max_{p_{k,n}, S_k^P} \sum_{k=1}^K \sum_{n \in s_k^P} (\varepsilon h_{k,n} p_{k,n} + \sigma^2)$$

$$s.t. \sum_{n \in s_k^I} \log(1 + \frac{h_{k,n} p_{k,n}}{\sigma^2}) \geq R_k, \forall k = 1, 2, \ldots K$$

$$\sum_{n \in s_k^P} (\varepsilon h_{k,n} p_{k,n} + \sigma^2) \geq B_k, \forall k = 1, 2, \ldots K \tag{4}$$

$$\sum_{k=1}^K \sum_{n \in N} p_{k,n} = P$$

If the "timesharing" condition [11] can be satisfied, the duality gap of the non-convex optimization problem is zero. So we can use the dual method to solve (4). The Lagrange equation of **P2** can be expressed as

$$
\begin{aligned}
L(p, \beta) = {} & \sum_{k=1}^{K} \sum_{n \in S_k^P} (\varepsilon h_{k,n} p_{k,n} + \sigma^2) \\
& + \sum_{k=1}^{K} \beta_{1,k} [\sum_{n \in S_k^l} \log(1 + \tfrac{h_{k,n} p_{k,n}}{\sigma^2}) - R_k] \\
& + \sum_{k=1}^{K} \beta_{2,k} [(\sum_{n \in S_k^P} (\varepsilon h_{k,n} p_{k,n} + \sigma^2)) - B_k] \\
& + \beta_3 [P - \sum_{k=1}^{K} \sum_{n \in N} p_{k,n}], k = 1, 2, \cdots K
\end{aligned}
\tag{5}
$$

where $\beta = \{\beta_{1,k}, \beta_{2,k}, \beta_3\}, \forall k = 1, 2, 3, \cdots K$, $\beta_{1,k} \geq 0$, $\beta_{2,k} \geq 0$, $\beta_3 \geq 0$ are Lagrange multipliers that are determined by the sub-gradient method below.

### 3.1    Dual Variables Optimizing

The dual function of the optimization problem in (5) can be expressed as

$$
g(\beta) = \max_{p, \beta} L(p, \beta)
\tag{6}
$$

and the dual optimization problem is

$$
\begin{aligned}
& \min_{\beta} g(\beta) \\
& s.t. \beta \succ= 0
\end{aligned}
\tag{7}
$$

According to [12], we can get sub-gradient easily given as

$$
\Delta \beta_{1,k} = \sum_{n \in S_k^l} \log(1 + \frac{h_{k,n} p_{k,n}}{\sigma^2}) - R_k
\tag{8}
$$

$$
\Delta \beta_{2,k} = \sum_{n \in S_k^P} (\varepsilon h_{k,n} p_{k,n} + \sigma^2) - B_k
\tag{9}
$$

$$
\Delta \beta_3 = P - \sum_{k=1}^{K} \sum_{n \in N} p_{k,n}
\tag{10}
$$

Denote $\Delta \beta = (\Delta \beta_{11}, \Delta \beta_{12}, \cdots \Delta \beta_{1,K}; \Delta \beta_{21}, \Delta \beta_{22}, \cdots \Delta \beta_{2,K}; \Delta \beta_3)$. The dual variables are updated as $\beta^{(t+1)} = \beta^{(t)} + \delta^{(t)} \Delta \beta$, where $\delta^{(t)}$ denote step size. Using the step size following the diminishing step size policy in [12], the optimal dual variable $\beta^*$ can be converged by this sub-gradient method.

### 3.2 Optimizing Primal Variables with Given Dual Variables

Next we will divide into two steps to find the optimal power allocation and the optimal subcarrier sets.

(1) Deriving the optimal power for fixed subcarrier sets:

Take the derivatives of $L(p, \beta)$ with $p_{k,n}(n \in S_k^I)$, $p_{k,n}(n \in S_k^P)$, respectively, so we can obtain

$$\frac{\partial L}{\partial p_{k,n}} = \frac{\beta_{1,k} h_{k,n}}{\sigma^2 + h_{k,n} p_{k,n}} - \beta_3, (n \in S_k^I) \tag{11}$$

$$\frac{\partial L}{\partial p_{k,n}} = (\varepsilon h_{k,n} + \varepsilon \beta_{2,k} h_{k,n}) - \beta_3, (n \in S_k^P) \tag{12}$$

According to Karush-Kuhn-Tucker (KKT) conditions [13], let (11), (12) be equal to zero, so we can obtain optimal $p_{k,n}(n \in S_k^I)$, $p_{k,n}(n \in S_k^P)$, respectively.

$$p_{k,n}^* = \left(\frac{\beta_{1,k}}{\beta_3} - \frac{\sigma^2}{h_{k,n}}\right)^+, (n \in S_k^I) \tag{13}$$

$$p_{k,n}^* = \begin{cases} p_{\max}, (\varepsilon h_{k,n} + \varepsilon \beta_{2,k} h_{k,n}) > \beta_3 \\ p_{\min}, otherwise \end{cases}, (n \in S_k^P) \tag{14}$$

where $p_{\max}$ and $p_{\min}$ represent the peak and lowest power constraints, and $[x]^+ \triangleq \max\{0, x\}$.

(2) Deriving the optimal Subcarrier sets:

Substituting the optimal $p_{k,n}(n \in S_k^I)$, $p_{k,n}(n \in S_k^I)$ into (5), so (5) can be rewritten as (15) and (16)

$$\begin{aligned} L(p, \beta) = &\sum_{k=1}^K \sum_{n \in S_k^P} [(\varepsilon h_{k,n} p_{k,n}^* + \sigma^2) + \beta_{2,k}(\varepsilon h_{k,n} p_{k,n}^* + \sigma^2) \\ &- \beta_{1,k} \log(1 + \tfrac{h_{k,n} p_{k,n}^*}{\sigma^2})] + \sum_{k=1}^K \sum_{n \in N} [\beta_{1,k} \log(1 + \tfrac{h_{k,n} p_{k,n}^*}{\sigma^2})] \\ &- \sum_{k=1}^K \sum_{n \in N} \beta_3 p_{k,n}^* + \beta_3 P - \sum_{k=1}^K (\beta_{1,k} R_k + \beta_{2,k} B_k), \\ &k = 1, 2, \cdots K \end{aligned} \tag{15}$$

$$\begin{aligned} L(p, \beta) = &\sum_{k=1}^K \sum_{n \in S_k^P} F_k + \sum_{k=1}^K \sum_{n \in N} [\beta_{1,k} \log(1 + \tfrac{h_{k,n} p_{k,n}^*}{\sigma^2})] \\ &- \sum_{k=1}^K \sum_{n \in N} \beta_3 p_{k,n}^* + \beta_3 P - \sum_{k=1}^K (\beta_{1,k} R_k + \beta_{2,k} B_k), \\ &k = 1, 2, \cdots K \end{aligned} \tag{16}$$

where

$$F_k = (\varepsilon h_{k,n} p^*_{k,n} + \sigma^2) + \beta_{2,k}(\varepsilon h_{k,n} p^*_{k,n} + \sigma^2)$$
$$- \beta_{1,k} \log(1 + \tfrac{h_{k,n} p^*_{k,n}}{\sigma^2}) \tag{17}$$

so the optimal subcarrier set $S^{P*}_k$ can be obtained to maximize $F_k$, i.e.

$$S^{P*}_k = \arg\max \sum_{n \in S^P_k} F_k \tag{18}$$

and the optimal $S^{I*}_k$ can be derived as

$$S^{I*}_k = N - S^{P*}_k \tag{19}$$

In this way, we obtain the optimal power allocation and the optimal subcarrier sets, and the above algorithm can be described as the following Algorithm 1.

---

**Algorithm 1**     Resource Allocation Algorithm for the Problem(3)

1 : **initialize** Lagrange multipliers $\{ \beta_{11}, \beta_{12}, L\ \beta_{1,K}; \beta_{21}, \beta_{22}, L\ \beta_{2,K}; \beta_3 \}$.

2 : **repeat**

3 :     Compute the optimal power allocation $p_{k,n}{}^*(n \in S_k{}^I)$, $p_{k,n}{}^*(n \in S_k{}^P)$ in(13) and (14).

4 :     Getting the optimal subcarrier allocation sets $S_k{}^{I*}$, $S_k{}^{P*}$ in (18) and (19).

5 :     Update $\beta$ by the sub-gradient method in (8), (9) and (10).

6 : **until** $\beta$ converge.

---

## 4  Simulation Results

In the simulation, we use Rice fading channel, the number of subcarriers set to 32, energy conversion efficiency $\varepsilon$ set to 1. Minimum required target rate of each user is set to uniform simplicity, Similarly, the minimum required energy is also set to the same.

Figure 2 compares the performance of our proposed algorithm with an algorithm shown as follows.

Algorithm 1: Each subcarrier is assigned the same power for information decoding and energy harvesting.

It can be seen from Fig. 2 that our proposed algorithm is superior to Algorithm 1. And we note that as the target rate increases, the amount of sum harvested energy decreases. This is because when the sum power (P = 0.5 W) and the minimum required energy ($B_k$ = 0.2 mW) remain unchanged, as the target rate increases, the power used to decode the information increases, so the power used to harvest energy decreases.

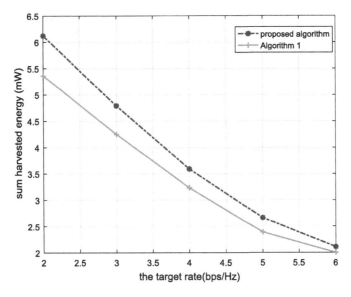

**Fig. 2.** The target rate versus sum harvested energy

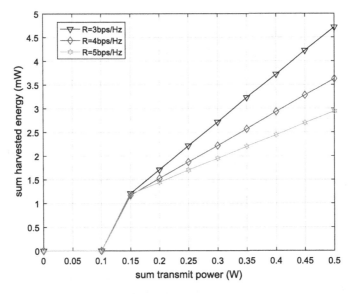

**Fig. 3.** Sum harvested energy versus sum power

Figure 3 presents that as the total transmission power increases, the sum energy also increases. The reason is that when the target rate and the minimum required energy remain unchanged ($B_k = 0.2$ mW), as the total power increases, the power used to decode information remains unchanged, so more power are used to harvest energy.

Also, the value of a curve in Fig. 3 is 0, indicated that the sum harvested energy is 0, this is because the sum transmit power is too small, the total energy collected by each user is lower than the minimum required energy.

From Fig. 4 we can see that when the minimum required energy increases, the sum harvested energy decreases.

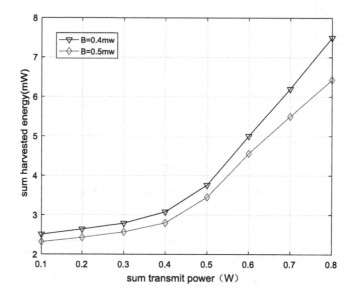

**Fig. 4.** Sum harvested energy versus sum power

## 5   Conclusion

In this article, we propose an algorithm that maximizes the sum harvested energy with a minimum harvested energy constraint and a minimum target rate constraint. The initial optimization problem cannot get the optimal solution directly, by transforming the original problem, we use Lagrange dual method to get the optimal power allocation and the optimal subcarrier sets.

## References

1. Grover, P., Sahai, A.: Shannon meets tesla: wireless information and power transfer. In: IEEE International Symposium on Information Theory, pp. 2363–2367, June 2010
2. Nasir, A.A., Zhou, X., Durrani, S., Kennedy, R.A.: Relaying protocols for wireless energy harvesting and information processing. IEEE Trans. Wirel. Commun. 12(7), 3622–3636 (2013)
3. Lu, W., Gong, Y., Wu, J., Peng, H., Hua, J.: Simultaneous wireless information and power transfer based on joint subcarrier and power allocation in OFDM systems. IEEE Access 5, 2763–2770 (2017)

4. Krikidis, I., Timotheou, S., Nikolaou, S., Zheng, G., Ng, D.W.K., Schober, R.: Simultaneous wireless information and power transfer in modern communication systems. IEEE Commun. Mag. **52**(11), 104–110 (2014)
5. Liu, L., Zhang, R., Chua, K.C.: Wireless information transfer with opportunistic energy harvesting. IEEE Trans. Wirel. Commun. **12**(1), 288–300 (2013)
6. Huang, K., Larsson, E.: Simultaneous information and power transfer for broadband wireless systems. IEEE Trans. Sig. Process. **61**(23), 5972–5986 (2013)
7. Liu, Y., Wang, X.: Information and energy cooperation in OFDM relaying: protocols and optimization. IEEE Trans. Veh. Technol. **65**, 5088–5098 (2015)
8. Li, Y., Wang, W., Kong, J., Peng, M.: Subcarrier pairing for amplify-and-forward and decode-and-forward OFDM relay links. IEEE Commun. Lett. **13**(4), 209–211 (2009)
9. Zhong, C., Suraweera, H., Zheng, G., Krikidis, I., Zhang, Z.: Wireless information and power transfer with full duplex relaying. IEEE Trans. Commun. **62**(10), 3447–3461 (2014)
10. Yin, S., Qu, Z.: Resource allocation in multiuser OFDM systems with wireless information and power transfer. IEEE Commun. Lett. **20**(3), 594–597 (2016)
11. Yu, W., Lui, R.: Dual methods for non-convex spectrum optimization of multicarrier systems. IEEE Trans. Commun. **54**(7), 1310–1322 (2006)
12. Boyd, S., Mutapcic, A.: Sub-gradient methods, notes for EE364, Standford University (2006)
13. Boyd, S., Vandenberghe, L.: Convex Optimization. Cambridge University Press (2004)

# Improved RSA Localization Based on the Lagrange Multiplier Optimization

Jiafei Fu[1], Jingyu Hua[1(✉)], Zhijiang Xu[1], Weidang Lu[1],
and Jiamin Li[2]

[1] College of Information Engineering, Zhejiang University of Technology,
Hangzhou 310023, China
eehjy@163.com
[2] National Mobile Communications Research Laboratory, Southeast University,
Nanjing 210096, China

**Abstract.** The non-line-of-sight (NLOS) error in wireless network is the main factor that affects the accuracy of positioning algorithm. Therefore, this paper proposes an improved range-scaling-algorithm (RSA) using the Lagrange multiplier method in the wireless sensor networks, where we account for two kinds of nodes, i.e., the static nodes (SN) and the mobile nodes (MN). The key of the proposed algorithm is to construct a composite cost function by the Lagrange multiplier method. Meanwhile, the SN grouping operation followed by a positioning combination is proposed to further improve the performance. Simulation results show that the proposed algorithm can effectively suppress the loss of positioning accuracy caused by non-line-of-sight error. Moreover, the proposed algorithm performs better with increasing number of SNs.

**Keywords:** Wireless localization · Non-line-of-sight error
Quadratic programming · Wireless sensor networks

## 1 Introduction

In the wireless sensor network (WSN) and the Internet of things, wireless positioning technology and location-based services such as vehicle-mounted mobile communication services have received wide attention [1]. Generally, the WSN may include three more static nodes (SN) and a number of mobile nodes (MN), in which the SN positions are known while the MN position requires to be estimated by the measurement information [2–5]. In order to realize the precise positioning, it is often divided into two steps, i.e., the localization parameter estimation and the position estimation. The localization parameter usually includes the time of arrival (TOA), angle of arrival (AOA) and their combinations [6–8].

The traditional positioning algorithm suffered from many uncertain factors in a real environment, such as measurement noise and non-line-of-sight error. These factors led to negative impacts for location [9–11]. Generally, the measurement noise is introduced in the measurement process, while the NLOS error is caused by obstacles blocking signal transmission. Unlike the Gaussian modeled measurement noise, the NLOS error usually cannot be modeled accurately. Therefore, researchers try to model the NLOS

© ICST Institute for Computer Sciences, Social Informatics and Telecommunications Engineering 2018
L. Meng and Y. Zhang (Eds.): MLICOM 2018, LNICST 251, pp. 632–640, 2018.
https://doi.org/10.1007/978-3-030-00557-3_63

localization as an optimization problem [12–14], where the geometric relationship of MN and SN is employed to construct the constraints. However, these optimization methods only limitedly suppressed the influence of NLOS error.

Based on the RSA location [15], an improved algorithm is proposed by addressing the composite costs, in which we construct a cost function accounting for both the original RSA cost and the new cost. Two costs are combined through the Lagrange multiplier method, and the optimal multiplier is derived analytically. Then, the new optimization problem is solved by the quadratic programming. Furthermore, we put forward a group positioning scheme to improve the positioning performance, where appropriate SN subgroups are employed to obtain the final position estimation. The simulations demonstrate the effectiveness of the proposed algorithm, and its superiority over other tested methods. In addition, we have found that the increased SN number also benefits the localization performance.

## 2  Original RSA Location Algorithm

### 2.1  Measurement Distance Model

The positioning algorithm based on TOA uses the measured distance between SN and MN, and the true distance between MN and SN can be expressed as

$$r_i = \sqrt{(x - x_i)^2 + (y - y_i)^2}, i = 1, \ldots, N \tag{1}$$

where $(x_i, y_i)$ represents the coordinates of SN, which is known to MNs. In (1), $(x, y)$ denotes the MN position to be estimated. If the corresponding measurement distance is $R_i$, then the relationship between the real distance and the measured distance can be established as

$$r_i = \alpha_i R_i \tag{2}$$

Since the signal is refracted or reflected, the measurement distance is greater than the true distance, then, $\alpha_i$ always falls between 0 and 1 in the NLOS environment. In addition to the influence of NLOS, there are errors caused by measurement noise far less than the NLOS error. According to (1) and (2), the following expression is obtained

$$(x - x_i)^2 + (y - y_i)^2 = \alpha_i^2 R_i^2, i = 1, \ldots, N \tag{3}$$

The definition of weight vector is as follows

$$\mathbf{v} = [v_1, \ldots, v_N]^T = [\alpha_1^2, \ldots, \alpha_N^2]^T \tag{4}$$

If the weight vector is known and perfect, the scaled distance equals the actual distance, then the equation group (3) must produces an accurate position estimation.

Hence, how to find the good solution of weight vector is the key issue of RSA and algorithms like RSA.

In [15], the optimization model of RSA follows

$$\begin{aligned} \underset{\mathbf{v}}{Minimize}\ F(\mathbf{v}) \\ s.t.\ \mathbf{v} \le \mathbf{v}_{max}, \ MN \in FR \end{aligned} \tag{5}$$

where FR denotes the feasible region and $\mathbf{v}_{max} = [1, 1, \ldots, 1]^T$. In (5), the cost function is defined as

$$F(\mathbf{v}) = norm(\mathbf{e} - \mathbf{X_A})^2 + \ldots + (\mathbf{e} - \mathbf{X_{last}})^2 \tag{6}$$

where the vertices of FR are represented as $\mathbf{X_k} = \{(x_k, y_k)\}_{k \in \{A,B,C,\ldots,LAST\}}$, and $\mathbf{e} = [x, y]^T$.

Once the optimal weight vector is found through solving (5), equation group (3) can be expanded as

$$\begin{cases} v_1 R_1^2 - K_1 = R - 2x_1 x - 2y_1 y \\ \quad \ldots \\ v_N R_N^2 - K_N = R - 2x_N x - 2y_N y \end{cases} \tag{7}$$

where $K_i = x_i^2 + y_i^2, R = x^2 + y^2$. The matrix form of (7) can be shown as

$$\mathbf{Y} = \mathbf{A}\mathbf{x} \tag{8}$$

where $\mathbf{Y} = \begin{bmatrix} v_1 R_1^2 - K_1 \\ v_2 R_2^2 - K_2 \\ \ldots \\ v_N R_N^2 - K_N \end{bmatrix}$, $\mathbf{A} = \begin{bmatrix} -2x_1, -2y_1, 1 \\ -2x_2, -2y_2, 1 \\ \ldots \\ -2x_N, -2y_N, 1 \end{bmatrix}$, $\mathbf{x} = \begin{bmatrix} x \\ y \\ R \end{bmatrix}$.

Using the least-squares principle, we have the final position estimation

$$\mathbf{x} = (\mathbf{A}^T \mathbf{A})^{-1} \mathbf{A}^T \mathbf{Y} \tag{9}$$

# 3 Improved RSA Algorithm Using Lagrange Multiplier Method

## 3.1 Cost Function from Lagrange Method

Equations (7) and (8) indicate the following relationship in the ideal environment

$$x^2 + y^2 = R \tag{10}$$

However, the measurement noise and NLOS error will break this relation, i.e., the solution of (9) cannot satisfy (10). Hence, we can use the following new object

$$x^2 + y^2 - R \tag{11}$$

This object will be approached if the NLOS influence is reduced.

Then, a novel cost function can be derived by Lagrange multiplier method, i.e.

$$L(x, y, \lambda) = F(\mathbf{v}) + \lambda(x^2 + y^2 - R) \tag{12}$$

Then, the matrix form of (12) can be shown as

$$L(\mathbf{v}) = F(\mathbf{v}) + \lambda(\hat{\mathbf{x}}^T \mathbf{p} \mathbf{x} + \mathbf{q} \mathbf{x}) \tag{13}$$

where $\mathbf{p} = \begin{bmatrix} 1 & 0 & 0 \\ 0 & 1 & 0 \\ 0 & 0 & 0 \end{bmatrix}$, $\mathbf{q} = [0 \quad 0 \quad -1]$, $\hat{\mathbf{x}} = [x', y', r']^T$, and $r' = x'^2 + y'^2$. Note that $(x', y', r')$ represents the least square estimate of MN position.

Then, the optimization problem of the improved RSA algorithm is changed as follows

$$\begin{aligned} &\underset{\mathbf{v}}{Minimize\ L(\mathbf{v})} \\ &s.t.\ \mathbf{v} \leq \mathbf{v}_{max},\ MN \in FR \end{aligned} \tag{14}$$

Let the partial derivatives w.r.t. x, y and r equal zeros, i.e.,

$$\begin{aligned} \nabla_x L(x, y, \lambda) &= 0 \\ \nabla_y L(x, y, \lambda) &= 0 \\ \nabla_\lambda L(x, y, \lambda) &= 0 \end{aligned} \tag{15}$$

Without tedious solving process, we present the following solution of Lagrange multiplier:

$$x = c * \sqrt{\frac{r'^2}{c^2 + 1}},\ y = \sqrt{\frac{r'^2}{c^2 + 1}},\ \lambda = \frac{x_A + \ldots + x_{last}}{x} - 3 \tag{16}$$

where $c = \frac{x_A + \ldots + x_{last}}{y_A + \ldots + y_{last}}$. Then, Substituting (16) into (14), the final optimization model can be obtained.

### 3.2  A Group Location Scheme

In our study, we have found that the proposed algorithm owns higher advantages with less SN numbers. For example, when the SN number is three, the proposed algorithm shows the largest superiority over other localization methods. Therefore, we need to group $M$ SNs into three-SN subgroups, viz., $M$ SNs are divided into $N$ groups $(N = C_M^3)$, and then, we can obtain $N$ position estimates for all subgroups. Again, we have found there are subgroups producing bad estimates, which should be eliminated. Finally, we propose the following localization process (Table 1).

**Table 1.** The improved RSA algorithm of lagrange multiplier.

| The algorithm starts | |
|---|---|
| Step1 | Divide SNs into $N$ subgroups |
| Step2 | Using formulae (9), (13)–(16) to estimate MN position for each SN subgroup |
| Step3 | Average all estimates of subgroup to obtain an initial position |
| Step4 | Check and choose subgroups if the initial position falls into the triangle of it |
| Step5 | Average all position estimates of chosen subgroups to obtain the final position estimation |

## 4   Simulation and Analysis

In this section, we use MATLAB to simulate the positioning performance, where the CLS method [13], RSA method [15], and LS method [16] are employed as the comparisons. Moreover, the classical seven-SN topology are exploited, i.e., the SN locates at $(0, 0)$, $(D, 0)$, $(\frac{D}{2}, \frac{\sqrt{3}D}{2})$, $(-\frac{D}{2}, \frac{\sqrt{3}D}{2})$, $(-D, 0)$, $(-\frac{D}{2}, -\frac{\sqrt{3}D}{2})$, $(\frac{D}{2}, -\frac{\sqrt{3}D}{2})$, respectively, where $D$ is 100 m in our study. Besides, the measurement error is modeled as a Gaussian variable with standard deviation (SD) of one meter, and the NLOS error is uniformly distributed in MIN and MAX. Each simulation runs 1000 times independently.

### 4.1   The Influence of NLOS Error

Figure 1 presents the cumulative distribution function (CDF) at the extreme serious NLOS environment, where the value of MAX equals 60% of $R$. From it, we explicitly see that the proposed algorithm outperforms all tested opponents. Moreover, the gap between the original RSA and the proposed one is significant.

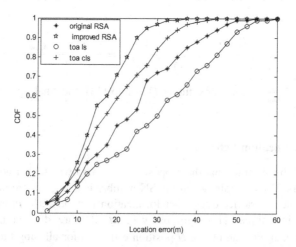

**Fig. 1.** The effect of NLOS error: MIN = 15 m, MAX = 60 m.

From Fig. 2, we clearly see the results agreeing with those of Fig. 1. When MAX = 40 m, i.e., a high but not extremely high NLOS error, the proposed produces the root-mean-square-error (RMSE) about 6.2 m, which is about 2.5 m lower than that of original RSA method.

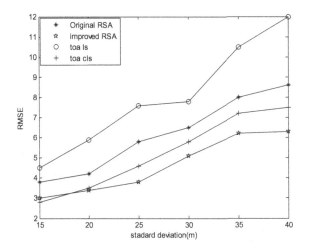

**Fig. 2.** The effect of MAX: MIN = 15 m, SD = 1 m.

### 4.2   Influence of Standard Deviation of Measurement Noise

In Fig. 3, we have seen an approximately flat curve for the proposed algorithm, which demonstrates the robustness of the proposed algorithm. By contrast, the tested opponents show the sensitivity to the SD variations. Yet, the proposed algorithm yields the best performance. Besides, when SD = 7 m, the RMSE gap between the proposed method and the original RSA method is about 2 m.

### 4.3   The Influence of SN Number

In addition to Fig. 1, here we further present the results of five SNs and nine SNs, where the SN topologies are shown as

(1)  Five SNs: $(0, 0)$, $(D, 0)$, $(\frac{D}{2}, \frac{\sqrt{3}D}{2})$, $(-\frac{D}{2}, \frac{\sqrt{3}D}{2})$, $(-D, 0)$.
(2)  Nine SNs: $(0, 0)$, $(D, 0)$, $(-D, 0)$, $(D, D)$, $(D, -D)$, $(-D, D)$, $(-D, -D)$, $(0, D)$, $(0, -D)$.

Moreover, the NLOS error varies from 15 m to 40 m, and the SD of measurement error is one meter.

Combining Figs. 1, 4 and 5, we can conclude that the proposed algorithm always performs best. Moreover, the increasing SN number helps to increase the CDF performance. When the SN number is nine, the localization error is about 7.5 m with probability 0.9, which is accurate for many WSN applications.

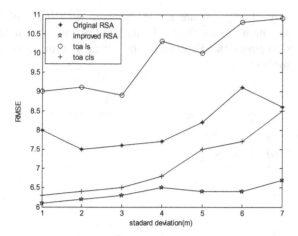

**Fig. 3.** Localization accuracy v.s. standard deviation of measurement noise: MAX = 40 m.

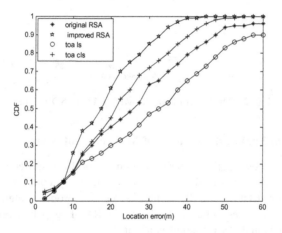

**Fig. 4.** CDF of five-SN case.

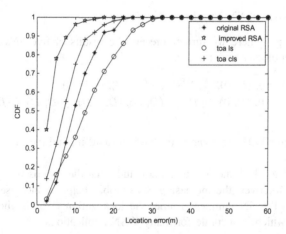

**Fig. 5.** CDF of nine-SN case.

# 5 Conclusions

Since the NLOS error significantly affects the localization performance in the WSN, this paper proposes an improved RSA method to suppress the influence of NLOS error. First, a Lagrange multiplier method is included to construct a composite cost function, and then the analytical multiplier is derived. Second, the grouping, choosing and averaging process is employed to enhance the localization performance. Finally, we can obtain accurate position estimation for the MN. The simulations demonstrate that the proposed algorithm is superior to the contrast algorithms, and the performance improves when the SN number increases.

**Acknowledgement.** This paper was sponsored by the National Natural Science Foundation of China under grant No. 61471322.

# References

1. Zhu, C., Leung, V.C.M., Yang, L.T., et al.: Collaborative location-based sleep scheduling for wireless sensor networks integrated with mobile cloud computing. In: GLOBECOM Workshops, pp. 452–457. IEEE (2014)
2. Zhang, Y., Ren, J., Chen, W.: A ToA-based location algorithm reducing the NLoS error under location-aware networks. In: International Conference on Wireless Communications, NETWORKING and Mobile Computing, pp. 1–4. IEEE (2011)
3. Al-Bawri, S.S., Jamlos, M.F., Aljunid, S.A.: Outdoor location estimation for mobile based on single base station scattering distance. In: RF and Microwave Conference, pp. 92–95. IEEE (2016)
4. Ding, T., Ding, M., Mao, G., et al.: Uplink performance analysis of dense cellular networks with LoS and NLoS transmissions. IEEE Trans. Wirel. Commun. **16**(4), 2601–2613 (2017)
5. Kong, F., Ren, X., Zheng, N., et al.: A hybrid TOA/AOA positioning method based on GDOP-weighted fusion and its accuracy analysis. In: Advanced Information Management, Communicates, Electronic and Automation Control Conference, pp. 29–34. IEEE (2017)
6. Wei, K., Wu, L.: Constrained least squares algorithm for TOA-based mobile location under NLOS environments. In: International Conference on Wireless Communications, NETWORKING and Mobile Computing, pp. 1–4. IEEE (2009)
7. Yang, K., An, J., Bu, X., et al.: A TOA-based location algorithm for NLOS environments using quadratic programming. In: Wireless Communications and NETWORKING Conference, pp. 1–5. IEEE (2010)
8. Zhang, Y., Ren, J., Chen, W.: A ToA-based location algorithm reducing the NLoS error under location-aware networks. In: International Conference on Wireless Communications, Network and Mobile Computing, pp. 1–4. IEEE (2011)
9. Chen, J., Yin, X., Tian, L., et al.: Measurement-based LoS/NLoS channel modeling for hotspot urban scenarios in UMTS networks. Int. J. Antennas Propag. **3**, 1–12 (2014)
10. Atzeni, I., Arnau, J., Kountouris, M.: Downlink cellular network analysis with LOS/NLOS propagation and elevated base stations. IEEE Trans. Wirel. Commun. **17**(1), 142–156 (2017)
11. Ding, M., Wang, P., López-Pérez, D., et al.: Performance impact of LoS and NLoS transmissions in dense cellular networks. IEEE Trans. Wirel. Commun. **15**(3), 2365–2380 (2016)

12. Liu, H., Bo, J., Liu, H., et al.: A cross-range scaling algorithm for range instantaneous doppler ISAR imaging. In: IEEE CIE International Conference on Radar, pp. 674–676. IEEE (2011)
13. Wang, X., Wang, Z., Dea, B.O.: A TOA-based location algorithm reducing the errors due to non-line-of-sight propagation. IEEE Trans. Veh. Technol. 52(1), 112–116 (2003)
14. Gao, J., Su, F.: A new cross-range scaling algorithm based on FrFT. In: IEEE, International Conference on Signal Processing, pp. 2043–2046. IEEE (2010)
15. Zheng, Z., Hua, J., Jiang, B., et al.: A novel NLOS mitigation and localization algorithm exploiting the optimization method. Chin. J. Sens. Actuators 26(05), 722–727 (2013)
16. Liu, L.J., Han, Y.: Newton iterated signal source localization algorithm based on the least squares method. J. Proj. Rocket. Missiles Guid. 26(3), 325–328 (2006)

# Particle Swarm Optimization Based Location Recommendation for D2D Communication Underlying LTE Cellular Networks

Chiapin Wang[1,2(✉)], Ming-Hsun Wu[1], and Te-Sheng Tsai[1]

[1] Department of Electrical Engineering, National Taiwan Normal University,
Taipei, Taiwan
chiapin@ntnu.edu.tw
[2] MOST Joint Research Center for AI Technology and All Vista Healthcare,
Taipei, Taiwan

**Abstract.** In this paper, we present a particle swarm optimization based location recommendation scheme (PSO-LR) for Device-to-Device (D2D) Communication underlying Long Term Evolution (LTE) cellular networks. The proposed scheme enables D2D users to move to new locations which provide better link qualities and a higher system capacity. Also, it can balance resource allocation between cellular users and D2D users. The simulation results illustrate that the proposed PSO-LR scheme can effectively improve the total system capacity by location recommendation for D2D users, and reduce both the distance and time of location recommendation by comparison with other location recommendation scheme [11].

**Keywords:** Device-to-Device (D2D) communication
3GPP Long Term Evolution (LTE) · Interference mitigation

## 1 Introduction

Recently, Device-to-Device (D2D) communication has been widely investigated for the growing demands of Internet of Things (IoT). Different from traditional D2D techniques like Bluetooth or Wi-Fi, D2D communication underlying Long Term Evolution (LTE) cellular networks is able to use operator legal license band for progressing high-speed and large-scale proximity discovery or direct communication [1]. D2D communication underlying LTE cellular networks can improve power-saving efficiency by enabling a direct data transmission between User Equipment (UE) within a short range without the relay by Base Station (BS). Furthermore, it can enhance the spectrum utilization by frequency reuse, and thus improve the total system capacity.

However, D2D communication might cause inter-interferences to cellular networks and degrade the overall system performance. The interferences in a D2D communication underlying LTE cellular networks can be classified into two types: cross-tiered (i.e., between the D2D communication and cellular networks) and co-tiered (i.e., solely between D2D communication) [2]. There have been some recent works on the mitigation of interferences and/or the cooperation of resource allocation between macrocell

© ICST Institute for Computer Sciences, Social Informatics and Telecommunications Engineering 2018
L. Meng and Y. Zhang (Eds.): MLICOM 2018, LNICST 251, pp. 641–651, 2018.
https://doi.org/10.1007/978-3-030-00557-3_64

user equipment (MUE) and D2D user equipment (DUE) [1–10]. In [3], the authors discuss the cross-tiered interference problem between the D2D communication and 3G Wideband Code Division Multiple Access (WCDMA) cellular networks. In [4–10], the authors investigate the interference problem of D2D communication underlying Long Term Evolution (LTE) cellular networks. [7] concludes that the a severe interference situation can be mitigated using orthogonal resource distribution. However, using orthogonal resource distribution restricts the frequency reuse and hence degrades spectrum utilization efficiency. [8] investigates that the mutual interference between D2D Communication and Cellular Networks can be limited to a certain area. It is mentioned that D2D Communication is similar to the secondary user in cognitive networks. The difference between D2D Communication and the secondary user is that the latter will not be controlled by the primary user whereas D2D communication can be controlled by cellular networks. [9] discusses that in downlink of LTE, all the resources can be divided into center part and edge part. Edge part is for partial frequency reuse. If D2D communication uses edge part of resources, the interference can be limited to this area.

In this paper, we tackle the cross-tiered interference problem between the D2D communication and cellular networks, and propose a particle swarm optimization (PSO) based location recommendation scheme for D2D Communication underlying cellular networks. PSO is often used in the field of automatic control [12, 13]. In this paper, we apply PSO in location recommendation for D2D users to reduce the interference between D2D communication and cellular networks and hence improve the link qualities of both MUE users and D2D users. The results of simulations show that comparing with our existing scheme [11], the proposed PSO location recommendation scheme effectively reduces both the cost and time of location recommendation. The rest of this paper is organized as follows. Section 2 illustrates the proposed PSO location recommendation scheme. Section 3 explains the simulation setup and results. Finally, the conclusion is given in Sect. 4.

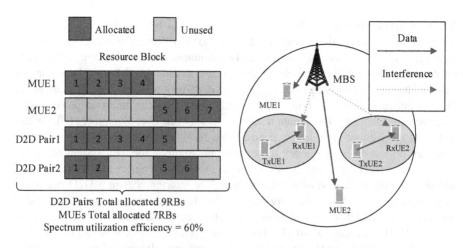

**Fig. 1.** Example of D2Ds with the proposed PSO LR scheme.

## 2  Proposed PSO Location Recommendation Scheme

To illustrate our resource allocation scheme and PSO Location Recommendation, consider the scenario shown in Fig. 1. The Transmission User Equipment (TxUE) of D2D communication can share the spectrum resources with cellular networks when it transmissions data to the Receiver User Equipment (RxUE). However, TxUE will produce mutual interference to MUE 2 because MUE 2 is within the transmission range of TxUE. Now, we consider the use of location recommendation for D2D users as shown in Fig. 2. When D2D communication pairs move, the interference from TxUE to MUE 2 is mitigated, and the total system capacity can be increased. The example illustrates that a location recommendation approach for D2D users can improve the overall transmission efficiency.

As Fig. 2 shows, location recommendation for D2D users can affectively increase the system capacity of cellular networks and D2D communication. In general, the location recommendation problem can be expressed as:

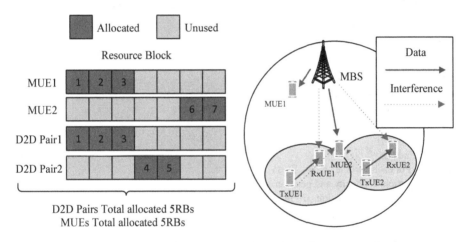

**Fig. 2.** Example of D2Ds in a co-channel interference scenario.

$$\hat{I} = F(I, \varphi, \psi) \tag{1}$$

where $\hat{I}$ represents the recommended location for D2D users; $I$ represents the current location of D2D users; $\varphi$ and $\psi$ represents the current and the desired system capacity of cellular networks and D2D communication, respectively. First, we mark $m$ coordinate points in the space of interest, measure the system capacity in each point, and record that in the database. Once the system capacity in the current point is inadequate, D2D users will be recommended to move to another location which provides sufficient system capacity. In this paper, the location recommendation approach is implemented based on a particle swarm optimization technique [13]. The fitness function in particle swarm optimization can be expressed as:

01: Construct and initialize the capacity map $\{(I_1,\varphi_1),(I_2,\varphi_2),.........,(I_m,\varphi_m)\}$

02: $D2D_h$ informs the serving $BS$ of $(I_h,\varphi_h)\rightarrow(\varphi_h,\psi_h)$

03: If $\varphi_h<\psi_h$

04: For k = 1 : m

05:     Export $(I_k,\varphi_k)$

06:     Set $\Lambda$ as the set of $\{(I_k^*,\varphi_k^*)\}$ in which $\varphi_k\geq\psi_h$

// $\varphi_k^*$ is adequate to the desired capacity level

07: End For

08: If $\Lambda\neq\phi$

//Calculate the moving distance from the current location $I_h$ to each location $I_k^*$ in $\Lambda$, $d_{h,k}$

09:     Initialize particles swarm optimization

10:     Repeat

11:         For each particle $i$ in $S$ do

// Construct and initialize the particle $S=\{(x_1,pd_1),(x_2,pb_2),..........,(x_i,pb_i)\}$

12:             If $f(x_i)<f(pb_i)$ then

//update the particle's best position by Fitness Eq. (5)

13:                 $pb_i=x_i$

14:             End If

15:             If $f(pb_i)<f(gb)$ then

//update the global best position

16:                 $gb=pb_i$

17:             End If

18:         End For

19:         For each particle $i$ in $S$ do

//update particle's velocity and position

20:             For each dimension $d$ in $D$ do

21:                 Execute Eq. (3) and (4)

22:             End For

23:         End For

24:         $n=n+1$ //advance iteration

25:     Until $n<MAX\_ITERATIONS$

26:     $\hat{I}=gb$

27: End if

28: Else $\Lambda=\phi$

29: Return $I_h$

30: Return $\hat{I}$

// Go to the new location $\hat{I}$

31: End if

32: End

**Fig. 3.** The proposed particle swarm optimization location recommendation algorithm (PSO-LR).

$$f(d_{\text{move}}) = \begin{cases} w_{\text{fit}}\left(C_{\text{D2D\_particle}}\right)\left(d_{\text{move}}\right)^{-1} & , C_{\text{D2D\_after}} - C_{\text{D2D\_before}} > C_{\text{D2D\_target}} \\ 0 & , \text{elsewhere} \end{cases},$$

(2)

where $w_{\text{fit}}$ is the fitness weight; $C_{\text{D2D\_particle}}$ is the system capacity where the particle locates; $C_{\text{D2D\_before}}$ is hypothetical system capacity before D2D users move; $C_{\text{D2D\_after}}$ is hypothetical system capacity after D2D users move; $C_{\text{D2D\_target}}$ is the target value of increased system capacity after a move. The objective of (2) is to provide a location recommendation which meets the situation $C_{\text{D2D\_before}} - C_{\text{D2D\_after}} > C_{\text{D2D\_target}}$. To combine PSO into the location recommendation approach, we use Eqs. (3) and (4) presented in [12],

$$v_{i,d}(n+1) = \xi v_{i,d}(n) + C_1\left(rnd_{0,1}\right)\left[pb_{i,d} - x_{i,d}(n)\right] \\ + C_2\left(rnd_{0,1}\right)\left[gb_d - x_{i,d}(n)\right],$$

(3)

$$x_{i,d}(n+1) = x_{i,d}(n) + v_{i,d}(n+1) \cdot T,$$

(4)

where $i$ represents the particle's index; $d$ represents the considered dimension; $n$ is the number of iteration; $C_1$ represents the acceleration constant for the cognitive component; $C_2$ is the acceleration constant for the social component; $T$ represents the systematic sampling time.

Once we complete the design of fitness function, the PSO-LR scheme will initialize all particles with random location $x_{i,d}$ and velocity $v_{i,d}$, and start to evaluate the fitness value of all particles. We divide our evaluation into two steps. In the first step, the current fitness value of each particle is compared with the best location $pb_{i,d}$ till now. If the current fitness value is better, $pb_{i,d}$ is updated with the current location. In the second step, the current fitness value of each particle is compared with the best overall location of particle swarm $gb_d$ till now. If the current fitness value is better, $gb_d$ is updated with the current location.

After updating particles' speed $v_{i,d}$ and location $x_{i,d}$ in Eqs. (3) and (4), PSO-LR will check whether the stop criteria is satisfied. If not, it will return to evaluation of the first phase, or select the position that has the shortest moving distance to D2D users.

Finally, since the shortest recommended distance does not represent the performance of the whole system, in order to get more accurate analysis to reinforce our proposed algorithm, we design a cost function for location recommendation, which can be expressed as Eq. (5),

$$LR_{\cos t}\left(w_{\cos t}, c_{ave}, r_{ave}, t_{ave}, d_{ave}\right) \\ = w_{\cos t}\left(c_{ave} \cdot r_{ave}\right)^{-1} \cdot t_{ave} \cdot d_{ave},$$

(5)

where $d_{ave}$ represents the average recommendation distance; $w_{\cos t}$ represents the cost weight; $c_{ave}$ represents the growth rate of system capacity; $r_{ave}$ represents the increasing rate of resource utilization; $t_{ave}$ represents the average calculation time. With the cost function, we can analyze the total effect of the advantages and disadvantages that PSO-LR produces. The pseudo code of the proposed PSO-LR scheme is shown in Fig. 3.

## 3  Performance Evaluation and Discussion

In this section, we conduct simulation scenarios of D2D communications underlying LTE cellular networks to demonstrate the effectiveness of the proposed PSO-LR schemes. The simulation is programmed using C++ by following the LTE standard [14]. The system parameters and their values are listed in Table 1. The simulation setup assumes a square area where the D2D users are randomly deployed. We compare the performance of the proposed PSO-LR scheme with that of our existing scheme [11] using brute force for producing location recommendation. The co-channel reuse scheme is used for resource allocation (i.e., the use of frequency spectrum will prevent interference as well as possible) to clearly examine the achieved performances with different LR schemes. The performance metrics are indexed as the recommended distance and recommended cost.

**Table 1.** Simulation parameters

| Notation | Parameter | Value |
|---|---|---|
| $D_{TxUE_j,RxUE_j}$ | The distance between D2D (meter) | 10 |
| $k$ | Number of MUEs | 30 |
| $h$ | Number of D2D pairs | 5 |
| $r$ | Number of resource block | 30 |
| $P_{MBS,RxUE_j}$ | Transmit power of BS (dBm) | 46 |
| $P_{TxUE_{j,k}}$ | Transmit power of TxUE (dBm) | 23 |
| $N$ | Noise power (dBm) | $-174$ |
| $\alpha$ | Path-loss exponent | 5 |
| $C_{D2D\_target}$ | Location recommendation capacity (bps) | 50 |
| $W_{fit}$ | Fitness weights | 10000 |
| $W_{cost}$ | Cost weights | 0.01 |
| $C_1$ | Constant value | 2 |
| $C_2$ | Constant value | 2 |
| $d$ | Dimensions $(x, y)$ | 2 |
| $i$ | Number of particles | 45 |
| $n$ | Iterations | 200–2000 |

According to our simulation scenarios, we respectively compare the data in different iteration number of brute-force LR with that of our PSO-LR scheme. We use both map sizes 1000 m * 1000 m (Case 1) and 2000 m * 2000 m (Case 2) with 5 pairs of D2D communication. The simulation results are illustrated with the average data in one thousand times.

The recommended distances using the proposed PSO-LR scheme and brute-force LR scheme [11] with different map sizes are shown in Fig. 4. As Fig. 4 shows, the recommended distance with PSO-LR is significantly lower than that with the brute-force LR scheme. Also, the more iteration number is, the shorter recommended distance is. Since the map size of Case 2 is bigger than that in Case 1, it has a slower convergence speed.

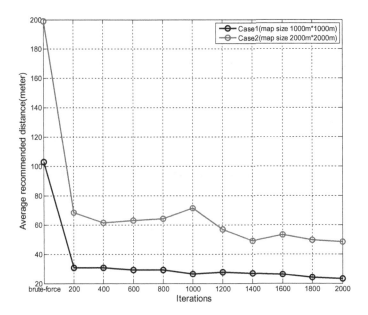

**Fig. 4.** Average recommended distance (meter).

The average execution time with different LR schemes are shown in Fig. 5. It is shown that the recommended times with PSO-LR are far less than that with the brute-force LR scheme. Also, in Case 2 with a bigger map, the advantage of shorter recommended time will be more obvious when using our PSO-LR scheme.

Figure 6 compares the average system capacity with the proposed PSO-LR scheme and brute-force LR scheme. It is shown that the system capacity with PSO-LR is merely lower than that brute-force LR (about 3.5% and 2.6% in Case 1 and Case 2, respectively). Although the increased system capacity with PSO-LR is beyond that brute-force LR, PSO-LR still can effectively increase the overall system capacity by location recommendation. Figure 7 shows the average resource reuse utilization ratio with the proposed PSO-LR scheme and brute-force LR scheme. It is shown that the resource reuse utilization ratio with PSO-LR is merely worse than that brute-force LR. The performance difference between PSO-LR and brute-force LR in Case 2 with a bigger map is less than that in Case 1.

Finally, we collect the recommended distance, execution time, capacity increase utilization ratio and resource reuse utilization ratio mentioned above to evaluate the cost in Eq. (5) to analyze the total effect of the advantages and disadvantages that PSO-LR produces. As Fig. 8 shows, our PSO-LR scheme is superior to brute-force LR scheme in terms of lower cost. From the simulation results shown in Figs. 4, 5, 6, 7 and

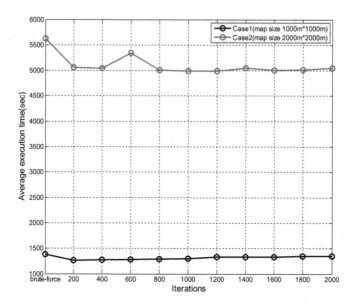

**Fig. 5.** Average execution time (sec).

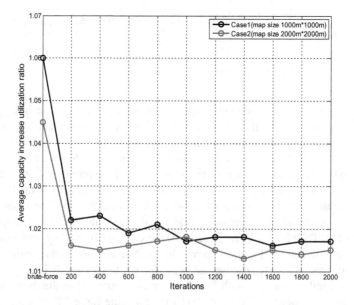

**Fig. 6.** Average capacity increase utilization ratio.

8, it is demonstrated that by comparison with brute-force LR scheme, the proposed PSO-LR scheme can effectively decrease the recommended distance and recommended time with a minor degradation of system capacity for D2D Communication underlying LTE cellular networks.

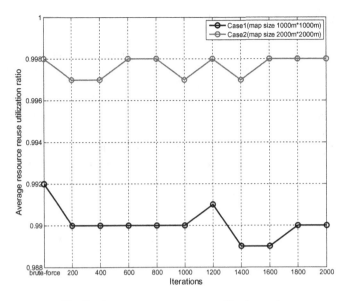

**Fig. 7.** Average resource reuse utilization ratio.

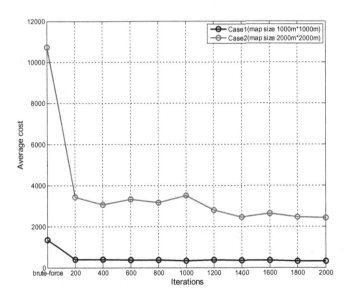

**Fig. 8.** Average cost.

# 4 Conclusion and Future Work

In this paper, we present a particle swarm optimization based location recommendation scheme (PSO-LR) for D2D Communication underlying LTE cellular networks. The proposed scheme enables D2D users to move to new locations which provide better link qualities and a higher system capacity. Also, it can balance resource allocation between cellular users and D2D users. The simulation results illustrate that the proposed PSO-LR scheme can effectively improve the total system capacity by location recommendation for D2D users, and reduce both the distance and time of location recommendation by comparison with other location recommendation scheme [11]. Our future research will investigate the joint problem of the location recommendation for D2D users combined with the deployment of cellular base stations.

**Acknowledgment.** The authors would like to thank the financial support provided by National Science Council (MOST 106-2221-E-003-023, and MOST 107-2634-F-155-001).

## REFERENCES

1. Cannon, M.J.: On the design of D2D synchronization in 3GPP release-12. In: IEEE International Conference on Communication Workshop (ICCW), pp. 633–638 (2015)
2. Fodor, G., et al.: Design aspects of network assisted device-to-device communications. IEEE Commun. Mag. **50**, 170–177 (2012)
3. Hakola, S., Chen, T., Lehtomaki, J., Koskela, T.: Device-to-device (D2D); communication in cellular network - performance analysis of optimum and practical communication mode selection. In: IEEE Wireless Communications and Networking Conference (WCNC), pp. 1–6 (2010)
4. Verenzuela, D., Miao, G.: Scalable interference coordination for device-to-device communications. In: IEEE Conference on Computer Communications Workshops (INFOCOM), pp. 348–353 (2015)
5. Yu, C.H., Doppler, K., Ribeiro, C., Tirkkonen, O.: Performance impact of fading interference to device-to-device communication underlaying cellular networks. In: IEEE 20th International Symposium on Personal, Indoor and Mobile Radio Communications (PIMRC), pp. 858–862 (2009)
6. Xu, C., Song, L., Han, Z., Li, D., Jiao, B.: Resource allocation using a reverse iterative combinatorial auction for device-to-device underlay cellular networks. In: IEEE Global Communications Conference (GLOBECOM), pp. 4542–4547 (2012)
7. Guo, B., Sun, S., Gao, Q.: Downlink interference management for D2D communication underlying cellular networks. In: IEEE/CIC International Conference on Communications in China - Workshops (CIC/ICCC), pp. 193–196 (2013)
8. Doppler, K., Rinne, M., Wijting, C., Ribeiro, C.B., Hugl, K.: Device-to-device communication as an underlay to LTE-advanced networks. IEEE Commun. Mag. **47**, 42–49 (2009)
9. Chen, X., Chen, L., Zeng, M., Zhang, X., Yang, D.: Downlink resource allocation for device-to-device communication underlaying cellular networks. In: 2012 IEEE 23rd International Symposium on Personal, Indoor and Mobile Radio Communications (PIMRC), pp. 232–237 (2012)

10. Hong, J., Park, S., Kim, H., Choi, S., Lee, K.B.: Analysis of device-to-device discovery and link setup in LTE networks. In: 2013 IEEE 24th Annual International Symposium on Personal, Indoor, and Mobile Radio Communications (PIMRC), pp. 2856–2860 (2013)
11. Wang, C., Fang, S.-H., Wu, H.-C., Chiou, S.-M., Kuo, W.-H., Lin, P.-C.: Novel user-placement ushering mechanism to improve quality-of-service for femtocell networks. IEEE Syst. J. **12**(2), 1993–2004 (2018)
12. Li, C., Yang, S., Nguyen, T.T.: A self-learning particle swarm optimizer for global optimization problems. IEEE Trans. Syst. Man Cybern. Part B (Cybern.) **42**, 627–646 (2012)
13. Shi, Y., Eberhart, R.: A modified particle swarm optimizer. In: IEEE International Conference on Evolutionary Computation Proceedings, pp. 69–73 (1998)
14. 3GPP and TR 36.912, Feasibility study for Further Advancements for E-UTRA (LTE-Advanced), V11.0.0 (Release 11) (2012)

# A Dual SIS Epidemic Model for Virus Spread Analysis in Cluster-Based Wireless Sensor Networks

Shensheng Tang[1](✉) and Chenghua Tang[2]

[1] Missouri Western State University, St. Joseph, MO 64506, USA
stang@missouriwestern.edu
[2] Guilin University of Electronic Technology, Guilin 541004, China
tch@guet.edu.cn

**Abstract.** In this paper, we propose a dual SIS epidemic model to study the dynamics of virus spread for a cluster-based wireless sensor network (WSN). The dual SIS model consists of two groups of general sensor nodes (SNs) and cluster heads (CHs) and describes the dynamics of virus spread through the interactions among the SNs and CHs. We transfer the proposed model to a nonlinear system of differential equations and perform detailed analysis about equilibrium points and stability. We develop the system stability conditions (i.e., $R_0$ and $R_1$) and draw the conclusions for the proposed system. Under specific conditions, the epidemic (virus spread) in both groups will either die out with any number of initial infectives or remain endemic and the number of infectives in each group will approach a nonzero constant positive level. We provide numerical results to validate our analysis. The proposed model and analysis is applicable to different types of networks with multiple groups of users.

**Keywords:** Wireless sensor network · SIS epidemic model · Susceptible node Infective node · Equilibrium point · Stability

## 1 Introduction

Recently, wireless sensor networks (WSNs) have received great attention due to their wide applications and the advances in micro-electro-mechanical systems (MEMS) technology. WSNs typically consist of a large number of sensor nodes (SNs) with limited signal transmission range. Cluster-based WSNs [1] can be managed locally by cluster heads (CHs). SNs in a cluster collect data and send them to its CH. An SN may exchange information with its neighbor SNs that are within its signal transmission range. Each CH manages the SNs in its cluster and relays the collected data to other CHs or the sink. A CH is located within the signal transmission range of all the sensors of its cluster and can communicate with its neighbor CHs at farther places. Thus in some applications, CHs may be more powerful than the SNs in terms of energy, bandwidth and memory [2] and provide inherent optimization and data aggregation/ fusion.

Sensors are resource-restrained devices with low defense capabilities and become vulnerable to software attacks such as sensor worm [3] or virus attack. Thus, security is

© ICST Institute for Computer Sciences, Social Informatics and Telecommunications Engineering 2018
L. Meng and Y. Zhang (Eds.): MLICOM 2018, LNICST 251, pp. 652–662, 2018.
https://doi.org/10.1007/978-3-030-00557-3_65

of great importance to WSNs. One promising method of analyzing virus spread in WSNs is to use the epidemiological models due to the similarity between software virus spread and epidemic disease transmission. In epidemic modeling, the total population is generally divided into three groups: susceptibles $S$, infectives $I$, and removed or immune $R$. Group $S$ are the individuals that may be infected with a desease. Group $I$ are the individuals that have been infected and can infect susceptibles. Group $R$ are the individuals that have recovered from the desease and are immune to further infection. A model composed of the above three groups is referred to as a susceptible-infective-recovered (SIR) model. For some deseases, such as malaria, the recovered individuals are not immunized and can be infected again. These deseases are usually described by susceptible-infective-susceptible (SIS) models, where there are only two groups of population: $S$ and $I$. Susceptibles become infectives due to infection, recovered after some infectious period due to medical or other factors, and become susceptibles again. Much research on epidemic modeling has been done for WSNs [4–9].

In [4], an SIR-M model was proposed to characterize the dynamics of virus spread process from a single node to the entire network. The proposed model can capture both the spatial and temporal dynamics of the virus spread process. In [5], a modified SIS epidemic model was proposed for virus spread analysis and an adjustable virus spread control scheme was developed to effectively restrain the virus outbreak. In [6], a susceptible-infected-quarantine-recovered-susceptible (SIQRS) model was proposed to describe the dynamics of worm propagation in WSNs. In [7], a hop-by-hop worm propagation model was proposed in mobile sensor networks and the worm infection capability was analyzed under a carryover epidemic model. In [8], a susceptible-infectious-quarantine-recovered (SIQR) model was proposed to describe dynamics of worms propagation with quarantine and to study the attacking behavior of possible worms in WSNs. In [9], an energy efficient susceptible-infected–terminally infected-recovered (SITR) model was formulated to analyze the attacking behaviour of worms in WSNs as well as the existence of equilibrium points and stability.

In this paper, we propose a dual SIS epidemic model to study the dynamics of virus spread for a cluster-based WSN. The dual SIS model describes the behavior of individual SNs and CHs and the interactions among them as well as incorporates specific WSN parameters such as number of neighbor nodes of an SN/CH. Based on the proposed model, we answer two basic questions under the occurrence of some initial viruses in SNs and/or CHs: (1) Under what conditions will the viruses in both SNs and CHs die out? (2) Under what conditions will the viruses in both groups of SNs and CHs remain endemic and if so, will the number of infectives in each group approach a constant positive level?

The remainder of the paper is organized as follows. Section 2 develops the modeling of a clustered-based WSN by the dual SIS model. Section 3 presents the detailed analysis and discussion. Section 4 presents numerical results. Finally, the paper is concluded in Sect. 5.

## 2 System Description and Modeling

The cluster-based WSN consists of a constant number of $N_1$ SNs and $N_2$ CHs, which are divided into two groups: susceptibles and infectives of SNs; susceptibles and infectives of CHs. Let $S_1(t)$ and $I_1(t)$ denote the number of susceptible and infective SN nodes at time t; $S_2(t)$ and $I_2(t)$ denote the number of susceptible and infective CH nodes at time t. Then, $S_1(t) + I_1(t) = N_1$, $S_2(t) + I_2(t) = N_2$. The $N_2$ clusters are deployed identically with m SNs and one CH in each cluster, i.e., $N_1 = mN_2$. SNs and CHs are installed with anti-virus programs that check the nodes periodically and equipped with omnidirectional antennas that have limited signal transmission range. Figure 1 shows a model of a cluster and some of its neighbor clusters. The data sensed from individual SNs can be transmitted to their respective CHs. Each CH can communicate with its neighbor CHs and with all the SNs inside its cluster. An SN can also communicate with its neighbor SNs for necessary information exchange if the neighbor nodes are inside the signal transmission range of the SN.

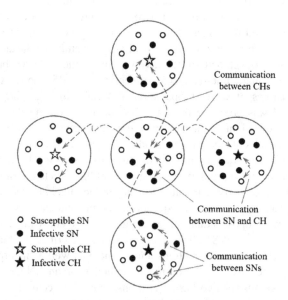

**Fig. 1.** A model of the cluster-based WSN.

In the dual SIS model without vital dynamics of population, i.e., no occurence of births and deaths of nodes, there are a constant number of susceptibles and infectives divided into two groups for the SNs and CHs respectively. The transition between different groups for a certain virus may be described as follows: a susceptible SN (in the first group, $S_1$) may become infected inside the same group ($I_1$) by contact with either an infective SN (in the first group, $I_1$) or an infective CH (in the second group, $I_2$), and after some infectious period, it is recovered by treatment and becomes a susceptible SN ($S_1$) again. Similarly, a susceptible CH (in the second group, $S_2$) may become infected inside its group ($I_2$) by contact with either an infective SN ($I_1$) or an infective CH ($I_2$), and after some infectious period, it is recovered by treatment and becomes a susceptible CH ($S_2$) again.

Assume that initially some SNs and/or CHs in the WSN become infected by viruses due to software attacks. The viruses can be spread together with normal data from the compromised node to its CH or its neighbor SNs through different communication protocols. As the virus spread process continues and the number of infected nodes increases, the virus spread might lead to endemic outbreak in a certain range, even the entire network failure due to insufficient workable nodes. On the other hand, anti-virus programs installed in SNs or CHs periodically check nodes and kill viruses for infective nodes. Thus, infective nodes (either SNs or CHs) can become susceptible (normal) from time to time and the viruses are possible to die out eventually in the network.

In order to formulate mathematical expressions, we make the following assumptions for the proposed model:

- The virus spread only happens through contact between a susceptible and an infective. Thus, contacting a neighbor does not necessarily lead to a new infective node. Only a susceptible neighbor of the infected node can become a new infective node. Contacting an infected neighbor by an infective obviously does not change the state of the system.
- The infection rate $\beta_{ij}$ represents the average number of infections per unit time of an infective in the jth group with the susceptible nodes in the ith group. For example, $\beta_{11}$ is the infection rate of an infectious SN with its susceptible neighbor SNs. Similarly, $\beta_{12}$ is the infection rate of an infectious CH with its susceptible SNs. $\beta_{21}$ is the infection rate of an infectious SN with its susceptible CH. $\beta_{22}$ is the infection rate of an infectious CH with its susceptible neighbor CHs. Clearly, $\beta_{ij}$ depends on the infectivity of a virus and the communication rate of a protocol since the virus spreads itself by piggybacking on normal data via regular communications. The larger the value of $\beta_{ij}$, the more susceptible nodes get infected every time.
- Infective nodes in group i (i = 1, 2) recover and are removed from the infective group at a constant rate $\gamma_i$ (called recovery rate) proportional to the number of infectives in the group. $\gamma_1$ is the recovery rate of infective SNs; $\gamma_2$ is the recovery rate of infective CHs. The probability of nodes that is infected at time $t_0$ and still remains infective at time $t_0 + t$ is exp($-\gamma_i t$), and the mean infectious period is $1/\gamma_i$.
- Each SN has $m_1$ neighbor SNs. Not all neighbors of an infective SN become infected every time. Let $p_0$ be the fraction of susceptible neighbor SNs infected by an infective SN every time; $p_1$ be the fraction of susceptible SNs infected by an infective CH every time.
- Similarly, each CH has $m_2$ neighbor CHs. Not all neighbors of an infective CH become infected every time. Let $p_2$ be the fraction of susceptible neighbor CHs infected by an infective CH every time.

For tractable analysis, we normalize the proper differential equations on $dI_1(t)/dt$ and $dI_2(t)/dt$ by dividing every $I_1(t)$ and $I_2(t)$ the population size $N_1$ and $N_2$ respectively, then the meanings of the variables $I_1(t)$ and $I_2(t)$ are changed to be the fractions of the total population in each group. Thus, the basic differential equations that describe the rate of change of the infective nodes in different groups are determined as:

$$I_1'(t) = \beta_{11}I_1\frac{p_0m_1}{m}S_1 + \beta_{12}I_2\frac{p_1}{N_1}S_1 - \gamma_1I_1, \tag{1}$$

$$I_2'(t) = \beta_{21}N_1I_1\frac{S_2}{N_2} + \beta_{22}I_2\frac{p_2m_2}{N_2}S_2 - \gamma_2I_2, \tag{2}$$

$$S_1 + I_1 = 1, \quad S_2 + I_2 = 1, \tag{3}$$

and initial condition

$$I_1(0) = I_{10}, \quad I_2(0) = I_{20}. \tag{4}$$

Note that in the above differential equations, we omit the parts of $S_1'(t)$ and $S_2'(t)$ due to the relationship in (3).

## 3 Analysis

We rearrange the above equations via a series of mathematics and obtain the following nonlinear system of differential equations:

$$I_1'(t) = aI_1 + bI_2 - (a+\gamma_1)I_1^2 - bI_1I_2, \tag{5}$$

$$I_2'(t) = cI_1 + dI_2 - cI_1I_2 - (d+\gamma_2)I_2^2, \tag{6}$$

where $a = \beta_{11}\frac{p_0m_1}{m} - \gamma_1$, $b = \beta_{12}p_1\frac{N_2}{N_1}$, $c = \beta_{21}\frac{N_1}{N_2}$, $d = \beta_{22}\frac{p_2m_2}{N_2} - \gamma_2$.

We can write the above Eqs. (5) and (6) in a vector form:

$$\vec{I}'(t) = A\vec{I}(t) + \vec{G}(t), \tag{7}$$

where $\vec{I}'(t) = \begin{bmatrix} I_1' \\ I_2' \end{bmatrix}$, $A = \begin{bmatrix} a & b \\ c & d \end{bmatrix}$, $\vec{I}(t) = \begin{bmatrix} I_1 \\ I_2 \end{bmatrix}$, $\vec{G}(t) = \begin{bmatrix} G_1 \\ G_2 \end{bmatrix}$, $G_1 = -(a+\gamma_1)I_1^2 - bI_1I_2$, and $G_2 = -cI_1I_2 - (d+\gamma_2)I_2^2$.

Therefore, the analysis of the virus spread in the proposed dual SIS model has been transferred to the analysis of a nonlinear system of differential equations represented by (7). In general, it may not be possible to find solutions for such a nonlinear system in terms of elementary functions. However, we can analyze some interesting questions without finding an explicit solution for the system. For example, what is the equilibrium point (or equilibrium solution) of the system? Is the equilibrium point stable? Under what condition does the equilibrium point converge to the origin or at a constant positive level on the phase plane?

### 3.1   Origin and Stability

An equilibrium solution of the nonlinear system (7) is a point $(I_1^*, I_2^*)$ on the phase plane (i.e., $I_1I_2$ plane) that makes $I_1'(t) = 0$ and $I_2'(t) = 0$, which is also called critical point, stationary point or rest point. By observation, it is easily determined that the point $(I_1^*, I_2^*) = (0, 0)$ is an equilibrium solution. This point denotes that no virus of SNs and CHs exists eventually (the viruses die out) and thus is referred to as a virus-free equilibrium. The proposed nonlinear system may have several equilibrium points. However, it is difficult to find them in terms of elementary functions. All the equilibrium points should be in the rectangular region D bounded by the $I_1$ and $I_2$ axes:

$$D = \{I_1, I_2 | 0 \le I_1, I_2 \le 1, I_1 + S_1 = 1, I_2 + S_2 = 1\}. \tag{8}$$

In order to find the local behavior of the proposed nonlinear system and determine the stability property of equilibrium points, one of the most useful methods is to approximate the nonlinear system with a linear system around the equilibrium points, which is referred to as linearization of the nonlinear system. We observe that the proposed system is almost linear system [10] since the vector $\vec{I}'(t)$ is a continuously differentiable function and the Jacobian matrix of the system at this equilibrium point is invertible (i.e., its determinant is not equal to zero). The Jacobian matrix is calculated by respectively differentiating (5) and (6) with respect to $I_1$ and $I_2$ [11]:

$$J\big|_{(I_1, I_2)=(0,0)} = \begin{bmatrix} \partial F_1/\partial I_1 & \partial F_1/\partial I_2 \\ \partial F_2/\partial I_1 & \partial F_2/\partial I_2 \end{bmatrix} = \begin{bmatrix} a & b \\ c & d \end{bmatrix}. \tag{9}$$

Equation (9) also verifies that J = A in the almost linear system [10]. The characteristic equation associated with (9) is

$$\lambda^2 - (a+d)\lambda + ad - bc = 0$$

with the characteristic roots are given by

$$\lambda_{1,2} = [(a+d) \pm \sqrt{(a-d)^2 + 4bc}]/2. \tag{10}$$

From the stability properties of differential equations [10, 11], if the characteristic roots are distinct and both are negative, then the equilibrium point is asymptotically stable. That is, if $\lambda_2 < \lambda_1 < 0$, $(I_1, I_2)$ approaches the equilibrium point $(0, 0)$ as t approaches infinity. The condition can be easily transferred to the following condition:

$$a + d < 0 \text{ and } ad - bc \ge 0. \tag{11}$$

From the above condition and substituting in (11) by the specific arguments of a, b, c and d, we derive the following theorem.

**Theorem 1.** For the dual SIS model in (7), if the two thresholds $R_0 < 1$ and $R_1 \le 1$, then the epidemic (virus) will die out in both groups for any number of initial infectives (i.e., the origin is asymptotically stable in the rectangular region D in (8)). The thresholds are defined as follows.

$$R_0 = \frac{\beta_{11} \frac{p_0 m_1}{m} + \beta_{22} \frac{p_2 m_2}{N_2}}{\gamma_1 + \gamma_2}, \tag{12}$$

$$R_1 = \frac{\beta_{11} \beta_{22} p_1}{(\beta_{11} \frac{p_0 m_1}{m} - \gamma_1)(\beta_{22} \frac{p_2 m_2}{N_2} - \gamma_2)}. \tag{13}$$

## 3.2   Endemic Equilibrium Point and Stability

If $ad - bc < 0$, we can check from (10) that the characteristic roots $\lambda_1$ and $\lambda_2$ will have one positive and one negative. Note that this result is obtained regardless of the sign of $(a + d)$. From the stability properties of differential equations [10, 11], if the characteristic roots have different signs, then the equilibrium system state will get away from the origin. In this case, the point $(0, 0)$ is called a saddle point and is obviously unstable. Then another question arises, under this condition (i.e., $ad - bc < 0$), is there any other equilibrium point at some positive level in the region D for the proposed system (7)?

We observe that in the system, the number of infectives in each group at a positive equilibrium point is impossible to be 1 (for example, if $I_1 = 1$ in (5), then $I_1'(t) < 0$). The only equilibrium point where the stable value is zero is the origin (for example, for $I_1'(t) = 0$ with $I_1 = 0$, we have $I_2 = 0$). Thus, we limit the analysis of equilibrium points to the region:

$$D_0 = \{I_1, I_2 | 0 < I_1, I_2 < 1, I_1 + S_1 = 1, I_2 + S_2 = 1\}. \tag{14}$$

Consider our analysis in the $I_1 I_2$-plane. For $0 < I_2 < 1$, applying $I_1 = 0$ to (7), we have $I_1'(t)|_{I_1=0} = bI_2 > 0$; applying $I_1 = 1$ to (7), we have $I_1'(t)|_{I_1=1} = -\gamma_1 < 0$. Therefore, there exists a value $I_1^* \in (0, 1)$ such that $I_1'(t)\big|_{I_1=I_1^*} = 0$ and the value is unique. The following gives the proof of uniqueness.

Assume that there is another nonzero equilibrium solution $K_1 \in (0, 1)$ in (7) that is not equal to $I_1^*$. Without loss of generality, we let $I_1^* < K_1$, then we have

$$0 = aI_1^* + bI_2 - (a + \gamma_1)(I_1^*)^2 - bI_1^* I_2 = aK_1 + bI_2 - (a + \gamma_1)K_1^2 - bK_1 I_2. \tag{15}$$

Multiplying $K_1/I_1^*$ on both sides of the first equation and noting that $a$, $b$, and $\gamma_1$ are all positive, we have

$$0 = aK_1 + bI_2 \frac{K_1}{I_1^*} - (a + \gamma_1)K_1^2 \frac{I_1^*}{K_1} - bK_1 I_2 > aK_1 + bI_2 - (a + \gamma_1)K_1^2 - bK_1 I_2. \tag{16}$$

There is a contradiction for (16) and (15), so there is only one equilibrium solution of $I_1(t)$ in (7) in $D_0$.

Similar result can be shown that there is a unique equilibrium solution $I_2^* \in (0, 1)$ of $I_2(t)$ in (7) in $D_0$. The earlier condition $ad - bc < 0$ can be converted as $R_1 > 1$. The expression of $R_1$ is referred to as (13). We give the following theorem to summarize the above analysis.

**Theorem 2.** For the dual SIS model in (7), if the threshold $R_1 > 1$, then the epidemic (virus) will remain endemic in both groups for any number of initial infectives and the number of infectives in each group will approach a nonzero constant positive level (i.e., a unique equilibrium point exists inside the region $D_0$ in (14)).

## 4   Numerical Results

In this section, we present numerical results to validate our analytic results for the dual SIS model. We study the phase portraits in the $I_1 I_2$-plane to visualize how the trajectories traced by the solutions of the proposed system would behave in the long run as well as the number of infective SNs and CHs $I_1(t)$ and $I_2(t)$ with respect to time $t$. The evaluation is performed under a WSN of m = 40 identical clusters with 25 SNs and one CH in each cluster. The values of other parameters are shown in individual figures. Note that all parameters are given in dimensionless units, which can be mapped to specific units of measurement.

Figure 2 shows the direction field for our system of differential equations along with two trajectories on the phase plane. Two starting points $(I_{10}, I_{20}) = (0.55, 0.25)$ and $(0.25, 0.15)$ are evaluated respectively. It is clearly observed that the equilibrium point $(0, 0)$ is asymptotically stable regardless of any starting points. The trajectories of two different starting points eventually converge to the origin. This verifies the result of Theorem 1. The thresholds under the given parameter configuration are obtained as $R_0 = 0.0145 < 1$; $R_1 = 0.1238 < 1$. Note that the arrows from the top left of the trajectories go down towards to the origin, while the arrows from the bottom right of the

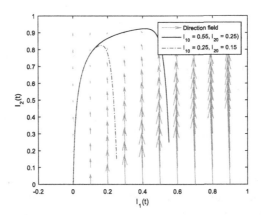

**Fig. 2.** A direction field and some trajectories for the dual SIS system with origin equilibrium point (Parameter values: $p_0 = 0.2$; $p_1 = 0.3$; $p_2 = 0.1$; $m_1 = 5$; $m_2 = 4$; $\beta_{11} = 0.3$; $\beta_{12} = 0.5$; $\beta_{21} = 0.7$; $\beta_{22} = 0.4$; $\gamma_1 = 0.5$; $\gamma_2 = 0.6$).

trajectories go up along with the trajectories to the origin. The arrows in the direction field [11] are tangents to the actual solutions to the differential equations, in which we can learn the solution property of the nonlinear system. The direction field can also be used to find information on the long term behavior of the solution.

Figure 3 shows the numerical simulations of the virus spread dynamics of $I_1(t)$ and $I_2(t)$ with respect to time for the dual SIS system with origin equilibrium point. We observe that under the current system configuration, $I_1(t)$ decreases with respect to time; while $I_2(t)$ first increases with respect to time and when it goes to a certain infection level, it begins to decrease. Both $I_1(t)$ and $I_2(t)$ eventually approach to the origin $(0, 0)$, which means the infectives eventually die out regardless of their initial conditions.

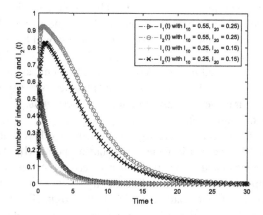

**Fig. 3.** The dynamics of $I_1(t)$ and $I_2(t)$ for the dual SIS system with origin equilibrium point (See Fig. 2 for the parameter values).

Figure 4 shows the direction field for the nonlinear system along with two trajectories on the phase plane. Two starting points $(I_{10}, I_{20}) = (0.55, 0.25)$ and $(0.10, 0.10)$ are evaluated respectively. It is observed that the system state approaches to a constant positive equilibrium point. Each group of SNs and CHs has a different constant value. The equilibrium point is asymptotically stable regardless of any starting point. This verifies the result of Theorem 2. The threshold condition in this case is obtained as $R_1 = 4.9205 > 1$.

Figure 5 shows the numerical simulations of the virus spread dynamics of $I_1(t)$ and $I_2(t)$ with respect to time for the dual SIS system with a positive equilibrium point. We observe that under the current system configuration, when the starting point is $(I_{10}, I_{20}) = (0.55, 0.25)$, $I_1(t)$ decreases from its initial value to a constant positive value (endemic of SNs); $I_2(t)$ first increases from its initial value and when it goes to a certain infection level, it begins to decrease to another constant positive level (endemic of CHs). When the starting point is $(I_{10}, I_{20}) = (0.10, 0.10)$, $I_1(t)$ increases from its initial value to a constant positive value (endemic of SNs); $I_2(t)$ also increases from its initial value to another constant positive level (endemic of CHs).

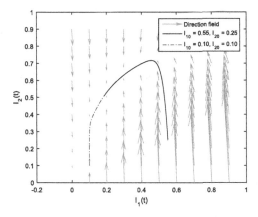

**Fig. 4.** A direction field and some trajectories for the dual SIS system with endemic equilibrium point (Parameter values: $p_0 = 0.8$; $p_1 = 0.8$; $p_2 = 0.1$; $m_1 = 5$; $m_2 = 2$; $\beta_{11} = 0.7$; $\beta_{12} = 0.8$; $\beta_{21} = 0.1$; $\beta_{22} = 0.15$; $\gamma_1 = 0.15$; $\gamma_2 = 0.45$).

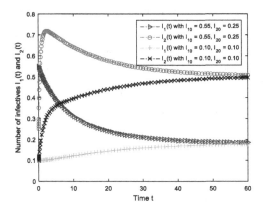

**Fig. 5.** The dynamics of $I_1(t)$ and $I_2(t)$ for the dual SIS system with endemic equilibrium point (See Fig. 4 for the parameter values).

## 5   Conclusions

We proposed a dual SIS epidemic model to study the dynamics of virus spread for a cluster-based WSN. The dual SIS model consists of two groups of SNs and CHs and describes the dynamics of virus spread through the interactions between SNs and CHs. We performed detailed analysis about equilibrium points and stability and developed the system stability conditions. Finally, we drew the conclusion for the proposed system: if the two thresholds $R_0 < 1$ and $R_1 \leq 1$, then the epidemic (virus) will die out in both groups for any number of initial infectives; if the threshold $R_1 > 1$, then the epidemic (virus) will remain endemic in both groups for any number of initial infectives and the number of infectives in each group will approach a nonzero constant positive level. We provided numerical results to validate our analysis. The proposed model and analysis is applicable to different types of networks with multiple groups of users.

**Acknowledgments.** This work was supported in part by the National Natural Science Foundation of China under Grant No. 61462020.

# References

1. Tang, S., Li, W.: QoS supporting and optimal energy allocation for a cluster-based wireless sensor network. Comput. Commun. **29**(13–14), 2569–2577 (2006)
2. Younis, M., Youssef, M., Arisha, K.: Energy-aware routing in cluster based sensor networks. In: Proceedings of 10th IEEE/ACM Symposium on Modeling, Analysis and Simulation of Computer and Telecom Systems (MASCOTS 2002), Fort Worth, TX (2002)
3. Wang, T., et al.: Propagation modeling and defending of a mobile sensor worm in wireless sensor and actuator networks. Sensors **17**(1), 139 (2017). https://doi.org/10.3390/s17010139
4. Tang, S., Mark, B.L.: Analysis of virus spread in wireless sensor networks: an epidemic model. In: 7th International Workshop on the Design of Reliable Communication Networks (DRCN 2009), Washington D.C., USA, 25–28 October 2009 (2009)
5. Tang, S., Myers, D., Yuan, J.: Modified SIS epidemic model for analysis of virus spread in wireless sensor networks. Int. J. Wirel. Mob. Comput. **6**(2), 99–108 (2013)
6. Mishra, B.K., Srivastava, S.K., Mishra, B.: A quarantine model on the spreading behavior of worms in wireless sensor network. Trans. IoT Cloud Comput. **2**(1), 1–12 (2014)
7. Ho, J.-W.: Hop-by-hop worm propagation with carryover epidemic model in mobile sensor networks. Computers **4**(4), 283–292 (2015). https://doi.org/10.3390/computers4040283
8. Khanh, N.H.: Dynamics of a worm propagation model with quarantine in wireless sensor networks. Appl. Math. Inf. Sci. **10**(5), 1739–1746 (2016)
9. Upadhyay, R.K., Kumari, S.: Bifurcation analysis of an e-epidemic model in wireless sensor network. Int. J. Comput. Math. (2017). https://doi.org/10.1080/00207160.2017.1336550
10. Brannan, J.R., Boyce, W.E.: Differential Equations: An Introduction to Modern Methods and Applications, 3rd edn. Wiley, Hoboken (2015)
11. Sanchez, D.A.: Ordinary Differential Equations and Stability Theory: An Introduction. Dover Publications, New York (2012)

# Communication-Efficient Decentralized Cooperative Data Analytics in Sensor Networks

Liang Zhao[1], Zhihua Li[2(✉)], and Shujie Guo[2]

[1] University of South Carolina Upstate, Spartanburg, SC 29303, USA
lzhao2@uscupstate.edu
[2] Jiangnan University, Wuxi 214122, Jiangsu, China
zhli@jiangnan.edu.cn, 1149165216@qq.com

**Abstract.** This paper presents a novel approach enabling communic-ation-efficient decentralized data analytics in sensor networks. The proposed method aims to solve the decentralized consensus problem in a network such that all the nodes try to estimate the parameters of the global model and they should reach an agreement on the value of the model eventually. Our algorithm leverages broadcasting communication and is performed in a asynchronous manner in the sense that each node can update its estimate independent of others. All the nodes in the network can run the same algorithm in parallel and no synchronization is required. Numerical experiments demonstrate that the proposed algorithm outperforms the benchmark, and it is a promising approach for big data analytics in sensor networks.

**Keywords:** Big data · Data analytics · Decentralized computing
Sensor networks · Asynchronous algorithm

## 1 Introduction

In the era of big data, the goal of transforming big data into actionable insights brings opportunities and also challenges into the community. High volume of data is generated from all over the world everyday. At the same time, data is coming in at a much higher speed, often close to real-time. Thus, there is a huge demand for efficient fast data analyzing approaches. In addition, to analyze big data, big model is always equipped in order to empower deep insights extraction. It is known that many big data analytics problems boil down to: How to apply advanced data analytics programs to large-scale problems with Big Data and Big Model. Essentially, convex optimization is at the core of solving many of these models. Convex optimization has applications in a wide range of disciplines, such as smart grid [1–3], seismic imaging [4,5], and sensor networks [6,7]. Recently, distributed optimization attracts a lot of attention in the optimization and computing society. It has shown potential to be a promising approach for designing scalable big data analytics solution. In general, distributed optimization can be

© ICST Institute for Computer Sciences, Social Informatics and Telecommunications Engineering 2018
L. Meng and Y. Zhang (Eds.): MLICOM 2018, LNICST 251, pp. 663–671, 2018.
https://doi.org/10.1007/978-3-030-00557-3_66

categorized into synchronous optimization and asynchronous optimization. In synchronous optimization, each node needs to wait for its slowest neighbor's information in order to proceed. On the contrary, asynchronous optimization can avoid this issues allowing each node to perform its decision independently and locally. Distributed optimization methods for asynchronous models have been designed in [8–10]. In [8,9], the alternating direction method of multipliers (admm) based algorithms have been proposed. Regarding their communication scheme, every node needs to wake up one of its neighbors randomly to exchange information in each iteration. However, the two works are based on unicast, which is much less preferable than broadcast communication, especially in real-world wireless sensor network scenario. Tsitsiklis [10] proposed an asynchronous model for distributed optimization, while in its model each node maintains a partial vector of the global variable. It is different from our goal of decentralized consensus such that each node contains an estimate of the global common interest. The first broadcast-based asynchronous distributed/decentralized consensus method was proposed in [11]. However, the algorithm is designed only for consensus average problem without "real objective function". Nedic [12] first filled this gap by considering general decentralized convex optimization under the asynchronous broadcast setting. It adopted the asynchronous broadcast model in [11] and developed a (sub)gradient-based update rule for its computation. By replacing (sub)gradient computation with full local optimization, an improved algorithm has been designed in terms of the number of communication rounds [13]. In this presenting work, we propose a novel method combing neighbors' (sub)gradient information in order to further speed up the algorithms in [13].

## 2   Problem Formulation

The formulation of the problem investigated in this paper can be described as follows. Consider an undirected connected network $\mathcal{G} = (\mathcal{V}, \mathcal{E})$ where $\mathcal{V}$ denotes the node set and $\mathcal{E}$ is the edge set. The size of network is $m = |\mathcal{V}|$ (cardinality of the set $\mathcal{V}$) and two nodes $i, j$ are called neighbors if $(i, j) \in \mathcal{E}$. Assume an objective $F_i : \mathbb{R}^n \to \mathbb{R}$ is only available to each node (sensor or agent) $i$. It is the data and acquisition process at node $i$. The goal is to find the global consensus solution $x \in X$ to minimize the optimization problem as follows.

$$\min_{x \in X} \left\{ F(x) := \sum_{i=1}^{m} F_i(x) \right\}. \tag{1}$$

Solving (1) in (wireless) sensor networks is nontrivial. First, data is generated in a distributed manner and it would be very costly and even infeasible to transmit all the data into a central place for post-processing due to bandwidth and energy constraints. Each node is able to access its local data only. Second, each node needs to exchange information with other nodes in order to obtain the optimal solution for the whole model. However, each node is assumed to communicate with its immediate neighbors only since multi-hop communication in the presenting application is very expensive and undesriable. In this work, we adopt broadcasting in our communication scheme. Third, the key challenge solving (1) in the network is the potential high communication cost because each node has only partial knowledge of the whole network. Hence, designing a communication-efficient algorithm would make decentralized data analytics in sensor networks feasible.

**Notation.** Let $x \in \mathbb{R}^n$ be a column vector in problem (1), and $x^i \in \mathbb{R}^n$ be the local copy held privately by node $i$ for every $i \in \mathcal{V}$. Without further remark, vectors are all column vectors. Subscript $k$ is outer iteration number, which is also the number of communication.

**Problem Setup.** Each sensor node is assumed to have its local clock that ticks at a user-customized Poisson rate for unit time, which is independent of the clocks of the other nodes. Each node broadcasts its current estimate to its neighbors at each tick of its local clock. During broadcasting, each sensor receives neighbors' information subject to link failures. For example, when node $i$ broadcasts, its neighbor $j$ will receive $i$'s iterate with probability $p_{ij}$. It is equivalent to consider a virtual global clock existing in the network for the algorithm analysis. Since the Poisson clock of each node (suppose rate $= 1$) is independent of each other, it is same as a global clock with Poisson rate $m$. We can then analyze the problem given that in each global iteration only one node broadcasts its value. There are several additional assumptions adopted in this paper as follows.

**Assumption 1.** *The gradient of function $F_i$ is bounded such that $\|\nabla F_i\| \leq G$, where $G > 0$ is some positive number.*

**Assumption 2.** *The solution set of (1) is nonempty. The private local objective function $F_i$, $i \in \mathcal{V}$ is (sub)differentiable and convex.*

**Assumption 3.** *The constraint set $X$ is bounded.*

**Assumption 4.** $\sum_{k=1}^{\infty} \frac{\rho_{i,k}}{k\alpha_{i,k}} < \infty$, $\sum_{k=1}^{\infty} \frac{\beta_{i,k}}{k\alpha_{i,k}} < \infty$ *almost surely.*

# 3   Proposed Algorithm

## 3.1   Local Full Minimization + Neighbor's (sub)gradient

The main computation steps in this proposed algorithm are:

$$y_k^i = \theta x_{k-1}^{i_k} + (1 - \theta) x_{k-1}^i,$$
$$x_k^i = P_X \left[ \operatorname*{argmin}_x \left\{ \frac{1}{2\alpha_{i,k}} \|x - y_k^i\|^2 + F_i(x) + \rho_{i,k} \left( \sum_{u \in \mathcal{N}_i} \tilde{\nabla} F_u(x_{\tau_{u,k}}^u)^T (x - y_k^i) \right) \right\} \right]. \quad (2)$$

The algorithm can be summarized as follows.

---

**Algorithm 1.** Decentralized Cooperative Data Analytics (DCDA) Algorithm

---

**Input:** Starting point $x_0^1, x_0^2, \cdots, x_0^m$.
**while** *each node* $i, i \in \{1, 2, \cdots, m\}$ *asynchronously* **do**
   **if** *node* $i_k$*'s local clock ticks now* **then**
      Node $i_k$ broadcasts its estimate $x_{k-1}^{i_k}$ and (sub)gradient $\tilde{\nabla} F_i(x_{k-1}^{i_k})$ to
      its neighbors; Node $i$ who receives node $i_k$'s broadcast updates its
      solution $x_k^i$ based on (2).
   **end**
**end**

---

*Remark 1.* In (2), neighbor's (sub)gradients $\left(\sum_{u \in \mathcal{N}_i} \tilde{\nabla} F_u(x_{\tau_{u,k}}^u)^T \left(x - y_k^i\right)\right)$ are incorporated in the update. Node $i$ then computes its next iterate by performing local minimization over all the terms in second equation of (2).

**Theorem 1.** *Let* $\left\{x_k^i\right\}, \forall i \in \mathcal{V}, k \geq 0$ *be the sequence generated by DCDA Algorithm and given that all the assumptions are satisfied. Then we can have:*

$$\sum_{k=1}^{\infty} \frac{1}{k} \|x_{k-1}^i - \bar{x}_{k-1}\| < \infty, \text{ and } \lim_{k \to \infty} \|x_k^i - \bar{x}_k\| = 0 \text{ almost surely.}$$

**Theorem 2.** *Let* $\left\{x_k^i\right\}, \forall i \in \mathcal{V}, k \geq 0$ *be the sequences generated by DCDA Algorithm and given that all the assumptions are satisfied. Then the sequences converges to a same optimal point almost surely for any node* $i$.

*Remark 2.* Theorem 1 implicates that all the nodes in the network will reach a consensus on the solution of the global model defined in (1). In addition, Theorem 2 indicates that the consensus solution is optimal. The attack plan for the proof is similar to the counterpart in [13]. The difference between our proposed algorithm and the local optimization based one in [13] is the extra item from neighbor's (sub)gradients $\left(\sum_{u \in \mathcal{N}_i} \tilde{\nabla} F_u(x_{\tau_{u,k}}^u)^T \left(x - y_k^i\right)\right)$. The main task is to bound this extra item and then we can use the proof framework in [13] to verify Theorems 1 and 2. We leave the details of the proof to the longer report due to page limit of this conference.

## 4    Interpretation of the Proposed Algorithms

### 4.1    Algorithm Interpretation

In this section, we will interpret and show the rationale of proposing DCDA algorithm. Now assume every node $i$ in the network can access all the local objective functions $F_i, i \in \{1, 2, \cdots, m\}$. The optimal strategy for every node $i$ to obtain the solution then becomes as follows.

$$x^i = \underset{x}{\operatorname{argmin}} \sum_{j=1}^{m} F_j(x), \forall i \in \{1, 2, \cdots, m\}. \tag{3}$$

That is, each node can directly try to minimize the summation of all the local objective functions as a "centralized" machine does (assuming all the data is available in this centralized node). To solve (3), we can evaluate a proximal operator as follows [14].

$$x^i = \mathbf{prox}_{\alpha F}(v) = \underset{x}{\operatorname{argmin}} \left\{ \frac{1}{2\alpha} \|x - v\|^2 + F(x) \right\}, \forall i \in \{1, 2, \cdots, m\}, \quad (4)$$

with certain constant $v$ (independent of decision variable $x$) and parameter $\alpha > 0$. Note that each node $i$ can obtain the optimal solution by evaluating (4), and more importantly there is no communication needed between nodes since $F(x)$ contains all the information in the network. However, this is under an ideal scenario (every node $i$ has the knowledge of all the local functions $F_j$) which will not be valid in our setting of decentralized sensor networks. Considering that $F_i$ is only available to node $i$ locally (according to our assumption in this paper), if we replace the term $F(x)$ in (4) with $F_i$ and let $v = y_k^i$ and $\alpha = \alpha_k^i$, the update rule for node $i$ in [13] is then derived as follows.

$$
\begin{aligned}
y_k^i &= \theta x_{k-1}^{i_k} + (1 - \theta) x_{k-1}^i, \\
x_k^i &= \mathbf{prox}_{\alpha_{i,k} F_i}(y_k^i) = \underset{x}{\operatorname{argmin}} \left\{ \frac{1}{2\alpha_{i,k}} \|x - y_k^i\|^2 + F_i(x) \right\}.
\end{aligned}
\quad (5)
$$

Further linearizing $F_i(x)$ in (5) yields Nedic's algorithm as follows [12].

$$
\begin{aligned}
y_k^i &= \theta x_{k-1}^{i_k} + (1 - \theta) x_{k-1}^i, \\
x_k^i &= \underset{x}{\operatorname{argmin}} \left\{ \frac{1}{2\alpha_{i,k}} \|x - y_k^i\|^2 + \left\langle \tilde{\nabla} F_i(y_k^i), x \right\rangle \right\} \\
&= y_k^i - \alpha_{i,k} \tilde{\nabla} F_i(y_k^i).
\end{aligned}
\quad (6)
$$

The deduction of the last step in (6) is based on the optimality condition described as follows.

$$\frac{1}{\alpha_{i,k}}(x_k^i - y_k^i) + \tilde{\nabla} F_i(y_k^i) = 0.$$

The first step in (5) and (6) takes the weighted average of node $i$'s solution and neighbor $i_k$'s solution which is the most recent broadcast received. This averaging step aims to mix the neighbor's information and enforce consensus of solutions among all the nodes in the network. Next, the proximal step in (5) forces the new solution $x$ to be close to $y_k^i$ (the weighted average) and optimizes the local objective function $F_i$ simultaneously. Parameter $\alpha_{i,k}$ controls the trade-off between the aforementioned two objectives. To speed up the process of decentralized consensus optimization, we are motivated to propose algorithms by adding the following item into the proximal steps in (5).

$$\sum_{u \in \mathcal{N}_i} \tilde{\nabla} F_u(x_{\tau_{u,k}}^u)^T (x - y_k^i) \quad (7)$$

The term in (7) contains node $i$'s neighbors' (sub)gradient information and it can be seen that (7) is a linear approximation to $\sum_{u \in \mathcal{N}_i} F_u$. Comparing (2) with (5) we can see that in (2) node $i$ is (approximately) optimizing $F_i(x) + \sum_{u \in \mathcal{N}_i} F_u(x)$ while (5) is optimizing local objective function $F_i(x)$ only. Hence, (2) is a better approximation to the ideal case in (4). In order to execute the computations in (2), node $i_k$ needs to broadcast its estimate $x_{k-1}^{i_k}$ and (sub)gradient $\tilde{\nabla} F_i(x_{k-1}^{i_k})$ to its neighbors.

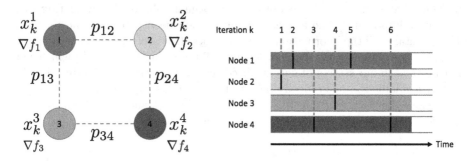

**Fig. 1.** Network model and asynchronous computing. Left: An example of decentralized sensor network. Right: Asynchronous computing model.

### 4.2  An Example of Executing the Proposed Algorithm

We assume the algorithms are performed in a decentralized sensor network illustrated in Fig. 1. There are four nodes in this cyclic network and it is clear to see that $\mathcal{N}_1 = \{2, 3\}$, $\mathcal{N}_2 = \{1, 4\}$, $\mathcal{N}_3 = \{1, 4\}$, $\mathcal{N}_4 = \{2, 3\}$. The algorithms run as follows.

**Iteration 1:** Node 2's clock ticks and it broadcasts $x_0^2$ and $\tilde{\nabla} f_2(x_0^2)$. Node 1 and 4 receive the broadcast and use $x_0^2$ and $\tilde{\nabla} f_2(x_0^2)$ to update $x_1^1$ and $x_1^4$ based on (2), respectively. Set $x_1^1 \leftarrow x_0^2$, $x_1^3 \leftarrow x_0^3$.

**Iteration 2:** Node 1's clock ticks and it broadcasts $x_1^1$ and $\tilde{\nabla} f_1(x_1^1)$. Node 2 and 3 receive the broadcast and use $x_1^1$ and $\tilde{\nabla} f_1(x_1^1)$ to update $x_2^2$ and $x_2^3$ based on (2), respectively. Set $x_2^1 \leftarrow x_1^1$, $x_2^4 \leftarrow x_1^4$.

**Iteration 3:** Node 4's clock ticks and it broadcasts $x_2^4$ and $\tilde{\nabla} f_4(x_2^4)$. Node 2 and 3 receive the broadcast and use $x_2^4$ and $\tilde{\nabla} f_1(x_1^1) + \tilde{\nabla} f_4(x_2^4)$ to update $x_3^2$ and $x_3^3$ based on (2), respectively. Set $x_3^1 \leftarrow x_2^1$, $x_3^4 \leftarrow x_2^4$.

**Iteration 4:** Node 3's clock ticks and it broadcasts $x_3^3$ and $\tilde{\nabla} f_3(x_3^3)$. Node 1 and 4 receive the broadcast and use $x_3^3$ and $\tilde{\nabla} f_2(x_0^2) + \tilde{\nabla} f_3(x_3^3)$ to update $x_4^1$ and $x_4^4$ based on (2), respectively. Set $x_4^2 \leftarrow x_3^2$, $x_4^3 \leftarrow x_3^3$.

It can be seen that after four iterations, each node has gathered all its neighbors' (sub)gradient information. As the algorithm goes on, the neighbors' (sub)gradient information will be updated for each node.

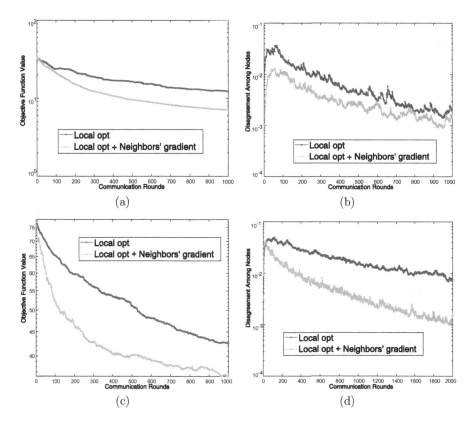

**Fig. 2.** Comparison of convergence speed. Application in decentralized regularized least-squares (a–b). Decentralized logistic regression problem (c–d).

# 5   Numerical Tests

In this section, we test and analyze the performance of the proposed DCDA algorithm. Two types of objective functions are adopted: regularized least-squares and logistic regression. Sensor networks are generated randomly with certain average node degrees (with 200 nodes in total). We investigate the performance of the proposed DCDA algorithm by showing the curve of average objective value and node consensus versus the number of communication rounds.

In decentralized regularized least-squares, node $i$'s local objective function is $F_i(x) = \frac{1}{2}\|\mathbf{A}_i x - \mathbf{b}_i\|_2^2 + \lambda_i \|x\|_2^2$, where the regularization parameter $\lambda_i$ is set to $1/200$, $\mathbf{A}_i$ and $\mathbf{b}_i$ (same dimension for each $i$) are data points available in node $i$. In this scenario, the size of $\mathbf{A}_i$ is $800 \times 3000$ and the dimension of $\mathbf{b}_i$ is set accordingly. In decentralized logistic regression, the local objective function (of node $i$) $F_i$ is set to $F_i(x) = \sum_{j=1}^{p_i} \left( \log \left[ 1 + \exp \left( \left( a_i^j \right)^T x \right) \right] - b_i^j \left( a_i^j \right)^T x \right)$ where $p_i = 10, n = 200$, $\left( a_i^j \right)^T$ represents $j$-th row of $\mathbf{A}_i$ and $b_i^j$ is the $j$-th entry of $\mathbf{b}_i$. We generate $\mathbf{A}_i \in \mathbb{R}^{p_i \times n}, \forall i$ randomly except the first columns are set to 1. Binary vector $\mathbf{b}_i \in \mathbb{R}^{p_i}$ is generated randomly.

In Fig. 2, we compare the performance of the proposed DCDA with the decentralized algorithm in [13]. It is clear that DCDA outperforms the benchmark in both applications, in terms of the speed to reach optimal objective function value as well as consensus among the nodes in the network.

## 6   Conclusion

We proposed a broadcast-based asynchronous decentralized optimization mechanism for data analytics in sensor networks. Our mechanism leverages the computational capability of each node and let all the nodes in the network cooperate to solve the problem of big data analytics with big model. Our future work includes evaluation of the proposed algorithm using more realistic measures.

## References

1. Zhao, L., Song, W.Z., Tong, L., Wu, Y.: Monitoring for power-line change and outage detection in smart grid via the alternating direction method of multipliers. In: 2014 28th International Conference on Advanced Information Networking and Applications Workshops, pp. 342–346, May 2014
2. Zhao, L., Song, W.Z.: A new multi-objective microgrid restoration via semidefinite programming. In: 2014 IEEE 33rd International Performance Computing and Communications Conference (IPCCC), pp. 1–8, December 2014
3. Zhao, L., Song, W.Z., Tong, L., Wu, Y., Yang, J.: Topology identification in smart grid with limited measurements via convex optimization. In: 2014 IEEE Innovative Smart Grid Technologies - Asia (ISGT ASIA), pp. 803–808, May 2014
4. Zhao, L., Song, W.Z., Ye, X.: Fast decentralized gradient descent method and applications to in-situ seismic tomography. In: 2015 IEEE International Conference on Big Data (Big Data), pp. 908–917, October 2015
5. Zhao, L., Song, W.-Z., Shi, L., Ye, X.: Decentralised seismic tomography computing in cyber-physical sensor systems. Cyber-Phys. Syst. **1**(2–4), 91–112 (2015)
6. Zhao, L., Song, W.-Z.: Distributed power-line outage detection based on wide area measurement system. Sensors **14**(7), 13114–13133 (2014)
7. Zhao, L., Song, W.Z.: Decentralized consensus in distributed networks. Int. J. Parallel Emergent Distrib. Syst. 1–20 (2016)
8. Wei, E., Ozdaglar, A.: On the o(1/k) convergence of asynchronous distributed alternating direction method of multipliers. arXiv:1307.8254 (2013)
9. Ciblat, P., Iutzeler, F., Bianchi, P., Hachem, W.: Asynchronous distributed optimization using a randomized alternating direction method of multipliers. arXiv:1303.2837 (2013)
10. Tsitsiklis, J.N., Bertsekas, D.P., Athans, M.: Distributed asynchronous deterministic and stochastic gradient optimization algorithms. IEEE Trans. Autom. Control **31**(9), 803–812 (1986)
11. Aysal, T.C., Yildiz, M.E., Sarwate, A.D., Scaglione, A.: Broadcast gossip algorithms for consensus. IEEE Trans. Signal Process. **57**(7), 2748–2761 (2009)

12. Nedic, A.: Asynchronous broadcast-based convex optimization over a network. IEEE Trans. Autom. Control **56**(6), 1337–1351 (2011)
13. Zhao, L., Song, W.-Z., Ye, X., Gu, Y.: Asynchronous broadcast-based decentralized learning in sensor networks. Int. J. Parallel Emergent Distrib. Syst. 1–19 (2018)
14. Parikh, N., Boyd, S.: Proximal algorithms. Found. Trends Optim. **1**(3), 127–239 (2014)

# Retraction Note to: A Method of Balanced Sleep Scheduling in Renewable Wireless Sensor Networks

Maohan Song, Weidang Lu, Hong Peng, Zhijiang Xu,
and Jingyu Hua

## Retraction Note to:
## Chapter "A Method of Balanced Sleep Scheduling in Renewable Wireless Sensor Networks" in:
## L. Meng and Y. Zhang (Eds.): *Machine Learning and Intelligent Communications*, LNICST 251, https://doi.org/10.1007/978-3-030-00557-3_30

The authors have retracted this article [1] because of the following errors which undermine the paper:

1. In Algorithm 1, the output of $S_{awake}$, $S_{sleep}$, TH and $E_u$ are depending on the input of $E_{h,u}$, $E_{c,u}$, $E_{res,u}$, u and $\eta$, in which $E_{h,u}$ and $E_{c,u}$ denote the harvesting energy and the energy consumption for the $u^{th}$ node, respectively. However, how to calculate and obtain the $E_{h,u}$ and $E_{c,u}$ are not given in the paper.

2. Equation (7) is not correct. $E_{h,u}$ denotes the harvesting energy for the $u^{th}$ node, which have already considered $\eta$. $\eta$ should not multiply with $E_{h,u}$ in equation (7). Thus, the result of $E_u$ is not correct, which will cause all the following results (the optimal $\tau$, the work mode of the nodes) not correct. It is a very serious problem.

3. In the simulation results and discussion, the side length of the network is assumed to be 480 m and the forder length is assumed to be 60 m. This assumption is wrong. It is impossible for the wireless sensor node to harvest energy through wireless energy transfer with such a long distance.

4. The range of $\tau$ shown in the paper is not correct. It should be $(0,1)$. If $\tau$ equals to 1, which means the node cannot harvest energy.

5. In the simulation results and discussion, the simulation is performed 100 times under the condition of $\tau = 0.5$. It is not correct. In the paper, $\tau$ needs to be optimized depending on TH and $E_u$. It should not equal to 0.5.

---

The retracted version of this chapter can be found at
https://doi.org/10.1007/978-3-030-00557-3_30

© ICST Institute for Computer Sciences, Social Informatics and Telecommunications Engineering 2020
L. Meng and Y. Zhang (Eds.): MLICOM 2018, LNICST 251, pp. C1–C2, 2020.
https://doi.org/10.1007/978-3-030-00557-3_67

In addition to the flaws identified above, the authors would also like to acknowledge the similarities with two publications by different authors [2, 3]which unfortunately were not been referenced in the published manuscript.

[1] Song, M., Lu, W., Peng, H., Xu, Z., Hua, J.: A method of balanced sleep scheduling in renewable wireless sensor networks. In: Meng, L., Zhang, Y. (eds.) MLICOM 2018. LNCS, vol. 251,pp. 293–302. Springer, Cham (2018). https://doi.org/10.1007/978-3-030-00557-3_30. Social Informatics and Telecommunications Engineering

[2] Fang, W., Zhang, Z., Mukherjee, M., Shu, L., Zhou, Z.: Energy-utilization aware sleep scheduling in green WSNs for sustainable throughput. In: 43rd Annual Conference of the IEEE Industrial Electronics Society, IECON 2017, pp. 4724–4727. IEEE, October 2017

[3] Fang, W., Mukherjee, M., Shu, L., Zhou, Z., Hancke, G.P.: Energy utilization concerned sleep scheduling in wireless powered communication networks. In: 2017 IEEE International Conference on Communications Workshops (ICC Workshops), pp. 558–563. IEEE, May 2017.

# Author Index

Printed in the United States
By Bookmasters